Effective Mainstreaming
Creating Inclusive Classrooms

Second Edition

Spencer J. Salend
The College at New Paltz, State University of New York

Macmillan Publishing Company
New York

Maxwell Macmillan Canada
Toronto

Maxwell Macmillan International
New York Oxford Singapore Sydney

Cover Image: Super Stock/Diana Ong
Editors: Robert Miller, Debra A. Stollenwerk
Production Editor: Laura Messerly
Art Coordinator: Ruth A. Kimpel
Phot Editor: Anne Vega
Text Designer: Debra A. Fargo
Cover Designer: Cathleen Norz
Production Buyer: Pamela D. Bennett

This book was set in Garamond by Carlisle Communications, Ltd. and was printed and bound by Book Press, Inc., a Quebecor America Book Group Company. The cover was printed by Phoenix Color Corp.

Printed in the United States of America.

Macmillan Publishing Company
866 Third Avenue
New York, New York 10022

Macmillan Publishing Company is part of the
Maxwell Communication Group of Companies.

Maxwell Macmillan Canada, Inc.
1200 Eglinton Avenue East, Suite 200
Don Mills, Ontario M3C 3N1

Library of Congress Cataloging-in-Publication Data

Salend, Spencer J.
Effective mainstreaming: creating inclusive classrooms/
Spencer J. Salend.
p. cm.
Rev. ed of: Effective mainstreaming. c1990.
Includes bibliographical references and index.
ISBN 0-02-405331-7
1. Handicapped children—Education—United States.
2. Mainstreaming in education—United States. I. Title.
LC4031.S244 1994
371.9'046'0973—dc20 92-44324
CIP

Printing: 1 2 3 4 5 6 7 8 9 Year: 4 5 6 7 8

Photo credits: Paul Conklin, p. 266; Robert Finken, p. 453; Barbara Schwartz/Macmillan, pp. 58, 65, 400; Ray Solomon/Monkmeyer Press Photo Service, p. 151; Anne Vega/Macmillan, p. 62; Tom Watson/Macmillan, pp. 1, 13, 115, 160, 203, 206, 269, 299, 311, 334, 344, 366, 387, 418, 469, 487; Gale Zucker, pp. 7, 32, 102, 158.

Chapter 4: Teaching Students to Accept Individual Differences offers guidelines for assessing and changing attitudes toward mainstreamed students. A variety of strategies and approaches for teaching students acceptance of individual differences based on disability, culture, language, gender, and socioeconomic status and for promoting friendships are discussed.

Chapter 5: Preparing Students for Success in Mainstreamed Settings offers guidelines for planning transitional programs to prepare students for success in mainstreamed settings. Strategies are presented for preparing students to deal with the critical factors that affect student performance in the regular classroom such as instructional format and materials, curricular demands, and teaching and learning style. Approaches for helping students make the transition from specialized schools, early education programs and bilingual/ESL programs as well as the transition to the world of work and independent living arrangements are discussed.

Chapter 6: Modifying Large- and Small-Group Instruction offers guidelines for adapting small- and large-group instruction. Strategies consistent with teacher-effectiveness data are reviewed, as are procedures for successfully implementing cooperative learning arrangements and academic games.

Chapter 7: Modifying Instruction for Diverse Learners offers guidelines for implementing instructional modifications to address the diverse learning needs of mainstreamed students. Strategies for modifying instruction for students with reading and writing difficulties, sensory disabilities, severe disabilities, and students from culturally linguistically diverse backgrounds are presented. The use of technology and adaptive devices to facilitate student performance are discussed.

Chapter 8: Modifying Reading, Writing, Spelling, and Handwriting Instruction offers guidelines for adapting reading, writing, spelling, and handwriting instruction for mainstreamed students.

Chapter 9: Modifying Mathematics, Science, and Social Studies Instruction offers guidelines for adapting mathematics, science, and social studies instruction for mainstreamed students, as well as strategies of creating a multicultural curriculum that is inclusive of and relevant to all students.

Chapter 10: Modifying Classroom Behavior and the Classroom Environment offers guidelines for promoting appropriate classroom behavior and modifying the classroom design to address the social and behavioral needs of mainstreamed students. Self-management strategies, affective education techniques, and group-oriented management systems are discussed.

Chapter 11: Evaluating the Progress of Mainstreamed Students offers guidelines for implementing a variety of formal and informal strategies for monitoring and assessing student progress. Strategies for adapting grading systems and teacher-made tests, as well as teaching test-taking skills to mainstreamed students are discussed. Suggestions for evaluating the effectiveness of instructional modifications, adaptive devices, and medical interventions are presented.

Interspersed within each chapter are vignettes and items to focus your thinking, called Think About It and Ideas for Implementation. To orient you, each chapter opens with a vignette and a series of questions related to the content presented in the chapter, which serve as an advance organizer. Vignettes also are presented throughout to provide you with practical examples depicting the actual application of the techniques and strategies presented in the book. Think About It, a series of questions or activities designed to help you reflect upon and interact with the material in the book, also appear in each chapter, as do Ideas for Implementation, which contain practical suggestions for teaching and providing services to students and parents.

As in the first edition, the second edition includes an instructor's manual, which has been prepared to assist instructors in using the text. Chapters in the manual parallel the organization and content of the text. Each chapter of the manual is divided into six parts:

Chapter objectives—a listing of the major learning outcomes and skills readers should acquire upon completing the chapter.

Chapter overview—a sequential listing of the major points contained in each chapter.

Key terms—a listing of terminology that readers should master.

Course learning activities—a series of suggested activities that can be used to promote mastery of information presented in the text and in class lectures.

Study guide questions—a study guide presenting questions in sequential order to assist the reader in identifying and outlining the important components of each chapter.

Test bank—a series of short answer and essay questions relating to the content presented in each chapter.

A computerized test bank also is available.

When writing a book, an author must develop a philosophy that serves as a framework for the text. Several philosophical assumptions concerning effective mainstreaming guided the development of this book. As you read and think about the following assumptions, you will learn about the book and its author.

Effective mainstreaming can improve the educational system for all students. Inherent in the concept of mainstreaming is the recognition of the need to individualize the educational system for *all* students. The result can be an educational system that is more able to accommodate and respond to the individual needs of *all* students. Thus, changes in the educational system designed to facilitate effective mainstreaming also can benefit *all* students, teachers, parents, ancillary support personnel, and administrators. For example, *all* students will benefit when a teacher modifies large-group instruction to facilitate the performance of a mainstreamed student. Similarly, as the educational system learns to respond to the needs of parents of mainstreamed students, it increases its ability to respond to all parents.

Effective mainstreaming involves a sensitivity and an acceptance of individual needs and differences. Educators cannot teach students without looking at the various factors that have and will continue to shape that individual and make him or her unique. Therefore, since race, linguistic ability, gender, socioeconomic status, and disability interact to create a complex amalgam that affects academic performance and socialization, educators and students must be sensitized to and accepting of individual needs and differences. Educators also must be willing to modify attitudes, instructional techniques, curriculum, and models of parental involvement to reflect these needs. Our ability to redefine the mainstream to be inclusive of the unique needs and differences of students and families, as well as incorporate their varied visions and contributions, is critical in expanding the educational, social, and cultural base of our educational system and promoting effective mainstreaming.

Effective mainstreaming involves collaboration among educators, parents, students, community agencies, and other available resources. When these forces are working in synergy, the likelihood for effective mainstreaming is increased. Thus, this book outlines the roles and responsibilities of educators, parents, mainstreamed students and their peers, and community agencies to promote effective mainstreaming and offers strategies for integrating these roles so that individuals work cooperatively. While all roles are important, it is the union of these roles that leads to effective mainstreaming.

In fact, this book is a result of the collaborative efforts of my students, colleagues, friends, and relatives. The book is an outgrowth of many ideas I learned from students in Woodlawn Junior High School (Buffalo, NY) and Public School 76 (Bronx, NY) and colleagues from PS 76: George Bonnici, Nydia Figueroa-Torres, Jean Gee, and Jean Barber. Similarly, much of the information presented was learned through interactions with teachers, administrators, and students in the Easton (PA) Area School District who both welcomed me and shared their experiences. Many of the examples and vignettes are based on the experiences of my students at the State University of New York, the College at New Paltz. I truly value my students who continue to educate me and add to my appreciation of the remarkable dedication and skill of teachers.

I also want to acknowledge my colleagues and friends who provided support and guidance through all stages of the book. I especially want to recognize Lee Bell, Meenakshi Gajria, Luis Garrido, Margaret Gutierrez, Karen Giek, Mark Metzger, Kathy Pike, George Roberts, Phil Schmidt, Lorraine Taylor, Margaret Wade-Lewis, Catharine Whittaker, and Jamey Wolff for supporting and inspiring me throughout the process. My deepest appreciation also goes to Connie D'Alessandro and Adam Cody for their invaluable assistance in coordinating various aspects of this book.

This book would not have been possible without the efforts of editors Robert Miller and Debbie Stollenwerk of Macmillan. I appreciate the work of copyeditor Robert Marcum and production editor Laura Messerly, whose skills have significantly enhanced many aspects of the book. I also am grateful to the reviewers, Deborah Gartland, Towson State University; Sandra H. Fradd, University of Miami; Carol Chase Thomas, The University of North

Carolina at Wilmington; Sandra B. Cohen, University of Virginia; Thomassine Sellers, San Francisco State University; Linda P. Thurston, Kansas State University; Barbara Ray, The University of Tennessee at Chattanooga; and Caryl Taylor, The University of Tennessee at Chattanooga. Their thoughtful and professional comments helped to shape and improve the book.

I want to acknowledge my father, Harry Salend, my son, Jack, and my mother-in-law Agnes Russ for their love and support. Finally, I want to dedicate this book to my collaborator in life, Suzanne Salend, in recognition of her love, intelligence, faith, encouragement, and strength.

To Suzanne
and in memory of my mother,
Anne Salend

Brief Contents

Contents

1 Understanding Mainstreaming as a Vehicle for Addressing the Needs of Diverse Learners

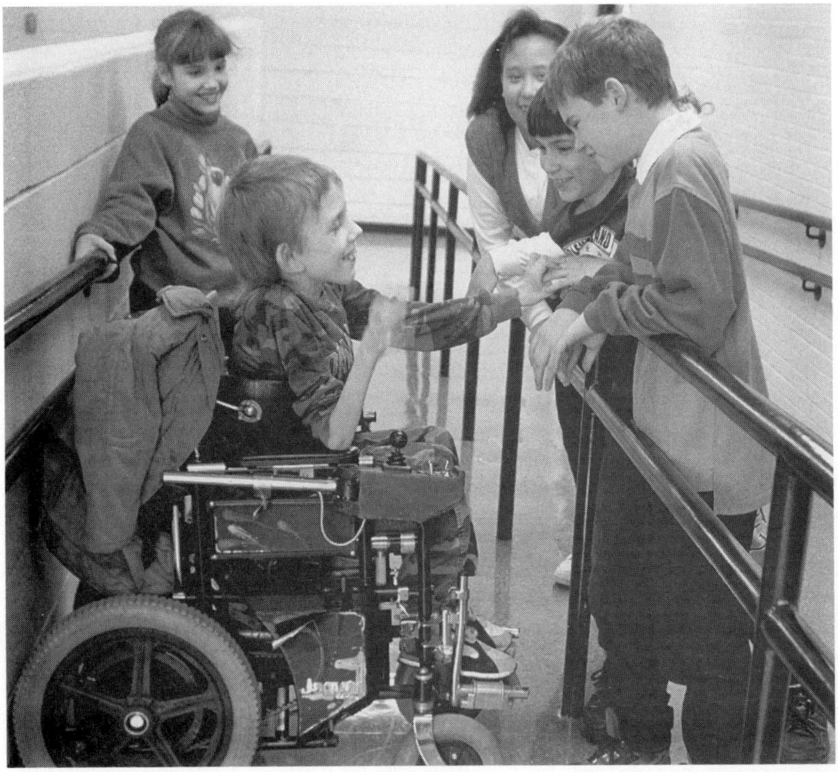

MARIE AND MARY

Marie was born in 1946. By age 3, her parents felt that she was developing slowly—little speech and late in walking. Marie's pediatrician told them not to worry, that Marie would grow out of it. After another year of no noticeable progress, Marie's parents took her to other doctors. One said she had an iron deficiency and another thought she had a tumor.

By the time Marie was old enough to start school, she was diagnosed as having mental retardation and was placed in a separate school for children with disabilities. She was doing well at the school when the school district sent Marie's parents a letter informing them that the school was being closed and that the district had no place for Marie and the other students. Marie's parents protested to school officials and their state legislator to no avail because by state law, the school district was not required to educate children like Marie. For a while, Marie attended a private program set up by parents whose children had cerebral palsy. Her parents knew this wasn't the right place for Marie, but there was no place else.

Concerned about her future, Marie's parents sent her to a large state-run program about 200 miles from their home. Initially, Marie's parents visited at least once a month. However, after two years, the visits became less frequent. During visits, Marie's parents found that Marie was often disheveled, disoriented, and incommunicative. Once she even had bruises on her arms and legs. After much debate, Marie's parents decided to bring her home to live with them.

Years later, Marie's parents were able to get her into a sheltered workshop program, where Marie was trained to place objects in plastic bags. Marie, although an adult, cannot perform daily living skills, and her parents are worried about what will happen to her when they are no longer able to care for her.

Mary, born in 1983, also was diagnosed as having mental retardation. Soon after birth, Mary and her parents were enrolled in an early intervention program. A professional came to their home to work with Mary and her parents. Parent training sessions were also available at the early intervention center. Mary's parents joined a local parent group that was advocating for services. When Mary was 4, she attended a preschool program with other children from her neighborhood. The school worked with Mary's parents to develop an Individualized Family Service Plan, to meet Mary's educational needs and assist her family in planning for the transition to public school. After preschool, Mary moved with the other children to the local elementary school. At that time, Mary's parents met with the school district's multidisciplinary team to develop an Individualized Education Program (IEP) for Mary. The multidisciplinary team recommended that Mary be educated in a self-contained special education class. However, Mary's parents felt that she should be in a setting that allowed her to interact with her peers who were not disabled. As a result of a due process hearing, Mary was placed in a mainstreamed setting for the majority of her school day. She also was to receive the services of a resource room teacher and a speech/language therapist. Mary had some teachers who understood her needs and others who did not, but she and her parents persevered. Occasionally, other students made fun of Mary, but she learned to ignore that and participated in many afterschool programs.

When Mary was ready to move to junior high school, the teachers and her parents worked together to help Mary make the transition. She was taught to change classes, use a combination lock and locker, and use different textbooks. Her IEP was revised to include grading and testing modifications as well as the use of word processing to help her develop written communication skills. Mary went to dances after school and bowling with her friends on Saturdays.

Mary graduated from junior high school and entered high school where her favorite subjects are social studies, science, and lunch. A peer helps Mary by sharing notes with her and Mary's teachers have modified the curriculum for her. She also is taking a course called "Introduction to Occupations" and participates in a work-study program. Mary hopes to work in a store or office in town when she graduates.

What events led Marie and Mary and their families to have such different experiences in school and society? After reading this chapter, you should be able to answer that as well as the following questions.

- How are the concepts of the least restrictive environment and mainstreaming related?
- What factors have contributed to the movement toward mainstreaming?
- How can schools change to address the societal shifts that have resulted in a growing number of

students whose needs are challenging the educational system?

- What are the advantages and disadvantages of mainstreaming?
- Based on the research, is mainstreaming a justifiable alternative for students?

The education and treatment of individuals with disabilities has undergone a metamorphosis. Prior to 1800, individuals with disabilities were feared, ridiculed, abandoned, or simply ignored. As educational methods were developed in the late 1700s that showed the success of various teaching techniques, society began to adopt a more accepting and humane view of individuals with disabilities. However, the nineteenth century saw the rise of institutions for individuals with disabilities that served to isolate them from society.

Although institutional settings played an important role in the education and treatment of individuals with disabilities until the 1970s, the early twentieth century also saw the rise of special schools and special classes within public school facilities for students with disabilities. The movement toward special programs and classes was followed by a period of advocacy and acceptance, which resulted in congressional enactment of PL 94-142, the Education for All Handicapped Children Act (1975), now renamed the Individuals with Disabilities Education Act (IDEA). Although PL 94-142 does not specifically mention mainstreaming, these acts established the concept of mainstreaming as one of the prevailing philosophical goals of the education of students with disabilities.

LEAST RESTRICTIVE ENVIRONMENT

Mainstreaming is rooted in the concept of the *least restrictive environment*. PL 94-142 mandates the placement of students with disabilities in the least restrictive environment in which their educational needs can be met. The least restrictive environment (LRE) concept requires educational agencies to educate students with disabilities as much as possible with their peers who are not disabled. The determination of the least restrictive environment is an individual decision that is based on the student's educational needs rather than the student's disability. While the least restrictive environment concept does not mean that all students with disabilities should be in regular classrooms, it does mean that students with disabilities should be removed to self-contained special education classes, specialized schools, and residential programs only when the severity of their disability is so great that the students' needs cannot be accommodated in the regular education setting. Data collected on the least restrictive environment concept since the inception of PL 94-142 indicate that the number of students with disabilities still being educated in separate facilities has not changed and that there is great variation from state to state in the use of separate facilities for these students (Danielson & Bellamy, 1989).

Tucker (1989) suggests that the least restrictive environment provision be service defined rather than location bound. A service-defined approach to the least restrictive environment focuses on providing services that meet students' educational needs and help them function successfully in the regular classroom setting. Wilcox and Sailor (1982) believe that the least restrictive environment must meet the following six criteria:

- include peers who are not disabled
- offer opportunities for interactions between students
- maintain a ratio of students with disabilities and students who are not disabled that is consistent with that of the larger population
- provide equal access to educational and nonacademic activities and facilities
- offer all students the same schedule for and organization of activities
- guarantee the delivery of high quality educational services

Some professionals have argued that the LRE concept should be discarded or revised because it impedes the total integration of all students into all aspects of society (Lipsky & Gartner, 1991). S. J. Taylor (1988) identified the following flaws in the LRE concept:

- gives credibility to restrictive environments
- promotes confusion between integration/segregation and the intensity of services
- facilitates placement in mainstreamed settings based only on professional determinations of readiness
- infringes on an individual's basic rights and access to community participation
- assumes that individuals should be moved as they grow and change
- emphasizes physical locations rather than the resources individuals need to be successfully mainstreamed

CONTINUUM OF EDUCATIONAL SERVICES

A continuum of educational placements ranging from the highly integrated setting of the regular classroom to the highly segregated settings of the residential program has been established to implement the least restrictive environment (E. Deno, 1970; Greer, 1988). Figure 1.1 presents the range from most to least restrictive educational placements for serving students, although variation exists within and among agencies. A student with a disability would be placed in one of the placement alternatives based upon that student's individual needs, skills, abilities, and motivation (Stephens, Blackhurst, & Magliocca, 1982). A student should move down the continuum to a less restrictive environment as quickly as possible and move up the continuum to a more segregated alternative only when such a move is indicated.

FIGURE 1.1
Continuum of educational services

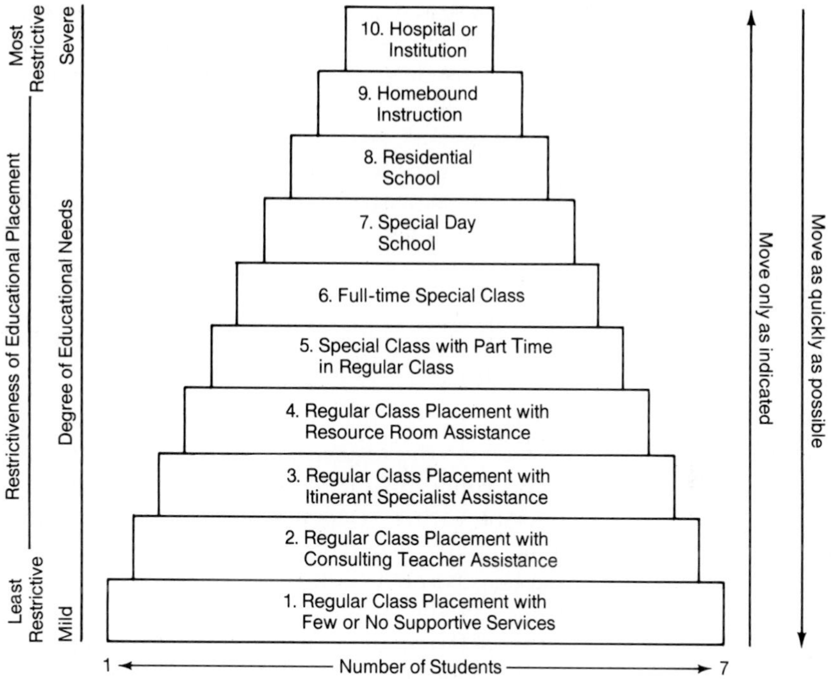

Source: Adapted from Blackhurst and Berdine (1981), Deno (1970), and Lewis & Doorlag (1987).

Option 1: Regular Class Placement with Few or No Supportive Services

The least restrictive environment within the placement alternatives is the regular classroom setting with few or no supportive services. In this option, the student is educated in the regular classroom, following the same schedule as other students. The regular classroom teacher has the primary responsibility for designing and delivering the instructional program to the student. The instructional program is adapted to the needs of the mainstreamed student, and students may use adaptive devices and alternative learning strategies. While no specialized services are provided to the student, indirect services such as inservice training to adapt the instructional program for mainstreamed students and to teach students about individual differences may be offered.

Option 2: Regular Class Placement with Consulting Teacher Assistance

This placement option is similar to option 1 in that the student is placed in the regular education setting for the entire day, and does not receive any direct special services. However, the regular classroom teacher receives consultative services from a special educator, school psychologist, guidance counselor, or other ancillary support personnel. The nature of the consultative services delivered will vary depending on the nature and severity of the student's needs as well as those of the teacher. Typically, consultative services include obtaining specialized curricula and instructional materials, adapting instructional strategies and teacher-made tests, designing behavior management programs, and promoting social interaction between students. Guidelines for implementing collaborative consultation services are provided in Chapter 3.

Option 3: Regular Class Placement with Itinerant Specialist Assistance

Itinerant teachers often travel from school to school to provide direct services to students. The regular education program is delivered in the regular classroom setting, and the student also receives weekly supportive services from itinerant teachers. Depending on the school district's arrangement, the itinerant teacher may deliver services to students within the confines of the regular classroom or in an area outside the classroom. For example, school districts in Wisconsin, New Mexico, and Vermont employ an integrated therapy model whereby supportive service personnel deliver their services in the regular education setting. Many speech/language therapists and other specialists deliver services to students within the regular classroom setting. Often they work collaboratively with the classroom teacher to integrate their services within the regular curriculum. Working within the regular classroom setting can help promote communication between professionals and establish links among skills taught by regular education and supportive services personnel. Occasionally, itinerant teachers working within the mainstreamed setting may provide remedial instruction to other students whose needs parallel those of the mainstreamed student.

Option 4: Regular Class Placement with Resource Room Assistance

Like the itinerant teacher, the resource room teacher offers direct services to students with disabilities. However, whereas the itinerant teacher often travels from school to school, the resource room teacher has a classroom within the school. Additionally, while itinerant teachers serve students who are not disabled, mainstreamed students, and students in self-contained special education classes, the resource room teacher usually serves only students who are mainstreamed for the majority of the school day. Resource room teachers provide individualized remedial instruction in specific skills (such as note taking, study skills, and so on) to small groups of students. In addition, resource teachers often provide supplemental instruction that supports and parallels the instruction the student is receiving in the regular classroom.

The resource room teacher also can help regular classroom teachers plan and implement instructional adaptations for mainstreamed students. For example, a teacher-made test adapted for mainstreamed students can be jointly constructed by the regular classroom and resource room teacher, and administered to the students in the resource room.

Option 5: Special Class Placement With Part Time in the Regular Class

In this option, the student's primary placement is in a special class setting within the same school building as their peers who are not disabled. The student's academic program is supervised by a special educator. However, some time is spent with students from the regular classroom. The amount of

Early intervention programs have been instrumental in promoting the development of young children.

time spent in the regular classroom may vary, and students in this option are placed in the regular setting only for subjects in which they can function successfully. Some students may enter the regular classroom for academic instruction, but most often the students in this option are integrated with their peers who are not disabled for art, music, industrial arts, and physical education.

Option 6: Full-Time Special Class

This placement alternative is similar to option 5. However, contact with peers who are not disabled takes place exclusively in a social rather than instructional setting. Students in this placement alternative share common experiences with other students on school buses, at lunch or recess, and during schoolwide activities (assemblies, plays, dances, and sporting events, and so on).

Option 7: Special Day School

Students in this placement alternative attend a school different from that of their neighborhood peers. Placement in a special school allows schools to centralize services (Lewis & Doorlag, 1987). Thus, students' needs for such services as physical and occupational therapy can be delivered more cost effectively. Students attending special schools may share the common experience of riding a bus to school (often students will take a different bus than will their neighborhood peers) and returning home after school, but this option is highly restrictive and is usually used with students with severe disabilities.

Option 8: Residential School

Residential programs also are designed to serve students with severe disabilities. Whereas students in a special day school return home at the end of the school day, students attending residential schools live at the school and participate in a twenty-four hour program. Students attend the residential school during the school year or all year, and see their families during holidays or family visits. In addition to delivering educational services, these programs offer the necessary comprehensive medical and psychological services that students may need.

Option 9: Homebound Instruction

Some students, such as those who are recovering from surgery or an illness or who have been suspended from school, may require homebound instruction. In this alternative, a teacher visits the home and delivers the instructional program in that setting. The teacher links homebound students with schools and classrooms by obtaining in-class assignments and delivering completed assignments to the classroom teacher.

Option 10: Hospital or Institution

Placing individuals with severe disabilities into hospitals and institutions has been lessened as a result of the deinstitutionalization movement, but such placements still exist. As with all the placement options, education must be a part of any hospital or institution program. These placements should be viewed as short term, and an emphasis should be placed on moving these individuals to a less restrictive environment.

MAINSTREAMING

Data from the 13th Annual Report to Congress on the Implementation of the Individuals with Disabilities Education Act *(1991b) indicate that 93% of the students with disabilities age 3–21 were educated in public school buildings.*

For many students with disabilities, the least restrictive environment has been interpreted as being mainstreamed into regular education classes (U.S. Department of Education, 1991b). The U.S. Department of Education, in evaluating the implementation of the IDEA, found that approximately 70 percent of the students with disabilities in this country receive their instructional program in regular education classrooms and resource room settings.

Figure 1.2 presents data on the types of students with disabilities and the settings in which they are educated. These data reveal that the extent to which students are mainstreamed varies by disability. Whereas approximately 78 and

FIGURE 1.2
Types of students with disabilities and the settings in which they are educated.

	EDUCATIONAL ENVIRONMENTS					
Disability Category	**Regular Class**	**Resource Room**	**Separate Class**	**Separate School**	**Residential Facility**	**Homebound/ Hospital**
Specific learning disabilities	19.6%	57.9%	20.9%	1.3%	0.1%	0.1%
Speech or language impairments	75.9	19.2	3.3	1.4	0.1	0.1
Mental retardation	5.9	22.4	58.9	11.3	1.2	0.4
Serious emotional disturbance	14.1	30.0	35.8	13.4	3.8	2.9
Hearing impairments	26.9	21.0	33.5	8.5	9.8	0.2
Multiple disabilities	7.0	14.1	46.2	25.9	4.0	2.8
Orthopedic impairments	29.3	18.6	33.5	11.1	0.7	6.9
Other health impairments	29.9	20.3	19.6	7.8	0.8	21.6
Visual impairments	52.0	17.9	21.5	3.4	4.9	0.3
Deaf-blindness	11.6	5.3	29.9	25.9	26.1	1.2
All disabilities	30.5	39.0	24.3	4.6	0.9	0.8

Source: The Thirteenth Annual Report to Congress on the Implementation of the Individuals with Disabilities Education Act (p. 27) by U.S. Department of Education, 1991, Washington, DC, Author.

95 percent of the students with learning disabilities and students with speech impairments, respectively, are placed in regular classroom or resource room settings, 59 and 36 percent of the students with mental retardation and emotional disturbance, respectively, were educated in separate classes. Students with hearing impairments are placed in regular classrooms (27%), resource rooms (21%), separate classes (34%), and residential programs (11%). Similarly, students with visual impairments are educated in regular classrooms (52%), resource rooms (18%), separate classes (22%), and residential programs (8%). While the vast majority of students with orthopedic and other health impairments receive their instruction in settings with students who are not disabled, 7 percent of the students with orthopedic impairments and 21 percent of the students with other health impairments also are educated in homebound/hospital environments. The most prevalent educational placement for students with multiple disabilities is the separate classroom (46%), followed by separate schools (30%), resource room (14%), and regular classroom (7%) placements.

Figure 1.3 shows data on educational environments in which students of various ages are placed. Generally, these data indicate that preschoolers and elementary-level students are more likely to be educated in regular settings than are students 12–17 and 18–21 years of age (U.S. Department of Education, 1991b). With resource room placement, the age pattern shifts; older students are more likely to be educated in resource room programs than younger students. Because a larger percentage of students who are still in school at age 18 are students with severe disabilities who require transitional programming not available in most regular education programs, students ages 18–21 are more highly represented in the more restrictive environments.

The scope of mainstreaming varies greatly from so broad as to be defined as any interactions between students who are not disabled and their peers who have disabilities (Lewis & Doorlag, 1987), to more specific integration of students with disabilities into the social and instructional activities of the regular classroom milieu (Kaufman, Gottlieb, Agard, & Kukic, 1975; Turnbull & Schulz, 1979). For example, the Kaufman et al. (1975) definition includes

FIGURE 1.3
Ages of students with disabilities and the settings in which they are educated.

	Age Groups			
Environment	**3–5**	**6–11**	**12–17**	**18–21**
Regular class	42.2%	41.0%	19.3%	14.2%
Resource room	16.1	34.8	45.0	35.0
Separate class	26.3	20.5	28.1	31.5
Separate school	12.9	3.1	5.1	14.6
Residential facility	0.4	0.4	1.2	3.3
Homebound/hospital	2.0	0.3	1.3	1.4

Source: The Thirteenth Annual Report to Congress on the Implementation of the Individuals with Disabilities Education Act (p. 25) by U.S. Department of Education, 1991, Washington, DC, Author.

the components of integration, educational planning and programming, and delineation of roles and responsibilities (MacMillan & Semmel, 1977). Figure 1.4 presents alternative definitions of mainstreaming.

This text defines *mainstreaming* as the carefully planned and monitored placement of students into regular education classrooms for their academic and social educational program. In this definition, the primary responsibility for the mainstreamed student's academic program lies with the regular education teacher. The academic component of the definition requires that the regular classroom environment be adapted to address the instructional needs of the mainstreamed student, while the social component requires that the mainstreamed student be assimilated into the social climate of the class and accepted by peers (Kaufman, Gottlieb, Agard, & Kukic, 1975).

This definition implies that mainstreaming is a dynamic, ongoing process that requires communication and sharing information between regular and special educators, ancillary support personnel, and parents. Since this definition emphasizes academic instruction and length of time spent in the regular classroom, the term *integration* will be used to refer to other planned interactions between students. Thus, the placement of students with mental retar-

FIGURE 1.4
Definitions of mainstreaming

Mainstreaming is

- the inclusion of special students in the general educational process. Students are considered mainstreamed if they spend any part of the school day with regular class peers (Lewis & Doorlag, 1987, p. 4).
- the social and instructional integration of handicapped students in a regular education class for at least a portion of the school day (Schulz & Turnbull, 1983, p. 49).
- the education of mildly handicapped children in the least restrictive environment. It is based on the philosophy of equal educational opportunity that is implemented through individual planning to promote appropriate learning, achievement, and social normalization (Stephens, Blackhurst, & Magliocca, 1982, p. 10).
- the temporal, instructional, and social integration of eligible exceptional children with normal peers based on an ongoing, individually determined, educational planning programming process, and requires clarification of responsibility among regular and special education administrative, instructional, and supportive personnel (Kaufman et al., 1975, p. 35).
- the carefully planned and monitored placement of students into regular education classrooms for their academic and social educational program. The academic program within the regular education classroom should be adapted to address the instructional needs of the mainstreamed student, and the social program should be designed so that the mainstreamed student is assimilated into the social climate of the class and accepted by peers. While the primary responsibility for the mainstreamed student's academic and social program lies with the regular classroom teacher, mainstreaming is a dynamic, ongoing process that requires communication and sharing information between regular and special educators, ancillary support personnel, and parents.

dation into a physical education class with their regular education peers twice a week would be an example of integration, while the placement of a student with mental retardation in a regular classroom for his or her academic program with supplemental assistance from a resource room teacher once a day would be considered mainstreaming.

Reynolds and Birch (1988) delineated three aspects of mainstreaming: physical, social, and instructional. Physical mainstreaming requires that students are educated in the same school facilities as their same age peers. While physical mainstreaming guarantees that all students attend and use the same facilities, it does not necessarily guarantee that there will be social and academic interactions between students. Social mainstreaming is implemented when school staff structure the learning environment so that students have opportunities to interact socially. Instructional mainstreaming occurs when all students receive their academic instruction in the same setting.

FACTORS CONTRIBUTING TO THE IMPETUS FOR MAINSTREAMING

Several factors have contributed to the impetus for mainstreaming. These factors include normalization, deinstitutionalization, early intervention, technological advances, advocacy, litigation, legislation, and efficacy studies. Societal changes have also occurred that have improved the public perception of mainstreaming as a viable and effective tool for educating diverse learners in regular education classrooms.

Normalization

The mainstreaming movement has its roots in the principle of normalization, a concept first formulated in Scandinavia (Kugel & Wolfensberger, 1969) and later brought to the United States (Wolfensberger, 1972). The normalization principle seeks to provide social interactions and experiences that parallel those of society to adults and children with disabilities (Nirje, 1969). Thus the

IDEAS FOR IMPLEMENTATION

Social mainstreaming can be implemented by encouraging interactions between students in a variety of situations.

- Using school facilities such as the gymnasium, play areas, lunchroom, and library
- Attending after-school activities such as dances and athletic events
- Joining clubs and teams
- Attending school events such as assemblies, school plays, and fairs
- Working cooperatively on classroom activities
- Volunteering to perform a school job
- Participating in field trips

Source: Biklen, Lehr, Searl, & Taylor (1987).

philosophy of mainstreaming rests on the principle that educational, housing, employment, social, and leisure opportunities for individuals with disabilities should resemble as closely as possible the patterns, opportunities, and activities enjoyed by their peers who are not disabled (Haring & McCormick, 1990). The normalization principle also serves as a guide to the delivery of services to individuals with disabilities (Bruininks & Warfield, 1978).

Deinstitutionalization

The normalization principle has contributed to the movement toward deinstitutionalization. The deinstitutionalization movement advocates eliminating large institutions for individuals with disabilities and placing them in smaller, community-based, independent living arrangements. The number of individuals with disabilities in institutions has decreased dramatically in recognition of the deplorable conditions in institutions and the negative effects of institutionalization. Several states, such as New Hampshire, have moved toward closing down all institutions. Unfortunately, there have been limited resources devoted to providing services to support individuals who have exited institutional programs. While the deinstitutionalization movement has encountered some resistance from local communities and a lack of funding, many examples of its successful implementation exist.

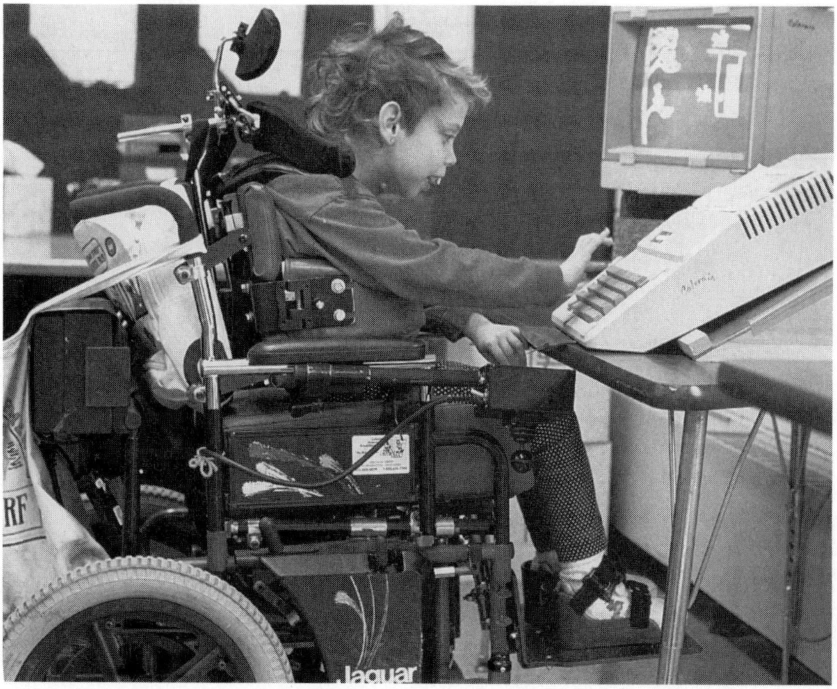

Technological advances are providing individuals with greater access to all aspects of society and schools.

Early Intervention

The effectiveness of early intervention for young children with or without disabilities aided the movement to mainstreaming. Early intervention—the delivery of a variety of intervention services to children from birth to 6 years of age—has been successful in promoting growth in terms of increased acquisition of physical, motor, cognitive, language, speech, socialization, and self-help skills. Early intervention also has lessened the likelihood that secondary disabilities will occur; has empowered parents and families so that they can be effective agents for promoting their child's development; and has decreased the probability that individuals will be socially dependent and institutionalized as adults (Heward & Orlansky, 1992). The characteristics of successful early intervention programs are delineated in Figure 1.5.

Technological Advances

Medical and assisted device technology have promoted the mainstreaming movement. Because of advances in medical technology, a growing number of individuals with severe disabilities and other problems at birth are surviving and living longer lives. Data indicate that in 1970, 33 percent of the infants born with severe disabilities lived to the age of 21; in 1990, 66 percent of the infants born with severe disabilities lived to the age of 21; and in 2000, it is anticipated that 83 percent of the infants with severe disabilities will live to the age of 21 (Council for Exceptional Children, 1991). Medical technology also is keeping individuals alive longer and forcing many families to confront the decision of whether to place their elderly family members in segregated

FIGURE 1.5
Characteristics of successful early intervention programs

Effective early intervention programs will perform the following functions:

Determine the needs of children and their families through assessment.

Address the needs, concerns, priorities, and goals of family members.

Provide a range of services to each child and family based on their individual needs.

Understand the family's linguistic, experiential, and cultural background.

Deliver services so that they maximize the child's independence and development in a variety of areas.

Educate the student in classrooms and other settings with peers.

Train family members in providing an appropriate learning environment for the child.

Help parents access relevant community services.

Evaluate the effectiveness of the services delivered.

Source: M. Wolery, *Exceptional Children* (1991).

settings such as nursing homes or to attempt to maintain them in more normalized, integrated settings.

Technological advances also have changed the quality of life for many individuals, facilitating their gaining access, independence, and achievement. Assistive and adaptive devices have empowered individuals with communication, physical, learning, and sensory disabilities by allowing them to gain more control over their lives and environment (Blackhurst & Shuping, 1991). These devices are providing individuals with disabilities greater access to all aspects of society and schools. While these devices were developed for individuals with disabilities, they have consequences and benefits for all members of society. Some examples of these new technological devices are as follows:

- a specialized soundtrack system that enhances television viewing for individuals with visual impairments by verbally describing events, character actions, and scenes during pauses in the dialogue
- a word-processing system that can listen to an individual talk and produce a printed copy
- a program that allows individuals with visual impairments to use more sophisticated computers by causing the computer to act as an interpreter that reads onscreen pictures, icons, and menus that portray instructions for using the machines
- an individually controlled, inexpensive adaptive powered mobility device
- a mechanical workstation that allows individuals with physical disabilities to perform various types of jobs
- an automated microwave oven that uses a laser reader to link a bar code to cooking time
- a bicycle that moves forward when the rider pedals backward
- talking thermometers and tape measures, and a braille monopoly set
- dual and multitrack audio for communicating simultaneously in two or more languages

In 1988, Congress enacted the Technology-Related Assistance for Individuals with Disabilities Act (PL 100-407), which is designed to help states develop and enact programs of technology-related assistance to individuals with disabilities. Many state education departments have established programs to link individuals with the devices they need. Academic Software, Inc. has developed the Adaptive Device Locator System, which is a microcomputer resource for elderly individuals, individuals with disabilities, and professionals searching for information about aids and devices related to Existence, Communication, In-Situ Motion, Travel, Rehabilitation, and Environmental Adaptation. Individuals can obtain more information regarding the Adaptive Device Locator System by contacting Academic Software at 800-842-2357. Additional information concerning adaptive devices can be obtained by contacting IBM's National Support Center for Persons with Disabilities at 800-426-2133 (voice), or 800-284-9482 (TDD); The National Special Education

Alliance (800-732-3131); or the Center for Special Education Technology (800-873-8255). Turnkey Systems, Inc. (703-536-2310) is compiling information concerning the use of adaptive technology to assist individuals from linguistically diverse backgrounds.

Advocacy Groups

The rise of organizations called *advocacy groups* for parents and professionals is also contributing to the mainstreaming movement. Parental groups provide a voice for parents and others interested in finding and developing services for individuals with disabilities. In addition to promoting public awareness of issues related to individuals with disabilities, these organizations lobby state and federal legislators and bring litigation on behalf of individuals with disabilities. Similarly, professional organizations, such as the Council for Exceptional Children, unite professionals and advocate for improving services to individuals with disabilities. As public awareness heightens and the needs of individuals with disabilities are recognized, the number of parental, professional and advocacy groups is increasing. A listing of some of these groups is presented in the Appendix.

In addition to advances in medical technology, various economic, political, and environmental factors have led to an increase in the number of Americans with disabilities; it is estimated that 43 million Americans have disabilities. Wars, for example, have led to an increase in the number of individuals with disabilities and have had the collateral effect of advancing the disability rights movement. Since one out of six Americans is disabled, most Americans have had direct contact with a friend or a relative who has a disability. These experiences have shaped the American public's views on mainstreaming and have influenced public policy makers. For example, former Senator Lowell Weicker (R, Connecticut) and Senator Tom Harkin (D, Iowa), who have relatives with disabilities, were instrumental in congressional enactment of federal mandates for early intervention services (PL 99-457) and the Americans with Disabilities Act, respectively.

Think About It

Think of a relative, friend or neighbor who has a disability. How has knowing that individual affected your views of individuals with disabilities? How has that individual affected you and others in your family and neighborhood?

Litigation

The movement toward mainstreaming has also been aided by legislation and litigation supporting the need for a free appropriate public education for students with disabilities in the least restrictive environment (Cartwright, Cartwright, & Ward, 1985). The precedent for much of the special education-related litigation and legislation was established by *Brown v. Topeka Board*

"Separate educational facilities are inherently unequal. This inherent inequality stems from the stigma created by purposeful segregation which generates a feeling of inferiority that may affect their hearts and minds in a way unlikely ever to be undone."

—*Earl Warren, Chief Justice of the Supreme Court*

of Education (1954) (Gearheart, Weishahn, & Gearheart, 1988). The decision in this landmark case determined that segregating students in schools based on race, even if other educational variables appear to be equal, is unconstitutional (Zirkel, 1978). This refutation of the doctrine of "separate but equal" served as the underlying argument in suits brought by parents to insure that their children with disabilities received a free appropriate public education.

In *Lau v. Nichols* (1974), the U.S. Supreme Court extended the concept of equal educational opportunity to include special language programs for students who speak languages other than English. In this case, the Court opined "that there was no equality of treatment merely by providing students with the same facilities, textbooks, teachers, and curriculum, for students who do not understand English are effectively foreclosed from any meaningful education." The Lau decision coupled with PL 94-142 also provided a mandate for the delivery of bilingual special education services. The Supreme Court's decision in *Lau v. Nichols* set the precedent for other federal and state legislation and litigation relating to meeting the educational needs of students who speak languages other than English (Baca & Cervantes, 1989).

Think About It

Recently, there has been a growing concern about the failure of mainstream schools to educate African American, Latino American, and Native American students effectively. For example, African American males (a) face a 1 in 10 chance of being murdered; (b) have high rates of dropping out and unemployment; (c) have seen their life expectancy decrease to under 65 years of age; (d) make up 25 percent of AIDS cases; (e) often reside in poverty; (f) account for 46 percent of the inmates in correctional facilities and are incarcerated in the United States at a rate four times higher than in South Africa; and (g) have high rates of suspensions and expulsions from school (Karp, 1991). In light of these statistics, several urban school districts have proposed separate schools to address the unique academic, emotional, and social needs of African American male students. These schools would offer a curriculum focusing on African American issues and the introduction of African American role models.

Do you think it is appropriate to separate students by gender or race? What are the implications of this school alternative for American schools? For students with disabilities?

In *Pennsylvania Association for Retarded Children (PARC) v. Commonwealth of Pennsylvania* (1972), PARC represented children with mental retardation. The suit questioned provisions of the Pennsylvania School Code that could be used to exclude students with mental retardation from school and another provision that established segregated education and training to these children. In a consent agreement approved by the court, the Commonwealth of Pennsylvania agreed that all students with mental retardation had a

"See, if I wouldn't have challenged them, there would be nothing. I was so disgusted; I almost had a nervous breakdown. But the lady from PARC said, 'Don't give up. When J gets on that bus and goes to that class, you're opening the door for kids like J in the whole state.'"
—A parent involved in the PARC case.

right to a free public education. The agreement further stated that placement in a regular public school classroom is preferable to more segregated placements and that parents had a right to be informed of any changes in their children's educational program.

While the PARC case resulted in a consent-agreement between two parties, *Mills v. Board of Education of the District of Columbia* (1972) was decided by a judge based on constitutional grounds. The Mills case extended the right to a free public education to all students with disabilities.

Several cases dealing with the education of students from diverse cultural and linguistic backgrounds have also had an impact on the mainstreaming movement. In *Meyer v. Nebraska* (1923), the Supreme Court ruled against statewide mandates banning instruction in non-English languages (Fradd & Vega, 1987). In *Hobson v. Hansen* (1967), it was ruled that the practice of tracking was unconstitutional and should be abolished as it served to segregate students based on race and/or economic status. *Lora vs. Board of Education of the City of New York* (1975) was a class-action suit involving African American and Mexican American students who had been placed in segregated day schools for students with emotional disturbance. The court ruled that these day schools were discriminatory and segregated students. The court also mandated that schools follow due process procedures in assessing and placing students (Meier, 1992). Other cases (*Diana v. State Board of Education* [1970], *Larry P. v. Riles* [1979]) dealing with nondiscriminatory testing changed evaluation procedures used to place students from diverse cultural and linguistic backgrounds in special education programs. These cases are reviewed in Chapter 11.

Several important cases have dealt with the implementation of PL 94-142. In *Irving Independent School District v. Tatro* (1984), the Supreme Court determined that catheterization was a related service because it enabled a student to benefit from special education. The Tatro decision also established the guideline that the decision of whether a medical service is related service is dependent on who provides the service rather than the service itself (Vitello, 1986). In *Board of Education vs. Rowley* (1982), the Supreme Court ruled that the intent of Congress in PL 94-142 was to provide students with disabilities with "reasonable opportunities to learn, but not assuring them an opportunity to reach their maximum potential" (Turnbull, 1986, p. 349).

Legislation

PL 93-112: Vocational Rehabilitation Act

The cases discussed above provided a background that helped shape several Congressional acts, the primary focus which was to integrate individuals with disabilities into the mainstream of society. In 1973, Congress passed the Vocational Rehabilitation Act (PL 93-112), which serves as a civil rights law for individuals with disabilities. Section 504 of this legislation forbids discrimination against individuals with disabilities in education, employment, housing, and access to public programs and facilities, and requires institutions to make architectural modifications that increase the physical accessibility of their buildings. Section 504 also provides all students with a right to have access to the regular education curriculum, extracurricular activities in their local schools, and instructional and curriculum adaptations.

PL 94-142: Education for All Handicapped Children Act

Two years later, Congress passed the Education for All Handicapped Children Act of 1975 (PL 94-142). PL 94-142 mandates that educational services be provided to all students with disabilities, and broadly identifies those services.

1. All students with disabilities, regardless of the nature and severity of their disability, must be provided with a free appropriate public education.
2. Each student with a disability will have an Individualized Educational Plan (IEP) which is based on and tailored to address the child's unique learning needs.
3. Students with disabilities will be educated in the least restrictive environment with their peers who are not disabled to the maximum extent appropriate.
4. Students with disabilities must have access to all areas of school participation.
5. Students with disabilities and their families are guaranteed rights with respect to nondiscriminatory testing, confidentiality, and due process.

One of the salient outcomes of PL 94-142 for students who speak languages other than English is the requirement that they be assessed in their native language or preferred mode of communication. Additionally, parents of these children must be informed, in their native language or preferred mode of communication, about their child's current level of functioning, instructional needs, and the implications of the participation in a special education program (Fradd, 1992).

PL 99-457: Education for All Handicapped Children Act Amendments of 1986

In 1986, Congress passed PL 99-457, which amended PL 94-142. PL 99-457 extends many of the rights and safeguards of PL 94-142 to children with disabilities aged birth to 5 years. PL 99-457 encourages the delivery of early intervention services and special assistance to students who are likely to experience educational failure without labeling them as having a disability (Fradd, 1992). PL 99-457 includes provisions for establishing a child-find system to identify eligible infants, toddlers, and preschoolers; conducting public awareness activities; training personnel; delivering related services; and developing an Individualized Family Service Plan (IFSP) for each child.

The IFSP, developed by a multidisciplinary team and the child's parents, details the early intervention services necessary to meet the developmental needs of eligible children. Eligible services, provided at no cost to families unless federal or state law requires payments by parents, include special education class placement, speech/language therapy, occupational and physical therapy, family training and counseling, service coordination, and some medical and health services. As a result, the IFSP must include the following information:

- a statement of the child's present levels of development
- a family-centered assessment that identifies the resources, priorities, and concerns of the family
- a statement of the anticipated outcomes for the child and family to be achieved by the program
- a listing of the criteria, techniques, and timelines for evaluating progress
- a statement of the early education services and their intensity and frequency that will be delivered in order to meet the child's and family's unique needs
- a statement of the natural environments where the early intervention services will be delivered
- the anticipated dates for initiating services and their duration
- the name of the individual who will serve as the service coordinator to supervise the implementation of the program
- procedures for promoting the transition from early intervention into preschool

The IFSP must be evaluated annually, and reviewed every six months or more often if necessary.

PL 101-476: Individuals with Disabilities Education Act

In 1990, PL 101-476 changed the title of PL 94-142 from the Education for All Handicapped Children Act to the Individuals with Disabilities Education Act (IDEA). The act was renamed to reflect "individuals first" language. Additionally, all references to the term *handicapped* are replaced by the term *disabilities.* IDEA continues the basic provisions outlined in PL 94-142, and initiated several other changes.

- The categories of children with disabilities were expanded to include autism and brain injury. While a separate category was not created for Attention Deficit Disorder, additional data on this condition is to be collected by the Department of Education.
- IEPs must include a statement of the needed transition services for students beginning no later than age 16 and annually thereafter. When appropriate for an individual student, the needed transition services should be specified for students beginning at age 14 or younger. *Transition services* are defined as "a coordinated set of activities for a student, designed within an outcome-oriented process, which promotes movement from school to postschool activities including postsecondary education, vocational training, integrated employment, continuing and adult education, adult services, independent living or community participation."
- Related services were expanded to include rehabilitation counseling and social work services.

- Early intervention programs should be implemented for children exposed to maternal substance abuse.
- Commitment to addressing the needs of linguistically and ethnically diverse youth with disabilities was increased.
- States can be sued by individuals if they violate the provisions of the IDEA.
- Each state should establish centers to offer parents training and materials on special education.

PL 101-336: Americans With Disabilities Act

In 1990, Congress enacted PL 101-336, the Americans with Disabilities Act (ADA), which has been referred to as a civil rights bill and the Emancipation Proclamation for individuals with disabilities. The ADA recognizes that individuals with disabilities are an oppressed group and equates denying an individual with a disability access to the social and economic mainstream of society with denying social and economic access to other groups based on their race, religion, or gender (Rasky, 1989). The ADA expands the rights of individuals with disabilities outlined in Section 504 of the Vocational Rehabilitation Act of 1973 by making the reasonable accommodations provision applicable to public schools, and addressing discrimination in programs not receiving federal funds (Miles, Russo, & Gordon, 1991). In addition to covering all individuals whose physical or mental impairments substantially limit one or more major life activities, the ADA also covers individuals with AIDS and those infected with HIV. The ADA addresses discrimination in the public and private sector. Figure 1.6 summarizes the provisions of the ADA.

FIGURE 1.6
Provisions of the Americans with Disabilities Act

- Forbids employers, employment agencies, labor organizations, or joint labor-management committees from discriminating against individuals with disabilities, and mandates that they make "reasonable accommodations" to the individual with a disability unless the accommodation would present an undue hardship to the business.
- Prohibits a state or local government from discriminating against a qualified person with a disability.
- Mandates specific requirements for access to public transportation.
- Forbids public facilities such as restaurants, hotels, shopping centers, and private transportation companies from discriminating in terms of access to goods, services, facilities, privileges, advantages, and accommodations.
- Mandates the creation of interstate and intrastate telephone relay systems for individuals with hearing impairments.
- Permits individuals to sue states in federal courts to enforce its provisions.
- Allows judges and courts to award attorney fees to provide individuals who are successful in their lawsuits to enforce the law.
- Mandates that the Architectural and Transportation Barriers Compliance Board establish guidelines for accessibility.

Source: Beach Center on Family and Disability (1989).

PL 90-247: Bilingual Education Act

To provide all children with an equal educational opportunity, Congress enacted the Bilingual Education Act in 1968. This act, also referred to as Title VII of the Elementary and Secondary Education Act, established guidelines and funding to encourage school districts to employ bilingual education practices, techniques, and methods to meet the educational needs of students who speak languages other than English. Since its inception in 1968, the Bilingual Education Act has been amended numerous times to extend the population served under the Act, establish new program alternatives, and place a greater emphasis on the learning of English (Baca & Cervantes, 1989).

PL 101-392: Carl Perkins Vocational and Applied Technology Education Act

While the federal commitment to vocational education services for individuals with disabilities and students from low socioeconomic backgrounds was established through the Vocational Education Amendments of 1968 (PL 90-576) and 1976 (PL 94-482), the Carl D. Perkins Vocational and Technical Education Act of 1984 (PL 98-524) encouraged educators to include vocational services in students' IEPs and deliver these services in mainstreamed settings (Berkell & Brown, 1989). In 1990, PL 98-524 was amended and renamed the Carl D. Perkins Vocational and Applied Technology Education Act of 1990 (PL 101-392). The 1990 Perkins amendment seeks to increase the participation of special populations in vocational programs. These special populations include individuals with disabilities, individuals from low socioeconomic backgrounds, individuals who speak English as a second language, migrants, and dropouts (Coyle-Williams, 1991).

Efficacy Studies

The reports of efficacy studies examining the value of special education services in the mid to late 1960s also provided an impetus for mainstreaming (Dunn, 1968; Goldstein, Moss, & Jordan, 1965). In a classic review, Dunn (1968) argued that special education classes for students with mild disabilities were unjustifiable in that they served as a form of homogeneous grouping and tracking. He supported this argument by citing efficacy studies that showed that students labeled as mildly disabled "made as much or more progress in the regular grades as they do in special classes" (p. 8), as well as studies that showed that labeling has a negative impact on self-concept and teacher expectations for success in school. He also noted that a disproportionate number of black students were placed in self-contained classes for the mentally retarded and that these classes served the purpose of segregating black students from white students.

Goldstein, Moss, and Jordan (1965) examined the effectiveness of carefully designed "ideal" special education and regular education placements on student performance. They found no differences between the two placements on arithmetic performance, and a slight difference on reading performance in favor of regular class placement. These findings led the researchers to the conclusion that regular class placements are a better educational alternative for students with mild disabilities.

However, several researchers have raised questions about the conclusions of efficacy studies (Gottlieb, Alter, & Gottlieb, 1983; Hallahan, Keller, McKinney, Lloyd, & Bryan, 1988; Tindal, 1985). They note that many efficacy studies have methodological flaws and (a) often failed to assign students to different classes randomly; (b) are dated in that they compared settings that used methods that are no longer comparable to current practices used in regular and special education settings today; (c) focused on physical placements rather than educational practices within these settings; and (d) did not support regular education placements over special education placements for students with mild disabilities (Hocutt, Martin, & McKinney, 1991).

Because schools are designed, in part, to prepare students to live independently and obtain meaningful employment, studies on the effectiveness of special education programs also have examined the employment rates of students with disabilities. Berkell (1991) noted that approximately 75 percent of the students with disabilities who leave schools each year are unemployed or underemployed. Most of those who found employment often work at part-time positions that pay at or below the minimum wage (Hasazi, Gordon, & Roe, 1985). The unemployment rate tends to be disproportionately high for females with disabilities (Hasazi, Johnson, Hasazi, Gordon, & Hull, 1989), individuals with severe disabilities (Kiernan, Thurlow, Lew, & Larson/Bruininks, 1988), and individuals from linguistically and culturally diverse backgrounds (William T. Grant Foundation, 1988).

SOCIETAL CHANGES

American society continues to undergo major metamorphoses. Society has been reshaped as a result of such factors as demographic shifts, economic conditions, changes in the structure of families, and increases in substance abuse. As a reflection of society, schools have been called upon to respond to these societal changes and meet the needs of increasingly diverse groups of students who challenge the existing school structure to change.

Factors such as learning English, being poor, homelessness, abusing drugs, prenatal exposure to drugs and AIDS, and being victims of abuse, neglect, or discrimination increase the likelihood that students may experience difficulties in school, be referred for and placed in special education, and drop out of school. For students with identified disabilities, these conditions often interact with the disability to place students in double jeopardy within the educational system. The movement toward mainstreaming means that increasing numbers of these students will be educated in regular education settings, and teachers must be trained and willing to create inclusive classrooms that address their diverse educational needs.

Demographic Shifts

There have been dramatic changes in the makeup of the American population, with the United States becoming a more linguistically and culturally diverse country.* Since 1980, the U.S. population has grown at a rate of approximately 9 percent. This growth has been characterized by a significant increase in the percentage of Asian and Pacific Islander (108%), Hispanic (53%), and Native American (38%) populations in the United States. During this time, the white and black groups in America grew at a rate of 6 and 13 percent, respectively.

While many of these groups share common traits, variety characterizes the American population. For instance, there are more than 300 independent Native American groups that do not share the same beliefs, customs, traditions, or languages. Similarly, whereas some Asian and Pacific Islander groups may hold some common beliefs, they come from more than 25 different countries that possess unique languages, religions, and customs. While Hispanic groups do speak different dialects of a common language, each group's identity is based on a separate set of beliefs, traditions, history, and social institutions.

Demographic data indicate that by the year 2000 students who were once referred to as minority students will make up the majority of students in many states.

Population projections suggest that school age children of color and native speakers of languages other than English will comprise 30 percent of the students in the United States in the year 2000, and 38 percent in 2020 (U.S. Bureau of the Census, 1987). Currently, these students either make up or approach the majority of students in many urban school districts in the states of California, Texas, Florida, and New York (Irvine, 1991). Because schools are structured to serve students who speak standard English and have cultural perspectives that allow them to feel comfortable in schools and classrooms, linguistically and culturally diverse students are likely to experience conflicts because schools are not sensitive to their culture, language, family background, and learning styles (Irvine, 1991).

Birthrates

A major factor in the demographic shifts in the United States is the changing birthrates of families who have resided in the United States for generations (Fradd, 1992). While the fertility rates for Americans from culturally and linguistically diverse backgrounds has not increased, the fertility rates for white Americans has decreased, resulting in a greater percentage of children from diverse, nonwhite backgrounds in the United States (Aramburo, 1989). Income levels also appear to affect fertility rates, with lower income women having higher fertility rates than middle and high income women (Williams, 1992).

Immigration

Another significant factor in the demographic changes in the population of the United States and the makeup of American schools has been immigration.

---

*For purposes of this text, *linguistically and culturally diverse* students are defined as those whose native or primary language is not English, and/or who are not native members of the Euro-Caucasian culture base currently dominant in the United States.

Census data indicate that during the last decade approximately 8.6 million people entered the United States (Barringer, 1992). This immigration, a result of a variety of global political, social, and economic factors, has contributed to demographic shifts in the United States. Many of these new immigrants are refugees who left their countries to escape political, religious, economic, or racial repression (Nahme Huang, 1989). In order to arrive in their new country, many refugees endured a long, arduous, and life-threatening journey characterized by malnutrition, disease, torture, and fear. Many refugees were forced to reside in overcrowded, makeshift, unsanitary, disease-ridden camps where food, clothes, and medical care were scarce (Borton, 1984). While some immigrants are well educated and held middle-class jobs, others come from rural areas and have limited education and employment skills. As new arrivals to America, they face an adjustment in learning a new language and culture and encounter negative and hostile reactions as they compete with others for jobs, housing, and governmental and community services.

Loescher and Scanlan (1986) estimate that there are 10 to 15 million refugees worldwide. Children make up approximately 50 percent of the refugee population (Nahme Huang, 1989). Many young refugees must cope with a type of post-traumatic stress disorder as a result of witnessing atrocities and torture, experiencing losses, and attempting to adjust to a new society (Carlin & Sokoloff, 1985). In school, they often encounter racial tension and rejection from peers that takes the form of physical altercations (fights, robberies, and so on), mimicking, and verbal harassment (Nahme Huang, 1989). Refugee youth also may fear individuals of authority such as the principal because the child or a family member has undocumented status (Harris, 1991; Vasquez, 1988). As a result, these youth may be reluctant to make friends with others, to seek assistance from and interact with professionals, to attempt to gain recognition or excel in programs, or to draw attention to themselves.

A particularly vulnerable group of refugees is those youth who migrated without their families. Nahme Huang (1989) and Nidorf (1985) noted that unaccompanied minors may experience depression, restlessness, attention and concentration difficulties, shame, despair, grief, survivor guilt, and alienation. These feelings make unaccompanied minors vulnerable to attempting suicide, engaging in maladaptive behaviors, joining youth gangs and dropping out of school.

Educational Rights of Immigrant Students. Based on the Supreme Court decision in *Plyler v. Doe* (1982), all undocumented students have the same rights as U.S. citizens to attend public schools. School personnel cannot take actions or establish policies that deny students access to public schools and have no legal obligation to implement laws regarding immigration. In delivering services to these students, schools cannot deny students from attending school based on their undocumented status, nor can they treat undocumented students in a different way when identifying their residency. School personnel may not engage in activities that may intimidate or threaten students and their families based on their immigration status, such as allowing Immigration and Naturalization Service (INS) on or near the school or requiring students or their families to identify their immigration status. They may not inquire about the immigration status of students or their families; ask students to provide schools with social security numbers which may indicate their immigration status; or inform outside agencies about the immigration status information contained in a student's school file without parental permission (National Coalition of Advocates for Students, *New Voices,* Spring 1991).

The National Coalition of Advocates for Students (1989) offers guidelines that teachers and administrators can follow to protect the legal rights of immigrant students and their families.

Racial Discrimination

Students from specific racial and linguistic backgrounds have historically been victims of racial discrimination in society and schools (Comer, 1989; Ogbu, 1978). While this discrimination is overtly manifested in the growing number of verbal and physical indicators of racial intolerance, it is more subtly seen in societal institutions such as schools. Kozol (1991) compared schools that serve students who are poor and predominantly African American and Hispanic with schools that serve students who are wealthy and predominantly white. In addition to almost complete segregation, he found severe inequalities in terms of funding, preschool opportunities, class sizes, physical facilities, resources, instructional materials and textbooks, teachers, technology, and expectations concerning student performance. He concluded that these inequalities reveal that economically poor students and students from nondominant groups are seen as inferior, and unworthy of being challenged and of attending adequately funded schools. This perceived inferiority provides the basis for differential treatment in the classroom based on race.

Despite the research findings that consistently and repeatedly indicate that tracking students has deleterious effects, poor and racially and linguistically diverse students are disproportionately placed in low-ability classes and therefore resegregated into two separate groups within the same school (Jones, Van Fossen, & Spade, 1987; Welsh, 1986). Once placed in lower track classes, students often encounter less effective and less relevant instruction, acquire negative self-concepts, develop antisocial behavior, and learn to react to teachers and peers with hostility (Irvine, 1990). They also experience lowered teacher expectations, which frequently impacts negatively on student academic performance, self-esteem, classroom behavior and interactions, educational and career goals, and motivation (Baron, Tom & Cooper, 1985; Brophy and Good, 1974).

Through subtle school-based experiences, students internalize perceptions of themselves that educators and other members of society hold. Positive perceptions about an individual's race and identity can promote increased self-esteem and readiness for success in school, whereas negative attitudes about race can create self-doubt and limit a student's potential for success in school (Comer & Poussant, 1975). Unfortunately, school curricula, teacher behaviors, assessment instruments, instructional materials and textbooks, parent involvement procedures, and peer relationships tend to be designed to address only the academic and socialization needs of students from the dominant culture whose parents have sufficient economic resources. As a result, economically poor students and students from nondominant groups suffer both covert and overt discrimination in schools that can cause underachievement and lead to eventual placement in special education classes (Cummins, 1989; Ogbu & Matute-Bianchi, 1986). Cummins (1989) summarizes the effects of discrimination on student performance as follows:

> When research results regarding minority student underachievement are examined internationally, a striking pattern emerges. The groups that currently perform poorly at school have historically been discriminated against and regarded as inherently inferior by the dominant group. For example, in the United States, Black, Hispanic, and Native American students have all experienced subjugation by the dominant group (see Ogbu, 1978). Several investigators have argued that the educational underachievement of these groups is, in part, a function of the fact that schools have traditionally reinforced the ambivalence and insecurity that many minority students tend to feel with regard to their own cultural identity (Cummins, 1986; Ogbu & Matute-Bianchi, 1986). The implication of this analysis is that prevention of academic difficulties among minority students, and genuine remediation, requires that educators adopt role definitions that challenge rather than reflect the values of the wider society. (p. 111)

Gender Bias

Researchers also have been exploring differences in the ways schools respond to female and male students. These findings indicate that schools tend to treat females differently from males and inadvertently reinforce stereotypic views of females in terms of behavior, personality, aspirations, and achievement, which may have a negative impact on the academic and social development of girls (Astin, 1977; Sadker & Sadker, 1990). Whereas boys and girls generally enter school with equal abilities and self-concepts, females usually lag behind their male counterparts in both areas when they graduate from high school. Researchers examining gender bias in predominantly white middle-class classrooms have found that many elementary and secondary classrooms are structured inequitably.

- Boys receive more active attention from teachers than do girls.
- Boys receive more detailed directions from teachers than do girls.
- Boys are asked to respond more than are girls.
- Boys talk more and are listened to more carefully in class discussions than are girls.
- Boys are interrupted when speaking less than are girls.
- Boys are asked more higher-level questions than are girls.
- Boys are encouraged to give opinions and take intellectual risks more than are girls.
- Boys receive more feedback from teachers than do girls.
- Boys are more likely to be acknowledged by teachers for their academic accomplishments than are girls, who are more likely to be acknowledged for their looks, their demeanor, and the neatness of their work.

- Boys are more likely to believe that their poor academic performance is due to lack of effort and can be corrected by greater effort than are girls, who tend to believe that their poor performance is an indication of their ability (Dweck, Davidson, Nelson, & Enna, 1978; Sadker & Sadker, 1985; Safilios-Rothschild, 1979; Sternglanz & Lyberger-Ficek, 1977).

While these studies have been conducted in predominantly white, middle-class classrooms, gender and race interact, making the experiences of black and Hispanic girls even more susceptible to bias in society and schools (Bell, 1991; Irvine, 1990).

There also appears to be a "self-esteem gap" in the ways society and schools respond to girls and boys. Whereas girls are taught by society to base their self-esteem on physical appearance and popularity, boys are encouraged to gain self-esteem through academic and athletic performance. Girls, particularly in adolescence, may be vulnerable to the negative consequences of peer pressure that encourages social success at the expense of academic performance. This fear of rejection and of being "smart" but not "popular" can result in pressure on female students to underachieve, to attempt to hide their success, to not enroll in advanced and challenging courses, and to select careers that are not commensurate with their skill levels (Bell, 1991; Fox, 1977). Frequently, when females do achieve at high levels or show an interest in a math or science career, they are "counseled" by advisors who ask questions of them that they would not address to males: "How will you handle your family if you're a doctor?" (Smithson, 1990, p. 2). Because girls generally don't act out and attract as much attention as boys, their needs are often overlooked and therefore programs to address these needs are not funded. Biased tests and textbooks also hinder the school performance and self-esteem of female students.

Hare (1985) reported that black males use social rather than academic experiences as the basis for high self-esteem.

Think About It

A disproportionate number of students from culturally and linguistically diverse backgrounds are referred to and placed in special education classes. Is this an example of discrimination in schools?

A disproportionate number of male students are in special education classes. Is this an example of gender discrimination in schools?

Gay and Lesbian Youth

Other learners who are targets of discrimination are gay and lesbian youth. While it is difficult to identify the number of homosexual youth in our nation's schools, it is estimated that approximately 10 percent of the adult population is gay and lesbian as well as hundreds of thousands of students in schools (McIntyre, 1992). These students face discrimination in schools and society that often takes the form of ridicule or a bias-related attack; it is estimated that 40 percent of homosexual youth have been victims of violent attacks (Hetrick & Martin, 1987). As a result, many gay and lesbian youth

IDEAS FOR IMPLEMENTATION

As teachers, you can start to eliminate gender bias and racial discrimination in your classrooms by enacting the following suggestions:

- Examine how you react to female and male students as well as students from the dominant and nondominant culture in terms of distribution of questions, types of questions, feedback, and opportunities to respond.
- Create a classroom environment that shows respect for all students.
- Refrain from grouping students based on gender and race such as by forming separate lines, separate teams, and separate academic learning groups.
- Assign students of both sexes and all races to class and school jobs on a rotating basis.
- Employ textbooks and materials that include the contributions of both sexes and all races.
- Use gender/race-inclusive and gender-neutral language.
- Provide male and female students with same-sex and -race role models who represent a continuum of perspectives and professions.
- Encourage students to explore a variety of career alternatives.
- Decorate the classroom with pictures of males and females from all races performing a variety of activities.
- Use cooperative learning groups and cross-sex and cross-race seating arrangements.
- Encourage and teach students to examine and discuss books, stories, movies, and other materials in terms of stereotypes and across race and gender perspectives.
- Provide students with the opportunity to talk in same-sex and same-race groups about the pressures that they face.
- Identify and eliminate gender and racial bias in the curriculum and standardized tests.
- Refrain from comparing students across gender and racial variables.
- Encourage female and male students of all races to take risks, make decisions, and seek challenges.
- Affirm effort and attributes that contribute to success in all students.

attempt to hide their sexual orientation from others (Fine, 1988), while others are disciplined and referred for placement in special education programs for students with emotional and behavioral disorders (McIntyre, 1992). They also face isolation, feelings of alienation, depression, self-hatred, and confusion about their sexual identity (Hetrick & Martin, 1987), which places them at greater risk for suicide and substance abuse problems (Flax, 1990). Data indicate gay and lesbian youths are involved in more than one-third of suicide attempts (Ramafedi, 1987) and deaths by suicide (Flax, 1990). Gay and lesbian youth also frequently encounter rejection and abuse from their families, which results in high rates of homelessness among homosexual youth (Tracy, 1990). In urban areas, it is estimated that between 30 to 50 percent of the homeless youth are homosexuals who have been thrown out on the streets by their families because they are gay (Green, 1991).

Economic Changes

Poor children comprise 20% of the children younger than 18 in the United States (Council for Exceptional Children, 1991).

The United States is also experiencing dramatic economic changes characterized by growing disparity between the wealthy and the poor, the old and young, and a shrinking middle class. These economic changes have had a profound effect on children. From 1982 to 1989, the number of children living in poverty increased by 2.1 million. If current trends go unabated, 25 percent of the children in the United States will be poor by the year 2000 (Children's Defense Fund, 1989).

Poverty affects all aspects of a child's life. The mothers of poor children often do not receive early prenatal care and it is estimated that by the year 2000, 20 percent of the births in the United States will be to mothers who have not had any prenatal care. This lack of prenatal care has contributed to the United States being ranked 23rd in terms of infant mortality among industrialized countries. From birth through adolescence, poor children also are more likely to suffer from illnesses and diseases and less likely to receive appropriate medical care. Poor children often reside in substandard housing; are victims of hunger, lead poisoning, child abuse, and neglect; usually enter school with fewer skills than their peers; and often attend schools that have limited funds. As a result, they are more likely to experience school failures, to be recommended and placed in remedial and special education programs, and to drop out than their middle- and upper-income peers.

While the majority of poor children in America are white, African American, Hispanic American, Native American, and Asian American children are more likely to live in poverty than are their white counterparts. For example, whereas approximately 42 percent of the African American and 35 percent of the Latino youths age 6 to 17 live in poverty, the poverty rate among their white counterparts is estimated at 14 percent (Children's Defense Fund, 1990). When families are both poor and members of nondominant linguistic and ethnic groups, the deleterious effects of poverty tend to be more pronounced and long lasting (Edelman, 1987).

Rural Poverty

The largest segment of poor Americans reside in rural areas, with as many as 60 percent of the the students whose needs challenge schools residing in rural and suburban settings (Council for Exceptional Children, 1991; National School Boards Association, 1989). Residents of rural areas face a variety of problems as they seek human services. These problems include limited availability and access to services, minimal resources, limited or no transportation, and failure to use existing services and agencies (Guy, 1991). The availability of services in rural areas also is affected by the population density and the topography of the area (Helge, 1987a). These same factors often result in school systems that are characterized by personnel and transportation problems, social and professional isolation, lack of supportive services and ancillary programs, poor student motivation, and funding problems and inequities (Helge, 1984). To overcome some of these problems, some rural areas employ distance learning programs, which allow them to beam educational programs to rural sites via satellite (Teltsch, 1991).

Think About It

Teaching in a rural area presents many unique professional and personal challenges. Some questions to consider when thinking about working in a rural area follow.

Could you cope with the remoteness to services and other resources?

Are you trained as a generalist who can deliver a variety of resources without the availability of specialists?

Could you cope with the remoteness from personal enrichment and stress reduction activities?

Do you feel comfortable working with rural families and communities?

Do you have information about rural subcultures?

Can you adapt to personal and professional transportation problems?

Are you trained to deal with transient populations?

Have you lived in a rural area before?

What personal and professional factors are important to you and how will they guide your selection of a geographic location for your job?

Source: L. W. Marrs, *Exceptional Children* (1984).

Children of Migrant Workers

"The sacks were getting heavier for Graciel. She had noticed for some time that it was becoming more difficult for her to lift them into the truck. Of all the field work she had done, the potato crop was her least favorite. It was one of the heavier crops. It had been an exceptionally hard summer in Idaho. But soon they would be heading home to the Texas Rio Grande Valley. A clinic doctor pinpointed her problem—myasthenia gravis. No one in her family had ever heard of it. She learned quickly that, with this crippling disease, she would not be able to work in the fields or anywhere else without additional training or education" (Sparks, 1991, p. 16).

One group of students who reside in rural areas are the children of migrant workers. Several factors associated with the migrant lifestyle increase the likelihood that migrant students may experience problems in school. Frequent mobility, irregular school attendance, and language and cultural differences seriously hinder access to and continuity of appropriate school and community services (Hunter, 1982). Poor sanitation in the fields and work camp facilities, overcrowded substandard housing and poor diets, exposure to pesticides and other hazards of agricultural work (in particular to pregnant women and young children), limited health care, and low wages make migrant youth particularly vulnerable for poor performance in schools.

The racial and ethnic distributions of migrant students is quite diverse. Of the total number of migrant students, 69 percent are Hispanic, 13 percent are white, 6 percent are African American, 3 percent are Asian/Pacific Islander and 1 percent are Native American or Native Alaskan (Interstate Migrant Education Council, 1987). Data concerning the educational performance of migrant students indicate that they are more likely than their nonmigrant peers to enter school behind the modal grade level; lag six to eighteen months below their expected grade level; fall significantly behind other students in achievement and grade levels by the time they reach third and fourth grade; and are less likely to graduate from school than any other group (Interstate Migrant Education Council, 1987). As they move from location to location, migrant students face isolation and economic, cultural, and social discrimination (Chavkin, 1991).

Many Native Americans reside in remote rural areas.

Native Americans

Many of the more than 1.5 million Native Americans also reside in remote rural areas (Guy, 1991). Because the economic opportunities in these areas are limited, Native Americans have an unemployment rate of 13.2 percent and a poverty rate of 27.5 percent, which are approximately twice the average for all other racial and linguistic groups. Similarly, the vast majority of Native Americans are poorly housed; many reside in homes that lack electricity, plumbing, and windows (Guy, 1991). They lack access to health care, have high rates of malnutrition, and have a life expectancy of 44 years, which lags significantly behind their non-Native American counterparts. These factors have an impact on Native American youth who have the lowest educational attainment of all groups in the the United States and high suicide and substance abuse rates (Guy, 1991).

Urban Poverty

Poverty is also prevalent in our nation's urban areas. Recent census data indicate that approximately 12 percent of the individuals living in the United States reside in urban areas. The Children's Defense Fund reports that over 25 percent of children living in urban areas are living in poverty. Poor urban children often live in crowded, run-down apartments; are victims of lead poisoning; encounter violence, crime, and drug trafficking in their neighborhoods; have limited access to health care; suffer malnutrition; and attend underfunded and dilapidated schools. Poor children in our nation's cities are less likely to receive immunization against diseases such as polio, diptheria, tuberculosis, and tetanus than children in such countries as Grenada, Uganda, North Korea, and Mexico (Lee, 1991).

Homelessness

While homelessness is prevalent in both rural and urban areas, one consequence of the changing economic climate has been the dramatic increase in homelessness in urban areas. Families with children make up the fastest-growing homeless group (Council for Exceptional Children, 1991). In 1989, the National Coalition for the Homeless estimated that there were one million homeless children in the United States (O'Connor, 1989). While federal law guarantees homeless children a right to a free, appropriate public education, approximately 28 percent of the homeless students in this country are not attending school (Pear, 1991). The major barrier preventing many homeless students from attending school is transportation, as they are often required to switch schools as they move from one residence to another. Other barriers include inappropriate class placement, lack of school supplies, poor health, immunization requirements, and failure to produce birth certificates, school files, and other important records and forms (Pear, 1991). As a result many students who are homeless have high absenteeism rates, perform poorly in school, and are often held over (Richardson, 1992). Many homeless youth are runaways who face a life of poverty, drug abuse, and violence on the streets

(O'Connor, 1989). Once homeless, some of these youths become involved in prostitution to earn money, and may become addicted to drugs and infected with HIV. Bassuk and Rubin (1986) found that a significant number of homeless children have impaired gross and fine motor functioning, exhibit emotional and behavior disorders, and suffer a series of ailments that include ear infections, asthma, and anemia. In addition, because they may lack washing facilities and adequate clothing, homeless students also may be the targets of ridicule from peers. Several school districts have developed unique strategies for educating homeless students, including using *mobiles* (motorized classrooms to deliver instruction in community locations), employing teachers and aides to tutor homeless students, and paying for taxis to transport homeless students to and from school (Pear, 1991).

Affluent Children

While there is awareness of the deleterious effects of poverty on children and adults, researchers also are examining the effects of affluence on children. Baldwin (1989) uses the term *Cornucopia Kids* to describe affluent children "who grow up with expectations (based on years of experience in the home) that the good life will always be available for the asking whether they develop personal accountability and achievement motivation or not" (p. 31). Baldwin notes that these children expect the best and the most expensive, demand constant stimulation, have difficulty completing projects, often form superficial relationships, fail to develop a sense of compassion for others, take little responsibility for personal property, mislead others when confronted with a demanding situation, and are present and pleasure oriented. As a result of being insulated from challenge, risk, and consequence, these youth suffer from boredom, low self-esteem, and a lack of motivation and may be susceptible to poor school performance, teenage sex, and substance abuse (Children's Defense Fund, 1988).

Individuals with AIDS

The last 15 years has seen an alarming epidemic of individuals and families affected by Acquired Immune Deficiency Syndrome (AIDS), a viral condition that destroys an individual's defenses against infections. Human immunodeficiency virus (HIV), the virus that causes AIDS, is passed from one person to another through the exchange of infected body fluids (U.S. Department of Education, 1988a). The virus is most often transmitted through unsafe sexual practices, the sharing of needles, and pregnancy. It also is rarely transmitted via transfusions of contaminated blood. A person infected with HIV often takes as long as ten years to be considered among the documented AIDS cases.

The Center for Disease Control estimates that over one million Americans currently have been infected with HIV and that between 50,000 and 100,000 new cases occur each year. Data indicate that a disproportionate number of poor people will contract AIDS. As a result women, children, and people of color are particularly vulnerable. Women with AIDS can transmit the

Data indicate that African American and Hispanic youth make up 52% and 80% of the youth with AIDS ages 5 through 19 and birth to 4, respectively (United States Department of Education, 1988a).

virus to their infants during pregnancy or through breastfeeding. As a result, approximately 2,000–4,000 newborns are infected each year. Adolescents are at risk for contracting AIDS because of the increasing number of teenagers who engage in sexual activity or drug abuse (Bartel & Meddock, 1989).

Researchers are beginning to explore the impact of AIDS on learning and child development. Initial findings indicate that children with AIDS may experience neurological problems, developmental delays, mental retardation, and motor abnormalities (Barnes, 1986; Diamond, 1989; Epstein, Sharer, & Goudsmit, 1988). As they grow older, many of these students may have learning problems. By the middle of the 1990s, it is anticipated that HIV infection may become the leading cause of mental retardation and brain damage in children (Council for Exceptional Children, 1991).

While there have been no known incidents of the transmission of AIDS in school settings, the delivery of educational services to students with AIDS continues to be debated. In *School Board of Nassau County, Florida et al. v. Arline* (1987), the Supreme Court ruled that individuals with infectious diseases including AIDS are covered under Section 504 of the Rehabilitation Act. Similarly, students with AIDS who have special education needs are entitled to a free appropriate education and all the provisions specified in the Individuals with Disabilities Education Act. Thus, students with AIDS should not be excluded from school unless they represent a direct health danger to others (i.e., engage in biting of others, have open sores). Decisions on the educational programs of students with AIDS should be made by a multidisciplinary team based on the student's educational needs and social behaviors as well as the judgments of medical personnel (U.S. Department of Education, 1988a).

Family Changes

"... remember Beaver Cleaver, his brother, Wally, and his best friend, Larry. They lived in a neat frame house in the suburbs, where Beaver's mother, June, cleaned and tended to the house and served her family selflessly and faithfully. Miss Landers, Beaver's teacher, seldom found it necessary to discipline Beaver but when he misbehaved (forgetting his homework or bringing his pet frog to school), Miss Landers quickly solved the problem by visiting Mrs. Cleaver who would assure Miss Landers that Beaver's *father* would speak to him as soon as he returned from work. Some educators have failed to clearly realize that Beaver Cleaver and ... two-parent families are an endangered species" (Jacqueline Jordan Irvine, Emory University).

Significant increases in the number of households with two wage earners have resulted in parents having less time to spend with their children.

During the last two decades, the structure of the American family has undergone compelling changes. High divorce rates, economic pressures necessitating two wage earners, and increases in teenage pregnancies have wrought dramatic changes in the composition, structure, and function of American families. These changes have had a profound effect on children in America.

IDEAS FOR IMPLEMENTATION

Students with AIDS have unique needs that schools should consider when designing educational programs for them.

1. Understand the symptoms of AIDS. The symptoms of AIDS include repeated incidents of fever, night sweats, diarrhea, weight loss, fatigue, swollen lymph glands, and skin rashes, and neurological disorders such as dementia, memory loss, partial paralysis, and loss of coordination.
2. Maintain confidentiality. Provisions of the Individuals with Disabilities Education Act and the Family Educational Rights and Privacy Act necessitate that medical information about individuals with AIDS be kept confidential.
3. Work closely with medical personnel. Because of their condition, students with AIDS may be more susceptible to common childhood infections (e.g., colds, measles, chicken pox) and serious contagious diseases (e.g., hepatitis or tuberculosis), and to contracting various diseases through vaccinations.
4. Work closely with the student's parents. Students with AIDS may be absent frequently. Educators should communicate with parents to minimize these and other disruptions in the student's educational program. Because AIDS has a psychological and economic impact on all the members of the family, teachers also can help families obtain assistance and information. Most states have agencies that assist family members through such services as crisis intervention, counseling, case management, advocacy, medical research information, and community education. Information about AIDS can be obtained by contacting such agencies as the National AIDS Hotline (800-342-7514), Public Health Service National AIDS Hotline (800-342-AIDS), AIDS School Health Education Subfile (800-468-0908), Lambda Legal Defense Fund (212-995-8585), AIDS Action Council (202-547-3101), National AIDS Network (202-347-0390), National Association of People with AIDS (202-429-2856), Association for the Care of Children's Health (301-654-6549), Multicultural AIDS Resources Center (415-861-2142) or a local AIDS project in your area.
5. Encourage the student to participate in all school activities. Limit, only if necessary, the student's participation in sports or other activities.
6. Remember that the social needs of students with AIDS may be greater than their academic needs.
7. Implement a curriculum to teach about AIDS.
8. Establish norms that encourage peer pressure to promote safe sex practices.
9. Learn more about AIDS. Bowd (1987) found that many teachers are not familiar with information about AIDS.

Source: U.S. Department of Education, *AIDS and the Education of Our Children* (1988).

One consequence of the changes in families in America is the growing number of children living in single-parent homes. Data indicate that high percentages of African American (51%), Hispanic (27%), and white (16%) children are residing in single-parent families (Council for Exceptional Children, 1991). Currently, it is estimated that 59 percent of all children will live in a single-parent household before they reach the age of 18. Projections for the future suggest that if current patterns persist, approximately 42 to 70 percent and 86 to 94 percent of the white and black children, respectively, will spend a part of their lives living in a one-parent household (Hofferth, 1987).

Divorce

I was four at the time. I was not aware of the divorce exactly but I was aware that something was out of the ordinary and I didn't like it. Dad was gone. There was a lot of anger and I had to listen to my mom constantly try to get me to agree with her that he was rotten to leave us. I didn't know what to think. I knew that I wanted him to come back. I'd ask her, "Where is Dad?" and she'd say, "Go ask him!" If I saw him, I'd say, "How come you don't live with us anymore?" and he'd say, "Go ask your mother." I couldn't bring my folks back together no matter how hard I tried. I just didn't know how. I thought if I just wished it, that wishing would be enough. (Michael, age 19).

Divorce has contributed to the increase in the number of children living in single-parent homes. It is estimated that 40 percent of American children are likely to experience the divorce of their parents while attending school (Quay & Werry, 1986), as nearly half of the marriages in the United States end in divorce (Hofferth, 1987). Approximately 90 percent of these children will reside with their mothers and have relatively little contact with their fathers (Quay & Werry, 1986). These mothers face many burdens as they assume many of the economic and social roles necessary to sustain the family unit. In the last three decades, there has been a nearly threefold increase in the number of single working mothers, to approximately 6 million, with about one-third of these families having incomes of between $10,000 to $20,000 (Dugger, 1992). As a result, many of these families are struggling to afford housing, health insurance, and child care.

The effects of divorce tend to vary from child to child; however, its effects on boys seem to be more profound and persistent (Hofferth, 1987). Initially, children whose parents have divorced may exhibit anger, anxiety, depression, noncompliance, and poor school performance (Quay & Werry, 1986; McLanahan, 1986). While some researchers note that the negative effects of divorce are short lived (Emery, Hetherington, & Fisher, 1984), others believe that the potential deleterious effects of divorce are long lasting (Wallerstein & Blakeslee, 1989). For some children, divorce may have positive effects—research shows that children raised in two-parent families where the parents are in conflict have more difficulties adjusting than children raised in supportive, conflict-free, single-parent homes (Hetherington, Cox & Cox, 1982).

Teenage Pregnancy

Teenage pregnancy is another factor affecting many American families. The Sex Information and Education Council of the United States estimates that

IDEAS FOR IMPLEMENTATION

Teachers can help students whose parents have divorced by enacting the following suggestions:

- Encourage students to participate in counseling sessions to talk with their peers who also are experiencing divorce. Many school districts have counseling programs (i.e., Banana Splits Program) for students experiencing divorce.
- Communicate with the student's parents concerning the child's social and academic adjustment.
- Acknowledge positive aspects of the student's behavior and academic performance.
- Provide consistent support by being available, accessible, tolerant and nonpunitive.
- Lessen sources of stress in school and making exceptions where possible.
- Use print and audiovisual materials that deal with divorce and single-parent families.
- Involve students in after school programs.

National data indicate that more than 50% and 70% of the girls and boys, respectively, have had sexual relations by the time they reach the age of 16.

over one million teens become pregnant in the United States each year resulting in more than 550,000 births, one of the highest rates of teenage pregnancy in the world. From 1980 to 1988, the percentage of unmarried teenagers having children increased in 40 states.

Census data indicate that two-thirds of the teenage mothers giving birth are not married. Teenage pregnancy has implications for both teen parents and their children. For parents, teenage pregnancy increases the likelihood of dropping out of school and being poor (Adolescent Pregnancy Prevention Clearinghouse, 1990). Almost 50 percent of the females who leave school prior to graduating drop out because of pregnancy. Similarly, teenage fathers are 40 percent less likely to graduate from school than their teenage peers who are not fathers.

Because teens have less access to health care and nutritional counseling, they are more likely to deliver low birthweight babies who have medical problems and developmental delays. These children may exhibit behavior problems and perform poorly in school (Hofferth, 1987). Many school districts and community agencies offer programs to address the needs of teenage parents. These programs often include training and assistance in stimulating their child's development, obtaining medical and nutritional care, being a parent, accessing community services, completing their education, and acquiring the vocational skills to obtain a job.

Latchkey and Unsupervised Children

The new American family also has been shaped by the increasing need for families to have two wage earners. Data indicate that approximately 65 percent of the females working are mothers. Of these working mothers, approximately 60 percent have children under the age of 6. As a result, many women and men are entering the labor force, working irregular hours and seeking appropriate child care. The shortage of economically feasible and adequate child care has resulted in many children spending large amounts of time unsupervised. Estimates of the number of these unsupervised "latchkey" children range from 10 to 12 million (Council for Exceptional Children, 1991). Many school districts and communities are funding afterschool programs to accommodate the needs of these children by providing increased afterschool care, and extending the school day and the instructional year.

Zero-parent Children

As a result of the rise of AIDS, substance abuse, child abuse, and teenage pregnancy, there has been a dramatic increase in the number of zero-parent children, those who do not reside with their parents. These children live with relatives, guardians, or others who assume a parental relationship, or in foster homes. Data indicate that approximately 10 percent of children in the United States resided in a household that was not headed by a parent. Many of these children are shuttled from one household to another, and often exhibit behavior problems in school. They also may be secretive about their home life, have a low self-esteem, and exhibit poor social and academic skills.

Child Abuse

Life crises, unemployment, poverty, marital problems, unwanted pregnancy, lack of support systems, low self-esteem, substance abuse, and prior history of being abused as a child have contributed to a significant increase in child abuse (Heward & Orlansky, 1992; Zirpoli, 1990). Reports of child abuse, which includes negligence, emotional and psychological harm, sexual molestation, and nonaccidental physical injuries, have been growing at an alarming rate (Zirpoli, 1990), with poor children particularly likely to be targets of child abuse and neglect (Wolock & Horowitz, 1984).

The American Association for Protecting Children noted that over two million cases of child abuse had been reported in the United States in 1987, and Harrison and Edwards (1983) suggested that as many as 20 percent of our nation's children may have been victims of some form of child abuse. However, the actual number of child abuse cases may be at least twice the number of reported cases as most incidents of child abuse go unreported (Straus, Gelles, & Steinmetz, 1980). Figure 1.7 shows the principal physical and behavioral indicators of child abuse.

Several factors increase the likelihood that some children will be victims of abuse. These factors include prematurity and dysmaturity, irritability, frequent crying, poor sleeping and eating habits, failure to respond to the expectations or demands of caregivers, and having a disability (Zirpoli, 1990). States have passed laws that require educators and other professionals who work with children to report suspected cases of child abuse. When reporting child abuse, educators should consider the following (see pp. 41 – 42):

FIGURE 1.7
Physical and behavioral signs of child abuse

PHYSICAL ABUSE

Physical Signs

Bruises, welts, and bite marks
Lacerations and abrasions
Burns
Fractures
Head injuries
Parentally induced or fabricated illnesses
Unexplained injuries

Behavioral Signs

Avoidance of interactions with parents and other adults
Anxiety when other children are injured or crying
Aggressiveness, shyness, and mood changes
Frequent attempts to run away from home
Fear of parents or going home
Talking about excessive parental punishment
Blaming self for reactions of parents
Habit disorders such as self-injurious behavior, phobias, and obsessions
Wearing inappropriate clothing to conceal injuries
Low self-image
Suicide attempts

NEGLECT

Physical Signs

Physical and emotional needs
Substance withdrawal symptoms
Delayed physical, cognitive, and emotional development
Attending school hungry
Poor hygiene and inappropriate dress
Speech/language problems
Limited supervision
Medical needs that go unattended for extended periods of time
Frequent absence from school

Behavioral Signs

Begging and stealing
Early arrival to and late departures from school
Frequent tiredness and falling asleep in class
Substance abuse
Thefts and other delinquent acts

FIGURE 1.7
(continued)

Talk about lack of supervision
Frequent attempts to run away from home
Stereotypic behaviors such as sucking, biting, and rocking
Antisocial behavior
Habit disorders such as phobias, obsession, and hypochondria
Extreme changes in behavior
Suicide attempts

SEXUAL ABUSE

Physical Signs

Problems in walking or sitting
Bloody, stained, or ripped clothing
Pain in or scratching of genitalia area
Bruises or bleeding in genitalia area
Evidence of sexual transmitted diseases
Pregnancy
Painful discharges
Frequent urinary infections
Foreign materials in body parts

Behavioral Signs

Avoiding changing clothes for or engaging in activities during physical education class
Engaging in withdrawn, fantasy, or infantile actions
Talk about bizarre, sophisticated, or unusual sexual acts
Difficulty making friends
Delinquent behavior
Running away from home
Forcing other students to engage in sexual acts
Fear of being touched by others
Absent from school frequently
Expressing negative feelings about self
Frequent self-injurious acts and suicide attempts

Source: New York State Department of Education, *The Identification and Reporting of Child Abuse and Maltreatment* (n.d.).

1. Review school policies for reporting.
2. Document and organize the data that leads you to suspect child abuse such as behavioral or physical indicators and observations of parent/child interactions.

3. Talk with other professionals concerning their viewpoints and knowledge of the child and the family.
4. Discuss with your administrator guidelines for making a report, how to deal with parental reactions to the report, and administrative support for individuals who make reports.
5. File the report. A completed report usually includes the following items:

   - names and addresses of the child, parents and/or caregiver
   - data relating to the child such as age, sex, and race
   - nature and extent of the alleged abuse
   - evidence of previous instances of abuse
   - explanations given by the child concerning the injuries
   - name(s) of the individual(s) suspected of the abuse
   - name, address, telephone number, and relation to the child of the individual making the report
   - action taken by the individual making the report including notifying medical personnel, taking x-rays or photographs, detaining the child
   - additional relevant information

6. Establish a group of educators, parents, and community members who can provide emotional support (New York State Education Department, n.d.; Tower, 1987).

In cases of suspected abuse of children from culturally and linguistically diverse backgrounds, educators also need to consider the family's cultural background. In many cultures, medial and spiritual cures may require the marking of the child's body, leaving bruises, and other marks that may be considered as abusive. For example, the custom of rubbing of hot coins on the forehead to alleviate an individual's pain may result in a bruise on the child's body, and therefore be interpreted by professionals as child abuse (National Coalition of Advocates for Students, 1991). For some families, confronting the parents with information or concerns about their treatment of their child can lead to further difficulties for the child. Therefore, teachers need to understand the family's cultural perspective and carefully select the most beneficial outcomes for their students, as well as the most appropriate course of action to comply with legal mandates regarding child abuse (Fradd, 1992).

Think About It

Kevin, a student in your class, has been misbehaving and failing to complete his homework. Your principal tells you to call his parents and talk to them. However, you are concerned about the parents' reaction as they frequently use physical punishment as the primary method for disciplining Kevin.

What would you do? What professionals might assist you in this situation?

Substance Abuse

"I felt depressed and hurt all the time. I hated myself for the way I hurt my parents and treated them so cruelly, and for the way I treated others. I hated myself the most, though, for the way I treated myself. I would take drugs until I overdosed, and fell further and further behind in school and work and relationships with others. I just didn't care anymore whether I lived or died. I stopped going to school altogether. . . . I felt constantly depressed and began having thoughts of suicide, which scared me a lot! I didn't know where to turn. . . ." A high school student, quoted in *What Works: Schools Without Drugs* (U.S. Department of Education, 1989, p. viii).

Data indicate that 54% of high school seniors have used an illegal substance by the time they graduate and that the percentage of students taking illicit drugs by the sixth grade has increased by 300% in the last 20 years (U.S. Department of Education, 1989).

During the last two decades, American society has experienced an explosion in the number of substance abuse cases, and the illegal use of drugs and alcohol. Substance abuse has become widespread among adults and students across all economic backgrounds, geographic regions, and ethnic backgrounds in the United States. While boys and girls tend to engage in substance abuse at equal rates, substance abuse tends to be more widespread among white students than among African American or Hispanic students and more widespread among students residing in suburban and rural areas than among students living in urban settings. Substance abuse problems are even more prevalent in adolescents with behavioral disorders who attend separate, self-contained schools (Leone, Greenburg, Trickett, & Spero, 1989). Many of the students buy and use their drugs at school.

A variety of factors have contributed to the growing trend in substance abuse among youth. These factors include dysfunctional families, stress, life events, anxiety, depression, peer pressure, boredom, low self-esteem, contact with adults who engage in substance abuse, and poverty (Newcomb & Bentler, 1989). In light of the growing incidence of substance abuse, educators should be aware of some of the signs that indicate possible substance abuse (see Figure 1.8).

While we often think of substance abuse as the use of cocaine, heroin, and other illicit drugs, alcohol appears to be the most frequently used drug, with 92 percent of high school seniors, 42 percent of sixth graders, and 26 percent of fourth graders reporting having used alcohol (U.S. Department of Education, 1989). It is estimated that 3 million youth have a serious drinking problem, and that approximately 7 million children under the age of 18 have a parent who has a problem with alcohol. Having a parent who has a substance abuse problem can have a significant impact on the child's behavior. Pressman (1991) delineated four survival roles children may assume in order to cope with dysfunctional family members who are substance abusers: hero, scapegoat, lost child, and family mascot.

Hero/Heroine. These students may react by becoming overachievers in order to compensate for and rescue the family. They attempt to excel in all areas

FIGURE 1.8
Signs of alcohol and other drug use

Signs of alcohol and other drug (AOD) use vary, but there are some common indicators of AOD problems. Look for changes in performance, appearance, and behavior. These signs may indicate AOD use, but they may also reflect normal teenage growing pains. Therefore, look for a series of changes, not isolated single behaviors. Several changes together indicate a pattern associated with use.

CHANGES IN PERFORMANCE

- Distinct downward turn in grades—not just from Cs to Fs, but from As to Bs and Cs
- Assignments not completed
- A loss of interest in school; in extracurricular activities
- Poor classroom behavior such as inattentiveness, sleeping in class, hostility
- Missing school for unknown reasons
- In trouble with school, at work, or with the police
- Increased discipline problems
- Memory loss

CHANGES IN BEHAVIOR

- Decrease in energy and endurance
- Changes in friends (secrecy about new friends, new friends with different lifestyles)
- Secrecy about activities (lies or avoids talking about activities)
- Borrows lots of money, or has too much cash
- Mood swings; excessive anger, irritability
- Preferred style of music changes (pop rock to heavy metal)
- Starts pulling away from the family, old friends, and school
- Chronic lying, stealing, or dishonesty
- Hostile or argumentative attitude; extremely negative, unmotivated, defensive
- Refusal or hostility when asked to talk about possible alcohol or other drug use

CHANGES IN APPEARANCE AND PHYSICAL CHANGES

- Weight loss or gain
- Uncoordinated
- Poor physical appearance or unusually neat. A striking change in personal habits
- New interest in the drug culture (drug-related posters, clothes, magazines)
- Smells of alcohol, tobacco, marijuana
- Frequent use of eye drops and breath mints
- Bloodshot eyes
- Persistent cough or cold symptoms (e.g., runny nose)
- Always thirsty, increased or decreased appetite, rapid speech
- AOD paraphernalia (empty alcohol containers, cigarettes, pipes, rolling papers, baggies, paper packets, roach clips, razor blades, straws, glass or plastic vials, pill bottles, tablets and capsules, colored stoppers, syringes, spoons, matches or lighters, needles, medicine droppers, toy balloons, tin foil, cleaning rags, spray cans, glue containers, household products)

Source: "School-based alcohol and other drug prevention programs: Guidelines for the special educator" by D. L. Elmquist, 1991, *Intervention in School and Clinic, 27,* 10–19, Copyright 1991 by PRO-ED, Inc. Reprinted by permission.

and may perform many of the roles that their parents are failing to perform. They tend to be nervous, and may suffer from depression and eating disorders.

Scapegoat. These students may react by acting up and diverting attention to themselves and away from the dysfunctional parent.

Lost Child. These students may react by becoming low achievers who avoid drawing attention to themselves. They may attempt to withdraw, avoid conflict with others, and live in a fantasy world.

Family Mascot. These students may react by becoming class clowns who fail to take anything seriously. They may be laughing on the outside and crying on the inside.

Approximately, 65,000 infants are born each year with alcohol-related problems, with many of these infants experiencing Fetal Alcohol Syndrome (FAS) or Fetal Alcohol Effect (FAE) (Heward & Orlansky, 1992). FAS, which is caused by alcohol use during pregnancy, often results in physical disabilities, sensory impairments, poor coordination, impulsivity, developmental lags, and learning problems. FAE, which affects children less dramatically, can lead to comprehension problems and difficulties controlling anger and other emotions.

Cocaine and crack use is accelerating at alarming rates and there is a growing number of cocaine-exposed and substance-abused newborns (Rist, 1990). Hospitals, using written surveys, found that 17 percent of the pregnant women self-report use of cocaine during pregnancy (Miller,

IDEAS FOR IMPLEMENTATION

Teachers can help students whose parents are substance abusers by enacting the following suggestions:

- Encourage students to differentiate events that they have control over (i.e., working hard in school, performing a class job, choosing a snack) and events that are beyond their responsibility.
- Acknowledge students' special talents and abilities.
- Praise and/or criticize an individual's behavior rather than the individual.
- Give the student meaningful assignments and responsibilities.
- Encourage students to socialize with others and participate in class activities.
- Teach students how to express their feelings in appropriate ways such as through art work and writing assignments.
- Use print and audiovisual materials that deal with substance abuse.
- Establish clearly defined expectations.
- Be consistent and predictable.
- Teach students to praise others and how to accept compliments.
- Contact agencies such as the National Association for Children of Alcoholics (714-499-3889) and other resources for assistance.

Source: Davis, Allen, & Sherman (1989).

1989). Since self-reporting of illegal drug use is likely to understate the problem, the actual incidence of cocaine use during pregnancy is probably much higher (Frank et al., 1988). As a result, it is estimated that as many as 50,000 cocaine-exposed and 300,000 substance-abused infants are born each year (Rist, 1990). Many of these infants are small and underweight, are born prematurely, have birth defects, suffer neurological damage, exhibit irritability, and experience difficulty relating to and forming attachments to others. Many are abandoned and are raised in institutional or foster care settings. Those that reside with their parents may encounter a life of poverty and physical and emotional neglect (Rist, 1990). In classrooms, they may have difficulty learning and socializing with others, can be easily frustrated or overwhelmed by the numerous visual and auditory stimuli, and may withdraw or become overly aggressive and difficult to manage. They also may exhibit communication and motor delays, organizational and processing problems, and difficulties in socializing and playing with others (Los Angeles Unified School District, 1990). Early intervention programs for cocaine-exposed children and their parents are needed; these programs should offer medical care, nutritional counseling, instruction in parenting skills and obtaining community services, and a structured and supportive learning environment. The Los Angeles Unified School District (1990) has developed a model program and guidelines for educating children who have been prenatally exposed to drugs/alcohol.

Dropouts

"By his sophomore year, Bill had become so disenchanted with his monotonous school program that he began cutting class regularly. He recalls that the year he dropped out he went to school no more than 60 days. Bill explains that since both parents worked, 'It was easy; I'd cut out and go home to watch TV, get high with friends, or sleep all day. Nobody did anything about it.' Bill's family had moved six times since kindergarten, and he reported that he had not yet found a school he considered worth going to. The times he was in school were, in his opinion, 'a waste of time.' He often asked, 'Why are we learning this?' In his two years of high school, Bill saw his counselor for one 10-minute interview, despite failing several classes each semester. 'At the end they called twice to tell me to come in and sign out, but I didn't.' No one tried to talk Bill out of dropping out" (Grossnickle, 1986, pp. 12–13).

In terms of ethnicity, dropout rates are 14%, 25% and 40% for white, black and Hispanic students, respectively (Yates, 1988).

Many of the changes in society have contributed to the failure of many students to complete their schooling. Wolman, Bruininks, and Thurlow (1989) estimate that 25 percent of our nation's students drop out of school. The dropout rate is particularly high in some urban and rural areas that serve large numbers of poor, and culturally and linguistically diverse students. The dropout rates for students with disabilities also are significantly higher than the dropout rates of students who do not have disabilities (Bruininks, Thurlow,

Lew, & Larson, 1988). Dropouts experience a difficult time obtaining employment and represent a high cost to society (McNergney & Haberman, 1988).

Several factors contribute to the likelihood of a student leaving school before graduating. Kuniswa (1988) and Cohen and deBettencourt (1991) outlined several factors that may lead to a student dropping out, including being poor, being nonwhite, having very low academic skills, having a disability, speaking a language other than English, being retained in school and separated from one's peer group, being a child of a single parent, holding a job, being pregnant, being a substance abuser, and being bored in or alienated from school. Attending schools that have limited resources and programs for motivating students and encouraging parental participation also is a major contributing factor to high dropout rates.

ALTERNATIVE PHILOSOPHIES FOR STRUCTURING SCHOOLS

While societal changes have resulted in a significant increase in the number of students whose needs challenge the system, and whose academic profiles resemble the performance levels of students with mild disabilities, many of these students are not disabled. However, the vagueness of the definitions of exceptionalities, imprecise and discriminatory identification procedures, limited funding resulting in a lack of appropriate services and the tendency of schools to resist change all increase the likelihood that these students may be inappropriately identified as in need of special education. Several alternative viewpoints for structuring schools to meet the needs of all students without labeling them have been proposed.

Multicultural Education

Multicultural education is a term that finds its origins in the post-civil rights efforts of diverse ethnic and linguistic groups to have their previously neglected experiences included in the structures and curricula of schools (Banks, 1987). For many, it has expanded to include concerns about class, disability, gender, and sexual orientation (Sleeter, 1991). Multicultural education is potentially the most profound movement for reforming schools since the original Supreme Court decision to desegregate schools (Suzuki, 1984).

Definitions of multicultural education vary (Sleeter, 1991). Sleeter and Grant (1987) identify the various definitions of the term, ranging from an emphasis on human relations and harmony to one that focuses on social democracy and empowerment. Suzuki (1984) offers the following inclusive definition of multicultural education:

> [It is] a multidisciplinary educational program that provides multiple learning environments matching the academic, social and linguistic needs of students. . . . In addition to enhancing the development of their basic academic skills, the program should help students develop a better understanding of their own

IDEAS FOR IMPLEMENTATION

As teachers, you can help students who are potential dropouts by enacting the following suggestions:

1. Understand the early warning signs of dropping out:
   - school avoidance as evidenced by frequent absenteeism, asking to be excused from classroom activities, stress-related symptoms (aches) during specific activities
   - discipline problems
   - difficulty in information processing as evidenced by problems in attention, memory, and organizational skills
   - motivation problems
   - poor self-concept
   - repeated school failure, such as grade retention
2. Refer students who exhibit early warning signs to programs that address their needs.
3. Encourage students to participate in afterschool activities.
4. Attend afterschool activities in which students participate.
5. Make instruction relevant and meaningful by explaining how the information or skill relates to daily activities and the world of work.
6. Pretest students to determine their mastery of the material.
7. Teach students to use learning strategies.
8. Involve students in evaluating their progress.
9. Create a sense of community in the classroom and the school through use of cooperative learning groups and peer mediated interventions.
10. Help students develop a sense of accomplishment and responsibility for their positive actions.
11. Focus students' attention on salient features of tasks by using verbal cues and highlighting.
12. Obtain more information about dropout prevention programs.

Additional information regarding dropout prevention programs can be obtained by contacting the Center for Dropout Prevention (305-284-3166), Center for Human Research (800-343-4705), National Center for Parents in Dropout Prevention (800-638-9675), National Dropout Prevention Center (800-443-6392) and National Dropout Prevention Network (707-257-8276).

Source: Cohen & de Bettencourt (1991).

> backgrounds and of other groups that compose society. . . . Finally, it should help them conceptualize a vision of a better society and acquire the necessary knowledge . . . to enable them to move the society toward greater equality and freedom. . . . (p. 305)

Banks, cited in Bullard (1992), identified the goals of multicultural education:

- to provide all students with an equal opportunity to learn in school
- to help all students understand and develop positive attitudes toward individuals from different groups

- to empower students by teaching them to use a variety of decisionmaking and social change skills
- to help students develop an appreciation of cross-cultural dependency, and examine themselves from the perspectives of others

Multicultural education and empowerment are inextricably linked (Sleeter, 1991). Ashcroft (1987) defined empowerment as "a state of belief in one's ability/capability to act with effect" (p. 145). Multicultural education seeks to make schools examine and address their role in either empowering or disabling students (Cummins, 1986). Empowering and disabling schools differ in terms of the extent to which (a) the students' cultural and linguistic backgrounds are integrated into or excluded from their school experiences; (b) the community works collaboratively with or is excluded from interacting with the school; (c) the teaching style in the classroom is one of reciprocal interaction among teachers and students or one of transmission of information from teachers to students; and (d) assessment of students is focused on advocacy or on documenting student failure (Cummins, 1986).

Proponents of multicultural education also seek to transform the language of schools (Roberts, Bell, & Salend, 1991). Terms such as *culturally disadvantaged, linguistically limited, at-risk, slow learners, handicapped,* and *dropouts* locate problems within students rather than within the educational structure (Freire, 1970). These labels present a view of students that often are discrepant with how they view themselves. These conflicting views can disable students academically and prevent the development of a positive self-esteem.

Think About It

We refer to students who have needs that challenge the school system as *at-risk, handicapped, culturally disadvantaged,* or *linguistically limited.* How might things be different if we referred to schools as *risky, disabling, disadvantaging,* and *limiting?*

Inclusion

Successful models for integrating individuals with severe disabilities have been implemented in various school districts throughout the United States, Canada, and other countries (Flynn & Kowalczyk-McPhee, 1989).

Inclusion is a movement of parents, educators, and community members that seeks to create schools and other social institutions that are based on acceptance, belonging, and community. Inclusionary schools welcome, acknowledge, and affirm all learners by educating them together in high quality, age-appropriate, regular education classrooms in their communities.

While the inclusion movement has focused on individuals with disabilities, it is designed to alter the philosophy for educating all students who challenge the system (Forest & Pierpoint, 1991). Rather than being structured based on a dual system that segregates students and teachers, advocates of inclusion seek to restructure schools to be a unified system based on the following principles:

- All students regardless of their race, linguistic ability, economic status, gender, age, ability, ethnicity, religion, and sexual orientation should be educated in the mainstream of regular education.

- All students are valued individuals who are capable of learning and contributing to society.
- All students are entitled to equal access to quality services that allow them to be successful in school and life.
- All students have access to individualization in terms of diagnostic services, curriculum accessibility, instructional strategies, and related services based on their needs.
- All students have opportunities to work and play together.
- All students are taught to appreciate and value human differences and similarities.
- All professionals, parents, peers, and community agencies work collaboratively to share resources, skills, and advocacy.
- All schools should involve parents and community members in the educational process. (Flynn & Kowalczyk-McPhee, 1989; Stainback, Stainback, & Bunch, 1989).

Inclusive programs adopt a zero rejection model, with all students being educated in age-appropriate regular education classrooms that are located in schools that students would attend if they did not have a disability. Rather than teaching students in self-contained special education classrooms, special educators work collaboratively with regular education teachers and support service personnel to educate students in the regular education classroom.

Regular Education Initiative

As a result of the special education efficacy studies and concern about the large numbers of students being labeled as disabled, some educators have proposed the *Regular Education Initiative (REI),* which calls for restructuring the relationship between regular, special, remedial, and compensatory education programs (Wang, Reynolds, & Walberg, 1986; Will, 1986). Proponents of the REI argue that the current educational service delivery system for students whose needs challenge the system is ineffective, inefficient, and costly; lessens communication between professionals; labels and stigmatizes students; ignores the needs of students with learning problems who are not identified as disabled; and is fragmented by numerous "pull-out" programs (such as special education, migrant education, Chapter 1 programs, and the like), and believe that these students should receive their education in regular education classes. They believe that student failure is related to problems in schools rather than problems in students and endorse the establishment of a partnership between regular and special education that results in a coordinated educational delivery system based on empirically validated practices. The REI also seeks to provide monies to support experimental trials of "more integrated forms of education for students who are unjustifiably segregated in separate programs" (Wang, Reynolds, & Walberg, 1986, p. 28).

Others have criticized the validity of the REI by arguing that it (a) is based on faulty assumptions; (b) represents policy advocacy rather than policy analysis; (c) lacks an adequate research base; (d) assumes that regular classroom teachers are willing and well trained to teach all students; (e) does not present a clear and detailed alternative; (f) competes with the goals of the excellence in education movement; (g) is inappropriate for certain disability groups; and (g) redirects monies away from students who are experiencing difficulties in school to affluent and high achieving students (Hallahan et al., 1988; Kauffman, 1989; Kauffman, Gerber, & Semmel, 1988; McKinney & Hocutt, 1988). Maheady and Algozzine (1991) have examined the system-level, school-level and child-level changes that must be addressed in order to implement the REI.

Semmel, Abernathy, Butera and Lesar (1991) noted that the discussion about the REI has been primarily within the special education policy and academic community. They surveyed special and regular education teachers concerning their opinions, attitudes, and perceptions of the salient dimensions of the REI. Their findings indicate that teachers are not dissatisfied with current special education practices.

Think About It

In response to concerns about the quality of our nation's schools and their ability to produce a workforce that can compete in world markets, many groups have produced reports outlining plans for reforming education. In 1991, the President and the National Association of Governors adopted six performance goals for the educational system as part of *America 2000: An Education Strategy.*

1. All children in America will start school ready to learn.
2. The high school graduation rate will increase to at least 90 percent.
3. American students will demonstrate competency in such areas as English, mathematics, science, history, and geography at grades four, eight, and twelve.
4. American students will be first in the world in science and mathematics achievement.
5. Every adult American will be literate and possess the skills necessary to compete in a global economy and exercise the rights and responsibilities of citizenship.
6. Every school in America will be drug and violence free and provide students with a disciplined environment that is conducive to learning (U.S. Department of Education, 1991a).

What are the implications of these goals for American schools? For you as a teacher? For students whose needs challenge the educational system?

ARGUMENTS FOR MAINSTREAMING

While the concept of mainstreaming is not new, the debate about its advantages and disadvantages continues. Proponents of mainstreaming support it for the following reasons, among others:

- Mainstreaming minimizes the deleterious effects of labelling.
- It allows students the opportunity to learn from and interact with each other.

- It prepares all students for their careers and lives in a setting that is more representative of society.
- It promotes the academic and social development of all students.
- It fosters the development of an understanding and appreciation of individual differences.
- It is consistent with the moral and ethical values of our culture.
- It provides for the delivery of services to students whose needs challenge the system without stigmatizing them.
- It infuses the skills of special educators into the school and curriculum.

Others attack special class placements as providing students with disabilities with a "watered down" curriculum that focuses on practical knowledge, social skills, and emotional adjustment rather than academic skills (Guskin & Spicker, 1968). Advocates of mainstreaming also question the over-reliance on standardized tests to label students as disabled, which results in a disproportionate number of students from culturally and linguistically diverse groups being isolated in special education classes (Mercer, 1973).

ARGUMENTS AGAINST MAINSTREAMING

"I've tried everything in my bag of tricks. I'm frustrated, he's frustrated and so are the other kids in the class."
—A first-grade teacher

However, others argue against mainstreaming:

- Regular educators are not trained to work with students with special needs.
- Students with special needs will require excessive amounts of teacher time, thereby impeding the progress of other students.
- Regular educators and peers have negative attitudes toward students with special needs, which will result in the isolation and stigmatization of students in the regular education milieu.
- Regular education is not structured to accommodate the needs of students with special needs.
- Students with special needs will be denied services and specialized instruction and fall further behind their peers.
- The emphasis on the excellence in education movement will create greater discrepancies between students with special needs and their peers.
- Research has not clearly established the efficacy of the mainstreamed setting.

Still others believe that special class placement is best for students with special needs because it will protect them from the harmful effects of repeated failures that they will experience in the regular education setting. Figure 1.9 presents commonly heard statements of opinion concerning mainstreaming.

MAINSTREAMING RESEARCH

Studies Supporting the Efficacy of Mainstreaming

Research on the efficacy of mainstreaming has reported mixed results (Caparulo & Zigler, 1983; Carlberg & Kavale, 1980; Polloway, 1984). The

FIGURE 1.9
Perspectives on mainstreaming

Different people have different views concerning mainstreaming. Here is a sampling of comments that have been heard regarding mainstreaming.

"I believe in mainstreaming, but I wasn't trained to teach these students. And the other students will make fun of the students."

"Some students need to be mainstreamed, but many of our students need special attention and individualized instruction, which only special education teachers can provide. What would special education teachers do if all students were mainstreamed?"

"Mainstreaming is a good idea, but we don't have enough money in the district to implement it. Those kids get all the money, anyway. What about the other kids?"

"I'm all for having a variety of students in the class, but won't these students take time away from the other kids?"

"Those kids will teach my child the wrong behaviors. He's not aware of drugs and sex—they'll teach him about it."

"Society is changing. All students need to know about and respect individual differences. All students benefit from learning about others. It helps prepare them for the world they will be inheriting."

"If people stopped to think about it, mainstreaming costs less. We can eliminate the need for large segregated buildings, excessive transportation costs and the duplication of services."

"Mainstreaming makes a lot of sense to me. It gives all students the chance to learn from one another."

"I think mainstreaming can work. Good teaching is good teaching and it works with all students."

"Mainstreaming sounds good to me. If I can get a special education teacher in the class, he or she might be able to help me with some of the other students who are having problems."

"I want my child to have the same experiences as other kids. J needs to be out of the house, on the school bus and with other people. J can learn from other kids and they can learn from him."

"Mainstreaming is the right thing to do. Segregating students makes them feel isolated, unwanted, and different."

results of mainstreaming studies should be interpreted with caution (MacMillan & Semmel, 1977; Reynolds & Birch, 1988). Because of the difficulties of conducting comparative field investigations in education (for example, insuring equal resources and equivalent students, teachers, and definitions of mainstreaming), it is not possible to conclude unequivocally that the results of these studies are correct (Reynolds & Birch, 1988). The relative newness of mainstreaming as an educational alternative and the recent changes and improvements in special education services also make mainstreaming a difficult concept to study empirically.

Several researchers have found that mainstreaming has promoted educational as well as social growth in students with disabilities (Guerin & Szatlocky, 1974; Haring & Krug, 1975; Macy & Carter, 1978; Madden & Slavin, 1983; Wang & Birch, 1984a). In carefully controlled studies, Calhoun and Elliot (1977) and Leinhardt (1980) found that randomly selected students placed in mainstreamed settings showed significantly greater gains in achievement than their counterparts educated in self-contained special education classes. In reviewing the comparative effectiveness of mainstreamed placements on social outcomes, Madden and Slavin (1983) found that "for outcomes as self-derogation, and self-concept, classroom behavior, and attitudes toward school, regular class placement with adequate supports typically is superior to full-time special class placement" (p. 536).

Wang, Anderson, and Bram (1985) performed a meta-analysis of 50 studies comparing regular and special education placements. The subjects of these studies included approximately 3400 students with various types of disabilities and grade-level placements ranging from preschool to high school. The results, found across all types of disabilities, indicated not only that the academic and social performance of students with special needs in mainstreamed settings were superior to those students educated in special classes, but also that the students who were mainstreamed on a full-time basis performed better than their peers who were mainstreamed on a part-time basis.

Reynolds and Birch (1988) reviewed several non-data-based reports on mainstreaming programs. They concluded that mainstreaming was a successful alternative, as evidenced by the positive reactions of teachers, parents, and students; the decrease in the number of students referred for special education services; and the increase in consultation services provided to regular educators. They also noted that many of the problems once associated with the implementation of mainstreaming had been resolved.

Adaptive Learning Environments Model

One successful mainstreaming program is the *Adaptive Learning Environments Model (ALEM),* which was developed at the University of Pittsburgh (Wang & Birch, 1984a, 1984b). ALEM is a full-time mainstreaming program that assists educators in adapting the instructional setting to accommodate the needs of special education students in the regular classroom. The program is designed to describe students in terms of their specific instructional needs rather than categorical labels, and provides for early identification of learning needs through an ongoing assessment of students' progress in relation to the program's curriculum. Individualized instructional programs are developed based on students' strengths and weaknesses, and students are encouraged to assume control of their learning (Wang & Birch, 1984b). ALEM is made up of three primary components; the Prescriptive component, the Exploratory component, and the Self-Schedule system. The Prescriptive component helps teachers to instruct students in basic skills. The Exploratory component focuses on the use of learning centers and activity areas to promote independent and small-group work. The self-schedule system seeks to promote student independence and responsibility.

Research shows that ALEM can be implemented in a variety of inner-city, suburban, and rural settings to facilitate student achievement (Wang & Birch, 1984a). Furthermore, a comparison between ALEM and a traditional resource room approach indicated that ALEM was superior in promoting interactions between mainstreamed students and their peers and teachers, improving basic academic skills, and increasing the positive attitudes of students (Wang & Birch, 1984b).

However, critics have raised concerns about the ALEM findings (Anderegg & Vergason, 1988; Fuchs & Fuchs, 1988). Such critics note that the studies examining its efficacy contain a variety of methodological limitations. These limitations include: (a) failing to provide descriptive information on program and student characteristics; (b) using a small number of students; (c) failing to provide data to verify the extent to which the ALEM procedures were implemented in the classes; and (d) using inappropriate statistical data analysis procedures (Hallahan et al., 1988; Fuchs & Fuchs, 1988). Clark and Bott (1991) noted that teachers may need extensive training to implement ALEM successfully in their classrooms.

Studies Questioning the Efficacy of Mainstreaming

While some researchers have found no differences between students placed in special education classes and those educated in regular education classes (Budoff & Gottlieb, 1976; Walker, 1974), others have found that mainstreaming has not been an effective educational alternative for students (Budoff & Gottlieb, 1976; Gottlieb, 1981; Gresham, 1982). Carlberg and Kavale (1980) analyzed special education versus mainstream placements and found that students labeled learning disabled, behaviorally disordered, and emotionally disturbed performed better in special classes. The results of several studies indicate that students with IQs between 70 to 75 who do not receive supportive services in the regular education setting perform better in structured special education classes (Goldstein, Moss, & Jordan, 1965; Myers, 1976). In related research, others have found that students with special needs in mainstreamed settings tend to be less popular (Bryan & Bryan, 1978; Gottlieb & Budoff, 1973; Siperstein, Bopp, & Bak, 1978).

Gresham (1982) reviewed the social skills literature and concluded that mainstreaming was a misguided approach because it was predicated on three premises that have not been empirically validated: (a) that mainstreaming will result in increased social interaction between mainstreamed students and their peers; (b) that mainstreaming will result in increased acceptance of mainstreamed students by their peers; and (c) that mainstreamed students will learn appropriate behavior through exposure to positive peer models in the regular education setting. Similarly, in reviewing the studies on mainstreamed placements for students with mild mental retardation, Gottlieb (1981) determined that mainstreaming was not fulfilling its promise.

Resolving the Discrepancy in Mainstreaming Research

Leinhardt and Pallay (1982) reviewed the literature contrasting special and regular education placements for students with special needs. They found successful examples of all types of placement alternatives for students. They resolved the discrepancy in the existing studies by concluding that

> the most significant point of view is that setting is not an important determinant of child or program success. When effective practices are used, then the mildly handicapped benefit. Therefore educators should focus less on debates of setting, and more on issues of finding and implementing sound educational processes. For moral and social reasons, the least restrictive environment is preferable, and this review indicates that most of the valuable practices can be implemented in either resource rooms or regular education settings. (p. 574)

Another explanation for these contradictory findings may lie in the variation of mainstreaming policies and their implementation from one school district to another (Gresham, 1982; Zigler & Muenchow, 1979). Others attribute inconsistent findings to the failure of schools to change their programs to facilitate mainstreaming (Bogdan, 1983; Stainback, Stainback, Courtnage, & Jaben, 1985). Zigler and Muenchow (1979) noted that because many school districts do not have clear guidelines for mainstreaming, their programs often become the least expensive rather than the least restrictive alternative for students. Similarly, Gresham (1982) criticized local and state education personnel for their failure to develop workable guidelines for mainstreaming.

Several studies have examined the mainstreaming procedures of school districts (Bogdan, 1983; Salend, Brooks, & Salend, 1987). Wang, Andersen, and Bram (1985) examined the program features that appear to be related to effective mainstreaming. They noted the following important mainstream program characteristics:

- ongoing assessment of student performance
- adaptive instructional techniques and materials
- individualized instruction
- student self-management strategies
- cooperative learning arrangements
- consultation and instructional teaming

Salend, Brooks, and Salend (1987) surveyed educators responsible for coordinating their school districts' mainstreaming programs to determine the extent to which their programs incorporated the factors that contribute to successful mainstreaming programs. They concluded that while districts have acknowledged a commitment to the philosophy of mainstreaming, few of the districts surveyed had systematic and viable procedures to insure its implementation. Furthermore, they reported that the implementation of mainstreaming appears to be based on informal networks between regular and special educators within individual schools rather than on established policies. These results are consistent with the findings of Bogdan (1983), who examined the mainstreaming policies of numerous school districts and found that few adaptations had been made to insure the successful implementation of mainstreaming programs. In light of these findings and the continued commitment to mainstreaming as the preferred educational alternative for students who challenge the system, this book is intended to provide educators with the skills to develop and implement effective mainstreaming programs.

SUMMARY

This chapter offered information for understanding mainstreaming as an educational philosophy for meeting the diverse needs of students. The chapter

- introduced the concepts of mainstreaming and the least restrictive environment
- outlined the educational placement options available to students
- reviewed the factors that contributed to the mainstreaming movement
- discussed how the concept of mainstreaming is being expanded and modified to address the societal changes that are challenging our nation's schools to adapt to the needs of a changing school population
- specified arguments for and against mainstreaming
- summarized the research on mainstreaming

RECOMMENDED READINGS

Biklen, D., Lehr, S., Searl, S. J., & Taylor, S. J. (1987). *Purposeful integration . . . Inherently equal.* Boston: Technical Assistance for Parent Programs.

Carlberg, C., & Kavale, K. (1980). The efficacy of special versus regular placements for exceptional children: A meta-analysis. *Journal of Special Education, 14,* 295–309.

Cohen, S. B., & de Bettencourt, L. V. (1991). Dropouts: Intervening with the reluctant learner. *Intervention in School and Clinic, 26,* 263–271.

Dunn, L. M. (1968). Special education for the mildly retarded—Is much of it justifiable? *Exceptional Children, 35,* 5–22.

Hasazi, S. B., Gordon, L. R., & Roe, C. A. (1985). Factors associated with the employment status of handicapped youth exiting high school from 1979 to 1983. *Exceptional Children, 51,* 455–469.

Kozol, J. (1991). *Savage inequalities: Children in American schools.* New York: Crown.

Lloyd, J. W., Singh, N. N., & Repp, A. C. (1991). *The regular education initiative: Alternative perspectives on concepts, issues and models.* Sycamore, IL: Sycamore Publishing.

National Coalition of Advocates for Students. (1991). *New voices: Immigrant students in U.S. public schools.* Boston: Author.

Stainback, S., Stainback, W., & Forest, M. (1989). *Educating all students in the mainstream of regular education.* Baltimore: Paul H. Brookes.

Williams, B. F. (1992). Changing demographics: Challenges for educators. *Intervention in School and Clinic, 27*(3), 157–163.

2 Determining the Diverse Educational Needs of Students

CAROL

I arrived from Jamaica when I was seven years old and my mother enrolled me in first grade. Though the work wasn't that hard, I had a difficult time adjusting. Even though I spoke English, there were many different ways of saying and doing things. One time we had a writing assignment and I made a mistake and wanted to use an eraser to correct it. Not knowing the word for eraser, I used the Jamaican term and asked the teacher and other students for a "rubber." No one responded to me, so I asked for a rubber again, and again I was ignored. Finally, I took an eraser (rubber) from a student's desk. He got upset and told the teacher, who scolded me. She never told me the correct word. Several months later, I learned the correct word when the teacher asked me to erase the board.

I could tell that the teacher thought I was slow. As a result, she treated me differently, which made me feel different. For example, she always asked me to read more than the other students because she said she liked to hear my accent. This made me withdraw from her and the rest of the class. However, my withdrawal was interpreted as being slow. The teacher would give directions to me by talking very slowly and down to me. Each question, was followed by the statement, "Do (pause) you (pause) understand?" Then the teacher asked peers to show me how to do everything. I was so embarrassed that I stopped talking completely and lost all interest in school.

The teacher must have referred me for special education or something. I remember being tested by several people. I asked my mother to talk to someone at the school, but she couldn't afford to take off from work. After the testing, they put me in another class. It wasn't a special education class but I knew it was a slower math and reading class. The work was so easy I soon became bored. Again, I felt embarrassed and isolated. They also decided I needed speech therapy to help change my accent. I was proud of my accent and wanted to keep it.

What factors should educators consider in designing an appropriate educational program for Carol? Should Carol have been placed in a special education class? After reading this chapter, you should be able to answer these as well as the following questions.

- What educational decisions are made by the multidisciplinary team?
- How do the definitions of and educational needs associated with the various types of disabilities differ?
- What are the components of an Individualized Education Program (IEP)?
- How do the cultural perspectives of students and teachers affect student performance in schools?
- How can educators plan to meet the needs of students who are learning English as a second language?

Educators make many important decisions concerning the education of students whose needs challenge schools. These decisions include assessing the effectiveness of prereferral strategies, determining a student's eligibility for special education, placing the student in appropriate educational environments, identifying educational and related service needs to assist teachers and parents in developing and implementing a student's Individualized Educational Program (IEP), determining the impact of students' cultural perspectives on school performance, and assessing the educational needs of students who are learning English as a second language.

ROLES AND RESPONSIBILITIES OF THE MULTIDISCIPLINARY TEAM

Prior to congressional enactment of PL 94-142, many educational decisions concerning a student's needs were typically made by the school psychologist.

However, the IDEA requires that a team of professionals and parents determine a student's eligibility for special education classes and the types of related services necessary to meet student needs and help the student benefit from special education. Although the makeup of the multidisciplinary team varies depending on the needs of the student in question and the decisions to be made (Hart, 1977), the team may be composed of individuals with training in regular education, special education, administration, school psychology, speech and language therapy, vocational education, physical therapy, occupational therapy, counseling, social work, and medicine (Golightly, 1987). In addition to these professionals, the team also should include a parent and, when appropriate, the student. For students with specific cultural or language needs, individuals who have experience with the student or an expertise in the specialized area should be a part of the team.

Parents

The child's parents are integral members of the multidisciplinary team. Because parents spend the most time with their child, they can provide the team with a variety of information related to the student's adaptive behavior, and medical, social, and psychological history. Parents also can assist the team in designing and implementing educational programs and determining appropriate related services. Additional information on the involvement of parents in the educational process is presented in Chapter 3.

School Administrator

The building principal or the special education coordinator usually serves as the chairperson of the multidisciplinary team. The chairperson is responsible for coordinating meetings and delivery of services to students and their families. The chairperson also ensures that all legal guidelines for due process, parental involvement, assessment, and confidentiality have been followed (Pasanella, 1980). Through their leadership and support, principals can foster a tone of acceptance and commitment to the concept of mainstreaming. For example, scheduling time for regular and special educators to meet, and planning in-service programs to prepare teachers to work with mainstreamed students can create a positive environment that can facilitate the success of mainstreaming.

Regular Educator

It is critical that the multidisciplinary team include a regular educator. Regular educators who have experience working with the student can offer information on the student's strengths and weaknesses, as well as data on the effectiveness of specific instructional approaches. In deciding on a mainstreamed placement, regular educators can provide team members with a perspective on the academic and social rigors of the regular education classroom. Involving the regular educator in the process also can allay the fears of the regular classroom teachers and facilitate their commitment to the success of the mainstreaming placement.

Special Educator

Another vital member of the multidisciplinary team is the special educator, who can assist the multidisciplinary team in developing an IEP by providing data concerning the student's academic and social skills, readiness for mainstreaming, and reactions to instructional techniques and materials. The special educator can offer information on the special education placement options within the school district. When a student is going to be mainstreamed, the special educator can consult with regular classroom teachers concerning instructional modifications, grading alternatives, prosthetic devices, and peer acceptance. The special education teacher also assumes the primary responsibility for preparing the student for entry into the mainstream.

School Psychologist

An important member of the multidisciplinary team is the school psychologist. In many instances, teams are chaired by the school psychologists because of their training and expertise in the administration and interpretation of standardized tests. In addition to carrying out test-related tasks, school psychologists also collect data on students by observing them in their classrooms and by interviewing other professionals who work with the student. Many school psychologists are trained to serve as consultants to assist classroom teachers in designing, implementing, and evaluating prereferral interventions and behavior management systems (Zins, Curtis, Graden, & Ponti, 1988). Occasionally, school psychologists provide counseling to parents and students.

Speech and Language Clinician

Information on the speech and language abilities of students can be provided by the speech and language clinician. Although these professionals have historically delivered services to remediate articulation problems and voice and fluency disorders, their responsibilities have been expanded to work with students with language problems. Speech and language clinicians are often the first persons to whom students who are learning English are referred to rule out or support the existence of a language disability. They also are available to offer teachers assistance in fostering the communication skills of students within the classroom environment.

Social Worker

The social worker serves as a liaison between the home and school and community agencies. In terms of the home-school relationship, the social worker counsels students and families, obtains information to assess the effect of the student's home life on school performance, and assists families during emergencies. In addition, the social worker can be instrumental in helping families obtain services from community agencies, and can contact agencies concerning the needs of the student and parents, and can evaluate the impact of services on the family.

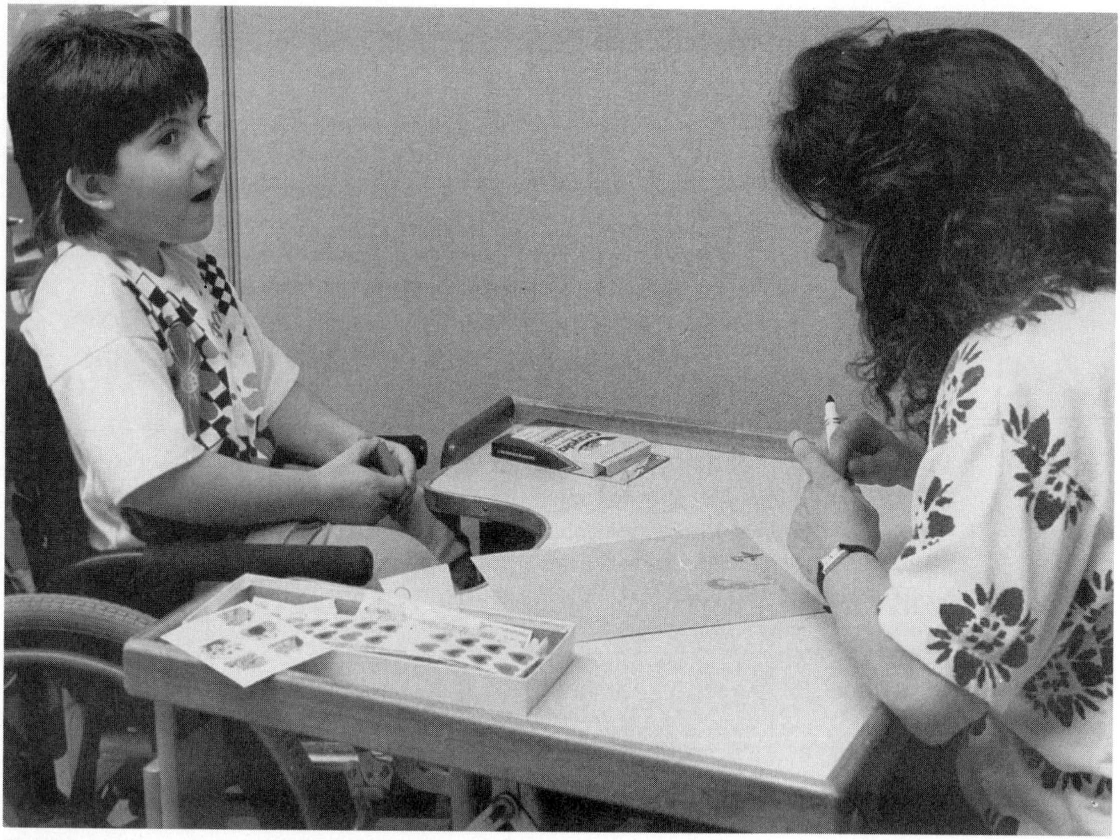

Speech and language clinicians help students develop their communication skills.

Guidance Counselor

Although more likely to work with secondary-level students, the guidance counselor can assist students at all levels. The counselor can provide the multidisciplinary team with insights concerning the student's social and emotional development including self-concept, attitudes toward school, and social interactions with others. In schools that don't have a social worker, the counselor may be the professional responsible for contacting parents and community agencies that provide services to the student and the family.

Frequently, counselors are given the responsibility of coordinating, assessing, and monitoring the mainstreamed student's program, as well as reporting the progress of the program to members of the team. The guidance counselor also may deliver counseling services to students and parents. For example, during the initial transition period, the mainstreamed student may need counseling to make the social and emotional adjustment to the regular education setting.

Vocational Educator

As part of the multidisciplinary team, the vocational educator offers valuable information concerning the student's work and career experiences and potential. Vocational educators are responsible for providing students with vocational and career education experiences, which requires vocational educators to collaborate with families and employers within the community (Brolin, 1982). Vocational education seeks to provide work experience and training to prepare students for specific careers. In addition, vocational educators can help teachers deliver career education programs that develop awareness, attitudes, habits, interests, and skills relative to employment options (Kokaska & Brolin, 1985).

Music and Art Therapist

Many students may benefit from the services of a music or art therapist. Music and art therapists use music or art to assess the student's emotional status, communication skills, socialization abilities, cognitive development and physical needs. They also employ art and music as interventions to address the student's unique needs. For example, music therapists use music improvisation, music listening, song writing, lyric discussions, and imagery when working with students.

Physician and Nurse

PL 94-142 established the need for greater involvement of medical and health-related personnel in the education of students with special needs (Guralnick, 1982). Levine (1982) noted that physicians can aid the multidisciplinary team by performing diagnostic tests to assess the student's physical development, sensory abilities, medical problems, and central nervous system functioning; by providing an understanding of nutrition, allergies, chronic illnesses, and somatic symptoms; by planning and monitoring the effectiveness of medical interventions; and by discussing the potential side effects of drug interventions.

Some students may require the services of a medical specialist, who can meet the specific medical and physical needs of students by providing diagnostic and treatment services within their area of specialization. For example, an ophthalmologist—who specializes in the treatment of conditions affecting the eyes—can provide information and assistance to students with specific visual impairments. Students with hearing impairments may need the medical services of an otologist, a physician with expertise in treating auditory disorders. Other specialists that can help students include psychiatrists, neurologists, orthopedic surgeons, and EENT (ears, eyes, nose and throat) specialists. Although they are not physicians, optometrists and audiologists can assist in the assessment and treatment of students with visual and hearing impairment, respectively.

Since physicians are costly, many medically related services may be provided by school nurses, who can screen students for sensory and physical problems; treat some illnesses; offer explanations of medical records; monitor the effects of pharmacological interventions; offer training in nutrition, dental care, and other health care-related skills; check the fit, maintenance, and functioning of prosthetic and adaptive devices; and help parents obtain medical and dental services.

Physical and Occupational Therapist

Students with fine and gross motor problems may require the services of physical and occupational therapists. These therapists can be a source of valuable information as part of the multidisciplinary team. The physical therapist usually focuses on the assessment and training of the lower extremities and large muscles, while the occupational therapist deals with the upper extremities and fine-motor abilities (Gearheart, Weishahn, & Gearheart, 1988). The physical therapist helps students strengthen muscles, improve posture, and increase motor function and range (Gloeckler & Simpson, 1988). The occupational therapist works with students to prevent, restore, or adapt to impaired or lost motor functions, and to develop the necessary fine-motor skills to perform everyday independent actions. In addition to providing direct services to students, the physical therapist serves as a consultant to the teachers, nurses, and adaptive physical educators who are responsible for implementing the therapy program. For students with impaired motor functions, occupational and physical therapists can offer recommendations concerning the use of adaptive equipment as well as suggestions for adapting materials and classroom environments (Haring & McCormick, 1986).

Special Considerations for Students Who are Learning English

In addition to the professionals described above, *Jose P. v. Ambach* (1983) mandated that multidisciplinary teams for students who are learning English and are referred for special education services include personnel who are fluent in the student's native language and bicultural in the student's home culture. Therefore, placement teams involved in the assessment and instruction process for these students should include such professionals as English as a second language teachers, bilingual educators, migrant educators, and language interpreters.

English as a Second Language (ESL) Teacher

English as a second language (ESL) teachers provide students with instruction in English. ESL teachers build on students' existing language skills and experiential backgrounds to enhance their acquisition of English skills.

Bilingual Educator

Many students come from backgrounds where English is not the language spoken; they will require the services of a bilingual educator (Baca & Cervantes, 1989). The bilingual educator performs a variety of roles:

Students with motor problems may require the services of physical therapists.

- teaching curriculum areas using two languages
- using the student's native language to teach reading
- teaching English as a second language
- helping students develop a positive self-concept
- instilling in students a sense of pride in their culture
- emphasizing positive attitudes toward cultural diversity
- assisting in the assessment of students from culturally and linguistically diverse backgrounds
- helping determine an appropriate placement for second language learners
- developing an instructional program that meets the needs of bilingual students
- evaluating the progress of bilingual students
- assisting parents in becoming involved in their child's education (Plata & Santos, 1981)

ESL and bilingual education programs are discussed later in this chapter.

Migrant Educator

To address the educational needs of migrant students, the federal government funds migrant education programs through the states. Typically, when a migrant family moves to a new area, it is certified as being eligible for migrant status and services by a recruiter from a local migrant education agency. After a family has been identified as eligible, a migrant educator is often charged with the responsibility of assisting the family in enrolling the children in school. The migrant educator also contacts local agencies, organizations, businesses, and other community resources that can provide assistance to migrant families.

Once the migrant students are in school, the migrant educator often gives them supplementary individualized instruction in small groups. The migrant educator is available to assist regular and special education personnel in meeting the unique needs of migrant students, to train parents, and to serve as a liaison between migrant parents and the school. Migrant educators often perform a variety of other roles, including acting as interpreters for parents; ensuring that students receive proper medical, dental, and health-related services; arranging transportation for families; and offering bilingual instruction, career education, and training in English as a second language.

Interpreter

Language and educational interpreters can be important members of multidisciplinary teams for students who are learning English, and students with hearing impairments, respectively, (Fradd & Wilen, 1990; Salend & Longo, in press). Interpreters can facilitate oral and written communications among students, their families, and school personnel. They also can provide culturally relevant insights into students' performance, classroom behavior and assessment data, and families' cultural perspectives.

PREREFERRAL STRATEGIES

While many referrals for special education placement are made by regular educators, referrals also may be made by parents, support personnel, administrators, physicians, significant individuals in the student's life, and the student. Most students referred for testing are placed in special education in the category in which they were referred.

Many school districts have instituted some type of prereferral system through the multidisciplinary team or a teacher assistance team to reduce the number of special education placements (Chalfant, Pysh, & Moultrie, 1979). In a *prereferral system,* a team of educators provides assistance to regular classroom teachers prior to considering a referral for a special education placement (Graden, Casey, & Christenson, 1985; Hayek, 1987). The team helps the regular education teacher devise and implement interventions to keep the student in the regular classroom. Possible interventions include behavior management systems, curricular and testing modifications, and instructional strategies adaptations. The effectiveness of these interventions are then assessed prior to formally evaluating the student for placement in special education. If the interventions are effective, the student remains in the regular classroom. If they are not effective, a formal evaluation is conducted.

Prereferral interventions have been successful in reducing the number of students placed in special education. Graden, Casey, and Bonstrom (1985) implemented a prereferral system that resulted in a decline in the number of students tested for and placed in special education. In addition to decreasing special education placements, prereferral systems provide data that assist placement teams in determining appropriate special education services, increase teacher knowledge of instructional alternatives, and help teachers examine the needs of their students (Schram & Semmel, 1984).

Because students from linguistically and culturally diverse backgrounds tend to be overreferred for special education services, prereferral strategies to address their unique needs in regular education classrooms are especially important (National Coalition of Advocates for Students, 1988). Second and third grades are especially critical for bilingual students in terms or referral for special education services (Figueroa, Fradd, & Correa, 1989).

Figueroa, Fradd, and Correa (1989) note that prereferral interventions with bilingual students occur infrequently and rarely include strategies for supporting the student's primary language.

Prereferral teams should include professionals who have expertise and experience working with culturally and linguistically diverse students. Such teams should attempt to determine whether the problems students are experiencing are due to sociocultural factors or specific learning and behavior disabilities, and should help educators and parents design and implement intervention strategies that address students' language acquisition and acculturation needs (Hoover & Collier, 1991). Ortiz and Wilkinson (1991) propose a six-step prereferral model for use with students from culturally and linguistically diverse backgrounds.

ELIGIBILITY FOR SPECIAL EDUCATION

When prereferral strategies are not effective, the multidisciplinary placement team determines if a student is eligible for special education placement based on a variety of both standardized and informal assessment procedures. Although problems with labeling students have been noted (Ysseldyke & Algozzine, 1982), state and federal funding formulas require the use of labels and definitions. However, educators must realize that no two students are alike and, therefore, each educational program must be based on individual needs rather than on a label (Haring & McCormick, 1986).

Students with special needs are categorized as being mildly disabled, sensory impaired, physically disabled, and severely disabled. Students with *mild disabilities* make up 94 percent of the students with disabilities and include students with learning disabilities, educable mental retardation, mild behavioral disorders, and speech/language impairments. Students with *sensory impairments* are those who have specific sensory disabilities and include students with hearing and visual impairments. Students with *physical disabilities* have a variety of unique physical needs, and include students who are orthopedically impaired or health impaired. Individuals who are deaf and blind, multihandicapped, seriously emotionally disturbed, or profoundly retarded are said to be *severely disabled.*

Students with Learning Disabilities

Bryce's early history included language and reading problems. Though a battery of tests revealed an individual intelligence quotient in the superior range, he was still not reading by the end of fourth grade. Attention and behavior began to be considered as problem areas during middle school.

Bryce's academic performance by ninth grade was midrange. He did well in most classes related to mathematics, science, and physics, and poorly in anything that was language based. His motivation fluctuated from applying himself to the point of making the honor roll to barely passing. His teachers tended to either really like him or really dislike him, and his parents were his sole source of emotional support and social outlet. Reports from the teachers included the fact that he had major problems assimilating information, organizing and compressing it, and presenting it in any sort of coherent form. His parents supported this, adding that when he would try to retell the theme of a movie, book, or television program, it was impossible for them to follow (Brandt & Berry, 1991, p. 300).

Forty-four percent of the students receiving special education services are students with learning disabilities, making them the largest group of students with disabilities (Sailor, 1991). Since 1976, the number of students with learning disabilities has increased by 160 percent. In addition to the term *learning disabilities,* these students also may be referred to as having perceptual problems, minimal brain dysfunction, hyperactivity, attention deficits, information processing problems, dyslexia, and developmental aphasia. The federal government estimates that approximately 5 percent of the students in our nation's schools are learning disabled (U.S. Department of Education, 1988b). However, some school districts report estimates as high as 20 percent of their school population (Tucker, Stevens, & Ysseldyke, 1983).

Ysseldyke (1987) noted that over 80% of our nation's students could be identified as having a learning disability using the current definitions of the term "learning disabilities."

This variation in the estimates is related to the vagueness of the definitions of learning disability as well as to differences in the assessment procedures used to identify students. Additionally, the comparative social acceptability of the learning disabilities label has led many school districts to categorize low-achieving students and other students with mild learning problems as having a learning disability (Mercer, 1986).

Although several definitions of the term have been proposed (Hammill, Leigh, McNutt & Larsen, 1981; Wallace & McLoughlin, 1979), most definitions of learning disabilities include students exhibiting a discrepancy between their intellectual ability and their academic achievement and exclude students whose learning problems are due to a sensory or motor handicap; mental retardation; emotional disturbance; or environmental, cultural or economic factors. The United States Office of Education (USOE) (1977) defines a specific learning disability as

> a disorder in one or more of the basic psychological processes involved in understanding or in using language, spoken or written, which may manifest itself

> in an imperfect ability to listen, think, speak, read, write, spell, or to do mathematical calculations. The term includes such conditions as perceptual handicaps, brain injury, minimal brain dysfunction, dyslexia, and developmental aphasia. The term does not include children who have learning problems which are primarily the result of visual, hearing or motor handicaps, of mental retardation, or emotional disturbance, or of environmental, cultural, or economic disadvantage.

Just as the definitions and estimates of students with learning disabilities vary, so do the explanations of the causes of learning disabilities. Some researchers believe that the etiology of learning disabilities is brain dysfunction. Initially, proponents of the brain dysfunction cause of learning disabilities focused on research to differentiate students with learning disabilities from their peers on the basis of hard and soft signs of neurological impairments (Gottesman, Croen, & Rotkin, 1982; Myklebust & Boshes, 1969). The results of these studies, however, were unclear as neurological irregularities were present in students both with and without learning disabilities. Although some researchers continue to identify neurological factors that distinguish individuals with learning disabilities (Ahn et al., 1980), many are now examining the relationship between learning disabilities and the hemispheric differences of the brain (Galaburda, 1983; Harness, Epstein, & Gordon, 1984).

Research also has been conducted to examine the role of heredity as a cause of learning disabilities. Studies show that learning problems often are common to several family members (Decker & Defries, 1980). Similarly, other studies support the finding that twins who have the same genetic makeup (identical twins) are more likely to have similar learning patterns than twins who do not have the same genetic makeup (fraternal twins) (Hermann, 1959). However, the results of these studies fail to take into account environmental factors such as economic status, cultural and linguistic differences, educational experience, and family interaction and child-rearing practices that can affect the ability to learn (Argulewicz, 1983; Coles, 1980; Kavale, 1980).

Characteristics of Students with Learning Disabilities

Because of the wide range of characteristics associated with learning disabilities, these students present many enigmas for educators. Despite the presumption that students with learning disabilities have normal or above normal intelligence, they often fail to perform academic tasks at a level commensurate with their potential or equal to their peers. This discrepant performance usually involves problems with reading, writing, spelling, and mathematics.

The characteristics and behaviors of individual students identified as learning disabled vary; many students with learning disabilities evidence problems in a variety of areas. These difficulties may manifest themselves in learning, language, perceptual, motor, social, and behavioral problems.

Learning Problems. Many students with learning disabilities have memory and attention problems that hinder their ability to master academic content (Bryan, Bay, Lopez-Reyna, & Donahue, 1991; Hallahan & Kauffman, 1982). Studies indicate that the performance of students with learning disabilities on school-related academic tasks lags behind their peers who are not learning disabled (Bryan, Pearl, Donahue, Bryan, & Pflaum, 1983) and that this gap increases with age (Cone, Wilson, Bradley, & Reese, 1985). Although most students with learning disabilities have reading problems, they may be proficient in some content areas but experience difficulties with others. Large numbers of students with learning disabilities also experience difficulties in mathematics as evidenced by problems in knowledge of basic facts and performing more complex procedures, and writing as evidenced by deficits in the areas of idea generation and text organization (Bryan et al., 1991). Students with learning disabilities also tend to use inefficient and ineffective strategies for learning (Alley & Deshler, 1979; Torgesen, 1977). For example, Wong (1982) noted that students with learning disabilities often fail to use appropriate metacognitive strategies to complete a task.

Language Problems. Language disorders are another common characteristic of many students with learning disabilities (Mercer, 1986). Research indicates that students with learning disabilities are less proficient than their peers who do not have learning disabilities on a wide range of phonological, semantic, syntactic, and communicative tasks (Donahue, 1987). Many educators believe that the language problems experienced by students with learning disabilities contribute to their difficulties in reading and acquiring information in the content areas (Wiig & Semel, 1984).

Perceptual and Motor Problems. Even though it appears that their senses are not impaired, many students with learning disabilities may experience difficulties recognizing, discriminating, and interpreting visual and auditory stimuli (Gearheart, Weishahn, & Gearheart, 1988; Morsink, 1981). For example, some students with learning disabilities may experience difficulty discriminating shapes and letters, copying from the blackboard, following multiple-step directions, associating sounds with letters, paying attention to relevant stimuli and working on a task for a sustained period of time. While some educators consider perception as an underlying factor in learning, others question its importance (Arter & Jenkins, 1979).

Students with learning disabilities also may have deficits in their gross- and fine-motor skills. Gross-motor deficits include awkward gaits, clumsiness, and an inability to catch or kick balls, skip, and follow a rhythmic sequence of movements. Fine-motor problems include difficulty cutting, pasting, drawing, and holding a pencil. Another motor problem found in some students with learning disabilities is hyperactivity, which results in constant movement and difficulty staying seated (Myers & Hammill, 1982).

Social and Behavioral Problems. Students with learning disabilities may have social and behavioral problems and may show signs of poor self-concepts, task avoidance, social withdrawal, frustration, and anxiety. Research also indicates that the poor social perception of learning disabled students results in students having difficulties relating to their peers (Bryan, 1977; Gresham & Reschly, 1986).

Another social-emotional trait often associated with students with learning disabilities is *learned helplessness,* or the inability to establish a locus of control. As a result, students with learning disabilities often are unable to attribute to themselves their own success or failure. While many individuals believe their success and failure is related to their efforts and ability, students with learning disabilities exhibit learned helplessness—they attribute academic success to factors beyond their control (Pearl, Bryan, & Donahue, 1980). Teachers can help students who exhibit learned helplessness by encouraging students to engage in adaptive attributions whereby students are taught how to respond to success and failure (Borokowski, Weyhing, & Carr, 1988).

Differentiating Cultural and Language Differences from Learning Disabilities

Students who are learning English as a new language may exhibit some behaviors that are similar to students with learning disabilities (Fradd, Barona, & Santos de Barona, 1988). These behaviors are presented in Figure 2.1. As a result, many of these students may be inappropriately placed in special education classes for students with learning disabilities.

Students with Emotional and Behavioral Disorders

Several different terms are used to refer to students with emotional and behavior problems. These terms include emotionally disturbed, behaviorally disordered, conduct disordered, and socially maladjusted (Cartwright, Cartwright, & Ward, 1985). These students make up 1 percent of the preschool and school-aged population (Jordan & Zantal-Weiner, 1987), with males significantly outnumbering females (Mendelsohn & Jennings, 1986). However, others note that students with emotional and behavioral disorders are underidentified and underserved and that traditional estimates of the prevalence rates of these students are extremely conservative (Walker & Bullis, 1991). Students with behavioral disorders tend to be identified as they enter the middle grades (Morse, Cutler, & Fink, 1964). The USOE (1977) defines a seriously emotionally disturbed student in the following terms:

1. Exhibiting one or more of the following characteristics over a long period of time and to a marked degree, which adversely affects educational performance:
   a. An inability to learn which cannot be explained by intellectual, sensory, or health factors;
   b. An inability to build or maintain satisfactory interpersonal relationships with peers and teachers;
   c. Inappropriate types of behavior or feelings under normal circumstances;
   d. A general pervasive mood of unhappiness or depression; or
   e. A tendency to develop physical symptoms or fears associated with personal or school problems.
2. The term includes children who are schizophrenic. The term does not include children who are socially maladjusted, unless it is determined that they are seriously emotionally disturbed.

FIGURE 2.1
Indicators of learning disabilities that are also characteristics of students in the process of learning English

Indicator	Cultural or Linguistic Explanation
Discrepancy between verbal and performance measures on intelligence tests	This discrepancy is predictable because those who are not proficient in the language of the test are often able to complete many of the nonverbal tasks correctly (Cummins, 1984).
Academic learning difficulty	Students in the process of learning a new language often experience difficulty with academic concepts and language because these terms and ideas are more abstract, less easily understood and experienced than ideas and terms that communicate social interactions and intents (Cummins, 1984).
Language disorders	When second-language learners enter into meaningful communication, they often appear as having language disorders because of disfluencies that are a natural part of second-language development (Oller, 1983).
Perceptual disorders	Even the ability to perceive and organize information can be distorted when students begin to learn a new language (DeBlassie, 1983).
Social and emotional problems	Students in the process of learning how to function successfully in a new language and culture predictably experience social trauma and emotional problems (DeBlassie and Franco, 1983).
Attention and memory problems	When students have few prior experiences on which to relate new information, they may find it difficult to pay attention and to remember (DeBlassie, 1983).
Hyperactivity or hypoactivity; impulsivity	When students have little prior knowledge or experiences on which to base present information, they frequently become restless and inattentive (DeBlassie, 1983).

S. H. Fradd and M. J. Weismantel, *Meeting the Needs of Culturally and Linguistically Different Students: A Handbook for Educators* (Austin, TX: PRO-ED, 1989), p. 78. Adapted from Mercer, C. D. (1987). *Students with learning disabilities.* (3rd ed.). New York: Merrill/Macmillan. Reprinted by permission of PRO-ED.

Several biological and environmental factors appear to affect an individual's behavior (Doorlag, 1988). Genetic, neurological, biochemical, and nutritional variables can contribute to a behavior disorder (Nicol & Erlenmeyer-Kimling, 1986). While such biological factors are thought to make an individual more vulnerable to behavior disorders (Thomas & Chess, 1984), environmental factors such as parent-child interaction, cultural background, and school experience also can influence the development of a behavior disorder (Hallahan & Kauffman, 1988).

Think About It

Professionals have debated whether the federal definition of seriously emotionally disturbed students should exclude students who are socially maladjusted. What do you think? Should the definition be inclusionary or exclusionary? What are the implications of an inclusionary definition? Of an exclusionary definition?

Regardless of the term used, these students are often categorized as mildly or severely disturbed depending upon their behaviors and the nature of their condition. Students who are *mildly emotionally disturbed* may resemble students with learning disabilities and mild retardation in terms of their academic and social needs (McCoy & Prehm, 1987). While the intellectual abilities of students with mild behavior disorders varies, many have IQ scores in the low average range (Hallahan & Kauffman, 1988). Their classroom behavior is often characterized by learning problems that cause poor academic performance and deficient social skills. They may exhibit high rates of inappropriate behavior such as temper tantrums, hitting and fighting with others, cursing, destruction of property, distractibility, attention seeking, and hyperactivity. They exhibit low rates of appropriate behavior such as attending to a task, working independently, interacting with peers, and following rules and directions (Cullinan & Epstein, 1986; Quay, 1979).

Students considered severely emotionally disturbed exhibit many deviant behaviors over a period of time. These students may exhibit cognitive, perceptual, speech, and language deficits. They also may lack daily living skills, engage in self-stimulatory and self-mutilatory behaviors, harm others, and fail to respond to others (Hallahan & Kauffman, 1988).

Students with Attention Deficit Disorders

Recently, there has been a growing recognition of the needs of students with attention deficit disorders (ADD) or attention deficit hyperactivity disorders (ADHD) whose school performance profiles are characterized by inattention, impulsivity, and hyperactivity, which can result in specific learning problems, low self-esteem, and poor socialization with peers. The U.S. Department of Education estimates that between 3 to 5 percent of the school-aged students have learning problems that may be related to ADD/ADHD, with boys being three times more likely to be affected than girls. While the causes of ADD are unknown at this time, possible causes are presumed to be metabolic abnormality in the brain, difficult prenatal/perinatal conditions, developmental delays, inner ear infections, lead poisoning, fetal alcohol syndrome, and food allergies (Children with Attention Deficit Disorders, n.d.).

The co-occurrence of ADD and LD ranges from 10 to 33%. The co-occurrence of ADD and ED ranges from 30% to 65% (Hallahan, 1989; Pelham & Murphy, 1986).

The term *ADHD* is included in the *Diagnostic and Statistical Manual of Mental Disorders* (DSM-111-R) (American Psychiatric Association, 1987). According to the DSM-111-R, individuals must exhibit on a continuing basis 8 or more of the following 14 behaviors for a period of at least six months with the onset of these behaviors prior to the age of 7.

IDEAS FOR IMPLEMENTATION

Educators can assist students with ADD/ADHD by enacting the following suggestions:

1. Work collaboratively with parents, medical personnel, school psychologists, and other ancillary support personnel.
2. Establish the proper learning environment by placing students in work areas that are free of distracting features, near positive role models, and close to the teacher.
3. Offer a structured program, follow classroom routines, and inform students in advance of deviations in the classroom schedule.
4. Give clear, concise, and simplified directions.
5. Monitor student performance and provide frequent feedback.
6. Adapt assignments and worksheets by breaking them into smaller chunks.
7. Allow students extra time to work on assignments.
8. Give students one assignment at a time.
9. Use a multimodality approach to learning.
10. Vary the types of activities that students are asked to do and the locations in which students perform them.
11. Employ technology (such as computers and calculators) and media (such as audiocassettes and videocassettes) to help students learn and to maintain student interest.
12. Use volunteers, peer tutors, and cooperative learning arrangements.
13. Teach social and organizational skills.
14. Involve students in afterschool activities.
15. Communicate regularly with parents, including use of a daily assignment notebook.
16. Employ behavior modification and self-monitoring strategies.
17. Monitor student reactions to medications.
18. Obtain more information by contacting the Attention Deficit Disorder Association (ADDA) (303-690-7548) and Children with Attention Deficit Disorders (C.H.A.D.D.) (305-792-8100).

Specific guidelines for implementing these recommendations are presented in subsequent chapters.

Source: Children with Attention Deficit Disorders, *Attention Deficit Disorders: A Guide for Teachers* (n.d.), R. E. Reeve, *Intervention in School and Clinic* (1990).

1. Often fidgets with hands or feet or squirms in seat (in adolescents, may be limited to subjective feelings of restlessness)
2. Has difficulty remaining seated when required to do so
3. Is easily distracted by extraneous stimuli
4. Has difficulty awaiting turn in games or group situations
5. Often blurts out answers to questions before they have been completed
6. Has difficulty following through on instructions from others (not due to oppositional behavior or failure of comprehension)
7. Has difficulty sustaining attention in tasks or play activities
8. Often shifts from one uncompleted activity to another

9. Has difficulty playing quietly
10. Often talks excessively
11. Often interrupts or intrudes on others
12. Often does not listen to what is being said to him or her
13. Often loses things necessary for tasks or activities in school or at home
14. Often engages in physically dangerous activities without considering consequences (American Psychiatric Association, 1987, pp. 52–53)

These behaviors also may be characteristic of children suffering from depression, living in chaotic homes, and experiencing health and nutrition problems and auditory processing difficulties (Reeve, 1990).

While not recognized as a separate category under the IDEA, the U.S. Department of Education notes that school districts are responsible for providing special education and related services to eligible students with ADD if the students are also found to be other health impaired, learning disabled, or seriously emotionally disturbed. Students with ADD who do not qualify for services under the IDEA can be eligible for these services under Section 504 (Small Special Education Program Caucus, 1991). When designing educational programs for students with ADD/ADHD, educators should collect information from a variety of sources, examine functioning in multiple settings, assess levels of inattention, impulsivity, and hyperactivity, and employ interviews, observations, rating scales, and psychoeducational tests (Reeve, 1990).

Students with Autism

Under the provisions of PL 101-476 (the 1990 amendments to PL 94-142), autism was added as a new disability category. Autism is usually characterized by a severe disorder in communication and behavior which usually occurs at birth or within the first two and one-half years of life. Students with autism may show the following physical symptoms:

- *Apparent sensory deficits*—acts deaf and may avoid making eye contact with others.
- *Severe affect isolation*—acts in an aloof manner, has difficulty interacting with others, uses people as objects, and reacts negatively to the touch of others.
- *Self-stimulation*—engages in repetitive stereotypic acts, such as body rocking, staring at spinning objects, flapping hands at the wrist, and laughing and giggling at inappropriate times.
- *Tantrums and self-mutilatory behavior*—exhibits a variety of inappropriate behaviors that may include aggression toward self and others.
- *Oral language difficulties*—fails to speak but may occasionally use simple verbalizations or echo the comments of others.
- *Learning problems*—has difficulty learning. Using traditional ways of assessing students, as many as 70 percent of the individuals with autism have IQ scores below 75.

- *Behavior deficiencies*—fails to exhibit a variety of age-appropriate behaviors such as feeding and dressing self and playing with toys. Shows no fear of common dangers, exhibits marked physical overactivity, and has difficulty with changes in routine (Lovaas & Newsom, 1976; Toscano, 1985).

While students with autism have traditionally been educated in institutional settings, residential programs, and special day schools, a variety of new findings are encouraging professionals and parents to place these students in less restrictive environments. Lovaas (1987) reported that half of the autistic children who received extensive early intervention services that included an individualized behavior modification program were mainstreamed into regular education classrooms. Similarly, Russo and Koegel (1977) were able to mainstream a student with autism successfully.

Facilitated Communication (FC)

One controversial technique that has far-reaching implications for individuals with autism is facilitated communication (FC). Originally developed by Rosemary Crossley in Australia, professionals in the United States are finding that individuals with autism, who were thought to have severe cognitive delays, are showing unexpected literacy and the ability to engage in conversations with others through facilitated communication (Biklen, 1990). *Facilitated communication* is a method that allows an individual with autism to communicate by using a word or letter board or electrified keyboard with the assistance of another person, called a facilitator (Biklen & Schubert, 1991; Wolff, 1991). The individual communicates his or her thoughts by pointing to a word or letter choice or typing on the keyboard while the facilitator provides a physical prompt, which may range from an encouraging hand on the shoulder, arm, or individual's clothing to hand or arm support to aid in isolating, stabilizing, or extending the index finger to point or type. Over time, the degree of physical assistance provided by the facilitator can be faded out; professionals report that some individuals with autism have eventually developed the ability to communicate manually without physical assistance from a facilitator (Wolff, 1991). These findings are causing professionals to hypothesize that autism may be related to a motor dysfunction that affects the ability to imitate, sustain, and inhibit a motor movement, rather than the traditional view of autism as a cognitive and communicative disorder (Biklen, 1990).

Concerns regarding the use of FC have been raised. These concerns include the intrusiveness of the facilitator and the extent to which the communication represents the facilitator's responses and cues rather than those of the individual being facilitated. Supporters of FC counter these concerns by noting that some individuals have learned to type independently, the individuals being facilitated exhibit concomitant signs such as laughter and facial expressions that are indicative of the person's understanding of communication, and the nature of the communications often relates to thoughts or facts of which the facilitator is not aware (Biklen, 1990). In addition, students who use facilitated communication often make unique typographical errors and phonetic spellings, and create unusual sentences and phrases that are peculiar to them.

Think About It

Kelly and Chris are two students with the physical symptoms associated with autism who attend the Children's Annex, a certified day school serving students with special needs in New York state. Kelly is a 9½-year-old girl who has been identified as being severely retarded and almost completely nonverbal. When tested at the age of 7½, she was found to be functioning at a mental age of 2 years. The Children's Annex staff provided Kelly with the opportunity to use facilitated communication and she wrote the following haiku while being facilitated by her teacher in a mainstreamed sixth-grade creative writing class.

KELLYS HAIKU

PEOPLE STOP AND STARE
I AM LOST
I CANT TELL WHY

Chris is a 12-year-old boy with autism. He has no oral language and had been functioning in the profoundly retarded range. After the Children's Annex staff provided him with the opportunity to use facilitated communication, he wrote the following:

THE GHOST OF THE CHILDRENS ANNEX

ONCE UPON A TIME A FRIENDLY GHOST NAMED GIERFOLD LIVED IN THE HALLS OF THE CHILDRENS ANNEX HE WAS A STUDENT FROM A LONG TIME AGO GIERFOLD WANTED TO LEARN WITH ALL THE OTHER KIDS BUT COULD NOT LEARN LIKE OTHERS HE WAS INVISIBLE AND DIDNT TALK ONE DAY A TEACHER TOLD THE OTHERS ABOUT GIERFOLD THEY DECIDED TO TRY AND HELP HIM THE TEACHERS FOUND A WAY TO TALK WITH GIERFOLD AND NOW HE COMES TO SCHOOL AND WORKS WITH THE KIDS

What do you think of facilitated communication? If individuals like Kelly and Chris can communicate like this, where should they receive their educational program? To what curriculum should they be exposed?

Students With Mental Retardation

Along with the significant increase in the number of students with learning disabilities, there has been a decrease in the number of students with mental retardation (Polloway & Smith, 1983; Reschly, 1988). Currently, these students comprise 1.2 percent of the preschool and school-aged students in the United States (U.S. Department of Education, 1991). The USOE (1977) defines students with mental retardation as having "significantly subaverage general intellectual functioning existing concurrently with deficits in adaptive behavior and manifested during the developmental period, which adversely affects a child's educational performance."

The causes of mental retardation can be categorized as biomedical and social-environmental (Lynch, 1988). Biomedical causes include genetic and chromosomal disorders, infectious diseases (e.g., congenital rubella, meningitis), gestational and obstetric disorders (e.g., prematurity, Rh incompatibility, lack of oxygen, perinatal injury), environmental hazards (for example, lead poisoning, fetal alcohol syndrome, head injuries), and neurocutaneous syndromes (Moore, 1982). However, biomedical factors account for the documented cause in only 20 to 30 percent of the cases (Garber & McInerney, 1982).

The predominant cause of mental retardation, particularly mild retardation, is thought to be social-environmental factors. Social-environmental factors that can affect a student's intellectual functioning and adaptive behavior performance include socioeconomic status, parenting style, health care and nutrition, and educational opportunities.

Depending on the degree of mental retardation, students may be classified as mildly, moderately, or severely/profoundly mentally disabled. Students with *mild retardation* make up approximately 85 percent of the total number of students with mental retardation (Gajria & Hughes, 1988). Their IQs range from above 50 to below 75 and they exhibit many of the behaviors of their counterparts with learning disabilities. However, while students with learning disabilities may show an uneven learning profile with strengths and weaknesses in different areas, students who are mildly retarded typically show a low learning profile in all areas.

Research indicates that students with mild retardation have difficulty learning material because of the following problems:

- paying attention to a task for an extended period of time
- attending to the important aspects of a task
- transferring and generalizing skills learned to new situations
- acquiring information through incidental learning
- remembering information that has just been taught
- using and understanding language
- thinking abstractly (Espin & Deno, 1988)

These problems often result in school performance that is significantly behind their peers who are not retarded. The frustration of repeated school failure may in turn lead to low self-esteem, an inability to work independently, and an expectancy of failure (Espin & Deno, 1988). Additionally, many students with mild retardation have poor social skills, which hinder their ability to interact with their peers (Strain & Shores, 1977).

Students with *moderate retardation* have IQ scores that range from 30 to 50 and compose between 6 to 10 percent of the individuals with mental retardation (Gajria & Hughes, 1988). Their performance levels tend to be slightly below those of students with mild retardation. Educational programs for students with moderate retardation often focus on the development of communication, vocational, daily living, and functional academic skills. As a result of these programs, many individuals with moderate retardation often learn basic reading and math skills and usually are employed and live independently in the community (Espin & Deno, 1988).

Students with *severe and profound retardation* have IQ scores below 30 and account for 4 percent of the individuals with mental retardation (Gajria & Hughes, 1988). These individuals may engage in inappropriate behaviors such as tantrums, headbanging, attacks against others, pica, and stereotypic and self-injurious behavior (Espin & Deno, 1988). Additionally, many of these students may have unique physical and health needs (Westling, 1986). Educational programs for these students help them learn appropriate behavior, develop functional living and communication skills, and obtain employment in a supervised work setting. While these students are often educated in self-contained classrooms or specialized schools, successful programs to integrate them into the mainstream of the school exist (Stainback & Stainback, 1988).

Fragile X Syndrome

A recently identified genetic disorder that causes mental retardation is *fragile X syndrome,* a chromosomal condition that is also thought to be associated with learning disabilities, language difficulties, attention deficit disorders, autism, and behavioral disorders (Santos, 1992). While fragile X affects females, the vast majority of individuals who exhibit the syndrome are males. Individuals with fragile X may have flat feet, strabismus, frequent ear infections, and other physical characteristics that may appear as individuals age (Santos, 1992). They also demonstrate a range of cognitive abilities, with female students being less affected than males (Reis, 1990). Behaviorally, individuals with fragile X may exhibit hyperactivity, attention difficulties, poor eye contact, and other behaviors associated with autism (Santos, 1992). Common speech and language difficulties include problems with word retrieval, poor eye contact, topic shifts, perseveration, overuse of common phrases, fluency, and voice quality (Hagerman & Sobesky, 1989; Scharfenaker, 1990).

Think About It

Review the definitions, characteristics, and ideas for implementation associated with students with learning disabilities, emotional disturbance, attention deficit disorders, and educable mental retardation. How do these categories overlap? How do they differ? What are the implications of these similarities and differences for planning educational programs for these students?

Students with Speech and Language Impairments

A growing number of students with special needs have speech and language impairments. Approximately 3 percent of preschool and school-aged children have been identified as having a speech or language impairment (Jordan & Zantal-Wiener, 1987). Most students with speech and language impairments are identified between the ages of 5 and 14 (Swift, 1988). A student with a speech/language impairment has "a communication disorder, such as stuttering, impaired articulation, a language impairment, or a voice impairment that adversely affects a child's educational performance" (USOE, 1977).

These students have receptive and expressive language disorders that hinder their performance in the classroom. *Receptive language* refers to the ability to understand spoken language. Students with receptive language problems may have difficulty following directions and understanding content presented orally.

Expressive language relates to the ability to express one's ideas in words and sentences. Students with expressive language disorders may be reluctant to participate in verbal activities. This lack of participation can have a negative impact on their academic performance and their social-emotional development. Expressive language disorders include articulation, voice, and fluency disorders. Students with articulation disorders comprise approximately 75 percent of the students with communication disorders (Swift, 1988). Articulation problems include omissions (for example, the student says *ird* instead of *bird*), substitutions (the student says *wove* instead of *love*), distortions (the student may distort a sound so that it sounds like another sound), and additions (the student says *ruhace* for *race*).

Students with voice disorders comprise approximately 6 percent of the school-age students identified as speech/language impaired (Moore, 1986). Voice disorders relate to deviations in the pitch, volume, and quality of sounds produced. Breathiness, hoarseness, and harshness, as well as problems in resonation are all indications of possible voice quality disorders.

Fluency disorders, which relate to the rate and rhythm of an individual's speech, account for 3 percent of communication disorders (Swift, 1988). Stuttering is the most prevalent type of fluency disorder; cluttering, which involves talking in a rapid, disorganized manner that is difficult to understand, is another type of fluency disorder (Hallahan & Kauffman, 1988).

Speech and language disorders may be caused by biological and environmental factors. Nervous system dysfunctions can impair speech production and language functions, while structural deviations (for example, cleft palates, loss of teeth) and obstructions in the nasal passages can cause disorders in speech production. Although it is difficult to identify the cause of most communication disorders, environmental factors such as vocal misuse, inappropriate language models, lack of language stimulation, and emotional trauma also may contribute to a speech or language impairment.

Taylor (1986) noted that speech and language abilities can be affected by race, ethnic background, socio-economic status, educational experience, geographical area, gender, peers, context, and exposure to language. Therefore, since students from various ethnic backgrounds and geographic regions may have limited experience with English or speak with a different dialect, educators should exercise caution in identifying these students as speech or language impaired. In fact, many of these students may have already mastered a language or dialect that has many sophisticated structures and rules (Bernthal & Bankson, 1988), and may be quite adept at code switching (Kirk & Gallagher, 1989).

Students with Physical and Health Needs

Students with physical impairments and/or health-related problems compose 1 percent of our nation's preschool and school-aged students (Jordan & Zantal-Wiener, 1987). The USOE (1977) recognizes two types of students with

IDEAS FOR IMPLEMENTATION

Teachers can assist students who stutter by enacting the following suggestions:

- Respond to the content of the students' verbalizations rather than how the students say it.
- Refrain from interrupting students or speaking for students when they pause or stutter.
- Make typical eye contact with students.
- Pause a few seconds before responding to students to help students relax.
- Refrain from hurrying students when they speak, criticizing or correcting their speech, forcing them to speak in front of others, and telling students to relax or slow down.
- Encourage students to express themselves and their ideas.
- Treat students who stutter in the same manner as other students.
- Ask students questions that can be responded to with relatively few words (Once students adjust, questions that require a more in-depth response can be introduced).
- Teach and encourage all students to take their time before responding to questions.
- Meet with parents and speech/language clinicians to learn about their concerns and expectations, and to get their suggestions.
- Teach other students how to respond when students stutter.
- Allow students who stutter to practice oral recitations.
- Refrain from bombarding the students with questions.
- Encourage students to make friends and participate in extracurricular activities.

Source: E. C. Conture & J. Fraser, *Stuttering and your child: Questions and Answers* (1990).

physical disabilities: orthopedically impaired and other health impaired. *Orthopedically impaired* students are defined as having the following:

> A severe orthopedic impairment which adversely affects a child's educational performance. The term includes impairments caused by congenital anomaly (e.g., clubfoot, absence of some member, etc.), impairments caused by disease (e.g., poliomyelitis, bone tuberculosis, etc.), and impairments from other causes (e.g., cerebral palsy, amputations, and fractures or burns which cause contractures). (USOE, 1977)

Other health impaired is defined as the following:

> having limited strength, vitality, or alertness, due to chronic or acute health problems such as a heart condition, tuberculosis, rheumatic fever, nephritis, asthma, sickle cell anemia, hemophilia, epilepsy, lead poisoning, leukemia, or diabetes, which adversely affects a child's educational performance. (Federal Register, 34, July 1, 1985)

In addition to their physical and medical needs, some of these students may have concomitant conditions such as learning disabilities, communication disorders, and mental retardation (Bigge & Sirvis, 1986).

Because of the wide range of conditions included in this category, it is difficult to generalize its specific characteristics. As a group, students with physical and health conditions tend to have IQ scores within the normal range. Although their IQ scores tend to be skewed toward the lower side of the IQ curve, many individuals with severe physical disabilities have above average IQ scores (Brady, 1988). However, their academic performance may be negatively affected by irregular school attendance caused by their need for medical care. In terms of social-emotional development, students with physical disabilities appear to be at risk for developing dependent behavior patterns (Brady, 1988). They also may have a lower self-concept and higher anxiety level than their peers without disabilities (Harvey & Greenway, 1984).

Students with physical and health needs are a heterogeneous group that includes a variety of conditions such as cerebral palsy, spina bifida, Tourette Syndrome, diabetes, convulsive disorders, cancer and other fragile medical needs.

Students with Cerebral Palsy

Cerebral palsy is caused by damage to the central nervous system and is not hereditary, contagious, progressive, or curable.

One of the most common physical impairments is cerebral palsy, a condition that affects voluntary motor functions of an estimated 700,000 children and adults in the United States. Students with cerebral palsy may experience seizures, perceptual difficulties, and sensory and speech impairments. There are several primary types of cerebral palsy: hypertonia, hypotonia, athetosis, and ataxia.

Hypertonia—An individual with hypertonia, also referred to as spasticity, exhibits movements that are jerky, exaggerated, and poorly coordinated.

Hypotonia—An individual with hypotonia has loose and flaccid muscles and may have difficulty maintaining balance.

IDEAS FOR IMPLEMENTATION

When working with students with cerebral palsy, teachers should enact the following suggestions:

1. Treat students as normally as possible without underestimating their capabilities.
2. Modify tasks based on the students' physical abilities.
3. Understand that they may need more time to complete a task.
4. Allow students more time to respond verbally.
5. Do not hesitate to ask students to repeat themselves if their comments are not understood by others.
6. Ask students if they need assistance.
7. Be sensitive to the social and emotional needs of students.
8. Learn how to position and transfer students who use wheelchairs. (Parette and Hourcade (1986) provide excellent guidelines for teachers to consider when positioning and transferring students.)
9. Seek more information by contacting the United Cerebral Palsy Association at 7 Penn Plaza, New York, NY 10001.

Athetosis—An individual with athetosis experiences uncontrolled and irregular movements.

Ataxia—An individual with ataxia experiences difficulties in balancing and using hands. (Heward & Orlansky, 1992).

Students with Spina Bifida

The Supreme Court, in Irving Independent School District v. Tatro *(1984), determined that catheterization was a related service that school districts were responsible to provide in order to maintain a student with spina bifida in the least restrictive environment.*

Another group of students with unique physical and medical needs is students with spina bifida. Spina bifida is a condition that is caused by a defect in the vertebrae of the spinal cord and usually results in some type of paralysis of the lower limbs as well as loss of control over bladder functions. Students with spina bifida often have good control over their upper body but may need to use some type of prosthetic device for mobility such as a walker, braces, or crutches. They also may require the use of a catheter or bag to minimize their bladder control difficulties.

Students with Tourette Syndrome

She is bright, friendly, anxious to please, generally well behaved and polite. However, for no apparent reason, she disrupts the class with snorting noises. She also blinks her eyes constantly, even though the eye doctor says she doesn't need glasses. She also persists in jumping around her seat. You have spoken to her and her parents about her behavior, but she has persisted. (Bronheim, n.d., p. 2).

IDEAS FOR IMPLEMENTATION

Teachers can help students with Tourette Syndrome by doing the following:

1. Be patient and react to the student's involuntary inappropriate behavior with tolerance rather than anger.
2. Allow students to leave the room for short periods of time when tics and verbalizations become uncontrollable and distracting.
3. Provide students with a quiet location to take tests.
4. Help other students understand the needs of students with Tourette Syndrome.
5. Employ alternative assignments to minimize the stress on students with Tourette Syndrome. For example, rather than giving a presentation to the whole class, students with Tourette Syndrome can make an audiocassette of an oral presentation or give the presentation to the teacher without other students present.
6. Monitor the side effects of medications the students may be taking.
7. Seek assistance from others such as counselors, school nurses, school psychologists, and parents.
8. Obtain additional information about Tourette Syndrome by contacting the Tourette Syndrome Association at 718-224-2999.

Source: Bronheim (n.d.).

The student described above does not have an emotional problem, rather she has Tourette Syndrome (TS). TS is a neurological disorder whose symptoms appear in childhood. These symptoms include involuntary multiple tics, uncontrolled repeated verbal responses such as noises (laughing, coughing, and throat clearing), words, or phrases. These symptoms occur and disappear at various times and change over time (Bronheim, n.d.). Students with TS also may have learning disabilities, language disorders, and obsessive-compulsive behaviors and difficulties in maintaining attention and controlling impulses.

Students with Diabetes

It is very likely that teachers will have students with diabetes in their classes as diabetes affects approximately 1 out of 600 school aged children (Winter, 1983). Students with diabetes lack enough insulin and therefore have difficulty gaining energy from food. Teachers should be aware of the symptoms of diabetes, which include the following:

- frequent requests for liquids
- repeated trips to the bathroom
- unhealthy skin color
- headaches
- vomiting and nausea
- failure of cuts and sores to heal
- loss of weight despite adequate food intake
- poor circulation as indicated by complaints about cold hands and feet
- pain in the abdominal area (Byrne, 1981)

Students who exhibit some of these symptoms should contact the school nurse or another trained medical professional.

For students who have been diagnosed as diabetic, teachers also should be aware of the signs of diabetic shock, which can result from excessive insulin, overexertion, or failure to eat. Heward and Orlansky (1992) note that the signs of diabetic shock are irritability, personality shifts, fatigue, dizziness, nausea, and double vision. Teachers can respond to diabetic shock by giving the student food or liquids that contain high levels of sugar such as orange juice, or a piece of candy or another substance that the student's doctor has recommended.

When a diabetic coma occurs, it indicates that the student's insulin level is too low and medical personnel should be contacted immediately (Heward & Orlansky, 1992). Signs of a diabetic coma are tiredness, excessive urination and thirst, hot skin, irregular breathing, and breath that has a sweet, fruity odor.

Students with Convulsive Disorders

Elaine was constantly being reprimanded by her teacher for not paying attention in school. Frequently, she would stare vacantly at the teacher, appearing not to understand what was occurring in the room. These expressionless, vacuous gazes became a serious concern for everyone involved with the child. The teacher noted that these short staring episodes were occurring more frequently, and the child often failed to acquire important information (Michael, 1992, p. 211).

Many individuals with physical disabilities and other health impairments may experience seizures. The Epilepsy Foundation of America (1987) estimates that over three-quarters of a million American youth have recurrent seizures. When these seizures occur on a regular basis, the individual is said to be suffering from a convulsive disorder or epilepsy. There are three types of seizures: generalized tonic-clonic seizure, absence seizure, and complex partial seizure.

Generalized Tonic-Clonic Seizure. Also referred to as grand mal, this type of seizure is characterized by a loss of consciousness and bladder control, stiff muscles, saliva drooling out of the mouth and violent body shaking. After a period of two to five minutes, the individual may fall asleep or regain consciousness in a confused manner.

Absence Seizure. Also referred to as petit mal, this type of seizure is characterized by a short duration in which the individual loses consciousness, appears to be daydreaming, looks pale, and drops any objects he or she may be holding.

Complex Partial Seizure. Also referred to as a psychomotor seizure, this type of seizure is characterized by a short duration in which the individual maintains consciousness but engages in inappropriate and bizarre behaviors. After a period of two to five minutes, the individual regains control and often does not remember what happened (Heward & Orlansky, 1992). Prior to these types of seizures, students may experience an *aura,* a sensation that indicates that a seizure is imminent.

Students who experience seizures will require few modifications in the mainstream setting, but the potential deleterious effects of a seizure can be minimized by carefully structuring the classroom environment. Teachers can help prevent students from hurting themselves during a seizure by staying composed and keeping the other students calm (it often helps to remind the class that the seizure is painless); by avoiding attempting to restrain the student, placing fingers or objects in the student's mouth, or giving the student anything to eat or drink; by making the student as comfortable as possible by helping him or her to lie down and loosening tight clothing; by protecting the student by placing a soft cushioned object under his or her head; by ensuring that the spaces around the student's work areas are large enough to thrash around in; and by keeping the area surrounding the student's desk free of objects that could cause harm to the student during the seizure. After the seizure, position the student's head to one side to allow the discharge of saliva that may have built up in the mouth, contact other necessary school and medical personnel and the student's parents, and briefly discuss the seizure with the class, encouraging acceptance rather than fear or pity. Since seizures often result in students being fatigued, a rest area with a cot may be necessary. Michael (1992) has developed a Seizure Observation Form that helps teachers document and share with others relevant information regarding a student's seizure. The components of the observation form are behavior before seizure, initial seizure behavior, behavior during seizure, behavior after seizure, student reaction to seizure, peer reactions to seizure, and teacher comments. Materials that provide guidelines for helping teachers and peers learn about epilepsy and seizures are available from the Epilepsy Foundation of America, 1828 L Street, N.W., Washington, DC 20036.

Students Treated for Cancer

Research indicates that one out of every 330 students is diagnosed as having cancer by age 19 (Karl, 1992). Because of a cure rate of approximately 70 percent, a growing number of students treated for cancer are attending our nation's schools (Karl, 1992). Schooling can provide a normalizing experience for students and enhance their quality of life. While some students who are treated for cancer may have special education needs, others will not.

Although there are a variety of causes of cancer, approximately 50 percent of the children diagnosed with cancer have a brain tumor or childhood leukemia, which can affect the central nervous system. Cancer treatments vary in terms of type and length of therapies. However, many treatments are toxic and can affect the student's cognitive, gross and fine motor, language, sensory, and emotional development (Karl, 1992). Frequent or lengthy hospitalizations resulting in erratic school attendance also can hinder learning and socialization. Teachers can help these students by using effective instructional procedures, providing emotional support, and obtaining assistance from hospitals, medical centers, and organizations that serve individuals with cancer.

Medically Fragile Students

A 9-year-old girl sustained a high cervical spinal cord injury, resulting in minimal head control and need for ventilator assistance in breathing. In her fourth-grade class, she requires mechanical ventilation, suctioning, positioning, catheterization, and assistance with equipment for eating and computer writing. She also requires immediate action in the case of an equipment breakdown or a health emergency (Sirvis, 1988, p. 40).

As a result of medical technology and legislation guaranteeing all students a right to a free appropriate education, school districts are serving an increasing number of students who are medically fragile. The Council for Exceptional Children's Task Force on Medically Fragile Students defines this group of students as those who "require specialized technological health care procedures for life support and/or health support during the school day. These students may or may not require special education" (Sirvis, 1988, p. 40).

The Office of Technology Assessment estimates that approximately 100,000 infants and students may require the use of medical technology to avert death or further disability. In classroom situations, these students may evidence limited vitality and mobility, tiredness, and attention problems. Decisions regarding their educational program and placement should be based on the student's medical needs and made in conjunction with parents and support personnel such as physical, occupational and respiratory therapists, doctors, and nurses.

Students with Traumatic Brain Injury

Tyler ... sustained a grade III injury at age eight when he was hit by an automobile while attempting to cross the street. He was in coma for five months and hospitalized for one year. Aside from a fused elbow, which limits

IDEAS FOR IMPLEMENTATION

Teachers can help students who have medically fragile needs by enacting the following suggestions:

1. Adjust schedules to address the student's unique medical needs.
2. Learn more about the student's condition by conferring with parents, the student and support personnel.
3. Develop a communication system with the student's parents.
4. Coordinate services with other agencies working with the student and the family.
5. Understand the student's home health care plan and the impact on the student of new treatments and medication.
6. Establish procedures for emergencies, problems with equipment, and minimizing interruptions to others for medical interventions that the student may need.
7. Become familiar with the student's equipment, ventilation management, and CPR.
8. Keep the equipment's oxygen source in a safe location away from electrical appliances, cigarettes, fire, products that are alcohol or petroleum based, and aerosols.
9. Check the equipment's tubing and settings.
10. Be aware of the signs that indicate a need for suctioning to clear secretions.
11. Create opportunities for the student to participate in social activities with peers.
12. Consider the social and emotional needs of the student.
13. Talk and encourage other adults and students to talk directly to the student rather than through the student's aide or nurse.
14. Modify curricula and testing procedures.
15. Understand the postioning needs of the student.
16. Set up a transportation schedule that minimizes time on the bus.

Source: Ahmann & Lipsi (1991); Rothstein & Levine (1992); Sirvis (1988); Lynch, Lewis, & Murphy (1992).

his range of motion, Tyler has no significant physical impairments. Cognitively, he has deficits in sustained attention, written arithmetic calculations, auditory memory, hypothesis testing and visual memory. Cognitive strengths include language ability and both written and oral communication skills. Reportedly, Tyler had been hospitalized in the recent past for depression and a suicide attempt. (West, Kregel, & Wehman, 1991, p. 25)

In addition to autism, the IDEA added traumatic brain injury (TBI) as a recognized disability category. Each year between 400,000 to 500,000 individuals are treated for a brain injury, with approximately 40 percent of these cases being children (Savage, 1987). Pieper (1991) defined traumatic brain injury as:

> an insult to the brain which results in a temporary *alteration of consciousness,* but does not necessarily result in a state of unconsciousness. The term Traumatic Brain Injury (TBI) is used both as an etiology and a diagnosis. TBI generally excludes conditions which are present at birth (congenital hydrocephalus, lack of oxygen) and those conditions which are progressive in nature (multiple sclerosis, etc.). (p. 6)

The characteristics of students with TBI vary from student to student depending on the nature of the brain injury (Jacobs, 1989), but may include the following:

- memory difficulties that may interfere with learning
- an inability to focus and maintain attention
- organizational problems
- mental and physical fatigue
- delays in processing and responding to information
- up and down performance profiles
- confusion and delay in selecting the correct words to use
- secondary social and emotional problems
- emotional swings and difficulty inhibiting

IDEAS FOR IMPLEMENTATION

Teachers can assist students with Traumatic Brain Injury (TBI) by enacting the following suggestions:

1. Use cooperative learning groups and peer tutoring.
2. Teach students strategies for remembering and organizing material.
3. Vary the types of learning activities.
4. Allow students to take breaks and have more time to complete tasks.
5. Provide immediate feedback and reinforcement.
6. Give clear and concise directions that include examples.
7. Teach students to use self-management techniques.
8. Contact the National Head Injury Foundation at 333 Turnpike Rd., Southboro, MA 01772 for additional information.

- loss of sensations and sensory abilities
- disorientation for time and space
- poor impulse control

Students with Hearing Impairments

Students with hearing impairments constitute slightly less than 2 percent of the school-aged population and approximately 8 percent of the general population. This category includes deaf and hard of hearing students. Students are considered *deaf* when they have "a hearing impairment which is so severe that the child is impaired in processing linguistic information through hearing, with or without amplification, which adversely affects educational performance" (USOE, 1977).

Hard of hearing is defined as "a hearing impairment, whether permanent or fluctuating, which adversely affects a child's educational performance but which is not included under the definition of "deaf" (USOE, 1977).

Approximately 0.2 percent of school-aged students have a severe or profound hearing disorder (Hoemann & Briga, 1981). While students with severe hearing impairments are usually identified and provided with special services, only about 20 percent of the hard of hearing students are receiving special services (Berg, 1986).

Trybus (1985) identified the primary causes of hearing impairments as heredity, maternal rubella, prenatal and perinatal complications, meningitis, and childhood diseases and injuries. However, the etiology of hearing impairments cannot be determined in approximately 20 percent of the cases (Moores, 1982).

A hearing loss can be unilateral (affecting one ear) or bilateral (affecting both ears), and may be categorized according to the type and degree of hearing loss (Gearheart, Weishahn, & Gearheart, 1988). There are two types of hearing losses: conductive and sensorineural (Lowenbraun & Thompson, 1986). *Conductive hearing losses* are impairments in the transmission of sound from the outer ear to the middle ear. Some conductive hearing losses can be corrected by surgery, while others can be minimized by use of a hearing aid. *Sensorineural hearing losses* are caused by damage within the inner ear and affect the conversion of sound waves into electrical impulses. Sensorineural losses tend to be permanent; they are not as amenable to correction through surgery or the use of a hearing aid. Both types of hearing losses can have an impact on the student's academic performance, speech/language development, and social skills.

The degree of hearing loss is assessed by giving the student an audiometric evaluation, which provides a measure of the intensity and frequency of sound that the student can hear. The intensity of the sound is defined in terms of decibel levels (db); the frequency is measured in hertz (hz). Based on the audiometric evaluation, the hearing loss is classified from mild to profound.

Some hearing disorders may not be detected prior to entry into school. Many students with hearing losses are identified by their teachers. A student with a hearing loss may do some or all of the following:

- have difficulty following directions and paying attention to auditory stimuli
- articulate poorly
- ask the speaker or peers to repeat statements or instructions
- avoid oral activities
- rely heavily on gestures
- turn up the volume when listening to audiovisual aids such as televisions, radios, and cassette recorders
- cock the head to one side (Gearheart, Weishahn, & Gearheart, 1988; Green, 1981)

If a hearing loss is suspected, the student should be referred to the school nurse or physician for an audiometric evaluation.

The intellectual abilities of students with hearing impairments parallel the intellectual capacity of students with hearing. However, the concomitant communication problems in learning an oral language system can create an experiential and informational deficit that hinders the intellectual functioning and academic performance of students with hearing impairments (Moores & Maestas y Moores, 1988). Research indicates that students with hearing impairments perform below their intellectual potential on traditional standardized tests measuring academic achievement (Moores & Maestas y Moores, 1988). Difficulties in communication also can affect the social-emotional development of students with hearing impairments resulting in difficulties establishing friendships, shyness, and withdrawn behavior (Loeb & Sarigiani, 1986).

Students with Visual Impairments

Students with visual impairments that require special services make up about 0.1 percent of the school-aged population (Hallahan & Kauffman, 1988). Definitions and types of visual impairments vary; the USOE (1977) defines a *visual disability* as "a visual impairment which, even with correction, adversely affects a child's educational performance. The term includes both partially seeing and blind children."

Heredity is the major cause of visual impairments. Other factors include infectious diseases, poisoning, diabetes, tumors, and prenatal complications. Aging has become a primary cause of blindness in the elderly.

Barraga (1983) identified three types of individuals with visual impairments: blind, low vision, and visually limited. *Blind* individuals have no vision or limited light perception. Individuals who have *low vision* can see objects that are close by but have difficulty seeing things at a distance. Individuals who are *visually limited* need aids or special lighting to see under normal conditions.

Most definitions of a visual impairment measure vision in terms of *acuity,* or clarity of vision, which is assessed through use of a Snellen Chart. The Snellen Chart measures acuity by comparing the individual's vision to a person with normal vision. For example, a visual acuity of 20/100 means that the individual can read a letter or symbol at 20 feet that a person with normal vision could read at 100 feet.

In addition to acuity, visual functioning and efficiency also are important (Barraga, 1983). *Visual efficiency* describes the ease, comfort, and time in which an individual can perform visual tasks; *visual functioning* relates to the ways individuals use the vision they possess. Students who are visually impaired should be encouraged to increase their visual efficiency and functioning.

As a group, individuals with visual impairments have IQ scores within the normal range. However, their cognitive and language development may be limited by their inability to obtain and understand abstract visual information from the environment (Terzieff, 1988). For example, students with visual impairments may have problems learning spatial concepts. Their language may be characterized by use of verbalisms, or words or phrases that are inconsistent with one's sensory experiences. Additionally, because of limited mobility, the motor development of some students with visual impairments may be delayed.

In terms of academic achievement, students with visual impairments may lag behind their sighted peers in learning abstract concepts during the middle school years. However, as they enter high school, their ability to understand these abstract concepts improves significantly (Terzieff, 1988). If isolated from peers, students with visual impairments may lack appropriate socialization skills and may develop a poor self-image.

Since visual impairments can hinder a student's cognitive, language, motor, and social development, early detection of visual impairments is important. Visual problems are indicated when the student does any or all of the following:

- holds reading material close to the eyes
- has difficulty seeing things from a distance
- blinks, squints, and rubs the eyes or tilts the head frequently
- covers or closes one eye
- has frequent swollen eyelids and inflamed or watery eyes
- complains of seeing double and having headaches
- exhibits irregular eye movements (National Society for the Prevention of Blindness, 1977)

Educators who suspect a visual problem should refer the student to the school nurse or physician.

Students with Severe Disabilities

Students with severe disabilities comprise 1 percent of school-age students and approximately 10 percent of students who are eligible for special education services (Sailor, Anderson, Halvorsen, Doering, Filler, & Goetz, 1989). The term *individuals with severe disabilities* often refers to individuals with profound retardation and concomitant sensory, communication, medical, motor, and emotional disabilities. The Association for Persons with Severe Handicaps (TASH) offers the following definition:

> These people include individuals of all ages who require extensive ongoing support in more than one major life activity in order to participate in integrated community settings and to enjoy a quality of life that is available to citizens with

> fewer or no disabilities. Support may be required for life activities such as mobility, communication, self-care, and learning, as necessary for independent living, employment and self-sufficiency. (Lindley, 1990, p. 1)

Because of the range of medical, cognitive, and social needs of students with severe disabilities, there is no common set of characteristics that are particular to this group of individuals. However, students with severe disabilities may exhibit some of the following:

- delayed receptive and expressive language abilities
- limited physical and motor abilities
- impaired self-help skills
- limited socialization and behavioral skills (Heward & Orlansky, 1992)

They also have difficulty learning new skills, maintaining skills previously learned, and applying skills to new situations (Alper & Ryndak, 1992).

Educational programs for students with severe disabilities should address these areas. While there is considerable debate in the field concerning the placement of students with severe disabilities, proponents of full integration for students with severe disabilities believe that educational programs for these students should incorporate best practices indicators (Thousand & Villa, 1990) (see Figure 2.2.).

Cayuga-Onondaga Assessment of Children with Handicaps (C.O.A.C.H.)

Giangreco, Cloninger, and Iverson (1990) developed the *Cayuga-Onondaga Assessment of Children with Handicaps* (*C.O.A.C.H.*) as a model to assist educators and parents in developing successful inclusion programs. C.O.A.C.H. serves as a family-based assessment instrument to identify and prioritize students' educational goals and management needs, with an emphasis on discipline-free goals that are student centered rather than discipline based. C.O.A.C.H. also includes strategies for meeting these identified goals and needs within the general education setting as well as a functional curriculum intended to add to the school's existing general education curriculum. The functional curriculum includes the following:

- cross-environmental activities designed to teach skills that occur across a variety of environments
- environmental-specific activities, which focus on skills that are unique to specific environmental situations
- sensory learning skills

Think About It

Some people believe that it may be easier to mainstream students with severe disabilities. Which categorical disability groups do you think would be most difficult to mainstream? Students with learning disabilities? Students with emotional and behavioral disabilities? Students with mental retardation? Students with autism? Students with physical disabilities? Students with sensory disabilities? Students with severe disabilities? Why?

INDIVIDUALIZED EDUCATION PROGRAM

If the multidisciplinary team decides that a student's needs require the provision of special education services, the team in concert with the student's teachers, parents, and wherever possible the student, also determines which educational services a student should receive. While teachers usually assume

FIGURE 2.2
Best practices indicators

- *Age-appropriate placement in local public schools*—Students are placed in regular education classrooms with their age-appropriate peers in schools within their local community.
- *Integrated delivery of services*—Instructional goals are integrated into students' school, home, and community activities. Students are provided with a functional curriculum within the regular classroom environment. Ancillary service personnel work with teachers and parents to fully integrate instruction on related service goals.
- *Social Integration*—Students are placed in integrated community and social environments, and activities to increase their social interactions within these environments are conducted.
- *Transition planning*—Plans to help students and families make the major transitions are included in students' IEPs, and are developed by parents, students, and professionals.
- *Community-based training*—Students are provided with the opportunities to acquire and demonstrate skills in community-based environments.
- *Curricular expectations*—The regular education curriculum is adapted to the students' needs, and students progress to full functioning as an adult in community settings.
- *Systematic data-based instruction*—Students are provided with instruction that includes a set of objectives, daily activities, and systematic data collection to monitor students' progress.
- *Team collaboration*—Decisions about students' programs are made and implemented collaboratively by teams of parents, students, ancillary support personnel, and administrators.
- *Home-school partnerships*—Parental involvement is an integral and ongoing part of students' programs through planning for the delivery of the educational and related services.
- *Systematic program evaluation*—All aspects of the program are evaluated on an ongoing basis by parents, teachers, ancillary support service providers, and administrators.
- *Staff development*—Professionals and parents receive training to work collaboratively and gain the skills necessary to promote student success.

Source: Hamre-Nietupski, McDonald, & Nietupski (1992); Thousand & Villa (1990).

IDEAS FOR IMPLEMENTATION

Teachers can create opportunities for full inclusion of all students by forming a collaborative team of educators, parents, aides, volunteers, peers and community members. The team can then plan a mainstreamed educational program by addressing the following:

1. What are the critical components of the classroom schedules, curriculum and routines?
2. What are the student's strengths and weaknesses?
3. What are the objectives and special accommodations as outlined in the student's Individualized Education Program (IEP)?
4. What ancillary support personnel are necessary for delivery of services? What services do they provide? What is the frequency and duration of these services?
5. What other schoolwide ancillary support personnel may be available to facilitate implementation of a more inclusionary program?
6. How can these objectives, accommodations and services be integrated into the classroom schedule?
   a. What classroom activities match the learning activities outlined in the student's IEP?
   b. What instructional strategies will be used to help the student learn the material?
   c. What individuals in the class will be responsible for guiding and assisting in the delivery of instruction? teacher? ancillary support staff personnel? aide? volunteer? peers?
   d. Where should the instruction take place?
   e. What accommodations and material adaptations are necessary to make the activities appropriate for students?
   f. How should the physical environment of the classroom be arranged to facilitate the student's performance?
7. How can the students' progress be measured and shared with others? How can the inclusionary program be modified to ensure its success?

a leadership role in designing an Individualized Education Program (IEP), in many states the multidisciplinary team provides information that assists in writing the student's IEP. The IEP includes (a) a statement of the student's present level of functioning; (b) a list of annual goals and the short-term objectives relating to these goals; (c) a projection concerning the initiation of services as well as the anticipated duration of the services; (d) a determination of the special education services that will be provided to the student as well as the necessary related services that the student will need to benefit from the provision of special education services; and (e) an evaluation procedure including objective criteria and a timeline for determining the student's progress in mastering the IEP's short-term objectives on at least an annual basis. The IEP also should contain a determination of the extent to which a student should be placed in special education programs. Additionally, as a result of the recent amendments to the IDEA, IEPs must include a statement of the needed transition services for students beginning no later than age 16 and for younger students when appropriate.

IEPs for students from linguistically and culturally diverse backgrounds should offer educators additional information to guide the instructional program for these students (Ortiz & Wilkinson, 1989). Professionals suggest that IEPs for students from culturally and linguistically diverse backgrounds should include the following:

- a summary of assessment results regarding the student's language proficiency in her or his native language and English
- the language(s) of instruction matched to specific goals and objectives
- the goals and objectives relating to the maintenance of the student's native language and the acquisition of English
- instructional strategies that relate to the student's linguistic ability, academic skill, cultural and socioeconomic background, and learning style
- instructional materials and curricula that address the student's linguistic and cultural background
- motivation strategies and reinforcers that are compatible with the student's cultural and experiential background (Ambert & Dew, 1982; Ortiz & Wilkinson, 1989)

Numerous computer programs are available to assist multidisciplinary teams in developing IEPs. Majsterek, Wilson and Mandlebaum (1990) have developed an evaluation form that educators can use to evaluate computerized IEP software programs. A sample IEP is presented in Figure 2.3.

UNDERSTANDING THE NEEDS OF CULTURALLY AND LINGUISTICALLY DIVERSE STUDENTS

Mrs. Jones, the teacher, passes out some dittos to her eighth-grade students. One young man, Cedric, shouts to her, "Mrs. Jones, ain't gon nam!"

She frowns and says, "What?" The children snicker.

Cedric mumbles, "Forget it."

A young female says to the teacher, "Ms. Jones, I need annurder one. This one tore up."

The teacher shouts, "What? I can't hear you."

Cedric interjects sarcastically, "Ms. Jones deef." Everyone laughs. Mrs. Jones stands in amazement, confused and frustrated. The lesson begins, and Mrs. Jones lectures.... The lesson deteriorates rapidly.

Cedric puts his head down on the desk and begins to fall asleep. Mrs. Jones shouts, "Wake up, Cedric, or you will be in trouble."

The student lifts his head slowly, stares angrily at the teacher and says, "What she be tripping about now?"

Mrs. Jones shouts, "What did you say?" The children laugh aloud. Mrs. Jones demands, "Cedric, get your textbook out and turn to today's lesson." Cedric reaches under the desk and fumbles with the many loose papers in his bookbag. Two minutes pass, and Cedric is still pretending to look for his work. Mrs. Jones interrupts the lesson and again warns Cedric, "If your work is not on your desk in the next minute, you'll be seeing me in detention hall." Cedric smiles, and Mrs. Jones grabs Cedric's new leather bookbag and throws it on the floor. "See me after class."

"Don't be putting my bag on the floor," the student shouts. "It brand new."

"I don't care," says Mrs. Jones. Cedric puts his head on his desk and stares out the window. A tired, dejected, and despondent Mrs. Jones goes home and decides to call Cedric's grandmother, his legal guardian. She carefully relays the day's events. She tells the grandmother, "Mrs. Washington, Cedric's negative attitude and lack of enthusiasm for school are preventing him from actively participating in the instructional activities. I'm afraid that he might be retained next year if he does not show dramatic improvement in these areas."

Source: Black Students and School Failure (pp. 21–22) by J. J. Irvine, 1990, Westport, CT: Greenwood. Reprinted by permission.

FIGURE 2.3
A sample individual education program (IEP)

Name: Jack S. **Sex:** Male **Grade of Reference Group:** 4th

Date of Birth: 12/25/84 **Chronological Age:** 10-3

Address: 1776 Main Street, New Cliff, NY **Telephone:** 555-1234

Parent, Guardian, or Surrogate Name: Agnes and Harry S.

Current Educational Placement: Self-contained special education class with part-time in regular class

Dominant Language:

* *Student:* English
* *Home:* English

Recommendation for Placement: Regular education class and with three hours of resource room per week. The resource room teacher will work with Jack in his regular classroom.

Percentage of time in the Regular Education Program: 100%

Rationale for Placement: Standardized assessment and curriculum-based assessment results indicate that Jack possesses the skills to perform in the regular classroom. However, he will need one hour per day of resource room instruction to support regular classroom instruction in the content areas and help him to make the transition to the regular classroom setting.

Related Services: Jack needs no adaptive devices or specialized transportation. He will participate in a career education program to increase his awareness of occupations and to promote an understanding of the importance of work.

Alternative Testing Techniques: Major unit tests in the content areas will be administered by the resource room teacher, who will read test directions when Jack experiences difficulty. Time limits will be waived.

Alternative Grading Systems: A mastery level grading system will be employed.

FIGURE 2.3
(continued)

Present Level of Functioning (Math): Performance on the *Keymath* and teacher-made, criterion-referenced tests indicate that Jack has mastered addition, subtraction, and multiplication facts and operations. However, he has not mastered division facts and operations.

Long-Term Goal: To improve division facts and operations.

Short-Term Objectives:

1. Given 40 problems with no remainders using one-digit dividends and one-digit divisors, Jack will write the correct answer to each problem within two minutes with no more than two errors.
2. Given 40 problems with no remainders using two-digit dividends with zero in the ones column and one-digit divisors, Jack will write the correct answer to each problem within three minutes with no more than two errors.
3. Given 40 problems with no remainders using three-digit dividends with zero in the ones and tens columns and one-digit divisors, Jack will write the correct answer to each problem within three minutes with no more than two errors.
4. Given 40 problems with no remainders using two-digit dividends and one-digit divisors, Jack will write the correct answer to each problem within three minutes with no more than two errors.
5. Given 40 problems with remainders using one-digit dividends and one-digit divisors, Jack will write the correct answer to each problem within three and one-half minutes with no more than two errors.

Evaluation Criteria: Daily time probes will be employed. When Jack demonstrates mastery of an objective on three consecutive probes, the next objective will be taught. Jack will check his answers using a talking calculator and will graph his performance daily.

Timelines:
Date IEP is effective: 1/25/94
Date IEP will be reviewed: 5/18/94

Multidisciplinary Team:

Name	Position	Signature
Ms. Agnes S.	Parent	____________
Mr. Harry S.	Parent	____________
Ms. Kris Dosharm	Principal	____________
Mr. Terry Feaster	Special Education Teacher	____________
Ms. Danielle Doyle	4th Grade Teacher	____________
Mr. John Walker	Resource Room Teacher	____________

Because of inappropriately used standardized tests, low socioeconomic status, and cultural and linguistic differences, a disproportionate number of students from culturally and linguistically diverse backgrounds tend to be referred to and placed in special education classes (Prasse & Reschly, 1986). Recent data on placements and ethnicity reveal that while students from diverse linguistic and cultural backgrounds comprise 30 percent of the students in schools in the United States, they make up 42 percent of the students who are identified as educable mentally retarded (Sailor, 1991). This finding is particularly true for African American students, who make up 16 percent of the general school population and 54 percent of the students with educable mental retardation (Williams, 1992). While Asian American students tend to be overrepresented in programs for the gifted and talented, African American, Native American, Native Alaskan, and Latin American students tend to be underrepresented in these programs (Williams, 1992). Many students who speak languages other than English who were previously placed in classes for the educable mentally retarded are now being categorized as having learning disabilities or communication delays (Figueroa, Fradd, & Correa, 1989). This designation is often related to whether the multidisciplinary team is influenced by the school psychologist or the speech-/language therapist (Rueda & Mercer, 1985). Therefore, when designing programs to address the academic and behavioral needs of students, educators should be sensitive to and adapt their services to take into account the cultural, linguistic, and economic factors that affect their students.

Cultural Considerations

Our schools and therefore the academic and social expectations for students are based on mainstream, middle-class culture (Almanza & Mosley, 1980; Gonzalez, 1974). It is important that educators be aware of this potential cultural bias and adjust their teaching behaviors and curricula to reflect differences within the classroom in terms of culture, experiential background, perception, and language. Because cultures differ in their views, philosophies, values, style, and language (Hilliard, 1980), employing the traditional methods, curriculum, and behavioral expectations with students not raised in the dominant culture can result in a cultural conflict (Aragon, 1974; Trueba, 1983). The cultural conflict that many students from diverse backgrounds experience may be particularly prevalent during *acculturation* when the student is trying to adapt to the new culture (Hoover & Collier, 1986). Research indicates that the cultural values of Hispanic Americans (Brischetto & Arciniega, 1980; Pediatric, Research and Training Center, 1988), Native Americans (Pepper, 1976), and Asian Americans (Leung, 1988; Morrow, 1987) differ from the perspectives of "mainstream, middle-class" Americans. These divergent views often result in differences in the behaviors and achievement levels of students from these cultures (Morrow, 1987).

Several cultural factors that may affect performance in schools are outlined below: time, respect for elders, individual versus group performance, nonverbal communication, and learning style. While this framework for contrasting the differences among students may be useful in understanding certain cognitive styles and associated behaviors, caution should be exercised in generalizing a specific behavior to any cultural group. Thus, rather than viewing these behaviors as characteristic of all members of a group, professionals should view them as a set of attitudes or behaviors that an individual may consider in learning and interacting with others (Anderson & Fenichel, 1989).

Time

Different groups have different concepts of time. The mainstream culture views timeliness as essential and a primary characteristic in judging competence. Students are expected to be on time and to complete assignments on time. Whereas other cultures may view time as important, it may be viewed as secondary to relationships and performance (Cloud & Landurand, n.d.). For instance, helping a friend with a problem may be given priority over completing an assignment by a certain deadline. Similarly, students who have different concepts of time may experience difficulties on timed tests or assignments. For example, LaFramboise and Graff-Low (1989) note that some Native American students may perform poorly on timed tasks because they are taught that perfection is important and therefore may work on tasks for long periods of time.

Respect for Elders

Cultures and therefore individuals have different ways to show respect for elders and authority figures such as teachers. In most cultures, teachers and other school personnel are viewed as prestigious and valued individuals who are worthy and deserving of respect. Respect may be demonstrated in a variety of ways such as not making eye contact with adults, not verbalizing to adults unless spoken to first, not asking questions, and using formal titles (Ramirez, 1989). For example, Nagata (1989) noted that out of respect for elders, Japanese American students may refrain from expressing opinions, speaking out, asking questions, seeking clarification, and making eye contact. Since the dominant culture does not always foster respect for elders and teachers in these ways, a monocultural viewpoint may interpret such behaviors as indicative of a communication or personality disorder that signals a need for special education rather than a behavior that is consistent with a cultural upbringing where such behaviors signify respect for elders.

Individual versus Group Performance

Whereas the American culture is founded on such notions as rugged individualism, many other cultures view group cooperation as more important than individual competition. For students from these cultures, social responsibility is perceived as an essential aspect of competence, and motivation to perform in the classroom is shaped by their commitment to group and community empowerment rather than by individual success (Roberts, Bell, & Salend, 1991). As a result, African American, Native American and Hispanic American students who are socialized in their communities to hold a "group solidarity" orientation, often face the conflict in school of accommodating to a competitive, individualistic orientation that they may view as "acting white" or "acting Anglo" (Fordham & Ogbu, 1986; Ramirez, 1989). Similar conflicts have been found in girls who identify a preference for cooperation over competition (Bell, 1991).

Humility is closely tied to a group's perceptions of the importance of group solidarity. Groups that value solidarity tend to value humility, whereas groups that emphasize individuality award status based on individual achievement. Students from cultures that view achievement in relation to the individual's contribution to the success of the group may perform better on tasks that are perceived as benefitting a group (LaFramboise & Graff-Low, 1989). They may avoid classroom situations that bring attention to themselves such as reading out loud, answering questions, gaining teacher praise, engaging in self-disclosure, revealing problems, or demonstrating expertise in class.

Nonverbal Communication

Nonverbal communication, which makes up 65 percent of all communication, also is culturally based (Irvine, 1991). Misinterpretations of nonverbal communications can result in miscommunication and conflicts between students and teachers. For example, whereas many teachers may judge students' readiness for learning by their making eye contact, nodding, and saying "um-hum," some African American students, particularly those from lower income levels, may not engage in physical gestures or verbal comments that show they have heard directions from teachers (Allen & Majidi-Ahi, 1989).

Cultural differences also are found in such aspects of nonverbal communication as touching and personal space (Anderson & Fenichel, 1989). Some cultures place a strong emphasis on establishing personal relationships with others through frequent physical contact and standing or sitting closely to others when communicating (Ramirez, 1989), while others value distance and place negative connotations on touching.

Learning Style

Westby and Rouse (1985) distinguish the differences between high-context and low-context cultures and their impact on school performance. (High-context cultures are those that offer overt cues to facilitate understanding. Low-context cultures do not.)

Cultural differences also have an effect on the way individuals process, organize, and learn material. Hilliard (in Hale-Benson, 1986) believes that most schools organize learning according to an analytic approach based on learning through rules, limited movement, convergent thinking, deductive reasoning, and an emphasis on objects. However, Irvine (1991) notes that many students from nondominant cultures employ a relational cognitive style that is based on variation, movement, divergent thinking, inductive reasoning, and an emphasis on people. Gilbert and Gay (1989) provide the following example to show how the stage setting behaviors of some African American students may be misinterpreted by teachers:

> Stage setting behaviors may include such activities as looking over the assignment in its entirety; rearranging posture; elaborately checking pencils, paper, and writing space; asking teachers to repeat directions that have just been given; and checking perceptions of neighboring students. To the black student these are necessary maneuvers in preparing for performance; to the teacher they may appear to be avoidance tactics, inattentiveness, disruptions, or evidence of not being prepared to do the assigned task (p. 277).

Another learning style factor that affects how classrooms are structured and how students function is the time ordering of the activities and classroom interactions (Cloud & Landurand, n.d.). In cultures that are polychronic oriented, individuals may engage in a variety of activities at the same time. For example, students with a polychronic orientation may converse with others while doing seatwork (Allen & Majidi-Ahi, 1989). Individuals from cultures that are monochronic in nature prefer to work on one task at a time.

Researchers also have found cross-cultural differences in terms of movement (Cloud & Landurand, n.d.). Students who are used to being active rather than passive may have difficulties in classrooms that are structured to limit movement. These differences also can impact on a teacher's perception of a student's academic and behavioral performance.

Think About It

How has your cultural background affected your learning style? Your teaching communication styles? How has your students' cultural background affected their learning style? How can you adjust your classroom to address these styles?

Linguistic Considerations

Educators also need to consider the impact of students' linguistic abilities on their educational performance. Over 2.8 million students in the United States speak languages other than English. It is estimated that this figure will exceed 3.4 million by the year 2000 (Oxford, Pol, Lopez, Stupp, Gendell, & Peng, 1981). These estimates are viewed as conservative in that they do not include the growing number of undocumented immigrants entering the United States each year (Cummins, 1984). Because these students often exhibit the usual problems associated with learning a second language such as poor comprehension, limited vocabulary, grammatical and syntactical mistakes, and articulation difficulties, these students tend to be overreferred to special education (National Coalition of Advocates for Schools, 1991). If they are placed in special education classes, these students often receive limited support in their native language, which can have a negative impact on their linguistic and academic development (Figueroa, Fradd, & Correa, 1989; Saville-Troike, 1991).

Understanding Second Language Acquisition

Referrals from teachers indicate that they do not understand the stages of second language learning (Figueroa, Fradd, & Correa, 1989). Research indicates that acquisition of a second language is facilitated when students have received a foundation for learning the new language through intensive instruction in their native language that teaches a variety of cognitive and academic skills (Cummins, 1984; Krashen, 1982). For example, Reyes (1987) found that students who learned to read in their native languages are able to acquire reading skills in English much more easily.

Proficiency in the second language is a long term process that involves two distinct stages of language proficiency (Cummins, 1981). *Basic interpersonal communication skills (BICS)*, or social language skills, are the language skills necessary to guide students in developing social relationships and en-

The language skills that guide social situations develop faster than the language skills that relate to classroom instruction.

gaging in casual conversations with others. Because BICS are context embedded and cognitively less demanding, they are often learned within two years. *Cognitive/academic language proficiency* (*CALP*) or academic language skills, are the language skills that relate to literacy, cognitive, and academic development in the classroom. Because CALP are context reduced and cognitively demanding, they often take up to seven years to develop. Collier and Kalk (1989) suggest that until students develop CALP in English, they should receive instruction primarily in their native language.

In learning a new language, second language learners' comprehension of the new language is usually greater than their production. Additionally, many second language learners go through a *silent period,* a stage in which learners process what they hear but avoid verbal responses (Maldonado-Colon, 1990). However, many educators often misinterpret this silent period as an indication of lack of interest, or shyness. Teachers can respond to students who are experiencing a silent period by showing respect for students, allowing students to respond in alternative ways such as through drawing, and creating a nonthreatening environment that encourages students to use English.

Assessing the Language Skills of Bilingual Students

To meet the needs of bilingual students, school districts are mandated to develop a pedagogically sound program that meets students' English language–learning needs, offers instruction in content areas so that learning is not hindered by language differences, assesses student progress regularly, and provides programmatic adjustments if assessment results reflect lack of educational process (Roos, 1984). Therefore, in addition to academic progress, educators also should assess the language skill development of bilingual students. Such an evaluation should examine the students' language proficiency, dominance, preference, and code switching.

Language *proficiency* relates to the degree of skill an individual possesses in the languages she or he speaks including receptive and expressive language skills. Proficiency in one language does not mean a lack of proficiency in another language. Measures of language proficiency can assist multidisciplinary teams in identifying students' language dominance. Language *dominance* refers to the language in which the individual is most fluent and implies a comparison of the student's language abilities in two or more languages to determine the student's stronger language and the language that should be given priority when teaching cognitive and academic skills (Ortiz, 1984). Language *preference* identifies the language in which the individual prefers to communicate. *Code switching* refers to "injecting or substituting phrases, sentences, or expressions from another language (Harris, 1991, p. 28)." Assessment data also should be collected to attempt to differentiate a language disorder from a bilingual or cross-cultural difference by comparing the student's performance in both the primary and secondary languages (Langdon, 1989).

Data relating to students' language performance can be collected through use of standardized tests, language samples, observations, questionnaires, and interviews (Baca & Cervantes, 1989). Langdon (1989) suggests that educators consider the following factors when assessing the language skills of bilingual students.

Length of Residence in the United States. How long and for what periods of time has the student resided in the United States? Students may have limited or interrupted exposure to English resulting in poor vocabulary, slow naming speed, and minimal verbal participation.

School Attendance Patterns. How long has the student been in school? What is the student's attendance pattern? Have there been any disruptions in school? Students may fail to acquire language skills because of failure to attend school.

School Instructional History. How many years of schooling did the student complete in the native country? What language(s) were used to guide instruction in the native country? What types of classrooms has the student attended (bilingual education, English as a second language, regular education, speech/language therapy services, special education)? What has been the language of instruction in these classes? What strategies and instructional materials have been successful? What language does the student prefer to use in informal situations with adults? formal situations with adults? What were the outcomes of these placements? Students may not have had access to appropriate pedagogical and curricular programs resulting in problems in language acquisition.

Cultural Background. How does the student's cultural background affect second language acquisition? Has the student had sufficient time to adjust to the new culture? Since culture and language are inextricably linked, lack of progress in developing a second language can be due to cultural and communication differences and/or lack of exposure to the new culture. For example, some cultures rely on the use of body language in communication as a substitute for verbal communication (Harris, 1991). Similarly, cultures have different perspectives on color, time, gender, distance, and space that affect language (Collier & Kalk, 1989).

Performance in Comparison to Peers. Does the student's language skill, learning rate, and learning style differ from those of other students from similar experiential, cultural, and linguistic backgrounds? Does the student interact with peers in the primary language and/or English? Comparisons of the student's performance should be made to students who have similar traits rather than students whose experiences in learning a second language are very different.

Home Life. What language(s) or dialect(s) are spoken at home? What language(s) are spoken by the student's siblings? Is the student's performance at home different from siblings? What language(s) or dialect(s) are spoken in the family's community? Is a distinction made among the uses of the primary language or dialect and English? If so, how is that distinction made? (For example, the non-English language is used at home, but children speak English when playing with peers.) In what language(s) does the family watch television, listen to the radio, and read newspapers, books, and magazines? What is the student's language preference in the home and community? Does the student experience difficulty following directions, understanding language and expressing thoughts in the primary language? In the second language? Important information concerning the student's language proficiency, dominance, and preference can be obtained by soliciting data from parents. Similarly, the student's acquisition of language can be enhanced by involving parents in the educational program (Cummins, 1989).

Health and Developmental History. What health, medical, sensory, and developmental factors have affected the student's language development? A student's difficulty in acquiring language may be related to various health and developmental variables.

Planning an Appropriate Educational Program

Language assessment data can then be used to plan instructional procedures, determine appropriate languages for instruction, and evaluate student progress. For example, if the student functions in the primary language in a number of domains (home, school, and community) and the skills in English are just starting to develop, then the student might benefit from academic instruction in the primary language and supplemental instruction in English as a second language (Wilkinson & Ortiz, 1986).

Bilingual Education

Research indicates that many bilingual students will benefit in terms of academic progress and acquisition of English skills from bilingual education programs (Cummins, 1989). When students receive instruction in their first language, they develop essential background knowledge, which facilitates their ability to learn a second language and perform academically in English (Cziko, 1992: Freeman & Freeman, 1992). A recent U.S. Department of Education study concluded that bilingual education programs help students make an easier and more successful transition to all-English instruction (Celis, 1991). Bilingual education programs offer content instruction in the student's primary language and English and instruction in language arts in the student's native language. Acquisition of English language skills is fostered through instruction in the student's primary language which provides a cognitive and academic background for learning a second language and instruction in English as a second language. As students acquire English language skills, more and more of the content area instruction is delivered in English.

Types of Bilingual Education Programs

Fishman (1979) delineates four categories of bilingual education programs: traditional bilingualism, monoliterate bilingualism, partial bilingualism, and full bilingualism. These programs differ in the degree to which they seek to maintain students' native culture and language.

Transitional Bilingualism. In transitional bilingual programs, the students' native languages are used initially to help them adjust to school and to begin to master classroom content. Rather than seeking to maintain the students' primary languages, the emphasis is on developing the students' English language skills and helping them make the transition to receiving all their instruction in English.

Monoliterate Bilingualism. In monoliterate bilingual programs, the objective is to develop the student's oral language abilities in both languages. However, reading instruction is conducted only in the second language. Thus, this type of program represents an intermediary position in the debate between language shift and language maintenance.

Partial Bilingualism. In partial bilingual programs, students develop fluency and literacy in the primary and second languages and some degree of cultural identity. However, literacy in the primary language is focused only on those content areas that relate to the students' culture.

Full Bilingualism. In full bilingual programs, students develop skills in both languages and in all content areas. These programs prepare students to function in both cultures and languages, and seek to help students develop pride in their cultural and linguistic identity.

Currently, the U.S. Department of Education's Office of Bilingual Education and Minority Language Affairs (OBEMLA) funds a variety of bilingual education programs, including Transitional Bilingual Education Programs (TBE), Special Alternative Instruction Programs (SAIP), and Developmental Bilingual Education Programs (DBE). TBE programs offer students content area instruction in their native language, language instruction in English, and a curriculum that is sensitive to the students' cultural heritage and the various ethnic groups that comprise American society. SAIP represent alternatives to traditional bilingual education programs, and offer specifically designed curricula to address the needs of students learning English. While instruction is usually delivered in English through English immersion, content area–based ESL, and sheltered English, a student's native language can be employed to promote learning (Tikunoff et al., 1991). DBE programs seek to assist students in developing competence in English and their native language while helping them master content area skills. DBE programs target classes that are made up of equal numbers of students who speak English and students who are learning English. One integrated example of this program type is the two-way bilingual education that mixes students who speak languages other than English with students who speak English. Students become bilingual and biliterate through instruction in both languages and exposure to a curriculum that teaches them about different cultures. Additional information regarding other bilingual education programs funded by the U.S. Department of Education can be obtained by contacting OBEMLA.

English as a Second Language (ESL)

An integral component of bilingual programs is instruction in English as a second language (ESL), sometimes referred to as English to Speakers of Other Languages (ESOL) (Ovando & Collier, 1985). ESL is a discipline that uses the students' native culture and language to systematically develop their skills in understanding, speaking, reading, and writing English (New York State Education Department, 1989). In ESL programs, instruction and communication are conducted exclusively in English. Yates and Ortiz (1991) suggest that ESL instruction should be comprehensible, interesting, and motivating; expose students to natural communication; facilitate comprehension before requiring expression; and use technology, media, and multisensory strategies.

Think About It

If you moved to another country that had a different language and culture when you were in fourth grade, what aspects of school would be difficult for you? Would you want to receive your academic instruction in English or the language of your new country? Would you want to be in a special education class? A transitional bilingual program? A monoliterate bilingual program? A partial bilingual program? A full bilingual program?

Black English

In addition to students who speak languages other than English, teachers also will work with students who speak various dialects of English, such as Black

English. It is estimated that between 80 and 90 percent of the blacks in the United States use some form of Black English (Smitherman, 1985). Black English also is the most popular language of the youth culture (Wade-Lewis, 1991).

Black English has maintained a number of vocabulary items from African languages. However, it employs for the most part the vocabulary of English with some phonology, morphology, syntax, nuance, tone, and gesture from African languages. Current research indicates that it evolved as a pidgin language either on the West Coast of Africa or the Caribbean during the slave trade, perhaps as early as 1500 A.D. (Alleyne, 1980; Hancock, 1986). A *pidgin* is a rudimentary language that evolves during situations of war, slavery, or trade when two groups of people with no language in common must learn to communicate too rapidly to learn each other's languages.

Between 1620 and 1865, Black English evolved into a creole language. A *creole* is a pidgin that has met two conditions: it has nativized, or become some group's native language; and it has stabilized, or developed stable norms. For example, Black English nativized when it became the native language of the children of African language speakers in the United States. Beginning around 1865, Black English decreolized and became a dialect of standard English, rather than a separate language. Today, Black English serves several important functions. It allows African Americans to connect with their cultural roots and express power and solidarity with each other, as well as to continually evolve new cultural forms based on the language, among them music (such as rap), creative imagery, and slang (O'Donnell, 1974; Smitherman, 1977). Simultaneously, it allows all Americans, especially youth, to participate in African American culture through use of Black English patterns in current music, movies, and commercials.

Black English has several distinct phonological, syntactic and lexical features that also are characteristic of other dialects of English (Alexander, 1985). Some phonological features of Black English include dropping the *t* when it is the final letter of a consonant cluster (*act* is pronounced *ak*), replacing the voiced *th* with *d* (*this* is pronounced *dis*), and substituting *i* for the *e* (*pen* is pronounced *pin*). Some syntactical features of Black English include using the verb *to be* to indicate ongoing action or a repeated occurrence and deleting *to be* when it is followed by a predicate, verb, adjective, or noun in the present tense ("The coffee be cold" indicates that the coffee is always cold while the statement, "the coffee cold" suggests that the coffee is only cold today.), employing *it* to indicate presence or to make statements, omitting *-ed* in the past tense, using double negatives in a single sentence, deleting plural markers when additional words in the sentence denote more than one ("He got three pencil" for "He got three pencils"), adding *s* to make plural forms of words (Peoples, womans, childrens), denoting possession through position and context rather than using the *'s* ("John car big" for "John's car is big"), and stressing subjects in a sentence by using subject/noun-pronoun redundancy ("My mother she be taking me to the hospital" for "My mother takes me to the hospital"). The grammatical and stylistic differences between Black English and standard English can be largely attributed to differences between African languages and English. For example, because West African languages from which Black English evolved are *vowel final* (generally lacking final consonants and consonant clusters), Black English tends to be vowel final (Assante, 1990). Lexical features include words that have meanings only to speakers of the dialect such as *bad* being the equivalent to *good* or *great* in standard English, and *half-stepping,* meaning getting by without doing your best. Stylistic elements of Black English include subtlety, angled body movements, and intonation (Alexander, 1985). Rhetorical elements include exaggeration through use of uncommon words and expressions and alliteration; mimicry of the speech and mannerisms of others; use of proverbs, puns, metaphors, and improvisation; displaying a sense of fearlessness; and use of innuendo and sound effects (Smitherman, 1977; Webb-Johnson, 1992). More extensive information concerning black English is available (Dillard, 1977; Smitherman, 1977).

Adger, Wolfram, Detwyler, and Harry (1992) found that while African American students use Black English in the classroom, they use standard English for reading, writing, and dictation activities and presentational actitivities.

Because of a lack of information regarding the history and importance of Black English, many teachers possess negative attitudes toward students who speak Black English. This lack of information and presence of negative attitudes often lead to lowered teacher expectations and the belief that these students have limited linguistic abilities (Smitherman, 1985). Negative expectations interact with standardized tests that are biased toward use of standard English and result in many students who speak Black English being identified as in need of special education (Newell, 1981).

Rather than making students who speak other dialects of English feel deficient and dysfunctional by interrupting and correcting them in midsentence, teachers should create a classroom that acknowledges and affirms the use of standard and other dialects of English as appropriate in various school and societal contexts. One effective approach for creating such a classroom is the *bridge system,* which encourages students to be bidialectal and to understand that different dialects are used in different situations. In this approach, teachers help students separate the context for use of language and understand when to use standard English and when it is appropriate to use other dialects of English. For example, when teachers need to prompt students to use standard English, they can ask students "how can you say that in school language?" (Adger, Wolfram, Detwyler, & Harry, 1992). In addition, teachers can help students become bidialectal by doing the following:

- Become aware of the dialects of students.
- Demonstrate respect for students' dialects and the cultures they reflect.
- Teach students about the power of language.
- Convey to students the belief that they can speak two or more dialects.
- Acknowledge the oral traditions of some students' cultures.
- Expose students to other English dialects through literature, books, songs, poetry, and films.
- Discuss and role play situations in which standard English and other dialects of English would be appropriate (Alexander, 1985; Thompson, 1990).

Migrant Students

One group of culturally and linguistically diverse students whose educational needs are beginning to be discussed is migrant students (Baca & Harris, 1988; Salend, 1990). For the purposes of federal eligibility requirements, migrant workers are classified according to their migratory status (currently migratory vs. formerly migratory), movement pattern (intrastate vs. interstate), and type of employment (agricultural vs. fishing). A currently migratory child, also known as a "true" migrant, is one "whose parent or guardian is a migratory agricultural worker or fisher; and who has moved within the past 12 months from one school district to another . . . to enable the child, the child's guardian, or a member of the immediate family to obtain temporary or seasonal employment in an agricultural or fishing activity" (Interstate Migrant Education Council, 1987, p. 2). A formerly migrant child, also referred to as a "resettled" migrant, is a "child who was eligible to be counted and served as a currently migratory child within the past five years, but is not now a currently migratory child" (Interstate Migrant Education Council, 1987, p. 2). Migrant families tend to travel in the same *streams,* or movement patterns, from year to year (Shotland, 1989).

Programs Serving Migrant Students

Several programs have been established to address the needs of migrant students (Reynolds & Salend, 1990a). The Migrant Students Record Transfer System (MSRTS) is designed to promote communication between educators serving migrant students. The MSRTS, a nationwide computerized communication system housed in Little Rock, Arkansas, collects and maintains health and academic records for migrant students throughout the United States. School personnel can request or start a file by contacting the local migrant education center or state education department.

The MSRTS also provides information on the delivery of special education services to migrant students. The special education component of the MSRTS includes prior information related to the existence of a disability, assessment results, previous services provided, and basic data regarding the student's IEP. Because the amount of special education information is limited by the space available in the system as well as by the quality of information entered, data are also provided in the MSRTS for directly contacting a migrant student's previous educational institutions to obtain more detailed information.

Because migrants travel intrastate and interstate, educators of migrant students have developed numerous programs other than the MSRTS to promote cooperation among educators. Migrant High School Equivalency Programs (HEP) are available to provide a variety of services to help migrant youth graduate from high school. Similarly, College Assisted Migrant Programs (CAMP) identify, recruit, and deliver services to migrant students in post-secondary educational settings.

The Portable Assisted Study Sequence (PASS) is designed to address the high dropout rate among migrant students that is related to the loss of credits because of frequent mobility and high absenteeism. The curriculum and corresponding materials are self-paced and portable, so they can be worked on as the student travels from state to state. Individualized tutoring is available to students who need it. School districts then award credits toward graduation based on completion of the PASS materials. Educators interested in more information about these programs should contact their local migrant education center or the office of their state director of migrant education.

Students Who Are Refugees

Thuy, a 12-year-old Vietnamese girl, was referred to the child and adolescent unit of a community mental health center by her teacher and counselor. Her teacher had noticed a marked deterioration in her academic performance and noted that she frequently complained of headaches and asked to leave the class, seemed to lack energy, showed a loss of appetite, and nonverbally conveyed a general feeling of hopelessness. During the past six months she had changed from a good student, actively involved with peers, to a withdrawn, depressed preadolescent. Most recently, for days at a time, she would not talk unless pressured to and frequently stared off into space.

Thuy was from a middle-class family in Saigon, where until the downfall of South Vietnam, her father had been a lower-level clerk with the army. He fled Saigon with his family, a wife and three children, in 1978; however, during the escape, the family became separated and the wife and two younger children remained in Vietnam. Thuy and her father escaped by boat. Their boat was intercepted by Thai pirates, and Thuy's father was beaten and several women were raped. Although Thuy observed this, she herself was not physically assaulted. Eventually they reached Malaysia, where they remained in a refugee camp for nearly a year until they located relatives in the United States. They have been in the United States for two years and reside in a small apartment with a cousin's family of five in the inner city of a West Coast metropolitan area.

Thuy's father has had a particularly difficult time adjusting to the United States. He struggles with English classes and has been unable to maintain several jobs as a waiter. He attributes these difficulties to the assault during his escape, saying blows to the head impaired his memory and crippled him physically.

Just before the onset of Thuy's problems, she received a letter from her mother informing them of the death of her 5-year-old brother. Complications from a childhood disease combined with malnutrition had contributed to his death. Thuy remained impassive on receiving this news, while her father wept uncontrollably, mourning the loss of his only son. Soon after that, her father was fired from yet another job, seemed to lose interest in English classes, and just languished around the small apartment.

Source: Children of Color: Psychological Interventions with Minority Youth (p. 307) by J. Taylor Gibbs and L. N. Huang, 1989, San Francisco: Jossey-Bass. Reprinted by permission.

A growing number of students who are immigrants or refugees are entering schools each year. These students face a myriad of problems as they enter and progress through school (Harris, 1991) (see Figure 2.4).

As a result of these factors, misplacement of immigrant students frequently occurs. Placements for these students often include special education, English as a Second Language, and vocational education programs. In designing educational programs that meet their needs, educators should consider the following questions.

- What are the major cultural influences on the student in the native country and the new country?
- What resources were available to the student's family in their homeland?
- Why did the student's family migrate?
- At what age did the student migrate?
- Did the student migrate with his or her family?
- What family members did not migrate?
- What events did the student and the family experience during migration?

FIGURE 2.4
Problems facing students who are immigrants

Students who are immigrants are likely to encounter several problems, including the following.

Learning a new language that differs from their native language in terms of articulation, syntax, and graphic features.

Adjusting to a new culture that values and interprets behavior in different ways.

Obtaining access to health care that addresses their needs such as mental health services to help them deal with their experiences in being tortured or seeing their relatives and friends tortured, raped, and executed.

Experiencing guilt as a result of their survival and concern about leaving others behind.

Facing economic pressures to work to support their family in the United States and family members in their native country.

Coping with sociocultural and peer expectations, such as self-hatred and youth gangs.

Dealing with cross-cultural and intergenerational conflicts and posttraumatic stress disorder.

Being targets of racism, violence, and harassment.

Developing a positive identity and self-concept.

Entering school with little, occasional, or no schooling in their native countries.

Being unfamiliar with schools in America.

Lacking school records and hiding relevant facts in order to avoid embarrassment, seek peer acceptance, and promote self-esteem.

Having to serve as cultural and language interpreters for their families.

Source: C. R. Harris, *Teaching Exceptional Children* (1991).

IDEAS FOR IMPLEMENTATION

Educators can facilitate the education of students who are immigrants by enacting the following suggestions:

- Allow students to tell their story.
- Offer language enrichment programs.
- Encourage students to do projects using materials in their native language.
- Be sensitive to the problems individuals face in learning a second language.
- Understand the cultural, economic, and historical factors that have had a significant impact on students.
- Establish communication with parents and extended family members.
- Employ narratives, role playing, and bibliotherapy.
- Teach students about their new culture.
- Use nonverbal forms of expression including music, dance, or art.
- Use peers and community members as a resource.
- Employ media in the students' native languages.
- Understand behavior with respect to the individual's culture and past experiences.
- Consider the student's educational background and learning potential.
- Encourage students to participate in extracurricular activities.
- Involve parents and knowledgeable community members in the student's educational program.
- Contact the Clearinghouse for Immigration Education (800-441-7192), the National Center for Immigrant Students (617-357-8507) or the National Coalition of Advocates for Students (617-357-8507), organizations that disseminate information about model school programs and organizations, teacher-made materials, relevant research, and resource lists addressing the needs of immigrant students and their families.

Source: C. R. Harris (1991); L. Nahme Huang (1989).

Think About It

You are a member of your school district's multidisciplinary planning team. A student who has recently moved to the United States from another country has been referred to the planning team. What factors would you consider in determining whether the student's difficulties in school are language, cultural, or learning based?

DEPRESSION AND SUICIDE

As the number of students whose needs challenge schools grows, there is a collateral increase in the number of students who suffer from depression and who attempt suicide. Poverty, cultural conflicts, stressful family conditions, substance abuse, and poor performance in school and other factors that produce emotional trauma, stress, and low self-esteem can contribute to individuals having a sense of worthlessness, helplessness, and hopelessness and make these individuals vulnerable to depression and suicide. Data indi-

Students with disabilities are particularly susceptible to depression and suicidal behavior. Peck (1985) reports that 50% of the children less than 15 years old who committed suicide in Los Angeles County had been diagnosed having a learning disability. The U.S. Senate Subcommittee on Juvenile Justice estimated that 60% of the teenagers who commit suicide are suffering from some type of mental disability (Blumenthal, 1985).

cate that approximately 500,000 youth attempt suicide each year (Brody, 1992). Ogden and Germinario (1988) estimate that from 4,000 to 5,000 teenagers commit suicide each year. The incidence of adolescent suicide has tripled in the last 30 years, making it the third leading cause of death among children and the second among older teenagers (Berman & Jobes, 1991; Brody, 1992). The adolescent suicide rate for males is five times greater than females, with approximately 90 percent of the adolescent male suicides being white (Guetzloe, 1989). As a result of their isolation and victimization, gay and lesbian youth are particularly susceptible to suicide—the attempted suicide rate for homosexual adolescents is three times higher than that of their heterosexual peers.

Data indicate that approximately 10 million Americans suffer from depression. Symptoms of depression may include the following:

- an overwhelming sadness, apathy, and hopelessness
- a loss of interest and enjoyment in everyday pleasurable activities
- a change in appetite, weight, and sleep pattern
- a continuous feeling of fatigue
- a pervasive difficulty in concentrating and making decisions
- a decrease in self-esteem and an increase in self-depreciation
- a slowness of movements or signs of hyperactivity
- a sense of inappropriate guilt
- a recurrence of thoughts of death or suicide (American Psychiatric Association, 1987)

While not all individuals who are depressed attempt suicide, there is a high correlation between depression and suicide (Robbins & Alessi, 1985). Therefore, teachers also should be aware of the following warning signs:

- an inability to get over the death of a relative or friend and the break-up of friendships
- a noticeable neglect in the student's personal hygiene, dress, and health care
- a significant change in sleep pattern or weight
- an increase in dangerous risk-taking behaviors and self-inflicted wounds
- an increase in the giving of valued items to others
- a dramatic change in school performance that is characterized by a drop in grades and an increase in inappropriate behaviors
- a radical change in personality
- an increased use of drugs or alcohol
- a growing tendency to engage in overt threats to take one's life

If teachers suspect that a student is depressed or suicidal, they should work with other professionals and parents to help the student receive the services of mental health professionals. If teachers encounter a student who is threatening suicide, teachers should do the following:

- Stay with the student, remaining calm and speaking in a clear, gentle, and nonthreatening manner.
- Introduce yourself to the student (if you are not known) and tell the student you are there to be of assistance.

- Show concern for the student.
- Ask the student to give up any objects or substances that can cause harm.
- Encourage the student to talk and acknowledge the student's comments.
- Avoid being judgmental and pressuring the student.
- Reinforce positive statements and comments concerning alternatives to suicide.
- Remind the student that there are others who care and are available to help (Guetzloe, 1989).

Guetzloe (1989) provides excellent guidelines that can assist educators in developing programs to counter suicide including assessing a student's suicide potential, counseling suicidal students, working with families, and dealing with the aftermath of suicide.

SUMMARY

This chapter provided information to help educators make important decisions regarding the diverse educational needs of students. The chapter

- outlined the roles and responsibilities of the multidisciplinary team and its members
- discussed the nature of prerefferal interventions
- reviewed information on the characteristics associated with specific disability categories
- outlined the components of an IEP
- examined some of the issues educators should consider in designing appropriate educational programs for students from culturally and linguistically diverse backgrounds
- offered suggestions for identifying and working with students who are depressed and suicidal

RECOMMENDED READINGS

Baca, L. M., & Cervantes, H. T. (1989). *The bilingual special education interface (2nd ed.)*. New York: Merrill/Macmillan.

Figueroa, R. A., Fradd, S. H., & Correa, V. I. (1989). Bilingual special education and this special issue. *Exceptional Children, 56,* 174–178.

Guetzloe, E. (1989). *Youth suicide: What the educator should know.* Reston, VA: Council for Exceptional Children.

Heward, W. L., & Orlansky, M. D. (1992). *Exceptional children (4th ed)*. New York: Merrill/Macmillan.

Mendelsohn, S. R., & Jennings, K. D. (1986). Characteristics of emotionally disturbed children referred for special education assessment. *Child Psychiatry and Human Development, 16,* 154–170.

Ortiz, A. A., & Wilkinson, C. Y. (1991). Assessment and intervention model for bilingual exceptional student (Aim for the Best). *Teacher Education and Special Education, 14*(1), 35–42.

Reeve, R. E. (1990). ADHD: Facts and fallacies. *Intervention in School and Clinic, 26*(2), 70–78.

Sailor, W., (1991). Special education in the restructured school. *Remedial and Special Education, 12*(6), 8–22.

Taylor Gibbs, J., & Nahme Huang, L. (1989) *Children of color: Psychological interventions with minority youth.* San Francisco: Jossey-Bass.

Thousand, J. S., & Villa, R. A. (1990). Strategies for educating learners with severe disabilities within their local home schools and communities. *Focus on Exceptional Children, 23*(3), 1–24.

3 Promoting Communication to Foster the Mainstreaming Process

THE SMITH FAMILY GOES TO SCHOOL

We knew it would be another rough year. Last year, Paul's teacher told us "he wasn't doing as well as the other students." Now after two months, Paul's new teacher, Mr. Rodl, called and said, "Paul is falling behind and we need to do something." Mr. Rodl asked us to come to a meeting with a team of professionals to discuss Paul's progress. He said we could schedule the meeting at a time that was convenient for us.

Going into the meeting was scary. There sat Paul's teacher, the principal, the school psychologist, and several other people we didn't know. Mr. Rodl started the meeting by introducing us to the others in the room. Then, he said, "Since I work closely with Paul, I'll lead the meeting and coordinate the decisions we make about Paul's program. We call that being the service coordinator." He asked each person in the room to talk about Paul. As different people spoke, others asked questions. When several people used words we didn't understand, Mr. Rodl asked them to explain it to us. When our turn came, Mr. Rodl asked us to talk about what was happening with Paul at home, what we thought was happening with Paul at school, and what we would like to see happen at school. At first, we felt very nervous. As people in the room listened to and discussed our comments, we became more relaxed. The group discussed several ways to help Paul. In the end, we all came up with a plan to help Paul learn better. Mr. Rodl summarized the plan and the roles each person would play to make it successful. We left the meeting feeling really good about being part of a team that was trying to help our son.

What factors made this meeting successful? What strategies could professionals and parents employ to help students such as Paul learn better? After reading this chapter, you should be able to answer these as well as the following questions:

- Why is interactive communication vital to the success of mainstreaming?
- What factors contribute to the development of a successful interactive communication mainstreaming network?
- How can educators facilitate communication and congruence regarding a student's educational program?
- How can collaborative consultation be implemented in schools?
- How can educators involve and communicate with parents?
- How can educators adapt their services to the needs of families from culturally and linguistically diverse backgrounds?
- What roles and services can be provided by paraprofessionals, volunteers, and community agencies in assisting students and families?

Successful mainstreaming depends on an ongoing process of good communication and cooperation among educators, parents, and community resources (Hundert, 1982). Mainstreaming means that educational programming for mainstreamed students, once the sole domain of the special or bilingual educator, is now a shared responsibility (Conway & Gow, 1988). Research suggests that the success of mainstreaming is often dependent on the quality of communication and support among educators, other professionals, and parents (Miller & Sabatino, 1978).

ESTABLISHING A COMMUNICATION NETWORK

One method of establishing ongoing communication is through the development of an interdisciplinary network of educators, parents, peers, mainstreamed students, and community resources. This network works cooperatively to provide appropriate services to students and their families (Cobb,

1978). The network can facilitate mainstreaming by establishing a team approach to solving problems that is based on communication and mutual obligation. The purposes of the network are to expand the range of services available to mainstreamed students and their teachers; to share the responsibility for implementing mainstreaming; and to coordinate the services provided to students and their families by the schools and the community. Maher and Hawryluk (1983) suggest a series of questions that can guide networks in designing effective mainstreaming programs, including the following:

1. What educational services and programs are to be provided to individual, group, and organizational clients?
2. In order to provide appropriate programs to these clients, what educational service delivery tasks need to be accomplished?
3. Within what period of time must task accomplishment occur?
4. Given the tasks that have been identified, which ones might be effectively and efficiently carried out by means of one or more versions of a team approach?
5. What specific kinds of teams might be utilized? (pp. 181–182)

For mainstreamed students, the network may consist of regular classroom teachers, administrators, ancillary support personnel such as special and bilingual educators, paraprofessionals, volunteers, parents, peers, local community resources, and professional and parent organizations, as shown in Figure 3.1 (Taylor & Salend, 1983). The components of the network will vary depending on the needs of mainstreamed students and their families. For example, a network for a student with a physical disability might be expanded to include medical and health professionals such as physicians, nurses, and physical therapists, while the network for a family that speaks a language other than English should include an interpreter.

Interactive Teaming

The mainstreaming network should function as an interactive team, sometimes referred to as a collaborative team (Thousand & Villa, 1990), where all members work together to achieve a common goal and reciprocally share their expertise and perceptions with others (Morsink, Chase Thomas, & Correa, 1991). Morsink et al. (1991) identified the following 10 dimensions of successful interactive teaming:

1. *Legitimacy and Autonomy*—Effective interactive teams have a recognized and supported function, and the freedom to operate independently.
2. *Purposes and Objectives*—Effective interactive teams have identified goals and work interdependently to share information and expertise to achieve these goals. Teams also are composed of individuals who have a common set of norms and values that guide the team's functioning (Friend & Cook, 1992).
3. *Competencies of Team Members and Clarity of Their Roles*—Effective interactive teams are comprised of members who are skilled in not only their discipline but also in collaborative problem solving, communication and leadership skills, and cultural diversity.

FIGURE 3.1
Sample mainstreaming network

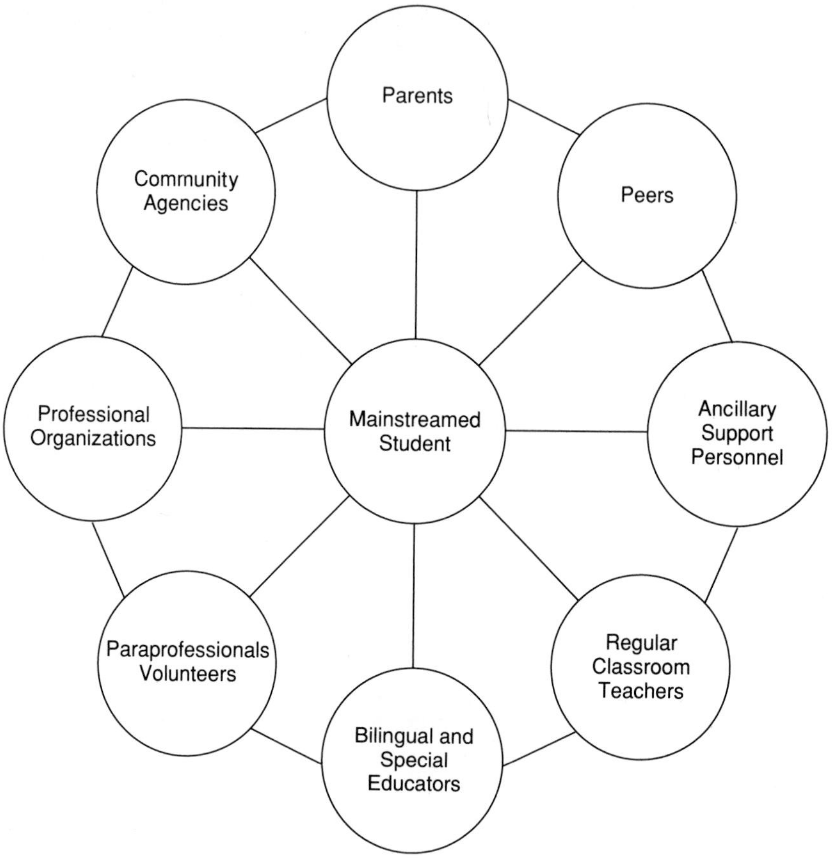

Source: Adapted from "Reducing stress-related burnout through a network support system" by L. Taylor and S.J. Salend, 1983, *The Pointer, 27*, pp. 5–9.

4. *Role Release and Role Transitions*—Effective interactive teams include members who can share their expertise with others; implement programs; use strategies from other disciplines; learn from others; and seek assistance and feedback from others.
5. *Awareness of the Individuality of Others*—Effective interactive teams contain members who recognize and accept the perspectives, skills, and experiences of others.
6. *Process of Team Building*—Effective interactive teams are committed to the process of working together and functioning as a team. Conflicts between team members are resolved through problem solving, communication, and negotiation (Friend & Cook, 1992).
7. *Attention to Factors that Impact Upon Team Functioning*—Effective interactive teams employ cooperative goal structures, create a supportive communication climate, share roles, and reach decisions through consensus.

8. *Leadership Styles*—Effective interactive teams rotate leadership responsibilities and expect leaders to solicit all points of view and involve all members in the decisionmaking process.
9. *Implementation Procedures*—Effective interactive teams consider a variety of factors when designing and implementing intervention techniques.
10. *Commitment to Common Goals*—Effective interactive teams have a shared commitment to collaborative goals and problem-solving techniques.

Case Manager/Service Coordinator

An essential component of the mainstreaming network is the *case manager,* or *service coordinator,* an individual who leads the team and coordinates the program. In interactive teams, the role of leader rotates among the members of the team. As a service coordinator, the leader performs several functions:

1. coordinating the services needed by the student/client and family
2. delegating responsibility for providing those services to the individuals best able to provide them
3. providing followup to ensure that goals are being met
4. guiding the contributions of paraprofessionals and volunteers who assist on the case (Morsink, Chase Thomas, & Correa, 1991)

Interpersonal and Communication Skills

Successful interactive teams must develop effective interpersonal and communication skills (Thousand & Villa, 1990). Landerholm (1990) summarized the interpersonal roles that team members can perform to facilitate the team's ability to function efficiently and establish a positive, trusting working environment:

- *Initiating*—All members identify problems and issues to be considered by the team.
- *Information gathering and sharing*—All members collect and share relevant information.
- *Clarifying and elaborating*—All members seek clarification and provide elaboration.
- *Summarizing*—All members review key points discussed by the team.
- *Consensus building*—All members participate in decisionmaking.
- *Encouraging*—All members encourage others to participate in the process.
- *Harmonizing and compromising*—All members seek to resolve conflict and compromise.

To help the team develop these skills, individual team members can be assigned roles such as facilitator, recorder, timekeeper, observer, and summarizer (Thousand, Fox, Reid, Godek, & Williams, 1986).

Map Action Planning System

The network can coordinate students' mainstreaming programs through use of the Map Action Planning System (MAPS), a systems approach to designing a plan for mainstreaming students (Forest & Lusthaus, 1990). In MAPS, mem-

IDEAS FOR IMPLEMENTATION	When communicating in interactive teams, individual team members should do the following: • Understand the purpose of the meeting. • Listen without interrupting others. • Consider the perspectives of others. • Avoid making judgments, assumptions, and interpretations. • Pay attention to the speaker's verbal and nonverbal behaviors. • Seek information and clarification by asking questions and paraphrasing the statements of others. • Reflect upon the speaker's message. • Categorize information presented by others. • Focus feedback on ideas rather than on the individuals who proposed the ideas. • Expand on the ideas of others. • Share credit for ideas and solutions with others. • Take notes. • Wait before speaking. • Refrain from showing anger, giving orders, moralizing, talking in a condescending way, asking excessive or inappropriate questions, and making threats. • Focus on commonalities rather than differences. • Avoid the use of jargon. • Seek feedback from others regarding their understanding of your comments. • Rephrase important and difficult to understand comments. • Use humor. • Use congruent nonverbal behaviors to support their message.

Source: Communication Briefings (1989); Deboer (1986); Friend & Cook (1992); Price (1990).

bers of students' mainstreaming networks including mainstreamed students, their families, and peers meet to develop a plan for successful mainstreaming by initially responding to the following questions.

1. *What is (the student's name) history?* This question provides the network with an understanding of the events that have shaped the student's life and family.
2. *What is your dream for (the student's name)?* This question allows the student and his or her family to share their visions and goals for the future.
3. *What is your nightmare?* This question helps the network with insights into the student's and his or her family's fears.
4. *Who is (the student's name)?* This question provides all members of the network with the opportunity to brainstorm descriptions of their perceptions of the student.
5. *What are (the student's name) strengths, gifts and talents?* This question helps the network focus on and identify the student's positive attributes.
6. *What are (the student's name) needs?* This question assists the network in defining the student's needs in a variety of areas.

7. *What would be an ideal day for (the student's name)? What do we need to do to make this ideal real?* These questions help the network plan the student's mainstreamed program by listing the student's schedule of activities, modifications needed to participate in these activities, and individuals responsible for implementing identified modifications (Forest & Lusthaus, 1989).

Think About It

Think about a situation in which you worked collaboratively with a team. How was the outcome affected by the collaboration? What problems did the team experience in working collaboratively? How did the team resolve these problems?

Involving Mainstreamed Students in the Network

Whenever possible, mainstreamed students should be involved in the networks' decisionmaking conferences. Mainstreamed students can provide the network with information about strengths and weaknesses, successful teaching strategies and materials, interests, hobbies and talents, and career goals (Van Reusen, Bos, Schumaker, & Deshler, 1987). Van Reusen and Bos (1990) propose that educators teach students to communicate in planning conferences through use of a learning strategy called I PLAN:

I = Inventory your strengths, weaknesses you need to improve, goals and interests, and choices for learning.

P = Provide your inventory information.

L = Listen and respond.

A = Ask questions.

N = Name your goals (p. 30).

They also note that educators can facilitate student participation in conferences by providing students with enough time to formulate and present their responses; by listening and paying attention to students' comments; by soliciting input and opinions from students; and by incorporating students' comments into the educational program.

FACILITATING COMMUNICATION AMONG EDUCATORS

Successful mainstreaming will require that educators work collaboratively throughout the process, determining a student's readiness for mainstreaming; preparing students for entry into the mainstream; implementing attitude change strategies with students; designing remedial instruction that parallels and supports regular education instruction; planning and implementing instructional, testing, and grading modifications; obtaining supportive services for mainstreamed students and their families; maintaining communication with parents and other members of the mainstreaming network; and evaluating student progress in the mainstream. For example, special and regular education teachers may jointly adapt a content area test for a mainstreamed student with the special education paraprofessional administering the test in the resource room.

Prior to mainstreaming, special and bilingual educators should provide regular educators with information concerning a student's academic achievement, social development, supplementary support services, medical needs, adaptive devices, and preparedness for entering the mainstream.

Communication and cooperation among educators should be initiated with the decision to mainstream a student into a specific classroom. Educators should work together to plan an orientation and instructional program for mainstreamed students. Safran and Safran (1985b) suggest that the initial communication between special and regular educators should clarify goals and achievement expectations, identify appropriate materials, delineate adapted instructional techniques, determine assignment modifications, plan for supportive instruction in the resource room, and establish grading options. For students with sensory impairments, the regular classroom teacher should receive information concerning the nature of the sensory loss as well as the amount of residual hearing or vision (Gearheart, Weishahn, & Gearheart, 1988). In the case of students with hearing impairments, teachers also should be informed of the student's communication abilities and needs and have an opportunity to meet with the student to establish a relationship. Similarly, for students who are learning English as a second language, teachers should be apprised of their linguistic abilities and the best approaches for helping students acquire English.

One method of communicating necessary information to the regular educator is the pre-entry questionnaire (Salend & Hankee, 1981). The pre-entry questionnaire is a written record of the sending teachers' responses to a series of questions and items concerning a mainstreamed student's performance. The completed questionnaire is sent to the regular education teacher prior to the entry of the mainstreamed student into the regular education class. A sample pre-entry questionnaire is presented in Figure 3.2.

Collaborative Consultation

Ms. Giek, a new collaborative consultation teacher, decides to keep a diary of her collaborative consultation experiences. At the end of three months, she looks back at some of the entries.

September 7: I can only be in one place at a time! Juggling teacher schedules and getting to students for assistance in their academic areas of need will be a feat worthy of a gold medal. And on top of that, time has to be set aside to conference with classroom teachers. I'm frustrated!!

September 8: I've worried about how junior high students would accept my presence in the classroom. . . . I discussed this with Mr. T, the building principal. During the grade level orientations, Mr. T introduced me as a teacher who would be in several different classes to assist students.

September 13: I did it! Schedules typed, all academic areas covered. I even managed to schedule time to conference with teachers (and it's not during lunch!) Mrs. C is not too keen on meeting with me on a regular basis, and voiced a great concern about how much work this would add to her already overloaded schedule. Copies of all schedules have been sent to teachers, administrators, and parents. I have contacted every parent by phone and explained the service.

September 14: Mrs. M came to see me. She blurted out to me that she didn't know if she could go through with having me work in her room. She indicated to me that she felt extremely intimidated and was worried about what I would think. My first reaction was, "Don't be silly." Thank goodness I didn't say that. It really wasn't silly, because, I, too, was very nervous. I told Mrs. M that I understood what she meant, and explained my own nervousness.

September 18: A pleasant surprise. Mr. K introduced me as a co-teacher. He told his students that if they had any questions they could ask either himself or Mrs. Giek. . . . I was wondering exactly how this would work out, when several different students raised their hands for assistance. In the end, I put together a small group of children to work with at the back table. How nice to see that the students I expected to work with, along with other students, accepted my presence and wanted my help.

September 20: I met with Mrs. E today. Together we worked on J's IEP and reviewed her entire curriculum, and decided on goals which should be included. It was wonderful having her input.

October 12: Mrs. C asked me if I would be willing to take a group of students for the social studies lesson and work on latitude and longitude. . . . We discussed the format and objectives of the lesson. During the class, we divided the room into groups and each taught a group. After the lesson, we were able to meet and discuss the results.

November 16: Ms. D, a first grade teacher approached me and asked if I could speak with her about one of her students. I do not have a student in her room. We met after school and discussed the difficulties this child was having. Ms. D then asked if I would sit in on a parent conference. I guess there is a lot more to this job than just working with my assigned students.

November 20: Today's consultation with Mrs K. centered on getting her feedback on a study guide I created. We went over all the points, and at the end of the conversation she asked me if I would mind if she duplicated the guide and gave it to all her students.

December 5: Mrs. M indicated that the whole class was having difficulty getting the concept of contractions. We discussed some strategies, and she asked if I would like to teach the lesson the following morning. At the end of the consultation session, she turned to me and said, "You know, I am still a little nervous, but I really do like this collaborative consultation.

Source: K. Giek, *The Forum,* Volume 16 No. 1 (New York State Federation of Chapters of the Council for Exceptional Children, 1990), pp. 5–6. Reprinted by permission.

FIGURE 3.2
Sample pre-entry questionnaire

What language(s) does the student speak? What language(s) do the parents speak?

What are the student's academic strengths?

What are the student's academic weaknesses?

What approaches and materials have been effective with the student?

What approaches and materials have not been effective with the student?

What instructional modifications does the student require?

What remedial activities are appropriate for use with the student?

What cultural factors should be considered in designing an educational program for the student? For involving parents in the educational program?

What social and behavioral skills does the student possess?

What social and behavioral skills does the student lack?

What are the student's hobbies and interests?

In what school clubs or extracurricular activities does/could the student participate?

How does the student get along with her or his peers?

How does the student feel about her or his disability?

What school personnel and community agencies will be working with the student? What services will they provide?

To what extent will the student's parents be involved in the mainstreaming process?

What communication system will be used to communicate between professionals? With parents?

What adaptive devices or medications does the student require?

Has the student been prepared for entry into the mainstream?

Collaborative efforts between educators should extend beyond the student's initial placement into the mainstream (Salend, 1984). Specifically, educators should work together to provide followup supportive services, such as collaborative consultation (West & Cannon, 1988). Collaborative consultation is a service delivery system to improve the quality of instruction for mainstreamed students educated in regular education settings (West & Idol, 1987). Idol, Paolucci-Whitcomb, and Nevin (1986) define collaborative consultation as

Collaborative consultation services are designed to prevent and remediate learning and behavioral problems and coordinate instructional programs (West & Idol, 1990).

> an interactive process that enables people with diverse expertise to generate creative solutions to mutually defined problems. The outcome is enhanced, altered and produces solutions that are different from those that the individual team members would produce independently. The major outcome of collaborative consultation is to provide comprehensive and effective programs for students with special needs within the most appropriate context, thereby enabling them to achieve maximum constructive interaction with their . . . peers. (p. 1)

Often, the consultation follows a triadic model in which the consultant, usually a special, bilingual, or multicultural educator or an ancillary support personnel member (a school psychologist, speech and language therapist, or physical therapist), works with the regular education teacher, who has primary responsibility for serving the student (Heron & Harris, 1987). Thus, the goals of collaborative consultation are to remediate problems and to assist and provide the classroom teachers with improved knowledge and skills to deal with like situations in the future.

Collaborative consultation differs in several ways from an expert approach to assisting teachers. These differences are summarized in Figure 3.3. In collaborative consultation, rather than the consultant supervising the consultee, the consultee has an equal status relationship with the consultant. However, based on prior experience, regular classroom teachers may view their roles as passive referral agents (Salend & Salend, 1984). Therefore, early in the consultation process, educators will need to clarify and agree upon their respective roles. Typically, classroom teachers provide a knowledge of the scope and sequence of the curriculum, child development, and instruc-

FIGURE 3.3
Comparison of consultation and expert systems

	RELATIONSHIP STYLE	
Dimension	**Collaborative**	**Expert/Authoritative**
Objectives/goals	Resolve presenting problem and improve consultee skills	Resolve presenting problem
Target of behavior change	Client and consultee	Client
Relationship	Equal partners	Superior/subordinate
Person responsible		
for client	Consultee	Consultee
for intervention development	Consultant and consultee	Consultant
Consultee involvement in problem solving	Extensive	Minimal
Amount of information generated about problem situation	Usually extensive	Minimal to extensive
Number of alternatives generated	Usually multiple	Often one
Assumption about consultee's involvement	Wants to be involved in problem solving	Wants consultant to solve problem
Time involved	Usually greater	Usually less
Person with problem-solving expertise	Consultant and consultee	Consultant

Source: J. E. Zins, M. J. Curtis, S. G. Graden, and C. R. Ponti. *Helping Students Succeed in the Regular Classroom* (San Francisco: Jossey-Bass, Inc., 1988). Reprinted by permission of the publisher.

tional procedures for large groups, while special and bilingual educators offer a knowledge of behavior management, assessment, second language acquisition, multicultural education, and instructional strategies and adaptations (West & Idol, 1987). Mutual clarification and understanding of roles can foster the establishment of a good relationship (Rodin & Janis, 1979), increased motivation (McClelland, 1977), and greater adherence to recommended interventions (Kasl, 1975).

The use of consultation has benefited students, teachers, and educational systems (Zins, Curtis, Graden, & Ponti, 1988). In terms of impact on students, consultation has led to a decrease in inappropriate behavior (Idol-Maestas, 1981), an increase in academic proficiency over an extended period of time (Jackson, Cleveland, & Merenda, 1975), and an improvement in the academic and social performance of nontargeted students (Jason & Ferone, 1978). With respect to teachers, consultation has led to an increase in their acquisition of teaching skills (Gutkin, 1980), positive attitudes toward working with mainstreamed students (Gutkin, Singer, & Brown, 1980), and knowledge and understanding of students who are experiencing difficulties in school (Curtis & Watson, 1980). Systemwide, consultation has resulted in a decrease in the number of students referred and tested for special education services (Ponti, Zins, & Graden, 1988).

Countering Resistance

Despite its effectiveness, professionals may be resistant to the use of consultation (Friend & Cook, 1992). Friend and Bauwens (1988) identified four sources of resistance to consultation: maintenance of the status quo, failure and frustration, professional pride, and varying perceptions of the process. They suggest that consultants can overcome this resistance by enlisting the support of administrators, involving classroom teachers in the whole process, providing incentives for teachers to participate, sharing data on the effectiveness of consultation, designing interventions that are consistent with the teacher's style, providing nonjudgmental feedback, and establishing a trusting relationship. Resistance to consultation also can be countered by educators demonstrating appropriate interpersonal and communication skills (Heron & Kimball, 1988).

Idol, Paolucci-Whitcomb, and Nevin (1986) and Friend and Cook (1992) provide guidelines for using positive nonverbal communication to implement collaborative consultation.

A major barrier to successful consultation is insufficient time for team members to meet and overwhelming caseloads (Johnson, Pugach, & Hammitte, 1988). West and Idol (1990) have identified a variety of strategies that schools have successfully implemented to provide classroom teachers and support staff with time to consult. Similarly, Idol (1988) has delineated guidelines for establishing collaborative consultation programs in schools that include suggestions for determining the caseloads and designing schedules.

The effectiveness of the consultation process can be enhanced by the extent to which individuals display *referent power,* an individual's ability to be liked, admired, and respected by others (Martin, 1978). Referent power is found in professionals who can develop a sense of empathy and rapport with others. Suggestions from professionals who possess referent power are more likely to be accepted than suggestions from professionals who are disliked or coercive.

IDEAS FOR IMPLEMENTATION	Educators can increase their referent power by enacting the following suggestions: • Demonstrate a desire to learn from others • Interact with teachers in noninstructional or social settings, such as the teacher's lounge • Emphasize similarities in beliefs, attitudes, and values • Display a positive attitude • Show respect for the consultee's profession and expertise • Listen actively • Maintain a nonauthoritarian supportive attitude • Limit the use of professional jargon • Solicit the support of influential school personnel • Give credit to others for their ideas and contributions

Source: Dorr, (1977), Hughes & Falk, (1981), Idol, Paolucci-Whitcomb, & Nevin, (1986), Rodin & Janis, (1979).

Steps in Collaborative Consultation

Bergan (1977) identified the steps in effective collaborative consultation as problem identification, problem analysis, plan implementation, and plan evaluation.

Problem Identification. The initial step in the consultation process is to identify the problem by meeting with the regular education teacher and/or observing the student in the mainstreamed setting. Factors to consider in identifying the problem include the curriculum, physical environment of the room, instructional strategies, teaching styles, peer relationships, student ability levels, family, and schoolwide policies and procedures (Zins, Curtis, Graden, & Ponti, 1988). Although teachers may want to focus on several problem areas at once, often it is best for the team to work on one situation at a time. If it is necessary to consider more than one situation, then it may be advisable to set priorities and select the most critical problems to work on first (Salend & Salend, 1984).

Once the problem has been identified and agreed upon by all professionals, it should be clearly defined in observable terms. For example, if professionals agree that the problem is inappropriate student comments during formal instruction and the goal is to decrease them, then the terms "inappropriate student comments" and "formal instruction" must be defined by their observable characteristics. The definition should include a statement of the student's current level of performance as well as a statement of the student's desired level of performance relative to the identified problem (Zins, Curtis, Graden, & Ponti, 1988).

Problem Analysis. In the second phase of the consultation process, professionals analyze the critical environmental features that appear to be related to the student's identified problem. Analyzing these aspects of the classroom will help in the planning of the intervention strategies. Classroom variables that may need to be examined include student behaviors, antecedents to and consequences of student behaviors, teacher behaviors, instructional format, classroom physical design, scheduling, peer socialization patterns, and unique classroom characteristics. To analyze these various components of the problem, educators should address the following questions:

1. What social and academic behaviors are difficult for the student(s)?
2. Which antecedent and consequence events seem to be affecting student behavior?
3. How does the teacher's behavior and style affect student performance?
4. Which classroom instructional and management strategies appear to be effective? Ineffective? Why?
5. What objects, events, or individuals could serve as potential positive reinforcers?
6. How do the presentation and response modes of the classroom material affect student performance?
7. How does the physical design of the classroom affect student performance? How does it affect the teacher's management system?
8. How do peers impact on the student's performance?
9. What unique characteristics of the classroom milieu appear to be affecting the student's and teacher's behaviors?

Educators also should consider the cultural and linguistic factors that impact student performance.

Plan Implementation. Information gathered during the problem analysis stage should help educators plan and select appropriate interventions to be implemented. During this step, educators should decide upon an appropriate intervention that addresses the identified problem as well as the concerns and context of the classroom. Professionals brainstorm and share their expertise in devising the interventions. When designing interventions, educators should consider such factors as practicality, effectiveness, effects on others, time demands, cost, and ease of implementation (Zins, Curtis, Graden, & Ponti, 1988).

Once the intervention has been selected, its specifics should be outlined. Educators also should determine and delineate responsibilities and timelines (West & Idol, 1990). The agreement among professionals also can be assessed by having them discuss the specifics of the intervention plan. For example, if the intervention is a positive reinforcement system to increase the student's interactions with peers, then educators can discuss the following:

1. What are the observable features that make up the behavior to be changed?
2. What are the daily and weekly goals of the intervention?
3. How will the change in behavior be measured?
4. What are the environmental conditions under which the program will be in effect?
5. What are the consequences of appropriate behavior? Of inappropriate behavior?

6. What reinforcers will be used? How frequently will they be delivered?
7. What is the teacher's role in the plan?
8. What is the consultant's role in the plan?

Plan Evaluation. Once the intervention has been implemented, periodic checks on its effectiveness should occur. Data on the effectiveness of the intervention in promoting changes in student performance can be obtained through direct observation, curriculum-based assessments, and analysis of student work samples.

In addition to monitoring student performance, followup evaluation should examine the implementation of the intervention and identify any problem areas that need change. Feedback should be an ongoing, interactive process focused on the intervention plan rather than on the individuals involved. To be helpful, feedback should be 1) based on observations rather than inferences and judgments; 2) presented in a direct, concise, clear, and nonevaluative manner; 3) designed to facilitate the sharing of ideas and information as well as the exploration of alternatives; 4) desired by and offered as valuable information for the receiver, not as a release for the provider; and 5) delivered at the appropriate time and place (Friend & Cook, 1992). In addition to evaluating the effect of the intervention on students, data also should be collected to assess its impact on educators and the school (West & Idol, 1990).

Think About It

Many people believe that the term *consultant teacher* should be changed to *collaborative teacher.* What do you think? Why?

Cooperative Teaching

Bauwens, Hourcade, and Friend (1989) delineate three types of cooperative teaching arrangements: complementary instruction, team teaching, and supportive learning activities.

Collaborative consultation also may involve *cooperative teaching,* whereby regular educators and supportive service personnel work jointly to develop and teach the instructional program in the mainstreamed setting (Bauwens, Hourcade, & Friend, 1989). Cooperative teaching allows for the infusion of specialized materials and teaching strategies into the regular education setting (Self, Benning, Marston, & Magnusson, 1991). Thus, rather than pulling a student out of the mainstream for supportive services, the supportive services are delivered in the regular classroom setting (Bean & Eichelberger, 1985). Successful cooperative teaching arrangements require educators to meet frequently to define roles and expectations, set schedules, select and transport appropriate materials if necessary, and determine space requirements and arrangements within the regular education setting (Bean & Eichelberger, 1985).

Several cooperative teaching programs have been successful in meeting the needs of mainstreamed students (Reynolds & Volkmar, 1984). Sargent, Swartzbaugh, and Sherman (1981) employed a cooperative teaching approach to mainstream students in English. The teaching team consisted of a reading specialist, a regular education English teacher, and a special educator. The team cooperatively designed an instructional program to teach reading, writing, listening, and speaking skills. For example, in the area of reading, students' needs were assessed by the teachers; the reading specialist then developed an instructional program that was implemented in the regular education setting by all three professionals. The team noted positive improvement in students' skills in all four content areas.

Multicultural Education Consultants

Recent demographic changes in our society have brought new challenges for schools such as the implementation of multicultural education. Because schools are slow to change and may lack the internal expertise in multicultural education, consultants are needed who can provide assistance to teachers and administrators attempting to respond to these new challenges. Roberts, Bell, and Salend (1991) propose a framework that consultants can use for communicating and negotiating multicultural education changes in schools. In this consultation model, consultants work with educators, community members and students to do the following:

- define terminology and agree upon the parameters of the consultation process
- recognize the impact of ideology
- transform the language of schools
- focus on group empowerment
- negotiate power conflicts
- involve the community
- transform staffing, decisionmaking and resource allocation
- re-create an inclusive classroom environment

Desegregation Assistance Centers located throughout the United States also provide technical assistance to help schools implement multicultural education.

PROMOTING CONGRUENCE

Ms. Rivera is concerned about Elisa, a migrant student, who leaves her classroom several times during the day to receive supplemental program services. To alleviate her concerns, Ms. Rivera meets with Mr. D'Allesandro, Elisa's migrant tutor, to coordinate their activities. Ms. Rivera and Mr. D'Alessandro discuss how to plan their programs so that Mr. D'Alessandro's tutoring sessions will reinforce what Ms. Rivera is teaching in the classroom.

They decide that Mr. D'Alessandro will preview stories with Elisa before they are read in Ms. Rivera's classroom. They also agree that Mr. D'Alessandro will review new words from the story and reread the story with Elisa. To coordinate these activities and check on Elisa's progress, Ms. Rivera and Mr.

D'Alessandro meet weekly. With this planning, Ms. Rivera feels better, and Elisa is better able to participate in class.

A goal of the mainstreaming communication system and network should be to insure *congruence,* the relationship between the curriculum, learning goals, instructional materials and strategies of the regular classroom, and the supportive services programs (Allington & Broikou, 1988). A congruent program is one in which supportive service personnel (special educators, reading specialists, speech and language therapists, bilingual and migrant educators) serving mainstreamed students are delivering a cohesive educational program based on common assessment results, goals and objectives, instructional strategies, and materials.

Johnston, Allington, and Afflerbach (1985) assessed the congruence between the reading programs used by reading specialists and regular classroom teachers and found that only one-third of the remedial reading specialists could identify the reading materials employed in the regular classroom, while only 10 % of the regular classroom teachers could identify the reading materials used in the remedial education setting.

However, rather than providing a program where the instruction in the remedial setting parallels the regular core curriculum, many supportive service personnel deliver fragmented educational programs based on divergent and conflicting curricula and instructional approaches (Idol, West, & Lloyd, 1988). These incompatible and conflicting educational programs appear to confuse students rather than facilitate their educational progress (Johnston, Allington, & Afflerbach, 1985). For example, confusion can occur when students receive remedial reading instruction using a phonetic approach in the resource room and a sight word approach in the regular classroom.

Allington and Shake (1986) propose two remedial instruction models for coordinating instruction so that the remedial program supports learning in the regular education setting, an a priori model and a post hoc model. In the *a priori* model, the supportive services personnel teach content that supports the content to be learned in the regular classroom. Instruction in the remedial class lays the foundation for instruction in the regular education setting. For example, the English as a second language educator might introduce the mainstreamed student to the spelling words on Monday that will be tested on Friday in the regular classroom.

The *post hoc* model ensures congruence by having the instruction in the remedial setting focus on reinforcing skills previously introduced in the regular education classroom. Thus, rather than introducing new content to the learner, the remedial teacher reviews and reteaches content previously covered in the regular education program. For example, while a student is receiving instruction in adding fractions in the mainstreamed setting, the resource room teacher would help the student understand the process and develop automaticity in responding to similar items.

Meetings

Meetings such as the IEP conference also can serve as a framework for establishing congruence by involving regular classroom teachers and supportive services personnel in the planning and implementation of instructional programs (Helge, 1987b). At the meeting, educators can align their instructional programs by agreeing upon a common set of objectives, appropriate instructional strategies and materials, and evaluation procedures to assess student mastery of objectives. As students master existing objectives, additional meetings can be held to revise the instructional program and evaluate congruence.

Student Interviews

Students can be a source for insuring and evaluating congruence. Both regular education teachers and remedial personnel can periodically discuss with students aspects of the instructional environment in other classes. Specifically, they can ask students, *What things are you learning in (class)? What type of activities do you do in (class)? What materials do you use in (class)? Does (class) help you in other classes?* (Johnston, Allington, & Afflerbach, 1985).

Notecard Systems

Congruence and communication between professionals serving mainstreamed students can be built into the network through use of a notecard system (Everston & Heshusius, 1985). Each professional working with a mainstreamed student completes a notecard that serves as an ongoing record of the student's performance in that class for a specified period of time. The information on the card could include a rating of the student's progress, a listing of the skills mastered and not mastered, upcoming assignments and tests, successful strategies, instructional materials being used, and skills other teachers should attempt to foster. An educator can be assigned the task of categorizing the information and sharing it with others to insure the continuity of instruction. Thus, if a resource room teacher were aware that a mainstreamed student was scheduled to have a test, time in the resource room can be devoted to preparing for that test. A sample notecard is presented in Figure 3.4.

Safran and Safran (1985b) have developed the Something's Out of Sync (SOS) form to facilitate communication between regular and special educators. The regular classroom teacher completes the SOS form to indicate that a student is having a problem in a specific content area. The regular classroom teacher can then request that the student receive additional work in the resource room in that area or that a meeting be held to discuss the problem.

Students Who Move During the School Year

Census data indicate that 18 % of United States households moved in 1989 with half the population changing address from 1985 to 1989.

In addition to such highly mobile members of our society as migrant workers, the homeless, foster children, and military personnel, many students move during the school year. Educators can facilitate the continuity and delivery of services to mainstreamed students who are moving to a new school by teaching parents to maintain current records and share relevant information with other school personnel. Available and up-to-date information can assist the new school district and the parents in determining an

FIGURE 3.4
Sample notecard

Student's Name:________________ Time Period:______________
Class/Supportive Service:_________ Educator:________________

Skills taught:

Instructional strategies and materials used:

Upcoming assignments/tests:
Assignment/Test *Date due*

Skills to be reinforced in other settings:

Suggested activities to reinforce skills:

Comments:

appropriate educational program quickly. Therefore, before the family moves, educators should encourage and help parents to obtain and update such relevant documents as birth certificates; immunizations records; lists of illnesses, accidents, special problems, and medications; papers from medical personnel; IEPs; report cards; transcripts; important correspondence between parents and school; and names, addresses, and phone numbers of medical and educational personnel who can provide information concerning the child's needs (Sarda et al., 1991).

School Administrators

School administrators can be instrumental in facilitating the communication between educators. Administrators can foster a sense of communication and congruence between school personnel through inservice training (Tymitz-Wolf, 1982).

IDEAS FOR IMPLEMENTATION

Educators can promote congruence by enacting the following suggestions:

- Supportive services personnel should align their assessment procedures, curriculum, and instructional strategies with those employed in the regular classroom program.
- Regular educators should assist in the design of supportive services programs.
- Regular classroom teachers and supportive service personnel should share lesson plans and materials.
- Administrators should schedule time for teachers to collaborate in the planning of the student's instructional program.
- Regular classroom teachers and supportive service personnel should observe each other's classrooms.
- Educators should use similar behavior management techniques so that they respond in the same manner to student behavior and promote the maintenance and generalization of the behavior change process.
- Supportive service personnel should teach study skills and learning strategies using the textbooks of the regular education program.
- Speech and language therapists should discuss with classroom teachers language concepts to be reinforced in the mainstreamed setting.
- Bilingual educators should share strategies for use with students who speak English as a second language.
- Social workers should contact community agencies to coordinate services.
- Educators should communicate instructional goals and student progress to parents.
- Educators should compile sharing folders containing student products.
- Educators should participate in staff development sessions that facilitate the coordination of services.

Inservice Training

Inservice programs can help educators involved in mainstreaming acquire the skills to work together and perform new roles. West and Idol (1990) suggest that inservice programs should provide educators with the communication and problem-solving skills to implement successful collaborative consultation programs. Effective inservice programs should address teacher-identified needs; employ competent personnel to deliver training; be coordinated by school districts, State Education Departments, teacher training institutions, and professional organizations; offer educators incentives to participate; deliver instruction using a variety of methods including demonstrations and activities that require active participation; provide teachers with feedback and the chance to experiment with the training in the classroom; and be evaluated based on teacher satisfaction, teacher and student change data, and acquisition of knowledge skills (Browder, 1983; Powers, 1983; Skrtic, Knowlton, & Clark, 1979).

Morsink, Chase Thomas, and Correa (1991) offer excellent guidelines for developing and implementing effective staff development programs.

Inservice training has been effective in promoting positive attitudes toward mainstreaming and helping teachers improve their skills (Hoben, 1980;

Johnson & Johnson, 1980). Hoben (1980) and Johnson and Johnson (1980) found that teacher attitudes could be positively influenced by providing inservice training that emphasized direct experiences with mainstreamed students. Similarly, results of field-based programs showed that teachers exited the training sessions with increased skills and more positive attitudes toward mainstreaming (Carlson & Potter, 1972; Yates, 1973).

Inservice training should be directed at promoting the necessary positive attitudes that teachers need to create the proper psychological and educational environment for mainstreamed students (Kauffmann & Hallahan, 1981). Donaldson (1980) identified several different modes for promoting attitude change that can be employed by inservice trainers. Because positive teacher attitudes toward mainstreaming appear to be related to the ability of teachers to instruct mainstreamed students (Salend & Johns, 1983), inservice training should also focus on skill acquisition, which should be directed at the competencies educators need in order to implement mainstreaming successfully. Redden and Blackhurst (1978) identified 6 functions and 32 competency statements relating to the skills necessary to teach students in mainstreamed settings.

Inservice instructional activities should be designed to address teachers' needs. Training should include interaction with peers who have been involved in successful mainstreaming efforts (Stokes & Axelrod, 1980), exposure to students who have been successfully mainstreamed, and contact with students (Noar & Milgram, 1980); followup in teachers' current work setting should be an integral part of the inservice program. Staff training also should focus on such topics as being sensitive to cultural and linguistic differences, understanding diverse learning styles, promoting parental involvement and sharing information with parents, employing culturally relevant instruction, working with interpreters, and working collaboratively with other professionals (Violand-Sanchez, Sutton, & Ware, 1991).

FOSTERING PARENTAL INVOLVEMENT

An essential component of a congruent mainstreaming network is the student's parents. Research indicates that when educators share information with parents, parents can be instrumental in promoting their children's academic and social progress (Peterson, 1989). Parental involvement also makes parents feel better about themselves and improves the working environment for teachers (Flaxman & Inger, 1991). McLoughlin, Edge, & Strenecky (1978) identified several ways to involve parents in the educational program. These include:

1. *Identification.* Often parents are the first ones to notice that their child is experiencing difficulty in a certain area.

2. *Assessment.* Because of their extensive experience with their children, parents are a valuable resource for assessing the student's educational and health-related needs.

IDEAS FOR IMPLEMENTATION

Administrators can encourage communication by enacting the following suggestions:

- Plan lunch and preparation periods so that regular and ancillary support personnel who work with the same mainstreamed students can meet to discuss and coordinate their work.
- Excuse teachers from duties so that they can meet with others.
- Schedule extra planning time for teachers who work with mainstreamed students.
- Hire a substitute to free teachers to attend meetings.
- Provide opportunities for teachers to collaboratively develop and implement lesson plans and instructional units.
- Request at the beginning of the school year that regular classroom teachers list the times that are most convenient for the students in their class to receive individualized supportive services.
- Ask supportive service personnel such as special and bilingual education teachers to give presentations at faculty meetings or inservice days.
- Maintain a file in which staff list the areas of expertise they would be willing to share with others.
- Limit the clerical and noninstructional tasks of teachers.
- Conduct a faculty meeting in a supportive service personnel member's classroom.
- Give faculty a tour of the school including a visit to the classrooms that house special programs.
- Encourage regular classroom teachers and supportive services staff to visit and observe each other's teaching activities.
- Ask faculty members to switch roles for a day.
- Designate an area of the teachers' lounge as a "materials table" where teachers leave certain materials that they think would be of value to others.
- Include all classes in all schoolwide activities.
- Send all school memos to all teachers.
- Have all teachers including supportive service personnel serve as coaches, school club advisors, and representatives of the school at community events.

Source: Salend (1980); West & Idol (1990).

3. *Programming.* Parents can provide input into the selection of educational goals, instructional procedures and modifications, testing adaptations, and related services.

4. *Teaching.* Parents can supplement the educational program by tutoring their child, assisting with homework assignments, and participating in behavior change projects.

The National Institute of Education (1985) also suggests that teachers involve parents as partners in their child's educational program in several ways, such as

- Ask the parents to read aloud to the child or listen to him or her read.
- Ask the parents to sign a child's homework.

- Encourage parents to drill students on math and spelling.
- Suggest the parents help the child with workbook and homework lessons.
- Encourage parents to ask the child to discuss his or her school day activities.
- Suggest things at home that parents can use to teach their children.
- Send home suggestions for game or group activities related to the child's schoolwork that can be played by parents and child.
- Invite parents to the classroom to watch how the child is taught.
- Encourage parents to take their child to the library regularly and frequently (National Institute of Education, 1985, p. 2).

5. *Evaluation.* Feedback from the parents' perspective on the effectiveness of the student's educational program can offer educators data to validate aspects of the program and identify program characteristics that need to be revised (McLoughlin, Edge, & Strenecky, 1978). Parents also can be involved in schools by meeting with teachers, providing transportation, observing in the classroom, conducting educational activities in the home, attending parent education groups, volunteering to work in the classroom, providing support to other parents, serving as advocates, working with administrators, raising funds, and sharing information with others (Cone, Delawyer, & Wolfe, 1985).

Individuals with Disabilities Education Act and Parents

In addition to being an educationally sound practice, involving parents in the educational program of students with disabilities is mandated by the Individuals with Disabilities Education Act (IDEA).

Due Process

To ensure parent awareness of and participation in the process, school districts must attempt to inform parents by telephone, written communication, or home visit in the parents' primary language or mode of communication of the parents.

The IDEA requires that parents be informed *and their consent solicited* when 1) a referral for placement in special education is initiated; 2) placement teams determine the need for testing to assess eligibility for special education services; 3) results of an assessment are available and being discussed; 4) IEPs are being formulated; 5) a recommendation for special education services is made by the placement team; 6) IEPs are reviewed; and 7) changes in the student's educational program are planned (McLoughlin & Lewis, 1986). Each attempt to inform parents should be documented and communicated.

Throughout each of these steps, parents should be aware of their right to *due process,* which offers parents the right to appeal and contest each decision made by the placement team. If parents and the placement team cannot agree on an aspect of the student's educational program, either party may initiate a due process hearing—a quasijudicial proceeding by which local and educational agencies and parents of special education students seek to resolve educational disputes. The hearing is conducted by an impartial hearing officer who makes a decision regarding the issues in question. The hearing officer is selected by the local educational agency from a list of qualified individuals. As part of their due process rights, parents have the right to have their case presented by an attorney or another knowledgeable representative, present evidence, subpoena witnesses, cross-examine witnesses, obtain a written or electronic transcript of the proceedings, and receive a copy of the hearing officer's decision. Either party can appeal the hearing officer's decision to the state educational agency. The decision of the state educational agency can be challenged through a civil action.

If a due process hearing is held, it is likely that professionals who work closely with the student will be called upon to give testimony. Before the hearing, professionals should ask questions so that they understand the relationship between their testimony and the issues of contention (Scandary, 1981). Because they may be called upon to testify to support the parent's case against the district, educators should seek information and advice from their local teachers' organization concerning potential conflicts and retaliation. Scandary (1981) has developed several guidelines to help educators prepare to serve as witnesses in a due process hearing. She suggests that educators be prepared to do the following:

- Establish their credibility by reviewing their professional credentials such as certification(s), years of experience, training, career experiences, professional awards, and recognition received.
- Outline the services they provide to the student and the student's response to these services.
- Describe in clear and observable terms the student's educational and behavioral strengths and weaknesses.
- Support statements by citing the formal and informal assessment methods used.
- Discuss the technical adequacy (reliability, validity, standardization, and so on) of the standardized assessment instruments used.
- Explain professional jargon so that all parties can understand it.

Think About It

You are a teacher of a student who has recently immigrated to the United States. The multidisciplinary team has determined that the student's needs can best be met in a special education class. As the student's current teacher, you feel that this placement is inappropriate because the student performs well in class when she can overcome her language difficulties. The student's parents are contesting the multidisciplinary team's recommendation and ask that you testify at the hearing. What would you do? Should an educator's allegiance be to the school district or to parents and students?

Confidentiality

The IDEA also provides parents and students with the right to confidentiality. In other words, those educators directly involved in delivering services to a student may have access to his or her records, but, before a school district can allow individuals not directly involved in a student's program to review a student's records, it must obtain parental consent. Confidentiality also guarantees parents the opportunity to obtain, review, and challenge their child's educational records. Parents can obtain their child's records by requesting a copy, which the school district must furnish upon request. However, parents may be responsible for the expenses incurred in duplicating their child's records. If parents disagree with the contents of their child's records, they can challenge them by asking school officials to correct or delete the information or by writing their own response to be included in the child's record.

Think About It

In light of the confidentiality rights of parents and students, what would you do in the following situations?

1. Teachers are discussing students and their families during lunch in the teacher's lounge.
2. A student teacher asks you to let him/her see a student's records.
3. You notice that the students' records in your school are kept in an unsupervised area.

Parent Conferences

Research indicates that parents are willing to and do attend meetings with educators (Turnbull, Strickland, & Brantley, 1982). However, although parents are interested in attending conferences with educators, they often are not satisfied with these interactions and characterize them as confusing, disorganized, and poorly attended by professionals (Hoff, Fenton, Yoshida, & Kaufman, 1978; McKinney & Hocutt, 1982; Scanlon, Arick, & Phelps, 1981). While parent input is mandated by the IDEA, parents tend to assume a passive role in conferences and appear to be intimidated by technical jargon and test scores (Knoff, 1983).

Educators can take several steps to improve the quality of parent/teacher conferences (de Bettencourt, 1987; Kroth & Simpson, 1977; Swick, Flake-Hobson, & Raymond, 1980). These steps are discussed here.

Plan the Meeting. Prior to conducting the meeting, educators should carefully plan for it (Price & Marsh, 1985). During the planning step, teachers should identify the objectives of the meeting and develop an agenda that corresponds to those objectives. McNamara (1986) suggests that teachers send a letter to parents soliciting their input concerning the meeting's agenda. The agenda should allow for enough time to discuss and resolve issues and address concerns of parents and educators. Therefore, it is helpful to share the agenda with parents and other educators before the meeting, and provide them with the necessary background information to participate in the meeting (Goldstein & Turnbull, 1982). Materials such as work samples, test results, and other teachers' comments that relate to agenda items should be organized and available before the meeting.

The planning phase also should ensure that the meeting time is appropriate for parents and professionals. They should be contacted early in the planning process to determine what times and dates are most appropriate for them. Once a meeting has been scheduled, teachers should contact parents and professionals in advance to inform them of the time, place, purpose, and duration of the meeting, and to confirm their participation (McNamara, 1986). Followup reminders to parents via mail or telephone as well can increase the likelihood that parents will attend the conference (Wolf & Troup, 1980).

Structure the Environment to Promote Communication. The room in which the conference will take place should be organized for sharing information (Kroth & Simpson, 1977). Comfortable, same-size furniture should be used by all participants and arranged to promote communication. Barriers, such as desks and chairs, should not be placed between parents and educators. Chairs should be seated around a table or positioned so that all participants can see each other (de Bettencourt, 1987). Lockavitch (1983) suggests that teachers arrange chairs so that they are no closer together than four feet and no farther apart than six to eight feet.

To make sure the meeting is not interrupted, teachers should post a note indicating that a conference is in session on the room's door. Additionally, distractions caused by the telephone can be minimized by taking the phone off the hook, asking the office to hold all calls, or using a room that does not have a phone (Kroth & Simpson, 1977).

Conduct the Conference. Educators should conduct the conference in a manner that encourages parent understanding and participation. Initially, review the agenda and the stated purpose of the meeting. To facilitate parental participation, teachers can ask parents if they would like pads and pencils to take notes (Humphrey, Hoffman, & Crosby, 1984).

The meeting should start on a positive note, with educators discussing positive aspects of the student's performance. Next, educators can review any concerns they have about the student. They should present data in a format that is understandable to parents and share with parents materials such as work samples, test results, and anecdotal records to support their comments (McLoughlin & Lewis, 1986).

They can solicit information from parents by asking them to discuss the issues or situations from their perspective (Swick, Flake-Hobson, & Raymond, 1980), or by asking parents to respond to open-ended questions (Cronin, Slade, Bechtel, & Anderson, 1992). Educators can increase parental sharing at meetings by listening attentively; by acknowledging and reinforcing parent participation ("That's a good point"; "I'll try to incorporate that"); by avoiding asking parents questions that have yes/no or implied answers; by asking parents questions that encourage them to respond rather than waiting for them to ask questions or spontaneously speak their minds; by informing parents that there may be several solutions to a situation; by refraining from criticizing parents; by speaking to parents using language that is understandable but not condescending; by checking periodically for understanding; by paraphrasing and summarizing parents' comments, and by showing respect for parents and their feelings (Goldstein & Turnbull, 1982; Cronin et al., 1992; Lockavitch, 1983; Swick, Flake-Hobson, & Raymond, 1980).

Teachers should adjust the structure of the meeting to meet the family's preferences. For families that value personal relationships teachers should create a friendly, open, and personal environment by demonstrating concern for family members and using close proximity, self-disclosure, humor, and casual conversation (Ramirez, 1989). Other families may be goal oriented and respond to professionals they perceive as competent (Nagata, 1989). These families may look to educators to provide a structure to the meeting, set goals, define roles, and ask questions of family members.

Families that have interdependent communication patterns may respond positively to a meeting that emphasizes collaboration and problem solving (Allen & Majidi-Ahi, 1989).

Conclude the conference with a summary of the issues discussed, points of agreement and disagreement, strategies to be taken to resolve problems, and roles to be assumed by parents and educators (Goldstein & Turnbull, 1982). At the end of the meeting, parents and educators should establish ongoing communications systems and determine appropriate dates for the next meeting (Schulz, 1987). A sample schedule of activities for a parent/professionals conference is presented in Figure 3.5.

Evaluate the conference. The conference should be evaluated by parents and educators. Feedback from parents and educators can be solicited by asking them to respond to a series of questions regarding the conference. Educators can be asked to respond to the following:

- Were the content and timelines of the agenda appropriate?
- Was the meeting organized appropriately?
- Did parents have enough information prior to the meeting to participate in and understand the conference?
- Did the room create the right atmosphere for sharing information?
- Were points communicated to parents in a clear, nonthreatening manner using jargon-free language?
- Was parent participation encouraged and supported?
- Were the parents' and/or their child's rights violated?

FIGURE 3.5
Sample schedule for parent/professionals conference

1. Welcome participants.
2. Introduce parents and professionals, including an explanation of the roles of each professional and the services they provide to the student.
3. Discuss the purpose of the meeting and review the agenda.
4. Review relevant information from prior meetings.
5. Discuss student's needs and performance from the perspective of the professionals. Educators support their statements with work samples, test results, and anecdotal records.
6. Provide parents with the opportunity to discuss their view of their child's progress and needs.
7. Discuss comments of parents and professionals attempting to meet a consensus.
8. Determine a plan of action.
9. Summarize and review results of meeting.
10. Determine appropriate dates for the next meeting.
11. Adjourn the meeting.
12. Evaluate the meeting.

Similarly, the parents' view of the conference can be obtained by asking them the following questions:

- Were you prepared for the meeting?
- Did the meeting address the issues you wanted to discuss?
- Did the room make you feel comfortable?
- Did you have sufficient time to present your opinion?
- Were you satisfied with the way the meeting was conducted?
- What aspects of the meeting did you like the best? Which did you like the least?
- Were you satisfied with the outcome(s) of the meeting?

Hudson and Graham (1978) provide additional guidelines for obtaining feedback from parents after IEP meetings.

WORKING WITH FAMILIES FROM CULTURALLY AND LINGUISTICALLY DIVERSE BACKGROUNDS

A Hispanic parent arrives in school, with a small child since she has no sitter, to attend a meeting.

The parent is confronted first with the security guard at the school entrance, an individual who usually does not speak Spanish. He manages to direct the parent to the principal's office.

When the parent arrives at the principal's office she is then confronted by the secretary, another individual who usually does not speak Spanish. If the secretary is on the telephone, the parent has to wait. When the secretary finishes her conversation, she asks aggressively: "Yes?" Or, "Can I help you?"

The parent is finally off to the meeting which, she is told, is in the conference room. (Where is the conference room?) The discussion is in English, and although she understands a little, she wishes someone would explain what is being said. (What is PAC? SSC?) She is given handouts, written in English, on her way out of the meeting. As she leaves the school building she wonders, what was the meeting about? (Nicolau & Ramos, 1990, p. 22)

Cultural Factors

Harry (1992) noted that parents from culturally and linguistically diverse backgrounds may possess cultural perspectives and expectations with respect to education that affect their ability to collaborate with educators and negotiate the special education system.

While parents of culturally and linguistically diverse students are interested in their children's education, divergent cultural perspectives can serve as barriers to establishing traditional school-family interactions. Therefore, in designing culturally sensitive programs to involve parents, educators should understand and adjust their services to the family's level of acculturation, prior history with discrimination, and behavioral and developmental expectations.

Levels of Acculturation

The family's level of *acculturation,* the extent to which members of one culture adapt to a new culture (Nahme-Huang & Ying, 1989), will affect a family's cultural perspective. Because children tend to acculturate faster than adults, children may perform some roles in the new culture that parents assumed in their native country, such as interacting with social institutions such as schools (Nahme-Huang & Ying, 1989). The time and stress associated with these roles and the dependence of parents on children can have a significant impact on the parent/child relationships and the student's academic performance.

Prior History with Discrimination

As a result of being targets of bigotry, many African American families teach their children to combat racism by encouraging self-confidence and self-esteem (Allen & Majidi-Ahi, 1989).

Many families from linguistically and culturally diverse backgrounds have been victimized by racism, which can impact on the family's behavior and attitudes (Nagata, 1989). These families may be reluctant to attend meetings at schools if they or others have been discriminated against or treated with disrespect at the school (Nguyen, 1987). Educators can enhance the likelihood that families will feel comfortable attending school related events by doing the following:

- inviting important extended family members to school events
- addressing elders first
- referring to parents by their titles, such as Mr., Mrs., Ms., Dr., Reverend)
- making school facilities available for community activities
- responding in a warm and caring way
- establishing a collaborative environment
- providing families with sufficient time to express their concerns
- decorating the school and classrooms with icons from various cultures (Allen & Majidi-Ahi, 1989; Anderson & Fenichel, 1989; Locust, 1990).

Family Structure

Most school-based strategies for involving parents have been designed to meet the needs of the nuclear family. However, many cultures emphasize the value of the extended family. For example, many Native American, African American, and Hispanic families live in a framework of collective interdependence and kinship interactions to share resources and services and offer emotional and social support (LaFromboise & Graff-Low, 1989; Ramirez, 1989; Taylor Gibbs, 1989). Rather than seeking assistance from schools in dealing with educational issues, these families may feel more comfortable relying upon community members or community-based agencies.

In many extended families, elders may play an important role in decisionmaking and child care. When working with families that value and rely upon extended family members, educators should involve all family members in the school program. For example, correspondence to parents could include a statement that all family members are welcome at educational meetings (Nicolau & Ramos, 1990).

Behavioral and Developmental Expectations

Cultures also differ in their perspectives on appropriate behavior and the importance of developmental milestones. For example, although many fam-

Harris (1985) found that parents from different cultural backgrounds had different interpretations of and reactions to the same behaviors of students.

ilies from the mainstream culture stress the importance of children reaching developmental milestones at age-appropriate times, many culturally diverse families may not ascribe the same importance to developmental milestones (LaFromboise & Graff-Low, 1989; Ramirez, 1989). Since the behavioral and developmental expectations of schools and families may conflict, teachers must work cooperatively with families to develop a culturally sensitive and relevant instructional program that includes agreed-upon bicultural behaviors, appropriate cultural settings for these behaviors, and cross-cultural criteria for measuring progress.

Families may have a variety of culturally based perspectives regarding the causes of problems their children are having. These causes may include reprisals for rule violations by family members, spirits, failure to avoid taboos, fate, choice, and lifestyle imbalances (Anderson & Fenichel, 1989; Locust, 1990; Nagata, 1989). They also may not accept Western views of medicine and technology. Educators may have to address these causes before families accept and respond to traditional educational strategies.

Cross-Cultural Communication Patterns

Cross-cultural communication patterns can limit the development of trusting relationships between educators and families. Therefore, educators need to understand differences in communication styles and interpret verbal and nonverbal behaviors within a social and cultural context. Anderson and Fenichel (1989) reported that communication variables such as eye contact, wait time, word meanings, facial and physical gestures, voice quality, personal space, and physical contact have different meanings in various cultures. For example, they note that in some cultures a "yes" connotes "I heard you" rather than agreement. Similarly, individuals from some cultures may interpret laughter as a sign of embarrassment rather than enjoyment.

Cultural perspectives also may hinder communication and the discussion of certain issues. Nagata (1989) noted that some Japanese American families may not feel comfortable discussing personal problems and concerns as they view that behavior as being self-centered or as losing face. Similarly, Locust (1990) reported that Native Americans who adhere to the concept of "Holding the Future," may refrain from discussing a person's future because they believe that negative or limiting comments about another person's future can cause it to happen. Community individuals who understand the family's needs and culture can help alleviate these communication barriers by assisting educators in understanding and interpreting cross-cultural communication behaviors, serving as liaisons between schools, families, and communities, and orienting new families to the school (Brandenburg-Ayres, 1990).

Think About It

Think about several individuals with whom you communicate regularly. How do these individuals' communication styles differ in terms of eye contact, wait time, word meanings, facial and physical gestures, voice quality, personal space, and

physical contact? How do these differences affect you? How do you adjust your communication style to accommodate these differences?

Linguistic Factors

Linguistic factors also may serve as barriers to communication between schools and families. Communication difficulties related to linguistic differences may be compounded by difficulties in comprehending educational terminology and practices that may not have counterparts in the parents' language and culture (Lynch & Stein, 1987). For example, based on their culture and language background, some parents believe that special education implies a program that is better than regular education (Garrido, 1991). Educators help alleviate this problem by providing parents with a survival list of key educational terminology in their native languages (Morsink, Chase Thomas, & Correa, 1991).

Interpreters are particularly important when educators need to communicate with families from cultures that do not have written language systems (Fradd & Wilen, 1990).

Interpreters can be used to promote communication between English-speaking educators and families who speak other languages (Fradd & Wilen, 1990). Interpreters should speak the same dialect as the family; maintain confidentiality; avoid giving personal opinions; seek clarification from parents and professionals when they experience problems communicating specific information; employ reverse translation when exact translations are not possible; show respect toward parents and professionals; and encourage parents and professionals to speak to each other rather than directing their comments to interpreters (Fradd & Wilen, 1990). Because it can be viewed as demeaning, the parents' child or other students should not interpret during meetings. Educators can enhance the effectiveness of the interpreter by discussing topics and terminology with the interpreter before the meeting, supplementing their speech with nonverbal communication, being aware of the nonverbal behaviors of family members, and soliciting feedback from the interpreter concerning the meeting (Cook, Tessier, & Klein, 1992).

Socioeconomic Factors

A variety of socioeconomic factors also can affect parental participation in schools. Lynch and Stein (1987) reported that lengthy work schedules, time conflicts, transportation problems, and child care needs can limit the involvement of families in their children's education. These barriers can be lessened by use of home visits. However, because many families may perceive a home visit as intrusive, educators should solicit the family's permission before visiting the home (Brandenburg-Ayres, 1990).

ONGOING PARENT COMMUNICATION SYSTEMS

Danny has been acting the part of class clown in school and failing to complete his homework. After observing this behavior for several weeks, his

IDEAS FOR IMPLEMENTATION	Educators can employ a variety of strategies to overcome economic barriers to parent participation, including the following suggestions: • Offer transportation and establish carpools for family members. • Conduct various activities and meetings at community-based sites. • Solicit the support and assistance of individuals, groups, and agencies from the community. • Provide child care. • Structure sessions so that parents and their children are not separated. • Schedule meetings at times that are convenient for parents. • Share information with families through community organizations. • Contact parents via the telephone.

Source: Lucas, Henze, & Donato (1990); Nicolau & Ramos (1990).

teachers contact Danny's parents, who ask for a meeting. At the meeting, Danny's behavior is discussed and the participants agree to implement a home-school contract. Each day, the teachers will rate Danny's behavior and list his homework assignments on a daily report card. Based on his daily report card, Danny will earn home privileges such as watching television, having a friend sleep over, going to the movies, and playing a video game. At the end of each week, Danny's parents and teachers will exchange feedback concerning the contract via a telephone answering machine.

Three weeks later, Danny has decreased his inappropriate classroom behavior and increased his homework completion rates. Through a telephone conversation, it is agreed that the system will be used on a weekly basis and homework assignments will be available to parents daily through a recording on a telephone answering machine.

Written Communication

Teachers often employ written communication to inform parents of their child's performance and needs. While this method can be effective, it is not suited for information that requires two-way communication. Because it is a time-consuming procedure, it is difficult for teachers to communicate detailed information that is tailored to the unique needs of students and parents.

Translators who aid in written communication and community members can help educators prepare culturally relevant and sensitively written documents (Fradd & Wilen, 1990).

Furthermore, correspondence from teachers may not reach parents if students fail to deliver them (Chapman & Heward, 1982). Teachers can improve the likelihood that parents receive messages by communicating positive comments to parents, sharing notes with students, and checking periodically to ensure that correspondence has been received.

One positive written communication device that some teachers employ is the *happygram,* a brief note that alerts parents to the positive accomplishments and improvements of their children (de Bettencourt, 1987). The value of positive notes and happygrams can be increased by pairing them with parental praise. Therefore, when parents receive positive notes from educators, they should be encouraged to read the note promptly; deliver praise to their child in the presence of family members and friends; put the note in a prominent location (such as the refrigerator door) where their child and others are likely to see it; and share their desire to receive additional notes of praise (Imber, Imber, & Rothstein, 1979).

Another form of written communication with parents is a newsletter, which can inform parents of school and classroom events, extracurricular activities, parent meetings, school policies, and lunch menus. Parent education also can be accomplished through a newsletter.

Daily Report Cards

The *daily report card,* a written record of student performance in school, has been effective in establishing communication with parents (Fairchild, 1987). This system also can be employed with teachers to share information and promote continuity. The content and format of the daily report card will vary depending upon the needs of students and teachers, and could include information on academic performance, preparedness for class, effort, behavior, peer relationships, and homework completion (Tracy & Mann, 1992). The format should be easy for teachers to complete and simple to interpret by parents. As students demonstrate success over a period of time, the report card can be shared with parents weekly, bimonthly, and then monthly. Two sample daily report cards are presented in Figures 3.6 and 3.7.

Teachers can communicate with parents by sending completed assignments home. Everston, Emmer, Clements, Sanford, & Worsham (1989) suggest that teachers send home work in a large envelope or folder that is taped closed. The envelope or folder should have the student's name on it as well as a place for parents' signatures, the date, and the number of assignments included.

FIGURE 3.6
Elementary level daily report card

SAMPLE DAILY REPORT CARD (PRIMARY GRADE)

Name: Joshua	Reading	Language	Math	Resource Room
Remains seated	★			★
Watches teacher when giving instructions	★	★	★	★
Follows directions	★		★	★
Avoids disrupting				★
Attends to lessons	★	★		
Finishes assignments	★	★		★
Sits up in seat	★	★	★	★
Lines up quickly and quietly				★

Source: T. N. Fairchild. *Teaching Exceptional Children,* Vol. 19 (Reston, VA: Council for Exceptional Children, 1987), p. 72. Reprinted by permission of the publisher.

FIGURE 3.7
Secondary level daily report card

SAMPLE DAILY REPORT CARD (INTERMEDIATE GRADE)

Date: 2/22/89 Name: Wendy

Class	Behavior	Effort	Homework	Teacher
English	2	2	none	LS
History	1	1	—	TNK
Crafts	3	3	project due	BL
Science	2	3	read chapter 5	RM
Art	3	2	—	CD
Math	1	2	quiz tomorrow	AR

Rating Scale: 1 = Poor 2 = Satisfactory 3 = Good

Source: T. N. Fairchild. *Teaching Exceptional Children,* Vol. 19 (Reston, VA: Council for Exceptional Children, 1987), p. 73. Reprinted by permission of the publisher.

Home-School Contracts

The daily report card system also has been used as part of a home-school contract (Fairchild, 1987). *Home-school contracts* allow parents to reinforce their children for improved academic performance or behavior in school. Teachers observe students in school and report their observations to parents. Parents then deliver reinforcers to their children. Involving parents through home-school contracts has several advantages, including promoting home-school communication, alleviating the demands on teachers in terms of time and finances, and lessening the likelihood that the student's peers will be affected by the provision of reinforcers to mainstreamed students.

Parents can provide a variety of reinforcers to their children. Edible and tangible reinforcers that parents can dispense include making special foods; buying clothes, records, or software programs; providing money toward the purchase of a desired item; and acquiring a pet. Parents can dispense activity reinforcers such as fewer chores, a family activity, trips, a party at the house, a rented video, or a special privilege (Reynolds, Salend & Beahan, 1989).

Before implementing a home-school contract, parents and teachers should meet to discuss the specifics of the program. This discussion should provide both parties with an understanding of the behavior to be changed, details of the communication system between home and school, potential reinforcers, and when and how to deliver the reinforcers. Once the system is implemented, followup communication is critical. It should address these questions:

- Are parents being promptly informed of their child's behavior?
- Are the reinforcers effective or do they need to be changed?
- Are parents delivering the reinforcement as planned?
- How is the system affecting the interaction between family members?

Telephones and Telephone Answering Machines

An alternative to conferences and written correspondence that educators can employ to communicate with parents is the telephone. Although the tele-

Chapman and Heward (1982) and Bittle (1975) found that recorded messages led to a significant increase in the number of parent-initiated contacts with teachers and improved spelling scores of students.

phone provides parents and teachers with direct access to each other, frequent telephone calls from and to parents can place an excessive demand on teacher time. However, telephone answering machines (TAM) can serve as an inexpensive, easy to use, effective communication strategy that minimizes the demands on teacher time. Parents like the system because it was readily available and kept them informed about their child's assignments.

In such a system, teachers record a daily message on a TAM. Parents then call and receive the message. The message could communicate to parents academic assignments (*Today in class we studied about weather. The homework assignment for today is to keep a calendar of the day's weather for a week. The assignment is due on ________.*); special events (*Next Tuesday, the class will be going on a trip to the Children's Museum. Please make sure your child brings ________.*); and reminders (*Tomorrow, please have your child bring a magic marker to school.*) (Chapman & Heward, 1982). Minner, Beane, and Porter (1986) propose that educators also use TAMs to provide parents with suggestions for teaching specific skills to their children; report on student performance in school; provide information to parents concerning their rights and specific programs; offer information on local events of interest for students and their families; encourage parents to attend parent meetings; and recommend movies, television shows, books, and other learning activities to parents.

Questions or comments parents have also can be recorded and played back by teachers. Teachers can respond to parents' concerns via followup phone calls, notes, or meetings. Individualized messages also can be communicated to parents by use of a coded system that protects confidentiality (Minner, Beane & Porter, 1986). Parents and their children can be assigned a code name or number and a message tailored to the parents can be recorded using the code. For example, a message for a parent of a mainstreamed student can be stated as *Student #5 is showing an improved effort. However, we need to continue to check that all homework assignments have been recorded and completed.*

Parental Observations

Communication between home and school can be enhanced by allowing parents to observe in the classroom. Observations allow parents to see and understand different aspects of the school environment and student behavior. This experience can help provide parents with the necessary background information for discussing school-related concerns with educators (McLoughlin & Lewis, 1986).

Teachers should carefully structure the observation to ensure that it provides parents with meaningful information. Initially, permission for parents to observe in the schools should be obtained from the appropriate school authorities and staff (McLoughlin & Lewis, 1986). Once permission is granted, parents should be prepared for the observation by reviewing ways to enter the room unobtrusively; locations in the room to sit; suitable times to observe; appropriate reactions to their child and other students; and the need to maintain confidentiality (McLoughlin & Lewis, 1986). Before the observation, parents and teachers should discuss the purpose of the observation and the unique aspects of the educational setting such as behavior management systems, reading programs, and the like. When the observation is completed, teachers should meet with parents to discuss what they saw.

Parent and Sibling Training

Parents may need training to perform varied roles in the educational process (McKinney & Hocutt, 1982). Many schools and community agencies offer parent training as part of their comprehensive delivery of services to students and their families. Calvert (1969) has identified several guidelines for setting up and evaluating parent training programs:

- *Who* should be involved?
- *What* is the content of the training program?
- *When* will training take place?
- *Where* will training occur?
- *How* do you train parents?

Who

May and Davis (1990) provide guidelines for working with fathers of children with special needs.

Although most programs train mothers, training should be available to both parents. Successful parent training programs for linguistically and culturally diverse families also offer training to extended family members. Religious organizations, social agencies, grassroots community organizations, and community leaders can help schools advertise training and recruit family members (Davies, 1991). Incorporating nonthreatening social and learning activities into training sessions and meetings can induce reluctant parents to attend these events.

Training should also be offered to siblings to help them understand the nature of their brother's or sister's disability and deal with the impact of having a brother or sister with special needs. Banta (1979) noted that the impact of a child with a disability on the family may affect siblings more than parents. Seligman (1983) reported that children's reactions to their siblings with disabilities depended upon the following variables:

1. the extent to which the sibling is held responsible for a handicapped brother or sister
2. the extent to which a handicapped sibling takes advantage of a normal brother or sister
3. the extent to which a handicapped sibling restricts one's social life or is considered a source of embarrassment
4. the extent to which a handicapped sibling requires time and attention from the parents
5. the extent to which the family's financial resources are drained by services for the handicapped child
6. the number of siblings

Having a child with a disability may affect the whole family—siblings as well as parents.

7. the overall accommodation parents have made to their special circumstances (p. 164)

Training for siblings can focus on providing information on the etiology and needs of the various disabilities; dispelling myths and misconceptions about disabilities; discussing ways of interacting with and assisting their siblings; responding to the reactions of their friends and other individuals; understanding human services; and understanding the long-term needs and future of their siblings (Meyer, Vadasy & Fewell, 1985). Training also should address the concerns siblings may have about their own children being born with a disability.

Summers, Bridge, and Summers (1991) have developed guidelines and a series of activities that educators can employ when developing sibling support groups.

Several formats for providing information to siblings have been developed. Meyer, Vadasy, and Fewell (1985) have written a book that parents and educators can use with siblings to help them adjust to life with a brother or sister with special needs. The book introduces siblings to disabilities, causes of disabilities, services for individuals and their families, and future considerations. Support groups for siblings have been established to offer information about disabilities and learn how to deal with the unique issues associated with having a sibling with a disability (Summers, Bridge, & Summers, 1991). Additional information on working with siblings can be obtained by contacting support groups for siblings (See Figure 3.8).

FIGURE 3.8
Sibling support groups

Sibling Information Network
Connecticut's University Affiliated Program
991 Main Street
East Hartford, CT 06108

Siblings Understanding Needs
Department of Pediatrics
University of Texas Medical Branch
Galveston, TX 77550

Siblings for Significant Change
823 United Nations Plaza
New York, NY 10017

Siblings Helping Persons with Autism through Resources and Energy
National Society for Children and Adults with Autism
Washington, DC 20005

Siblings of Disabled Children
535 Race Street, Suite 200
San Jose, CA 95126

Think About It

Do you have, or know someone who has, an individual with a disability in the family? What has been the impact of this individual on family members? What types of training would benefit the family?

What

The content of the training program should focus on parents' needs. Generally, training should provide parents with the skills to teach their child in the home; the ability to interact with professionals serving their child; information relative to the delivery of educational services; counseling to provide emotional support and develop a positive self-image; and information to assist them in obtaining services for their child. Parents of younger children may desire training in child care and development, early intervention, discipline, and schoolwide expectations (Violand-Sanchez, Sutton, & Ware, 1991). Parents of adolescents may prefer training about services and agencies that can assist them and their children in making the transition to postsecondary settings and employment opportunities. Parents also may seek training in such issues as AIDS, teen pregnancy, child abuse, and drug prevention (Nicolau & Ramos, 1990). Parents who speak languages other than English may benefit from family-based ESL classes and instruction in the policies and practices used by the school district (Garate, Sen, Thien, & Chaleunrath, 1987).

When

The frequency of training also will depend on the parents' needs and teachers' time. However, parent training should be ongoing, as should evaluation of the training.

Where

Training can occur in the home or in the school. Home-based training, which occurs in the parents' and child's natural environment, can promote the maintenance and generalization of skills learned. Home-based training programs are especially appropriate for parents who have difficulty attending school meetings because of transportation problems or work schedules. School-based training allows parents to be trained as a group, which can facilitate the sharing of information and experiences with parents. Additionally, school-based programs provide parents with the opportunity to meet and interact with a wide variety of professionals (Heward & Orlansky, 1992).

Davies (1991) and Nicolau and Ramos (1990) suggest that training for parents be conducted in nonintimidating, community-based sites such as religious establishments, social clubs, community centers, restaurants, and shopping malls.

How

Educators can use a variety of strategies to train parents including lecture, group discussion, role playing, simulations, presentations by service providers and other parents, and demonstrations. Additionally, print materials and training programs for parents are available from state education departments, local organizations serving families and professional organizations. Vanderslice, Cherry, Cochran, and Dean (1984) offer excellent suggestions for designing and implementing workshops for parents. Parent training programs and materials can be previewed by contacting various parental organizations (see the Appendix).

Other programs that teach parents how to interact with their children are available, including Parents as Teachers (Becker, 1971), Games People Play (Berne, 1964), Systematic Training for Effective Parenting (Dinkmeyer & McKay, 1976), Between Parent and Child (Ginott, 1965), and Parent Effectiveness Training (Gordon, 1970).

IDEAS FOR IMPLEMENTATION

In delivering training to parents, educators should enact the following suggestions:

- Conduct training in the primary language of the families.
- Use terminology that parents can understand.
- Share personal experiences that relate to their own families.
- Avoid putting parents in embarrassing positions.
- Acknowledge the contributions and efforts of parents.
- Offer opportunities for parents to share their experiences, skills, and talents.
- Provide parents with materials written in their native language.
- Give parents materials that they can share with others.
- Offer families refreshments.

Source: Lucas, Henze, & Donato (1990); Nicolau & Ramos (1990).

Because some parents may have difficulty with the readability of print materials, videocassettes are an excellent format for presenting content to parents. Video presentations have the advantages of providing a visual image and model for parents; allowing parents and teachers to stop the video at any time to discuss, review, or replay the content; and being available to parents to view in school or at home. Sarda et al. (1991) have developed a series of nontechnical videocassettes for training parents. Three of the videos focus on infants and introduce parents to infant development, early intervention, and working with professionals to obtain and deliver services. Other's in the series deal with developmental stages of school aged children; services, agencies, and educational alternatives; participation of parents in the multidisciplinary team process; and the impact of a disability on the individual and the family.

Experienced and skilled parents of mainstreamed students can be a valuable resource for training other parents (Ball, Coyne, Jarvis, & Pease, 1984; Kroth, 1980). These parents can share their knowledge and experience with other parents and provide emotional support and information on the availability of services in the local community (Berger, 1981). In selecting parents to serve as trainers, educators should ask the following questions:

- Do parents respect and trust this individual?
- Does the individual have the time and skills to communicate and work with other parents?
- Does the individual possess the necessary skills to facilitate group interactions?
- Does the individual have a good understanding of school policies, school curriculum, teaching strategies, and services within the local community?
- Has the individual completed any training to serve as a trainer of other parents?
- Will the individual seek assistance when he or she confronts a problem that he or she cannot solve? (Heward, Dardig, & Rossett, 1979).

ENLISTING COMMUNITY RESOURCES

For some students, the mainstreaming network should include community agencies that assist in everyday school and community activities. Through these agencies and activities, needs identified by educators and parents can be remedied. For example, if a student with a visual impairment must have an adaptive device to function in the mainstreamed setting, a community agency can be contacted to assist in purchasing the equipment. Therefore, educators should be aware of the supportive organizations, agencies, institutions, and resources available in their communities (Coballes-Vega & Salend, 1988). Community agencies which may comprise a network for mainstreamed students include the following:

- community and governmental agencies that specifically address the needs of students and their families
- organizations providing crisis intervention and counseling services

- job training and career counseling centers
- organizations assisting families from culturally and linguistically diverse backgrounds
- child care agencies
- local hospitals, clinics, mental health and rehabilitation centers
- service-oriented agencies
- local volunteer groups
- national service and fraternal organizations
- college or university centers, which may offer assessment and remediation clinics and other services (Coballes-Vega & Salend, 1988)

In enlisting the support of community organizations, educators should consider the unique medical, behavioral, and social needs of students as well as the financial resources of the student's family (Taylor & Salend, 1983). Since many students may require similar services from agencies, it may prove helpful for educators to maintain a file of community agencies and the services that they provide. A sample file card is presented in Figure 3.9.

Paraprofessionals and Volunteers

A community resource that many mainstreamed students may benefit from is the service of paraprofessionals and volunteers (Boomer, 1981; Platt & Platt, 1980). Hedges (1972) noted that the use of volunteers allowed elementary school teachers to increase their performance of higher level functions by approximately 20 percent and increase threefold the amount of attention provided to students.

Working Effectively with Paraprofessionals and Volunteers

Blalock (1991) and McKenzie and Houk (1986) offer several steps educators can employ to effectively work with paraprofessionals and volunteers.

Determine the Roles of the Paraprofessionals and Volunteers. The roles paraprofessionals and volunteers perform in the classroom should be directly related to the needs of teachers and mainstreamed students.

Recruit Them. Potential volunteers can be recruited by contacting principals, parent-teacher associations, service organizations, and senior citizen

FIGURE 3.9
Sample community organization file card

Name and Address of Community Organization:

Services Provided:

Contact Person: Phone:

IDEAS FOR IMPLEMENTATION

Paraprofessionals and volunteers can assist teachers and mainstreamed students by enacting the following suggestions:

- Prepare individualized learning materials and modify written materials.
- Provide remedial instruction and reinforce concepts taught previously.
- Assess learning needs.
- Administer teacher-made tests.
- Monitor seatwork activities.
- Deliver small-group instruction.
- Assist students with motor and mobility problems.
- Read to students.
- Play educational games.
- Listen to problems and offer guidance.
- Correct and grade papers.
- Complete paperwork and perform clerical duties.
- Work with media.
- Assist students with health and physical needs.
- Supervise students during activities outside the classroom.
- Assist with behavior management.
- Observe and record behavior.

Source: Blalock (1991); Boomer (1980); Buffer (1980); Cuninggim (1980); McKenzie & Houk (1986); Platt & Platt (1980).

groups. When contacting potential paraprofessionals or volunteers, educators should carefully interview them to determine their suitability for the job (Boomer, 1980) and provide them with a job description including roles to be performed, time commitments, and schedules.

McKenzie and Houk (1986) identify a variety of resource materials that can be used to train paraprofessionals and volunteers.

Train Them. Paraprofessionals and volunteers need to be prepared for the roles they will perform. They therefore need an orientation and training program that should include a tour of the school; introduction of key school personnel; description of relevant programs; explanation of the need for and rules relating to confidentiality; delineation of the roles and responsibilities inside and outside the classroom; review of the dress code and other standards of decorum; identification of the specialized medical, social, and academic needs of and equipment used by mainstreamed students; a review of the communication system; demonstration of how to operate media and other necessary equipment; and discussion of scheduling, major school events, school calendars, absences, approaches to emergencies, and other school procedures (Boomer, 1980, 1981; Buffer, 1980; Cuninggim, 1980). Paraprofessionals and volunteers also can acquire skills by attending workshops and inservice presentations and reading relevant articles and books (McKenzie & Houk, 1986).

Meet Regularly. Periodically, educators and paraprofessionals should meet to jointly plan and coordinate activities, monitor student performance, and resolve problems (Blalock, 1991).

Acknowledge their Accomplishments. Educators can acknowledge the contributions of paraprofessionals and volunteers by showing appreciation via notes from students and teachers, graphs or examples that depict student progress, certificates of appreciation, and verbal comments.

Evaluate their Performance. Educators should observe paraprofessionals and volunteers in action, and provide them with feedback on their performance. Evaluation should focus on performance of duties as well as rapport with students and other school personnel. Information on how to improve job performance also should be provided. Additionally, the perceptions of the paraprofessionals and volunteers concerning their roles in the school should be solicited.

Working with Students from Culturally and Linguistically Diverse Backgrounds

Paraprofessionals and volunteers who are trained or have experiences with students' languages and cultures can play an important role in educating students from culturally and linguistically diverse backgrounds. Miramontes (1991) has developed the Multilingual/Multiethnic Instructional Services (MMIS) team to coordinate services to students through collaboration among educators and paraprofessionals. In this model, paraprofessionals assist in developing and delivering students' educational programs; incorporate students' primary languages and cultures into their education; meet with professionals and parents to share information and plan instructional strategies; serve as positive ethnic and linguistic role models; and serve as school-community liaison.

Think About It

What would you do in the following situations?

1. You expect your paraprofessional to work independently with little supervision, but your paraprofessional seeks your guidance frequently and prefers a predictable schedule.
2. You assign your paraprofessional to perform mostly clerical tasks, however your paraprofessional would like to be working directly with students.
3. You observe your paraprofessional violating confidentiality.
4. You notice a paraprofessional inadvertently coaching a student during a test.

Professional and Parent Organizations

Many professional and parent organizations offer a variety of services to professionals and parents that can assist them in meeting the needs of mainstreamed students. Local chapters of national organizations can provide teachers with information on techniques and materials for working with mainstreamed students, and help parents function as advocates for their children. For example, national organizations such as the March of Dimes, Fed-

Paraprofessionals and volunteers can assist teachers and students.

eration of the Blind, Epilepsy Foundation, Council for Exceptional Children, and the Association for Children with Learning Disabilities offer instruction on new developments in the field, showcase new materials, organize parent groups, provide small grants to stimulate the development of innovative programs, and assist individuals in acquiring specialized aids and prosthetic devices. A listing of national organizations is given in the Appendix.

SUMMARY

This chapter provided guidelines for establishing a network of professionals based on communication and congruence. The chapter

- presented suggestions for establishing an interactive network of communication
- discussed strategies for promoting communication and congruence regarding a student's educational program
- offered guidelines for employing collaborative consultation in schools
- presented a variety of strategies for foster communication with and the involvement of parents

- outlined issues and strategies in working with families from culturally and linguistically diverse backgrounds
- discussed the roles of paraprofessionals and volunteers and services community agencies can provide in assisting students and their families

RECOMMENDED READINGS

Bauwens, J., Hourcade, J. J., & Friend, M. (1989). Cooperative teaching: A model for general and special education integration. *Remedial and Special Education, 10*(2), 17–22.

Blalock, G. (1991). Paraprofessionals: Critical team members in our special education programs. *Intervention in School and Clinic, 26,* 200–214.

Forest, M., & Lusthaus, E. (1990). Everyone belongs with MAPS action planning system. *Teaching Exceptional Children, 22*(2), 32–35.

Fradd, S. H., & Wilen, D. K. (1990). *Using interpreters and translators to meet the needs of handicapped language minority students and their families.* Washington, DC: National Clearinghouse for Bilingual Education.

Harry, B. (1992). *Culturally diverse families and the special education system.* New York: Teachers College Press.

Lynch, E. W., & Stein, R. C. (1987). Parent participation by ethnicity: A comparison of hispanic, black, and anglo families. *Exceptional Children, 54,* 105–111.

Morsink, C. V., Chase Thomas, C., & Correa, V. I. (1991). *Interactive teaming: Consultation and collaboration in special programs.* New York: Merrill/Macmillan.

Price, B. J., & Marsh, G. E. (1985). Practical guidelines for planning and conducting parent conferences. *Teaching Exceptional Children, 17,* 274–278.

Schulz, J. B. (1987). *Parents and professionals in special education.* (1987). Boston: Allyn & Bacon.

West, J. F., & Idol, L. (1990). Collaborative consultation in the education of mildly handicapped and at-risk students. *Remedial and Special Education, 11*(1), 22–31.

4 Teaching Students to Accept Individual Differences

MS. GEE'S CLASS

Though her students are doing well academically, Ms. Gee is concerned about the social interaction patterns in her class. She decides to observe her students' interactions inside and outside the class for one week. At the end of the week, she examines her notes and finds the following entries:

> Kyesha wouldn't play with Linh because "She talks funny."
>
> Several boys would not let Suzanne play basketball because "She's a girl."
>
> Hector didn't want to sit next to James because "James is an Indian and I saw a movie last night where Indians kill people."
>
> Several students called Nathan "fatty."
>
> Delbert stayed to himself, and several students made fun of his "old and lame clothes."
>
> Mary called John a "retard."
>
> Chris didn't want Lee in his cooperative learning group because "Lee is slow."
>
> Stacy told a demeaning joke about girls with blond hair.
>
> No one wanted Danny on their baseball team because he's in a wheelchair;
>
> White and black students sat at separate tables in the lunchroom.

What factors contributed to these student behaviors? How can Ms. Gee help her students change these behaviors? After reading this chapter, you should be able to answer these as well as the following questions:

- What roles can students perform to facilitate the success of mainstreaming?
- What factors contribute to the development of attitudes toward mainstreamed peers?
- How can educators assess students' attitudes toward mainstreamed students?
- How can educators teach students acceptance of individual differences related to disability?
- How can educators teach students acceptance of individual differences related to culture, language, gender, and socioeconomic status?
- How can educators facilitate the development of friendships and peer support groups?

Regular education classroom students can play a significant role in determining the success or failure of mainstreaming (Plumb & Brown, 1990; Westervelt & McKinney, 1980). The process can be facilitated when these students interact positively with their mainstreamed peers (S.J. Salend, 1984) and aid them in adjusting to and functioning in the mainstream by serving as role models, peer tutors, and friends (Salend & Moe, 1983). Stainback, Stainback, and Wilkinson (1992) noted that regular education classroom peers can help mainstreamed students feel accepted and can provide support and encouragement in academic and social settings. Additionally, regular education classroom students can be instrumental in implementing adaptations, such as peer tutoring or note taking, that can help mainstreamed students perform successfully. However, the ability and willingness of regular education students to help make mainstreaming successful may be influenced by their attitudes toward their mainstreamed peers.

RESEARCH ON PEER ATTITUDES TOWARD MAINSTREAMED STUDENTS

Research indicates that by the age of 4, students are cognizant of and curious about cultural and physical differences (Derman-Sparks, Higa, & Sparks,

1980). Unfortunately, due to environmental influences, many students enter school holding misconceptions and stereotypic views about individuals whom they perceive as different (Pang, 1991).

While some studies suggest that students view their mainstreamed peers positively (Perlmutter, Crocker, Corday, & Garstecki, 1983; Prillaman, 1981; Randolph & Harrington, 1981), the majority of studies indicate that students who do not have disabilities demonstrate negative attitudes toward their peers who do (Horne, 1985). Several studies suggest that mainstreamed students are rejected by or less accepted than their regular education peers (Gerber, 1977; Goodman, Gottlieb, & Harrison, 1977). These unfavorable attitudes can have a negative impact on mainstreamed students' goals and school achievement (Glick, 1969; Ide, Parkerson, Haertel, & Walberg, 1981), social-emotional adjustment (Hansell, 1981), in-class behavior (Horne & Powers, 1983), and attitudes toward school and self (Horne, 1985).

While regular education classroom students hold less-than-favorable attitudes toward students with all types of disabilities, they tend to be more accepting of students with sensory and physical disabilities and less accepting of students with learning and emotional problems (Horne, 1985; Miller, Hagan, & Armstrong, 1980).

Several variables may influence perceptions of individuals with disabilities (Horne, 1985). Factors such as cultural background, gender, and socioeconomic status may interact with disability to influence the acceptance of students. Monroe and Howe (1971) found that mainstreamed students from higher socioeconomic status backgrounds are viewed more positively by their classmates than those whose socioeconomic status is low. Bryan (1974) and Scranton and Ryckman (1979) reported that female students with learning disabilities were more likely to be rejected by their peers than male students with learning disabilities. However, female students tend to hold more favorable attitudes toward mainstreamed students than their male counterparts (Sandberg, 1982; Voeltz, 1980). Generally, older students possess less favorable attitudes toward individuals with disabilities than do younger students (Simpson, 1980).

Pepper (1976) noted that textbooks, movies, and television shows typically portray Native Americans and Native Alaskans in ways that demean their dignity and heritage.

Numerous factors contribute to the development of negative attitudes toward mainstreamed students. Many childrearing practices limit interactions between children based on disability, race, and linguistic abilities. Attitudes toward individuals with disabilities and those from linguistically and culturally diverse backgrounds also are shaped by the media, which, unfortunately, tend to portray these groups in a negative manner.

Chavez (1985) found an ethnic and gender bias in cartoons printed in daily newspapers. Donaldson (1981) analyzed 85 randomly selected 30-minute segments of prime time television shows and found few individuals with disabilities represented. She further noted that when they *are* on television, they are often portrayed in a negative role. Similarly, Weinberg and Santana (1978) found that characters with disabilities in comic books are often presented as evil.

Think About It

When you were growing up, did you have opportunities to interact with children and adults who were disabled? With those from a different race? With those who spoke a different language? How did these experiences shape your understanding and acceptance of individual differences?

Examine books, television shows and commercials, cartoons, and movies. How are individuals with disabilities, women, and individuals from diverse cultural and linguistic backgrounds portrayed? How do these media contribute to your understanding and acceptance of individual differences?

ASSESSING ATTITUDES TOWARD MAINSTREAMED STUDENTS

Before employing an attitude change strategy, educators should assess their students' attitudes toward mainstreamed students as well as their understanding, knowledge, and acceptance of individual differences. If the assessment reveals that students' attitudes toward individual differences and mainstreamed students are accepting, teachers can forego such strategies; in this case, these activities may inadvertently highlight differences students either have not discovered or have considered unimportant. However, if the assessment indicates that mainstreamed students are being isolated and segregated, educators should implement a training program to teach students about individual differences.

Observation

Direct observation of interaction between mainstreamed students and their regular education classroom peers can be an excellent way of assessing acceptance of individual differences (Ford & Jones, 1990; Horne, 1985). For example, Dunlop, Stoneman, and Cantrell (1980) examined the relationship between mainstreamed preschoolers and their peers by observing their play and classroom interactions, and Marotz-Ray (1985) used an observational recording system to record the peer-interaction skills of mainstreamed students. Mercer and Denti (1989) employed observation and teacher anecdotal reports to document changes in attitudes toward mainstreamed students. They reported that one teacher, after observing peer interactions, wrote, "The kids initially had some difficulty understanding him because of his poor articulation. But relationships were formed. The teams were very protective. They would rehearse outside the classroom before going in and then would stand back and coach each other" (p. 35). Fritz (1990) used the *Educational Assessment of Social Interaction (EASI)* observation recording system to record interactions between mainstreamed students and their peers.

Because interactions occur in a variety of settings, teachers should examine the interaction patterns of their students in locations other than the classroom, such as the lunchroom and the playground. In observing interactions, teachers should consider these questions:

- How often are mainstreamed students interacting with their peers?
- What is the nature of these interactions?
- Who is initiating the interactions?
- How many students are interacting with their mainstreamed peers?

- What events seem to promote interactions?
- What events seem to limit interactions?
- Do the mainstreamed students possess the requisite skills to interact with their peers?
- What are the outcomes of these interactions?

Educators can obtain data relative to these factors by using EASI or another observation recording system. Keep in mind that it is difficult to measure attitudes in a reliable and valid manner; direct observation yields information on behavior that may or may not be related to attitudes and acceptance. Teachers can also gather information on the extent to which mainstreamed students are accepted by their peers from parents, other teachers, guidance counselors, and lunchroom and playground aides.

Sociometric Measures

Ms. DeVries, a middle school teacher, has structured her class so that students spend a great deal of time working in groups. However, she notices that the students have difficulty interacting with each other, particularly those students from the two different elementary schools that send students to the middle school. Her observations indicate that students from Hamilton Elementary School and those from Burr School mostly socialize with their peers from the same school.

To confirm her suspicions, Ms. DeVries decides to have the class do a sociogram. She tells the students that she "wants to find out certain things about the classroom." She explains to students that people have preferences about different things and asks them to identify their favorite foods, records, colors, movies, and television shows.

After soliciting the students' preferences on these items, Ms. DeVries tells them, "Now we are going to examine preferences in the classroom." She gives each student a handout that lists each student's name, and a number. Students from Hamilton Elementary School are assigned even numbers and students from Burr School are assigned odd numbers. Next, she explains the importance of using numbers rather than names and has students practice by asking them to write down the numbers of three students who are wearing blue shirts or blouses and then write down the numbers of three students whose last name begins with *S*. When she feels that students understand the directions, Ms. DeVries asks them to write down the numbers of three students they would like to sit next to on the next school trip, and write down the numbers of three students they would not like to sit with during lunch. She circulates around the room to assist students and to answer their questions.

Ms. DeVries then collects the students' responses and scores each question separately by arranging the students' numbers in a circle and drawing solid- and broken-line arrows to indicate positive and negative selections. The results indicate that only one student from Hamilton School made a positive choice of students from Burr School and students from Burr School made no positive choices of students from Hamilton School. Using these findings, Ms. DeVries plans a series of activities to teach students about each other and promote class cohesiveness.

Sociogram results can be employed to determine the extent to which mainstreamed students are being integrated into the social fabric of the classroom.

The most widely used technique for measuring peer acceptance is sociometric measurement (Horne, 1981). One sociometric strategy that many educators employ to assess peer relationships is peer nomination, in which students complete a sociogram (Asher & Taylor, 1981). A *sociogram* is a technique for assessing classroom interaction patterns and students' preferences for social relationships by asking students to identify the peers with whom they would like to do a social activity (Cartwright & Cartwright, 1974; Gronlund, 1976). In addition to providing data on the acceptance of mainstreamed students, sociograms can offer educators information that can assist them in identifying students who need to improve their socialization skills and in grouping students for instruction (Wallace & Larsen, 1978).

The first step in implementing a sociogram is to devise questions that will accurately elicit the desired data. Teachers should consider the following when devising sociogram questions:

- What kind of information do I want to gather?
- What do I suspect about the classroom interactions?
- What are the ways students segregate themselves from others?
- What are the ways students show they like each other?
- What skills do the most popular students have?
- What skills do the least popular students lack?

Because it is important to obtain information on both stars and isolates in the class, teachers should include both acceptance and rejection questions. (As shown in Figure 4.1, questions may also be *directives,* statements requiring student response.) Questions should be phrased in language the students can understand. To encourage confidentiality, each question should begin with a stem such as "Write down the numbers of the students . . ." Sample sociogram questions are presented in Figure 4.1.

After formulating the questions, teachers construct a handout listing each student's name and number. To make scoring easier, teachers should assign

FIGURE 4.1
Sample sociogram questions

1. Write down the numbers of three students whom you would like to sit next to on the next school trip.
2. Write down the numbers of three students whom you would not like to sit with during lunch.
3. Write down the numbers of three students whom you would like to play with during recess.
4. Write down the numbers of three students whom you would like to invite to your birthday party.

numbers based on the variables they are interested in measuring. For example, if teachers want to examine interactions between female and male students, then female students can be assigned even numbers and male students odd numbers. To encourage confidentiality, teachers should explain to students the importance of using numbers rather than names. Teachers also should review with students the list of names. Teachers can help students who cannot read the names on the list by administering the sociogram to them individually, having them raise their hands to obtain teacher assistance, putting numbers on each students' back, and creating a bulletin board that has the students' pictures and numbers.

Initially, teachers should help students understand the concept of the sociogram. Teachers can introduce the sociogram to the class by providing practice sessions where students demonstrate mastery of the concept by responding to nonsense questions. For example, teachers can offer students practice by asking them to list the numbers of all the students in the class who are wearing sneakers, whose first name begins with *S,* or whose hair color is red.

Scoring sociograms allows teachers to develop a picture of classroom interactions by graphing each question separately—arranging the students' numbers in a circle on a piece of paper, then drawing lines indicating choices from number to number to represent the students' responses. A solid line ( ) indicates a positive choice, while a broken line ( ) denotes a negative choice. Figure 4.2 shows a sample sociogram. In examining the sociogram, teachers should attempt to identify students who are rejected, isolated, and accepted. Rejected students are those who receive several negative choices, while students who receive several positive choices are considered accepted. Students that are not selected as either positive or negative choices are considered isolated. If mainstreamed students are rated as rejected or isolated, then the teacher should initiate a program to increase social interactions.

The sociogram can be adapted by using pictorial representations. For example, instead of rating classroom peers, students can answer sociogram questions by rating pictures showing students with different types of disabilities or from varying ethnic and racial groups. Using pictures makes this strategy a viable technique for assessing the attitudes of young children.

Several structured sociometric rating procedures have been developed for educators. These techniques provide educators with specific questions to ask students and standardized procedures to follow when administering the sociometric procedure. For example, *How I Feel Toward Others* (Agard, Veldman, Kaufman, & Semmel, 1978) is a fixed-choice sociometric rating scale where each class member rates every other class member as *likes very much* (friend), *all right* (feels neutral toward), *don't like* (does not want as a friend), or *don't know.* Other structured sociometric rating scales include the *Peer Acceptance Scale* (Bruininks, Rynders, & Gross, 1974) and the *Ohio Social Acceptance Scale* (Lorber, 1973).

Attitude Change Assessment Instruments

Several instruments have been developed to assess attitudes toward individuals with disabilities. These instruments can be adapted to assess attitudes toward individuals from culturally and linguistically diverse backgrounds by

FIGURE 4.2
Sample sociogram

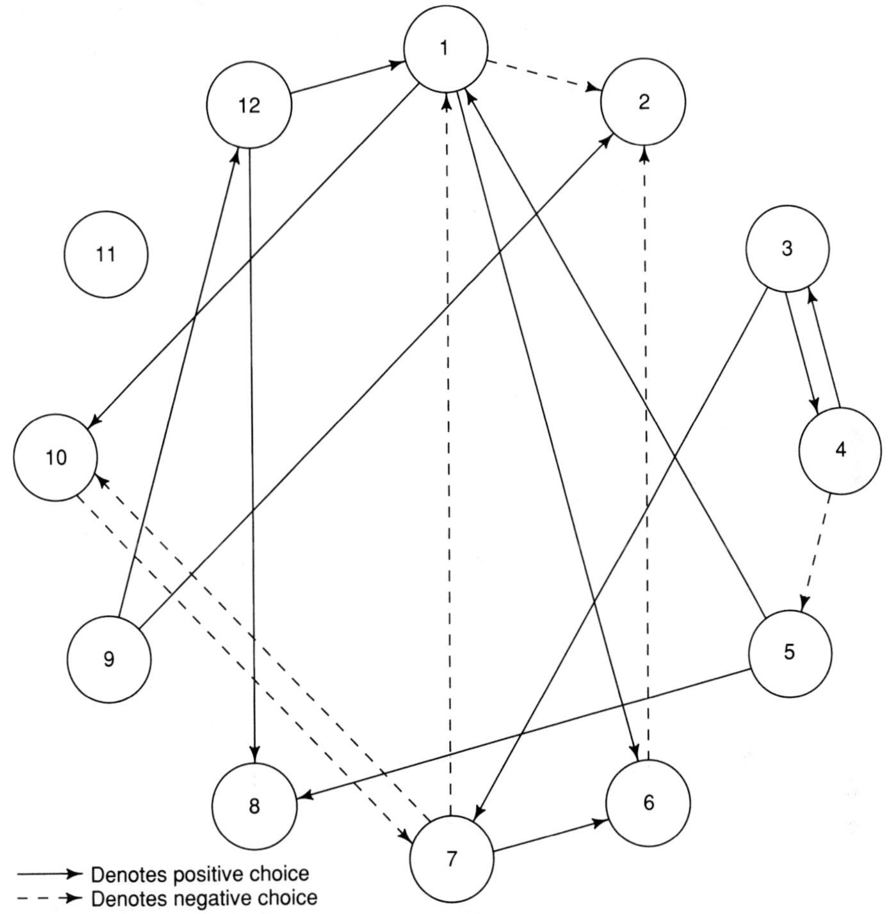

changing the directions so that they focus on attitudes related to cultural and linguistic variables rather than to various disabilities. For example, the *Attitudes Toward Disabled Persons (ATDP)* instrument can be adapted by asking students to complete each item with respect to individuals who speak a language other than English rather than individuals with disabilities.

Yuker, Block, and Young (1970) developed the ATDP, which is comprised of 30 statements about individuals with disabilities (such as *Disabled persons are often unfriendly*) that are rated on a Likert-type scale, from *strongly agree* to *strongly disagree*. High scores on the scale indicate positive attitudes. Since the language used in the ATDP can be confusing to students (Falty, 1965), teachers should provide time to answer questions and explain the meaning of certain statements. Teachers can adapt the scale by simplifying the language and phrasing items in a true-false format (Lindsey & Frith, 1983). An adapted form of the ATDP is the *Attitudes Toward Handicapped Individuals,* which contains only 20 items and uses the term *handicapped* in place of *disabled* (Lazar, Gensley, & Orpet, 1971). The *Scale of Attitudes Toward Disabled Persons* represents an updated alternative to the ATDP (Antonak, 1981).

The *Acceptance Scale* includes four levels to assess attitudes toward individuals with disabilities (Antonak & Livneh, 1988). In all four levels, students indicate their agreement (*Yes, I agree*), disagreement (*No, I disagree*) or uncertainty (*Maybe, I'm not sure*) with negatively (*I wouldn't spend my recess with a handicapped kid*) and positively (*I believe I could become close friends with a special education student*) phrased items. The Lower Elementary and Upper Elementary versions are given to students in grades one and two and three through six, respectively. Students in grades seven through twelve complete either the secondary Level A or B version; the A version is designed for students who experience problems with reading.

Another assessment instrument that has been used to measure students' attitudes toward the others and self is the *Personal Attribute Inventory for Children (PAIC)* (Parish, Ohlsen, & Parish, 1978; Salend & Moe, 1983). The PAIC is an alphabetically arranged adjective checklist consisting of 24 negative and 24 positive adjectives. The students are asked to select 15 adjectives that best describe a particular student or group of students. The scores are computed in terms of the total number of negative adjectives chosen (Parish & Taylor, 1978).

Bagley and Greene (1981) developed the *Peers' Attitudes Toward The Handicapped Scale (PATHS)* to assess the attitudes of students in grades four through eight toward students with various disabilities. Students read 30 statements describing a student with a physical, behavioral, or learning disability and a problem that the student is experiencing. Then they determine where the student depicted in the description should work. Choices include *Work with me in my group, Work in another group, Work in no group, Work outside of class,* or *Stay at home.*

Esposito and Peach (1983) and Esposito and Reed (1986) used the *Primary Student Survey of Handicapped Persons (PSSHP)* to assess the attitudes of young children and nonreaders. The PSSHP contains six questions, which are administered to each child orally to minimize the need for reading and writing:

1. Tell me everything you know about a handicapped person.
2. Do you like handicapped people?
3. Do you have any handicapped friends?
4. Can you get sick playing with handicapped people?
5. Are you afraid of handicapped people?
6. Do you think that handicapped people seem a lot different from you?

Each of the student's responses can be recorded verbatim by the examiner or on audiocassette and later transcribed on to a score sheet. Negative responses are scored a 0, neutral responses are scored a 1, and positive responses receive a 2. The PSSHP manual contains guidelines for rating student responses and information on technical adequacy.

Another instrument that has been used to measure attitudes toward individuals with disabilities is the *St. Joseph Curriculum-Based Attitude Scale (STJCBAS)* (Fielder & Simpson, 1987). This attitude measurement scale is made up of 25 items that are rated on a six-point Likert scale from *very much like me* to *very much unlike me.* Higher scores suggest more propitious attitudes toward individuals with disabilities.

Several attitude assessment instruments employ pictures to sample attitudes. Picture-oriented attitude scales are especially appropriate for assessing attitudes toward males and females and individuals from diverse racial backgrounds, and for measuring the attitudes of young students (Chigier & Chigier, 1968; Jones & Sisk, 1967). Richardson, Goodman, Hastorf, and Dornbusch (1961) assessed students' attitudes by having them rank a series of drawings depicting male and female, black, Puerto Rican, and white students who do not have disabilities; who have a leg brace and use crutches; who use a wheelchair; and who have only one hand. Billings (1963) developed a two-step procedure that uses pictures to measure attitudes. Initially, students view a picture, then write a story about the child in the picture. In the second step, students again write a story, but this time are told that the child in the picture has a disability.

The *Scale for Children's Attitudes Toward Exceptionalities (SCATE)* uses graphics to measure students' attitudes (Miller, Hagan, & Armstrong, 1980; Miller, Richey, & Lammers, 1983). Students read a narrative depicting a student with a disability and look at a picture of students with and without disabilities. Attitudes are then assessed by students predicting the responses of both groups to situations involving social distance (being in a group with a student with a disability), friendship (desire to be friends with a student with a disability) and subordination-superordination (acceptance of students with disabilities in leadership roles) (Miller & Loukellis, 1982).

Other attitude assessment techniques that can be used include *The Perception of Closeness Scale* (Horne, 1981), *Disability Social Distance Scale* (Tringo, 1970), *Mental Retardation Attitude Inventory* (Harth, 1971), and *Attitudes To Blindness Scale* (Marsh & Friedman, 1972).

Knowledge of Individual Differences Probes

In order to command a more comprehensive perception of student views of Native Americans, I asked a fifth-grade class to complete the following sentences:

1. Long ago Indians were . . .
2. Long ago Indians lived . . .
3. Today Indians are . . .
4. Today Indians live . . .
5. Words or phrases that I would use to describe Indians today are . . .

The children's responses demonstrated a romanticized view of Native Americans as people of the past who lived on the Plains. One child wrote,

"Long ago Indians were people who never cut their hair and ate buffalo and fish, rabbits, corn, and berries and were probably smarter than todays indians (sic)." . . . Another student indicated that Indians today are "very unique and not at all like we are. They hunt different, they talk different and they also cook different. They don't cook their food all the way like chicken. They cook hamburger only part way and it would give us stomach aches but is doesn't (sic) to them." . . .

The children held inaccurate and idealistic perceptions. They saw Native Americans as a powerful group whose present-day lives are easier because of an abundance of food. All the students in this class of twenty-seven except one provided a narrow and stereotypic conception of Native Americans. . . . None of the students demonstrated knowledge of issues like poverty, political disenfranchisement, and mental health (Pang, 1991, pp. 184–185).

Teachers can assess students' knowledge of information about individual differences and various groups via a probe that queries the students' understanding of differences and factual knowledge about the groups (*What does it mean to have a learning disability? What is AIDS?*); stereotypic views of others (*True or false: People in wheelchairs are retarded. True or False: Homeless people are adults who don't work and choose to be homeless.*); needs of other individuals (*What are three things that you would have difficulty doing if you were blind? What are three things that you would have difficulty doing in this classroom if you didn't speak English?*); ways to interact with and assist (if necessary) (*If you were hearing impaired, how would you want others to treat you?; If you had difficulty speaking English, what are some ways that others could help you?*); and devices and aids designed to assist individuals (*What is a device that a student with one arm could use?*) A sample quiz on disabilities developed by Barnes, Berrigan, and Biklen (1978) is presented in Figure 4.3.

Student Drawings

Students' acceptance and knowledge of others can be revealed in the ways they depict and describe others. Having students draw a picture of a scene depicting other individuals can be a valuable way of assessing their attitudes. To obtain an accurate assessment of the students' feelings, students also should write a story explaining the picture.

For example, examine the picture in Figure 4.4. How would you rate the attitude of the student who drew this picture toward individuals with disabilities? An initial assessment of the drawing may suggest that the student possesses a negative attitude. However, upon reading the story accompanying this picture, the student's attitude becomes much clearer: The student explained the picture by stating "People with disabilities are almost always made fun of. This picture shows a person with a disability crying because of the way other people laugh at him. Put yourself in his position."

FIGURE 4.3
Quiz on disabilities

YES ☐ NO ☐ NOT SURE ☐		1. Is a person with a disability usually sick?
YES ☐ NO ☐ NOT SURE ☐		2. Can a person who is blind go to the store?
YES ☐ NO ☐ NOT SURE ☐		3. If someone can't talk, do you think he's retarded?
YES ☐ NO ☐ NOT SURE ☐		4. Were people with disabilities born that way?
YES ☐ NO ☐ NOT SURE ☐		5. Do you feel sorry for someone who is disabled?
YES ☐ NO ☐ NOT SURE ☐		6. Can blind people hear the same as other people?
YES ☐ NO ☐ NOT SURE ☐		7. If a person is retarded, does it mean that he/she will never grow up?
YES ☐ NO ☐ NOT SURE ☐		8. Are all deaf people alike?
YES ☐ NO ☐ NOT SURE ☐		9. Can a person in a wheelchair be a teacher?
YES ☐ NO ☐ NOT SURE ☐		10. Do all children have a right to go to your school?

Source: E. Barnes, C. Berrigan, and D. Biklen, *What's the Difference? Teaching Positive Attitudes Toward People with Disabilities* (Syracuse, NY: Human Policy Press, 1978), p. 5. Reprinted by permission of the publisher.

ATTITUDE CHANGE STRATEGIES

When students possess negative attitudes toward individuals whom they view as different, positive attitudes can be fostered through a variety of *attitude change strategies* (Conway & Gow, 1988; Donaldson, 1980). An essential factor in the success of attitude change strategies is the establishment of an *equal status relationship,* a relationship in which both parties view each other as equal in terms of social, educational, or vocational status (Donaldson, 1980). To be successful, attitude change strategies should provide students with information that counters their stereotypic views toward and decreases their feelings of uneasiness about others they perceive to be different. Addi-

FIGURE 4.4
Student drawing depicting an individual with a disability

tionally, effective attitude change strategies give individuals a structured experience with individuals who they perceive as different and teach students to accept individual differences (Donaldson, 1980). Teachers can use a variety of strategies to change attitudes and teach students about individual differences. In choosing an attitude change strategy to use with students, teachers should evaluate each strategy using the guidelines presented in Figure 4.5.

Teaching students to accept and appreciate the value of individual differences can facilitate the acceptance of mainstreamed students and establish a sense of community within the classroom (Simpson, 1980). Individual differences instruction should promote the belief that individuals are more similar to each other than different, and should facilitate an understanding of one's strengths and weaknesses and likes and dislikes. Teachers can supplement individual differences instruction by serving as a role model to show that all students are valued and accepted.

Strategies to teach students to accept individual differences related to disability and culture, language, gender, and socioeconomic status are discussed here. Many of these strategies overlap and can be adapted to teach students about individual differences related to a variety of issues.

FIGURE 4.5
Attitude change strategy checklist

Several attitude change strategies exist. Teachers can determine the appropriate strategy to use in the classroom by evaluating the strategy in terms of the following questions:

Is the strategy appropriate for my students?

What skills do I need to implement the strategy? Do I have these skills?

What resources will I need to implement the strategy? Do I have these resources?

Does the strategy teach critical information about the group and the acceptance of individual differences?

Does the strategy present positive nonstereotypic examples of the group?

Does the strategy provide for establishing an equal status relationship?

Does the strategy offer students a structured experience in which to learn about the group and individual differences?

Does the strategy facilitate followup activities and additional opportunities for learning about the group and individual differences?

TEACHING ACCEPTANCE OF INDIVIDUAL DIFFERENCES RELATED TO DISABILITY

Attitude change strategies designed to modify attitudes toward individuals with disabilities have four goals:

1. provide information about disabilities
2. increase the comfort level with people who have disabilities
3. foster empathy with disabled people
4. facilitate accepting behavior toward people with disabilities (Barnes, Berrigan, & Biklen, 1978, p. 19)

Simulations

A unique and effective way to teach positive attitudes toward individuals with disabilities is through the use of disability simulations (Ward, Arkell, Dahl, & Wise, 1979; Hallenback & McMaster, 1991), which provide students with experiences that give them an idea of how it feels to have a disability. In addition to introducing students to the problems encountered by individuals with disabilities, Wright (1978) recommends that simulations also expose students to methods of adaptation that individuals with disabilities use. Jones, Sowell, Jones, and Butler (1981) found that a training program that included simulations to sensitize students to the needs and experiences of students with disabilities led to an increase in positive attitudes toward the disabled. Clore and Jeffrey (1972) noted that attitude change via disability simulations were long lasting, especially when the simulation allowed students to view the reactions of other individuals who do not have disabilities.

IDEAS FOR IMPLEMENTATION

When using disability simulations, teachers should do the following:

1. Select and design the simulation activities so that they are as realistic as possible.
2. Provide clear, practical, and detailed directions to students.
3. Inform students that they must take the simulation seriously and that they cannot quit the simulation until the activity is completed.
4. Ensure the safety and comfort of students performing the simulations.
5. Assign an observer to watch and, if necessary, assist the students participating in the simulation.
6. Follow the activities with group discussions to provide additional information concerning such issues as causes, severity, and feelings.
7. Have students write about and discuss their experiences including their feelings about the experience, the reactions of others, and the adaptations they made.

Wesson and Mandell (1989) have developed a participant reaction form and an observer reaction form that can be used to guide students in reflecting upon their experiences (see Figures 4.6 and 4.7).

Source: Jones, Sowell, Jones, & Butler (1981); Popp (1983); Wesson & Mandell (1989); Hallenback & McMaster (1991).

Additional simulation activities are available in Hallenback and McMaster, 1991; Raschke & Dedrick, 1986; and Wesson and Mandell, 1989).

Simulations of varying disabilities and sample corresponding followup questions follow (Bookbinder, 1978; Glazzard, 1979; Hochman, 1979; Israelson, 1980; Popp, 1983; Ward, Arkell, Dahl, & Wise, 1979).

Visual Impairment Simulations

Activity: Blindfold students and seat them at a desk. Give them an empty cup and a pitcher of water. Have them fill the cup with water. So that other students may observe the activity, use a see-through plastic cup.

Followup Questions:

1. How did you approach the task?
2. How did you know when to stop?
3. What other activities would be difficult to do if you couldn't see?

Activity: Set up an obstacle course using several chairs and desks. Group students into pairs, with one of each pair blindfolded and the other not blindfolded. The blindfolded student must negotiate the obstacle course and find a designated chair at its end without touching any of the obstacles, by following directions given by the student who is not blindfolded.

Followup Questions:

1. What was it like to give directions? To receive directions?
2. What other senses did you use? How did they help you?
3. How does an individual with a visual impairment move around without knocking into things?

FIGURE 4.6
Simulation participant reaction form

PARTICIPANT REACTION FORM

Participant's Name ______________________________
Activity ____________________ Date ____________________

I. Describe your reactions to this activity by completing the following:
1. Describe your behaviors during the activity. What did you do?
2. Describe your emotions during the activity. How did you feel after the activity?
3. How were your reactions to this experience different than what you expected? Explain.

II. Rate your reactions to the activity on the scale provided:
SD = strongly disagree D = disagree A = agree SA = strongly agree

1. This activity made me feel incompetent.	SD	D	A	SA
2. This activity was easier to do than expected.	SD	D	A	SA
3. One of the worst things in the world would be to do this activity every day for the rest of my life.	SD	D	A	SA
4. This activity made me feel dumb.	SD	D	A	SA
5. This activity was fun to do.	SD	D	A	SA
6. This activity made me think a long time about this disability.	SD	D	A	SA
7. This activity made me feel helpless.	SD	D	A	SA

III. Rate your reactions to persons with this disability by completing the following.
SD = strongly disagree D = disagree A = agree SA = strongly agree

1. A person with this disability would have a hard time having a boyfriend or girlfriend.	SD	D	A	SA
2. A person with this disability could never have a professional occupation.	SD	D	A	SA
3. A person with this disability would have a very hard time being a parent.	SD	D	A	SA
4. A person with this disability would have a hard time liking him or herself.	SD	D	A	SA
5. A person with this disability needs a lot of assistance keeping house.	SD	D	A	SA
6. A person with this disability has few riends.	SD	D	A	SA
7. A person with this disability would probably never be able to vote in national elections.	SD	D	A	SA
8. A person with this disability cannot keep track of their own finances.	SD	D	A	SA
9. A person with this disability has few leisure activities he or she really enjoys.	SD	D	A	SA
10. A person with this disability would enjoy coming to visit me at my house.	SD	D	A	SA

Source: C. Wesson and C. Mandell, *Teaching Exceptional Children,* vol. 21 (Reston, VA: Council for Exceptional Children, 1989), p. 34. Reprinted by permission of the publisher.

FIGURE 4.7
Simulation observer reaction form

OBSERVER REACTION FORM

1. Name of Person Observed__________
2. Name of Activity Observed__________
3. Handicap being simulated__________
4. Dates of observation__________
5. Time observed __________to__________
6. Number of observations of the handicap simulation__________

Observer's Rating of the Activity

SD = strongly disagree D = disagree A = agree SA = strongly agree

1. This activity was difficult for the participant to do.	SD	D	A	SA
2. I'd like to try this activity myself.	SD	D	A	SA
3. This activity made the participant feel frustrated.	SD	D	A	SA
4. This activity required a lot of effort on the part of the participant.	SD	D	A	SA
5. This activity made the participant feel like s/he really had this handicap.	SD	D	A	SA
6. Watching this activity made me feel uncomfortable.	SD	D	A	SA

Source: C. Wesson and C. Mandell, *Teaching Exceptional Children,* vol. 21 (Reston, VA: Council for Exceptional Children, 1989), p. 35. Reprinted by permission of the publisher.

Activity: Have students wear blindfolds during part of the school day. Blindfold one student and assign another student as a helper to follow the blindfolded student around the room and building. Periodically, have the helper and the blindfolded student change roles. Structure the activity so that students must move around in the classroom, eat a meal, go to the bathroom, and move to other classes. Have the blindfolded student complete a form with the helper providing verbal assistance only.

Followup Questions:

1. What problems did you have during the activity? What problems did you observe as a helper?
2. What did you do that helped you perform the activities without seeing?
3. What did the helper do to help you perform the activities?
4. What changes could be made to assist students who can't see in school? At home?

Hearing Impaired Simulations

Activity: Give students a new pair of ear plugs and have them wear them for several hours during the school day. Try to structure the school day so that they have a variety of experiences that require listening and talking, such as following directions for class assignments, ordering lunch in the cafeteria attending an assembly program in the auditorium, and hearing a message over the loudspeaker system.

Followup Questions:

1. What problems did you experience? How did these problems affect you?
2. What strategies did you use to help you understand what was being said?

Activity: Give directions to students by mouthing the words. The students must try to determine the directions by reading your lips.

Followup Questions:

1. What were you being asked to do?
2. What problems did you have in lipreading?

Activity: Show a movie or video without the sound. Ask students questions that can only be answered by having heard the sound. Show the same film or video again with the sound and have students respond to the same questions.

Followup Questions:

1. How did your answers differ?
2. What information did you use to answer the questions after the first viewing?

Physical Disabilities Simulations

Activity: Put a dowel rod in the joints of the students' elbows while their arms are positioned behind their backs. First, give the students a comb and have them attempt to comb their hair. Then untie their shoes and ask them to tie them.

Activity: Place stockings or rubber wash gloves on the students' hands and have them do a puzzle, sort small objects, or draw a picture.

Activity: Place a splint on the back of each finger on the student's writing hand or a bandage on the student's dominant hand. Have the student perform activities that require the use of that hand including eating, writing, cutting, drawing, and pouring.

Followup Questions:

1. Were you successful at combing your hair? Tying your shoes? Doing the puzzle? Sorting? Drawing? Eating? Writing?
2. What other activities would you have difficulty doing if you had limited use of your hands?
3. Are there any strategies or devices that you could use to perform the tasks?

Activity: Place a low balance beam on a gym mat. Have the student spin around ten times and then try to walk across the balance beam. (To prevent injury to students, it is essential that the floor surface be cushioned where this activity is being performed.)

Activity: Tape rulers and sandbags to students' legs and assign tasks that require them to move around the room.

Followup Questions:

1. What happened after you spun around? Were you able to walk across the balance beam?
2. How would it feel if walking was that difficult for you all the time?
3. How could you play with someone who couldn't walk?

Activity: Place students in wheelchairs and have them maneuver around the classroom and the school. Structure the activity so that students attempt to drink from a water fountain, write on the blackboard, make a phone call, go to the bathroom, and transfer themselves onto a toilet. Because of the potential architectural barriers in the school, have a same-sex peer assist and observe the student in the wheelchair.

Followup Questions:

1. What problems did you encounter in maneuvering around the school?
2. How would you feel if you couldn't go to the bathroom alone because you use a wheelchair?
3. What were the reactions of other students who saw you in the wheelchair? How did their reactions make you feel?
4. What are some barriers that would make it hard for a wheelchair-bound person to move around on a street? In a store?
5. What modifications can make it easier for wheelchair-bound individuals to maneuver in schools? In streets, stores, or homes?

Speech Impaired Simulations

Activity: Assign students in pairs. Have one student try to communicate messages to the other by using physical gestures only, by talking without moving their tongues, and by employing a communication board.

Followup Questions:

1. Were you able to communicate the message to your partner?
2. What strategies did you use to communicate the message?
3. How did you understand the message your partner was trying to give?
4. How did it feel to try to understand the speaker?
5. If you had difficulty talking, how would you want others to talk to you?
6. How would you feel if you talked like that all the time?

Learning Disabilities Simulations

Activity: Place a mirror and a sheet of paper on the students' desks so that students can see the reflection of the paper in the mirror. Have the students write a sentence and read a paragraph while looking in the mirror. Then have the students do the same tasks without looking in the mirror. Compare their ability to do the tasks under the two different conditions.

Followup Questions:

1. What problems did you experience in writing and reading while looking in the mirror?
2. How did it feel to have difficulty writing and reading?
3. What other tasks would be hard if you saw this way all the time?

Think About It

Simulate several disabilities for a whole or part of a day. How did the various simulations make you feel? How did others treat you? What problems did you experience? What did you learn? How did you adapt to the various disabilities?

Successful Individuals with Disabilities

Many famous, highly successful individuals had some type of disability. Lessons on these individuals' achievements and how they overcame their disability can help students who do not have disabilities see such individuals in a more positive light. Lazar, Gensley, and Orpet (1971) found that they could promote positive attitudes toward individuals with disabilities by delivering an attitude change program that included a unit on individuals with disabilities who have made a significant contribution to society.

One effective way to introduce students to the achievements of individuals with disabilities is through a matching activity, in which students are given a list of famous athletes, writers, musicians, politicians, and historical figures with disabilities, and are required to match the individual to his or her disability. This activity can be followed by a discussion of the individuals' lives, including the factors that helped them overcome their disabilities. Figure 4.8 shows a sample matching activity.

Book reports on the lives of famous individuals with disabilities also can be a valuable activity to introduce students to the achievements of many such individuals. Discussions and reports should focus attention on how these historical figures were able to develop as individuals and adjust to their disability (Simpson, 1980). The report could include the following information:

Aaron, Phillips, & Larsen (1988) have done interesting research concerning individuals with disabilities that can help guide students' reports.

- the nature of the handicap and how it occurred
- how the handicap affected the person's education, home life, friends, job
- what problems were encountered as a result of the handicap
- what are/were the accomplishments, contributions, goals, and/or future hopes of that person (Research for Better Schools, 1978, p. 25)

Teachers can have students write about a friend or relative who has a disability or complete a research report on the causes of different disabilities (Barnes, Berrigan, & Biklen, 1978). The Research and Training Center on Independent Living (1987) offers guidelines for writing about individuals with disabilities that teachers can share with students, including the following:

FIGURE 4.8
Sample individuals with disabilities matching activity

In the space next to each individual's name, indicate the letter of the disability they possess(ed).

Individual	**Disability**
_____ Franklin Roosevelt, U.S. President	a. blind
_____ Ludwig van Beethoven, composer	b. deaf-blind
_____ Helen Keller, author	c. paralyzed in both legs
_____ Stephen W. Hawking, physicist	d. speech impediment
_____ Winston Churchill, British Prime Minister	e. dyslexia
_____ Albert Einstein, mathematician	f. deaf
_____ Earvin "Magic" Johnson, professional basketball player	g. learning disabled
_____ Stevie Wonder, musician	h. born without a hand
_____ Jim Abbott, major league pitcher	i. hearing impaired
_____ Marlee Matlin, Academy Award–winning actress	j. HIV
	k. ALS (amyotrophic lateral sclerosis)

- Don't focus on the individual's disability unless it is essential to the piece.
- Don't create false expectations about individuals with disabilities by portraying them as superhuman.
- Focus on the individual rather than the disability by using the term *individuals with a specific disability* (individuals with mental retardation) rather than by describing individuals as being part of a specific disability group (the retarded).
- Highlight abilities rather than limitations.

Guest Speakers

An attitude change strategy that provides students with direct exposure to individuals with disabilities is inviting to class guest speakers who have disabilities (Hallenback & McMaster, 1991; Froschl, Colon, Rubin, & Sprung, 1984). Teachers can find potential guest speakers by contacting local community agencies, parent groups, professional and advocacy organizations, special education teachers, and special education schools. Numerous persons may be available; teachers should meet with any potential speakers to determine how relevant and appropriate it would be to invite them.

Once a speaker has been selected, teachers should meet with them to help plan their presentation (Bookbinder, 1978). Speakers may want to address such topics as the problems they encounter now as well as those they experienced when they were the students' age; school experiences; hobbies and interests; family; jobs; a typical day; future plans; causes of their disability; ways to prevent their disability (if possible); adaptations they need; ways of interacting with others; and adaptive devices they use. Speakers should be encouraged to use short anecdotes and humorous stories that portray positive examples of their lives.

IDEAS FOR IMPLEMENTATION

In selecting a guest speaker, teachers should consider the following:

1. Is the individual comfortable with his or her disability?
2. Does the individual have an independent lifestyle?
3. Does the individual have a range of experiences to share with students?
4. Does the individual represent a positive role model for students?
5. Does the individual have the skills to talk to students at a language level they can understand?
6. Does the individual possess a sense of humor and warmth that will appeal to students?
7. Can the individual deal with the questions your students may ask?

Source: Bookbinder (1978).

To assist speakers in tailoring their remarks to students, teachers should provide speakers with background information about the class (age level, grade level, exposure to and understanding of disabilities) and possible questions students may ask. Prior to the speaker coming to class, teachers should have students identify the questions they have about the disability to be discussed, so that they can then be shared with the speaker. Because some students may hesitate to ask questions, the teacher can help overcome their reluctance by initially asking the speaker some of the questions the students have previously identified.

Films and Books

The first-grade curriculum mandates that Mr. Monroig teach his students how to interact with, understand, and accept others. In his teaching Mr. Monroig uses the book, *Easy or Hard? That's a Good Question* (Tobias, 1977), a children's book that makes the point that all people are similar in some ways and different in other ways, and that some things are easy for some people and hard for others.

Mr. Monroig begins the lesson by asking his students to identify two things that are easy and two things that are hard for them to do. He then divides the class in half, with one side of the room labeled the easy side (he puts an "EZ" sign on that side of the room) and the other side the hard side (he puts a sign with a rock on that side of the room). After reading each "easy" or "hard" sequence in the book, he has students indicate whether the behavior or task mentioned in the book is easy or hard for them by moving to the easy or hard side of the classroom. Periodically, he notes the similarities and differences between the students' responses.

After completing the book, Mr. Monroig asks students to share the two things they feel were easy and the two things that were hard to do. Again, he notes the similarities and differences in their responses. He then discusses with the class some of the factors that affect the ease with which one can perform a task. He asks them to identify things that would be easy or hard to do if they had the following disabilities:

- had a reading problem
- were in a wheelchair
- didn't understand English
- couldn't hold a pencil
- couldn't see
- couldn't hear

Mr. Monroig then has the students perform various tasks with and without a simulated disability. For example, he has students attempt to watch a movie with and without the sound, and walk around the classroom blindfolded. He concludes the lesson by asking students, "If you knew someone who found something hard to do, what could you do to show that person that you understand that some things are hard?"

Numerous films and videos depicting the lives of individuals with disabilities are available (Barnes, Berrigan, & Biklen, 1978; McGookey, 1992; Research for Better Schools, 1978). Westervelt and McKinney (1980) found that viewing a film about a student with disabilities led to an increase in the students' attraction to a wheelchair-bound student. However, because the attitude change via the film was shortlived, Westervelt and McKinney suggest the pairing of films with other attitude change strategies (group discussions, guest speaker). The Mad Hatters Educational Theatre for the Understanding of People with Special Needs or Disabilities, in Kalamazoo, Michigan, uses drama to teach students, adults, and professional educators about individual differences (McGookey, 1992).

McGookey (1992) offers guidelines for using drama in the classroom to teach students about disabilities.

Books about individuals with disabilities can promote positive attitudes and can teach students about individual differences and disabilities (Greenbaum, Varas, & Markel, 1980; Litton, Banbury, & Harris, 1980). Leung (1980) examined a literature program consisting of 10 short stories and discussions concerning individuals with disabilities to determine its effect on the social acceptance of mainstreamed students. The findings indicated that, after exposure to the program, the number of positive and neutral interactions among mainstreamed students and their regular classroom teachers and peers increased, while the number of negative interactions involving mainstreamed students decreased. In addition, students possessed more propitious attitudes toward individuals with disabilities. The sociometric ratings of mainstreamed students remained unchanged; regular classroom teachers held high opinions of the program.

Reeves (1990), Hildreth and Candler (1992), and McGookey (1992) have compiled helpful lists of books about disabilities that teachers can use with their students across a range of age and grade levels. Similarly, Gropper and Schuster (1981), Froschl, Colon, Rubin, and Sprung (1984) and Slapin, Lessing, and Belkind (1987) have identified and rated children's books about disabilities. Crosby's (1963) five-phase strategy can be used after students have read books about individual differences. The five steps are as follows:

- retelling the story
- helping students explore changes in the characters' feelings, behaviors, and interactions with others
- examining with students similar events that they have experienced or read about
- having students discuss consequences related to various behaviors and feelings depicted in the story
- asking students to draw conclusions and generalizations concerning the story

Salend and Moe (1983) compared the effects of two situations. In one, students were exposed to books about disabilities only by listening to a teacher reading them. In the second, the teacher read the books to the students and highlighted the main points to be learned through discussion, simulations, and explanations. The results suggested that while the books-only situation did not lead to a significant change in attitudes, the books-and-activities combination did.

IDEAS FOR IMPLEMENTATION

In choosing appropriate books to use to teach students about individual differences, teachers should consider several factors, including the following:

1. Are the language and style of the book appropriate?
2. Is the book factually correct and realistic?
3. Is the individual with disabilities depicted in the book shown in a variety of situations and settings?
4. Does the book portray individuals with disabilities as positive, competent, and independent?
5. Are individuals with disabilities depicted as being multidimensional and as having ideas and feelings not associated with their disability?
6. Does the book introduce the readers to the adaptations and devices that individuals with certain disabilities need?
7. Does the book allow the readers to develop an equal-status relationship and learn about the similarities and differences between individuals with disabilities and individuals who do not have disabilities?
8. Do the illustrations facilitate discussion and the sharing of information?
9. Will the book stimulate questions and discussions about individuals with disabilities?

These guidelines can be adapted and used to evaluate books that teach about individual differences related to race, gender, culture, linguistic ability, and economic status.

Source: Moe (1980); Slapin, Lessing, & Belkind (1987).

Older students can be introduced to individuals with disabilities via literature. *The Handicapped in Literature: A Psychosocial Perspective* (Bowers, 1980) includes selections from H. G. Wells, Carson McCullers, Somerset Maugham, and Kurt Vonnegut; *The Exceptional Child Through Literature* (Landau, Epstein & Stone, 1978) contains short stories by Joyce Carol Oates, John Steinbeck, and Alfred Kazin. Both can be used to give students insights into the experiences and feelings of individuals with disabilities. Followup questions to guide the discussion also are included with both books. Landau, Epstein, and Stone (1978) offer a bibliography of adult books dealing with individuals with disabilities. Guidelines for using folktales to promote a greater understanding of disabled individuals also are available (Barnes, Berrigan, & Biklen, 1978).

Think About It

Think about a book that you have read regarding an individual with a disability. What insights did you gain? What did you learn about individual differences?

Obtain a children's book about disabilities and evaluate it using the guidelines presented. Would you recommend using the book with students?

Instructional Materials

Litton, Banbury, and Harris (1980) compiled a descriptive list of commercially developed attitude change materials.

A drawback in the use of simulations, children's books, and other attitude change strategies is the time it takes teachers to prepare the activities. Teachers can minimize the time required in planning attitude change activities by using commercially developed instructional materials for teaching students about their peers with disabilities. These programs usually include a variety of activities, materials necessary to implement the activities, and a teacher's manual. For example, Froschl, Colon, Rubin, and Sprung (1984) have developed a curriculum for teaching preschoolers about various disabilities, while Barnes, Berrigan, and Biklen (1978) have identified numerous activities for use with elementary and secondary students.

The Smallest Minority: Adapted Regular Education Social Studies Curricula for Understanding and Integrating Severely Disabled Students is a curriculum program that teaches students about the needs and feelings of students with disabilities and the value of individual differences. The curriculum is divided into three levels: lower elementary, upper elementary, and secondary grades. *The Lower Elementary Grades: Understanding Self and Others* (Brown, Hemphill, & Voeltz, 1982), designed for K–3 students, introduces them to similarities and differences among all people, prostheses, and adaptive methods of communicating. *The Upper Elementary Grades: Understanding Prejudice* (Brown, Fruehling, & Hemphill, 1982), which targets students in grades 4 through 6, examines the effects of prejudice and focuses on group dynamics. *The Secondary Grades (7–12): Understanding Alienation* (Hemphill, Zukas, & Brown, 1982) explores the effects of physical and programmatic barriers on the alienation of individuals with disabilities. Additional activities for infusing an understanding of students with disabilities into the curriculum are available in *Special Alternatives: A Learning System for Generating Unique Solutions to Problems of Special Education in Integrated Settings* (Fruehling, Hemphill, Brown, & Zukas, 1981).

Teachers also can promote acceptance by introducing other materials in their classrooms. Posters and photographs depicting individuals with disabilities in typical situations can be used to stimulate discussions and decorate the walls of the room. *Feeling Free Posters,* a resource material that includes three color posters of individuals with disabilities, is available from Human Policy Press, P.O. Box 127, Syracuse, NY 13210.

Resource Photos for Mainstreaming, an adult and children's series of black and white photographs depicting individuals with disabilities in a variety of situations, can be purchased from Women's Action Alliance, Inc., 370 Lexington Avenue, New York, NY 10017.

Positive Images, a video that portrays the lives of three women with disabilities and the social, economic, and political barriers they encounter, is available from Women Make Movies/Box SE, 225 Lafayette St., New York, NY 10012.

Puppets, dolls, and stuffed animals that have disabilities can be used to teach students about disabilities. *New Friends* provides educators with three make-your-own patterns to follow in creating multiracial dolls that depict individuals with disabilities. The dolls can be used to introduce students to various disabilities and the adaptive equipment that different disabled individuals employ (Froschl, Colon, Rubin, & Sprung, 1984). The doll patterns are available from Chapel Hill Training Outreach Project, Lincoln Center, Merritt Hill Road, Chapel Hill, NC 27514.

Similarly, *Special Friends,* stuffed animals with disabilities (for instance, an elephant who uses a hearing aid) can be obtained for classroom use by contacting Pediatric Projects, Inc., P.O. Box 1880, Santa Monica, CA 90406.

Kids on the Block presents information about a range of disabilities through puppet shows that portray life-size puppets of students with disabilities in real-life situations. The vignettes encourage the audience to explore their feelings toward individuals with disabilities and to ask questions concerning individuals with specific disabilities. In addition to programs about disabilities, Kids on the Block offers programs on medical differences (AIDS, diabetes) and social concerns (aging, divorce, teen pregnancy, child abuse, substance abuse, and cultural differences). Additional information on Kids on the Block groups in local areas can be obtained by contacting Kids on the Block, 9385-C Gerwig Lane, Columbia, MD 21046.

Kids on the Block has developed two disability awareness programs including activities, stories, stickers, and posters to promote the acceptance and appreciation of individual differences: "Each and Every One" for primary grades and "Each and Every One" for intermediate grades. A series of books for children based on the Kids on the Block puppets and supplementary materials (chatabout cards, buttons, activity books, audiocassettes, and videocassettes) also are available.

Information on Disabilities and Characteristics

The National Information Center on Deafness at Gallaudet University has developed two series of materials to teach students grades 3–4 and 5–12 about deafness and hearing loss.

Fielder and Simpson (1987) found that either a categorical or noncategorical curriculum concerning information related to individuals with disabilities could promote positive student attitudes toward their mainstreamed peers. The categorical curriculum focused on categories of exceptionality, and included a review of standard definitions, characteristics, and causes for each of the disabilities (learning disabilities, mental retardation, visual and hearing impairments, and so on). The noncategorical curriculum examined the problems with labeling, an understanding of the use of language to describe individuals, an acceptance of individual differences, a review of the benefits of acceptance and mainstreaming, and the need for self-advocacy, advocacy, and independence.

Adaptive Device Instruction

Many mainstreamed students may require the use of devices, aids, materials, and appliances in order to function successfully in the mainstreamed setting. These aids include talking books, hearing aids, speech synthesizers, wheelchairs, and Braille. A program to prepare students for the entry of these students into the mainstream should introduce them to these aids and devices (Aiello, 1979; Bookbinder, 1978). Wherever possible, it would be best for the mainstreamed students to introduce and explain the aids and devices they use. Students should be shown the devices and allowed to touch and experiment with them. For example, a student with a hearing impairment could explain the parts and maintenance of the hearing aid, and then have students use a hearing aid for a brief period of time. If mainstreamed students do not feel comfortable showcasing and explaining the aids they use, a professional—a physical therapist, teacher, or guidance counselor—or parent can do so.

Aiello (1979) proposed that adaptive devices be obtained from a variety of sources and placed in a central location within the room. Students can then experiment with and explore the devices at different times during the school day.

Alternative communication systems, such as Braille, sign language, and fingerspelling can be introduced to students in a variety of ways that simultaneously promote academic skills. Teachers can teach students the manual alphabet, then have them practice their spelling words by spelling them manually. Teachers can include hand signs for numbers as part of a math assignment. For example, rather than writing the numbers of a division computation on the board, the numbers can be presented using numerical hand signs. Basic signs can be introduced to students and used by teachers to give directions for assignments. Students who have learned Braille can be assigned the task of reading Braille books, and writing their names or compositions in Braille.

Reverse Mainstreaming

McCann, Semmel, and Nevin (1985) suggest that increased acceptance of students with disabilities can be promoted through *reverse mainstreaming*. Reverse mainstreaming can take the form of visits to special education classes, or students may perform a function such as serving as a peer tutor. These reverse mainstreaming activities can lessen the stigma that is often related to placement in special education classes by promoting a greater understanding of their purpose and function. Reverse mainstreaming also can provide opportunities for friendships that can carry over into the regular classroom.

Group Discussion

Providing students with the opportunity to discuss issues related to students with disabilities can be an effective attitude change strategy (Gottlieb, 1980). Gottlieb (1980) found that structured group discussion resulted in a significant improvement in student attitudes toward peers with disabilities. Since Siperstein, Bak, and Gottlieb (1977) found that an unstructured group discussion can have a negative effect on students' perceptions of the students with disabilities, teachers should carefully structure the discussion so that it relates to specific questions and highlights positive features about individuals with disabilities. The success of this technique can be enhanced by the teacher or peers modeling positive responses and attitudes toward individuals with disabilities (Donaldson & Martinson, 1977). When using group discussion, teachers should create an open environment that allows students to ask questions and explore and examine their feelings.

Communicating with Mainstreamed Peers

The various sensory, speech and cognitive abilities of mainstreamed students can limit social interactions with others and serve as a barrier to establishing friendships. Therefore, teachers should provide students with guidelines for communicating with individuals with disabilities (see Figure 4.9).

Hypothetical Examples

Overall, Ms. Bell has been pleased by her students' reactions to their new classmate, Lee, a wheelchair-bound student. However, she notices that many of the students are assisting Lee when she doesn't need assistance. Ms. Bell is concerned that these well-meaning but overly sympathetic behaviors will limit Lee's independence and prevent equal-status relationships between Lee and her peers.

Ms. Bell decides to teach her students when and how to assist students in the class by having them brainstorm various solutions to classroom problems. She presents the class with the following hypothetical examples:

1. The class is returning from physical education class and recess and is getting drinks at the water fountain. Lee, in her wheelchair, is thirsty but cannot reach the fountain. What could be done?

2. While everyone is playing together during recess, Nydia, a student who is learning to speak English, often plays by herself. What could be done?

3. While the class is playing team games during recess, Stacy, a student who is not athletic, is always the last one picked. What could be done?

After each hypothetical example is presented, Ms. Bell guides the students in brainstorming and evaluating solutions to the situations. For the situation with Lee, one student suggests that a peer be assigned to go to the classroom and get Lee a glass from which she can drink. Ms. Bell asks the students to consider the consequences of that solution. They decide that the solution is not fair as it might take time away from the students and makes Lee dependent on other students. One student also says that, "the glass could break and hurt someone." This discussion leads another student to suggest that Lee carry a foldable cup, like the one her family uses when they go camping and someone from the class can fill it up. The class agrees that this is a good solution.

One cognitively based attitude change strategy that sensitizes students in when and how to aid their mainstreamed peers is to present hypothetical examples that illustrate the problems mainstreamed students are likely to encounter in the regular classroom (Salend & Knops, 1984). After the hypothetical examples are presented, students discuss them and brainstorm possible solutions. For example, the following hypothetical example can be presented to the class:

> During class discussions Jack, a student with a hearing impairment, has difficulty understanding what we are talking about and knowing who is talking. What can we do so that Jack will understand better?

Following a discussion of this scenario, students can discuss solutions such as allowing Jack to leave his work area to facilitate lipreading or having a peer point to speakers to indicate changes in the flow of the conversation.

Salend and Knops (1984) examined the effectiveness of hypothetical examples and found that hypothetical examples were easy to use, effective strategies for promoting positive attitudes. Salend (1983d) has developed a six-step model for generating and implementing hypothetical examples in the classroom:

Step 1: Determining Students' Strengths and Weaknesses. Teachers should determine the strengths, weaknesses, and unique needs of mainstreamed students to determine the areas in which they will need assistance, as well as those areas in which they will not.

Step 2: Specifying the Environmental Demands. Teachers pinpoint problem areas by analyzing the total classroom environment (social and academic activities, special routines, architectural barriers) in relation to the students' disability.

Step 3: Identifying Problem Areas. Based on information gathered in steps 1 and 2, teachers specify the content of the hypothetical examples, which relate to existing discrepancies between the mainstreamed students' unique needs and the characteristics and demands of the regular classroom.

Step 4: Phrasing Problem Areas as Hypothetical Examples. Teachers translate problem areas identified in step 3 into hypothetical examples, which should be stated so that information about the problem is presented,

FIGURE 4.9
Guidelines for communicating with individuals with disabilities

COMMUNICATING WITH INDIVIDUALS WITH DISABILITIES

1. View the individual as a person, not as a disability.
2. Refrain from "talking down" or speaking in a condescending way.
3. Talk directly to the individual even if the individual uses an interpreter.
4. Relax, be considerate, and treat the individual with respect.
5. Talk using language and about topics that are age appropriate.
6. Don't apologize for using common expressions that may relate to the individual's disability such as, "I've got to run" or "Have you seen Mary?"

COMMUNICATING WITH INDIVIDUALS IN WHEELCHAIRS

1. Respect the individual's space by refraining from hanging on to the wheelchair.
2. Sit or kneel at the individual's eye level when the conversation is going to continue for an extended period of time.
3. Don't assume that the individual wants you to push the wheelchair.

COMMUNICATING WITH INDIVIDUALS WITH VISUAL DISABILITIES

1. Introduce yourself and any companions when encountering the individual.
2. Speak in a normal voice.
3. Direct communications to the individual by using the individual's name.
4. Tell the individual that you are leaving or ending the conversation.

COMMUNICATING WITH INDIVIDUALS WITH HEARING DISABILITIES

1. Make sure you have the individual's attention before speaking.
2. Speak clearly and in short sentences.
3. Avoid raising your voice or exaggerating your mouth movements.
4. Refrain from repeating yourself. If the individual doesn't understand, rephrase your message in simpler language or write it out.
5. Use facial expressions, physical gestures, and body movements.

COMMUNICATING WITH INDIVIDUALS WITH SPEECH/LANGUAGE DIFFICULTIES

1. Focus your attention to the individual.
2. Refrain from correcting or speaking for the individual.
3. Be encouraging and patient.
4. Seek clarification when you don't understand by repeating what you did understand.

Source: Mid-Hudson Library System (n.d).

phrased in language that is consistent with the age and grade level of the class, and posed as a question.

Step 5: Presenting the Hypothetical Examples. Teachers explain the purpose of and describe the activity, and train students in the process by presenting other hypothetical examples and modeling possible solutions.

Teachers should assume the role of facilitator and encourage students to respond in an honest and positive fashion. Pity and other responses that would produce overdependence can be discouraged by including some examples that portray situations where students will not need any assistance. Introducing the activity by presenting examples that relate to generic problems that any class member might experience (for example, students who are picked last in games, or name calling) can establish an open, positive environment for brainstorming realistic solutions.

Step 6: Brainstorming Solutions. Students discuss the hypothetical examples and identify and evaluate possible solutions. Teachers guide the discussion and provide additional information when necessary. The class can evaluate all potential solutions by examining each solution with respect to its completeness, its ability to solve the problem, and its impact on peers, teachers, mainstreamed students, and class and school rules.

Think About It

Think about how you would present the following hypothetical examples. What solutions do you think students would suggest?

1. The class is having a spelling bee. Mack, a student with a hearing impairment, is a good speller but is having difficulty hearing the spelling words. What could be done?
2. Nydia, a visually impaired student, uses large print and Braille. Because these books are heavy and cumbersome, she has difficulty carrying them during class changes. What could be done?
3. As part of social studies class, students are required to take notes from lectures. Some of the students have difficulty taking notes. What could be done?

Teaching Students About AIDS

Students frequently learn about various conditions such as AIDS through television and other media. Unfortunately, these media sources provide only minimal information regarding AIDS-related prevention, transmission, and testing procedures (Wysocki & Harrison, 1991). As a result, many students have misconceptions about AIDS and are fearful of being in classrooms with students who have AIDS (Fassler, 1990; Jones, 1991).

Teachers can use several strategies to overcome these negative attitudes and misconceptions about AIDS. A trained professional or an individual with AIDS can be invited to speak about the social and medical factors associated with AIDS (Colson & Colson, 1992). Additionally, students can role play what it feels like to have AIDS, or be a family member or a friend of someone who has AIDS. A variety of curriculum materials is available to teach students about AIDS (Byrom & Katz, 1991). These materials often include print and video materials that teach students specific content pertaining to AIDS, help

IDEAS FOR IMPLEMENTATION

In planning and implementing AIDS education programs, teachers will benefit from enacting the following suggestions:

- Establish ground rules, such as no preaching, putdowns, personal questions, or discussions outside of class.
- Obtain information about AIDS and AIDS education strategies and curricula.
- Involve parents and community organizations in the design and delivery of the program.
- Use mixed-gender groups.
- Include training related to factual information about AIDS, sexuality, physical growth, sexual abuse, and the skills necessary to make good decisions.
- Teach students to respect self and others and how to form and value personal relationships.
- Provide students with a knowledge of sexual responsibility and safe sex practices.
- Include desensitization activities to help students feel comfortable talking about sex.
- Define relevant terms in language students can understand and use concrete and visual aids.
- Focus the program on risk activities rather than on risk groups.
- Encourage students to discuss their experiences and ask questions.
- Answer students' questions in an honest, matter-of-fact fashion, using language that is appropriate to the students' ages and levels of sophistication.
- Admit it when you don't know the answer to a question and inform students you will get more information to answer the question.
- Inform students that there is no confidentiality for illegal or dangerous information.
- Evaluate and check students' understanding of the information.

Source: Colson & Colson (1992); Tiffany, Tobias, Raqib, & Ziegler (1991).

students understand the impact of their health habits and choices, and assist students in acquiring the decisionmaking, assertive communication, and self-esteem–enhancing skills necessary to take control of their lives and resist peer pressure. For example, the National Coalition of Advocates for Students (1990) has developed a bilingual curriculum on AIDS and HIV prevention, *On the Road to Healthy Living.* Similarly, Byrom and Katz (1991) have compiled a list of resources that teachers can use to teach students with special education needs about HIV prevention and AIDS education. The American Foundation for AIDS Research disseminates *Learning AIDS,* a comprehensive listing and critique of over 2000 videos, books, brochures, monographs, and instructional materials about AIDS, which professionals and parents can obtain by contacting

The American Foundation for AIDS Research
1515 Broadway
New York, NY 10109-0732

Professional Organizations

Numerous organizations exist that provide information to assist individuals with disabilities. Many of these organizations provide resources that can be used as part of a training program to promote positive reactions to individuals with disabilities. A listing of some of these organizations is presented in the Appendix.

TEACHING ACCEPTANCE OF INDIVIDUAL DIFFERENCES RELATED TO CULTURE, LANGUAGE, GENDER, AND SOCIOECONOMIC STATUS

Teachers also should provide students with learning activities that teach them to understand, accept, and appreciate individual differences related to cultural, language, gender, and socioeconomic status. These activities should provide students with a multicultural perspective that allows them to identify and acknowledge underlying similarities and obvious differences among various groups. For example, Mack (1988) identified several activities that teachers can use to promote an awareness of the cultures of African American, Hispanic, Asian/Pacific Islander and Native Americans. When employing these activities, teachers should highlight the various ways in which these and all groups are similar. Teachers also should establish a positive classroom environment that discourages harassment of students by their peers.

Teachers also should counter any *ethnocentrism,* misunderstanding and negative attitudes toward other cultures, that they perceive students to have. Martin (1987) defined two types of ethnocentrism that teachers may encounter:

1. *Cultural absolutism.* When children respond to some foreign cultural behavior with a statement such as, "How awful—how could anyone do that?", they are looking at their own culture as superior.
2. *Cultural relativism.* If the same children look at the same foreign behavior and say, "Well, we have our ways, and they have theirs," they are missing the idea of the unity that underlies all human behavior (p. 5).

Promoting Acceptance of Cultural Diversity

Creating an environment of multicultural acceptance can enhance the self-esteem and learning performance of students from culturally and linguistically diverse backgrounds by affirming their cultures, languages, and experiences.

Many regular education students may view students from culturally and linguistically diverse backgrounds as different, and limit their interactions with them because of their unique language, clothes, and customs (Lewis & Doorlag, 1987). Teachers can help students overcome these attitudes by teaching them about the different culture and the value of cultural diversity (Garcia, 1978; Chinn & McCormack, 1986; Schniedewind & Davidson, 1983).

Derman-Sparks (1989) has developed an antibias curriculum to educate students regarding issues of color, language, gender, and disability. The curriculum includes a variety of activities to teach students to be sensitive to the needs of others, think critically, interact with others, and develop a positive self-identity based on one's strengths rather than on the weaknesses of others. When teaching students about cultural diversity, teachers should consider the following guidelines:

- Examine cultural diversity with the belief that all individuals have a culture that is to be valued and affirmed.
- Teach initially about cultural diversity by citing the diversity of students and adults in the classroom and then extending the discussion beyond the parameters of the classroom.

IDEAS FOR IMPLEMENTATION

Teachers can create an environment of acceptance and understanding of cultural diversity by employing a variety of strategies that can sensitize students to different cultures:

- Share information about the teacher's cultural background.
- Ask students and their parents to discuss the unique characteristics of their cultures.
- Discuss the similarities and differences among cultures including music, foods, customs, holidays, and languages.
- Make cultural artifacts from different cultures.
- Listen to music from different cultures and learn ethnic songs in music class.
- Teach students words, phrases, and songs in other languages.
- Construct bulletin boards that introduce students to a multicultural perspective—for example, a new bulletin board related to a different culture each month.
- Make a class calendar that recognizes the holidays and customs of all cultures—for example, the Iroquois celebrate the Maple festival in early spring, which includes singing and dancing.
- Celebrate holidays that are common to several cultures in a way that recognizes each culture's customs.
- Plan multicultural lunches, where students and their parents work together to cook multiethnic dishes, and compile a class cookbook comprised of these recipes.
- Develop a mural that has elements of many cultures.
- Take field trips that introduce students to the lifestyles of different cultures.
- Show movies and videos that highlight aspects of different cultures.
- Read ethnic folktales to students.
- Teach students ethnic games.
- Encourage students to use cross-cultural and gender toys and other objects.
- Provide students with multicolored paints, paper, and other art materials, and skin-tone crayons.
- Display artwork that represents various cultures and perspectives.
- Decorate the room with pictures and symbols that offer a multicultural perspective.
- Have students maintain an ethnic feelings book that summarizes their reactions to multicultural awareness activities and their experiences with their culture and other cultures.

Source: Chinn & McCormick (1986); Derman-Sparks (1989); Ford & Jones (1990); Garcia (1978); Schniedewind & Davidson (1983).

- Help students view the similarities among groups through their differences.
- Have cultural diversity activities be an ongoing and integral part of the curriculum rather than a one-day "visit" to a culture during holidays or other special occasions.
- Relate cultural diversity experiences to real life and give students hands-on experiences that address their interests.
- Teach students about the variance of individual behavior within all cultures and emphasize the notion that families and individuals experience and live their culture in personal ways (Derman-Sparks, 1989; Martin, 1987).

A variety of music examples, lesson plans, audiocassettes, videocassettes, and practical teaching strategies for teaching music from a multicultural perspective are available by contacting the Music Educators National Conference Publication Sales, 1902 Association Drive, Reston, VA 22091 (800-828-0229).

Incorporating Cultural Diversity into the Curriculum

Teachers also can incorporate an acceptance of cultural diversity into their curricula. They should carefully examine textbooks and other materials for inclusion of all groups and the roles they play in the specific content area. A list of several commercially developed multicultural awareness materials are presented in Figure 4.10.

Reviews and lists of children's literature about various cultures across a wide range of grade levels are available (Cox & Galda, 1990; Derman-Sparks, 1989; Galda & Cotter, 1992; Hickman, 1989; McMath, 1990; Reimer, 1992; Stalker, 1990).

In examining books and other instructional materials, teachers should consider the following:

- Is the language of the material free of cultural and sexist biases?
- Are individuals from diverse groups portrayed in a positive, nonstereotypic way?
- Does the material recognize and include the contributions of individuals from diverse groups?
- Does the material offer examples that depict individuals from diverse groups in a variety of situations and settings?
- In what proportion are individuals from different groups shown in pictures and illustrations? (Schniedewind & Davidson, 1983.)

Additional guidelines for selecting bias-free textbooks and storybooks are available (Council on Interracial Books for Children, 1980).

Teachers can supplement the instructional materials they use to ensure that the contributions of members of different groups are infused into the content areas (Garcia, 1978). For example, celebrating holidays in recognition of the accomplishments of African American scientists or Hispanic poets in science and English classes, respectively, can teach students about the contributions of those ethnic groups (Schniedewind & Davidson, 1983). Additionally, students can be assigned to read books about different cultures and biographies of women who have made significant contributions to society.

Teaching about Linguistic Differences

As their teacher begins reading a story in Spanish to an English-speaking group, a few children begin to giggle. The teacher stops reading and tells the children, "I am stopping because some children are giggling while I am reading. That is not OK—it is rude. I know Spanish is a new language to some of you. Sometimes we are not comfortable with something we do not know and we laugh to make ourselves feel better, but laughing at how people talk is hurtful and unfair. Laughing is not OK, but it is OK to raise your hand and ask me questions about what I am reading" (Derman-Sparks, 1989, pp. 69–70).

FIGURE 4.10 Commercially developed multicultural awareness materials

Available from Council on Interracial Books for Children, 1841 Broadway, New York, NY 10023:

Thinking and Rethinking US History—Examines what textbooks teach about racism and offers strategies to help teachers and students identify bias and omissions in history texts.

Unlearning "Indian" Stereotypes—A booklet and 15-minute filmstrip that teaches elementary students information about Native Americans.

Winning Justice for All: A Supplementary Curriculum Unit on Sexism and Racism: Stereotyping and Discrimination—A curriculum including filmstrips, student workbooks, and teacher guides that deals with stereotypes and race and sex discrimination in history, books, and work.

From Pluralism to Racism—A filmstrip that examines the concept of pluralism and racism.

Available from the Education Development Center, 55 Chapel St., Newton, MA 02106:

Elementary Curriculum Guide for Integrating Cultural Diversity into Non-Sex-Biased Curriculum—A curriculum that teaches students about racism and sexism.

Available from Peaceworks, P.O. Box 19-1153, Miami Beach, FL 33119:

Fighting Fair: The Legacy of Dr. Martin Luther King—A curriculum and video that shows how Dr. King nonviolently confronted racism and offers nonviolent ways for students to cope with conflicts.

Available from the Anti-Defamation League of the B'nai Brith, 823 United Nations Plaza, New York, NY 10017:

Teacher They Called Me a ________: Prejudice and Discrimination in the Classroom—A curriculum designed to help students understand differences, bigotry, and stereotyping.

Being Fair and Being Free—A series of lessons to help secondary students understand and confront discrimination.

The Wonderful World of Difference and *A World of Difference*—Two series of lessons to teach students in grades kindergarten through eight about individual differences.

Available from Teaching Tolerance, 400 Washington Ave., Montgomery, AL 36104:

Teaching Tolerance—A free magazine that features effective programs, materials, and strategies to introduce issues of tolerance and diversity across the curriculum.

Language is important as it reflects cultural variation and symbolizes group and personal identities that students bring to schools (Roberts, Bell, & Salend, 1991). In light of the importance of language, schools should foster an environment that promotes an understanding of cultural diversity through the acceptance of linguistic differences. Schools can acknowledge and affirm an acceptance of linguistic differences by doing the following:

- having bilingual signs throughout the school that reflect the different languages spoken in the community
- encouraging students to use their native language in school
- asking students to explain customs, games, or objects from their culture in their native language
- offering students the opportunity to speak their native language with others in school
- enlisting the assistance of community members who can speak the students' native languages to serve as volunteers
- using teacher aides fluent in students' native languages to provide instruction
- displaying books and materials written in several languages in classrooms and in the school library
- incorporating students' native languages into the instructional program
- using various languages in school newsletters and other forms of written communication
- having students write journal entries in their native languages
- asking students to contribute pieces to the school newspaper or magazine that are written in their native languages
- inviting speakers and storytellers who speak various languages to address the class
- developing and delivering lessons on various languages
- teaching students about the various dialects of English, and the reasons for and importance of these dialects
- showing respect for all languages and dialects
- establishing a pen pal system of letters written in students' native languages
- giving awards and recognition for excellence in speaking languages that may not be part of typical foreign language courses offered at the school
- showing videos and playing music in various languages (Alexander, 1985; Freeman & Freeman, 1992; New Zealand Department of Education, 1988; Tikunoff et al., 1991)

Teaching about Dialect Differences

Since all English-speaking students speak a dialect, they also will benefit from learning about dialect differences. Adger, Wolfram, Detwyler, and Harry (1992) have developed a proactive curriculum for dialect education that teaches students about dialect and language awareness and variation. Students learn how language works and the roles and functions of language by studying and comparing some of the different dialects of English, such as New England speech, Southern speech, Appalachian English, and African American English in terms of dialect differences, cultural and linguistic conventions, and historical developments. For example, students listen to and contrast the stories of *Cinderella* told in a "standard" English dialect such as New England or Midwestern, and *Ashley Lou and the Prince* told in Appalachian English. For younger students, an awareness of dialect differences can be fostered by reading and listening to stories, poems, and songs in different dialects.

Teaching about Sex Equity

Bell (1991) outlines a program to teach multiracial groups of girls to challenge gender bias.

An effective program to teach students about cultural diversity should include activities designed to promote an understanding of the importance of sex equity. Sex equity activities help male and female students expand their options in terms of behaviors, feelings, interests, career aspirations, and abilities (Shapiro, Kramer, & Hunerberg, 1981). These activities make all students aware of the negative effects of gender bias on females and males, and of ways to combat sexism (Schniedewind & Davidson, 1983; Sprung, 1975). A variety of curriculum activities, media, books for children and adults, photographs, posters, toys, games, and professional organizations that teachers can use as resources for teaching students about sex equity are available (Schniedewind & Davidson, 1983; Shapiro, Kramer, & Hunerberg, 1981; Sprung, 1975).

Teaching about Homelessness and the Migrant Lifestyle

Because frequent changes in schools can result in homeless and in migrant students being targets of ridicule by peers, teachers should teach students about the lifestyles of homeless and migrant students (Salend, 1990). This should be done carefully, as teachers do not want to stigmatize these students. Information about the homeless and about migrant lifestyles can be presented to students through presentations from speakers by showing film or video documentaries and dramatic programs. Similarly, teachers can use the information and pictures in the monograph, *Homeless Children* (O'Connor, 1989) to describe the life of children in shelters and homeless programs.

Teachers can introduce students to the value and importance of the work of migrants by having migrant students and their parents discuss their experiences and the places where they have lived; by developing a map that traces the path of migrant families; by establishing a pen pal system where full-year students write to their migrant classmates who are traveling around the country; by discussing the importance of migrant workers to our society; and by planting and harvesting a class garden. In addition, teachers can show the video documentary, *Old Harvest New Shame* (Corporation for Public Broadcasting, 1990), which traces a migrant family's journey as they travel from state to state in search of agricultural employment, or may expose students to

IDEAS FOR IMPLEMENTATION

Teachers can promote a classroom environment that promotes sex equity by enacting the following suggestions:

- Help students recognize when they are responding in a sexist manner.
- Model a commitment to sex equity by challenging students' stereotypic behavior and by using gender-inclusive language.
- Teach students how their attitudes and behavior relating to sex roles are affected by television, movies, music, books, and the behavior of others.
- Examine how language that ignores, categorizes, and stereotypes can be changed.
- Use nonsexist instructional materials.
- Modify sexist instructional materials.
- Modify the curriculum to include the contributions of women to society.
- Help male and female students understand and respect the importance of work inside and outside the home and the various work possibilities that are available to them.
- Encourage male and female students to participate in a variety of physical education and extracurricular activities.
- Integrate sex equity instruction into all content areas.
- Teach students to challenge sex-role stereotyping that occurs in school and society.

Source: Shapiro, Kramer, & Hunerberg (1981).

books about the migrant lifestyle such as *Migrants, Sharecroppers, Mountaineers* (volume 2 of *Children of Crisis* [Coles, 1971]), and *The Effects of Migration on Children: An Ethnographic Study* (Diaz, Trotter, & Rivera, 1989).

Teaching Students about Stereotyping

Freedman, Gotti, and Holtz (1981) and Pecoraro (1970) reduced stereotypic attitudes by presenting examples of "counterstereotypic" behavior by individuals from various cultural groups, and by exposing students to the positive contributions of members of ethnic groups, respectively.

Because many students gain negative perceptions of others through stereotypes, it is important that teachers help students to understand and challenge the process of stereotyping in addition to learning about the group's experiences and history (Martin, 1987). Teachers can counter the deleterious effects of stereotyping by doing the following:

- inviting individuals who challenge stereotypes to speak to the class
- assigning students to read books and view videos that challenge stereotypes and address discrimination
- displaying pictures and materials that challenge stereotypes
- discussing and critiquing how language, books, television shows, commercials, cartoons, toys, and common everyday items (such as lunch boxes) create and foster stereotypes
- comparing items, images, and words and expressions regarding their portrayal of various groups
- discussing how stereotyping impacts perceptions and decisionmaking

- listing and discussing stereotypes that students have about others as well as the stereotypes that others have about them
- affirming and supporting students' awareness of stereotyping (Derman-Sparks, 1989; Martin, 1987)

Think About It

Think about a situation in which you were the target of stereotyping. What factors contributed to others holding that view about you? How did it make you feel? How did it affect the outcome of the situation?

Think about a situation in which you stereotyped someone. What factors contributed to you holding that stereotype? How did it make you feel? What would you do differently?

Teaching about Discrimination

An important aspect of learning about cultural diversity is learning about discrimination and its deleterious effects (Banks, 1991a; Schniedewind & Davidson, 1983). Teachers can help students learn about discrimination by having students experience it. For example, teachers can group students according to some arbitrary trait (e.g., hair color, eye color, type of clothing) and can then treat the groups in different ways in terms of rules, assignments, compliments, grading procedures, privileges, homework, and class jobs. Similarly, teachers can show students what it means to be discriminated against by assigning several groups the same task, while varying the resources each group is given to complete the task, so that the differential performance of the groups is related to resources rather than ability (Schniedewind & Davidson, 1983). Following these activities, teachers and students can discuss the effects of discrimination on individuals.

Banks (1991a) identifies a variety of resources and activities for teaching students about discrimination.

Group Discussions

Teachers also can help students learn about cultural diversity and the impact of discrimination and stereotyping through group discussion (Houlton, 1986). Case studies and short stories regarding various cultures and instances of discrimination can be used to stimulate group discussions (Vanderslice, Cherry, Cochran, & Dean, 1984). Through group discussion, students are exposed to a variety of perspectives, experiences, and ideas that help them reach conclusions, question and affirm their viewpoints, and value the contributions of others (Vanderslice et al., 1984). For example, Reissman (1992) used group discussions to help students learn about the ways newspapers cover various cultural and linguistic groups. Vanderslice et al. (1984) provide guidelines for leading group discussions, including initiating the discussion by presenting several key questions to students; establishing a comfortable environment that respects the contributions of all group members; asking students to respond to the comments of others; linking students' comments to the topic and to comments previously made by others; determining when to end the discussion; and summarizing the discussion. When using group discussions, teachers should establish several ground rules to guide the discussion, including be honest and open; avoid blaming others; speak for yourself; listen carefully to and be supportive of others; and challenge and disagree respectfully.

Responding to Stereotyping and Discrimination

"I'm going to make my eyes straight and blue," 4-year old Kim tells her teacher. "Why do you want to change your lovely eyes?" her teacher asks wonderingly. Kim: "It's prettier." Teacher: "Kim, I don't think straight eyes are prettier than yours are. Your mommy and daddy and grandpa don't think so either. We like you just the way you are, with your beautiful, dark brown eyes shaped just as they are. Why do you think straight and blue eyes are prettier?" Kim: "Sarah said I had ugly eyes, she likes Julie's better." Teacher: "Sarah is wrong to say you have ugly eyes. It's not true and it is unfair and hurtful to say so. In this classroom we respect how everyone looks. Let's go and talk with her about it" (Derman-Sparks, 1989, p. 34).

Once students learn about the negative effects of prejudice, they should be taught how to respond to stereotyping and discrimination. Teachers can establish an inclusive classroom environment by modeling acceptance of all students and by establishing a rule that an individual's gender, race, ethnicity, language skills, religion, dress, or socioeconomic status is not a reason for excluding or teasing them. If someone breaks the rule, teachers should act immediately to offer support to the student who has been discriminated against and help the student to articulate his or her reaction to the student(s) who are engaged in the exclusionary behavior, as well as help the excluding student(s) understand the detrimental effects of prejudice (Derman-Sparks, 1989).

Teachers also may encounter situations where students express a desire to change physical characteristics such as their color, sex, body size, hair texture, or eye color and shape. When encountering this, teachers should respond immediately by telling students that they are fine; by assuring students that others love them the way they are; by explaining to students that others who do not like them that way are wrong; by explaining to students that there are many people who have the same traits; and by confronting others who made negative statements that triggered the students' reactions (Derman-Sparks, 1989).

Teachers can use role playing to help students learn how to respond to instances of discrimination and stereotyping (Ford & Jones, 1990). For example, students can be presented with a situation that depicts a bias-related incident and asked to role play their responses to this situation. Following the role play, the students can discuss their experiences and reactions. Vanderslice et al. (1984) present guidelines for using role plays:

- Emphasize that there is no right or wrong behavior in a role play; everyone is acting. Remind participants that the goal is to enact a situation and to talk about the results.
- State the goal of and reason for using the technique. ("By acting out this situation, you will have the opportunity to observe and express some of the behaviors we have been discussing.")
- Describe the situation to be enacted clearly and in detail.
- Never force someone into assuming a role.
- Give the players written or verbal descriptions of their roles and provide observers with specific tasks such as watching the verbal and nonverbal responses of particular characters.
- Begin the action.
- Stop the action when enough has happened to stimulate discussion, the situation has been adequately illustrated, or the action has become dull or repetitive. When role plays become boring, their impact is diminished.
- Debrief the actors and observers. Ask each actor to describe his or her experience, response to particular behaviors, and feelings. Asking actors for their feelings before discussing the role play with the group lessens their anxiety about criticism. Ask the observers to report on what happened and encourage them to ask questions. Encourage the group members to discuss what happened in the role play, why it turned out the way it did, and whether they are satisfied with the way it turned out (pp. 49–50).

Think About It

Think about how you would respond to the following situations:

A student refuses to drink chocolate milk because she is afraid that it will turn her skin black.

Students are telling anti-Semitic jokes.

Students are using terms such as *Indian giver.*

Students are mimicking a student's accent.

Students are denying their racial, ethnic, or religious identities.

Students are teasing a male student who likes to sew.

ESTABLISHING FRIENDSHIPS

Stainback, Stainback, and Wilkinson (1992) suggest several strategies teachers can employ to establish classroom friendships and support systems.

A desired outcome of mainstreaming is the development of friendships and peer supports (Stainback, Stainback, & Wilkinson, 1992). Because mainstreamed students may have few friends and limited peer support (Gottlieb & Leyser, 1981), teachers and parents need to encourage the development of friendships and peer support systems for mainstreamed students who are isolated in their regular education classrooms (Perske & Perske, 1988; Strully & Strully, 1989).

Circles of Friends

Forest and Lusthaus (1989) suggest that teachers use *circles of friends* to encourage students to understand their support systems and to develop "a network that allows for the genuine involvement of children in a friendship, caring, and support role with their peers" (p. 47). To implement the circle of friends, teachers should do the following:

1. Give students a sheet with four concentric circles, with each circle progressively larger and farther away from the center of the sheet, which contains a drawing of a stick person. Tell students that the stick figure represents them.
2. Explain to students that each circle will represent a particular type of friendship.
3. Direct students to fill in the first circle (the one closest to the stick figure) by listing the people who they love and are closest to them.
4. Direct students to fill in the second circle by listing the people that they like, such as their best friends.
5. Direct students to fill in the third circle by listing groups that they like and do things with, like members of their teams or community organizations.
6. Direct students to fill in the fourth circle by listing individuals who are paid to be in their lives, such as doctor or teacher.
7. Ask students to share their circles and tell what roles people in each circle perform.
8. Describe the mainstreamed student and share the mainstreamed student's circle with the students.
9. Sensitize the students to the mainstreamed student's need for friends by having them compare their circle with the mainstreamed student's circle. Discuss how a student might feel if he or she had only a few names in the circles.
10. Ask students to suggest ways they could help the mainstreamed student.
11. Discuss the meaning and importance of friendship and peer support groups and how to make friends and establish peer support groups (Forest & Lusthaus, 1989; Fritz, 1990; O'Brien, Forest, Snow, Pearpoint, & Hasbury, 1989).

Friendships also can be promoted through use of cooperative learning groups (see Chapter 6).

Think About It

Make a circle of friends for yourself. How have your friends and support group assisted you during stressful times? What additional supports would be helpful? What other insights did you have about your support network?

Peer Support Committees

Some teachers have instituted peer support committees to address classroom social interaction problems and promote peer acceptance of mainstreamed students (DiMeo, Ryan, & Defanti, 1989). Peer support committees are charged with the responsibility of ensuring that all students are valued and accepted as contributing members in the class. The peer support committee identifies problems individual class members or the class as a whole are experiencing and devises strategies to alleviate these problems such as establishing buddy systems, peer helpers, and study partners. In addition, the committee brainstorms strategies for promoting friendships in the classroom (Stainback, Stainback, & Wilkinson, 1992). Typically, the membership on the committee is rotated so that each member of the class has an opportunity to serve.

Vaughn, McIntosh, and Spencer-Rowe (1991) suggest that peer support committees place a problem-solving box in the classroom. When students encounter a problem, they write it on a piece of paper, which is placed in the box. The peer support committee meets to offer solutions and alternatives to identified problems and shares these suggestions with other members of the class.

Class Cohesiveness

Friendships and acceptance of students also can be fostered by activities that promote a sense of class cohesiveness. These group activities facilitate acceptance by creating a class identity that recognizes the unique contributions of each class member. A list of activities that educators have used to promote class cohesiveness (Canfield & Wells, 1976) is provided in Figure 4.11.

Namecalling

Mainstreamed students may be the targets of namecalling. Ford and Jones (1990) observed that students were more likely to engage in ethnic name-

Teachers can use books to teach students about individual differences.

FIGURE 4.11
Activities to promote a sense of class cohesiveness

1. Create a class scrapbook that includes the work of or recognition of everyone in the class.
2. Make a class mural, having each student complete a part of the mural.
3. Construct a class tree. Each branch of the tree can contain a picture of a student or work produced by a student.
4. Compile a who's who in the class book. Each child can have a page in the book devoted to interests, achievements, etc.
5. Leave space in the room for a "Proud Of" bulletin board where students can hang up work they are proud of.
6. Set up a tutoring center. Students can advertise something that they can teach to others in the class.
7. Include student's names as spelling words.
8. Have a "class applause" where the whole class acknowledges the accomplishments or improvements of individual classmates.
9. Publish a class newspaper, with each student in the class contributing a piece or drawing during the school year.

Additional guidelines for implementing these and other activities can be obtained by consulting J. Canfield and H. C. Wells, *100 Ways to Enhance Self-Concept in the Classroom* (Englewood Cliffs, NJ: Prentice-Hall, 1976).

calling when they were experiencing academic and social problems. While mainstreamed students can learn to ignore namecalling, ignoring often results in the namecallers escalating their ridicule (Salend & Schobel, 1981). Additionally, teachers can discipline namecallers, but this method of dealing with namecalling emphasizes the negative and usually has only temporary results. Salend and Schobel (1981) have developed a positive approach to namecalling that teachers can employ, which involves implementing a series of activities to teach students the importance, meaning, derivation, and function of names as well as teaching the negative effects of calling others names.

SUMMARY

This chapter offered educators a variety of strategies for teaching students to accept individual differences. The chapter

- outlined the roles students can perform in facilitating the success of mainstreaming
- reviewed the research on peer attitudes toward mainstreamed students
- presented suggestions for strategies to assess attitudes toward mainstreamed students
- provided guidelines for teaching students to accept individual differences related to disability
- provided guidelines for teaching students to accept individual differences related to culture, language, gender, and socioeconomic status
- presented strategies for establishing friendships and peer support groups

RECOMMENDED READINGS

Antonak, R. F., & Livneh, H. (1988). *The measurement of attitudes toward people with disabilities: Methods, psychometrics and scales.* Springfield, IL: Charles C. Thomas.

Barnes, E., Berrigan, C., & Biklen, D. (1978). *What's the difference? Teaching positive attitudes toward people with disabilities.* Syracuse, NY: Human Policy Press.

Derman-Sparks, L. (1989). *Anti-bias curriculum.* Washington, DC: National Association for the Education of Young Children.

Diaz, J., Trotter, R., & Rivera, V. (1989). *The effects of migration on children: An ethnographic study.* Harrisburg, PA: Pennsylvania Department of Education, Division of Migrant Education.

Froschl, M., Colon, L., Rubin, E., & Sprung, B. (1984). *Including all of us: An early childhood curriculum about disability.* New York: Educational Equity Concepts.

Mack, C. (1988). Celebrate cultural diversity. *Teaching Exceptional Children, 21,* 40–43.

O'Brien, J., Forest, M., Snow, J., Pearpoint, J., & Hasbury, D. (1989). *Action for inclusion: How to improve schools by welcoming children with special needs in regular classrooms.* Toronto: Inclusion Press.

Pang, O. (1991). Teaching children about social issues: Kidpower. In C. Sleeter (Ed.), *Empowerment through multicultural education* (pp. 179–197). Albany, NY: State University of New York Press.

Schniedewind, N., & Davidson, E. (1983). *Open minds to equality: A sourcebook of learning activities to promote race, sex, class and age equity.* Englewood, NJ: Prentice-Hall.

Tiffany, J., Tobias, D., Raqib, A., & Ziegler, J. (1991). *Talking with kids about AIDS.* Ithaca, NY: Department of Human Services Studies at Cornell University.

5 Preparing Students for Success in Mainstream Settings

NICK

Nick is about to be mainstreamed into Mr. Roberts's sixth-grade class. Nick's special education teacher, Ms. Thomas, contacts Mr. Roberts to plan a program to help Nick make a successful transition to Mr. Roberts's class. They discuss and compare the essential components that contribute to success in their respective classrooms. Based on these similarities and differences, they target several skills and information that Nick will need to make a smooth adjustment to Mr. Roberts's class.

Although Nick will not enter Mr. Roberts's class for several weeks, Ms. Thomas and Mr. Roberts agree that they should begin the orientation program immediately. In her class, Ms. Thomas introduces Nick to the textbooks and assignments he will be encountering in Mr. Roberts's class. She starts to give Nick homework assignments and tests that parallel those given in Mr. Roberts's class.

They also have Nick visit Mr. Roberts's class and make a videocassette recording of a typical instructional session. Ms. Thomas reviews the video with Nick to discuss classroom procedures and other critical elements of the classroom environment. In addition to introducing Nick to the routines and expectations of the mainstreamed setting, Ms. Thomas uses the video to encourage Nick to discuss any questions and concerns he has about the new setting.

Ms. Thomas also uses the video to teach Nick appropriate note-taking skills. Initially, Nick and Ms. Thomas watch the video together while Ms. Thomas models how to take notes. To make sure Nick understands the different note-taking techniques and when to apply them, Ms. Thomas periodically stops the video and reviews with Nick why certain information is or is not recorded and why a specific format is used. As Nick's note-taking skills improve, Ms. Thomas attempts to have Nick apply his new skills in Mr. Roberts's class. Both she and Nick visit Mr. Roberts's class and take notes. After the class, they compare their notes, emphasizing the critical factors that make for good note taking.

What additional factors should educators consider when planning a transitional program to prepare students such as Nick for success in the mainstream? After reading this chapter, you should be able to answer this as well as the following questions.

- What is transenvironmental programming?
- How can educators determine the content of a transitional program?
- How can educators teach students to use learning strategies and textbooks?
- How can educators prepare students for the text comprehension, listening, note-taking, memory, independent work, organizational, behavioral, social, and language demands of mainstreamed settings?
- How can educators plan a program to help students who speak primary languages other than English make the transition to mainstreamed settings?
- How can educators promote generalization of skills?
- What factors should educators consider in helping students from specialized schools and early education programs make the transition to mainstream schools within their community?
- How can educators promote the successful transition of students who are exiting schools?

Beginnings are difficult. Mainstreaming means a new beginning for students. Students moving from one setting to another must learn to adjust to different instructional formats, curriculum demands, teaching styles, behavioral expectations, physical designs, and student socialization patterns (Anderson-Inman, 1986; Fuchs, Fuchs, Fernstrom, & Hohn, 1991). For example, a student is much more likely to receive individualized instruction in a special education or bilingual education class than in a regular education class and therefore may encounter difficulties in moving from one setting to another (Rose, Lesson, & Gottlieb, 1982). Similarly, a student moving from a special day school to an integrated program within the community's public school system or a postsecondary program will encounter new rules, extracurricular activities, and personnel at the new school (Salend, 1981b). Thus, learning the rules and schoolwide procedures prior to entering a new school can help avoid a potentially confusing and troublesome adjustment. It is essential, then, that students be prepared for entry into mainstream settings (Hundert, 1982; Lowenthal, 1987). This chapter offers a variety of strategies for helping students make the transitions to mainstreamed settings. While these strategies are appropriate for mainstreamed students, they also can be used to help all students function in mainstreamed settings.

TRANSENVIRONMENTAL PROGRAMMING

Anderson-Inman's (1986) four-step transenvironmental programming model can serve as an excellent framework for planning and delivering a program to prepare students for success in mainstreamed settings. The four steps in the model are environmental assessment, intervention and preparation, generalization to, and evaluation in the target environment. *Environmental assessment* involves determining the content of the training program by identifying the skills that facilitate success in the regular classroom. In the *intervention and preparation* phase, the objectives identified in the environmental assessment are taught to students using a variety of instructional strategies. After the skills have been learned, the next two steps are to *promote and evaluate* use of the skills in the regular classroom. Each step necessitates communication between special and mainstreamed educators. A sample transenvironmental programming model for a student is presented in Figure 5.1.

Determining Content of the Transitional Program

The transitional program developed from the environmental assessment should teach students about their new class placement and make their adjustment as easy as possible. The teacher should establish the content of the orientation program by analyzing the critical environmental features of the new learning environment. Salend and Viglianti (1982) have provided educators with a useful format to identify the dimensions of classrooms that affect student performance.

- instructional materials and support personnel
- presentation of subject matter
- learner response variables
- student evaluation
- classroom management
- social interactions
- physical design

For students from linguistically and culturally diverse backgrounds, educators also should consider the language used to deliver instruction as well as the cultural factors that affect performance.

FIGURE 5.1
Sample transenvironmental programming model

Regular Class	Special Class
Ms. G. uses textbooks, computers, and other instructional media.	Mr. K. should teach the student to use the textbooks and instructional media.
Ms. G. requires students to complete worksheets.	Mr. K. should teach the student to work independently and be familiar with the format of the worksheets.
Students interact with each other during recess.	Mr. K should teach the student to initiate and engage in play with others.
Ms. G. expects students to raise their hands before speaking.	Mr. K. should teach the student to follow the rules of the regular class.
Ms. G. gives an hour of homework three times per week.	Mr. K. should give the student an hour of homework three times per week.
Ms. G. gives weekly spelling tests that include dictated sentences.	Mr. K should make sure the student can write dictated sentences.
Ms. G. occasionally praises students for appropriate behavior.	Mr. K. should wean the student from his token system and praise the student periodically.
Ms. G. presents information through lectures and expects students to take notes.	Mr. K. should teach the student listening and note-taking skills.

An educator can complete the form presented in Figure 5.2, observing a variety of variables related to the mainstreamed setting. Although educators can obtain most of the information to complete the form by observing the future learning environment, they can acquire some background material by meeting with classroom teachers. Educators also should assess additional characteristics of the regular program such as routines in the cafeteria and at assemblies, movement between classes, and expectations in physical education, art, and music classes.

Wood and Miederhoff (1989) and George and Lewis (1991) have developed checklists that can help teachers plan the transition to mainstreamed settings.

The determination of the content and sequence of the transitional program should be a shared responsibility among educators. The program should be individualized to address the skills of the mainstreamed student as well as the characteristics of the regular education milieu. Some students may need instruction in numerous transitional skills; others may require training in a limited number of areas. In planning the preparation program, educators also may need to prioritize the skills to be taught and identify which skills will be taught prior to and after the student has been placed into the mainstreamed setting.

Some schools have included a classmate on the placement team to assist in identifying the content that should comprise the transitional program

FIGURE 5.2
Classroom Variables Analysis Form

Teacher:____________________ **Subject:**____________________
Grade:____________________ **Date:**____________________
Teacher Completing the Observation:____________

A. INSTRUCTIONAL MATERIALS AND SUPPORT PERSONNEL

1. What textbooks are used in the class? What are the grade levels of the texts?

2. What supplementary materials are used in the class? What are the grade levels of the supplementary materials?

3. What types of media are frequently used in the classroom?
   _____television
   _____films
   _____filmstrips
   _____slides
   _____overhead projector
   _____record player
   _____audio tapes
   _____others (please list)
   ____
   ____
   ____

4. What type(s) of support personnel are available in the classroom? How often are they available?
   _____aide
   _____volunteer
   _____peer tutor
   _____others (please list)
   ____
   ____
   ____

B. PRESENTATION OF SUBJECT MATTER

1. How often does the teacher . . . *% of time*
   a. lecture? ________
   b. use the blackboard? ________
   c. use individualized instruction? ________
   d. use small group instruction? ________
   e. use large group instruction? ________
   f. use individual centers? ________
   g. others (please list) ________
   ________________ ________
   ________________ ________
   ________________ ________

2. What is the language and vocabulary level used by the teacher?

C. LEARNER RESPONSE VARIABLES

1. How often is the student required to . . . *% of time*
   a. take notes? ________
   b. copy from the board? ________
   c. read aloud in class? ________
   d. do independent work? ________
   e. participate in class? ________
   f. others (please list) ________
   ________________ ________
   ________________ ________
   ________________ ________

2. In what ways can a student request assistance in the classroom?

FIGURE 5.2
(continued)

3. How are directions given to students? How many directions are given at one time?

D. STUDENT EVALUATION

1. How often and in what ways does the teacher evaluate student progress?
2. How are grades determined?
3. What types of tests are given?
   ______essay
   ______true/false
   ______multiple choice
   ______matching
   ______completion
   ______oral
   ______simple recall
   ______fill in
   ______other
4. Does the teacher assign homework?
   a. What type?
   b. How much?
   c. How often?
5. Does the teacher assign special projects or extra-credit work? Please explain.

E. CLASSROOM MANAGEMENT

1. Does the teacher have a management system? Briefly describe it.
2. What are the stated rules in the classroom?
3. What are the unstated rules in the classroom?
4. What are the consequences of following the rules? What are the consequences of not following the rules?
5. In what ways and how often does the teacher reinforce the students?
6. Does the teacher follow any special routines? What are they?

F. SOCIAL INTERACTIONS

1. How often are student interactions . . . *% of time*
   a. individualistic? __________
   b. cooperative? __________
   c. competitive? __________
2. What are the student norms in this class concerning . . .
   a. dress?
   b. appearance?
   c. interests?
   d. acceptance of individual differences?
   e. other unique relevant characteristics? Please list.

FIGURE 5.2
(continued)

3. What are the students' attitudes toward the handicapped?

4. What is the language and vocabulary level of the students?

5. What personality variables does the teacher exhibit that seem to affect the class?

G. PHYSICAL DESIGN

1. What, if any, architectural barriers are in the classroom?

2. How does the design affect the students' . . .
   a. academic performance?
   b. social interactions?

Source: S. J. Salend and D. Viglianti, *Teaching Exceptional Children* (Reston, VA: Council for Exceptional Children, 1982), pp. 138–139. Reprinted by permission of the publisher.

(McNeil, Thousand, & Bove, 1989). The student member of the team can provide input in such areas as books and materials needed, social interaction patterns, class routines, and student dress. Peers also can be instrumental in welcoming and orienting students to their new environment.

Think About It

Think about your transition from high school to college. How are those two educational settings different? What problems did you experience in making the transition to college? How did peers help you in making the transition? What should be the content of a program to help students make the transition from one school setting to another?

Teaching Transitional Skills

Once educators have determined the objectives of the training program, they should implement the orientation program. The objectives could be specified in the student's IEP and instruction should begin prior to the student's placement in the mainstream. Additionally, once the student is placed in the mainstream, teachers should continue to monitor them, teaching new and reviewing old transitional skills as necessary.

Learning Strategies

Ms. Washington, a seventh-grade teacher, has noticed that several of her students are not physically and mentally prepared for class. She observes the students closely for several days to determine exactly what skills and strategies they employ successfully and what ones they appear to lack. She then meets with the students to talk about her concerns, and how their current approaches are affecting their performance. Though initially reluctant, the students indicate that they aren't pleased with their classroom performance and "would like to do better." She discusses with them a strategy that she thinks would help them called PREP and explains to students how it might help them. PREP, a learning strategy, involves students executing four stages:

*P*repare materials

- Get notebook, study guide, pencil, and textbook ready for class
- Mark difficult-to-understand parts of notes, study guide, and textbook

*R*eview what you know

- Read notes, study guide, and textbook cues
- Relate cues to what you already know about the topic
- List at least three things you already know about the topic

*E*stablish positive mind set

- Tell yourself to learn
- Suppress "put-downs"
- Make a positive statement

*P*inpoint goals

- Decide what you want to find out
- Note participation goals (Ellis, 1989, p. 36)

After reviewing the strategy and briefly explaining each step to the students, Ms. Washington asks the students to decide if they are willing to make a commitment to learning this strategy. One student says, "No" and Ms. Washington tells her she does not have to learn it but if she changes her mind, she can learn it another time. The other students indicate that they were willing to try to learn the strategy. To increase their motivation and reinforce their commitment to learning the strategy, Ms. Washington has the students set goals.

Ms. Washington begins by modeling and demonstrating the strategy by verbalizing and "thinking out loud" so that students can experience the thinking processes they would need to engage in when implementing the strategy. She models the procedure several times using a variety of materials from the class and reviews how she uses the PREP acronym as an mnemonic to remember the steps in the strategy. Students discuss how the PREP strategy compares with their current approaches to learning as well as the overt and covert behaviors necessary to implement the strategy.

Next, Ms. Washington has the students attempt to learn the steps of the strategy. She divides them into teams and has each team rehearse and memorize the strategy and its proper sequence. To help some students learn the strategy, she gives them cue cards. As students memorize the steps, Ms. Washington gives them cue cards with less information on them. When the students can verbalize the steps in their proper sequence, Ms. Washington has students practice applying the strategy with materials from the classroom. Students work in cooperative learning groups to practice the strategy and receive feedback from their peers. She circulates around the room and observes students using the strategy and also provides feedback to students. She encourages the students to concentrate on becoming proficient and fluent in using the strategy and not to be concerned about the accuracy of the instructional content. As students increase their proficiency in performing the steps in the strategy, Ms. Washington gives them other materials so that they can apply the strategy in a variety of situations. When students are able to apply the strategy across a variety of materials, Ms. Washington gives them a test to check on their mastery of the material.

Once students master the strategy, Ms. Washington encourages them to use it in her class. She observes her students to see if they are employing the strategy and keeps records of their academic performance. Periodically, Ms. Washington reviews the strategy procedures. She cues students to use the strategy through verbal reminders, cue cards, listing the strategy on the board, and reviewing the components of the strategy. Because the strategy has led to a significant positive increase in the students' performance, Ms. Washington is working with some of the other teachers to help students use the strategy in their classrooms.

Much of the content of the training program may include the teaching of learning strategies. *Learning strategies* are "techniques, principles, or rules that will facilitate the acquisition, manipulation, integration, storage, and retrieval of information across situations and settings" (Alley & Deshler, 1979, p. 13). Rather than teaching a specific content area, learning strategy instruction teaches students how to learn. For example, DISSECT, a word identification learning strategy, can be taught to students to help them determine the meaning of unknown words (Lenz, Deshler, Schumaker, & Beals, 1984). The steps in DISSECT are as follows:

D = Discover the context

I = Isolate the prefix

S = Separate the suffix

S = Say the stem

E = Examine the stem using the rules of 2s and 3s: If a stem or part of the stem begins with a vowel, divide off the first two letters; if it begins with a consonant, divide off the first three letters

C = Check with someone

T = Try the dictionary (Ellis & Lenz, 1987, p. 101)

In determining if a specific learning strategy should be included in the transitional program educators should ask the following questions:

- Is the strategy critical for success in the regular classroom?
- Is the strategy required in multiple settings?
- Does the strategy enable the student to solve problems independently? (Crank & Keimig, 1988)

Clark, Deshler, Schumaker, Alley, and Warner (1984) and Mutch (1989) provide a model for teaching learning strategies that educators can employ to prepare students for success in mainstreamed settings. The model includes the following:

- allowing students to perform a task without instruction to assess the student's skill level
- assisting students in realizing the problems associated with their current strategy
- explaining the new strategy and its advantages as compared to the old strategy
- demonstrating the strategy for students
- teaching students to verbally rehearse the strategy
- providing the students with the opportunities to practice the strategies with materials written at their level and then with materials used in the regular classroom setting
- offering feedback on the student's use of the strategy
- posttesting students to ensure mastery of the strategy

Specific guidelines for implementing these steps and promoting generalization in the use of the strategy are available (Ellis, Lenz, & Sabornie, 1987).

Attribution Training

Attribution training also can promote student effort and persistence (Dweck, 1975).

The effectiveness of learning strategies can be enhanced by combining learning strategy instruction with attributional training (Borkowski, Weyhing, & Carr, 1989). Attribution training involves teaching students to analyze the events and actions that contribute to successful and unsuccessful outcomes. Students who understand attribution recognize and acknowledge that their positive performance is due to effort (*I spent a lot of time studying for this test.*), ability (*I'm good at social studies.*), and other internal factors, whereas students who fail to understand attribution often interpret their poor performance as a result of bad luck (*I got the hardest test.*), teacher error (*The teacher didn't teach that.*), low ability (*I'm not good at math.*), or other external factors. Teachers can help students learn to engage in attribution training by teaching them 1) to understand the importance of attributions and effort on performance, 2) to view failure as an initial aspect of learning and a sign to increase effort, and 3) to assume responsibility for successful outcomes (Fulk & Mastropieri, 1990).

Think About It

What learning strategies do you use? Are they successful? How did you learn these strategies?

Preteaching

Anderson-Inman (1986) suggests that students can be prepared for the academic expectations of the regular classroom through preteaching. *Preteaching* entails the special or bilingual educator employing the curriculum, teaching style, and instructional format of the regular classroom in the special or bilingual education classroom. The transitional program should introduce the student to the content of the regular education curriculum as well as the instructional formats (commercially produced instructional programs, media, software) that are employed in the mainstreamed setting. Therefore, as part of the transitional program, educators should obtain and review the objectives, sequence, learning activities, and other relevant parts of the regular education curriculum. Similarly, a meeting with the regular education teachers should be convened to discuss the skills currently covered in the curriculum, as well as the assignments and materials used to teach these skills.

USING REGULAR CLASSROOM TEXTBOOKS

Students should be exposed to the textbooks and the instructional materials used in the regular classroom. In addition to using the textbook as part of the instructional program in the present student's educational setting, educators can prepare students to use the text by carefully analyzing several dimensions such as content, method of presentation, supplementary materials, and format (Burnette, 1987). Teachers should examine the vocabulary and concept development that students will need to use the book and teach students how to identify and define these terms. For example, the teacher and the student can review chapters from the book, selecting key terms and concepts that they can define by using the book's glossary or another resource, such as a dictionary or an encyclopedia. When students demonstrate proficiency at this task, they should be encouraged to perform the steps without teacher assistance.

Allen, Wilson, Cefalo, and Larson (1990) suggest that students learn a keywords strategy that involves the following steps:

Read the statement

Identify the important words using clues such as

- Is it a person, place or thing?
- Does it describe or emphasize the content and/or explain what to do?
- Are the words or phrases highlighted (italicized, underlined, in quotes, boldfaced, or enumerated)?

Mark the important words and/or phrases

Self-check by asking

- Do the keywords and/or phrases contain critical information?

An understanding of the organization of textbooks can assist students in effectively and efficiently comprehending the information presented (Meyer, Brandt, & Bluth, 1979). Because information is presented in a similar fashion from chapter to chapter in a textbook, reviewing the organization of the textbook also can help students. This task can be accomplished by reviewing and explaining the functions of and the interrelationships among the book's components (the table of contents, text, glossary, index, appendices) and the elements of the book's chapters (titles, objectives, abstracts, headings, summary, study guides, followup questions, references, alternative learning activities). Because students will be working with several books that may have different formats, students should be exposed to the components of different books they will be using (Gleason, 1988).

In learning about a textbook, it may be helpful to teach students the strategies employed by the author(s) to present content (Spargo, 1977). Vaca, Vaca, and Gove (1987) suggest that students should receive instruction to help them identify five patterns that are typically used by authors: enumeration, time order, comparison-contrast, cause-effect, and problem solution. These strategies are often repeated throughout the book, so students can be taught to analyze a book by examining: the numbering (*1, 2, 3*), lettering (*a, b, c*) or word (*first, second, third*) system used to show the relative importance of information as well as the order of ideas; the typographic signs (*boldfacing, underlining, color cuing, boxing*) employed to highlight critical information; and the word signals that indicate the equal importance of information (*furthermore, likewise*), elaboration (*moreover*), rebuttal and clarification (*nevertheless, however, but*), summarization (*therefore, consequently*), and termination (*finally, in conclusion*) (Spargo, 1977).

Many textbooks often have accompanying supplemental materials such as student activity worksheets and overviews. Therefore, students should receive some training in completing the activity worksheets and interpreting information presented in graphic displays. Archer (1988) and Allen et al. (1990) suggest that teachers can help students learn to complete end-of-chapter questions by training them to do the following:

- read each question to determine what is being asked
- identify words in the question that can guide the reader to the correct answer
- determine the requirement of the question and the format of the answer
- convert appropriate parts of the question into part of the answer

IDEAS FOR IMPLEMENTATION	Teachers can help students identify and use the organization of a textbook by enacting the following suggestions:
	• Discuss with students relationships in everyday situations. • Explain how relationships are established and information is organized in textbooks. • Teach the key words that indicate relationships. • Question students to show how information is interrelated. • Teach students to ask questions that identify relationships. • Offer time for practice. • Orient students to the sequence, repetition, and length of the material presented in the chapters of the text. • Teach students to examine the directions given and objectives specified as well as the internal and end-of-chapter assignments. • Have students under the direction of the teacher identify the relationship between the objectives, content, and study questions in a chapter and predict some study questions based on the objectives.

Source: Meyer (1984).

- identify the paragraphs of the chapter that relate to the question
- locate the answer to the question by reading the chapter
- write the answer to the question
- check the answer for accuracy and form

Learning to look for highlighted information that is usually italicized or boldfaced also can help students identify main points that often contain answers to study questions.

Visual Aids

Additionally, textbooks provide information in the form of graphs, charts, tables, and other illustrations. Pauk (1984) suggests that teachers can show students how to gain information from visual displays by previewing the graphics to obtain a general idea of its purpose; by reading the title, captions, and headings to determine relevant information about the graphic; by identifying the units of measurement; and by relating and generalizing graphical information to the text. Barry, cited in Ellis and Lenz (1987), developed the *Reading Visual Aids Strategy* (*RVAS*) to assist students in gaining information from graphic presentations. The strategy involves the following activities:

R = Read the written material until you are referred to a visual aid or until the material is not making sense

V = View the visual aid using CLUE:
- C = Clarify the stated facts in the written material
- L = Locate the main ideas (global) and details (specific parts)

U = Uncover the signal words (look for captions or words in the visual aid)
E = Examine the logic (Does what you "read" make sense with what you read in the material?)

A = Ask yourself the relationship between the visual aid and the written material using FUR:
F = Ask how the visual aid and the written material" fit" together
U = Ask how the visual aid can help you "understand" the written material
R = Ask how the visual aid can help you "remember" the written material

S = Summarize most important information (Ellis & Lenz, 1987, p. 98)

Think About It

How is this book organized to present information to the reader? What strategies does the author use to highlight information? What aspects of the textbook help promote student learning?

Text Comprehension Strategies

Many text comprehension strategies require students to identify the main ideas of the reading selections.

Because many mainstreamed students may have difficulty reading the textbooks used in the regular education setting, teachers will need to train them in comprehension skills. Since many students may need training in finding the main idea (Baumann, 1982), teachers can foster an ability to identify main ideas.

- Have students select the best title for short and then longer selections.
- Discuss how to identify the main idea in a paragraph.
- Assign students the task of writing headlines for passages and newspaper articles.
- Teach students the relationship between headings, subheadings, topic sentences, and main ideas.
- Encourage students to focus on information presented in introductory and summary paragraphs (Harris & Sipay, 1985).

Because the main idea of a paragraph is usually embedded in the topic sentence, students should be taught to identify the topic sentence by locating the initial sentence of the paragraph. However, sometimes the topic sentence is located in the middle or at the end of the paragraph, so students also should learn to identify main points by looking for repetitions of the same word or words throughout the paragraph (Crank & Keimig, 1988).

Anderson-Inman (1986) suggests several steps for teaching textbook comprehension skills to mainstreamed students:

- Prioritize with the student the textbooks to be used.
- Discuss with the regular classroom teacher and analyze the textbooks to determine the most important comprehension skills needed.
- Employ appropriate instructional materials and strategies to teach the necessary skills.
- Provide training in the skill with the textbooks the student will be using in the regular classroom.

Several strategies that teachers can employ to overcome difficulties in acquiring information from print materials are available and are described here.

Surveying

Surveying a reading assignment from the textbook can facilitate understanding of the content of the passage. The *SQ3R* technique can assist students in surveying reading material (Robinson, 1969). This technique consists of five steps: survey, question, read, recite, and review.

Survey. Surveying allows the reader to look for clues to the content of information presented in the chapter. In surveying, the reader should do the following:

- Examine the title of the chapters and try to anticipate what information will be presented.
- Read the first paragraph to try to determine the objectives of the chapter.
- Review the headings and subheadings to identify main points.
- Analyze visual aids to determine relevant supporting information and related details.
- Read the final paragraph to summarize main points.

Question. Questioning helps the reader to continue to identify important content. Students can formulate questions by restating headings and subsection titles as questions as well as basing them on their own reactions to the material.

Read. Reading enables the learner to examine the section more closely and to answer the questions composed in the questioning phase.

Recite. Reciting assists the student in recalling the information for further use. In this step, students should be encouraged to study the information they have just covered.

Review. Reviewing also aids the student in remembering the content of the book. This can be accomplished by having the students prepare an oral or written summary of the main topics presented in the section.

Bradstad and Stumpf (1987) provide excellent guidelines for training students to learn each step involved in using SQ3R.

Multipass

A modified version of SQ3R that has been employed successfully by students with learning disabilities is multipass (Schumaker, Deshler, Denton, Alley, Clark, & Warner, 1982). The multipass technique encourages students to review the content of a reading selection three times. The first, or *survey* pass, orients the reader to the structure and organization of the selection. In making the first pass, the student previews the material by examining the chapter title, introductory and summary paragraphs, headings, visual displays, and organization of the chapter. The survey pass concludes with the student paraphrasing the content of the selection.

The second review, the *size-up* pass, is designed to help the student identify the critical content to be learned from the chapter. The student reads the chapter questions; those that the student can answer after the initial pass are checked off. The student then surveys the material to locate the answers to those questions that do not have checkmarks by paying attention to cues, phrasing cued information as a question, skimming paragraphs to determine the answers, and paraphrasing the answer and all the material that can be remembered.

In the final, or *sort-out* pass, the student once more reads the selection and answers the accompanying student questions. Again, the student checks off each completed question and moves on until all questions are answered.

Other similar techniques, such as SOS (Schumaker, Deshler, Alley, & Warner, 1983), PANORAMA (Edwards, 1973), OK5R (Pauk, 1984), and PQST (Pauk, 1984), also can be taught to students.

Self-Questioning

Several self-questioning procedures have been effective in promoting comprehension skills (Reetz & Crank, 1988; Wong & Jones, 1982). Wong and Jones (1982) increased the comprehension abilities of students with learning disabilities by training them to use a self-questioning technique that involved determining the reasons for studying the passage, identifying by underlining the passage's main ideas, generating a question associated with the main idea and writing it in the margin, finding the answer to the question and writing it in the margin, and reviewing all the questions and answers. Similarly, an adapted version of self-questioning, whereby students paraphrase the main idea and identify essential details after underlining the main idea, also was successful in promoting the comprehension skills of students (Wong, Wong, Perry, & Sawatsky, 1986).

Another self-questioning technique was developed and evaluated at the Institute for Research in Learning Disabilities at Kansas University (Clark et al., 1984). In applying this procedure to written material, students are taught to compose and give symbols for who, what, where, when, and why questions; and find and denote the correct answers to the questions by placing the corresponding symbol in the correct location of the text.

Reetz and Crank (1988) propose another type of self-questioning strategy. In this technique, students read a part or title of a section and devise questions based on what they have read, continue reading the rest of the section to find the answer to their questions, and repeat the answers to their questions to ensure retention. Upon completion of the self-questioning phase, the teacher checks students' comprehension of the material.

Cohen et al. (1973) propose using a main-idea questioning strategy to facilitate text comprehension. This questioning strategy requires students to identify the main point of a paragraph and phrase it as a question, the answer to which summarizes the relevant information presented in the selection. Cohen and her colleagues provide excellent activities for teaching students how to generate questions. Other self-questioning techniques include identifying several questions related to a reading selection that students might ask a friend, and asking questions that relate to the structure of the text, such as "What is the setting?" (Graham & Johnson, 1989).

Paraphrasing

Another learning strategy that can assist students to acquire information from print materials is paraphrasing (Herr, 1988). Schumaker, Denton, and Deshler (1984) found that teaching students with learning disabilities to paraphrase significantly improved their correct responses to grade-level appropriate comprehension questions. Paraphrasing requires the student to read a section of text, ask questions about the section to determine the main idea and corresponding relevant information, and paraphrase the responses to these questions in their own words. Paraphrased statements should be communicated in a complete sentence; be correct and logical; provide new and useful information; and be stated in the student's words (Schumaker et al., 1984).

Scanning

Scanning abilities can help students learn to respond to review and preview questions in textbooks. To help students develop scanning skills, teachers should teach them how to search out and interpret key content, such as graphic displays, titles, headings, introductory and summary paragraphs, and italicized information.

Outlining

Students can gain information from textbooks by learning to outline chapters. Outlining allows students to identify, sequence, and group main and secondary points so they can better understand what they have read. Students should learn to use a separate outline for each topic, delineate essential parts of a topic using Roman numbers, present subtopics by subdividing each main heading using capital letters, and group information within a subdivision in a sequence using numbers (Fisher, 1967), as shown in Figure 5.3. Spargo (1977) offers an outline format where the left-hand margin contains all the main points with a brief explanation. Students record and easily review supporting information relative to each main point as an indented subheading. Teachers can train students to outline by having students complete a teacher-generated partially completed outline (Roe, Stodt, & Burns, 1983). As students become successful, the teacher can decrease involvement in creating the outline as the student takes over the task.

FIGURE 5.3
Sample outlining format

I. Main Point
  A. Subtopic
  B. Subtopic
II. Main Point
  A. Subtopic
    1. Supporting information
    2. Supporting information
    3. Supporting information

Summarizing

Another approach to teaching text comprehension skills recently found to be effective with students is summarization (Gajria, 1988). Brown, Campione, and Day (1981) and Gajria (1988) identified several basic rules students can employ in summarizing text:

- identify and group main points
- eliminate information that is repeated or unnecessary
- find the topic sentence
- devise topic sentences for paragraphs that are missing one
- delete phrases and sentences that fail to present new or relevant information

When students are working on complex textual material, Malone and Mastropieri (1992) suggest that they use a self-monitoring card to prompt their use of summarization. Thistlethwaite (1991) provides a six-phase model for teaching students to use summarization.

Paragraph Restatements

Another form of summarization that students can learn is paragraph restatements, which Jenkins, Heliotis, Stein, and Haynes (1987) found significantly improved students' reading comprehension of narrative passages. Paragraph restatements help students actively process reading material by encouraging them to devise original sentences that summarize the main points of the reading selection. The sentences should include the fewest words possible, and can be written in the textbook, recorded as notes on a separate sheet, or constructed mentally. Jenkins et al. (1987) provides guidelines for teaching students to use paragraph restatements.

Critical Thinking Maps

Critical thinking maps can help students interpret and comprehend textbook information. Idol (1987a) improved the skills of students with reading comprehension problems by teaching them to use a critical thinking map. Students complete the map during or after reading the selection by listing the following:

- the main point(s) of the selection
- the important facts, actions, examples, events, or steps that lead to and support the main point(s)
- their interpretations, opinions, and prior knowledge with respect to the content of the chapter as well as any additional viewpoints of the author
- their conclusions concerning the information presented
- the relationship between the information presented and events and issues in society and their lives

Guidelines for teaching students to use this procedure are available (Idol, 1987a).

Guided Probing

Idol-Maestas (1985) increased students' comprehension of factual, sequential, and inferential questions by teaching them to apply a guided probe technique called *TELLS Fact or Fiction.* The TELLS Fact or Fiction procedure involves the following questions and activities:

T	Title	What is the title? Does it give a clue as to what the story is about?
E	Examine	Look through each page of the story. Skim for clues.
L	Look	Look for important words. Talk about what they mean.
L	Look	Look for hard words. Practice saying them and talk about what they mean.
S	Setting	What is the setting of the story? When did it take place? Where did it take place?
Fact or Fiction		Is it a true story (Fact) or is this a pretend story (Fiction)? (Idol-Maestas, 1985, p. 246).

After implementing the guided probe, students read the selection and answer corresponding comprehension questions.

Visual Imagery

Some students may be able to improve their reading comprehension skills by using visual imagery (Clark, et al., 1984; Rose, Cundick, & Higbee, 1983). Visual imagery requires the student to read a section of a book, create an image for every sentence read, contrast each new image with the prior one, and evaluate the images to make sure they are complete. Rose et al. (1983) improved the text comprehension skills of students with learning disabilities by using a visual imagery strategy that taught them to "pause after reading a few sentences, close their eyes, and make pictures ... in their mind about what they had read." (p. 353). Fredericks (1986) offers a sequence of activities that teachers can use to instruct students in learning how to use visual imagery, including asking students to create visual images for concrete objects, having students visualize familiar objects and settings, asking students to create images while listening to high imagery stories, and having students devise images as they read.

Verbal Rehearsal

Verbal rehearsal also can improve students' text comprehension skills (Rose et al., 1983). Verbal rehearsal involves students pausing after reading several sentences to themselves and verbalizing to themselves the selection's content. Initially, teachers can cue students to engage in verbal rehearsal by placing red dots at various places in the selection.

Think About It

Apply the various text comprehension strategies presented using material in this textbook or a textbook that corresponds to the grade(s) and subject matter you would like to teach. Which strategies were the easiest to implement? Which strategies were most effective?

Note Taking from Textbooks

Proper note-taking skills from textbooks also can be an invaluable aid for students in acquiring information from their textbook. A good method to teach students to take notes from their textbooks is to set up a margin, about two inches from the left side of the paper, into which they can jot questions based on the information presented in the chapter, on chapter subheadings, and on discussion/study questions. Students also should use this column to list vocabulary words and their definitions. They should use the rest of the page to record answers to the identified questions and other critical information from the chapter.

If allowed by the school, highlighting information in a textbook can increase the student's ability to comprehend, evaluate, and remember information presented (Spargo, 1977). This form of note taking can help the student identify parts of a chapter that are critical for class sessions and can assist in studying for exams. Examples of these guidelines for highlighting are presented in Figure 5.4.

Think About It

Look back at the notes you have taken for this book. What note-taking strategies did you employ? How well do you use these strategies? Which note-taking strategies do you find to be most efficient?

TEACHING STUDY AND BEHAVIORAL SKILLS

Listening Skills

Gearheart and Weishahn (1984) estimated that students spend 66% of their school time engaged in listening activities.

Students in elementary and secondary education classrooms spend much of their school day listening. Good listening skills help students follow oral directions and receive information from teachers and their peers. However, many students may initially lack the necessary listening skills to participate

FIGURE 5.4
Guidelines for highlighting textbook information

Explanation and Description	Symbols, Markings, and Notations
1. Use double lines under words or phrases to signify main ideas.	Radiation can produce mutations . . .
2. Use single lines under words or phrases to signify supporting material.	comes from cosmic rays . . .
3. Mark small circled numbers near the initial word of an underlined group of words to indicate a series of arguments, facts, ideas—either main or supporting.	Conditions change . . . ① rocks rise . . . ② some sink . . . ③ the sea dashes . . . ④ strong winds . . .
4. Rather than underlining a group of three or more important lines, use a vertical bracket in the margin.	had known . . . who gave . . . the time . . . of time . . .
5. Use one asterisk in the margin to indicate ideas of special importance, and two for ideas of unusual importance. Reserve three asterisks for principles and high-level generalizations.	*When a nuclear blast is . . . **People quite close to the . . . ***The main cause of mutations . . .
6. Circle key words and terms.	The genes are the . . .
7. Box words of enumeration and transition.	fourth, the lack of supplies . . . furthermore, the shortage . . .
8. Place a question mark in the margin opposite lines you do not understand as a reminder to ask the instructor for clarification.	? The latest . . . cold period . . . about 1,000,000 . . . Even today . . .
9. If you disagree with a statement, indicate that in the margin.	Disagree Life became . . . on land only . . . 340 million years . . .
10. Use the top and bottom margins of a page to record ideas of your own that are prompted by what you read.	Why not use carbon dating? Check on reference of fossils found in Tennessee stone quarry.
11. On sheets of paper that are smaller than the pages of the book, write longer thoughts or summaries; then insert them between the pages.	Fossils Plants : 500,000,000 years old Insects : 260,000,000 " " Bees : 100,000,000 " " True Fish : 330,000,000 " " Amphibians : 300,000,000 " " Reptiles : 300,000,000 " " Birds : 150,000,000 " "
12. Even though you have underlined the important ideas and supporting materials, still jot brief cues in the side margins.	Adapt – . . . . fossil – . . . . layer – . . . .

IDEAS FOR IMPLEMENTATION	In highlighting information from written material, the student should be taught to employ the following strategies: • Be selective. • Employ a double underline system to identify relevant main points and a single underline to denote supporting statements. • Summarize information from visual displays by writing a brief synopsis in the margin. • Delineate important sections by using brackets. • Use a symbol to identify essential facts (*) or information that needs further clarification (?). • Number items presented in a list or series. • Write abbreviations in the margins to identify definitions (*def.*) or content relating to visual displays (*vis.*). • Indicate that a similar point has already been made by placing vertical line segments in the margin. • Circle key terminology. • Record reactions and questions in the margins.

Source: Adler (1969); Pauk (1984); Spargo (1977).

fully in the regular education program (Loban, 1976). Consequently, an orientation program for students also should promote the development of listening skills. Research indicates that listening skills can be taught to a wide range of students using a variety of strategies (Alley & Deshler, 1979). Several of these strategies are described here.

Paraphrasing

Students can be taught to receive and follow directions by learning to paraphrase oral information (Wallace & Kauffman, 1986). Paraphrasing requires students to receive the information, then convert it into words that they can understand. Paraphrasing skills can be taught by asking students to paraphrase directions, assignment instructions, or peer comments. As students improve their paraphrasing skills, the complexity of the verbal message should be increased to match the levels used in the regular classroom.

Questioning

Students will need to ask questions to help clarify information missed during a verbal presentation. Therefore, students should be taught the appropriate times to ask questions; the correct ways to ask questions; and the value of meeting with the teacher after class to discuss material (Alley & Deshler, 1979).

Using Cues

Both nonverbal and verbal cues can aid listening skills (Alley & Deshler, 1979). *Nonverbal* cues, such as eye contact and gestures, as well as awareness of the reactions of others in the audience, are skills that can increase a student's ability to gain verbal information. For example, if a student observes others in the class looking intently at the teacher, it should indicate the need to listen carefully to the teacher's comments. Similarly, students should be taught how to respond to *verbal* cues, such as pacing, inflection, and loudness. Additionally, students should learn the words and statements that teachers use to highlight and organize key points. Alley and Deshler (1979) suggest that teachers use a videocassette recorder to teach these skills because it allows students to experience different speaking styles, and can be stopped and replayed to demonstrate key points.

Screening

An efficient listener knows how to distinguish relevant from nonessential points of a verbal presentation. Successful listening involves the ability to learn to listen for ideas in addition to facts, to judge the speaker's comments rather than the speaker's style, to be flexible, and to concentrate and pay attention and avoid being distracted by extraneous stimuli (Communication Briefings, 1989a).

Students can learn to screen information by listening for phrases that suggest critical information ("This is important."; "Do you understand?"; "I want you to remember this."). Alley and Deshler (1979) noted that teachers can use several activities to help students identify main points.

1. Have the student listen to a short selection and suggest a title.
2. Tell a short story and have students summarize it in one sentence.
3. Give three statements, one containing a main idea and two containing subordinate ideas. Have students identify each statement.
4. Have students listen to a class presentation on videotape and identify the main ideas. In the beginning, students should be presented with a worksheet from which they can choose the main idea. Students should discuss why each of the other choices is not a main idea (too general, too specific, irrelevant, inaccurate, and so on) (pp. 295–296).

TQLR

Tonjes and Zintz (1981) recommend a technique called *TQLR:* students are taught to listen by *t*uning in, *q*uestioning, *l*istening, and *r*eviewing. Tuning in involves being ready to listen, alertly focused on what the speaker is saying. Questioning involves asking oneself questions based on the speaker's statements to determine the meaning and direction of the message. Reviewing entails conducting a mental review at the end of the presentation to remember key points.

Cue Cards

Gloeckler and Simpson (1988) suggest that students' listening skills can be enhanced by using a cue card that lists the guidelines for listening. For example, a cue card can remind students to do the following:

1. keep alert
2. be quiet

3. don't be distracted by others or noises
4. don't touch or play with objects
5. concentrate on what teacher/students are saying
6. avoid daydreaming or thinking about other things

Class Participation Intervention

Ellis (1989) has developed the *Class Participation Intervention* (*CPI*), a series of metacognitive learning strategies to promote listening and participating in mainstreamed settings. The CPI helps students learn to prepare for class, listen during classroom instruction, and reflect upon content presented in class.

Listening Materials

Many instructional materials that help teach listening skills have been developed for elementary and secondary students (Robinson & Smith, 1983). These materials are designed to teach a variety of listening skills including discriminating and attending to auditory stimuli; using memory strategies such as visualization, rehearsal, and grouping; following directions; determining sequence, main ideas, and details of verbally presented content; identifying supporting information; and making inferences and predicting outcomes.

Listening to Lectures

Many secondary-level mainstreamed students will need to develop their listening skills to improve their ability to obtain information from lectures. Masters and Mori (1986) offer the following strategies that students can use to maintain their attention during oral presentations of information.

1. Take notes.
2. Draw small simple pictures that provide a general explanation of the content that is presented.
3. Try to anticipate what will be said next.
4. Actively employ memory strategies during the presentation.
5. Restate the main idea to yourself during the presentation and try to tie in the related or supporting points.
6. Formulate questions and ask them either during or immediately after the presentation (p. 130).

Lecture Note-Taking Skills

Because information in the regular classroom is often conveyed through large-group presentation or lecture, mainstreamed students should have the skills to record information for later use. There are many ways to record information. The type of note-taking strategy selected depends on the content being presented; therefore, students should be taught to match their strategy to the material. One way to determine which strategy to employ is to teach the student to identify words and phrases that indicate the type of note-taking technique to use. For example, terms such as *in comparison, whereas,* and *on the other hand* indicate that information is being contrasted or compared.

Bradstad and Stumpf (1987) present key terminology that students should be taught in learning the type of note-taking technique to employ. A *chart* method of note taking is used when the speaker is contrasting information, such as the advantages and disadvantages of using a certain note-taking system (Bradstad & Stumpf, 1987). When information is presented according to the date of occurrence, the student should learn to use a *timeline* approach to note taking, whereby students make a horizontal line across the page and record the events and dates in sequence (Bradstad & Stumpf, 1987). If content of the lecture is presented in steps, then it is appropriate to take notes in *step-wise,* or numerical fashion. Examples of these three systems are presented in Figure 5.5. Note-taking skills also can be facilitated by teaching students to use symbols to represent phrases and relationships. For example, the symbol = can be used to indicate a relationship between two concepts.

Saski, Swicegood, and Carter (1983) provide additional information on other note-taking formats.

Another note-taking system that some students may prefer is the *2-5-1* format (Learning Resource Center, n.d.). In this system, the page is divided into three columns. In the first column, which should be two inches wide, students summarize concepts presented in class. In the second column, five inches wide, they list the critical points offered by the teacher. In the last column, one inch wide, students can reflect and expand on the ideas discussed.

FIGURE 5.5
Three methods of note taking

Chart Method

	Hamilton	*Jefferson*
Cabinet Position	Secretary of the Treasury	Secretary of State
Political Party	Federalist	Republican
Constitutional	Supported England	Supported France

Timeline Method

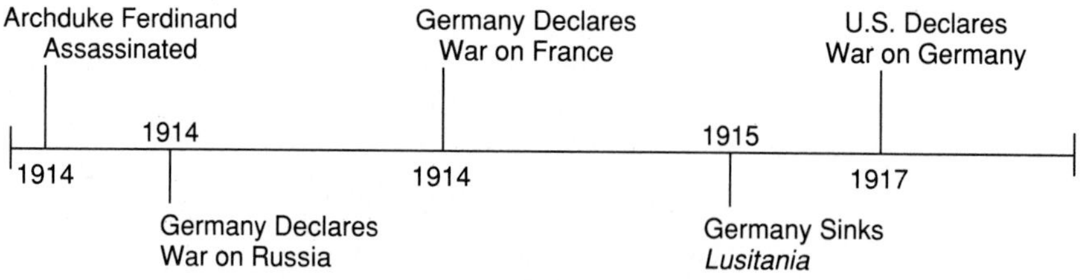

Step-Wise Method

The three principles underlying Roosevelt's "Good Neighbor" Policy:

1. Noninterference in affairs of independent countries
2. Concern for economic policies of Latin American countries
3. Establishment of inter-American cooperation

IDEAS FOR IMPLEMENTATION	Teachers can assist students in developing their note-taking skills by teaching them to do the following: • Select a seat near the speaker. • Realize the importance of bringing writing utensils, notebooks, and a tape recorder if necessary. • Skip a line to indicate transitions between material. • Record notes in their own words. • Indent to indicate main points and establish a structure to the notes. • Mark important information or information that has been missed with a symbol. • Jot down a key word or leaving a blank when there is not enough time to record a whole thought. • Ask the teacher or a peer to provide missed information immediately after the class is completed. • Delineate and label the student's thoughts and peer comments from those of the teacher. • Record the teacher's examples to clarify information. • Listen for key phrases that indicate important information and transitions from one point to another. • Highlight points the speaker emphasizes. • List the name or content area of the class, page number, and date on each page to ensure continuity. • Write complete statements rather than unconnected words or phrases. • Indicate an overlap between the textbook and the teacher's comments. • Record in their class notes the length of time spent on a topic. • Highlight information the teacher might identify as being on the next test.

Source: Adler (1969); Bradstad & Stumpf (1987); Learning Resource Center (n.d.); Masters & Mori (1986); Spargo (1977).

Students can improve their note-taking skills by engaging in several behaviors before, during, and after the lecture (Bradstad & Stumpf, 1987). Before the lecture, students should read the corresponding material that has been assigned; review notes from previous classes; anticipate the material the teacher will cover in class; have the necessary materials and writing utensils; and organize the pages into two columns, one on the left for checking comprehension and the other on the right for recording notes. During the lecture, students should pay attention and avoid being distracted by extraneous stimuli, listen to and watch for verbal and nonverbal cues from the speaker and the audience, write legibly, jot down only critical points and essential details, and use note-taking techniques appropriate to the content being presented. Following the lecture, students should add any missing words, incomplete thoughts, or original ideas; summarize the main points using a ***noteshrink*** technique, which involves surveying the notes, identifying and highlighting main points, and listing these points in the quiz column; review notes; and assess mastery of the content. Sometimes, students should rewrite notes after class; doing so allows them to organize and easily review their notes (Adler, 1969).

The use of abbreviations can help students take complete notes in a timely fashion. Pauk (1984) has identified several rules for using abbreviations and symbols in note taking. However, abbreviations should be used with caution; overusing them can result in notes that are hard to decipher.

Think About It

What skills and strategies do you use to pay attention and take notes in class? Are they successful? How do they compare with the strategies presented in this book?

Memory Skills

Mr. Contreras had just completed his first year as a fourth-grade teacher. Although the year had many successes, he was most surprised by the difficulty many students had in memorizing information. He was pleased with his efforts to teach students a variety of strategies to remember information presented in class. For instance, during science instruction, he taught students to use a first-letter mnemonic strategy to memorize the colors of the spectrum. By using the first letter of each word in the list, students created a word, name, or sentence that helped them remember and retrieve information. One group of students devised the mnemonic "Roy G. Biv," a name composed of the first letter of each color of the light spectrum. Another time, when students were having difficulty memorizing the names of the states in the United States, he taught students to categorize states according to geographic location and then memorize each geographical cluster. Looking back, Mr. Contreras had many good memories of the school year.

Because students also need to retain large, diverse amounts of information, training in developing memory skills will be helpful. Students should learn to apply a variety of effective strategies to increase their memory skills (Leal & Raforth, 1991).

Rehearsal

One strategy for increasing information retention is rehearsal (Levin & Allen, 1976). Rehearsal involves the student repeating essential facts that have just been presented. However, since rehearsal requires concentration, it is more likely to be implemented after class or when the teacher is not presenting additional information. Students also can work with a partner to rehearse critical information and check each others' memory of the material. Since research indicates that reviewing material is a significant factor in remembering content, students should be taught to engage in frequent and spaced reviews of material after it is presented, rather than trying to memorize large amounts of information at once (Bradstad & Stumpf, 1987).

Categorization

Memory of specific information can be increased by teaching students to categorize information (Pauk, 1984). Rather than trying to memorize a series of facts or a list of terms individually, students should try to cluster them before memorizing. Additionally, since research shows that the items at the beginning and ending of a list are more readily remembered, students should give careful attention to learning items from the middle of the list.

Chunking

Studies indicate that the average individual's memory span is approximately seven "bits" of content (Miller, 1956). Because the size of these bits does not appear to affect memory, it is recommended that students memorize information by creating seven broad areas, and supplementing these areas with additional bits of information. This information can then be recalled by associating it with the broad areas (Pauk, 1984).

Mental Visualization

Some students' memory skills may be enhanced by the use of mental visualization (Paivio, 1971), a technique in which they conjure up a mental visual display of the content to be remembered. Later, students recall the mental picture to prompt their memory. Visual rehearsal, where students repeatedly review visual images, also can be used to enhance memory (Ellis & Lenz, 1987).

Mnemonics

Students also can learn to improve their memory skills by using mnemonics, which aid memory by providing the learner with visual or word-related aids that facilitate information retrieval. For example, students can be taught to memorize a list of items that go together by remembering a word or sentence, the letters of which represent the first letters and sequence of each item to be remembered. In devising word or sentence mnemonics, students should be taught to determine the key word in each item that will trigger memory of the main point; record the first letter of the words so identified; and compose an easy-to-remember word or sentence from these letters (Pauk, 1984). If there is an order to the items to be remembered, this should be reflected in the mnemonic. Nagel, Schumaker, and Deshler (1986) have developed a learning strategy for teaching students to use mnemonics.

Narrative Chaining

A similar memory aid that some students find effective is narrative chaining, a technique in which students devise a story that includes the items to be remembered. Bradstad and Stumpf (1987) offer a use of this technique to assist in remembering the biological classification system:

> The **kingdom** was in chaos, so the knights sharpened their weapons. "File 'em!" **(phylum)** they were directed. The peasant **class** had revolted and the knights were to impose **order**. Every **family**, even those containing **geniuses** (genus), was to be investigated to eradicate traitors from the **species**. (p. 57)

Teachers should teach students to apply several guidelines that are associated with successful mnemonic devices. Masters and Mori (1986) identify these guidelines:

1. Always encourage the students to make up their own images and/or pictures as they will be more powerful than any the teacher might impose.
2. Images that are linked should use the *HEAR* rule, which includes the following:

   *H*umor—images should be created that are humorous to their creator.

   *E*xaggeration—enlarging the size or proportion of the pictures will add a unique quality of the image.

   *A*ction—make the image perform movements such as making things fly, hop, or crawl when they do not normally do so.

   *R*idiculous—create images that are unusual or nonsensical.

3. When possible add the dimension of sound, taste, smell, and touch to the images.
4. When memorizing a list of more than four objects it is best to break the items into "chunks" of three (p. 116).

Independent Work Skills

Although students may be able to receive frequent teacher assistance in smaller education classes, the number of students in regular education classes may limit the assistance mainstreamed students may receive from their teachers. Therefore, an important skill for success in the regular classroom is the ability to work independently. Teachers should use a gradual approach to teaching students to work without teacher assistance (Cohen & de Bettencourt, 1988). Initially, teachers should require students to work without teacher assistance for short periods of time. As students are able to work independently for a specific interval, the length of the interval should be increased.

A *job card* can help students learn to function independently (Cohen & de Bettencourt, 1988). The job card structures the students' performance of each task by having them determine the materials needed to do the assignment, the best ways to obtain the necessary materials, the appropriate location in which to complete the assignment, the amount of time allocated to finish the task, and the procedures for handing in their work and finishing assignments early.

Written Assignments

Students in mainstreamed classrooms are expected to complete many written assignments. In addition to evaluating content and writing skills, teachers often grade these assignments based on appearance. Therefore, mainstreamed students should be taught to hand in neat assignments that follow the format the teacher requires. The *HOW* technique, outlined here, provides students with a structure for producing papers that fit the expectations of the teacher (Archer 1988).

How should your paper look?

H = HEADING

1. Name
2. Date
3. Subject
4. Page number if needed

O = ORGANIZED

1. On the front side of the paper
2. Left margin
3. Right margin
4. At least one blank line at the top
5. At least one blank line at the bottom
6. Good spacing

W = WRITTEN NEATLY

1. Words or numbers on the line
2. Words or numbers written neatly
3. Neat erasing and crossing out (p. 56)

Seatwork

Mainstreamed students also will be required to complete many seatwork assignments. In addition to working within the time frame established by the teacher, students will need to develop the skills to complete the assignment successfully. Archer (1988) has proposed a model for training students to complete seatwork:

Step 1: Plan it.
Read the directions and circle the words that tell you what to do.
Get out the material you need.
Tell yourself what to do.

Step 2: Complete it.
Do all items.
If you can't do an item go ahead or ask for help.
Use HOW.

Step 3: Check it.
Did you do everything?

Did you get the right answers?
Did you proofread?
Step 4: Turn it in. (p. 56)

Proofreading

Proofreading skills also can help maximize mainstreamed students' performance on writing tasks. Students should be taught to review their written products to check for misspelled words, sentence fragments, and errors in punctuation, capitalization, and grammar. To strengthen their students' proofreading skills, teachers can show them how to review their products and identify all spelling errors, check that capital letters are used to begin all sentences and proper nouns, include punctuation marks at appropriate places and at the end of sentences, and ensure that paragraphs are indented (Tompkins & Friend, 1988). One strategy that trains students to use these proofreading skills in a systematic way is *COPS* (Schumaker, Nolan, & Deshler, 1985). In the COPS procedure, students learn to proofread their papers by checking *c*apitalization, *o*verall appearance, *p*unctuation, and *s*pelling. Additional strategies such as *DEFENDS* and *WRITER* also employ COPS to monitor the quality of written language products (Ellis & Lenz, 1987).

Students' proofreading skills also can be enhanced by employing proofreader's marks as they review their papers (Tompkins & Friend, 1988). Teachers can train students to use these marks by teaching students the system and modeling its use when giving feedback on written assignments. Additionally, teachers can give students a handout of editing symbols paired with examples of their use, as shown in Figure 5.6 (Whitt, Paul, & Reynolds, 1988).

Organization Skills

"I can't find it. I know I put my math paper in my desk, but it's not here now. I did it yesterday and put it right in my desk and now it's gone." Harry is now digging furiously in his desk. Papers, notebooks, books, and assorted rubbish begin to fall to the floor around him. All eyes in the room are intently on Harry. A neighboring student starts picking up debris and hands it to Harry. Harry takes it, thanks his friend, and attempts to stuff it back into his desk. (Haman & Issacson, 1985, p. 45).

Notebooks

In most regular education classrooms, students take notes and record information in their notebooks. Therefore, students should be taught to maintain a notebook according to the specifications of the regular education teacher(s). For secondary students, this procedure often entails use of a three-ring looseleaf binder divided by subject and a writing utensils pouch (Archer, 1988). An 8½ by 11-inch binder allows duplicated materials to be inserted

FIGURE 5.6
Editing symbols form

EDITING SYMBOLS

Mark	Explanation	Example
⬭	Circle words that are spelled incorrectly.	My freind and I went to the zoo last Sunday.
/	Change a capital letter to a small letter.	Mary and Jim watched Television for one hour.
≡	Change a small letter to a capital letter.	bob loves the way I play horn.
∧	Add letters, words, or sentences.	My friend lives in the ∧ house next door. (brick)
⊙	Add a period.	My dog, Frisky, and I are private detectives⊙
ℓ	Take out letters, words, or punctuation.	Last summer Bob went and flew an airplane in Alaska.
∧	Add a comma.	Bob visited Alaska Ohio and Florida.

Source: J. Whitt, P. V. Paul, and C. J. Reynolds, *Teaching Exceptional Children, vol. 20,* (Reston, VA: Council for Exceptional Children, 1988), p. 38. Reprinted by permission of the publisher.

easily. Elementary-level students usually need training in using two folders; one for in-class work and the other for work that goes home (Archer, 1988). When notebooks become crowded, students should remove the oldest notes and place them in a separate notebook or folder. Teachers can encourage students to organize their notebooks by periodically evaluating notebooks in terms of neatness, organization, completion, and currency (Spector, Decker, & Shaw, 1991).

Students need to learn to use an assignment notebook. Usually, the assignment notebook can be a small pad, which can be kept in the binder or the pencil pouch, on which they can record homework assignments. Students should be trained to list assignments in the notebook including page numbers, dates the assignments are due, and relevant information needed to complete the task (Reetz & Crank, 1988). Spector et al. (1991) suggest that teachers can help students learn to use assignment pads by periodically checking students' pads, and reminding students to use their pads to record important assignments, projects, and tests. Teachers also can have students use a homework buddy, a peer who can be contacted regarding missed assignments and for further clarification (Chiapetta, Budd, & Russo, 1990).

Assignment Logs

Shields and Heron (1989) suggest that students learn to use an assignment log to keep track of assignments. The log consists of two pocket folders with built-in space to store assignment sheets that contain the name of the assignment, a description of the assignment, the date the assignment was given and is due, and a place for a parent's signature. When assignments are given to students, they complete the information on the assignment sheet and place it into the pocket folder labeled "To Be Completed." Upon completing the assignment, the assignment sheet is updated (signed by the parent) and put in the "Completed Work" pocket folder.

Time Management

Josh, a ninth grader, is having a tough time adjusting to high school. When he does an assignment, he usually receives a good grade. However, far too often, he forgets to do his assignments and to study for tests. In addition to his classes, Josh actively participates in extracurricular activities and occasionally works at a local restaurant.

His parents and teachers are frustrated by his erratic performance and decide that a weekly schedule will help Josh organize his activities and complete his school work. Initially, each Monday Josh meets with Ms. Gates, one of his teachers, to plan his schedule. They divide each day into hourly time slots, list class assignments and tests, and outline after school and home activities as well as job related commitments. They then determine which activities have specific time commitments and record them in the schedule. Next, they list Josh's weekly assignments and due dates and estimate the amount of time that should be allocated to complete them. Josh and Ms. Gates then establish priorities and enter items in the schedule based on their priority. Finally, they review the schedule to see that all desired activities have been allocated sufficient time and that there is a balance among activities. Throughout the week, Ms. Gates checks Josh's progress in following the schedule. As Josh masters the steps in planning and implementing his schedule, Ms. Gates encourages him to develop his own schedule and monitor his own performance.

Students also learn how to keep track of the numerous activities that make up life in the mainstreamed setting by maintaining a monthly calendar onto which teachers can train students to list their homework, exams, long-term assignments, and classroom and school activities (Archer, 1988). Students also should be trained to look at the calendar every day to determine daily activities and plan for long-term projects.

In addition to the monthly calendar, students can increase their productivity by charting their daily schedules, including listing the time of day and the activity that should and did occur during that time period (Reetz & Crank, 1988). Students also should be taught to review the daily schedule at different times during the day to ensure that they are following the schedule (Masters & Mori, 1986). Initially, teachers can guide students in planning their schedules. However, as students develop skill in planning and following the schedule, they should be encouraged to plan their own schedules and determine the obstacles they encounter in successfully following those schedules (Alley & Deshler, 1979). In developing their schedules, students should be encouraged to do the following:

- consider and allot time for all types of activities
- allocate a sufficient amount of time to study for each class
- avoid studying material from one class for extended periods of time
- divide study time into several short study periods rather than having one lengthy study period
- consider their attention span in planning study periods
- prioritize school tasks based on due dates, importance of task, and time demands
- schedule time for relaxation
- reward studying by planning other activities (Mercer & Mercer, 1985; Pauk, 1984)

Pauk (1984) proposes the use of a time reminder system that combines elements of the monthly calendar and the daily schedule. The time reminder system requires the student to record all essential daily and long-term activities on an index card.

Another valuable planning system is the assignment-oriented weekly schedule, which helps students determine a schedule for completing weekly assignments (Pauk, 1984). Students list their weekly assignments including subject area, approximate length of time needed to complete the assignment, and the due date. They use this information to develop a weekly schedule, allotting time from each part of the day to work on assignments. A sample schedule is presented in Figure 5.7.

Establishing Priorities

Students' use of time can be improved by learning how to establish priorities. Lakein (1973) has developed an *ABC* system that students can learn to accomplish this goal. The ABC system requires students to list all the critical activities that need to be accomplished; assign each task a value with *A, B,* and *C* indicating high, medium, and low values, respectively; rank order items given the same letter value using a numbering system (*A-1, A-2*); and complete the activities according to the established priorities.

Homework

One instructional strategy that regular classroom teachers often employ is homework. Since mainstreamed students are likely to encounter more frequent and greater amounts of homework in the regular classroom, educators can prepare students for regular education placements by approximating the homework demands of the mainstreamed milieu in their classrooms (Salend & Schliff, 1988). Thus, if the regular classroom teacher requires 45 minutes of homework four days a week, the other educators can assign the same amount of homework in their educational settings.

FIGURE 5.7
Sample weekly schedule

TIME MANAGEMENT CALENDAR, THE UNCALENDAR

WHAT NEEDS TO BE DONE THIS WEEK?

SCHOOL TASK	DUE	TIME TO DO IT
Book report	Friday	6 hrs.
Math Homework	Monday & Wednesday	2 hrs.
Social Studies	Tuesday & Thursday	2 hrs.

HOME

TASK	DUE	TIME
Clean Car	Sat.	1 hr.

WORK

TASK	TIME
McDonald's	4-8 M-F

WEEK-END	MONDAY DATE	TUESDAY DATE	WEDNESDAY DATE	THURSDAY DATE	FRIDAY DATE
SCHEDULE	SCHEDULE	SCHEDULE	SCHEDULE	SCHEDULE	SCHEDULE
	7-8am bus ride (Homework) 8-3pm School 4-8pm Work 8:30-10:00 Homework	→	→	→	→
Tasks: Time:	Tasks: Time:	Tasks: Time:	Tasks: Time:	Tasks: Time:	Tasks: Time:
Book Report 2 hr.	Math 1 hr. Book Report (w/Patty) 1 hr.	Soc. St. 1 hr. Book Report 1 hr.	Math 1 hr. Book Report (w/Patty) 1 hr.	Soc. St. 1 hr. Book Report 1 hr.	Clean Car 1 hr.
Comments:	Comments:	Comments:	Comments:	Comments:	Comments:
Need help outlining Book Report- See Patty		Have Patty proofread book report			

Source: J. M. Shields and T. E. Heron, *Teaching Exceptional Children,* vol. 21 (Reston, VA: Council for Exceptional Children, 1989), p. 11. Reprinted by permission of the publisher.

Library Skills

Mainstreamed students will need certain library skills to be successful in the regular classroom (Mastropieri & Scruggs, 1987). Students should be taught the type of information that can be obtained, as well as how to locate information in reference sources that are used by students in the mainstreamed setting (dictionary, encyclopedia, thesaurus, and so on). For example, students should learn that the dictionary can assist them in defining, spelling, and pronouncing words. Similarly, instruction in how to use the dictionary should include looking up words alphabetically, using the guide words that indicate the first and last words located on a page, and selecting the correct meaning of a word (Spargo, 1977). Students should be introduced to the library, including how to use the card catalogue, computer terminals, the Dewey Decimal system, and the Library of Congress book classification system, as needed.

IDEAS FOR IMPLEMENTATION

Teachers can increase their students' ability to complete their homework by teaching them how to do the following:

- Choose a distraction-free location.
- Schedule and budget time.
- Organize materials.
- Use resources.
- Seek assistance from others when necessary.
- Ask questions to make sure the directions and expectations of a homework assignment are understood.
- Organize their homework by using notepads for recording assignments.
- Use separate folders for transporting homework to and from school.
- Store homework assignments before and after they are completed.
- Review their skill at receiving the directions for homework assignments by checking with a peer.

Behavioral Skills

An important part of success in the regular classroom is the ability to demonstrate the requisite behavioral skills (Wilkes, Bireley, & Schultz, 1979). Because students with disabilities often engage in inappropriate behaviors, they may need instruction in how to comply with the behavioral expectations of the regular classroom teacher's management system. While many special educators use a management system based on the delivery of frequent, systematic reinforcement, many regular education teachers view techniques based on behavioral principles as difficult to implement within the confines of the regular classroom (Lovitt, 1975). Therefore, students who are being prepared for entry into a regular education setting should be weaned from any specialized management systems and taught to respond under the management system employed in the mainstreamed setting, or to use self-management strategies. For example, rather than using a token reinforcement system, a soon-to-be mainstreamed student can be taught to monitor his or her "talking out" through use of a self-managed technique. A variety of self-management strategies are presented in Chapter 10.

Teaching Social and Basic Interpersonal Communication Skills

Since the language that guides social interactions and instruction in the classroom is English, many students will need to receive instruction to develop the necessary basic interpersonal communication skills (BICS) to be successful in the mainstreamed setting. Observing the mainstreamed students' interaction patterns in a variety of settings (such as recess, cafeteria, and afterschool activities) can help teachers determine the appropriate BICS and social skills that students need to learn to interact with their peers. These skills can then be taught by providing students with the opportunities to use and practice these skills. Furthermore, BICS and other social skills can be taught to students using a variety of strategies that provide students with experiences in the language and settings that structure social interactions. Some of these strategies are described here.

Modeling. Modeling allows students to view appropriate examples of language and social interaction patterns. For example, the student can observe other students in the mainstreamed setting during a social interaction activity or view a video of such an activity. The teacher can then review the observation with the student, emphasizing language, behaviors, and cues that promote social interactions—specifically, strategies and language for initiating and maintaining social interactions.

Teachers also can introduce peers into the self-contained classroom to serve as models to stimulate the development of language and social skills (Carter & Sugai, 1988). These students can be matched with mainstreamed students during socialization activities, providing mainstreamed students with exemplars they can imitate. Schoen (1989) provides excellent guidelines for teaching students to learn through modeling.

Role Playing. Students can develop BICS and social skills through role playing social interaction situations (Hoover & Collier, 1986). Where possible, the role play should take place in the environmental milieu in which the behavior is to be implemented. Following the role play, teachers should give students corrective feedback concerning their performance.

Prompting. Teachers can employ prompting to help students learn relevant cues that can assist them in engaging in appropriate interpersonal skills (Carter & Sugai, 1988). In prompting, the student is taught to use environmental stimuli to acquire new skills. For example, in promoting the use of BICS on the playground, the student and the teacher can visit the playground, identify stimuli, and discuss how these stimuli can be used to promote socialization. Specifically, playground equipment, such as the slide, can serve as a prompt to elicit statements such as "Do you want to play?"; "This is fun!"; and "Is it my turn?"

Coaching. Carter and Sugai (1988) suggest the use of coaching to guide students in recognizing appropriate behaviors and when to exhibit them. They describe a coaching technique to teach students how to engage in conversation in various settings; the teacher coaches students to verbalize and follow the rules for conversations in that setting.

Scripting. Since much of the dialogue that comprises social conversation is predictable and often redundant, teachers can show students the language and structure of social interactions through scripts that outline conversations that might occur in a specific environmental setting (Gaylord-Ross & Haring,

1987). For example, a typical conversation at lunchtime can be scripted to include questions and responses relating to the day's events (*How are you doing today?*), menus (*Are you buying lunch today?; What kind of sandwich do you have?*), and school or class events (*Are you going to the game after school?*). Gaylord-Ross and Haring (1987) suggest guidelines for scripting, which include identifying topics, sequence, structure, and language of the script through considering the cultural and environmental setting in which the interaction will occur; observing typical, naturally occurring interactions and interviewing peer participants to determine verbalizations and topics that are reflective of the ecology of the interaction; teaching students the script and how to expand on it; and providing opportunities to practice in the setting where the script will be used.

Additional strategies for teaching social skills to students are presented in Chapter 10.

Teaching Cognitive Academic Language Proficiency Skills

The strategies for teaching BICS also can be employed in teaching Cognitive Academic Language Proficiency (CALP) skills. CALP can be facilitated through providing students with techniques for understanding the instructional terminology used in the mainstreamed setting. Students can maintain words and concepts used in the classroom discussions, textbooks, and assignments in a word file for retrieval as needed (Alley & Deshler, 1979).

For quick retrieval, the file should be organized alphabetically or by content area. As the student demonstrates mastery of specific terminology, those terms can be deleted or moved to an inactive section of the file. The student can also maintain a record of key words and concepts by using the *divided page* method (Bradstad & Stumpf, 1987). Students divide a page into three columns. In column one, the student lists the term, phrase, or concept. The context in which the term is used is then presented in column two, and the word is defined concisely in the third column. Students can then keep a separate list for each new chapter or by subject area. These methods of listing difficult terminology can be adapted for students who are learning English by recording information in their dominant language. For example, the primary language equivalent of words and phrases can be included in a word list or as separate sections of the divided page.

TRANSITIONAL PROGRAMS FOR LINGUISTICALLY AND CULTURALLY DIVERSE STUDENTS

A transitional program for students who speak primary languages other than English should prepare these students for movement from bilingual or English as a second language (ESL) classrooms. While many of the transitional strategies previously discussed will be appropriate for linguistically and culturally diverse students, bilingual education and ESL teachers should work together with mainstreamed teachers to plan and implement the orientation program for second language learners. Initially, they should plan the goals and content of the transitional program. Chamot (1985) suggests that a transitional program for students who speak languages other than English should include an understanding of the technical terminology related to each content area; an ability to delineate the appropriate language functions that guide academic and verbal interactions; and a mastery of the language skills necessary for acquiring academic content, such as listening, reading, speaking, and writing. Handscombe (1989) proposes that students' language program should prepare them for the language demands necessary for success with the curriculum, and in social interactions with peers and adults. Toward this end, teachers should begin to align their curriculum and instructional materials with those used in the mainstreamed setting, to rely more on English to guide instruction, and to use the student's primary language to check comprehension when necessary. Instructional materials and programs, such as *Macmillan's Transitional Reading Program,* can be used to help students in making the transition from reading in their primary language to reading in English (Calderon, Tinajero, & Hertz-Lazarowitz, 1992). Teachers also should teach students *pragmatics,* the functional and cultural aspects of language. For example, the Special Alternative Instructional Program (SAIP) in Hillsboro, Oregon integrates English-language development with science, social studies, and health courses that parallel the regular education curriculum to prepare students for mainstream content courses (Tikunoff et al., 1991).

The orientation program should teach students the accepted cultural norms and communication skills that guide social and academic classroom interactions (Li, 1992). For example, whereas some teachers may expect students to raise their hands to seek teacher assistance, some students may be reluctant to do so because they are taught not to draw attention to themselves. Educators can help students learn these different cultural behaviors by doing the following:

- acknowledging and understanding the student's cultural perspective
- explaining to the student the new perspective and the environmental conditions associated with it
- using modeling, role playing, prompting, coaching, and scripting to teach new behaviors
- understanding that it may take some time for the student to develop bicultural competence

A transitional program for these students also should include opportunities for these students to have informal, natural conversations with peers and to work with peers in cooperative learning groups (Supancheck, 1989).

Cognitive Academic Language Learning Approach

Chamot and O'Malley (1989) have developed the *Cognitive Academic Language Learning Approach* (*CALLA*) to help students make the transition from bilingual and ESL programs to mainstreamed settings and develop the cognitive academic language proficiency skills necessary for success in mainstreamed academic programs. While CALLA was designed for students who speak primary languages other than English, it can be used to plan a transitional program for all students. CALLA has three components: content-based curriculum, academic language development, and learning strategy instruction.

Content-Based Curriculum

In the content-based curriculum component of CALLA, students are gradually introduced to the curriculum of the regular classroom in the bilingual education or ESL program through use of the authentic content-related materials used in the mainstreamed setting. It is recommended that students be introduced to the content areas in the following sequence: science, mathematics, social studies, and language arts.

Academic Language Development

In this component, students practice using English as the language of instruction while teachers provide contextual support through use of concrete objects, visual aids and gestures. Possible activities include the following:

- Developing an academic vocabulary in different content areas.
- Understanding academic presentations accompanied by visuals and demonstrations.
- Participating in hands-on science activities.
- Using manipulatives to discuss and solve math word problems.
- Making models, maps, graphs, and charts in social studies.
- Participating in academic discussions and making brief oral presentations.
- Understanding written texts through discussion, demonstration, and visuals.
- Using standard formats as supportive structures for writing simple reports in science and social studies.
- Answering higher-level questions orally (Chamot & O'Malley, 1989, p. 115).

Learning Strategy Instruction

In the third component of CALLA, students learn techniques that facilitate the acquisition of language and subject matter content. These learning strategies are presented in Figure 5.8.

Newcomer Programs

To help immigrant students adjust to American schools, many school districts have instituted *newcomer programs,* which offer students a variety of academic and support services designed to help them make the transition to and succeed in mainstream classrooms (Friedlander, 1991). The services offered by newcomer programs include: (a) activities and classes to orient students to the school and society; (b) a specialized curriculum that promotes the learn-

FIGURE 5.8
Learning strategies taught in the cognitive academic language learning approach (CALLA)

METACOGNITIVE STRATEGIES	
Advance organization	Previewing the main ideas and concepts of the material to be learned, often by skimming the text for the organizing principle.
Advance preparation	Rehearsing the language needed for an oral or written task.
Organizational planning	Planning the parts, sequence, and main ideas to be expressed orally or in writing.
Selective attention	Attending to or scanning key words, phrases, linguistic markers, sentences, or types of information.
Self-monitoring	Checking one's comprehension during listening or reading, or checking one's oral or written production while it is taking place.
Self-evaluation	Judging how well one has accomplished a learning task.
Self-management	Seeking or arranging the conditions that help one learn, such as finding opportunities for additional language or content input and practice.
COGNITIVE STRATEGIES	
Resourcing	Using reference materials such as dictionaries, encyclopedias, or textbooks.
Grouping	Classifying words, terminology, numbers, or concepts according to their attributes.
Note taking	Writing down key words and concepts in abbreviated verbal, graphic, or numerical form.
Summarizing	Making a mental or written summary of information gained through listening or reading.
Deduction	Applying rules to understand or produce language or solve problems.
Imagery	Using visual images (either mental or actual) to understand and remember new information or to make a mental representation of a problem.
Auditory representation	Playing in back of one's mind the sound of a word, phrase, or fact in order to assist comprehension and recall.
Elaboration	Relating new information to prior knowledge, relating different parts of new information to each other, or making meaningful personal associations with the new information.

FIGURE 5.8
(continued)

Transfer	Using what is already known about language to assist comprehension or production.
Inferencing	Using information in the text to guess meanings of new items, predict outcomes, or complete missing parts.
SOCIAL AND AFFECTIVE STRATEGIES	
Questioning for clarification	Eliciting from a teacher or peer additional explanation, rephrasing, examples, or verification.
Cooperation	Working together with peers to solve a problem, pool information, check a learning task, or get feedback on oral or written performance.
Self-talk	Reducing anxiety by using mental techniques that make one feel competent to do the learning task.

Source: J. M. O'Malley and A. U. Chamot, *Learning Strategies in Second Language Acquisition* (New York, Cambridge University), pp. 198–199. Reprinted by permission of the publisher.

Friedlander (1991) reviewed various newcomer programs and offered guidelines for developing newcomer programs.

ing of English, multicultural awareness, and academic content; (c) support services such as counseling, tutoring, parent training, information, medical and referral services, career education, and transportation; and (d) individualized and innovative instruction from specially trained teachers (Friedlander, 1991).

Roles of the Regular Classroom Teacher

Regular classroom teachers can help students who speak a primary language other than English by structuring the learning environment to provide students with the opportunity to gain new information through *context embedded tasks,* which facilitate students' understanding of language through use of physical gestures, movements, objects, graphic representations, and manipulatives (Supancheck, 1989). Therefore, regular classroom teachers should use some of the same approaches to facilitate language acquisition as those used by bilingual and ESL teachers, including Total Physical Response and Sheltered English.

Total Physical Response

One effective approach for teaching a second language is *Total Physical Response* (*TPR*), a technique that seeks to enhance students' vocabulary through modeling, repeated practice, and movement (Asher, 1977). In TPR, the teacher models the message through use of emphasized physical gestures and objects. (The teacher states the message, models, and physically emphasizes movements related to the concept of, say, sharpening a pencil.) Next, the class as a group responds to the teacher's directions. (The teacher asks the students to sharpen their pencils and the students, as a group, make the motion of sharpening their pencils.) Finally, individual students respond to verbal commands given by the teacher and peers. (Individual students are asked by the teacher and peers to sharpen a pencil.) As students develop skills, the complexity of the language skills taught increases. Adaptations of TPR include having students write statements, or comply with statements that are written (Freeman & Freeman, 1992).

Sheltered English

Hamayan and Perlman (1990) offer educators guidelines for helping second language learners make the transition to mainstreamed settings.

Another approach used by many bilingual and ESL educators is *Sheltered English*, a technique that employs cues, gestures, media, manipulatives, drama, and visual stimuli to teach new vocabulary and concepts (Northcutt & Watson, 1986). When using a Sheltered English approach, the teacher provides instruction in the terminology needed to understand the concepts associated with specific content areas. Teachers present information orally and visually, and assist students in learning by restating, paraphrasing, simplifying, and expanding the material being presented (Tikunoff et al., 1991).

PROMOTING GENERALIZATION

Diana, an eleventh-grade student, is having difficulty in her science and social studies classes because those classes rely on presenting information through textbooks. Her social studies, science, and resource room teachers meet to discuss Diana's performance and agree that she would benefit from learning SQ3R, a text comprehension strategy. Diana's resource room teacher introduces her to the strategy and helps her learn it in that setting. However, her teachers notice that Diana frequently fails to apply the strategy in their classrooms. Diana's teachers decide to give her a self-monitoring checklist that presents the skills Diana should demonstrate when implementing the strategy in social studies and science. They give Diana the following self-monitoring checklist:

STEPS	YES	NO
1. Did I survey the chapter?	_____	_____
a. headings and titles	_____	_____
b. first paragraph	_____	_____
c. visual aids	_____	_____
d. summary paragraphs	_____	_____
2. Have I made questions?	_____	_____

3. Did I read the selection? ____ ____
4. Did I recite the main points? ____ ____
5. Did I produce a summary of the main points? ____ ____

Diana's use of the strategy increases, as does her performance in science and social studies.

Transfer of training to other settings does not occur spontaneously; educators must have a systematic plan for the generalization of behavior (Stokes & Baer, 1977).

Once a transitional skill has been learned in one setting, educators should take steps to promote *generalization,* which ensures the transfer of training to the mainstreamed setting (Anderson-Inman, 1986). In planning a generalization program for mainstreamed students, teachers must consider the students' abilities as well as the nature of the regular classroom including academic content, activities, and teaching style (Vaughn, Bos, & Lund, 1986).

Goodman (1979) suggests that teachers can promote generalization by approximating the new environment—in other words, by training the mainstreamed student to perform under the conditions and expectations that they will encounter in the regular classroom. This goal can be achieved by introducing dimensions of the regular classroom into the special education or bilingual education classroom and by providing students with the opportunity to experience sufficient exemplars (Stokes & Baer, 1977).

For example, if the regular classroom situation requires students to do vocabulary homework by defining words on Mondays, using words in sentences on Tuesdays, and spelling words on Wednesdays, then the special education teacher should strive for the same work demands in the special education setting. Similarly, a student who is going to be placed in the regular classroom should be trained to perform under the natural circumstances of the mainstreamed milieu.

Teachers can use several generalization strategies to prepare students for the demands of the mainstreamed setting, including changing reinforcement, cues, materials, response set, dimensions of the stimulus, settings, and teachers (Vaughn et al., 1986). Descriptions and examples of these generalization techniques are presented in Figure 5.9.

Generalization also can be fostered by employing components of the orientation program in the regular classroom (Alberto & Troutman, 1990). Students can be instrumental in ensuring that elements of the training program are transferred to the regular education setting (Anderson-Inman, 1986). For example, a list developed in the resource room of difficult terms used in the regular classroom and their meanings can be brought into the mainstreamed setting to assist students.

Classroom Procedures

As students move to regular education settings, they will need to be taught the procedures and routines of the mainstreamed classroom. Therefore, before students are placed in the mainstream, they should be introduced to several

IDEAS FOR IMPLEMENTATION

Regular classroom teachers can help students adjust to a new language environment by enacting the following suggestions:

- Show respect and acknowledge the value of the students' cultural background and primary language.
- Encourage all attempts at language including students' use of their first language.
- Serve as a model for appropriate language.
- Motivate students to acquire a second language by relating learning to their feelings, needs, interests and to real-life situations.
- Provide a low-anxiety language learning environment that encourages students to take risks, limits anxiety, and promotes self-confidence and self-esteem.
- Keep students active in the learning process.
- Encourage and facilitate socialization with peers.
- Make language meaningful, relevant, and interesting to students.
- Enlist the support of school personnel, parents, and community members who understand the students' language and culture.
- Give and review directions step by step.
- Use materials and events that relate to the students' experiences and cultural backgrounds.
- Integrate language development with content area instruction.
- Teach important vocabulary and concepts in advance.
- Introduce new concepts through use of simple and familiar vocabulary, concrete examples, and hands-on demonstrations.
- Encourage students to expand appropriate responses by requesting them to provide additional information and by modeling elaboration.
- Ask higher-level questions.
- Evaluate responses for ideas expressed.
- Check periodically to ensure comprehension.
- Provide feedback related to intended meanings rather than only to correctness of English.
- Facilitate students' comprehension by articulating clearly, pausing often, limiting the use of idiomatic expressions and slang, and using simple vocabulary and shorter sentences.
- Provide students with adequate wait time.
- Highlight critical words and phrases through variations in volume and intonation.
- Encourage students to use bilingual dictionaries.
- Pair less fluent students with fluent peers during instructional and social activities.
- Have an aide fluent in the student's native language assist the student.
- Talk and socially interact with students before and after class.
- Use visuals to supplement oral presentations.
- Employ cues to convey the meaning of new words.
- Pair language with appropriate body language and movement.
- Use self-talk and parallel talk to explain what you and others are doing and thinking, respectively.
- Foster students' self-image.
- Offer frequent summaries of the important concepts and material in a lesson.

Source: Bos & Vaughn (1991); Hamayan & Perlman (1990); Krashen (1982); Short (1991); Supancheck (1989); Tikunoff et al. (1991); Terrell (1981); Westby & Rouse (1985).

IDEAS FOR IMPLEMENTATION

Teachers can seek to promote transfer of training by enacting the following suggestions:

- Encourage students to try the new techniques in additional settings.
- Discuss with students other milieus in which they could employ the strategy.
- Identify with students similarities and differences between settings.
- Role play the use of the strategy in other situations.
- Request that regular education teachers assist students in using the strategy.
- Establish with students an understanding of the link between the strategy and improved performance in the mainstreamed setting.
- Provide opportunities to practice the skill in the regular education classroom.
- Allow students time to review use of strategies periodically.
- Use cue cards or self-monitoring checklists to guide and monitor the use of strategies in the mainstreamed setting.

Source: Ellis, Lenz, & Sabornie (1987); Gleason (1988).

aspects of the regular classroom milieu. The orientation should include an explanation of the class rules, class jobs, and special events, as well as class routines such as lunch count, homework, attendance, and the like (Kansas-National Education Association, 1984). The class schedule should be reviewed, and necessary materials and supplies for specific classes should be identified. Teachers should explain procedures for storing materials; using learning centers, media, materials, and other equipment; working on seatwork activities and in small groups; obtaining assistance; handing in completed assignments; seeking permission to leave the room; and making transitions to activities and classes (Everston, Emmer, Clements, Sanford, & Worsham, 1989). They should also conduct a tour of the classroom to acquaint students with the design of the room and the location of instructional materials. Once students are moved into mainstreamed classrooms, classmates can be peer helpers to assist new students in learning about the class and school routines, schedules, rules, instructional materials, and facilities (Goodman, 1979).

Get-Acquainted Activities

Once a student is placed in the mainstreamed setting, teachers should use icebreaking activities to acquaint students with their peers (Salend & Schobel, 1981, October). Salend and Schobel (1981, October) and Schniedewind and Davidson (1987) outline a variety of cooperative activities that teachers can use to introduce new students to the group and give all students a common experience on which to build future friendships.

TRANSITION FROM SPECIAL DAY SCHOOLS AND EARLY INTERVENTION PROGRAMS

Students moving from special day schools to self-contained classrooms within a local school district building and from early intervention programs to

FIGURE 5.9
Transfer of training techniques

CHANGE REINFORCEMENT

Description/Methods	Examples
Vary amount, power, and type of reinforcers.	
• Fade amount of reinforcement.	• Reduce frequency of reinforcement from completion of each assignment to completion of day's assignments.
• Decrease power of reinforcer from tangible reinforcers to verbal praise.	• Limit use of stars/stickers and add more specific statements, e.g., "Hey, you did a really good job in your math book today."
• Increase power of reinforcer when changing to mainstreamed setting.	• Give points in regular classroom although not needed in resource room.
• Use same reinforcers in different settings.	• Encourage all teachers working with student to use the same reinforcement program.

CHANGE CUES

Description/Methods	Examples
Vary instructions systematically.	
• Use alternate/parallel directions.	• Use variations of cue, e.g., "Find the . . ."; "Give me the . . ."; "Point to the . . ."
• Change directions.	• Change length and vocabulary of directions to better represent the directions given in the regular classroom, e.g., "Open your book to page 42 and do the problems in set A."
	• Move from real objects to miniature objects.
• Use photograph.	• Use actual photograph of object or situation.
• Use picture to represent object.	• Move from object/photograph to picture of object or situation.
• Use line drawing or symbol representation.	• Use drawings from workbooks to represent objects or situations.
• Use varying print forms.	• Vary lower and upper case letters; vary print by using manuscript, boldface, primary type. • Move from manuscript to cursive.

CHANGE MATERIALS

Description/Methods	Examples
Vary materials within task.	
• Change medium.	• Use unlined paper, lined paper; change size of lines; change color of paper. • Use various writing instruments such as markers, pencil, pen, typewriter.
• Change media.	• Use materials such as films, microcomputers, filmstrips to present skills/concepts. • Provide opportunity for student to phase into mainstream.

FIGURE 5.9
(continued)

CHANGE RESPONSE SET

Description/Methods	Examples
Vary mode of responding. • Change how student is to respond.	• Ask child to write answers rather than always responding orally. • Teach student to respond to a variety of question types such as multiple choice, true/false, short answer.
• Change time allowed for responding.	• Decrease time allowed to complete math facts.

CHANGE SOME DIMENSION(S) OF THE STIMULUS

Description/Methods	Examples
Vary the stimulus systematically. • Use single stimulus and change size, color, shape.	• Teach colors by changing the size, shape, and shade of "orange" objects.
• Add to number of distractors.	• Teach sight words by increasing number of words from which child is to choose.
• Use concrete (real) object.	• Introduce rhyming words by using real objects.
• Use toy or miniature representation.	• Use miniature objects when real objects are impractical.

CHANGE SETTING(S)

Description/Methods	Examples
Vary instructional work space. • Move from more structured to less structured work arrangements.	• Move one-to-one teaching to different areas within classroom. • Provide opportunity for independent work. • Move from one-to-one instruction to small-group format. • Provide opportunity for student to interact in large group.

CHANGE TEACHERS

Description/Methods	Examples
Vary instructors. • Assign child to work with different teacher.	• Select tasks so that child has opportunities to work with instructional aide, peer tutor, volunteer, regular classroom teacher, and parents.

Source: S. Vaughn, C. S. Bos, and K. A. Lund, *Teaching Exceptional Children,* Vol. 18 (Reston, VA: Council for Exceptional Children, 1986), pp. 177–178. Reprinted by the permission of the publisher.

Beckoff and Bender (1989) and Pinkerton (1992) offer guidelines that can assist educators in designing programs that help students and families make the transition from early intervention programs to schools.

school also will require transitional programs to prepare them for entry into their new school (Fowler, Schwartz, & Atwater, 1991; Mental Retardation Institute, 1991). Johnson, Cook, and Yongue (1990) developed the Capstone Transition Process to serve as a model for planning and implementing a transitional program. Activities in the model include developing a transition timeline, preparing participants for transition, collecting data on student performance, establishing communication procedures, sharing information, holding meetings, and evaluating the process. Salend (1981b) noted that such a transitional program should introduce students to the new school's personnel and the roles these individuals perform; to the school's physical design, including the location of the cafeteria, gymnasium, auditorium; and to important rules, procedures, and extracurricular activities. For example, if students learn the location of and the rules for the school cafeteria before the first day in school, they can avoid a potentially confusing and troublesome situation. Teachers can orient students to the new setting by giving them a map of the school with key areas and suggested routes highlighted, assigning a reliable student to help the new student learn how to get around the school, and color coding the student's schedule (Gillet, 1986).

Goodman (1979) has developed a model for integrating students from specialized schools to schools within their community that also can be adapted to plan transitions from early intervention programs to school. The model involves:

1. *Deciding on Placement.* Initially, educators determine the appropriate community school placement based on location, attitudes of school personnel, availability of services, and needs of the students.

2. *Approximating the New Environment.* Educators in the special school help students adjust to the new placement by attempting to replicate the demands, conditions, and strategies of the new setting.

3. *Leveling of Academic Skills.* Students are prepared for the academic requirements of the new setting, and transitions to the new placement's textbooks, instructional materials, and assignments are established.

4. *Building Skills in the New School.* Staff from the special school setting meet with teachers, administrators, and support staff from the new school to discuss strategies that have been successfully employed with the students.

5. *Visiting the School.* Students visit and tour the new school.

6. *Starting with Small Units of Time.* Initially, some students may attend the new setting for a brief period of time to help them gradually adjust to the new placement. As students feel comfortable in the new setting, the length of time in the new school increases until the student spends the whole school day in the new setting.

7. *Accompanying the Child.* A staff member from the sending school initially may accompany the student to the new school to serve as a resource for the student and the staff.

8. *Structuring Social Acceptance.* Teachers in the new setting structure the environment to promote the social acceptance of the new students by locating their work area near class leaders or assigning them an important class job.

9. *Opening Lines of Communication.* Ongoing communication systems between personnel from the sending and receiving schools are established.

10. *Scheduling Followup.* As part of the communication system, followup meetings to discuss the students' progress and to resolve areas of conflict are conducted.

School Administrators

School administrators can be instrumental in orienting and welcoming students to their new school. Principals can help assimilate students into the new school by doing the following:

- referring to the class as they would any other class by room number or teacher's name
- acknowledging the classes' achievements over the intercom system
- having the class design a class symbol, such as a mural
- ensuring that the class participates in all schoolwide activities
- giving the class a guided tour of the school
- encouraging students to participate in clubs and organizations
- having the class run a school contest or conduct a school poll
- assigning school jobs to the class or to class members (Salend, 1979b)

TRANSITIONAL PROGRAMS FOR STUDENTS EXITING SCHOOL

The Individuals with Disabilities Education Act (IDEA) requires that multidisciplinary teams develop and implement services to help students make the transition from school to adult life. These services must be delivered to students no later than 16 years of age. Students with severe cognitive and/or multiple disabilities should be provided these services no later than 14 years of age. In designing transitional programs, multidisciplinary teams should develop a transition plan that includes the following:

- an ecological assessment of the new environment to identify the physical, social, emotional, and cognitive skills necessary to perform effectively in the new setting
- a listing of the related services and adaptive devices that can affect success in the new environment as well as any potential barriers such as availability of transportation
- a statement of the goals and objectives of the transitional program
- a listing of instructional strategies, approaches, materials, and adaptations as well as the supportive services necessary to achieve the stated goals of the transitional program

- a description of the communication systems that will be used to foster information sharing among professionals and between school and family members
- a system for evaluating the success of the transition program (Mental Retardation Institute, 1991)

Johnson and Thompson (1989) provide guidelines for enhancing parental participation in planning transitional programs. A sample transitional plan is presented in Figure 5.10.

Transitional programming for students exiting schools often addresses three areas: employment, living arrangements, and leisure (Chadsey-Rusch, Rusch, & O'Reilly, 1991; Halpern, 1985).

Employment

An important outcome for many youth leaving high school is employment including earning money, interacting with others, and advancing in one's career (Chadsey-Rusch et al., 1991). In recognition of the importance of this outcome, the Office of Special Education and Rehabilitation Services established the transition from school to work as a priority for schools (Will, 1984). Despite this priority, current estimates indicate that the unemployment rate for non-college-bound youths is as high as 15.8 percent (William T. Grant Foundation, 1988).

The unemployment and underemployment rate is tragically high for African American youth and youth with disabilities (Mithaug, Martin, Agran, & Rusch, 1988; William T. Grant Foundation, 1988).

Competitive Employment

Youth who are exiting schools will need assistance in making the transition to competitive and supported employment. *Competitive employment* involves working as a regular employee in an integrated setting with coworkers who are not disabled, and being paid at least minimum wage (Berkell & Gaylord-Ross, 1989). Individuals usually find competitive employment through participating in a job training program, obtaining the assistance of a network of family and friends, and receiving the services of a rehabilitation agency.

Supported Employment

While some individuals with mild disabilities may find competitive employment, many individuals will benefit from supported employment (Rusch, 1990). Encouraged by the Rehabilitation Act Amendments of 1986, *supported employment* provides individuals with ongoing assistance as they learn how to obtain, perform, and hold a job; travel to and from work; interact with coworkers; work successfully in integrated community settings; and receive a salary that is commensurate with the prevailing wage rate (Heward & Orlansky, 1992; Powell & Moore, 1992). Lagomarcino, Hughes, and Rusch (1989) compiled a list of performance, adaptability, and social skills measures that educators can use in helping prepare individuals for success in competitive and supported employment settings. Powell and Moore (1992) provide an overview of agencies and programs providing services to employees and

FIGURE 5.10
Sample individualized transition plan

INDIVIDUALIZED TRANSITION PLAN

PLANNING MEETING DATE ______
DATE OF BIRTH 16 years old at time of meeting

NAME OF STUDENT Alan

PLANNING TEAM Alan, Alan's mother, Mrs. Thomas (classroom teacher), Jeff R. (job coach), Mr. Jones (school administrator) and John M. (paraprofessional)

TRANSITION OPTIONS	GOAL	SCHOOL REPRESENTATIVES AND RESPONSIBILITIES	PARENT/FAMILY RESPONSIBILITIES	AGENCIES INVOLVED RESPONSIBILITIES AND CONTACT PERSON	SUPPORTIVE IEP GOAL(S)/OBJECTIVE(S)
VOCATIONAL PLACEMENTS Competitive Supportive Sheltered Specify the above or other It is unclear whether Alan will be better able to perform in a competitive or supportive work environment 5 years from now, but both options are being explored. Identify current and past vocational experiences Alan currently spends 2 hours each week working at a local nursery.	 X X X	1. Teacher will increase from 2 hrs. weekly to 5 hrs. weekly the time Alan spends working at the nursery. 2. Job coach will expand the types of jobs Alan performs from maintenance tasks to more nursery trade related tasks. 3. Job coach will introduce two additional vocational experiences for Alan each of the next 3 years so that Alan can, in his last 2 years of school, choose a vocational area of preference and refine his skills in these.	1. Alan's mother will begin to give Alan a regular, weekly allowance. 2. Mother will begin to explore vocational options/interests by: a) checking with friends who own businesses to see if any have training opportunities for Alan; and b) spending time with Alan visiting different places and talking with Alan about the different jobs observed on these "exploration trips." 3. Mother will assign Alan some household "jobs" so Alan has the opportunity to be responsible for chores.	1. Job coach/teacher will arrange Alan's schedule next year to include more community-based vocational experiences. 2. School administrator will initiate canvass of local businesses to explore potential vocational training sites for Alan including: a) local automotive parts refurbishing site b) local shipping company c) local supermarket chain d) local restaurant 3. Contact at local VESID office will visit school to provide overview training to staff re: job-related skills development. 4. Job coach/teacher will perform functional assessment at each worksite to identify areas in which Alan needs support.	—communication —identify job(s) he likes —behavior relaxation, identification of feelings —money management —skill mastery in designated tasks/jobs. —grooming via uniform care and laundry, etc. —functional time telling —learning how to use staff lounge for break/meal times —social skills training (co-workers)

FIGURE 5.10
(continued)

INDIVIDUALIZED TRANSITION PLAN

NAME OF STUDENT Alan

PLANNING MEETING DATE ____

DATE OF BIRTH 16 years old at time of meeting

PLANNING TEAM Alan, Alan's mother, Mrs. Thomas (classroom teacher), Jeff R. (job coach), Mr. Jones (school administrator) and John M. (paraprofessional)

TRANSITION OPTIONS	GOAL	SCHOOL REPRESENTATIVES AND RESPONSIBILITIES	PARENT/FAMILY RESPONSIBILITIES	AGENCIES INVOLVED RESPONSIBILITIES AND CONTACT PERSON	SUPPORTIVE IEP GOAL(S)/OBJECTIVE(S)
LIVING ARRANGEMENTS With family Semi-independent living Community residence Specify the above or other Alan expressed the desire to live with his friend—a coworker who resides in an ICF. Identify current living arrangements Alan lives at home with his mother.	 ____ ____ X X	1. Alan's teacher will work with the school assistant principal to redesign Alan's class activities to allow for more community-based instructional activities. Prioritized inclusions are: a) shopping and money management b) clothing maintenance and grooming c) food preparation d) recreation and leisure e) household cleaning chores 2. School social worker will complete and send out a referral packet on Alan highlighting his need for residential placement.	1. Alan's mother will, with assistance from school social worker, process appropriate paperwork to "register" Alan with the local OMRDD office and will place Alan's name on a waiting list for resident placement. 2. Alan's mother will begin to visit different residential programs (e.g., ICF, CR, supervised apartment) to become acquainted with the varying levels of care available. 3. Alan's mother will provide opportunities for Alan to perform some household tasks, e.g., laundry, some simple food preparation and some cleaning chores.		—food preparation and menu planning —weight maintenance group —functional counting —money skills

FIGURE 5.10
(continued)

INDIVIDUALIZED TRANSITION PLAN

PLANNING MEETING DATE ______

NAME OF STUDENT Alan

DATE OF BIRTH 16 years old at time of meeting

PLANNING TEAM Alan, Alan's mother, Mrs. Thomas (classroom teacher), Jeff R. (job coach), Mr. Jones (school administrator) and John M. (paraprofessional)

TRANSITION ISSUES	GOAL	SCHOOL REPRESENTATIVES AND RESPONSIBILITIES	PARENT/FAMILY RESPONSIBILITIES	AGENCIES INVOLVED RESPONSIBILITIES AND CONTACT PERSON	SUPPORTIVE IEP GOAL(S)/OBJECTIVE(S)
RECREATION AND LEISURE Use of integrated, community facilities and programs	X	1. Teacher will meet with gym teacher to explore sporting activities (other than basketball) to which Alan can be exposed. 2. Teacher's aide will spend 1 afternoon weekly with Alan visiting various sites (including museums, parks, toy stores, craft supplies stores) in an effort to expose Alan to various types of leisure-/hobby activities and elicit any interests Alan may have. 3. Teacher will include Alan in weekly "club" activities (run by other teachers) during which students are taught various board and card games and encouraged to participate in tournaments. 4. Teacher and social worker will look for an appropriate activity—based on Alan's preferences—in which Alan can participate with same age peers from school's mainstream population.	1. Mother will set aside time on weekends to "play" with Alan the games he learned in school. 2. Mother will contact the group home where Alan's friend lives and she will arrange for Alan to visit periodically and join in on some of the home's leisure activities. 3. Mother will look at neighborhood sponsored programs to see if any might be of interest to Alan (e.g., local YMCA, library).		—communication —functional math —turn-taking skills —learning new games —identify preferences
Use of specialized facilities and programs	____				
Specify the above or other	____				
Identify current recreation and leisure programs being used Alan occasionally goes bowling with his mother. Also, he occasionally goes to the movies with her.					

FIGURE 5.10
(continued)

INDIVIDUALIZED TRANSITION PLAN

NAME OF STUDENT Alan
PLANNING MEETING DATE ____
DATE OF BIRTH 16 years old at time of meeting
PLANNING TEAM Alan, Alan's mother, Mrs. Thomas (classroom teacher), Jeff R. (job coach), Mr. Jones (school administrator) and John M. (paraprofessional)

TRANSITION ISSUES	GOAL	SCHOOL REPRESENTATIVES AND RESPONSIBILITIES	PARENT/FAMILY RESPONSIBILITIES	AGENCIES INVOLVED RESPONSIBILITIES AND CONTACT PERSON	SUPPORTIVE IEP GOAL(S)/OBJECTIVE(S)
TRANSPORTATION Provided by family Public transportation Specialized tranportation Orientation and mobility assistance Specify the above or other	 X ___ ___ ___ ___	1. Teacher will work with job coach to begin travel training with Alan on using public bus to/from the nursery. 2. Speech/language therapist will work with teacher and Alan in developing a travel-specific communication card system for Alan to use when he travels in the community.	1. Mother will occasionally ride public bus with Alan during the weekends to further expose Alan to this mode of travel. 2. Mother will walk with Alan in their neighborhood to help Alan develop his sense of direction and orientation. 3. Mother will apply for 1/2 fare ID card for Alan's use when using public transportation.		-communication -mobility training in community using public transportation
Identify current modes of transportation used School bus; family car					

Source: J. O'Neill, C. Gothelf, S. Cohen, L. Lehman, and S. B. Woolf, *Supplement for Transition Coordinators: A Curricular Approach to Support the Transition to Adulthood of Adolescents with Visual or Dual Sensory Impairments and Cognitive Disabilities.* (New York, NY: Hunter College of the City University of New York and the Jewish Guild for the Blind, 1990. ERIC Documentation Reproduction Service No. EC 300 449-453).

work incentives to employers to support the establishment of supported employment placements.

Heward and Orlansky (1992) identified four supported employment models: the work enclave or clustered placement, the mobile work crew, the entrepreneurial model, and individual placement.

Work Enclave. In the *work enclave* or *clustered placement* model, individuals work in groups at an integrated community work setting. The group, which is made up of no more than ten workers, is supervised by a trained, experienced professional and receives wages based on its productivity (Rhodes & Valenta, 1985). A variation of the work enclave is the *dispersed enclave,* where the group is divided into smaller groups that perform various job functions at locations dispersed throughout the job site (Mental Retardation Institute, 1991).

Mobile Work Crews. In this model, individuals work in groups with each group member performing a specific job (Mental Retardation Institute, 1991). Often the crew travels from site to site and is supervised by a supported employment specialist.

Entrepreneurial Model. In the *entrepreneurial* model, a business hires small groups of individuals with disabilities as well as groups without disabilities and contracts out their services to other businesses within the community (Heward & Orlansky, 1992).

Individual Placement. In *individual placement,* individuals are placed in employment situations and receive the services of a job coach. Wehman and Kregel (1985) have developed a model for placing individuals in supported employment that includes four phases: job placement, job-site training and advocacy, ongoing evaluation of the individual's performance, and followup services and job retention planning.

Job Coach

An essential component of all supportive employment models is the services of a *job coach* or a supported employment specialist (Wehman & Kregel, 1985). While the functions of the job coach depend on the supported employment model, the job coach may perform a variety of roles, including the following:

- providing assistance to and working collaboratively with educators, parents, and employers
- assessing the student's job skills and preferences for employment
- identifying and placing students in jobs in the community that relate to the student's job skills and interests
- training students in the job-related, travel, and interpersonal skills necessary to be successful on the job
- working with employers and coworkers to obtain their assistance in helping the individual function successfully

- helping families and community members enhance the employment-related skills of their child and friends
- evaluating the progress of the individual
- providing on the job assistance and feedback to individuals
- monitoring the satisfaction of the individual, employer, coworkers, and parents
- fading out their services and providing periodic followup services (Rehder, 1986; Wehman & Kregel, 1985)

Career Education

A developmentally appropriate career education program can be instrumental in helping students make the the transition to work. Beginning in the elementary school years, career education should occur throughout students' schooling and include career awareness, orientation, exploration, preparation, and placement (Grennan).

Elementary School Years. During the elementary school years, students' career education programs should focus on *career awareness,* an understanding of the various occupations and jobs available to workers, the importance of work and an initial self-awareness of career interests (Greenan, 1989). Career education programs at the elementary level also introduce students to daily living skills, attitudes, values, and concepts related to work through classroom jobs, homework, and money (Clark & Kolstoe, 1990; Mental Retardation Institute, 1991).

Junior High/Middle School Years. During the junior high school years, students' career education programs should focus on *career orientation,* an identification of career interests through practical experience and exposure to a variety of occupations (Greenan, 1989). Through field trips, speakers, special vocational classes, and integrated curricula, students develop greater familiarity with work settings, attitudes, job-related and interpersonal skills, and an appreciation of values associated with working.

High School Years. During the high school years, students' career education programs should focus on career exploration, preparation, and placement (Greenan, 1989). *Career exploration* activities provide students with simulated and direct experiences with a range of occupations to assist students in determining their career goals and interests. Vocational guidance and counseling also is provided to help obtain information about a variety of jobs. *Career preparation* helps students make the adjustment to work by offering instruction, support and work experiences through vocational education programs. A career preparation program includes training in the specific job-related skills and the opportunity to demonstrate mastery of these skills in simulated or real work settings. *Career placement,* the placement of students in jobs or other postsecondary opportunities, often occurs as students are ready to exit from high school.

While in high school, students may participate in work experience programs such as cooperative work education or work-study (Clark & Kolstoe, 1990). In *cooperative work education programs,* students attend school and work on a part-time basis. Through a cooperative agreement between schools and employers, students' educational and employment experiences are coordinated so that students are encouraged to complete school while obtaining the necessary training and experiences for future employment (Greenan, 1989). *Work-study programs* also help students complete high school by providing them with economic assistance through a part-time job. In addition to economic assistance, students' jobs offer them the opportunity to acquire job-related skills and experiences.

Career Education Models

A variety of career education models is available to educators (Clark & Kolstoe, 1990). A brief description of some of these models follows. The *Life-Centered Career Education (LCCE)* model targets 22 life-centered competencies within the domains of daily living skills, personal-social skills, and occupational guidance and preparation that are designed to be infused into the regular education curriculum (Kokaska & Brolin, 1985). Clark and Kolstoe (1990) have developed the *School Based Career Education Model,* which offers a framework for delivering career education services from preschool through adulthood and includes the areas of values, attitudes, habits, human relationships, occupational information, and job and daily living skills. Larson (1981) developed the *Experience-Based Career Education (EBCE)* model, which provides students with the opportunities to work in community-based settings while taking classes in school. The *School-Based Comprehensive Career Education* model seeks to transform the regular education curricula through career education information and the availability of guidance, counseling, consultation, and curriculum guides that outline modifications and innovative strategies (Goldhammer & Taylor (1972). Gillet's (1981) *Career Education for Exceptional Children and Youth,* offers educators a developmental model for teaching students about a variety of jobs and helping students develop appropriate work habits and skills.

Career Education for Students from Culturally and Linguisitically Diverse Backgrounds and for Female Students

Data indicate that students from culturally and linguistically diverse backgrounds and female students are often channeled into less challenging careers. For example, when female students express an interest in a medical career, they are often encouraged to explore nursing rather than being a doctor. Educators should provide all students with an understanding of the following:

- the importance of work
- sex-role and cultural stereotyping and its impact on career choices
- the preparation they need for the variety of careers that are available to them
- the importance of jobs inside and outside the home (Shapiro, Kramer & Hunerberg, 1981)

Walker (1991) outlines a multicultural model that can help educators understand the impact of an individual's cultural perspectives on their career choices.

Think About It

How did you become interested in teaching as a career? What career education programs assisted you in making that decision? What job-related and interpersonal skills do you need to be an effective teacher? What career education experiences have helped you develop those skills? How did your cultural background and gender affect your career choice?

Living Arrangements

As students exit school, they also may need assistance in making the transition to residing in community-based living arrangements. Clark and Kolstoe (1990) identified the most common community-based living arrangements:

1. Independent living (alone or with a spouse, significant other, or roommates) in a house, mobile home, or apartment
2. Semi-independent living (alone or with someone else) in a house, mobile home, or apartment with periodic supervision
3. Living at home with one or both parents or other relatives with minimal or no supervision
4. Group home living with 6 to 10 other residents under minimal but continuous supervision
5. Family care or foster home living with close and continuous supervision (pp. 349–350)

To successfully make the transition to these residential settings, students will need training to overcome negative attitudes, environmental constraints (such as the availability of transportation, shopping and leisure activities), and socioeconomic barriers (Clark & Kolstoe, 1990). In addition to addressing these barriers, programs to prepare students for the transition to various residential settings should help them learn how to be self-sufficient and take care of their needs, maintain the property, and seek assistance from others when necessary (Salend, Michael, Veraja, & Noto, 1983). Curricula and training programs to teach housekeeping and other independent living skills are available (Bauman & Iwata, 1977; Crnic & Pym, 1979).

Salend and Giek (1987) propose that schools and agencies establish the position of an independent living specialist to coordinate placing individuals in independent living arrangements. The independent living specialist would serve as a liaison between landlords, tenants, tenants' families, and agencies and schools. Independent living specialists can assess an individual's readiness for independent living arrangements; assist the individual in finding an appropriate residence in terms of cost, location to work, recreation, shop-

ping, transportation, and community services; assist the individual
the adjustment to the new residential setting; and offer training in bas
skills.

Leisure

Though often overlooked, leisure is another important component in providing transitional services to students (Chadsey-Rusch et al., 1991; Ludlow, Turnbull, & Luckasson, 1988). Dattilo and St. Peter (1991) define *leisure* as "a person's perception that he or she is free to choose to participate in meaningful, enjoyable and satisfying experiences" (p. 420). Through leisure and recreation activities, individuals can develop satisfying social and interpersonal relationships with others (Halpern, 1985). Unfortunately, followup studies on the leisure activities of individuals with disabilities reveal that they are less likely to belong to school or community groups than their peers who are not disabled (Wagner, 1989).

Wagner (1989) found that the rate of participation in leisure activities of students with disabilities significantly decreased upon their exiting school.

Leisure Education

In light of the recognition of the importance of leisure for all members of society, there has been a growing movement toward providing leisure education services to students. Leisure education services provide individuals with an awareness of recreation and the skills necessary to interact with others in a range of community leisure activities throughout one's life (Center for Recreation and Disability Studies, 1991; Howe-Murphy & Charboneau, 1987). Leisure education teaches students to function independently during free-time activities at school, at home, and in the community; participate in leisure and recreation activities with others; and engage in positive free-time activities.

Dattilo and St. Peter (1991) suggest that effective leisure education programs should include the following components:

The Center for Recreation and Disability Studies (1991) has developed a list of leisure education and recreation resources that can guide educators in developing leisure education programs. Durgin, Lindsay, and Hamilton (1985) have compiled a listing of sports and recreation groups and national clearinghouses serving individuals with disabilities.

- an awareness of leisure
- a knowledge of one's preferences for recreation activities
- an appreciation of leisure and its importance
- an understanding of the distinction between leisure and work
- an ability to participate in specific recreation and leisure activities
- an ability to select appropriate, realistic, and acceptable leisure-time activities
- an understanding of the skills, costs, equipment, other individuals, and resources necessary to participate in various leisure activities
- an ability to exhibit the social skills necessary to interact and develop friendships with others

Dattilo and St. Peter (1991) also suggest that leisure education programs employ a *leisure coach,* a therapeutic recreation specialist or an individual with expertise in leisure education. The leisure coach works with teachers, parents, community members, and multidisciplinary team members to inte-

grate leisure education goals into students' educational and transitional programs. Dattilo and St. Peter outline the roles of the leisure coach.

Postsecondary Opportunities

The American Council on Education (1987) reported that 6.8% of the first-year college students identified themselves as having a disability.

A growing number of students with disabilities is exploring college as a postsecondary opportunity. In particular, students with learning disabilities appear to be interested in attending college (White, Alley, Deshler, Schumaker, Warner, & Clark, 1982).

Brandt and Berry (1991) and Grasso-Ryan and Price (1992) offer guidelines for transitioning students with disabilities to college that include suggestions for planning and goal setting, promoting academic preparation, and developing social skills. Aune and Ness (1991) have developed *Tools for Transition* for use by educators who are helping students make the transition to postsecondary education. The eight units of Tools for Transition are (a) Un-

IDEAS FOR IMPLEMENTATION	Teachers can promote the leisure skills and attitudes of their students by enacting the following suggestions: • Allow and encourage students to select their own free-time activities. • Provide students with the opportunities and skills to try new activities and toys. • Teach students how to initiate play with others. • Model how to contact community-based leisure resources to get information about available activities. • Invite members of community-based leisure groups to speak to students about their groups' activities. • Discuss and visit leisure activities available in the community. • Share and read in class materials about community leisure activities such as newspaper articles, flyers from parks and museums, and newspaper and magazine movie, music, and dance reviews and sports pages. • Have students write and talk about their leisure activities. • Role play leisure situations. • Encourage students to participate in afterschool activities. • Teach scoring for a variety of recreational games. • Seek the assistance of others such as a therapeutic recreation specialist, physical educator, community recreation personnel, and parents.

Source: Center for Recreation and Disability Studies (1991).

derstanding My Learning Style; (b) Using Study Strategies; (c) Planning Accommodations in School; (d) Self-Advocacy; (e) Exploring Careers; (f) Choosing a Type of Postsecondary School; (g) Choosing and Applying to a Postsecondary School; and (h) Interpersonal Skills.

Peer Mentors

Peer mentors, adults with disabilities who guide and assist younger individuals with disabilities, can be a valuable resource in helping students make the transitions to adulthood (Driscoll, 1989). Partners are selected based on shared interests, disabilities, goals, and personalities. By sharing their experiences and meeting with students with disabilities on a regular basis, peer mentors serve as role models for working in competitive employment situations, living independently, participating in community recreation activities, and having a family life. Same-race and -language peers, and personnel who understand the students' language and culture also can be instrumental in helping students from culturally and linguistically diverse backgrounds make the many school- and society-based transitions they face.

SUMMARY

This chapter was designed to offer guidelines for planning and implementing transitional programs to prepare students for success in a variety of mainstreamed settings. The chapter

- offered a framework based on Anderson-Inman's transenvironmental programming model for preparing students to function successfully in mainstreamed settings
- provided guidelines for teaching students to use a variety of strategies for obtaining information from regular classroom textbooks; for listening to information from teachers and peers; for taking notes from lectures and textbooks; for remembering specific information; for working independently; and for developing appropriate behavioral, social, and language skills
- reviewed guidelines for developing transitional programs for students who speak English as a second language
- presented strategies to promote the generalization of skills to mainstreamed settings
- outlined a model for moving students from special day schools to public schools, and from early intervention programs to school
- discussed factors to consider in designing transitional programs for students who are exiting school

RECOMMENDED READINGS

Anderson-Inman, L. (1986). Bridging the gap: Student-centered strategies for promoting the transfer of learning. *Exceptional Children, 52,* 562–572.

Archer, A. L. (1988). Strategies for responding to information. *Teaching Exceptional Children, 20,* 55–57.

Berkell, D. E., & Brown, J. M. (Eds.) (1989). *Transition from school to work for persons with disabilities* White Plains, NY: Longman.

Bradstad, B. J., & Stumpf, S. M. (1987). *A guide book for teaching study skills and motivation* (*Second edition*). Boston: Allyn & Bacon.

Chamot, A. U., & O'Malley, J. M. (1989). The cognitive academic language learning approach. In P. Rigg & V. G. Allen (Eds.), *When they don't all speak English: Integrating the ESL student into the regular classroom* (pp. 108–125). Urbana, IL: National Council of Teachers of English.

Clark, G. M., & Kolstoe, O. (1990). *Career development and transition education for adolescents with disabilities.* Boston: Allyn & Bacon.

Hamayan, E. V., & Perlman, R. (1990). *Helping language minority students after they exit from bilingual/ESL programs: A handbook for teachers.* Washington, DC: National Clearinghouse for Bilingual Education.

Masters, L. F., & Mori, A. A. (1986). *Teaching secondary students with mild learning and behavior problems: Methods, materials, strategies.* Rockville, MD: Aspen.

Mental Retardation Institute (1991). *Assessment and educational planning for students with severe disabilities.* Valhalla, NY: Author.

Vaughn, S., Bos, C. S., & Lund, K. A. (1986). . . . But they can do it in my room: Strategies for promoting generalization. *Teaching Exceptional Children, 18,* 176–180.

6 Modifying Large- and Small-Group Instruction

REVISING MANNY'S INSTRUCTIONAL PROGRAM

Manny's teachers have been concerned about his academic progress. In particular, he is doing poorly in classes where teachers use lectures and require students to take notes. His motivation seems to vary depending on the assignment, and several of his teachers feel he has difficulty following directions and paying attention. They note that he does perform quite well when he works with others in cooperative learning groups.

After fully discussing the conditions that affect Manny's performance, his teaching and planning team brainstorms and develops a list of potential instructional modifications to be used with Manny. The team then discusses and evaluates each suggested modification with respect to its potential impact on Manny and other students, prior effectiveness, and ease of implementation. They agree to try writing main points on the board, providing lecture outlines, and summarizing main points at the end of the class to assist Manny in following oral presentations and taking notes. To help him in following directions and paying attention, they decide to place Manny with a peer who can maintain attention and serve as a homework buddy.

What other instructional modifications would be appropriate for Manny? After reading this chapter, you should be able to answer this as well as the following questions.

- What procedures should planning teams use in determining appropriate instructional modifications for students?
- How can educators modify large-group instruction to meet the needs of mainstreamed students?
- How can educators modify small-group instruction to meet the needs of mainstreamed students?
- What are the elements of direct instruction?
- How can educators successfully implement cooperative learning arrangements and academic games?

Teachers teach in many different ways. They use large- and small-group instruction to convey new information to their students. Whereas Chapter 5 discussed a variety of strategies that *students* can use to benefit from instruction in the mainstreamed setting, this chapter offers strategies that *teachers* can employ to facilitate students' mastery of classroom content presented through large- and small-group instruction.

DETERMINING INSTRUCTIONAL MODIFICATIONS

The types of instructional modifications mainstreamed students will need can be determined and specified by the multidisciplinary planning team. Since teachers are more likely to implement instructional modifications that they help design, teachers should be included in planning instructional modifications for their mainstreamed students (Margolis & McGettigan, 1988). Additionally, whenever possible, mainstreamed students should participate in planning adaptations; they can be a reliable source of information concerning which modifications they have found to be most useful and effective.

While a variety of techniques exist for adapting the learning environment to promote the optimal performance of mainstreamed students, the selection of an appropriate modification will depend on several factors, including the students' learning needs and the teachers' instructional styles. Cohen and

Lynch (1991) offer an excellent model for selecting appropriate instructional modifications for students. The model has seven steps:

Step 1: Clarification of Elements Under Teacher Control. The planning team identifies the variables under the teacher's control, including the physical and social environment of the classroom, the organization and objectives of the lesson, the choice of instructional activities, materials and media, the availability of ancillary support personnel, the classroom management strategies, and the evaluation techniques.

Step 2: Development of a Modification Menu. The planning team lists potential modifications that can be employed with the student.

Step 3: Decision about Whether a Problem Exists. The planning team meets with teachers to determine the extent of the problem.

Step 4: Development of Problem Statement. The planning team agrees upon and states the problem in a clear and understandable manner.

Step 5: Selection and Grouping of Modifications. The planning team reviews the modification menu delineated in step 2 and selects a number of alternatives that address the problem(s) stated in step 4.

Step 6: Ranking of Modification Options. The planning team ranks each alternative suggested in step 5 according to potential impact, prior effectiveness, teacher's ability, and number of outside resources and time demands necessary to implement the modification.

Step 7: Modification Implementation. The planning team selects an instructional modification based on the rankings computed in step 6, which is then implemented and evaluated for its impact on the problem.

Treatment Acceptability

Another important factor that teachers and planning teams should consider in adapting instructional techniques to address the needs of mainstreamed students is *treatment acceptability,* the extent to which teachers view a specific instructional strategy as easy to use, effective, appropriate for their settings, and reasonable (Kazdin, 1980; Martens, Peterson, Witt, & Cirone, 1986). Brown (1988) noted that reasonableness can be assessed by examining the instructional modification in terms of how much extra time it will take to implement, whether it will require significant changes in the teachers' styles, and how much it will cost. In general, teachers are more likely to implement an instructional strategy that is practical, easy to use, immediately effective, and not disruptive to their classroom routine and teaching style (Margolis & McGettigan, 1988).

A second aspect of treatment acceptability examines the impact of the proposed intervention on the mainstreamed students and their classroom peers. Bacon and Schulz (1991) reported that teachers were more likely to employ strategies that benefit all students. Additional dimensions of treatment acceptability related to students include age appropriateness, risks such as student embarrassment or isolation, intrusiveness into the student's personal space, and student cooperation (Epps, Prescott, & Horner, 1990). For example, placing a mainstreamed student who has difficulty attending to seatwork in a cubicle, or assigning a mainstreamed student a math assignment while the other students are working on social studies, can have the negative effect of isolating a student within the mainstreamed setting. Care must be taken to ensure that proposed modifications do not adversely impact either the mainstreamed student or his or her classmates. Therefore, in selecting, designing, and implementing modifications of the students' and teachers' needs, placement teams should consider the following:

- What are the strengths, weaknesses, and unique needs of the student?
- How does the presentation mode of the teacher and the course content affect the student's performance?
- How does the response mode of the teacher and the course content affect the student's performance?
- Does the student require specialized material or adaptive devices?
- Are there any architectural barriers that affect the student's performance?
- Is the modification compatible with the student's cultural perspective?
- Is the modification consistent with the student's linguistic abilities?
- Does the modification adequately address the problem(s)?
- Does the modification protect the integrity of the course and the grading system?
- What are the implications of the modification on the teacher, the mainstreamed student, other students, and the staff?

Think About It

What factors do you consider when choosing an instructional strategy to implement with students? Use these factors to evaluate the instructional strategies presented in this book.

Oral Presentations

Data indicate that the instructional strategy most frequently used by teachers is lecturing (Wood, 1988). Teachers can employ a variety of strategies to help students gain and understand information presented through oral presentations.

Pausing

Hawkins (1988) and Hughes, Hendrickson, and Hudson (1986) found that pausing periodically during lectures facilitated information retention.

Teachers can help students retain lecture content by pausing for two minutes after every five to seven consecutive minutes of lecturing (Guerin & Male, 1988; Ruhl, Hughes, & Schloss, 1987). During the two-minute pause, students should be directed to discuss and review content presented and their notes, jot down questions, rehearse important points, associate the lecture information with their experiences and interests, and engage in visual imagery. To ensure that students are active during the instructional pause, teachers can structure the pause by using a cue card that focuses students to engage in activities related to specific lecture content (Hawkins, 1988).

Cooperative Learning Groups

The amount of information gained from teacher-directed oral presentations can be enhanced through use of a variety of cooperative learning arrangements, such as collaborative discussion teams, Numbered Heads Together, and Think-Pair-Share.

Collaborative Discussion Teams. Teachers also can use collaborative discussion teams at various intervals throughout the lecture. After a specific amount of time, usually at 10- to 15-minute intervals, teams can respond to discussion questions, react to material presented, or predict what will happen or be discussed next. Teams can then be called upon to share their responses. At the end of the lecture, teams can summarize main points and check each other's comprehension.

Numbered Heads Together. Numbered Heads Together can be used to help students review, and check comprehension of orally presented information (Kagan, 1990). Teachers can implement Numbered Heads Together by doing the following:

1. Rank students by ability and assign them to heterogeneous groups of three or four.
2. Assign a number (1, 2, 3, or 4) to each student within each group.
3. Break up the oral presentation by periodically asking the class a question and telling each group to "put your heads together and make sure that everyone in your group knows the answer."
4. Inform the groups to end their discussion, call a number, ask all students with that number to raise their hands, select one of the students with that number to answer, and ask the other students with that number to agree with or expand upon the answer (Mallette, Pomerantz, & Sacca, 1991).

Think-Pair-Share. Think-Pair-Share is another cooperative learning strategy that teachers can employ to assist students in mastering content presented in oral presentations. In Think-Pair-Share, teachers do the following:

1. Randomly pair students.
2. Present students with a question, problem, or situation.
3. Ask individual students to think to themselves about the question posed by the teacher.
4. Have students discuss their responses with their partners.
5. Select several pairs to share their thoughts and responses with the class (Lyman, 1987; Mallette, Pomerantz, & Sacca, 1991).

Guided Lecture Procedure

Teachers can also use a guided lecture procedure to help the mainstreamed student benefit from lectures (Kelly & Holmes, 1979). In this procedure, teachers review the objectives of the lecture and allow students to record them in their notes before beginning the lecture; focus students' attention on the lecture by periodically reminding them to listen carefully and by not allowing them to take notes; pause midway through the lecture to offer students the opportunity to take notes on the content presented; place students in small groups at the end of the lecture to review content and share and develop notes; offer assistance to the small groups; and provide time for students to study and verbally summarize their notes. Because this technique requires students to be able to retain information for a period of time, it may not be effective with students who have memory deficits unless more frequent pauses are made during the lecture to allow for note taking.

Overhead Projector

Teachers can supplement their lectures with transparencies projected on an overhead projector (Wood, 1988). Transparencies can help students by providing visual support (charts, graphs, lists) during an oral presentation. For example, it is often helpful for teachers to begin by presenting the lecture's outline on a transparency as an advance organizer to orient students to the main and supporting points to be presented. The overhead projector allows teachers to present content and highlight main points and key vocabulary simultaneously on the overhead while maintaining eye contact with students. When presenting information using prepared transparencies, it is best to focus the students' attention by covering the transparency with a piece of paper and presenting one piece of information at a time.

Encouraging Questions

In order to benefit from oral instruction and understand assignments and directions, students should ask questions to clarify teacher comments and instructions. However, many mainstreamed students may be reluctant to ask questions (Alley & Deshler, 1979). To help these students overcome their fear of asking questions, teachers can do the following:

- reinforce student questioning through using praise (*I'm glad you asked that question. That's a good question. It shows you're really thinking.*)
- listen attentively and make eye contact
- offer students time to write down and ask questions during class
- provide students with the correct response and ask them to state the corresponding question
- teach students when and how to ask questions (Alley & Deshler, 1979; Fraenkel, 1973)

Note-Taking Skills

Mr. Goss, a seventh-grade social studies teacher, is concerned that although his students claim that they are studying, they are doing poorly on his tests. He asks them how they study for tests. They tell him that they study notes from class and the textbook. He examines their notes from class and notices that the students' notes are often incomplete and focused on material that he does not consider relevant.

The class is beginning a unit on the Civil War. To assist students in their note-taking skills, Mr. Goss prepares a series of listening guides for them, one of which is shown in Figure 6.1. As he lectures, he covers each of the main points listed in the outline. He periodically pairs students to check each others' listening guides and sometimes he collects their listening guides to check students' responses. Prior to the test, he reminds his students to use their listening guide to study. Mr. Goss is pleased when he discovers that students' grades on the test increase significantly.

The amount of information gleaned from lectures also will depend on the students' ability to take notes. Teachers can engage in several behaviors that can help students take quality notes (see Chapter 5 for a discussion of teaching students skills for better note taking).

IDEAS FOR IMPLEMENTATION

In preparing and delivering lectures, teachers can help students follow along by enacting the following suggestions:

- Initially state the objectives, purpose, and relevance of the lecture.
- Review prerequisite information and define key terminology needed to understand the main points.
- Explain the relationship between the new material and material previously covered in class.
- Organize the lecture so that the sequence of the presentation of information is appropriate.
- Use ordinal numbers and temporal cues (*first, second, finally*) to organize information for students.
- Emphasize important concepts and critical points by varying voice quality and by using cue words—speaking them with emphasis, writing them on the blackboard, and repeating them.
- Employ examples, illustrations, charts, diagrams, advance organizers, and maps to make the material more concrete.
- Use visual aids to supplement oral material.
- Refer to individuals, places, or things using nouns rather than pronouns.
- Employ specific numerical quantification terms instead of ambiguous ones (using *two* instead of *a couple*).
- Decrease the use of vague terms (*these kinds of things, somewhere*) and avoid phrases (*to make a long story short, as you all know*).
- Reduce extraneous information and stimuli.
- Ask students questions that require them to think about information presented and that assess comprehension and recall.
- Discuss and summarize all main points.
- Assign readings and other assignments that prepare students for class.
- Provide the opportunities for questions during and after the class.
- Offer students time at the end of class to review, summarize, and organize their notes.

Source: Bos & Vaughn (1988); Carman & Adams (1972); Chilcoat (1987); Wallace, Cohen, & Polloway (1987).

FIGURE 6.1
Listening guide for Civil War unit lecture

Civil War

A. The sides
   1. The Union:
   2. The Confederacy:
   3. The Border States:
      a. c.
      b. d.

B. Advantages of each side
   1. The Union:
      a. d.
      b. e.
      c. f.
   2. The Confederacy:
      a.
      b.

C. The strategy of each side:
   1. The Union:
      a.
      b.
      c.
      d.
   2. The Confederacy:
      a.
      b.
      c.

D. Key individuals to know
   1. Abraham Lincoln
   2. Jefferson Davis
   3. Stonewall Jackson
   4. Robert E. Lee
   5. Ulysses S. Grant
   6. Clara Barton

Source: Developed by Peter Goss, Social Studies Teacher, New Paltz Central Schools, New Paltz, New York.

Outlines

Giving students a teacher-prepared outline of the class session can provide them with a foundation for notes. Initially, the outline should include headings with main points as well as subheadings with supporting information. It should be read and discussed with the class. As students develop note-taking skills, teachers should introduce a skeletal outline of main points with enough space after each main point to record supporting information.

If providing students with outlines is not feasible, then teachers can facilitate note taking by listing the major points of each lecture on the blackboard or the overhead (Devine, 1981). Teachers also can structure students' notes at the beginning of class by listing questions on the blackboard relating to the day's class, and then discussing answers to them at the end of class (Hoover, 1986).

Teachers can provide students with a framework for note taking by using a listening guide or a slot/frame outline. Shields and Heron (1989) note that a *listening guide,* a list of important terms and concepts that parallels the order in which they will be presented in class, can facilitate identification and retention of key terms and major concepts. Students then add to the guide by writing supplemental information and supportive details. Some students may need a *slot/frame outline,* a sequential overview of the key terms and main points of the class or textbook chapter presented as an outline made up of incomplete statements (Lovitt, Rudsit, Jenkins, Pious, & Benedetti, 1986; Wood & Rosbe, 1985). Students listen to the lecture or read the textbook chapter and fill in the blanks to complete the outline, which then serves as the students' notes.

Highlighting Main Points

To help students in determining important points to be recorded in their notes, teachers can emphasize these points by pausing for attention, using introductory phrases *(I want you to remember this. This is critical to you.),* and changing inflection (Spargo, 1977). Another method that can aid students in identifying important classroom content is *oral quizzing,* in which the teacher allots time at the end of the class session to respond to student questions and to ask students questions based on the material presented in class (Spargo, 1977). Similarly, end-of-class time can be devoted to summarizing and reviewing main points from class content and discussing what points should be in the students' notes (Lock, 1981). Pairing students to check each others' notes after class also can ensure that mainstreamed students' notes are in the desired format and include relevant content (Mercer & Mercer, 1985). Additionally, teachers can check the accuracy, completeness, usability, and style of student notes by periodically collecting and reviewing them.

Peer Note Takers and Audiocassette Recorders

When selecting peer note takers, teachers should consider the peer note takers' mastery of the class content, sensitivity to mainstreamed students, and ability to work independently (Wilson, 1981).

The notes of students who have difficulties recording verbal information can be supplemented by the aid of peers or with audiocassette recorders. Teachers or mainstreamed students can ask classmates who are proficient at note taking to share their notes with others. Reproducing the notes can be facilitated by providing the peer with carbon paper or by using a photocopying machine.

Students also can record class sessions on an audiocassette, which can be replayed after class to allow students to take notes at their own pace (Devine, 1981). As with other notes, teachers periodically should review notes from tape-recorded classes. Since the replaying of audiocassettes can be time consuming, students with access to one can use a *harmonic compressor,* which can play back the recording at a faster speed without distorting the speech. Whether mainstreamed students are using peer note takers or audiocassettes, they should be required to take notes during class sessions. This will allow them to practice their note-taking skills and keep alert in class. It also can help prevent resentment from other students who may feel that the mainstreamed students have to do less work.

Think About It

What strategies do your instructors use to facilitate your note taking in class?

Listening Skills

A skill critical to taking notes is the ability to listen. Since communication is a two-way process, the speaker can assist students in developing their listening skills (see Chapter 5 for a discussion of teaching students skills to facilitate listening).

One strategy is to offer students some incentives for listening. For example, students can be given extra credit, free time, or no homework when they identify a carefully placed contradiction or a mistake in a teacher presentation. Motivation to listen also can be fostered by teachers' using gestures, eye contact, facial expressions, pauses, and voice changes. Keeping students actively involved in learning also can motivate them to listen. Teachers can actively involve students in the lesson by doing the following:

- teaching them to ask questions of their peers
- expanding upon and using students' responses
- employing activities that require students to use objects or work in small groups
- relating lesson content to the students' lives and interests
- using high-interest materials
- varying the schedule so that students are not passive for long periods of time (Jones & Jones, 1986)

Teachers also can promote listening skills during class presentations. Students can be asked to repeat or paraphrase instructions, assignments, and important statements. Teachers can periodically intersperse questions relating to critical content into class presentations, and have students try to predict what will be discussed next (Wallace & Kauffman, 1986). Listening also can be facilitated by supplementing oral statements with visual aids, varying the pace of the oral presentation to emphasize critical content, moving around the room, placing the student near the speaker, and minimizing nonessential and distracting noises and activities (Robinson & Smith, 1981).

Gaining Attention

Students spend much of their classroom time listening. An important aspect of listening to and following directions is paying attention. However, because many mainstreamed students may have difficulty focusing their attention (Lerner, 1985), teachers may have to use several attention getting strategies, such as the following:

- directing them to listen carefully (*Listen carefully to what I say.*)
- giving clear, emphatic instructions (*Put your finger on the top of the page.*)
- pausing before speaking to make sure all students are paying attention
- limiting distractions by having students remove unnecessary materials from their desks
- eliminating noise and visual distractions (Jones & Jones, 1986; Wallace & Kauffman, 1986)

Jones and Jones (1986) suggest that teachers use a cue, such as a verbal statement or physical gesture (raising hand, blinking the lights, ringing a bell), to alert students of the need to pay attention. To motivate students to respond to the cue, teachers can involve students in determining the cue and changing it on a monthly basis.

Attention also can be maintained by using color. Zentall and Kruczek (1988) found that color could enhance the performance of students with attention problems. However, they caution that color should focus attention to the salient features of the task rather than just increasing the attractiveness of the task.

Giving Directions

Research indicates that most teachers give over 200 instructional statements each day (Lovitt & Smith, 1972). Attention and listening skills are therefore important if students are to understand and follow directions to complete their assignments. Teachers can modify the ways they give instructions to help the class attend to and follow directions for assignments.

In general, instructions should inform students about the content of the assignment; the rationale for the assignment; the type of assistance allowed

IDEAS FOR IMPLEMENTATION

Teachers can maintain students' attention by enacting the following suggestions:

- Employ a fast-paced delivery of material.
- Have students respond frequently.
- Use repetition by asking students to answer the same questions several times during a class period.
- Reinforce correct responses and appropriate behavior with descriptive statements.
- Cue correct responses.
- Supplement statements with visual aids.
- Decrease distractions from extraneous stimuli.
- Place students closer to the speaker.
- Assign one activity at a time.
- Group students with peers who can maintain attention.
- Maintain eye contact with all students.
- Create suspense.
- Select students randomly to respond.
- Remind students that they may be called on next.
- Ask students to add information to or explain an answer given by a peer.
- Supplement the presentation or discussion with a visual display.
- Change activities frequently and vary the presentation and response modes of instructional activities.
- Decrease the complexity and syntax of statements.

Source: Everston, Emmer, Clements, Sanford, & Worsham (1989); Gearheart, Weishahn, & Gearheart (1988); George (1986); Robinson & Smith (1981).

from adults, peers, reference materials, and other aids; the amount of time allowed to complete the assignment; the format of the assignment; and the way the teacher will evaluate the assignment. Teachers can help students remember the materials they will need to complete the assignment by listing them on the assignment sheet (Cohen & de Bettencourt, 1988). Additionally, students should be told where and when to hand in a completed assignment and be given guidance on activities that they can work on if they complete a task early.

Teachers should use specific techniques for giving directions to students. When explaining assignments, make certain all students are attentive, pausing when students are not. Present directions to students visually via the blackboard, overhead projector, or flip chart, and review them orally using terminology that the students understand. When giving directions orally, teachers should simplify the vocabulary, decrease the use of extraneous words and irrelevant information, and use consistent terminology from assignment to assignment (Gillet, 1986). Students should copy the directions in their notebooks. If some students have difficulty copying from the blackboard or writing, the assignment can be given via a teacher-prepared handout using the writing style (manuscript or cursive) to which students are accustomed. Directions for completing assignments can also be recorded on audiocassette. Students who have difficulty can copy at their seat using the teacher's or a peer's notes, or a peer can copy the assignment. In presenting directions that have several steps, teachers should number and list the steps in sequential order. For example, an assignment using dictionary skills can be presented to students by listing the steps:

1. Use the dictionary guide words.
2. Check the pronunciation of each word.
3. Write the definition.

Teachers also can facilitate the students' understanding of the directions by providing students with a model of the assignment, encouraging students to ask questions concerning the assignment, and having students paraphrase and explain the directions to the rest of the class. Similarly, the teacher may question students to assess their understanding of the instructions (*What steps are you required to follow in doing this assignment? Can you anticipate any problems in doing this assignment? If you have a problem, who should you ask for help? What can you do if you finish early?*). Finally, to ensure understanding, students can complete several problems from the assignment under teaching supervision before beginning to work independently.

For students who continue to experience problems in following directions, teachers should break directions into shorter, more meaningful statements (Wallace, Cohen, & Polloway, 1987). When possible, teachers should give no more than two instructions at a time. These students should work on one part of the assignment at a time, and should check with the teacher before advancing to the next phase of the activity. Long assignments can be divided into several shorter ones, with students completing one part before working on the next.

Teachers can help students with reading and language problems understand written directions via a *rebus* system, wherein pictures represent important words in the directions (Cohen & de Bettencourt, 1988). Recurring direction words and their corresponding rebus can be placed in a convenient location in the room so that all students can see it. A sample rebus direction list developed by Cohen and de Bettencourt (1988) is presented in Figure 6.2.

Teachers also can help students follow directions on assignments by periodically providing time for students to receive teacher assistance. A signup sheet posted in the classroom can serve as a means of scheduling teacher-student meetings. The times teachers are available to provide assistance can be listed, and students can request assistance by signing their names next to the desired time.

Since teachers in the regular classroom may not be available to check students' work, independent work skills also can be fostered through use of self-correcting materials (Cohen & de Bettencourt, 1988). Potential self-correcting materials in the classroom include flash cards, puzzles, matching cards, tape-recorded answers, and transparency overlays.

Motivating Students

Ms. Whilemson, an eleventh-grade math teacher, notices that her students are not as enthusiastic as they were earlier in the school year. Some students are failing to complete their assignments and fewer students are participating in class. The number of yawns and notes passed in class seem to be increasing.

To reverse this cycle, Ms. Whilemson decides to change the major assignment for her upcoming unit on spreadsheets. She observes her students for a few days and notes that they spent a lot of time talking about getting jobs and buying a car and clothes. Based on these observations, she decides to have her students research a career and develop a spreadsheet that outlines their expenditures during the first year of employment. She also asks them to write a narrative answering the following questions: Why did you choose this career? What education or training is needed to enter this profession? What is the anticipated demand for this career? What is the beginning salary for this profession?

She asks students to share their spreadsheets and narratives with the class. All of the students complete the assignment and seem to enjoy sharing their findings with the class.

Motivation is an important aspect of learning, listening, and following directions. Because of their past history of negative experiences, mainstreamed students may lack the motivation necessary to be successful learners.

Organizing Notebooks and Work Areas

In addition to helping students take notes, pay attention, and listen, teachers may need to assist students in organizing and maintaining their notebooks.

FIGURE 6.2
Sample rebus directions list

	Direction Word	Picture Stimulus
1.	circle	
2.	cross out	
3.	book	
4.	read	
5.	page	P.
6.	cut	
7.	color	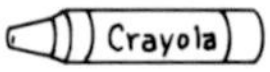
8.	look (at, over)	
9.	listen	
10.	underline	written
11.	do	do
12.	write	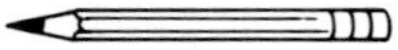
13.	think	
14.	tape (record)	
15.	remember	

Source: S. Cohen and L. de Bettencourt, "Teaching Children to be Independent Learners: A Step by Step Strategy," in E. L. Meyen, G. A. Vergason, and R. J. Whelan, *Effective Instructional Strategies for Exceptional Children* (Denver, CO: Love, 1988) p. 322. Reprinted by permission of the publisher.

IDEAS FOR IMPLEMENTATION

Teachers can help to motivate students by enacting the following suggestions:

- Have students identify what they would like to learn during the upcoming school year or semester.
- Develop a unit or several lessons based on students' interests.
- Survey students at the beginning of a unit to determine what their existing knowledge base is and what questions they have concerning the content of the unit.
- Integrate popular characters, items, and trends into classroom examples and assignments.
- Solicit feedback from students concerning innovative ways to demonstrate mastery.
- Ask students to assess their mastery of content.
- Establish high but realistic goals for students.
- Display enthusiasm for learning and for the material being presented.
- Use activities that arouse students' curiosity.
- Employ suspense and fantasy when presenting activities.
- Use games, simulations, and novelty.
- Acknowledge students' achievements.
- Teach students to set goals, and recognize the relationship between effort and performance.
- Allow students to demonstrate mastery through role play, skits, cartoons, and art projects.
- Devote class time periodically to student-selected content areas.
- Allow students to select learning and practicing activities from a variety of options.
- Offer activities that require students to be active rather than passive.
- Vary the instructional format and grouping arrangements.
- Ask open-ended, low-risk questions.
- Relate content to students' interests and to their lives.
- Use high-interest, culturally relevant materials.
- Employ examples that are relevant to students' cultural perspectives and life-styles.
- Create sensory curiosity.
- Teach content that is appropriate to the students' skill levels.
- Personalize instruction by using the students' names, interests, and experiences in the lesson.
- Provide students with choices, and with a range of options in terms of content and process.
- Reward students and teach them to reward themselves for work completion.

Source: Adelman & Taylor (1983); Brophy (1987); D'Zamko & Hedges (1985); Fuhler (1991); Jones & Jones (1986); Okolo, Bahr, & Gardner (1992).

Teachers can help students who have difficulties in organizing their notebooks by doing the following:

- monitoring notebooks and desks periodically
- offering class time to review notebooks, folders, and desks to reorganize them and throw out unnecessary materials

- providing students with the space to store materials
- giving students cartons to help them organize desk material
- teaching students to use folders and how to organize their notebooks and desks
- using incentives to motivate students to keep organized
- marking a notebook page about 20 pages from the last sheet to remind students to purchase a new notebook
- training peers to provide feedback to mainstreamed students on organizing their materials and desks (Archer, 1988; Glazzard, 1980)

To help prevent the loss of notebooks when taken back and forth between home and school, teachers can encourage the use of folders to transport assignments and other relevant necessary materials and information and can remind students to put their names in and cover all textbooks.

Some students also may need assistance in keeping their work areas neat and orderly. A weekly work area cleanup can help students eliminate unnecessary papers and materials and make sure they bring papers home to their parents. Baskets they can keep in their desks can store important materials that students need such as pencils, pens, scissors, and tape (Terranova, 1984).

DIRECT INSTRUCTION

Mr. Armstrong begins his lesson by reminding students that "we have been learning about nouns and verbs," and asking them to tell him something they did over the weekend. Students reply, "I went camping with my family," "I went to the movies," and "I played with my friends." Mr. Armstrong repeats these sentences and asks students to identify the nouns and verbs in the sentence, pausing for several seconds before randomly picking a student to respond.

Mr. Armstrong tells the students, "Today, we are going to learn about adjectives." He then defines an adjective and models finding the adjectives in a series of sentences. Then, using sentences he has written on the blackboard, he asks students to identify the nouns, verbs, and adjectives. Sometimes he asks a peer if he or she agrees with a student's response.

Next, he asks students to open their books to a page containing a series of sentences. He has students read a sentence and think about which words in the sentence are nouns, verbs, and adjectives. Then, he picks a word from the sentence and has students indicate whether the word is a noun, verb, or adjective by arranging their fingers in the shape of an *N* (noun), *V* (verb) or *A* (adjective). Occasionally, he asks students to justify their responses (*Why do you think that word is an adjective?*).

Mr. Armstrong concludes the lesson by giving students a handout of sentences and having them identify the nouns, verbs, and adjectives. As students work on the assignment, he circulates around the room, praising students, providing feedback, and assisting students. For homework, he asks them to write five sentences containing nouns, verbs, and adjectives and place an *N* over the nouns, *V* over the verbs, and *A* over the adjectives.

Elements of Direct Instruction

There has been a growing emphasis on identifying effective teaching behaviors that promote student mastery of content (Englert, 1984). A major focus of the teacher effectiveness research has been an examination of the components of effective lesson presentation (Hunter, 1981; Rosenshine, 1983; Stevens & Rosenshine, 1981). The elements of successful lessons for teaching concepts and skills include the following:

- Establish the purpose by explaining goals and objectives.
- Review prerequisite skills.
- Perform task analysis and introduce content in discrete steps followed by practice.
- Give clear directions, explanations, and relevant examples.
- Provide time for active and guided practice.
- Check for comprehension.
- Give prompt and specific feedback.
- Offer time for independent seatwork activities.
- Summarize main points and evaluate mastery (Rosenshine, 1986).

When using direct instruction techniques with second language learners, teachers should provide students with contextual cues and should integrate tasks into a meaningful whole (Ortiz & Yates, 1989).

These elements, which can be used effectively to guide both large- and small-group instruction, are discussed here.

Element 1: Establish the Purpose by Explaining Goals and Objectives

Teachers should begin the lesson by identifying its purpose so that students can focus their attention on the new information (Rosenshine, 1986). Research indicates that students' achievement increases when they understand their teachers' goals, the importance of the content, and its relationship to information previously learned (Kennedy, 1968).

Teachers should start the lesson with an *anticipatory set,* a statement or an activity that introduces the students to the content and offers some motivation to students to learn the material (Hunter, 1981). Usually, teachers then establish the purpose of the lesson either by telling students the objectives and goals of the lesson, or by writing them on the blackboard and establishing a relationship between the new content and previously learned material (Anderson, 1984). Teachers also can motivate students to learn the new material by relating the goals of the lesson to students' interests and relevant future life events (Wood, 1992). It also is helpful for students if teachers offer a review of the schedule of activities in the daily lesson and discuss the value of learning the material to students (Englert, 1984).

Element 2: Review Prerequisite Skills

After the lesson's purpose has been communicated to students, it is important for teachers to start the lesson with a review of previously learned, relevant skills. The review should be a five- to ten-minute synopsis of prerequisite skills that they will need to learn the new material in the lesson (Rosenshine,

1986). For example, in learning to tell time it might help students if the teacher reviews such skills as discriminating the big and small hands of the clock, and identifying the numerals 1 through 12. Effective teachers typically review prerequisite skills by correcting and discussing the previous night's homework, asking students to define key terms, requiring students to apply concepts, or assigning an activity that requires students to demonstrate mastery of prior relevant material (Englert, 1984; Rosenshine, 1986).

Element 3: Perform Task Analysis and Introduce Content in Discrete Steps Followed By Practice

Once the review of prerequisite skills has been completed, specific points should be presented to students in small, incremental, and sequential steps (Hunter, 1981; Rosenshine, 1986). Task analysis can aid teachers in identifying the sequential discrete steps that make up mastery of a skill. *Task analysis* is a systematic process of stating and sequencing the salient components of a specific task to determine the subtasks students should perform in order to master the task. A task analysis can help teachers 1) identify skills that need to be taught, as well as superfluous skills that are not essential to learning a task; 2) establish a sequence of instruction; 3) define the prerequisite skills needed to master the task; 4) record data and pinpoint errors; 5) understand the inherent difficulties associated with tasks; 6) individualize the lesson to meet the multiple skill levels of students; and 7) fill in the gaps in the curriculum. A sample task analysis is presented in Figure 6.3.

Teachers can follow several steps in performing the task analysis.

Determine Terminal Goal and Present Level of Functioning. Initially, teachers should identify the behavior that they want the students to learn (ask yourself, *What do you want the students to be able to do at the end of the lesson?*) and determine the students' present level of functioning on the skill (*What skills related to the task can students perform?*) to decide the last and first steps of the task analysis, respectively.

Identify Prerequisite Skills. Teachers can begin to analyze the task by examining the prerequisite skills needed to perform it. For example, a prerequisite skill related to the task of telling time is the ability to distinguish the numbers 1 through 12. Prerequisite skills mastered by students should be introduced in the daily review section of the lesson, while those skills not mastered should be incorporated into the task.

Determine the Components of the Behavior and Their Sequence. Next, teachers should determine the subskills that comprise the behavior and list them in sequential order from easiest to hardest. Depending upon the behavior, teachers can determine the components and the appropriate sequence by performing the task, consulting print materials, and examining the presentation and response modes.

Perform the Task. Some linear tasks, such as motor tasks, can be broken down into their component parts by performing the task, verbalizing the

FIGURE 6.3
Task analysis of telling time

Each skill completes the statement *The student will*

1. verbally identify the clock and its function.
2. verbally identify the numbers on the clock.
3. discriminate the big hand as the hour hand and the little hand as the minute hand.
4. state the number of minutes in an hour and number of seconds in a minute.
5. state the time when the time is set
   a. on the hour.
   b. on the half-hour.
   c. on the quarter-hour.
   d. in 10-minute intervals.
   e. in 5-minute intervals.
   f. in 1-minute intervals.
6. position the hands of the clock when given a specific time
   a. on the hour.
   b. on the half-hour.
   c. on the quarter-hour.
   d. in 10-minute intervals.
   e. in 5-minute intervals.
   f. in 1-minute intervals.
7. write the time when the time is set
   a. on the hour.
   b. on the half-hour.
   c. on the quarter-hour.
   d. in 10-minute intervals.
   e. in 5-minute intervals.
   f. in 1-minute intervals.

steps, and writing them down. For example, the steps in tying a shoe can be identified by performing the task and recording each step. Similarly, observing others who perform the task well or interviewing them can help identify the sequence of steps necessary to be proficient in the task.

Consult Print Materials. Teachers can consult professional publications to supplement information on the order of skills to be presented in learning a new task. Technical manuals, commercially developed instructional materials, criterion-referenced tests, developmental scales, and behavioral checklists frequently contain skill sequences for a variety of content areas.

Examine the Presentation Modes. Teachers can determine and vary the task's level of difficulty by examining the different ways that the task can be presented. Therefore, in performing a task analysis, teachers should consider complexities related to the presentation of the content. For example, in a bingo game that requires students to match colored shapes, the task's level of difficulty can be varied from showing students the colored shape and simultaneously verbalizing it (*Who has the yellow circle?*) to verbalizing the colored shape only (*Who has the red square?*).

Cues and prompts also can affect the level of difficulty in which material is presented. For example, when initially introducing addition of fractions, the visual cue of a shaded portion of a shape can be paired with a corresponding numerical representation of a fraction (such as $\frac{1}{2} + \frac{1}{2} = 1$). Similarly, the types of devices that students are allowed to use to assist them in performing a task (ruler, calculator, dictionary, compass, numberline) also should be considered in the task analysis. For example, the level of difficulty of a simple addition task will be affected by the use of a numberline. However, since the goal of instruction often is for students to master skills without cues or aids, gradually fading out their use should be part of the task analysis.

Teachers' behavior during the presentation of the content also can be varied to promote student performance. Teachers can structure the presentation of the task so that they initially model it or guide students in their performance. As students demonstrate proficiency, the teacher's role should fade. Figure 6.4 presents an example of a task analysis based on varying the teacher's role.

Examine the Response Mode. Another teaching variable that should be considered in performing a task analysis is the type or level of response mode associated with the task. In other words, analyze the memory, language, and motor requirements of the response. In addition to the complexity of the response, teachers also should examine the time limits associated with the

FIGURE 6.4
Task analysis based on varying the teacher's role

Skill to be taught: When given one to five objects and asked, *How many do you have?,* the student will state correctly the number of objects given.

Step 1. Teacher Guidance
Teacher takes one object and says, "I have one." Teacher gives student one object and says, "You have one."

Step 2. Teacher Modeling without Student Failure
Teacher takes one object and says, "I have one." With only one object available so that the student can't fail, teacher says to student, "You take one."

Step 3. Teacher Modeling with Possible Student Failure
Teacher repeats step 2 with more than one object available.

Step 4. Fade Out Teacher Modeling
Teacher repeats step 3 without the teacher serving as a model.

Step 5. Student Responds Receptively to Teacher Requests
Teacher asks student to find or make a specific number of objects on command. For example, teacher asks a student to show a chair, show two fingers, draw three circles, erase four letters, and so on.

Step 6. Student Responds Expressively to Teacher Requests
Teacher gives student the similar objects from one to five, and asks student, "How many do you have?"

Note: Each step should be repeated using different types of objects and numbers so that students don't associate the object name as a number.

task. This is especially true when automaticity is important in such skills as number facts and phonetic rules.

Think About It

How would you task analyze a motor skill such as brushing your teeth? How would you task analyze a cognitive skill such as measuring the length of a line using a ruler?

Element 4: Give Clear Directions, Explanations, and Relevant Examples

Research indicates that teachers who give longer and more detailed explanations and examples of content are more successful in promoting learning in their students (Everston, Emmer, & Brophy, 1980). Thus, when explaining points to students and giving directions on tasks, teachers should present content and activities with clear and explicit statements. Instructions and directions should be directly related to the objectives of the lesson and should vary in length and language used at the beginning of the statement (Lovitt & Smith, 1972). Teachers should avoid using confusing wording (*you know, a lot, these things*) and try to use terminology that students can understand (Smith & Land, 1981). While the rate of presentation of the materials will depend upon the students' skills and the complexity of the content, it is suggested that teachers try to maintain a swift pace for instruction (Englert, 1984). However, to ensure understanding, teachers should repeat key points, terminology, and concepts (Mastropieri & Scruggs, 1987), and adjust the pace of the lesson to allow for reteaching and repetition if students appear confused or bored (Jones & Jones, 1986).

Element 5: Provide Time for Active and Guided Practice

Students need opportunities to practice what they have learned. Therefore, it is often best for teachers to structure time for practice after they introduce small amounts of difficult or new material. Since high rates of success during practice are associated with student learning, teachers should strive for a practice success rate of at least between 75 to 80 percent, and should prepare practice activities that require students to respond to items that have various levels of difficulty (Rosenshine, 1986). Some good practice activities include responding to teacher-directed questions, summarizing major points, and engaging in peer tutoring (Rosenshine, 1986). Practice activities should be directed to provide all students with the chance to respond overtly so that the teacher can ensure that all students have mastered the skill. Rosenshine (1986) lists a variety of student response strategies that teachers can use to encourage all students to become actively involved in practice.

Carnine (1989) outlined several factors teachers should consider when designing practice activities.

Model-Lead-Test. When introducing new concepts, teachers can model the new concept or strategy for students, carefully identifying and emphasizing the salient features of each point (Englert, 1984). One effective modeling procedure is the *model-lead-test* strategy, which requires teachers to model and orally present the task or concept, guide students in understanding the process through prompts and practice, and test student mastery (Carnine & Silbert, 1979). When modeling new content, teachers should make the demonstration very clear and exaggerate the salient features of the task. It also is desirable to offer specific examples as well as nonexamples (Rosenshine, 1986). Examples should be relevant to the experiences of the students and help make abstract information more concrete.

Physical Guidance. When introducing skills that require a motor response, it is sometimes necessary for the teacher to physically guide students through the steps of the skill (Deutsch-Smith, 1981). Teachers also should simultaneously verbalize the steps being executed during the physical guidance. For example, in teaching the cursive letter *a,* a teacher could place her or his hand over the student's hand holding the writing utensil and physically guide the student in the formation of the letter while verbalizing the stroke by saying *Start at the top . . . go around . . . and down . . . back up to the start . . . down again.*

Physical guidance is highly intrusive and should be used only during the initial stages of learning a skill, then faded quickly (Deutsch-Smith, 1981). Teachers can begin to fade out physical guidance by providing students with *picture task analysis,* a pictorial depiction of the sequential steps learners should follow to successfully complete a task (Roberson, Gravel, Valcante, & Maurer, 1992).

Time-Delay. Another strategy that has been successful in promoting mastery of spelling words, reading sight words, computing math facts, and defining vocabulary words is *time-delay* (Stevens & Schuster, 1988). The steps in time-delay are as follows:

- The teacher presents the task to the student(s) and requests the student(s) to respond—for example, the teacher shows a card with the addition problem 11 + 5 = _____ and says, *How much is 11 + 5?*
- The teacher prompts the student(s) immediately (zero-second delay) by providing the correct answer during several trials—for instance, after presenting the problem, the teacher shows a card with the answer 11 + 5 = 16 and says, *Eleven plus five equals sixteen.*
- Students respond and receive feedback based on their response.
- Students repeat prior steps while increasing in increments the amount of time between the presentation of the content and the teacher's providing the correct response.
- The teacher fades out assistance so that the students can respond quickly and independently.

Stevens and Schuster (1988) provide additional guidelines for using time-delay.

Element 6: Check for Comprehension

Rather than asking students if they have questions, teachers should check for understanding after presenting each new point (Rosenshine, 1986). When checking for understanding, teachers should sample behaviors from all students in the class by having them identify main points or state agreement or disagreement with the comments and responses of their peers (Rosenshine, 1986).

Questioning. Teachers can check for comprehension by asking students questions, which should be stated so that they direct all students to respond in an overt manner (Mastropieri & Scruggs, 1987). Thus, rather than targeting a question for a specific student by linking the question with a student's name (*Jack, who was the president during the Civil War?*), teachers should start a question using such terms as *Everyone listen and then tell me* or *I want you all to think before you answer.* Also, teachers should randomly select students to respond to questions, giving them at least from 5 to 10 seconds to formulate their answers (Rowe, 1974), and ask students to respond to answers given by their peers (Jones & Jones, 1986). If students fail to respond to the question, teachers should ask them if they know the answer, probe their related knowledge, ask the question to another student, or provide the student with the correct answer (Robinson & Kasselman, 1990).

To encourage full participation and the review of content that needs to be overlearned, teachers can use *choral responding,* in which students answer simultaneously on a cue from the teacher, such as *Everyone whisper the answer when I say three* (Mastropieri & Scruggs, 1987), or have students write down their answer and then check each student's response. Similarly, group physical responses that allow each member of the group to indicate a response through an overt physical gesture also are desirable (Englert, 1984). For example, students can respond to a question that elicits a *yes* or *no* answer by placing their thumbs up or down, respectively. It can be motivating for students to plan with teachers different ways to indicate their responses using physical gestures. When questioning students, teachers should not promote student inattention by repeating questions, vitiate the need for students' responses by answering questions for students, or supplement students' incomplete answers (Hoover, 1976).

Teachers should adjust their questions to meet the level of difficulty of the content and the skill levels of the students. To check understanding of simple facts or basic rules, teachers can use questions that ask students to restate information and procedures such as *What is the "i before e" rule?* (Mastropieri & Scruggs, 1987). To survey students' ability to apply complex skills, teachers should use questions that require students to apply basic rules or generalizations (Rosenshine, 1986). For example, asking students to spell *receive* is a more complex skill than merely asking students to repeat the rule. Sanders (1966) has developed a hierarchy of questions that teachers can use to tailor their questions to the ability levels of the students. The hierarchy, sequenced from easiest to hardest, includes seven levels of questioning: memory, translation, interpretation, application, analysis, synthesis, and evaluation.

Teachers also should adapt their questioning techniques for students who are learning English. Teachers can encourage these students to respond to questions by providing students with visual supports such as pictures and words; by asking students questions that can be responded to in one- or two-word answers; and by repeating and elaborating upon student responses (Fradd, 1987).

Element 7: Give Prompt and Specific Feedback

Students' responses during comprehension checks, practice activities and other lesson phases should be followed by feedback from the teacher. The type of feedback should be related to the nature of the students' responses. Therefore, in determining what type of feedback to employ, teachers should categorize the students' responses as *correct and confident, correct but unsure, partly correct,* or *incorrect.* If the answer is correct and presented with a degree of certainty, teachers should confirm the response with praise and ask additional questions at the same or a more difficult level (Mastropieri & Scruggs, 1987; Rosenshine, 1986). If the answer is not correct and confident, another type of feedback should be delivered.

Process Feedback. While teachers can acknowledge a correct student response with praise, students who are unsure of their correct responses may need to receive *process feedback* (Good & Grouws, 1979), a technique that allows teachers to praise students verbally and reinforce their response by restating why the answer was correct. For example, if a student correctly answers a question by applying a rule of possessives, the teacher would confirm the answer by stating it was correct and repeating the possessive rule that was applied successfully by the student.

In addition to responding to correct answers, it is also important for teachers to provide feedback to students whose responses are partly correct. Teachers should confirm the aspect of the response that is correct, then restate or simplify the question to address the incorrect part of the answer.

Teachers also can respond to students' errors with a variety of techniques including corrective feedback, prompting, and cuing. If these strategies are not effective, teachers can call on other students to provide the answer, and recheck understanding of the question later in the session (Mastropieri & Scruggs, 1987).

Corrective Feedback. *Corrective feedback* guides students on how to perform the task more effectively (Wallace & Kauffman, 1986). When using corrective feedback, teachers identify errors and offer instructional support to assist students in modifying these errors (Cohen, Perkins, & Newmark, 1985). Research suggests that corrective feedback is more effective in promoting learning than *general feedback,* in which responses are identified for students simply as correct or incorrect; *right-only feedback,* where only correct responses are identified for students; or *wrong-only feedback,* where only incorrect responses are identified for students (Kulhavy, 1977; Mims & Gholson, 1977).

When students fail to respond, or give an incomplete or incorrect response, teachers can deliver corrective feedback by restating the question, rephrasing the question, or changing the question to activate the students' knowledge about the content (Robinson & Kasselman, 1990). If the students' responses are obviously incorrect, and extensive teacher assistance will not help the students determine the correct answer, teachers can respond by clarifying the directions, rechecking mastery of prerequisite skills, teaching a lower-level skill from the task analysis, providing additional practice, and modifying the presentation style (Mastropieri & Scruggs, 1987). When the students' incorrect answers appear to be caused by a lack of effort, attention, or preparation, teachers should emphasize the need to improve in these areas.

Prompting. Teachers can assist in correcting errors by using a variety of prompting procedures. Schloss (1986) defines *prompting* as "visual, auditory, or tactile cues that assist the learner in performing a subskill of the terminal behavior" (p. 181). Prompts can be categorized from most to least intrusive, including *manual prompts,* during which the student is physically guided through the task; *modeling prompts,* in which the student observes another individual perform the task; *oral prompts* that provide students with a description of how to perform the task; and *visual prompts,* whereby the student is shown the correct process or answer via a graphic presentation (Schloss, 1986). Teachers should use prompts in a sequential fashion depending on the skill level of the students and the degree of complexity of the task.

Highly intrusive prompts should be coupled with more natural prompts (Schloss, 1986).

Cuing. One type of prompt is *cuing,* which can increase students' abilities to deal with a difficult task because it relates the task or the components of the task to the students' existing skill repertoire (Salend, 1980, October). Deutsch-Smith (1981) suggests the use of movement, position, and redundancy cues when students need assistance on worksheet assignments. *Movement cues* require the teacher to physically indicate the response. For example, when working on a reading comprehension worksheet with multiple-choice responses, the teacher might indicate the correct response by pointing, touching, or circling it. When using *position cues,* teachers ensure that the correct response is located nearest to the student. *Redundancy cues* allow teachers to highlight the correct response through use of such variables as color, shape, size, and position. Other cuing strategies include highlighting salient features of a task, modeling correct answers, and cuing verbally using words, phrases, and sounds (George, 1986).

Effective use of praise can promote self-esteem in students, establish a greater bond between teachers and students, reinforce appropriate behavior, and create a positive environment in the classroom.

Praising. Research indicates that while teachers are very likely to acknowledge a correct and appropriate response, they are less likely to use praise frequently in their classrooms (Sadker & Sadker, 1985). Because many students tend to rate their performance in negative terms (Meunier & Rule, 1967), praise coupled with comments concerning strengths and weaknesses can provide valuable feedback to students and increase their proficiency (Page, 1958).

Despite the fact that praise is more effective with lower-achieving students and students from lower socioeconomic backgrounds, they are less likely than their peers to receive teacher praise (Brophy & Everston, 1976). Teachers can increase their use of praise with these students by recording the number of praise statements they direct to students. Additionally, displaying a cue in a location of the room that teachers frequently see (for example, a smiling face on the back wall of the classroom) and finding a student to praise each time eye contact is made with the cue can promote an increase in the use of praise.

In addition to verbal statements, praise also can be delivered through use of nonverbal gestures such as a smile, a hug, a pat on the back, the O.K. sign, or the thumbs up sign. Since some researchers have shown that frequent praise can minimize students' independence, self-confidence, and creativity (Brophy, 1981), teachers should distribute praise evenly and examine its effect on students. Thus, rather than just praising on-task behavior and task correctness, praise should be delivered to encourage independence, determination, and creativity.

Student-Directed Feedback. Students also can be a valuable source of feedback. Students can be encouraged and taught to use self-monitoring techniques to record and analyze their progress. They can chart their mastery of a specific skill by graphing their percentage or number correct every day. In addition to graphing performance, it may be desirable for students to identify the variables that led to their being successful (Jones & Jones, 1986). Identifying these factors can help students learn to attribute their success to competence and effort rather than believing that they had little control over the outcome. Additionally, students can be taught to exchange papers and offer feedback to peers on each others' performance.

Element 8: Offer Time for Independent Seatwork Activities

Teachers often conclude successful lessons by giving students seatwork activities that allow students to demonstrate mastery of the material presented

IDEAS FOR IMPLEMENTATION

When using praise in the classroom, teachers should enact the following suggestions:

- Deliver praise after the appropriate response has occurred.
- Describe the specifics of the behavior that is being praised. (Rather than saying *This is a good paper,* the teacher should say, *You really did a good job of using topic sentences to begin your paragraphs in this paper.*)
- Increase the credibility of the praise by using diverse and spontaneous statements.
- Consider the age, skill level, and cultural background of the students when phrasing praise statements.
- Distribute praise so that all students are acknowledged.
- Acknowledge effort as well as specific outcomes.
- Focus students on the behaviors that helped them to be successful.
- Individualize praise so that the students' achievements are evaluated in comparison to their own performance, rather than the performance of their peers.

Source: Brophy (1981).

(Rosenshine, 1986). Seatwork activities should be directly related to the content provided in the lesson so that students are developing automaticity of the skill (Brophy, 1987). Teachers should direct students (*Now I want to see you do these math problems.*) rather than ask students to perform a task (*Would you like to do these math problems?*) when presenting assignments (Wallace & Kauffman, 1986). Because students frequently exhibit off-task behaviors during seatwork (Berliner & Rosenshine, 1977), teachers can do several things to keep their students actively engaged in the task:

- Inform students of the purpose of the assignment and its objectives (Wong, Wong, & Lemare, 1982).
- Explain the relationship between the seatwork assignment and the material covered in the lesson (Anderson, 1984).
- Give clear directions concerning expectations (Mastropieri & Scruggs, 1987).
- Peruse the room to monitor student behavior (Englert, 1984).
- Walk around the classroom to help students in need of assistance (Englert & Thomas, 1982).
- Provide prompt feedback (Rosenshine, 1980).
- Review seatwork after it is completed (Englert, 1984).

Teachers also can improve student completion levels of seatwork by establishing, communicating, and enforcing their expectations in terms of accuracy, time, format, and appearance (Englert, 1984). If students fail to complete an assignment according to the teacher's expectations, they should be required to rework the product until it complies with the teacher's standards (Everston & Emmer, 1982). Levels of accuracy demonstrated by students are especially important for promoting learning; so, it is recommended that teachers strive for seatwork accuracy levels of 90 percent of higher (Rosenshine, 1983).

Teachers also can modify seatwork by providing students with assistance or with access to peer tutors. Students can indicate that they need help by placing a help sign or card on their desks, raising their hands, or signing a list for students needing assistance (Everston, Emmer, Clements, Sanford, & Worsham, 1989). Initially, teachers should provide students with assistance by asking questions and making statements that help students assume responsibility for figuring out answers, such as *Where can you find the answer? What things can help you figure out the answer?* (Beirne-Smith & Johnson, 1991). Although it is appropriate to modify the seatwork tasks, it would not be appropriate to have mainstreamed students work on a content area that is different from the rest of the class; this differentiation might isolate them within the class.

Element 9: Summarize Main Points and Evaluate Mastery

At the end of the lesson, teachers should summarize the main points and evaluate students' mastery of the content. The summary can be a brief review of the main points and procedures presented in the lesson. Following the summary, teachers should assess students' mastery of content via a one- to five-minute probe. Since maintenance of skills is critical for establishing a foundation for learning additional skills, weekly and monthly maintenance

IDEAS FOR IMPLEMENTATION

For mainstreamed students, it may be appropriate for teachers to adapt seatwork assignments by enacting the following suggestions:

- Decrease the number of items they are required to answer.
- Intersperse items relating to content that has been mastered previously with items addressing the new material.
- Give clear and concise directions.
- Present directions in a list of sequential steps.
- Offer examples of correct response formats.
- Provide cues to highlight key parts of directions, details of items, and changes in item types.
- Use a similar worksheet format repeatedly.
- Employ color cues to note starting and ending points.
- Divide worksheets into sections by folding, drawing lines, cutting off parts of the page, boxing, and blocking out with an index card or with a heavy crayon.
- Provide sufficient space for students to record their answers.
- Shorten the assignment.
- Limit the amount of distracting visual stimuli presented.
- Modify the content of the assignment to meet the skill levels of the students.
- Give several shorter assignments rather than a single lengthy one.
- Provide students with additional time to complete the assignment.

Source: Chalmers (1991); Gillet (1986); Humphrey, Hoffman, & Crosby (1984).

probes also are desirable (Mastropieri & Scruggs, 1987). Additional guidelines for evaluating student mastery and progress are presented in Chapter 11.

Think About It

Try to plan and write a lesson using the elements of direct instruction.

STUDENT-DIRECTED SMALL-GROUP ACTIVITIES

There are several techniques for modifying instruction that are particularly valid for use with student-directed small-group activities. These techniques include cooperative learning arrangements and academic games.

Cooperative Learning

After reading and attending several inservice sessions on cooperative learning, Ms. Johnson decides to try it with her students. She divides students into groups and gives each group an assignment to work on together. She then circulates throughout the room and observes the groups. In one group, Luis, a new student from the Dominican Republic, sits quietly and does not participate in his group's project. Luis does not speak throughout the activity and no one speaks to him. In another group, students rely on Maria to do the assignment while they talk about the upcoming school dance. In still another group, students fight over who will draw a picture that will be part of the group's project.

Frustrated, but not one to give up, Ms. Johnson realizes that she needs to help her students learn to work collaboratively. She decides to start by having pairs of students study for a quiz together and receive their average grade score. Next, she has students work together in peer tutoring dyads; she arranges it so that all students serve both as tutors and tutees.

She also teaches her students how to develop specific collaborative skills. For example, she has the students discuss the need for encouraging participation from all group members. They then brainstorm, role play, and practice ways to encourage others to participate. Another lesson focuses on the need for and use of quiet voices, speaking softly.

After several lessons to teach collaborative skills, Ms. Johnson asks students to perform a science experiment and write a report while working in cooperative learning groups. She tells them they will be working cooperatively, and asks "How will I know if you're cooperating? What will I see and hear if you're working cooperatively?" The students' responses are listed on the blackboard and discussed.

To ensure the participation of all students, she assigns shy and quiet students like Luis to groups that contain supportive peers. To make sure all students contribute to and understand the group's project, she tells the class that she will randomly select group members to explain parts of the group's report. To help groups work efficiently, she assigns one student in each group to be the group's recorder and another student to make sure that each member of the group participates.

As the groups work on their projects, Ms. Johnson monitors their progress and observes their use of collaborative skills. When students demonstrate such skills, she acknowledges them. Periodically, she praises a group to the whole class, and asks groups to model various collaborative skills. She also asks each group to keep a record of the skills they use. At the end of the class session, she and the students discuss and reflect upon their collaborative skills.

Cooperative learning has been highly effective in simultaneously promoting academic and affective skills of all students and facilitating the mainstreaming of students (Aronson, Blaney, Stephan, Sikes, & Snapp, 1978; Johnson & Johnson, 1986; Slavin, Madden, & Leavey, 1984).

Teachers usually structure learning so that students work individually or competitively (Johnson & Johnson, 1986). However, teachers can adapt their instructional program by employing cooperative learning. Cooperative learning arrangements have been recommended for promoting the academic and social performance of students with disabilities, students from culturally and linguistically diverse backgrounds, and female students.

Cooperative learning refers to a method for organizing learning, in which students are working with their peers toward a shared academic goal rather than competing against or working separately from their peers. Teachers structure the learning environment so that each class member contributes to the group's goal. When learning is structured cooperatively, students are accountable not only for their own achievement but also for the performance of other group members, as the group's evaluation is based on the group's product. Cooperative learning is especially worthwhile for heterogeneous student populations because it encourages mutual respect and learning among students of various academic abilities, linguistic, and racial and ethnic backgrounds (Sharan, 1980; Slavin et al., 1985).

Cooperative learning activities should contain three important components: positive interdependence, individual accountability, and face-to-face interactions. *Positive interdependence* is established when students understand that they must work together to achieve their goal. *Individual accountability,* the understanding that each group member is responsible for contributing to the group and learning the material, is often established by giving individualized tests or probes, adding individual group members' scores together, assigning specific parts of an assignment to individual group members, randomly selecting group members to respond for the group, or asking all members of the group to present a component of the project (Whittaker, 1991). Building individual accountability into cooperative learning groups helps to lessen the potential for the "free-rider" effect, which happens when some members fail to contribute to the group and allow others to do the majority of the work (Slavin, 1990). *Face-to-face interactions* occur when students encourage and assist each other in learning the material. Both social and group processing skills are necessary to help the group function smoothly (Taylor, Stefanisko, Peck, & Schlissel, 1991).

Schniedewind and Salend (1987) have reviewed several guidelines for implementing cooperative learning. These guidelines are discussed here.

Selecting a Cooperative Learning Format

Teachers can begin to implement cooperative learning in their classrooms by selecting a format for structuring the cooperative learning experience. The format teachers choose for their classes will depend on the unique needs and characteristics of their students and classrooms, as well as their experiences in working cooperatively. For example, a teacher might choose to introduce peer tutoring first because it is easy to manage. Another teacher may elect to begin with Student Teams-Achievement Divisions (STAD). Groups with varying levels of ability who need structure might do best with the jigsaw technique, which ensures that all students actively participate. Finally, when working with students who have had practice with cooperative learning, teachers should consider using Learning Together, a group project that optimizes student responsibility.

Kagan (1990) outlines the academic and social functions of the various cooperatively structured learning arrangements.

The type of cooperative learning format selected also will depend on the content of the assignment. According to Maheady, Harper, and Mallette (1991) peer tutoring, Classwide Peer Tutoring (CWPT), and Student Teams-Achievement Divisions (STAD) are best for teaching basic skills and factual knowledge in content areas; jigsaw is appropriate for text mastery; and Learn-

Students benefit academically and socially from working in cooperative learning groups.

ing Together is the desired format for teaching higher-level cognitive material and having students learn how to work together and reach consensus on controversial material.

Peer Tutoring. One widely used cooperative format that has been effective in increasing the amount of time students are engaged in learning, promoting educational progress, and fostering positive attitudes toward school and learning is peer tutoring (Jenkins & Jenkins, 1981; Osguthorpe & Scruggs, 1986). In addition to benefiting tutees, peer tutoring can promote a greater sense of responsibility and improved self-concept, as well as increased academic skills in tutors (Gerber & Kaufman, 1981). In *peer tutoring,* one student tutors and assists another in learning a new skill. When using peer tutoring, teachers should do the following:

- Establish specific goals for the sessions.
- Plan particular learning activities to meet the identified goals.
- Select tutors who have demonstrated proficiency in the content to be taught.
- Train students to function as successful tutors.
- Match tutors and tutees.
- Schedule sessions for no longer than thirty minutes and no more than three times per week.

- Monitor periodically the tutoring process and provide feedback to both members of the dyad.
- Allay potential parental concerns by explaining to parents the role and the value of peer tutoring.

Teachers should carefully plan tutoring sessions so that mainstreamed students are not always the ones being tutored. For example, if a mainstreamed student performs well in math, the teacher could structure the peer tutoring format so that this student would teach math to a student who provided tutoring to him or her in learning capitalization rules. Students who are not capable of teaching academic skills can teach nonacademic skills related to their hobbies or interests.

Jones and Jones (1986) propose two ways that peer tutoring systems can be incorporated into classrooms on a continuing basis. Students can be given symbols that are displayed on their desks to indicate whether they need or can provide help. For example, they suggest using a red card to indicate the need for assistance and a green card to announce that the student is willing to aid others. Similarly, recording on the blackboard the names of students who are available to provide assistance for a specific assignment can guide students in selecting peer tutors.

Classwide Peer Tutoring. *Classwide Peer Tutoring (CWPT)* is a novel peer tutoring system that has been effective in teaching reading, spelling, vocabulary, math, and social studies to a wide range of students educated in a variety of instructional settings (Greenwood, 1991; Maheady, Harper, & Sacca, 1988). Teachers randomly divide their class into two groups and assign tutoring dyads within the groups. During the first 10 to 15 minutes of the period, one student tutors the other. The members of each dyad then reverse their roles and continue for another equal time period.

Teachers train students to tutor using a set instructional procedure that involves the following:

1. Tutors present material that requires a response from tutees (*Spell the word ______. Answer the question, ____________?*).
2. Tutees "say and write" their responses. A correct response earns two points. An incorrect response prompts tutors to offer the correct response, ask tutees to write the correct response three times, and award a point to tutees for correcting their errors.
3. Teachers circulate around the classroom to give bonus points for appropriate tutee and tutor behavior.

After this procedure is repeated throughout the week, students take individually administered tests and receive points for each correct response. All points earned by the groups are totaled at the end of the week, and the group with the most points is acknowledged through badges, stickers, certificates, public posting of names, and access to additional free time (Maheady, Harper, & Mallette, 1991).

Student Teams-Achievement Divisions. Another cooperative learning structure that teachers can use is *Student Teams-Achievement Divisions (STAD)* (Slavin, 1980). Kagan (1988) outlines the steps in implementing STAD:

1. Content is presented to students by the teacher.
2. Teams are formed, work on study sheets, and prepare for quizzes related to the content presented.
3. Students take quizzes individually; their improvement above an individually assigned "base score" earns points for their respective teams (base scores are averages of the students' two latest quizzes).
4. Teachers recognize team and individual improvement by distributing a newsletter concerning the teams' performance or providing special activities to teams.

A variation of STAD is *Teams-Games-Tournaments (TGT),* where triads work together and compete with other teams in weekly tournaments (Slavin, 1990).

Jigsaw. The *jigsaw* format divides students into groups, with each student assigned a task that is essential to the accomplishment of the group's goal (Aronson, Blaney, Stephan, Sikes, & Snapp, 1978). Every group member contributes an individualized part that is integrated with the work of others to produce the group's product. When teams are working on the same task, expert groups can be formed by having a member of each group meet with peers from other groups who have been assigned the same subtask. The expert group members work together to complete their assignment, then share their results with their original jigsaw groups.

Teachers should structure the students' assignment so that each group member can succeed. For example, one regular classroom teacher taught a lesson about Dr. Martin Luther King, Jr. by giving each student one segment of Dr. King's life to learn about and teach to others in their group. Students who had the same aspect of Dr. King's life met in expert groups to complete their part; then the original group answered questions on all segments of Dr. King's life.

Variations of the jigsaw have been developed. Slavin (1980) has developed Jigsaw 2, which incorporates elements of STAD into the jigsaw format. Kagan (1990) suggests several modifications in using expert groups that teachers can employ when using jigsaw. Gonzalez and Guerro (cited in Kagan, 1990) have adapted jigsaw for use with bilingual students.

Learning Together. A cooperative learning format that places more responsibility on the group members is Johnson and Johnson's (1986) *Learning Together Approach.* In this format, students are assigned to teams; each team is given an assignment. Teams decide whether to divide the task into its component parts or approach the task as a whole group. All group members are involved in the team's decisions by offering their knowledge and skills and seeking assistance and clarification from others. Every group produces one product, which represents a composite of the contributions of every group member. The teacher grades this product, with each student in the group receiving the group grade. For example, one teacher used a group project to teach students about mammals. The teacher divided the class into groups and assigned each group the task of developing part of a bulletin board display containing descriptive information and artwork about a particular mammal. Individual students within each group then contributed to the group's display by reporting information, doing artwork, or dictating material about mammals.

Team-Assisted Instruction. *Team-Assisted Instruction (TAI)* is a cooperative learning system whereby heterogeneous groups of students work to master individualized assignments (Slavin, Madden, & Leavey, 1984). While other cooperative learning formats are group paced, TAI is unique in that it combines cooperatively structured learning with individualized instruction. In TAI, individual group members work on their own assignments and assist other group members with their assignments. Group members are then rewarded if their team's performance meets or exceeds a pre-established criteria.

To implement TAI in their classrooms, teachers initially develop individualized units of instruction for each student. These units contain a list of instructions, skillsheets, quizzes, and answer sheets. Team members exchange answer sheets and work on the skillsheets in their individualized units, seeking assistance from their teammates when necessary. When a student completes a skillsheet, a teammate checks the answers using the unit answer sheet. If the answers are correct, the student proceeds to the other skillsheets in the unit. If the problems are answered incorrectly, the student reworks them.

After completing the unit and obtaining the consent of all teammates, students take a practice test, and then a final test on content that parallels the content of the student's unit skillsheets. If teammates do not give the student approval to take a test, the teacher gives the student additional skillsheets and assistance if necessary. When each member of the team has taken at least one final test, the team's average is computed. If the team's average meets or exceeds a set criteria established by the teacher, reinforcement is delivered to the whole group (Salend & Washin, 1988).

Establishing Guidelines for Working Cooperatively

Teachers and students should establish guidelines for working cooperatively. Johnson (1988) outlines several classroom guidelines that can help students work cooperatively:

- Each group will produce one product.
- Each group member will assist other group members to understand the material.
- Each group member will seek assistance from her or his peers.
- Each group member will stay in his or her group.
- No group member will change her or his ideas unless logically persuaded to do so.
- Each group member will indicate acceptance of the group's product by signing her or his name.

Maheady, Harper, and Mallette (1991) note that teachers may encounter several problems when using cooperative learning arrangements: increased noise levels, complaints about partners, and cheating. They suggest that noise levels can be minimized by developing rules, providing rewards for groups that follow the rules, and teaching students to use their quiet voices; complaints can be dealt with by ignoring them and by reinforcing students who work collaboratively; and cheating can be lessened by random checks of the groups' work. Teachers also should remind students that the standard classroom expectations of behavior will be followed during cooperative learning lessons.

Forming Cooperative Groups

Teachers should assign students to heterogeneous groups, considering such variables as sex, race, ethnicity, linguistic ability, disability, and academic and social skill level. When assigning students to groups, teachers also should consider various student characteristics such as personality and motivation. For example, shy students who sit quietly and fail to participate could be assigned to a team whose members are highly supportive. Whittaker (1991) identified a variety of strategies for dealing with students with reading and/or learning problems, behavior and emotional disorders, short attention spans, and auditory and visual perceptual difficulties.

Dishon and O'Leary (1991) offer guidelines for assigning students to heterogeneous groups.

Another factor to consider in forming groups is the students' ability to work together. Information on how well students can work together can be obtained through observation and/or by administering a sociogram (see Chapter 4). While it is possible to change groups for each cooperative lesson, keeping the students in the same group for several weeks can provide the continuity that is helpful in developing cooperative skills. The length of time a group remains together should depend on the students' ages, the nature of the task, and the group's interpersonal skills. Initially, teachers should use small groups of two or three students, increasing the size to no more than five when students become accustomed to cooperative learning (Johnson & Johnson, 1986). When forming new groups, teachers should start with a series of activities that help students get acquainted (Edwards & Stout, 1990).

Arranging the Classroom for Cooperative Learning

Teachers can structure their classrooms for cooperative work by arranging the students' desks or tables in clusters, placing individual desks in pairs for peer tutoring, or blocking off a carpeted corner of the room. For larger groups, desks should be placed in circles rather than rectangles, which can prevent eye contact and communication (Johnson & Johnson, 1986). Bookshelves, screens, movable chalkboards, and easels can divide the classroom into discrete areas. Since the time required to complete cooperative projects may vary, teachers should provide the groups with a safe area to store in-progress projects and other necessary materials.

Developing Cooperative Skills

Whittaker (1991) identified eleven specific interpersonal skills that enhance students' ability to work cooperatively.

Many students may have only limited experience in working cooperatively, so teachers may have to devote some time to helping students learn to work cooperatively (Reynolds & Salend, 1989). Johnson and Johnson (1990) delineated several interpersonal skills that students must develop to collaborate effectively and efficiently including getting to know and trust peers, communicating in a direct and clear manner, supporting others, accepting differences, and resolving conflicts. They outline a series of steps teachers can take to develop these skills that include helping students do the following:

- understand the need to employ the skill
- define the skill
- determine when the skill should be used
- practice and master the skill
- evaluate and reflect upon their use of the skill

Cooperative learning skills should be taught gradually, building on the students' experiences with cooperative learning. Teachers can vary the complexity of the cooperative learning activity by modifying the task to meet the students' needs. For classes with little experience with cooperative learning, it is best to start with small groups of two on a short-term, discrete, cooperative learning task with well-defined roles.

Teachers can also help students learn to work cooperatively by providing opportunities for them to practice specific skills. For example, putdowns of group members can hinder cooperation. Because mainstreamed students may be the targets of negative statements from peers, teachers could help the class practice how to respond appropriately to putdowns. First, teachers should have their students brainstorm all constructive ways to respond to putdowns directed at themselves or other group members. Students should be given time to practice responding to putdowns. As followup, teachers can lead their students in a discussion of the most effective responses to putdowns, possibly listing them on a chart for further reference.

Another method of helping students gain the skills necessary for productive group functioning is *role delineation,* whereby each member of the group is assigned a specific role to enable the group to work cooperatively. For example, for tasks involving written products, a team might need a reader, a discussion leader to promote brainstorming and decision making, a secretary to record all contributions, and a writer to edit the product. Other students might be assigned the roles of keeping the group on task, explaining word meanings, managing materials, encouraging all group members to participate and assist others, and providing positive comments. Periodically, students can complete evaluation sheets that ask them to react to the roles and contributions of group members as well as what the group could do to improve (Morton, 1988).

Monitoring groups and providing feedback can build cooperative skills in classes. Therefore, it is important for teachers to observe groups, model appropriate cooperative skills, intervene as a consultant, and provide feedback regarding group processing skills (Reynolds & Salend, 1989). After students complete a cooperative lesson, they can be encouraged to reflect on their experience by responding to such processing questions as the following:

Gillespie (1976) has identified several processing questions that can be used to help students assume greater responsibility and improve their cooperative skills.

- What did group members do to help your group accomplish its goal?
- What did group members do that hindered your group in achieving its goal?
- What will your group do differently next time to work together?

Students also can offer their perspectives on how well the group is working collaboratively through writing. To ensure shared responsibility, the group could maintain a process journal that specifies the roles and contributions of each group member (McCormick, 1988). The journal can be reviewed periodically to determine whether the group is working cohesively and to identify any problems that may need to be resolved.

Evaluating Cooperative Learning

Teachers should evaluate groups based on their mastery of subject matter as well as on their ability to work together. To promote peer support and group accountability, students are evaluated as a group, and each student's individual learning contributes to the group's evaluation. A popular method for evaluating cooperative learning is the *group project/group grade* format. The group submits for evaluation one final product (a worksheet, report, oral presentation) that is a composite of the individual group members' contributions. Teachers then evaluate the product and assign each group member the same grade.

In another evaluation format, *contract grading,* groups contract for a grade based on the amount of work they agree to accomplish according to a set of criteria. Thus, group members who have differing skill levels can perform different parts of the task according to their ability. For example, a cooperative lesson might contain five activities of varying degrees of difficulty, with each activity worth 10 points. The contract between the teacher and the groups might then specify the criteria the groups must meet to achieve an A (50 points), B (40 points), and C (30 points). Once a contract for a grade is made, group members can divide the tasks, choosing tasks commensurate with their abilities. Additional guidelines for using contract grading are discussed in Chapter 11.

One evaluation system that provides students with particular incentives to assist others in learning the material is the *group average.* Individual grades on a quiz or part of a project are averaged into a group grade. Each group member receives the average grade. For example, each group member could be given an individualized test tailored to his or her unique abilities in math. Thus, one student might be tested on addition, while other students might be tested on subtraction and multiplication. During the week, group members help each other master their assignments and prepare for their tests. Some students initially may be resistant to the concept of group grades.

Teachers can minimize their resistance by assuring students that group members will only be assigned work that is possible for them to complete. Inform students that if all group members do their best and assist others, they will all receive high grades.

In addition to evaluating the group in terms of mastery of content, teachers also might grade students in terms of effort and ability to work together by assigning each member of the team a percentage grade that represents a measure of their efforts and ability to work together. Since team members will have a greater idea of the relative contributions of each group member, the group can determine the effort and teamwork grade for each of its members. However, since students may feel uncomfortable rating their peers, teachers should exercise caution in requiring an effort grade. Kagan (1988) has developed several forms that teachers can employ to solicit evaluations from teammates.

Some additional useful resources to help teachers learn more about cooperative learning are Dishon and O'Leary (1985), Johnson, Johnson, Holubec, and Roy (1984), Kagan (1988), Slavin (1990), and Schniedewind and Davidson (1987).

Think About It

You have recently started to implement cooperative learning arrangements in your classroom. Several parents have called you to complain that their children are in groups with others who have not done the work. They feel that their children did the work for the group, and still received a poor grade because others did not do their share. What would you say to these parents?

Academic Games

One small-group instructional format that is particularly motivating for students is the learning game (Jones & Jones, 1986). Salend (1979a) defines an *academic learning game* as "a pleasure invoking, rule based interaction between at least two persons, with successful movement toward an agreed upon goal dependent on mastery of academic skills" (p. 4). Academic games may take several formats. When space is limited, a gameboard format (Regional Support and Technical Assistance Centers Coordination Office, 1976) would be a feasible alternative; if a space is available, a movement oriented format is appropriate (Cratty, 1971; Humphrey, 1969).

An important facet of academic games, which make them particularly suitable for mainstreaming, is that the academic component is controlled by the teacher, who can vary the level of the skill, the presentation, and the response mode to match the needs and levels of a wide variety of students. Thus, students of varying abilities can interact within the same instructional format, yet perform skills differing in complexity. For example, the academic content for several students in the game can be addition of fractions with a common denominator, while other students' movement toward the winning criteria may involve solving problems requiring the division of fractions.

Salend (1979a) identified four phases in developing academic games for mainstreamed settings:

Phase 1: Foundation. The foundation phase allows teachers to develop a framework from which the game can evolve, and determine the game's rules. Rules should specify the criteria for completion of the game, penalties or bonuses, criteria for movement toward an agreed end point, order of participation, nature of player exchanges, use of materials, schedule of events, recordkeeping, and game modifications.

Phase 2: Formulation. The formulation phase requires teachers to match the game's characteristics to the specific abilities of their students. Questions and activities related to the students' academic skills and needs are formulated to constitute the academic component of the game.

Phase 3: Experimentation. In the experimentation phase, teachers initially focus on the construction of the game and its materials. During this phase, teachers train students in the rules and prerequisite skills needed to play the game.

Phase 4: Evaluation. The evaluation phase is a feedback mechanism. Evaluation data regarding rules, prerequisites, learner response variables, academic content, and other game variables are gathered, analyzed, and interpreted.

Games should stress cooperation rather than competition (Salend, 1981a). One cooperative goal strategy requires players to strive for a common goal. In this technique, winning is not confined to one player who arrives at the terminal goal first; rather, winning occurs when the whole group arrives at the terminal goal. Devising game movers as puzzle pieces also can foster the cooperative effect of an academic game. For example, each player's mover can be part of a puzzle that is completed when each player reaches a specified terminal goal. Competition with self can be built into common-goal games by setting individualized time limits or increasing the level of difficulty of the content. The time limits and content levels should be based on a previously established standard or a prior level of performance.

Teachers can increase the cooperation between players by phrasing questions so that they require the input of more than one player to be completed correctly. For example, the academic question *Add the number of players on a baseball team to the number of eggs in a dozen, then multiply that number by the number of players on a basketball team, and then divide that number by the number of students in this class* can be answered by having players collaborate.

Rules can be designed to optimize cooperation among players. A rule that requires players to periodically change teams or movers during the game can promote cooperation. Similarly, a rule that periodically requires one player to move toward the goal dependent on the academic performance of another player will tend to foster a coalition of game participants. Another cooperative rule allows a player who has reached the terminal goal to aid the other players by helping to answer questions put to them.

Think About It

Identify a game you or your students like to play. How can you apply the principles presented above to make this activity a cooperative learning game?

HOMEWORK

Homework can be an effective and valuable instructional tool that supplements large- and small-group instruction (Coulter, 1980; Keith, 1982). Teachers can use homework with mainstreamed students to individualize instruction, facilitate learning through practice and application, complete work not finished in school, teach independent study skills and work habits, and communicate to parents the skills and materials that are being covered in school (Turner, 1984).

Teachers should pay attention to the amount of homework they assign to students. It should depend on the students' ages and educational placement. As students proceed beyond third grade, the amount of homework should be increased to two to four nights each week, for 30 minutes to an hour per night. Because mainstreamed students may be taught in several settings, teachers should attempt to coordinate homework assignments—particularly for secondary level students who may have different teachers in each content area. Mainstreamed students also may need the assistance of a homework buddy, a peer who can be contacted to provide information on and assistance with homework assignments (Chiappetta, Budd, & Russo, 1990).

A critical factor in making homework meaningful is the content of the assignment. Not only *what* but *how* teachers teach the material should be incorporated into the assignment. Many mainstreamed students may have difficulty with generalization, so applying skills to other conditions should not be assigned as homework unless it has been taught in class. For example, students instructed in how to solve addition problems presented in the vertical format should not be given homework in horizontal form until specifically taught the procedure.

The type of homework also will depend on the instructional purpose in giving the assignment. Lee and Pruitt's (1979) homework taxonomy delineated four possible instructional purposes of homework: practice, preparation, extension, and creativity. If the goal of homework is to practice material learned in class, teachers can assign some type of drill-oriented assignment (*Rewrite these sentences using commas*). When the instructional purpose of homework is to prepare students for upcoming lessons, assignments should be structured to provide students with the prerequisite information necessary to perform successfully in class (*Read pages 45–53 and define the terms* weathering *and* erosion). Assignments requiring abstract thinking and transfer of prior knowledge to different conditions should be employed when the teacher's intention is to extend and apply skills mastered to more complex and varied situations (*Based on what you learned, read the following paragraph and write down all the reasons this location is a good site for a city*). Finally, when teachers seek to foster creativity in their students, they should use long-term assignments that require the integration of many skills and processes (science projects, book reports, historical timelines, oral reports, term papers).

The type of homework assignments given also should be related to the manner in which students acquire the content. Material taught via analysis, synthesis, or problem-solving techniques would best be reviewed by creative open-ended homework assignments (such as responding to essays), whereas homework on factual and rote-memory material should use a drill format.

Some mainstreamed students may need to be motivated to complete their homework (Salend & Schliff, 1988). Teachers can motivate these students by making homework as creative and enjoyable as possible. For example, an assignment relating to computing averages may be made more interesting by using the scoring record of the members of the school's basketball team. Teachers also can increase motivation to complete homework by grading it and displaying exemplary homework assignments. Similarly, motivation to complete homework can be fostered by praising students, granting students free time or extra computer time, and giving tangible rewards such as stickers or erasers to students who successfully complete their homework.

Frequent evaluation by teachers also can motivate students to complete their homework. Therefore, teachers should provide immediate feedback to students on their homework assignments. Feedback should encompass recognition of correct responses as well as identification of responses in need of further refinement. Teachers can deliver feedback through daily reviews of homework during class time or by teacher comments on the students' products. Homework evaluation also should include homework grades, which should then become part of a report card grade.

Parents can be instrumental in monitoring and assisting with their children's homework. Make them a part of the homework process by periodically communicating with them about the purpose of homework and the amount and type of homework given. Teachers could offer parents suggestions on how to help their children complete their homework, including how to give feedback, employ positive reinforcement, schedule time to do homework, establish a proper distraction-free environment, deal with frustration, and avoid completing homework for the child (Salend & Schliff, 1988).

Clary (1986) developed a checklist that can help parents monitor the homework and study behaviors of their children.

SUMMARY

This chapter was designed to offer guidelines for adapting small- and large-group instruction for mainstreamed students. The chapter

- offered a framework that planning teams can use in determining appropriate instructional modifications for students
- provided guidelines for modifying large-group instruction to meet the needs of mainstreamed students

- provided guidelines for modifying small-group instruction to meet the needs of mainstreamed students
- outlined the elements of direct instruction
- described procedures for successfully implementing cooperative learning arrangements and academic games

RECOMMENDED READINGS

Brophy, J. E. (1981). Teacher praise: A functional analysis. *Review of Educational Research, 5,* 301–318.

Chalmers, L. (1991). Classroom modifications for the mainstreamed student with mild handicaps. *Intervention in School and Clinic, 27*(1), 40–42, 51.

Cohen, S. B., & Lynch, D. K. (1991). An instructional modification process. *Teaching Exceptional Children, 23*(4), 12–18.

Englert, C. S. (1984). Measuring teacher effectiveness from the teacher's point of view. *Focus on Exceptional Children, 17* (2), 1–14.

Fuhler, C. J. (1991). Searching for the right key: Unlocking the doors to motivation. *Intervention in School and Clinic, 26,* 217–220.

Gillet, P. (1986). Mainstreaming techniques for LD students. *Academic Therapy, 21,* 389–399.

Johnson, D. W., & Johnson, R. T. (1986). Mainstreaming and cooperative learning strategies. *Exceptional Children, 52,* 553–561.

Kagan, S. (1988). *Cooperative learning: Resources for teachers.* Riverside, CA: University of California.

Madden, N., & Slavin, R. (1983). Mainstreaming students with mild handicaps: Academic and social outcomes. *Review of Educational Research, 53,* 519–659.

Maheady, L., Harper, G. F., & Mallette, B. (1991). Peer-mediated instruction: A review of potential applications for special education. *Reading, Writing, and Learning Disabilities International, 7,* 75–103.

7 Modifying Instruction for Diverse Learners

TOM

Tom, a student with severe disabilities, has been fully mainstreamed and is included in all classroom activities in Ms. Taravella's sixth-grade class. Ms. Taravella's students have been reading books and sharing them with their classmates through a variety of activities. After completing their books, students choose a strategy for sharing their books from a list of activities that vary in both level of difficulty and learning style. The activities include writing a letter or summary about the book, acting out or reading a part of the story, and making a poster or drawing related to the book. To make sure that students select activities that are appropriate to their cognitive levels, Ms. Taravella limits the choices available to students. She also maintains a record of student choices and encourages them to try new activities. While Tom's peers work on activities like composing a unique ending to their books, writing a short play, or making a diorama about the book, Tom and the teacher's aide work together to read a big book and draw pictures of scenes from the book.

What other instructional modifications would be appropriate for Tom? After reading this chapter, you should be able to answer this as well as the following questions.

- What strategies can educators employ to modify instruction from textbooks and other print materials?
- What strategies can educators use to modify instruction for students with sensory disabilities and students with written language difficulties?
- How can technology and adaptive devices facilitate the learning and performance of students?
- What strategies can educators use to modify instruction for students with severe disabilities?
- What strategies can educators employ to modify instruction for students from culturally and linguistically diverse backgrounds?

Research indicates that when teachers make adaptations in their instructional practices, mainstreamed students are often successful learners in the regular classroom (Madden & Slavin, 1983; Wang & Birch, 1984b). This chapter offers proven adaptations of instructional techniques that address the unique needs of mainstreamed students. Additionally, most of the instructional accommodations for mainstreamed students presented here can aid the performance of other students in the regular classroom (Stainback, Stainback, Courtnage, & Jaben, 1985). For example, while multi-level teaching is presented within the context of adapting instruction for students with severe disabilities, it may be used to modify lessons to ensure the participation of all students.

LEARNING STYLES

In addition to employing instructional modifications that are consistent with the teacher's teaching style and that address issues of treatment acceptability (see Chapter 6), Dunn and Dunn (1978) note that when selecting and implementing instructional strategies for students, educators should consider students' learning styles. The work of Carbo, Dunn, and Dunn (1986) suggests that matching instructional strategies to students' learning styles improves students' academic performance and classroom behavior. Proponents of learning styles instruction seek to adapt instruction to address the ways in which individuals learn best. Dimensions of learning styles instruction include the following:

Dunn (1990) and Kavale and Forness (1990) debate the research and merits of instruction based on learning styles.

- environmental considerations such as background noise levels, lighting, temperature, and seating arrangements
- emotional considerations such as individual levels of motivation, persistence, conformity, responsibility, and need for structure
- grouping considerations such as learning alone or in groups, and with or without adults present
- physical considerations such as learning modality preferences, time of day, and need for food, drink, and mobility while learning
- psychological considerations such as approaching a task globally or analytically (Dunn & Dunn, 1978; Carbo & Hodges, 1991)

Guidelines for identifying students' learning style preferences and designing instructional strategies and environments to address these preferences are available (Dunn & Dunn, 1978; Dunn, Dunn, & Price, 1989; Carbo & Hodges, 1991).

Learning and teaching styles also have been delineated as either *field independent* or *field sensitive* (Gollnick & Chinn, 1990). Field independent students appear to work best on individually oriented tasks such as independent projects, and seek formal relationships with teachers; field sensitive students prefer to work in groups, and establish personal relationships with others including teachers (Morsink, Chase Thomas, & Correa, 1991). Field independent teachers use techniques that foster academic performance through competition and independent assignments; field sensitive teachers tend to employ personal and conversational instructional techniques.

Another important learning style consideration is *locus of control,* an individual's belief concerning the relationship between one's efforts and achievements (Ortiz & Yates, 1989). Individuals who view their actions as contributing to their success or failure are said to have an *internal* locus of control, while individuals who believe that circumstances they do not control affect their performance are referred to as having an *external* locus of control. Vasquez (1975) delineated differences between individuals with internal and external loci of control in terms of self-reliance, achievement motivation, expectations of success, intensity of effort, and performance under skill conditions. Hoover and Collier (1989) noted that because of the effects of acculturation, many students from culturally and linguistically diverse backgrounds may exhibit behaviors that indicate an external locus of control. They note that teachers can help these students by training them to view mistakes as temporary, and as correctable through hard work.

Cornett (1983) noted that learning styles can be affected by cultural factors. For example, some cultures emphasize learning through use of verbal rather than visual descriptions, whereas other cultures emphasize physical modeling over the use of pictorials (Collier & Kalk, 1989). In addition, students' socioeconomic status can impact their learning and cognitive styles (Garcia & Ortiz, 1988).

Think About It

Examine the dimensions of learning and teaching styles. How would you characterize your learning style? Your teaching style? What are your learning and teaching style preferences? How do you adapt when the instructional strategy and environment do not accommodate your learning strategy preference?

Should teachers match instruction to students' learning styles all of the time? Some of the time? Should students learn to adapt their learning styles to the various teaching styles they will encounter in schools?

STUDENTS WHO HAVE READING DIFFICULTIES

Teachers present much educational content to students using print materials such as textbooks. However, since many mainstreamed students may have difficulty reading and gaining information from print materials, teachers may need to modify reading selections to assist students in benefiting from instruction via textbooks and other print materials (Burnette, 1987; Meese, 1992). Chapter 5 discusses strategies that students can learn to facilitate their text comprehension skills.

Modifying Instruction Via Textbooks and Other Print Materials

Text Comprehension

Before assigning a selection for reading, teachers should review new vocabulary and word pronunciation. Scanning the selection and discussing the meaning of boldfaced or italicized terms within the context of the chapter also can aid students. New vocabulary words can be placed in a word file of index cards by chapter, each new term placed on a separate card that includes its definition and the page number on which it appears (Wood & Wooley, 1986).

Previews, structured overviews, and prereading organizers can direct students' attention to the relevant information in the selection and assist students in identifying what they know about the selection's topic. For example, teachers can give an outline of the selection's main points to students and discuss it prior to reading; or, they can give students an outline to complete as they read the selection (Bos & Vaughn, 1988). As students read the assignment, teachers emphasize key points by underlining, repeating, and discussing them, and by questioning students about graphs, pictures, and diagrams. Students' memory and understanding of key terms and concepts also can be facilitated by doing the following:

- giving students copies of definitions of important vocabulary and major concepts
- limiting the amount of new material presented
- establishing the purpose of the reading selection
- setting goals for reading
- summarizing main points
- discussing the content and writing style of the selection after reading the material
- assigning study questions (Bos & Vaughn, 1991)

Activating students' prior knowledge before reading the selection also can facilitate text comprehension. Teachers can activate students' background knowledge by using brainstorming, by employing Pre Reading Planning (Langer, 1981) and a *K-W-L* strategy: *K* (assessing what I *K*now) *W* (determining what I *W*ant to learn) *L* (recalling what I did *L*earn) (Ogle, 1986), and by discussing and predicting components of the story through a schema activation strategy (Hansen, 1981).

Teachers can improve students' text comprehension skills by having students perform a writing activity related to the reading assignment before they actually read the passage (Marino, Gould, & Haas, 1985). Learning logs, written summaries, and questions related to readings can be used to help students understand the material by allowing them to organize their thoughts (Barclay, 1990).

Questioning

A frequently used strategy for guiding text comprehension, having students respond to questions about the text (Beck & McKeown, 1981), can focus the students' attention on the purpose of the reading assignment. Questions also can be used to have students make predictions about the text, and activate students' prior knowledge (Graham & Johnson, 1989). Manzo and Manzo (1990) delineated various types of questions that teachers employ:

- *Predictable questions*—Questions that address the factual components of the selection (who, what, where, when, why, and how questions).
- *Mind-opening questions*—Questions related to the written and oral language components of the selection.
- *Introspective questions*—Questions that cause students to reflect upon the material.
- *Ponderable questions*—Questions that portray dilemmas or situations that have no right or wrong answer.
- *Elaborative knowledge questions*—Questions that ask students to incorporate their prior knowledge with information presented in the selection.

Teachers can help students answer chapter questions correctly by modifying the type and timing of the questions. In varying the type of question, teachers should initially present questions that deal with factual information and move to those that require inference and more complex skills. Rather than using open-ended questions, teachers can rephrase questions, using simpler language or employing a multiple choice format. Teachers can help students gain information from textbooks by using *prequestions,* those posed before the selection is read, and *postquestions,* those posed after the materials have been read (Beck, 1984). Postquestions are particularly effective in promoting recall by establishing the need for review (Harris & Sipay, 1985). Teachers should exercise some caution in using prequestions; their use can result in students focusing too much on information related to the answers and ignoring other content in the text (Tierney & Cunningham, 1984).

Teachers can promote text comprehension skills by having students generate their own questions and paraphrase a selection's content in their own words. Students can be taught to compose their own questions through a procedure call *REQUEST,* which involves students reading silently, asking questions about the text, responding to teacher questions, repeating the procedure with other parts of the selection, making predictions about what will happen, reading silently, and discussing their predictions (Manzo, 1969).

Reciprocal Teaching

Text comprehension skills also can be strengthened through *reciprocal teaching,* a procedure that establishes a dialogue between teachers and students to understand the meaning of a text (Palinscar & Brown, 1983). Reciprocal teaching involves the teacher assigning students to read a selection silently, summarizing the content, discussing and clarifying problem areas, using questions to check student comprehension, and providing students with the opportunity to predict future content. After students observe the teacher modeling these strategies, students assume the role of the teacher while the teacher provides assistance through prompting (*What type of question would a teacher ask in this situation?*), instructing (*A summary is a short statement that only includes essential information*), modifying the activity (*If you can't predict what's going to happen, summarize the information again*), praising students (*That was a good prediction*), and offering corrective feedback (*What information could help you make your prediction?*).

Palincsar and Klenk (1991) outline guidelines to prepare teachers and students to use reciprocal teaching.

Guided Reading

Teachers can use *guided reading* to help students comprehend material presented in a reading passage (Manzo, 1975). The steps in implementing guided reading are as follows:

1. Students read the selection and attempt to remember as much as possible.
2. Students share the information they remember with the class and the teacher records their responses on the chalkboard.
3. Students review the selection and correct inconsistencies or errors in information presented on the chalkboard, then add new information.
4. Students organize the information on the chalkboard into an outline or pattern.
5. Teachers promote understanding of the material by questioning students about the information.
6. Teachers assess the students' short term memory of the information.
7. Repeat steps 1 through 6 as needed (Manzo, 1975).

Semantic Feature Analysis

Bos, Anders, Filip, and Jaffe (1989) suggest that teachers use *semantic feature analysis* to increase their students' text comprehension skills. Initially, teachers delineate the content into superordinate, coordinate, and subordinate concepts and vocabulary. A relationship chart is then developed by listing the superordinate concept as the title, the coordinate concepts as important ideas across the top of the chart, and the subordinate concepts down the left margin of the chart. Before reading the selection, students define key terminology and important ideas in their own minds. Then, using the relationship chart, students predict the relationship between the key terms and the main ideas as positive (+), negative (−), none (0), or unknown (?).

Story-Mapping

Some students may benefit from the use of *story-mapping,* a strategy where teachers help students identify the major elements of a selection through use of a pictorial story map (Idol & Croll, 1987). Teachers can implement this strategy by giving students story-maps that contain spaces for them to list the setting (characters, time, and place), the problem, the goal, the action, and the outcome. As students read information related to the components of the story-map, teachers ask them to discuss the information and write the correct response on their story-map. As students develop proficiency, they can complete the story-map independently.

Modifying Materials

Teachers also can facilitate students' comprehension of reading matter by modifying the actual materials. Framing the page and highlighting critical information via underlining can help students identify main points, locate essential content, and foster reading anticipation (Burnette, 1987). Cues linking a chapter question with the location of the answer in the selection can help students learn how to find correct answers to reading assignments. For example, teachers can color code study questions and their corresponding answers in the text. Similarly, pairing chapter questions with the page numbers that contain the answers, simplifying vocabulary by paraphrasing questions, defining important and difficult to understand terms, breaking multiple-part questions into separate questions, or recording questions on cassettes and including the corresponding pages of the correct response can assist students (Chalmers, 1991; Wood & Wooley, 1986).

Audiotapes

In addition to using reading selections with lower readability indices, teachers can supply students with audiotapes of the text that are commercially produced or volunteer made (volunteers can be peers, parents, teacher aides, community group members, drama club members, honor society members, and others) (Smith & Smith, 1985). For example, groups of students from the class can be assigned the creative cooperative task of preparing an audiocassette of a textbook chapter. So that tapes can be used repeatedly by many students, they can be stored in the library and checked out when needed (Smith & Smith, 1985).

IDEAS FOR IMPLEMENTATION

The readability of the text can be enhanced by teachers enacting the following suggestions:

- Decrease the number of words in a sentence.
- Break long sentences into two or three sentences.
- Convert complex language into language the students can understand.
- Eliminate extraneous sections that may distract students.
- Use coordinate and subordinate conjunctions to establish cohesive ties between concepts.
- Use clear pronoun reference and word substitution to contribute to the understanding of relationships.
- Establish the order inherent in concepts by using signal words, such as *first, second,* and *third.*
- Use words that show relationships, such as *because, after, since.*
- Rephrase paragraphs so that they begin with a topic sentence followed by supporting details.
- Present a series of events or actions in chronological order.
- Cluster information that is related.
- Use words that are known to students.
- Embed the definition of new words in paragraphs and selections.
- Refrain from using different words that have identical meanings.
- Insert text and examples to clarify main points.

Source: Beech (1983); Reynolds & Salend (1990b); Wood & Wooley (1986).

Think About It

Obtain a book that you might use with students. Pick a selection from the book and try to apply the principles for adapting the readability of books to the selection.

When preparing tapes of written materials, the quality of the tape can be improved by the speaker reading in a clear, coherent voice, at a rate of between 120 to 175 words per minute with pauses appropriate to punctuation (Deshler & Graham, 1980). The clarity of the tape can be enhanced by recording in a quiet location, keeping the microphone in a fixed position approximately six inches from the speaker's mouth, and adjusting the volume so that clicks are minimized (Mercer & Mercer, 1985). Cassette players also can be adapted through use of specialized circuits to adjust the playback speed, and auditory cues may be placed on the tape (Wisniewski & Sedlak, 1992).

Each tape should begin with a statement of the title of the textbook, the authors' names, and the chapters or sections recorded. The beginning of the tape can include study questions or an advance organizer to orient the listener to the important points of the selection (Bos & Vaughn, 1988; Mercer & Mercer, 1985). In preparing audiotapes for students, it is often helpful for the teacher to limit the amount of information presented, emphasize vocabulary words, and explain graphic information. Teachers can encourage students to rehearse or apply the content presented by including study questions on the tape. For example, a reminder to the listener, such as *Stop here, and list three changes in America that were a result of the Industrial Revolution,* can guide students. At strategic points throughout the tape, teachers also should provide students with a summary of the information.

Deshler and Graham (1980) suggest the use of a marking system to help students follow along in the text while they are listening to the tape. They propose that teachers place symbols in the text that relate to a specific section of the tape. For example, a # in the text may indicate that this section has been paraphrased. To enhance the motivational aspect or the dramatic effects of the audiocassettes, some teachers and commercial producers add music, sound effects, and other strategies (Burnette, 1987). Audiocassettes adapting several history books and including supplemental print materials are available commercially from

DLM Teaching Resources
DLM Park, P.O. Box 4000
Allen, TX 75002

Audiocassette readings of textbooks also are available to students with learning disabilities, and students with visual and print impairments. Educators can obtain these materials by contacting

The National Library Service for the Blind and Physically Handicapped
Library of Congress
1291 Taylor Street, N.W.
Washington, DC 20542
202-287-5100

American Printing House for the Blind
1839 Frankfort Avenue
Louisville, KY 40206
502-895-2405

Recording for the Blind, Inc.
20 Roszel Road
Princeton, NJ 08540
609-921-6534

Franklin County Special Education Cooperative
Box 44
Union, MO 63084
314-583-8936

Some of these organizations charge a registration fee, which can be paid by the school district if the student's IEP states that the student needs recorded textbooks. Time delays are common before students receive the cassettes, so it is important that teachers inform in advance the individuals responsible for obtaining the cassettes, so that they are available to students at the appropriate time in the school year (Vogel, 1988). Commercially recorded books are quite popular: in fact, many novels are available on cassette in local stores.

Previewing

An alternative to audiotapes, *previewing,* has been defined as "any method that provides an opportunity for a learner to read or listen to a selection or passage prior to instruction and/or testing" (Rose, 1984b, p. 544). The most popular previewing strategies employed by teachers include *oral previewing,* where students read the passage aloud prior to the whole-class reading session; *silent previewing,* where students read the passage silently before the reading session; and *listening previewing,* in which students listen and follow along as an adult reads the passage aloud (Hansen & Eaton, 1978).

Research indicates that oral previewing is superior to silent previewing in promoting the reading skills of students with disabilities (Rose, 1984a; Rose, 1984b; Rose & Sherry, 1984).

One type of listening previewing that has been effective with mainstreamed students is *peer previewing* (Salend & Nowak, 1988). In this system, mainstreamed students listen to and follow along while peer previewers read the selection. Before using peer previewing, teachers should train the previewers by modeling effective previewing and emphasizing that previewers should read clearly and at a rate that the listener can follow.

Computer Software

Some students with poor reading comprehension skills may benefit from using computer-presented texts, which allow teachers to incorporate effective strategies for reading comprehension into the reading passage via strategy prompts (Keene & Davey, 1987). Strategy prompts can be placed throughout the selection to remind students to engage in effective reading comprehension practices. Strategy prompts can remind students to review material, look ahead to preview material, ask questions about the material, repeat words silently to themselves, pay attention to underlined or highlighted information, and construct mental pictures (Keene & Davey, 1987).

Print materials, including textbooks, have been adapted into computer software (Burnette, 1987). These software programs introduce students to the textbook material by defining terms and reviewing prerequisite skills; demonstrating concepts; individualizing the lesson through help menus, self-pacing, sound effects, and pauses; involving students actively in the lesson through games and simulations using computer-generated graphics; providing corrective feedback; and assessing mastery of the content. In addition to providing printouts of student progress, these programs also include supplementary materials for teachers and strategies that teachers can use to modify each student's disk to meet her or his specific needs. Information on software programs modifying textbooks is available by contacting

D.C. Heath and Company
2700 N. Richardt Avenue
Indianapolis, IN 46219

MODIFYING INSTRUCTION FOR STUDENTS WITH SENSORY DISABILITIES

Students with sensory disabilities have unique needs that teachers must address. For students with visual disabilities, teachers must emphasize presenting information orally; for students with hearing disabilities, teachers must focus on the use of visual stimuli to provide meaningful instruction. At all times, teachers should encourage their independence.

Educational Interpreters

Students with hearing impairments and students who are learning English as a second language may need the services of an *educational interpreter,* sometimes referred to as an educational transliterator, a professional who facilitates the transmission of information between individuals who do not communicate with a common language or code (Commission of the Education of the Deaf, 1988; Massachusetts Commission for the Deaf and Hard of Hearing, 1988). Because preferred modes of communication for students with hearing impairments may vary, a variety of educational interpreting methods exist. A signed system interpreter translates spoken language directed toward a student with a hearing impairment into a signed system such as Conceptually Accurate Signed English (CASE). An oral interpreter facilitates the student's understanding of verbal messages by silently mouthing the complete verbal message or its paraphrased equivalent (Castle, 1988). In either of these methods of interpreting, the interpreter employs voice interpretation if the student needs assistance in converting his or her responses into the preferred mode of understanding of others communicating with the student.

Salend and Longo (in press) offer guidelines and suggestions related to the educational interpreter's relationship with mainstreamed students, teachers, the student's peers and parents, supportive service personnel, and administrators.

An educational interpreter can facilitate the student's academic performance in the mainstreamed setting by translating directions, content, and assignments presented orally by teachers and the comments of peers, as well as sharing the student's responses and questions with teachers and peers. Early in the school year, the teacher and interpreter should agree on their responsibilities with respect to such issues as grading, contacting parents, working with other students, assigning and assisting with homework and other assignments, designing and administering tests, arranging for peer note takers, communicating with other professionals, and disciplining students. Generally, roles should be defined so that the teacher has primary responsibility and the interpreter serves in a supportive role (Salend & Longo, in press).

Since interpreters may not have prior exposure to the content and instructional strategies employed in the classroom, it is helpful for teachers to provide interpreters with an orientation to the curriculum, and with textbooks and other relevant instructional materials. A knowledge of class routines, projects, and long-term assignments can assist interpreters in helping students understand and prepare for assignments. When a unit of particularly difficult material is to be covered that includes technical vocabulary and other

IDEAS FOR IMPLEMENTATION

Teachers can modify instruction for students with visual disabilities by enacting the following suggestions:

- Provide experiences that allow students to learn by doing and using manipulatives.
- Give test directions, assignments, notes, and important directions verbally.
- Use *o'clock* directions to describe the location of an object on a flat surface, such as *Your book is at three o'clock and your pencil is at nine o'clock.*
- Guide the student's hand to an object if it is near and in danger of being knocked over.
- Hand the student objects by gently touching his or her hand with the object.
- Avoid use of purple dittos and multicolored chalk; they are often difficult for students with visual impairments to see. Tracing over the letters, numerals, and pictorials with a felt tip marker can facilitate the viewing of dittos. Placing a piece of yellow acetate over a page of print serves to enhance the contrast and darken the print.
- Provide students with writing paper that has a dull cream-colored finish, a rough texture, and wide-spaced green lines. Felt or nylon tipped markers, black ball-point pens, and thick pencils with soft lead are helpful for writing.
- Make letters and numerals on the chalkboard, and on flash cards, handouts, and assignments larger. The distance between lines of print should be equivalent to the height of the tallest letter in the line.
- Use tactile illustrations and graphics that avoid clutter and emphasize contrast. Students with visual impairments will find it difficult to read print surrounded by small pictures and print superimposed over pictures.
- Provide additional time to students with visual impairments to complete assignments and tests. Be aware that students may suffer from visual fatigue during activities that require continuous use of visual skills. Visual fatigue can be minimized by reducing the number and length of activities that require visual concentration.
- Use, and allow students to use, typewriters with large, clear type when preparing written assignments.
- Record assignments or present information on an audiocassette.
- Teach manuscript writing first as it helps some partially sighted students differentiate between letters and words that look similar. Students also may benefit from having a larger space in which to write.
- Phrase questions and comments directed to students with visual impairments to include their names.
- Identify yourself by name or voice when walking up to students with visual impairments. Don't leave a room without telling the student that you are leaving.
- Give directions to specific destinations within the classroom or school by using non-visual statements. Directions for going left and right should be in relation to the student's body rather than yours.
- Initially assign students a buddy to facilitate their movement through the school. When students become proficient in traveling around the school, ask them to

Source: Torres & Corn (1990).

material that may be hard to explain in alternative forms of communication, the teacher and the interpreter should meet to discuss these terms. For example, when teaching a unit about the geological history of the earth, teachers might provide interpreters with a list of key terms and copies of lesson plans so that interpreters can plan in advance how to translate and explain such terms as Paleozoic era, Oligocene epoch, and Jurassic period.

perform errands and class jobs. Peers also can read directions and materials, describe events in the classroom, take notes, and assist these students during fire drills and other emergencies.

- Facilitate students' acquisition of information by giving students a copy of notes, verbalizing notes as they are being written on the board, sharing notes with students' resource teachers, and allowing students to take notes using a laptop computer.
- Provide students with desk copies of important visual stimuli such as charts or maps.
- Show videos and television programs on a stereo television or videocassette recorder that can receive an additional broadcast signal that includes a sound track describing the action and body language in the show.
- Be aware that with some students with visual impairments, particularly those born blind, their facial expressions may not accurately indicate their feelings. The way they hold their hands and fingers may give a better indication of their feelings.
- Provide audible warning signals accompanied by simultaneous visual signals to alert students with visual impairments to dangerous situations and fire drills.
- Use cues to help students develop proper posture.
- Consult with others in how to deal with some mannerisms that blind students may exhibit such as placing their fingers in their eyes, rocking, drooping their heads, engaging in excess or rhythmic motor responses, and making inappropriate noises.
- Obtain additional information and specialized materials by contacting the following organizations.

The American Printing House for the Blind
1839 Frankfort Avenue
Louisville, KY 40206

American Foundation for the Blind
15 West 16th Street
New York, NY 10011

Division for the Blind and Physically Handicapped
Library of Congress
1291 Taylor Street
Washington, DC 20542

Association for the Education of the Visually Handicapped
919 Walnut Street
Philadelphia, PA 19107

National Association for the Visually Handicapped
3201 Balboa Street
San Francisco, CA 94121

Teachers and interpreters also should discuss procedures for maximizing the effectiveness of the interpreter. Teachers with an interpreter in their class should alter their behavior accordingly.

- Be sensitive to the processing time delays that are associated with interpreting.
- Talk to the students and not to the interpreter.

- Refrain from directing comments to the interpreter during class time. Signals can be used to indicate the need to discuss concerns after the class is completed.
- Encourage the interpreter to seek clarification when communication problems arise during class that affect the translation process.

MODIFYING INSTRUCTION FOR STUDENTS WITH WRITTEN LANGUAGE PROBLEMS

Many teachers require students to respond to and demonstrate mastery of specific content by producing a written product. However, while many mainstreamed students may master the content of the assignment, their writing difficulties can interfere with their performance. In addition to allowing students to respond by other means (orally, via audiocassette, or artistically), teachers can help students improve their written products by doing the following:

- scheduling and audiotaping writing conferences with students to clarify and develop ideas, outline responses, and provide feedback
- encouraging students to use the dictionary and the thesaurus
- providing checkpoints during the process to monitor student's work
- allowing students to redo assignments for an improved grade by responding to teacher comments
- giving separate grades for content, grammar, and spelling (Vogel, 1988)

Teachers can provide mainstreamed students with writing samples that depict the correct format, writing style, and organization of content as a model for their written product. The value of the model can be enhanced by reviewing it with students and marking it with comments that direct students to the qualities that contribute to making it an excellent product. For example, the topic sentence can be emphasized by the teacher circling it and writing the comment *This is a good topic sentence. It introduces the reader to the content in the paragraph.* Similarly, the inclusion of specific sections that make up the report (hypothesis, procedures, results, or discussion) can be noted to ensure that the student's paper includes all the necessary sections.

In addition to providing students with a model, teachers also can facilitate writing by providing a checklist of items the teacher will use in evaluating the paper. The checklist can then guide students in evaluating their papers before handing them to the teacher. A checklist also can be given to students to help them proofread their written products (Wood, 1988). A sample proofreading checklist is presented in Figure 7.1.

Peers also can assist with assignments that require written language proficiency. A peer proofreader can check a mainstreamed student's grammar, punctuation, and spelling. When only the content of an assignment is important, mainstreamed students can dictate their response to a peer scribe, who will then write it with correct grammar, spelling, and punctuation (Perreira, Franke, & Woych, 1988).

FIGURE 7.1
Sample proofreading checklist

FORM

_____ 1. I have a title page with centered title, subject, class, name, and date.
_____ 2. I have a thesis statement telling the main idea of my paper.
_____ 3. I have an outline that structures the major topics and minor subheadings.
_____ 4. I have footnoted direct quotes and paraphrased material.
_____ 5. I have made a footnote page using correct form.
_____ 6. I have made a bibliography, using correct form, of all reference materials.

GRAMMAR

_____ 1. I have begun all sentences with capital letters.
_____ 2. I have put a period at the end of each sentence and a question mark at the end of questions.
_____ 3. I have used other punctuation marks correctly.
_____ 4. I have checked words for misspelling.
_____ 5. I have reread sentences for correct noun–verb agreement and awkward phrasing.
_____ 6. I have checked all sentences to be sure each is complete.

CONTENT

_____ 1. I have followed my outline.
_____ 2. I have covered each topic from my outline thoroughly and in order.
_____ 3. Each paragraph has a topic sentence.
_____ 4. The paper has an introduction.
_____ 5. The paper has a conclusion.
_____ 6. I have proven my thesis statement.

Source: J. W. Wood and K. W. Rush, *Academic Therapy,* vol. 23 (Austin, Texas: Pro-Ed), p. 244. Reprinted by permission of the publisher.

Technology

Today, teachers can modify instruction for mainstreamed students through use of technology. They can apply technology to individualize instruction, modify the ways in which material is presented and responded to, facilitate writing, and create adaptive devices for individuals with physical and sensory disabilities.

Microcomputers

Teachers can supplement and individualize instruction for mainstreamed students by using microcomputers and computer-assisted instruction. Microcomputers can

- individualize instruction by branching students to items that relate to their skill levels
- allow students to work at their own pace
- provide opportunities for automaticity through constant drill, repetition, and practice

IDEAS FOR IMPLEMENTATION

Teachers can modify instruction for students with hearing impairments by enacting the following suggestions:

- Use an overhead projector to present material; it simultaneously allows the student to view both the material and the teacher's lips.
- Assign a peer to take notes using carbon paper, and to point to speakers during a group discussion. A peer also can ensure that the student is following along in the correct place when the class is working on an assignment.
- Speak clearly with a normal tone of voice and at a moderate pace.
- Use visual signals to gain the student's attention.
- Ask questions to check understanding of orally presented directions and content.
- Rephrase content or questions to be more understandable.
- Supplement information presented orally with visual aids.
- Give test directions, assignments, and lecture outlines in writing.
- Use visual cues to indicate that someone is talking over the intercom, and make sure that someone explains the intercom message to students with hearing impairments.
- Provide the student with outlines, assignments, vocabulary lists, and the like prior to introducing new material. Encourage the student's parents to review these materials with their child.
- Remember to present all spelling and vocabulary words in sentences, as many words presented in isolation look alike to lip readers.
- Establish a visual signal to alert students to dangerous situations.
- Shine a light on the speaker's face when the room is darkened for films or slides.
- Provide the student with the script of a record or a filmstrip to help the student follow along.
- Try to limit movement and unnecessary gestures when speaking to students with hearing impairments.
- Repeat and summarize main points of orally presented information.
- Provide written models to aid students in checking the accuracy of their assignments.
- Teach the student to look up difficult-to-pronounce words in the dictionary.
- Use an interpreter to help students coordinate the visual and auditory messages associated with the class presentation. Waldron, Diebold, and Rose (1985) suggest that the interpreter sit slightly in front of the student without blocking the view of the chalkboard or the teacher, focus the student's attention by pointing with one hand to the visuals as the teacher refers to them, and use the other hand to communicate the dialogue of the teacher or the other students.

- offer multisensory presentations of content
- deliver direct instruction to teach new concepts and multistep processes
- facilitate problem-solving skills
- provide immediate feedback and delivery of reinforcement
- offer instruction in a nonthreatening manner (Ellis & Sarbonie, 1988; Lerner, 1985; Taber, 1984)

McCormick and Haring (1986) and Polloway, Payne, Patton, and Payne (1985) identified five types of computer-assisted instruction:

1. Drill and practice programs, which seek to promote mastery of content through repetition and feedback
2. Tutorials, which are designed to introduce new material, concepts, and skills
3. Simulations, which teach problem solving within a realistic context
4. Problem-solving programs, which provide students with a systematic approach to solving problems
5. Tool application programs, such as word processing programs, which help students with their writing

However, the effectiveness of computer-assisted instruction is dependent on the software program used. Many software programs are open to criticism; teachers should carefully evaluate the software programs they use with students (Majsterek & Wilson, 1989). A form for evaluating software programs is presented in Figure 7.2.

Edyburn (1990/1991) provides guidelines that teachers can use to obtain information about software programs.

Word Processing

The computer's word processing capabilities can be especially helpful in assisting with students' writing. While the superiority of word processing over handwriting as a vehicle for improving the quality of student writing has not been clearly established (Vacc, 1987), word processing has several advantages over handwriting that can facilitate the writing process for mainstreamed students, such as allowing students to focus on the writing process; minimizing spelling errors; facilitating publication; overcoming handwriting problems so that all students produce a neat, clean copy; providing students with a novel experience that motivates them to write; making text revision easy by allowing students to move text around and insert words; improving the variety of words used in writing through use of a thesaurus program; eliminating the tedious process of copying; and searching for word repetitions (Smith, 1988; Vogel, 1988). Additionally, though in their infancy, programs that check text for punctuation, capitalization, usage, and style are available and can be helpful (Kaufman, 1988).

Mainstreamed students may experience some difficulties using word processing. Degnan (1985) noted that students with memory problems may have difficulty remembering functions that require multiple key presses or syntax codes. MacArthur and Shneiderman (1986) found that the keyboarding skills of students with learning disabilities were characterized by inefficient cursor movements and inappropriate use of deletion procedures. Students also experienced problems in saving and loading files and using the return key to organize text on the monitor. Therefore, teachers should have students use word processing programs that have safeguards to prevent the loss of documents, that offer easy to read manuals and directions for use, and that contain obvious pictures and cues to prompt students (Majsterek, 1990).

Messerer and Lerner (1989) analyzed and described three word processing programs that teachers can use with mainstreamed students.

To benefit from word processing, students may need to receive some instruction in keyboarding skills and the word processing program. Morocco and Newman (1986) suggest that students receive instruction in keyboarding

FIGURE 7.2
Computer software evaluation form

LEARNER/TEACHER NEEDS	YES	NO
1. Does the program reach the target population for which it was designed?	☐	☐
2. Will the program motivate the students to learn?	☐	☐
3. Is the content relevant to the instructional needs of the students?	☐	☐
4. Will the material be effective with individual learning styles?	☐	☐
5. Does the format appeal to the students?	☐	☐
6. Is the material relevant to daily living experiences?	☐	☐

INSTRUCTIONAL INTEGRITY	YES	NO
1. Does the program state behavioral/instructional objectives?	☐	☐
2. Is the teaching/learning mode identified (drill and practice, diagnosis, tutorial, simulation, inquiry, game, problem solving)?	☐	☐
3. Is the program organized and presented in a sequential manner and in appropriate developmental steps?	☐	☐
4. Is the material presented at a concrete level and in a variety of ways?	☐	☐
5. Is the content presented clearly?	☐	☐
6. Does the program use a multisensory approach?	☐	☐
7. Are the use of graphics, sound, and color appropriate?	☐	☐
8. Does the program provide meaningful interaction for the students?	☐	☐
9. Does the program provide for user self-pacing?	☐	☐
10. Does the material require the purchase of accompanying printed material, or is it self-sufficient?	☐	☐
11. Does the material prescribe to a number of sources or just the publisher's own materials?	☐	☐
12. Does the material provide direct instruction?	☐	☐
13. Does the material provide immediate feedback?	☐	☐
14. Does the material provide a variety of built-in reinforcements?	☐	☐
15. Does the program offer supplementary materials or suggested activities for reinforcement?	☐	☐
16. Does the content use past learning or experiential background?	☐	☐
17. Is the material presented on a meaningful and appropriate lanugage level?	☐	☐

skills using the computer daily for brief periods of time. Schloss and Sedlak (1986) note that word processing instruction should teach students to enter and save text, return to the menu, print copies, load disks, clear memory, center, justify, add, delete and move text, skip lines, and move the cursor. Teachers should monitor student progress, initially emphasizing accuracy and correct hand placement rather than speed.

	YES	NO
18. Is the required reading presented at the students' level of functioning?	☐	☐
19. Does the program provide "flexible" branching so the content and reading levels meet the needs of individual student levels?	☐	☐
20. Does the program allow the student adequate time to complete learning segments?	☐	☐
21. Is the program designed to alert the teacher to a student who is experiencing difficulty with the content?	☐	☐
22. Does the material meet race, sex, and cultural distributions of the student population?	☐	☐

TECHNICAL ADEQUACY AND UTILITY	YES	NO
1. Are the teacher's instructions well organized, useful, and easy to understand?	☐	☐
2. Does the material require extensive preparation or training on the teacher's part?	☐	☐
3. Is the material of high quality?	☐	☐
4. Is the material reusable?	☐	☐
5. Is the material durable for repeated and prolonged use?	☐	☐
6. Is the size of the print clear and well spaced?	☐	☐
7. Does the speed of presentation match individual learning styles?	☐	☐
8. Does the student need typing skills to use the program?	☐	☐
9. Is it "kid-proof?"	☐	☐
10. Can a student use the program without supervision?	☐	☐
11. Is a printout of student performance available, if desired?	☐	☐
12. Is the initial cost of this nonconsumable material reasonable?	☐	☐
13. Is the program packaged so that it can be easily and safely stored?	☐	☐
14. Can the program be used in a regular classroom, resource room, media center, agency, or institution?	☐	☐
15. Does the publisher provide a policy for replacement of parts?	☐	☐
16. Does the publisher provide for preview and/or demonstration of the program?	☐	☐
17. Has the publisher produced the program so that it is available for use on at least two different models of microcomputer hardware?	☐	☐

Source: A. Hannaford and E. Sloane, *Teaching Exceptional Children,* vol. 14 (Reston, Virginia: Council for Exceptional Children, 1981), p. 56. Reprinted by permission of the publisher.

Keyboarding skills also can be taught to students through use of typing programs (Kaufman, 1988). Several educators recommend that teachers select a typing program that accepts only correct responses, provides numerous practice activities, introduces skills gradually, contains graphics for finger positions, and offers frequent feedback (Ellis and Sarbonie, 1988; Majsterek,

1990). Prompt cards that display the keys and their functions help students to remember key functions and patterns of multiple key pressing. The program to train students to use word processing also should teach students how to load, save, and exit the program.

Talking word processors, which have synthesized speech output capabilities, may benefit mainstreamed students (MacArthur, 1988). Talking word processors allow students to detect syntax errors, receive feedback on spelling as they enter words, and hear their text read. Rosegrant (1986) found that students who used a talking word processor spend more time writing, revise more, and write longer pieces of a higher quality than those using a nontalking word processor.

Talking word processors and enlarged print systems can enhance the writing capabilities of students with visual disabilities (Shell, Horn, & Severs, 1989). Word processors that have voice output systems can provide verbal feedback to users concerning keystrokes and various commands, as well as orally reviewing content appearing on the screen. A variety of special monitors and print enlargement programs also are available for students who would benefit from word processing through use of enlarged print (Shell et al., 1989).

Talk-type word processing programs based on computerized speech recognition also are being developed. In these programs, individuals talk, pausing briefly after each word. The individual's comments then appear on a video monitor and may be revised or printed. Researchers are developing voice recognition systems that are not speaker dependent, and are able to recognize continuous speech.

Hypertext/Hypermedia

One relatively new computer-based instructional tool is *hypertext* or *hypermedia,* a computerized instructional delivery system that provides learners with alternative formats for mastering content including additional text, specialized graphics, animated presentations, and computer-produced speech and sound effects (Higgins & Boone, 1990). Whereas most traditional print materials present content in a linear fashion, hypermedia allows teachers to link information presented via television monitors, videodisks, and videocassettes controlled by a microcomputer into a unified lesson based on students' needs and interests (Byrom, 1990). In hypertext, information presented on one screen such as words, letters, numbers, sentences, paragraphs, and pictures are linked to supplemental, related content on other screens that students access based on their needs and interests. Fitzgerald, Bauder, & Werner (1992) offer guidelines that teachers can employ to develop hypermedia-authored programs.

Higgins and Boone (1990) describe several uses of hypertext and identify several hypertext authoring programs that educators can use.

Videocassettes

Videocassette recorders (VCRs) can help teachers in presenting information. The taping, stopping, and starting capabilities of videocassettes allow demonstrations, experiments, and other classroom activities to be taped and then played back for students to highlight or repeat key parts or information. Videocassettes also can facilitate modeling, and can help establish an environment that promotes simulation activities or group discussions. For example, a videocassette of a student giving an oral presentation can serve as a model that mainstreamed students can take home to help them master the task.

Videocassettes of shows, movies, or documentaries can be used as teaching tools. For example, a video of excerpts from a television show on the homeless can stimulate a discussion on the plight of the homeless. Some video rental stores offer videocassettes at no cost on such topics as AIDS and drug education that teachers can use in their classrooms.

Videos also can serve as advance organizers (Walla, 1988). For example, a video of the film *West Side Story* can introduce and orient students to the characters and plot of *Romeo and Juliet.* In addition, this use of videocassettes can motivate students to pursue further study.

Teachers can have students demonstrate mastery of content through video-based projects, such as writing, producing, and recording a news program, play, or video; role playing a reading selection; simulating an activity; or explaining how to solve a problem or perform an experiment (Rosenthal & Tetel-Hanks, 1981). Similarly, videocassette recordings of sessions can help students and teachers evaluate the implementation of new instructional formats. For example, a videocassette of a cooperative learning group working successfully can be viewed and discussed to focus student attention on the behaviors and roles that help groups work collaboratively.

Videodiscs. Teachers can present content via *videodiscs* connected to a computer (Thorkildsen & Friedman, 1986). Kelly, Carnine, Gersten, and Grossen (1986) used videodisc-guided instruction to teach basic fractions concepts to a group of remedial students and students with mild learning problems. Each disc can present up to 30 minutes of, or 54,000, realistic computer graphic displays, videocassette segments, slides, or motion pictures and sound effects (Woodward & Gersten, 1992). With remote control, teachers can quickly access visual and auditory stimuli randomly or continuously, and can pause the presentation to highlight critical information or to ask students questions. Thus, videodisc instruction allows students to hear explanations; interact with colorful and expressive visual displays and demonstrations, computer graphics, and sound effects that accurately depict concepts and material in a gradual and systematic way; and practice mastery of the material (Gersten, Carnine, & Woodward, 1987; Woodward & Gersten, 1992). For example, a lesson on the Civil War can be supplemented through a videodisc that portrays actual battles, presents interviews with soldiers, and displays maps and important documents. While several videodisc programs have been developed, availability is currently limited by their high cost (Cartwright, Cartwright, & Ward, 1985).

Adaptive Devices

Computer technology has been used to develop many adaptive devices to promote the independence of students with various disabilities.

Students with Physical Disabilities. Students who have difficulty making the motor responses necessary to produce intelligible speech may find microcomputers with speech synthesis capabilities invaluable. Computer programs and output devices are available that can transform word input into speech. The student can input a phrase or press a key that activates the computer's speech capabilities. Because these students also may have problems inputting information into the computer in traditional ways (such as pressing more than one key at a time), alternative methods have been developed (See Figure 7.3).

Brandenburg and Vanderheiden (1987) describe a variety of augmentative communication systems that can be used with a wide range of individuals.

Computer technology can be used to help students with speech and language impairments remediate articulation, fluency, and voice disorders (Wisniewski & Sedlack, 1992). Devices such as videos, audiocassette recorders with an "s" meter, a pitch meter, and phonic mirror can offer feedback to students to correct their speech (Levitt, 1989; Wisniewski & Sedlack, 1992). Software programs that use game formats to reinforce appropriate pitch, rhythm, and sound quality and to provide feedback are available.

Computer technology has also helped increase the range of movements and thus the independence of individuals with physical disabilities. For example, Schneider, Schmeisser, and Seamone (1981) developed a computer-

FIGURE 7.3
Alternative methods of inputting information into computers

1. **Voice recognition.** The computer recognizes speech of user and converts speech into action.
2. **Key guard.** A device that modifies the traditional keyboard to change the size and spacing of the keys. May include a key lock that automatically toggles specialty keys.
3. **Keyboard alteration programs.** Programs that modify the keyboard in terms of key accept time and key repeating.
4. **Graphics tablet.** A small slate that may be covered by templates of words, pictures, numerals, and letters that are input when touched by a special stylus.
5. **Adapted switches.** The student activates the system by using an adapted switch controlled by pressure or body movements. Switches can be activated by foot, head, cheek, chin, and eye movements.
6. **Scanning systems.** An array of letters, phrases, and numerals are displayed on the screen at a rate that is adjusted to the student's need. The student selects the message from the scanner by use of the keyboard or a switch.
7. **Touch screens/light pens.** Devices that allow the student to activate the computer by touching or writing on the screen.
8. **Joysticks.** The student controls the movement of the cursor by moving a stick in different directions.
9. **Mouthsticks.** A tool that is placed in the mouth and used to press buttons and activate switches.
10. **Headbands.** The student wears a headband that allows control of the computer through head or eye movements.
11. **Sip & puff systems.** The student sucks on a long command tube attached to a computer or wheelchair.
12. **Skateboard.** A block of wood on rollers attached to the student's arm that is moved in different directions to control cursor movements.
13. **Mouse.** A mouselike object that is moved in different directions to control the computer. Adaptations of the mouse can be controlled by use of the numeric pad of the keyboard (keyboard mouse) or through a headsetlike device, such as a headband, that conveys directions to the computer via head movements.

controlled robotic arm that attaches to a worktable. The arm allows individuals with physical disabilities to perform a variety of motor activities, such as feeding themselves and using a typewriter. Personal robots can also perform manual functions for individuals with physical disabilities. Computerized systems in the home can be programmed to perform such activities as turning on the oven, shutting off lights, locking doors, and adjusting the sound of the television so that these individuals can live on their own.

Students with Visual Disabilities. Although expensive, several adaptive devices have been developed to help visually and print-impaired students acquire information from print materials. The *Kurzweil Reading Machine* is programmed to recognize letters, group letters into words, pronounce words, and provide the correct pronunciation of words in a sentence in several different languages. Printed materials are placed on the glass top of a machine that resembles a photocopy machine. Students then punch buttons on a panel that allows them to pause the machine; rewind to hear one or more lines read again; move ahead to a particular section; find a specific word and spell it out; and control volume, pitch, and speech rate.

Another device that can help students read print materials is the *Optacon.* As the student moves a cameralike device along a printed page, the Optacon translates the image to a tactile Braille-type representation or converts it to synthesized speech. The *Talking Terminal* also provides students with visual disabilities with access to large bodies of information by reading aloud computerized material.

A variety of optical aids including hand-held magnifiers, magnifiers mounted on a base, and magnifiers that are attached to eyeglass frames or that are part of the lenses magnify printed materials for individuals with visual disabilities. One technology-oriented optical aid, the *Apollo Laser Electronic Aid,* employs a closed-circuit television system that enlarges visual stimuli aimed through its lens. It helps students obtain information presented on the chalkboard by enlarging white lettering on a black background, or gain information from a book by enlarging black lettering on a white background. The visual acuity of students varies, so the Apollo Laser allows the student to adjust the size of print on the screen.

Technology also has been developed to establish communication systems for individuals with visual disabilities. The *Tele-Braille* facilitates communication for deaf and blind individuals by converting a message typed on a Braille keyboard into print on a video monitor, which is read by a sighted person. The sighted person then types a response, which is converted into a Braille display. Similarly, *VersaBraille,* a device that produces a Braille readout of information presented on a computer screen, allows individuals with visual impairments to communicate with others. Computers with large print, Braille, and voice output capabilities also have facilitated the communication process for individuals with visual disabilities.

Electronic travel aids can increase the independent mobility skills of students with visual disabilities. The *Mowat Sensor* is a hand-held electronic device that uses vibrations to alert students to barriers in their path and

Adaptive devices can promote the independence of students with various disabilities.

indicate the distance to obstacles. Similarly, the *Laser Cane* emits three laser beams that provide auditory feedback to sensitize the user to objects, dropoffs, or low-hanging obstacles in the individual's path. Information about the environment to facilitate an individual's mobility also can be obtained through the *Sonicguide* and the *Pathsounder* (Wisniewski & Sedlak, 1992).

Students with Hearing Disabilities. Technology is having a profound impact on improving adaptive devices for individuals with hearing disabilities. For some individuals whose hearing loss is related to damage to the cochlea, a small microprocessor can be implanted into the ear to improve hearing. The microprocessor translates auditory stimuli into electrical signals, which are transmitted to the nerve fibers leading to the brain. Following the implant, individuals must be taught to convert the sounds into meaningful messages.

Systems that convert verbal statements to print can promote communication between individuals with hearing disabilities and individuals who do not have hearing disabilities. The *teletypewriter* can translate speech into a visual display on a screen that can be read by individuals with hearing disabilities. The dialogue that accompanies closed-caption television shows and films can be presented visually on the screen via a device that receives closed-caption signals connected to the television. Telecommunication Devices for the Deaf (TDD) allow individuals with hearing disabilities to communicate using the telephone.

A student's ability to communicate with others through lip reading can be enhanced through the *Upton Eyeglass,* a device that uses microprocessors to identify, transform, and present five critical features of speech that aid lip readers (Compton & Kaplan, 1988). During conversations, microprocessors analyze speech, and an array of diodes light up in sequence based on the phonemes heard to indicate the word(s) spoken.

Students From Linguistically Diverse Backgrounds. Students who are learning English as a second language may benefit from the use of several devices. The *Language Master* is an electronic dictionary, thesaurus, and grammar and spell checker that pronounces words, gives definitions and synonyms, corrects spelling of phonetic words, and offers educational word games for over 83,000 words. Similarly, the Claris Corporation of Santa Clara, California has developed a word processing program for individuals whose native language is Spanish.

Think About It

What technological aids have you used to enhance your skills as a learner? To make your life easier?

MODIFYING INSTRUCTION FOR STUDENTS WITH SEVERE DISABILITIES

Teachers can use a variety of instructional and curricular adaptations to modify and individualize instruction for students with severe disabilities, including individualized adaptations, multi-level teaching, and curriculum overlapping (Ayres, Belle, Green, O'Connor, & Meyer, n.d.). While these modifications have been suggested for use with students with severe disabilities, they also can be employed to adapt instruction for all students.

Individualized Adaptations

Individualized adaptations involve modifications in the ways information is presented to students or the ways students respond. Frequently, instructional modifications are used to help students who are learning the same material as their classmates. Individualized adaptations include using materials, equipment, and technology, delivering verbal cues and physical prompts, employing a modified skill sequence, and adjusting classroom rules (Ayres et al., n.d.).

Multi-Level Teaching

Individualization across all lessons and curricular areas can be achieved through use of *multi-level teaching* (Murray, 1991). In multi-level teaching, students participate in lessons that address the same curricular areas as their peers but at varying levels of difficulty (Ayres et al., n.d.). For example, a student with a severe disability might practice writing numbers by copying the same problems that students are using to practice addition of decimals. Collicutt (1991) delineated a four-step process for designing multi-level instructional lessons:

Step 1—Identification of Underlying Concepts. Teachers identify and examine the objectives and materials of the lesson and determine potential content and skill level differences.

Step 2—Consider the Methods of Teacher Presentation. Teachers consider the different learning styles, and cognitive and participation levels of students as well as the various presentation modes that can be used to present the lesson.

Step 3—Consider Methods of Student Practice and Performance. Teachers consider the different ways students can practice and show mastery of skills and concepts. Teachers also employ methods for teaching students to accept the differing response modes for demonstrating skill mastery and understanding of concepts.

Step 4—Consider Methods of Evaluation. Teachers consider a variety of ways to individually assess students' mastery.

Think About It

Think about a mathematics lesson. How could you use multi-level teaching to adapt the lesson to the needs of a student with a severe disability? A student with a mild disability?

Curriculum Overlapping

Teachers also can adapt instruction for students with severe disabilities by employing *curriculum overlapping,* which involves teaching students individualized skills in an integrated setting while classmates are working on a different curricular area (Ayres et al., n.d.). In curriculum overlapping, instruction in a specific skill related to the student's instructional program is embedded within the classes' learning activities across the curriculum. For example, while classmates are working on social studies and science lessons, a student with a severe disability can be working on following multiple-step directions.

MODIFYING INSTRUCTION FOR STUDENTS FROM CULTURALLY AND LINGUISTICALLY DIVERSE BACKGROUNDS

In addition to using cooperative learning arrangements and the other strategies presented in this chapter, teachers also should consider the following guidelines when designing instructional modifications for students from culturally and linguistically diverse backgrounds.

Use Culturally Relevant Instructional Strategies and Curriculum Modifications

Instructional strategies and curriculum adaptations should be consistent with the students' background of experiences, cultural perspectives, and developmental ages (Collier & Kalk, 1989; Foulks, 1991). Instructional strategies and activities should validate students' cultural backgrounds through use of language, dialect, readings, and music that reflect students' cultures (Freeman & Freeman, 1992).

Hale-Benson (1986) has developed a culturally relevant curriculum for African American students that addresses the areas of language/communication, mathematics, African American studies, and attitudes toward self, learning, and school.

Irvine (1990) noted that there should be a synchronization between the instructional strategies that teachers employ with students and students' cultural background and learning style preference. For example, because many Native American students are socialized by and learn traditions through observation, imitation, and listening (Henry & Pepper, 1990), these students may perform better when teachers use observational learning (Franklin, n.d.). Teachers can implement observational learning by offering students opportunities to work on experiential activities, use manipulatives, and view concrete examples and models of new and difficult-to-learn skills (Franklin, n.d.).

Franklin (in press) examined the research on effective strategies for teaching students from culturally and linguistically diverse backgrounds and identified several strategies that appear to be successful with African American students and other groups of students:

Emphasizing Verbal Interactions—Teachers use activities that encourage students to respond verbally to the material in creative ways such as group discussions, role plays, story telling, group recitations, choral and responsive reading, and rap (Holliday, 1985).

Teaching Students to Engage in Self-talk—Teachers encourage and teach students to learn new material through self-verbalizations (Willis, 1989).

Facilitating Divergent Thinking—Teachers encourage students to explore and devise unique solutions to issues and problems through activities such as brainstorming, group discussions, and cooperative learning groups (Boykin, 1982).

Using Small-group Instruction and Cooperative Learning—Teachers provide students with the opportunities to work in small groups, and use cooperative learning arrangements including peer tutoring and cross-age tutoring (Hale-Benson, 1986).

Employing Verve in the Classroom—Teachers employ active, movement-oriented activities such as dancing, hand clapping, singing, as well as multisensory teaching methods (Boykin, 1982; Hale-Benson, 1986). Teachers can introduce *verve,* a high level of energy and exuberance, into the classrooms through moving around the classroom, using their bodies to act out and demonstrate content, varying their voice quality, and employing facial expressions (Irvine, 1990).

Focusing on Real-world Tasks—Teachers introduce content, language, and learning by relating it to students' home, school, and community life (Willis, 1989).

Promoting Teacher–Student Interactions—Teachers use instructional procedures that are based on interactive exchanges between students and teachers. Teachers ask frequent questions, affirm students' responses, give feedback, offer demonstrations and explanations, rephrase, review, and summarize material (Irvine, 1990).

Enhance the Skills of Second Language Learners

Employ Reciprocal Interaction Teaching Approaches

Teaching models that promote the transmission of information through task analysis, structured drills, and independent seatwork may not be effective with second language learners because they fail to provide a language context for students (Figueroa, Fradd, & Correa, 1989; Ortiz & Yates, 1989). Therefore, when instructing these students, teachers need to employ *reciprocal interaction teaching models,* approaches that foster empowerment and learning through verbal and written exchanges between students and teachers, and among students (Cummins, 1984). In implementing reciprocal interaction approaches, teachers use students' prior knowledge and experiences to add sufficient context to promote comprehension, incorporate language use across all activities and content areas, and target higher level critical thinking skills rather than basic skills. Teachers also use student-centered instruction, student-to-student interactions, problem-solving situations, tasks that promote internal motivation, and guided questioning to help students gain control over their learning (Wiig, Freedman, & Secord, 1992). Teachers also employ *scaffolding,* breaking down a comment a student doesn't understand or a task a student has difficulty performing into discrete components that facilitate student comprehension or mastery.

When using interactive approaches teachers should adjust their communication style to the student's needs and style by doing the following:

- speaking clearly in a typical conversational tone
- using high-frequency words that are familiar to students
- controlling the use of idiom and difficult-to-understand vocabulary, as well as sentence length and complexity
- examining language in terms of precision, pace, and word choice
- previewing relevant vocabulary, phrases, and expressions

- previewing topics, graphics, pictures, titles, and subheadings
- highlighting new and important words through variations in volume and intonation
- restating or paraphrasing key terms and phrases
- giving examples of new words and concepts
- asking questions to assess student comprehension
- focusing feedback on meaning and language use rather than on grammatical correctness (Beaty, 1990; Chamot & O'Malley, 1989; Maldonado-Colon, 1990)

Teachers also can promote these teacher-student interactions through use of confirmation checks (*Are you saying ________?*), comprehension checks (*Do you understand what I just said? Tell me in your own words what I'm saying*), clarification requests (*Can you explain that again? In a different way?*), repetitions, and expansions (Beaty, 1990; Fradd, 1987).

Jones and Warren (1991) identified three interactive teaching strategies to teach language skills: incidental teaching, the mand-model technique, and systematic commenting. *Incidental teaching* occurs when the teacher introduces a new skill by seeking a more elaborate response from a student who has initiated an interaction with the teacher. If the student responds appropriately, the teacher delivers reinforcement, and continues the conversation. If the student fails to respond appropriately, the teacher models the correct response and reinforces the student for engaging in successful imitation. The *mand-model technique* is similar to incidental teaching, except that teachers initiate it by prompting students, asking them to verbalize about a topic or situation. Teachers can use *systematic commenting* by making descriptive comments directed to the student to solicit a response.

Teach New Vocabulary and Concepts

Several of Mr. Taylor's first grade students are experiencing difficulty understanding concepts that he uses to give directions. When Mr. Taylor gives directions, he notices that they act confused and look to students around them for help. Today, when he asks students to point to the animal at the top of the page, several students point to the bottom. Mr. Taylor decides that learning about opposites would help his students follow directions better. Initially, he explains to students the meaning of the concept of opposites, and allows students to experience a variety of opposites by having them touch hot and color water, carry heavy and light things, and measure big and little objects. Next he presents word pairs that are examples or nonexamples to students, and asks them to tell if the word pairs are opposites. Finally, students work in dyads to act out opposites. Dyads are given word pairs, and asked to act them out and indicate if they are opposites. For example, one student pantomimes being happy, while her partner mimicks being sad. The dyad then identifies the word pair as an opposite.

IDEAS FOR IMPLEMENTATION

Teachers can facilitate instruction for second language learners by enacting the following suggestions:

- Establish a low-anxiety learning environment that encourages students to take risks and attempt to use their new language.
- Introduce new skills and assignments through use of modeling, demonstration, hands-on experiences, and audiovisual materials.
- Begin new lessons with reviews of relevant previously learned skills.
- Rephrase important points, directions, and questions.
- Relate new material to students' experiences.
- Use real-world language and experiences.
- Be descriptive.
- Use cultural referents and student experiences during instruction.
- Delineate relationships between concepts and new material.
- Provide students with multiple experiences.
- Allow students to use manipulatives.
- Facilitate understanding of statements and new words through use of rephrasing, pictorials, and pantomimes, and by writing key words.
- Teach students how to use dictionaries in class.
- Encourage students to share their opinions, ask questions, and expand on the comments of others.
- Use meaningful and functional activities.
- Integrate language development activities into content area instruction.
- Assign vocabulary and spelling words that are related to content areas.
- Facilitate students' understanding of visual and written work.

Effective instruction for second language learners requires that teachers help them learn new vocabulary and concepts. When introducing new vocabulary and concepts to students, teachers should consider the following sequence:

Step 1: Highlight the salient features associated with understanding the concept.
Step 2: Introduce and label the concept in a variety of different situations. Where possible, present the concept by using concrete materials and manipulatives.
Step 3: Show and discuss examples and nonexamples of the concept. Use the concept in a variety of naturally occurring situations.
Step 4: Contrast the concept with other related concepts.
Step 5: Allow students to practice use of the concept (Boehm, 1986; Bos & Vaughn, 1991; Nelson & Cummings, 1981).

Teach Figurative Language

Second language learners may experience difficulty learning figurative language, words and expressions that have various meanings depending on the context in which they are used (Billows, 1977). Manning and Wray (1990) suggest several guidelines that teachers can employ to facilitate students' acquisition of figurative language, including the following:

- Use repetition to help students acquire the rhythm, pitch, volume, and tone of their new language.Use gestures, facial expressions, visuals, props, and other cues to provide contextual support to convey meanings of new terms and concepts.
- Introduce new material in context, discussing changes in the context while it is occurring.
- Develop students' language competence through use of art forms, drama, simulations, role plays, storytelling, music, and games.
- Supplement oral instruction with accompanying visual stimuli such as charts, maps, graphs, and pictures.
- Use audiocassettes and videocassettes to supplement instruction.
- Provide students with the opportunities to work together in cooperative learning groups.
- Provide opportunities for all students to serve as tutors.
- Encourage all students to seek feedback and assistance from peers.
- Establish a learning environment where all students are proud of their accomplishments and share them with peers.
- Show respect for and encourage the maintenance of all languages that students speak.
- Label objects in the classroom in several languages.
- Offer activities that are both bilingual and multilingual.
- Encourage students to speak their native languages when the development of English language proficiency is not the focus of the activity.
- Note that being bilingual is an asset.
- Preview and review important content through use of students' native language.
- Employ nonverbal strategies to indicate acceptance.

Source: Gutierrez, Whittington-Couse, & Korycki (1990); Foulks (1991); Freeman & Freeman (1989); Maldonado-Colon (1990).

- Cue students to key concepts by varying voice intonation.
- Introduce figurative language through use of stories that provide a background and context for the expression.
- Use manipulatives and demonstrations to facilitate students' understanding of the figurative expressions.
- Use illustrations to depict the meanings of figurative language.
- Alert students to the physical properties of the figurative expressions.
- Isolate terms by asking questions to cue students to the meanings of important words within figurative expressions.
- Teach students to analyze the semantic and syntactic contexts of key words.
- Compare literal and figurative interpretations with respect to common and different features.

Books and stories also can be an effective strategy for teaching figurative language (Westby, 1992).

Encourage Second Language Learners to Respond

Teachers may need to encourage students who are learning English and students with speech and language difficulties to respond verbally. Wood

(1976) noted that teachers can aid these students in responding by creating an atmosphere that facilitates speaking, by offering numerous chances for students to engage in oral discussions, by allowing students to use gestures initially until they develop language competence, and by acknowledging the student's contribution and seeking additional information when necessary. Teachers should provide students with enough time to interact and discuss material before formulating their responses. Teachers also can stimulate the use of language by providing experiences that encourage verbalizations such as introducing new objects into the classroom; making periodic changes in the classroom environment; allowing students to work and play cooperatively; conducting interviews; sending students on errands; creating situations whereby students need to request assistance; asking students to recount events, talk about doing something while doing it, or present an account of a personal experience; asking students questions; and employing visuals that display pictorial absurdities (Spekman & Roth, 1984; Westby, 1992).

Think About It

Watch a television show or film in a second language. What factors assisted you in understanding the content of the show or film?

SUMMARY

This chapter was designed to offer guidelines for planning and implementing instructional modifications to address the specific learning needs of mainstreamed students. The chapter

- presented strategies to modify instruction from textbooks and other print materials
- presented strategies to modify instruction for students with sensory disabilities and students with written language difficulties
- outlined how technology and adaptive devices can facilitate the learning and performance of students
- presented strategies for modifying instruction for students with severe disabilities
- provided guidelines for modifying instruction for students from culturally and linguistically diverse backgrounds

RECOMMENDED READINGS

Bos, C. S., & Vaughn, S. (1991). *Strategies for teaching students with learning and behavior problems* (2nd ed). Boston: Allyn & Bacon.

Brandenburg, S. A., & Vanderheiden, C. G. (1987). *Rehab/education technology resource book series: Communication, control and computer access for disabled elderly individuals, Resource book 1: Communication aids.* Boston: College-Hill Press.

Carbo, M., Dunn, R., & Dunn, K. (1986). *Teaching students to read through their individual learning style* (2nd ed.). Reston, VA: Reston Publishing Co. (ERIC Document Reproduction Service No. ED 281 171).

Collicott, J. (1991). Implementing multi-level teaching: Strategies for classroom teachers. In G. L. Porter & D. Richler (Eds.), *Changing Canadian schools: Perspectives on disability and inclusion* (pp. 191–218). Toronto: The Roeher Institute.

Commission on the Education of the Deaf (1988). *Toward equality: Education of the deaf. A report to the President and the Congress of the United States.* Washington, DC: U.S. Government Printing Office.

Cummins, J. (1984). *Bilingualism and special education: Issues in assessment and pedagogy.* Clevedon, Avon, England: Multilingual Matters.

Hale-Benson, J. E. (1986). *Black children: Their roots, culture, and learning styles (2nd ed.).* Baltimore: Johns Hopkins University Press.

Higgins, K., & Boone, R. (1990). Hypertext: A new vehicle for computer use in reading instruction. *Intervention in School and Clinic, 26*(1), 26–31.

Irvine, J. J. (1990). *Black students and school failure: Policies, practices and prescriptions.* New York: Praeger.

Palinscar, A. S., & Klenk, L. J. (1991). Learning dialogues to promote text comprehension. In B. Means & M. S. Knapp (Eds.), *Teaching advanced skills to educationally disadvantaged students—Final Report* (pp. 20–34). Washington, DC: U.S. Department of Education.

8 Modifying Reading, Writing, Spelling, and Handwriting Instruction

MS. PIKE'S CLASS

Ms. Pike's students slowly begin to arrive at school. When they arrive at Ms. Pike's class, they start working on either independent reading or journal writing. After about 20 minutes, all her students have arrived, and the class meets to discuss such topics as important school, community, or current events, or a review of a new movie or book.

Following the class meeting, Ms. Pike shares a book with students. Today, she is reading the African folktale, *Why Mosquitoes Buzz in People's Ears,* which is part of a theme on understanding people from diverse cultures. Before reading the story, Ms. Pike discusses the African reverence for nature, and the use of animals in folk tales to represent human traits. Also as part of the theme, students are reading and writing about female and male scientists and mathematicians from diverse ethnic backgrounds, and examining historical events from the perspectives of different groups.

As a followup activity to her lesson on folktales, Ms. Pike asks her students to work in groups to write and illustrate a short folktale using animals as the characters in the story, to be read or performed for the class in a week. Before assigning students to groups, Ms. Pike conducts a lesson and discussion on folktales. While the students work, Ms. Pike circulates around the room to observe and conference with individual students and groups. One group conference focuses on why that group selected a camel to be their main character, while another conference deals with creating a storyline.

The group activity is followed by individualized reading. Students independently read books about individuals from various cultures that they have selected from a list prepared and previewed by Ms. Pike and the class. Students who select the same book to read are grouped together, and meet with Ms. Pike to discuss the book and work on group projects. Occasionally, Ms. Pike teaches a minilesson to help students learn a specific reading or writing strategy.

The students and Ms. Pike also read these books during the afternoon sustained silent reading period. After working in their literature groups, students react to what they have read by making entries in their reading journal. Ms. Pike periodically collects and reads the journals and responds to students' entries via written comments or individual conferences.

What philosophical approach is Ms. Pike using to promote the literacy skills of her students? After reading this chapter, you should be able to answer this as well as the following questions.

- What approaches and strategies can educators use to adapt instruction of reading and word recognition skills?
- How can educators implement a process-oriented approach to teach writing to students?
- What approaches and strategies can educators use to adapt spelling instruction?
- What approaches and strategies can educators use to adapt handwriting instruction?

In addition to adapting textbooks (see Chapters 7 and 9) and teaching text comprehension strategies (see Chapter 5), teachers may need to help mainstreamed students develop literacy skills. This chapter offers guidelines for teaching reading, writing, spelling, and handwriting.

READING

Word recognition, the ability to establish the relationship between the printed word and its correct pronunciation, is an important component of reading comprehension (Harris & Sipay, 1985).

Selecting an Appropriate Reading Approach

Teachers can choose from among a variety of different approaches to teach students word recognition skills. Most reading programs are based on a

Cohen and Plakson (1978) provide guidelines for examining the advantages and disadvantages of different reading approaches with mainstreamed students.

particular teaching philosophy; therefore, they differ in their instructional approach. Teachers should select a reading approach appropriate to the student's learning needs and characteristics. While there are few guidelines for matching a student with a specific reading approach (Zigmond, Vallecorsa, & Leinhardt, 1980), Harris and Sipay (1985) suggest that the student's rate of learning and emotional responsiveness be the guides for determining appropriate instructional procedures.

Phonetic Approaches

Phonetic approaches provide students with a strategy for decoding new, unknown words. Phonics instruction is geared toward teaching students the relationship between letters and sounds. It also teaches students to focus on the letter sequences and sounds within words. The curriculum of most phonics programs includes auditory discrimination of sounds in words; letters and their corresponding sounds; initial and final consonant sounds; consonant blends and digraph sounds; vowel sounds; vowel digraphs, double vowels and dipthong sounds; sounds of vowels followed by the letter *r;* sounds related to the final *e;* and final *y* sound (Heilman, Blair, & Rupley, 1981).

Phonics approaches are categorized as synthetic or analytic. The *synthetic* approach develops phonetic skills by teaching students the specific symbol to sound (grapheme to phoneme) correspondence rules. Once students learn the sound and symbol rules, they are taught to synthesize the sounds into words through blending. When using this approach, teachers do the following:

1. Introduce letters and their names to students.
2. Instruct students in the corresponding sounds that are associated with each letter.
3. Provide students with opportunities to develop automaticity in grapheme-phoneme relationships.
4. Teach students how to blend sounds into words.
5. Offer activities that allow students to apply their skills to unknown words (Vaca, Vaca, & Gove, 1987).

In an *analytic* approach to phonics instruction, grapheme-phoneme correspondence is learned by teaching students to analyze words. These word analysis skills help students develop an understanding that letters within words sound alike and are written in the same way (Vaca et al., 1987). When using the analytic approach, teachers do the following:

1. Present students with a list of words that share a common phonic element.
2. Question students concerning the similarities and differences in the look and sound of the words.
3. Help students determine the common phonetic patterns in the words.
4. Have students state the rule concerning the phonetic pattern (Vaca et al., 1987).

An alternative analytic method uses a *linguistic* approach to teach reading. Based on the work of Fries (1963) and Bloomfield and Barnhart (1961), students learn to read and spell word families that share the same phonetic patterns. Through repeated presentations of these word families, students learn the rules of sound and symbol correspondence. For example, the *at* family would be introduced together, using such words as *bat, cat, fat, hat, rat,* and *sat.* In a linguistic approach, blending is not taught; little emphasis is placed on meaning and comprehension during the early stages of reading.

Phonetic approaches may present some problems for mainstreamed students (Cohen & Plakson, 1978). Students taught using these phonetic approaches tend not to guess words that do not follow phonetic rules; read more regular words than irregular words; and tend to pronounce words based on graphic and phonetic cues rather than semantic and syntactical cues (Barr, 1975; Dank, 1977). Students may have difficulty both in differentiating words that do not follow phonetic patterns and in isolating and blending sounds, so teachers may need to supplement phonics instruction with other approaches.

Lewandowski (1979) found that only 41% of high-utility words followed phonetically regular patterns.

Whole Word Approaches

Whole word approaches help students make the link between whole words and their oral counterparts. In the whole word approach, meaning also is emphasized. New words are taught within sentences and passages, or in isolation. Teachers can modify whole word approaches for mainstreamed students by decreasing the number of words to be learned, offering spaced practice sessions, and providing opportunities for overlearning and delivering more frequent reinforcement (Harris & Sipay, 1985). Students taught through whole word methods tend to attempt to read unfamiliar words, use context cues rather than graphic cues, and substitute familiar words for new words (Biemiller, 1970).

Basal Readers

Perhaps the most widely used whole word approach is the basal reader (Britton, Lumpkin, & Britton, 1984). Students learn to recognize, read, and define the common words that comprise the basal reader. More complex words are introduced gradually as students progress through the series.

Basal readers cover a wide range of reading levels, usually from readiness kindergarten materials to eighth grade, allowing students to work at different levels within the regular classroom (Vaca et al., 1987). Students progress throughout the series to develop reading proficiency (Heilman, Blair, & Rupley, 1981). Each level may have several books that correspond to specific skills within the skill sequence on which the series is based. The skill sequence usually follows a continuum of reading readiness, word identification, vocabulary, comprehension, and study skills. As students develop their skills, phonics and word analysis skills are taught to increase word recognition skills.

The content of the series is controlled so that vocabulary and new skills are introduced in a gradual, logical sequence. Teachers guide groups of students through a story using *directed reading,* which includes three components: preparation, reading, and discussion (Harris & Sipay, 1985). During the preparation stage, the teacher stimulates students' interest and presents new words and concepts from the selection. Next, the students read the selection silently after participating in a discussion about the story title and the accompanying pictures. After silent reading, the group discusses the story; then each member takes a turn reading the story aloud. Students then practice skills and words introduced in the story through some type of followup activity.

In addition to the readers themselves, basal reader programs also include criterion-referenced tests to assess mastery; alternative followup activities such as comprehension questions, workbooks, ditto masters, and games; media such as films, videocassettes, filmstrips, and audiocassettes; a teacher's manual to guide and train educators to use the program; and recordkeeping forms to chart student progress.

Language Experience Approach

Another reading strategy that incorporates reading, listening, speaking, and writing is the *language experience* approach, a program based on the belief that what students think about, they can talk about; what students can say, they can write or have someone write for them; and what students can write, they can read (Vaca et al., 1987). Language experience approaches are highly individualized; they use the students' interests, hobbies, and experiences to compose their reading materials (Hall, 1981). The incorporation of students' experiences can maintain a high level of motivation and can foster creativity.

Teachers provide students with guided and varied experiences and encourage students to share their thoughts, ideas, and feelings through artwork, speaking, and writing. In the younger grades, students share their reactions and experiences by dictating stories to the teacher, which then form the core of the reading program. Teachers guide the formation of the story, helping students make revisions and instructing them about grammar, punctuation, spelling, syntax, and vocabulary. As students develop a sufficient number of words they can recognize, easy books are introduced. They also are encouraged to write and then read their own stories, poems, and plays.

Whole Language Approach

One philosophy for promoting literacy that may be particularly appropriate for students from linguistically and culturally diverse backgrounds is *whole language* which employs students' language and experiences in and out of school to increase their reading and writing abilities (Freeman & Freeman, 1992; Goodman, 1986; Weaver, 1990). A whole language approach seeks to immerse students in a supportive, stimulating, natural learning environment that promotes their literacy. In a whole language approach, reading, writing, listening, speaking, and thinking are integrated as part of each lesson and activity (Butler, n.d.). Rather than teaching students specific skills, whole language programs seek to teach students strategies that help them control their learning (Holdaway, 1979; Edelsky, Altwerger, & Flores, 1991).

In a whole language approach, the emphasis is on reading for meaning rather than learning decoding skills in isolation. Students are motivated to read and improve their reading by reading real, relevant, and functional materials. Rather than using basal readers or skill development programs, whole language reading materials are fiction and nonfiction books and resources the students need or want to read (Goodman, 1986). Thus, the whole language classroom is stocked with books of varying degrees of difficulty and content such as novels, short stories, dictionaries, and encyclopedias.

The whole language curriculum may be organized around themes and units that serve to increase language and reading skills. Teachers and students develop and structure curricula to offer instructional experiences relating to real problems and ideas. Initially, students start to read meaningful, predictable whole text. Next, they use these familiar words to begin to learn new words and phrases. While learning to read, students also are learning to write. Students are encouraged to write about their experiences through composing letters, maintaining journals, making lists, labeling objects in the classroom, and keeping records.

Butler (n.d.) delineates the ten components of a balanced, whole language program. These components are discussed here.

Reading to Students. Teachers read quality literature and books from a variety of genres to students to introduce them to the enjoyment and excitement of reading. Reading to students also allows teachers to model good oral reading and to offer background knowledge on such areas as story structure and content. Story reading also promotes good reading habits and student writing. In reading to students, teachers should do the following:

- Discuss the title and cover of the book.
- Ask the students to make predictions about the book.
- Introduce the author and illustrator of the book.
- Talk with students about other books they have read by the author or on a similar topic or theme.
- Relate the book to students' experiences.
- Provide students with background information necessary to appreciate the book.

Shared Book Reading. Students and teachers sit in close proximity and share in reading a variety of reading materials. Often, teachers read a new or familiar piece, students react to the piece through arts and crafts, drama, reading or writing, and students then reread the story on their own. Big books with large print and pictures are particularly appropriate for shared book reading as they allow teachers to display the words that they are reading.

An important part of shared book reading is giving students insights into the reading process. Teachers therefore generally make one or two teaching points when implementing shared book reading. For example, for older students, teachers might emphasize how to use context to figure out a word that is difficult to read.

Sustained Silent Reading. Teachers, students, and other members of the classroom read self-selected materials for an extended period of time. Typically, the rules for sustained silent reading are 1) read silently, 2) do not interrupt others, and 3) do not change books.

Guided Reading. Teachers work with students in small groups to explore books and ideas. During the guided reading, teachers also demonstrate reading strategies and help students learn how to use them. For example, teachers may demonstrate for and discuss with students successful strategies for selecting a book, using context clues, or reading with purpose.

An important component of guided reading is the *group reading conference,* a time when groups discuss books or selections that they have been reading independently. Teachers structure the conference by asking open-ended questions that require students to think, express an opinion, and relate the selection to their own experiences. For example, Bos (1991) described the use of *literature circles,* small groups of students who work collaboratively to share their reactions to and discuss various aspects of books that all group members have read.

Harste, Short, and Burke (1988) and Bos (1991) offer guidelines for implementing literature circles.

Individualized Reading. Students learn to exert control over their literacy by reading selections addressing their individual needs and instructional levels. They keep records of books read and their responses to these books.

Teachers monitor student progress and help students select appropriate reading material. Periodically, teachers help students reflect on various aspects of the material they are reading, and provide them with assistance when they encounter difficulties in reading or comprehending material.

Language Experience. Teachers promote students' literacy by using students' language generated during both planned experiences organized by the teacher and spontaneous experiences that happen within the day. Students' responses to these experiences are recorded and presented to students in a written format.

Children's Writing. Students write in a variety of genres.

Modeled Writing. Teachers model writing, providing students with the opportunity to observe composing and other elements of the writing process.

Opportunities for Sharing. Students share their products with others through such activities as writers' circle, author's chair, or literature response groups.

Content Area Reading and Writing. Teachers provide students with opportunities to read and write across the curriculum. They also use *thematic units,* which integrate reading, writing, speaking, and listening to help students master content area material (Swicegood & Parsons, 1991). Swicegood and Parsons offer guidelines to assist teachers in developing thematic units.

In the whole language approach, teachers perform a variety of roles to facilitate students' literacy. They motivate students, structure the environment,

IDEAS FOR IMPLEMENTATION	Teachers can begin to implement a whole language approach in the classroom by enacting the following suggestions: • Maintain a classroom environment that is print rich through use of charts, mobiles, logos, signs, flashcards, and posters. • Encourage students to talk about their ideas and reactions. • Create opportunities for students to verbally interact with their peers. • Establish a risk-free environment where students are encouraged to explore and investigate. • Establish centers for reading and writing. • Make students aware of the meaning of written language by sharing and explaining written messages with them. • Take and discuss school trips to expand their range of experiences. • Label objects and areas of the classroom. • Read to students and encourage them to follow along, and provide them with the opportunity to predict events within a story. • Role play and discuss situations. • Have students make and read recipes. • Display work on bulletin boards, blackboards, doors, and walls that has been written and read by students. • Ask students to dictate stories to an adult and then read them. • Have students read in unison big book editions of popular books. • Provide students with access to material written by adults and peers. • Create a comfortable environment for learning through use of bean bag chairs, couches, and carpeted areas. • Maintain a classroom library of books and materials that relate to students' interests and cultural backgrounds. • Encourage students to follow along while listening to audiocassettes of books. • Use predictable books that contain repetitive language, an interesting story line, pictures that relate to the text, and a predictable structure. • Have students maintain a reading log of books read.

Source: Goodman (1986); Franklin (1992); Hollingsworth & Reutzel (1988).

evaluate progress, supply and expose students to relevant and meaningful materials and experiences, serve as models for students, and involve students in learning.

Working with Students from Culturally and Linguistically Diverse Backgrounds

In addition to using a whole language approach, many students from culturally and linguistically diverse backgrounds may benefit from use of a variety of instructional strategies and curricular adaptations. Fradd and Bermudez (1991) suggest that in adapting instruction for such students, teachers should use the *POWER* model, which includes process-oriented instruction, whole language, cooperative learning, cognitive mapping, and reading and writing across the curriculum.

Curricular Adaptations

Environmental Print. Environmental print in the form of labels and posters in the classroom can help students who are learning English give meaning to printed symbols. Environmental print can be used to promote literacy through role plays, journals, and copying (Fradd, 1987).

Storytelling. Storytelling can promote listening comprehension and vocabulary skills, and can motivate students to read. While all students will benefit from exposure to storytelling, it is a particularly good instructional technique for students whose cultures have an oral tradition, and students who are learning a second language (Maldonado-Colon, 1991). Teachers can increase the effectiveness of storytelling by doing the following:

- encouraging students to assist in storytelling
- asking students to clarify events in, or make predictions about the story
- encouraging students to create mental images as they listen to the story
- asking students to dramatize or draw a part of the story (Maldonado-Colon, 1990)

Frames. Frames outline important components of stories and provide students with cues to assist them in writing and comprehending a variety of genres (Maldonado-Colon, 1991). One frame that has proven to be effective is the circle story, which is developed by plotting a story's important components in sequence clockwise on a circle diagram.

Story Grammars. Story grammars can motivate students to read and develop a variety of cognitive skills (Feldman, 1985). Story grammars allow students to expand on their experiences by generating stories with teachers and peers (Fradd, 1987).

Repeated Reading. Repeated reading of a book or a selection can increase students' fluency (Bos & Vaughn, 1991). Repeated reading also aids students in learning the rhythm, volume, tone, and language patterns of the students' second language (Hough, Nurss, & Enright, 1986; Petty, Petty, & Becking, 1985). Repeated reading involves rereading relatively short and meaningful selections. After students master the selection, the procedure is repeated with a new selection.

Choral Reading. Choral reading involves the students and teachers reading together. It can promote students' fluency, vocabulary development, diction, self-confidence, and motivation to read, and can help establish the relationship between oral and written language (McCauley & McCauley, 1992). Initially, teachers read and discuss a selection. As students feel comfortable, they are given the opportunity to read the selection with the teacher and their peers.

Drama. Drama can improve students' reading and language acquisition (Hernandez, 1989). Through drama, students can act out stories and more quickly acquire reading, writing, and oral language skills.

Optimal Learning Environment Curriculum

The *Optimal Learning Environment (OLE)* curriculum was developed to provide teachers with effective strategies for teaching language arts to second language learners (Ruiz, 1989). The OLE curriculum is based on the following principles:

1. *Take into account students' sociocultural backgrounds and their effects on oral language, reading, writing, and second language learning.* The OLE curriculum provides teachers with guides for promoting students' oral language uses, knowledge about print, background knowledge, and sense of story.

2. *Take into account students' possible learning problems and their effects on oral language, reading, writing, and second language learning.* The OLE curriculum offers explicit instruction in reading and writing strategies.

3. *Follow developmental processes in literacy acquisition.* The OLE curriculum develops students' literacy in developmental phases.

4. *Locate curriculum in a meaningful context where the communicative purpose is clear and authentic.* The OLE curriculum stresses the use of meaningful oral and written communication through reading and writing whole texts, and collaborative learning to solve problems.

5. *Connect curriculum with students' personal experiences.* The OLE curriculum provides students with the opportunity to talk, read, and write about their personal experiences.

6. *Incorporate children's literature into reading, writing, and ESL lessons.* The OLE curriculum uses literature to help students learn to negotiate various meanings.

7. *Involve parents as active partners in their children's instruction.* The OLE curriculum offers strategies for establishing equitable parent-school partnerships (Ruiz, 1989).

Cooperative Integrated Reading and Composition

Cooperative Integrated Reading and Composition (CIRC) is a program designed to teach reading and writing skills that includes use of basal readers, direct instruction, integrated reading and writing, and cooperative learning arrangements (Slavin, Madden, & Stevens, 1990). Initially, teachers assign students to dyads or triads within reading groups. These dyads are then placed in teams made up of dyads from two other reading groups. Teachers conduct direct instruction lessons with dyads, groups, and individuals, and meet daily to lead reading groups, while students complete assigned activities by working in dyads or with the whole team. The instructional sequence usually includes the following elements:

- The teacher introduces and discusses a story from the students' regular basal readers.
- Students work in their dyads, read the story silently, and then read it aloud, alternating readers after each paragraph.

- Students are asked to respond to various story-structure tasks, such as identifying main characters, describing the setting, and making predictions about the story. After reading the story, students work as a team to produce a written product on a topic relating to it.
- Students work in dyads or with the whole team to learn to read and define a list of new or difficult words from the story.
- Students retell the main points of the story, which is checked by their partners who have a list of essential story elements.
- Students test each other on a list of spelling words until all words are spelled correctly.
- Partners sign an assignment sheet to indicate that their peer has completed the task(s) successfully.
- Students take tests to assess their mastery of the reading material.
- Teams are rewarded at the end of the week based on the whole team's performance on quizzes, compositions, and other related activities (Slavin et al., 1990).

Calderon, Hertz-Lazarowitz, and Tinajero (1991) adapted the CIRC model for use in multiethnic and bilingual classrooms.

Remedial Reading Strategies

Because many mainstreamed students have difficulty with reading, teachers may have to supplement their reading programs with remedial reading strategies.

Multisensory Strategies

Multisensory strategies teach letters and words using combinations of visual, auditory, kinesthetic, and tactile modalities. Several multisensory strategies are available including writing the words in chalk, spelling the word after saying it, tracing three-dimensional letters with students' eyes shut, and tracing letters on the students' backs (Blau & Blau, 1986; Witman & Riley, 1978).

Fernald Method. A multisensory, whole word, language experience strategy that was developed for students with learning problems is the *Fernald method,* which involves four steps (Fernald, 1943). The step at which students begin depends on their reading level.

Step 1: Tracing. The teacher presents a model of the word. Students simultaneously touch trace the model with a finger while stating aloud each syllable of the word. Students also are encouraged to visualize the word while tracing it, and write a story using the new word. Step 1 is continued until students can write the word from memory. At that time, the word is filed alphabetically in a word list.

Step 2: Writing without trace. Rather than tracing new words, students attempt to write the word after viewing the model and visualizing it with eyes closed. The students' written products are compared with the model; and words mastered are placed in the word list.

Step 3: Recognition in print. Students attempt to read and write the word after looking at it in print, hearing the teacher read it, and repeating it several times. Teachers provide books and encourage students to read them.

Step 4: Word Analysis. Students attempt to read new words by comparing them to familiar words previously mastered.

Gillingham-Stillman Strategy. The *Gillingham-Stillman strategy* employs a multisensory synthetic phonics approach to teaching reading (Gillingham & Stillman, 1973). Initially, students are taught letter and sound symbol correspondence using a visual-auditory-kinesthetic methodology, whereby students view the letters, hear the sounds they make, link the letters to their sounds and write the letters. Once 10 letters (*a, b, f, h, i, j, k, m, p, t*) are mastered, blending of the sounds is taught. Blending is followed by story writing, syllabification, dictionary skills, and instruction in spelling rules.

Additional classroom activities based on the Gillingham-Stillman strategy have been developed by Slingerland (1976) and Traub (1982).

Programmed Reading Materials

A highly structured approach to the teaching of reading involves use of *programmed materials,* which are designed to present information in small, discrete steps that follow a planned sequence of skills. Each skill within the skill sequence is presented so that students have an opportunity to review, practice, overlearn, and apply the skill while receiving feedback. Errors are corrected before they can proceed to the next skill. Teachers follow the presentation sequence by adhering to the directions outlined in the manual.

Neurological Impress Method

A remedial listening strategy that has been effective in promoting the word recognition and comprehension skills of poor readers is the *Neurological Impress Method* (Bos, 1982; Heckelman, 1969). In this method, the student and the teacher read aloud in unison for 15 minutes each day. The student is positioned in front of the teacher so that the teacher's voice is directed into the student's ear. Initially, the teacher reads louder and faster than the student, with the student focusing on keeping up with the teacher. Both the teacher and the student slide their fingers along as they read each word. As the student becomes more proficient in oral reading, he or she is encouraged to read louder and faster. Individualized and group adaptations of the Neurological Impress Method are available (Henk, 1983; Henk, Helfedt, & Platt, 1986).

Cuing Strategies

Cuing can help mainstreamed students read difficult or unfamiliar words. Cues can be divided into two types: teacher cues and student cues. *Teacher cues* are strategies initiated by the teacher to help a student make the correct response; *student cues* are strategies used by students to determine the correct response.

Salend (1980, October) identified three types of cues that are readily available to teachers for remediating reading errors: language cues, visual cues, and physical cues. Students can improve their reading by employing configuration and context cues.

Language Cues. Language cues use the students' language skills as the base for triggering the correct response. For example, if a student had difficulty decoding the word *store,* a vocabulary cue, such as *You go to buy things at a* ___________, might elicit the correct response. Other language oriented cues include rhyming (*it rhymes with door*), word associations (*Choo! Choo!* to cue the word *train*), analogies (*Light is to day, as dark is to* _________ for *night*) and antonyms (*It's the opposite of hot* for *cold*).

Visual Cues. Visual cues can help students focus their attention on important stimuli within words. For example, attention to medial vowels can be fostered visually by color cues (make the medial vowel a different color than the other letters), size cues (make the medial vowel enlarged while the other letters are kept constant, such as *cAt*) or graphic cues (accentuate the medial vowel by underlining or circling it, such as *cat*).

Visual cues can be valuable in remediating reversals. For example, difficulty discriminating *b* and *d* can be lessened by graphically cuing one of the letters. Similarly, picture cuing, where pictures depicting words are drawn above words that are difficult to read, is especially helpful in reading nouns and prepositions. For example, if a student typically read the word *saw* as *was,* a drawing of a saw above the word *saw* would help the student make this discrimination. Finally, visual cues, such as pointing to an object in the classroom or showing a numeral, can be used to prompt the reading of words that correspond, respectively, to objects in the classroom and number words.

Physical Cues. Physical cues are most effective in communicating words or concepts that possess perceptually salient features. These words can be cued by miming the distinct qualities or actions associated with them. For example, the word *safe* can be cued by assuming the position of an umpire who has just declared a runner safe on a close play. In addition to pantomiming, teachers can use finger spelling as a cue to elicit a correct response.

Think About It

How could you use cues to help students who have difficulty reading the following words?
laugh bee floor know ate yellow jump seven quiet why small

Configuration Cues. Configuration cues relate to the outline of the word, and can be useful when there are noticeable differences between words in terms of shape and length. While research on the effectiveness of configuration cues is inconclusive (Haber, Haber, & Furlin, 1983), it appears that they are most effective when used with context and other cuing strategies (Haber & Haber, 1981).

Context Cues. The context in which the word is presented in the sentence or selection can provide useful cues to students that can assist them in determining the pronunciation of unknown words. Potential context cues that students can use include syntactical, semantic, and picture features of the text. When using context cues, teachers should ensure that the syntactical and semantic structures of the sentence or passage is consistent with the students' skill level and background of experience (Duffelmeyer, 1982). To provide students with the necessary syntactical and semantic information, context cues are best suited for words that are embedded near the middle or the end of the sentence (Duffelmeyer, 1982).

Syntactical Cues. Syntactical cues deal with the grammatical structure of the sentence in which the word is embedded. They are dependent on the students' knowledge of word order and the nature of words (Harris & Sipay, 1985). The syntactical structure of English dictates that only certain words can fit into a particular part of a sentence or statement. Thus, students can be taught to use parts of sentences to figure out difficult words.

Semantic Cues. Semantic cues, available by examining the meanings of sentences, can help students improve their word recognition skills. Students can be taught to use semantic cues by having them closely examine the sentence containing the unknown word, as well as the chapter or story plot in which the word appears. These cues are particularly appropriate when students are learning to read abstract words (Durkin, 1978).

Pictorial Cues. Many reading passages contain illustrations that are designed to promote comprehension and facilitate student motivation. These pictorial cues also can help students recognize new words by helping them establish the context of the story (Arlin, Scott, & Webster, 1979; Denburg, 1976). To maximize the effects of illustrations on word recognition, the students' attention should be directed to the word and the illustration (Ceprano, 1981).

Think About It

What cuing strategies do you use when you encounter a word you don't know?

Error Correction Techniques

When students make word recognition errors, teachers can use a variety of error correction techniques, including phonic analysis correction, word supply, and drill (Jenkins, Larson, & Fleisher, 1983). *Phonic analysis correction* involves encouraging students to sound out the word that was read incorrectly (Rose, McEntyre & Dowdy, 1982). In *word supply,* teachers provide students with the correct pronunciation of the word after the word has been misread (Jenkins, Larson, & Fleisher, 1983). The *drill* correction procedure involves simultaneously applying the word supply technique and writing each misread word on an index card; having students attempt to read each of the words on the index cards after the selection has been read; separating the correct and incorrect readings of the words on the index cards into two piles; reviewing the incorrect word pile by providing students with the correct word and having them repeat it two times; and concluding the procedure when students can read correctly all words recorded on the index cards for two consecutive trials (Jenkins, Larson, & Fleisher, 1983).

WRITTEN LANGUAGE INSTRUCTION

Ms. Rogers notices that many of her third graders are having difficulty with writing assignments. A review of their work reveals that students' written products are extremely short and disorganized, lack important elements, and include irrelevant information. To correct these problems, Ms. Rogers decides to try a different approach to teaching students to write.

Ms. Rogers begins by writing a description of herself, reading it to her students, and asking them to guess who is being described in the piece. After the students guess that the individual is Ms. Rogers, Ms. Rogers explains how she wrote it. She draws a semantic map on the board and demonstrates how she used it to list the important characteristics she wanted to mention in her description. She then provides her students with a semantic map outline and asks them to complete it using the characteristics that best describe themselves.

The next day, Ms. Rogers asks students to use their semantic maps to write a five-sentence draft that describes themselves. After students complete their drafts, Ms. Rogers collects them, selects students to read them to the class, and has the class guess who wrote each piece. Ms. Rogers concludes the day's writing lesson by telling students that tomorrow they will work on revising their descriptions.

Ms. Rogers begins the next day's lesson by explaining the purpose of revising a draft. Using her description of herself, Ms. Rogers asks students to identify things they liked about it. After students identify the positive aspects of the piece, she asks them to identify ways the description could be improved. Following this discussion, Ms. Rogers reviews several guidelines for giving and accepting feedback. Ms. Rogers selects a student's draft and role plays giving feedback with the student.

Ms. Rogers then places students in dyads, gives each group member a checklist to guide the feedback process, and asks them to read each other's papers and share their reactions. While students work collaboratively, Ms. Rogers monitors their progress and assists them in developing collaborative skills. During the last 15 minutes of the period, Ms. Rogers and the whole class discuss how it feels to give and receive feedback.

The next day's writing period is devoted to revising students' drafts based on the feedback they have received. Ms. Rogers works on her draft and circulates around the room to monitor student progress and to conference with individual students. After students revise their writing, they type their product on the computer, and share their printout with their dyad partner. They then make final revisions, and a copy of each student's description is printed out and compiled into a class book called *Who's Who,* which is shared with parents, other teachers, and the principal.

One content area directly related to reading that cuts across all aspects of the school curriculum is written language. However, rather than assume that students are improving their writing skills by writing about reading and content area assignments, instruction in written expression should be an ongoing part of the students' instructional program (Graham & Harris, 1988). Instruction in writing should allow students the opportunities to write for social, creative, recreational, and occupational purposes, as well as to share opinions and express factual information (Graham & Harris, 1988). Graham (1992) suggests that students be provided with the opportunity to perform meaningful writing tasks. He defines *meaningful* tasks as those that have an authentic audience, are of interest to the author, and serve a real purpose. Teachers can make writing meaningful by doing the following:

- allowing students to select the topics of their writing tasks
- teaching students to set goals for their writing
- having students share their work with others
- allowing students to work on the same product for an extended period of time
- integrating writing into other activities
- asking students to perform writing projects that have specific and real purposes (Graham, 1992)

Calkins (1986) believes that at least 45 minutes of each school day should be devoted to writing; Graham and Harris (1988) propose that students receive writing instruction a minimum of four times a week. Calkins (1986) also suggests that students work on the same writing product over a period of time (writing sessions). Bos (1988) advocates the use of individual folders to facilitate the writing process and promote independence in students. Individual folders could include works in progress, completed products, ideas for future products, student- and teacher-selected goals, graphs of progress, and writing aids (a list of spelling demons, word-processing programs).

Process-Oriented Instruction

Although there is considerable overlap of stages in writing (Englert & Raphael, 1988), many researchers advocate teaching writing by using a process-oriented approach (Calkins, 1986; Flower & Hays, 1981; Graves, 1983). A process-oriented approach to writing, integral to whole language instruction, is divided into four subprocesses: planning, drafting, revising and editing, and publishing (Bos, 1988; Englert & Raphael, 1988).

Planning

During the planning phase, students determine the purpose of the writing task, generate and group ideas, and plan how to present the content to the reader (Englert & Raphael, 1988). Thomas, Englert, and Gregg (1987) observed that students with disabilities often use a knowledge-telling strategy, an inefficient technique for generating ideas for writing. In applying the knowledge-telling strategy, students typically list all the information they possess on a topic without screening for irrelevant details or ordering the sequence of the content. This strategy often results in a written product that is disorganized and difficult for the reader to follow (Scardamalia & Bereiter, 1986).

Teachers can help students plan their writing in several ways. They can model and verbalize the steps involved in planning writing, share written products, offer instruction in writing strategies, and solicit feedback from students (Graham & Harris, 1988). Teachers also can discuss with students the different rationales for writing and can present examples of the different writing formats (Whitt, Paul, & Reynolds, 1988).

Idea Generation. Allowing students to work on self-selected topics can foster idea generation because students will probably choose topics with which they feel familiar (Graves, 1985). When students select the topics of their writing activities, and make decisions about content, they develop a sense of ownership toward writing in the classroom (MacArthur & Schwartz, 1990). Similarly, a journal, in which students write about their personal reactions to events and their experiences, can be a good way to facilitate writing. For students who have difficulty generating journal entries, a *dialogue journal* may be appropriate (Graham & Harris, 1988). The dialogue journal, in which students and teachers write responses to each other, can motivate students to write while promoting a positive relationship between teachers and students.

Simulations, trips, interviews, pictorial representations, music, sensory explorations, speakers, demonstrations, brainstorming, and researching can be used to inspire the selection of topics (Tompkins & Friend, 1986; Whitt et al., 1988). Reading and discussing passages before writing can help students select topics and add details to their writing (Graham, 1982). Englert et al. (1988) suggest that teachers use oral questions to promote topic generation and supporting ideas to be covered in the written product.

Because writing is linked to reading, students can obtain ideas for writing from reading (Whittaker & Salend, 1991). Younger students can write stories by changing the characters or action in a story they have just listened to or read. Predictable books can be used as vehicles for stimulating such story writing since they often follow repetitive story lines (Newman, 1985).

Story Starters/Enders. Some students may benefit from use of *story starters* or *story enders,* whereby students are given the first or last paragraph of a story, or the initial or ending sentence of a paragraph, and asked to complete the story or paragraph. Music, pictures and videos also can serve as starters. Similarly, Duques (1986) suggests that teachers use paragraph organization worksheets and paragraph draft outlines to help students plan and organize their writing.

Outlines and Semantic Maps. Ideas generated can then be organized by assisting students in developing an *outline,* which should include the main topics and supporting ideas grouped together, as well as the sequence in which they will be presented. Students also can be taught to organize their writing by developing a *semantic map,* a diagram or a map of the key ideas and words that make up the topic (Tompkins & Friend, 1986; Whitt et al., 1988). Mapping allows students to identify main points and to plan the interrelationship between these parts. In introducing semantic maps to students, teachers should ask questions that assist students in understanding their own decisionmaking processes and in learning from others (Whittaker & Salend, 1991). A sample semantic map is presented in Figure 8.1.

Tompkins and Friend (1986) provide excellent, practical activities for generating ideas and organizing them prior to writing.

Goal Setting. An important part of the planning process is goal setting, which helps students to channel their efforts and attention on the writing task (Graham, MacArthur, Schwartz, & Page-Voth, 1992). Graham et al. (1992) propose that teachers help students establish writing goals by teaching them to use a planning strategy called *PLANS*:

*P*ick goals,

*L*ist ways to meet goals,

*A*nd make

*N*otes.

*S*equence notes.

Write and say more.

Check to see if goals are met (Graham, 1992, p. 141).

Narrative Stories. Graham and Harris (cited in Graham, Harris, & Sawyer, 1987) have developed a self-instructional strategy for teaching students to write a narrative story. After learning to apply the strategy, the quality of the

FIGURE 8.1
A sample writing map

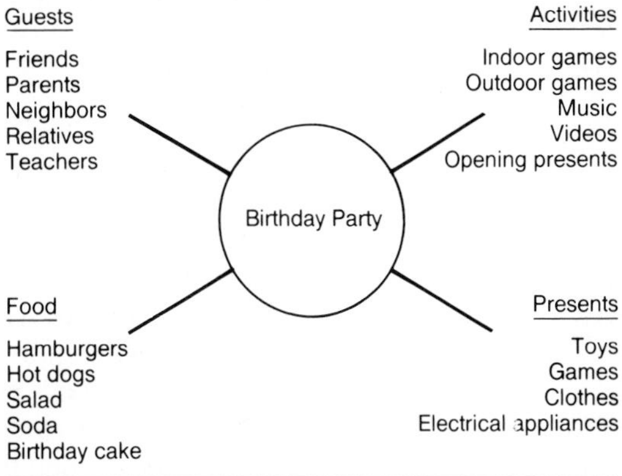

stories written by students with learning disabilities who applied the strategy was similar to that of their age-appropriate peers who were skilled writers. The self-instructional strategy involved five steps:

1. Look at the picture (stimulus item).
2. Let your mind be free.
3. Write down the story part reminder (W-W-W; What = 2; How = 2).
4. Write down story parts for each part reminder.
5. Write your story; use good parts and make sense (Graham, Harris, & Sawyer, 1987).

The mnemonic *W-W-W; What = 2; How = 2* helps students remember the following:

1. Who is the main character? Who else is in the story?
2. When does the story take place?
3. Where does the story take place?
4. What does the main character want to do?
5. What happens when he or she tries to do it?
6. How does the story end?
7. How does the main character feel? (Graham et al., 1987, p. 7)

A similar strategy has been successful in helping students plan for writing narrative compositions (MacArthur, Schwartz, & Graham, 1991; Montague, Graves, & Leavell, 1991), and short stories on material they have just read (Harris & Graham, 1988). Montague et al. (1991) suggest that teachers teach students to use a story grammar cue card, a listing of the elements of the strategy in sequential order.

Opinion Essays. Graham and Harris (1989) developed and tested a three-phase strategy to assist students in planning and composing opinion essays. In this strategy students are taught to:

- Think, who will read this, and why am I doing this?
- Plan what to say using *TREE* (note *T*opic sentence; note *R*easons, *E*xamine reasons; note *E*ndings).
- Write and say more (Graham & Harris, 1989, p. 204).

Drafting

In the drafting phase, writers transform their plans into printed sentences and paragraphs. They make attempts to establish a relationship and order between these sentences and paragraphs, and make appropriate word choices. While it should not be emphasized in the drafting stage, some attention to the rules of grammar, punctuation, and spelling may be appropriate (Bos, 1988). In a writing process approach, these skills are taught within the context of the students' writing products through individualized or group lessons. During this step, teachers encourage students to plan, and provide time to revise their draft. To facilitate revision, teachers should encourage students to skip lines when writing their drafts.

Teachers can facilitate drafting in several ways. They can ask questions to help students explore alternatives, offer suggestions, encourage students, and focus attention on the writing task (Whitt, Paul, & Reynolds, 1988). Research indicates that use of self-evaluation questions during writing is more valuable to students than criteria applied after completion of the written product (Benton & Blohm, 1986), so teachers can help students to monitor their drafts by providing them with self-evaluation questions (Moran, 1988). Additionally, teachers should encourage students to use the self-evaluation guidelines throughout the writing process. Since the criteria for judging the effectiveness of a written product will vary depending on the type and purpose of writing the task, tailor the self-evaluation questions to the specific writing task students will be asked to perform. For example, the questions used for an opinion essay will be very different from those applied to a business letter or a creative writing task. Sample self-evaluation questions for writing stories adapted from the work of Graham & Harris (1986) and Issacson (1988) are presented in Figure 8.2.

Harris and Graham (1985) improved the writing skills of students with learning disabilities by teaching them to apply a *self-control strategy*, designed to teach students to "look at the picture and write down good action words; think of a good story idea to use my words in; write my story—make sense and use good action words; read my story and ask, 'Did I write a good story? Did I use action words?'; fix my story; 'Can I use more action words?' " (p. 29).

Revising and Editing

In this phase, students edit their drafts by making revisions, additions, and deletions to ensure that their products adequately address their writing goals (Englert & Raphael, 1988). Teachers can introduce students to revision by reviewing a sample paper as a group (Tompkins & Friend, 1988). The class can identify the positive aspects of the product as well as the problems a reader would have in reading the paper. The discussion should focus on the content, organization, and word choices rather than on mechanical errors. The class can complete the revision by correcting the problems identified in

FIGURE 8.2
Sample writing evaluation questions

- Does each paragraph start with a topic sentence?
- Does each paragraph include relevant supporting information?
- Are the paragraphs organized appropriately?
- Are the main characters introduced and described?
- Is the location of the story presented and described?
- Is the time of the story introduced?
- Does the story include a starting event?
- Does the story include the main characters' reactions to the starting event?
- Does the story present actions to resolve conflicts?
- Does the story have an ending?
- Does the ending include the outcome's effects on the main characters?

the paper as a group. For example, students and the teacher can help the writer generate a list of synonyms that can replace nondescriptive words (such as *nice, great, fine, good*) that have been used repeatedly (Fagen, Graves, & Tessier-Switlick, 1984). The Find (Search) and Replace functions of many word-processing programs can then be used to locate the nondescriptive word and replace it with the new word.

Research suggests that many mainstreamed students may have poor revision skills (MacArthur, Graham, & Skarvoed, 1986), which can be improved by auditory feedback. Espin and Sindelar (1988) found that students who listened to a written passage read to them were able to identify more errors in the passage than students who read the passage themselves.

Collaborative Groups. While a collaborative writing group can be an excellent source for assisting students and promoting a positive environment for writing (Weiner, 1988), it also is a particularly valuable methodology for promoting the writing skills of students from linguistically and culturally diverse backgrounds. Students can work in collaboration by reading their products to the group or to individual group members; editing the products of group members; brainstorming ideas for writing; developing outlines as a group; and producing a group product, such as a class newsletter (Graham & Harris, 1988).

Fleming (1988) proposed three models for employing collaboration in the drafting process: the chunk model, the blended model, and the raisin bread model. In the *chunk* model, each group member contributes a specific part of the written product. *Blended* writing requires the group to reach consensus in composing and discussing each sentence in a writing assignment. The *raisin bread* model allows one group member to transform the contributions of individual group members into a larger group draft.

Bernstein and McGuire (1992) established the effectiveness of a peer tutoring program on the acquisition of writing skills of students learning English as a second language. Tutors were trained to assist second language learners in their daily writing activities by sounding out words, using pictorials, talking about writing, delivering praise, and finding a comfortable place to work. Tutors also were instructed *not* to spell, write, or copy words for tutees, ask another student to interpret, offer negative feedback, or force tutees to write.

Collaborative groups can be particularly helpful in revising written assignments. One collaborative strategy is the *author's chair* (Graves & Hansen, 1983). In this technique, upon completing their product, students read it aloud to their peers, who discuss the positive features of the text and ask questions concerning the author, strategy, meaning, and writing style.

MacArthur, Schwartz, & Graham (1991) developed a peer-revising strategy to assist students working in dyads to provide feedback to each other. The strategy requires students to do the following:

Listen to each other's papers and read along.

Tell what your partner's paper is about and what you liked best.

Reread your partner's paper and make notes:
Is everything clear?
Can any details be added?

Discuss your suggestions with your partner.

Revise your own paper and correct errors.

Exchange papers and check for errors in sentences, capitalization, punctuation, and spelling (Graham, 1992, p. 141).

Students can work together in groups to offer feedback on content, sequence, and vocabulary, and to edit drafts (Isaacson, 1988). Taylor (1989) suggested that peers begin to offer feedback by using a *say-back* technique, asking each group member to repeat a word or say a phrase that he or she remembers or likes. Perl (1983) proposed that peers be encouraged to provide feedback to writers concerning clarity by paraphrasing their view of the author's message. Moore, Moore, Cunningham, and Cunningham (1986) established guidelines for peer writing groups, including focusing on initial feedback that emphasizes the positive aspects of the product; phrasing negative reactions as questions; giving reactions orally or in written form, and providing writers with time to respond to the reactions of their peers. Teachers also can facilitate feedback by providing peer reviewers with a response key that lists criteria to use in evaluating written products (Copeland & Lomax, 1988).

Mohr (1984), Ronan (1991), Russell (1983), and Tompkins and Friend (1986) provide some specific guidelines and questions teachers can use to guide students in giving feedback to their peers.

Tsujimoto (1988) advocates the use of *peer editors,* students who work individually to edit their classmates' writing assignments. Each student's products are edited by two peers and the teacher. Peer editors edit the papers using different colored pens and sign their names at the bottom of the paper. Their comments are then reviewed by the teacher and the author. The teacher grades both the writer and the peer editors.

Editing groups are similar to peer editors; however, the editing is done by the group rather than by individual students (Herreman, 1988). In editing groups, each group member reads his or her product aloud while peer editors follow along on a photocopy. Peer editors record their reactions and comments on their photocopy and then present and discuss the written product as a group. Herreman (1988) modified editing groups so that each group focuses on a specific aspect of the written product.

In addition to training peers to give constructive and specific feedback, teachers can guide students in learning how to accept feedback constructively (Copeland & Lomax, 1988). Teachers can help students accept feedback from others by establishing rules for accepting reactions from others, including the following:

- Listen carefully to all comments from others.
- Ask for feedback from as many people as possible.
- Do not dispute or dismiss feedback from others.
- Seek further clarification or examples when you don't understand another person's reaction.
- Check your understanding of another person's reaction by paraphrasing the statements in your own words (Elbow, 1981).

Collaborative writing groups can foster students' writing.

Writers' Workshop. Another collaborative writing strategy is the Writers' Workshop, where students write on a daily basis and receive feedback from peers and teachers on topics which they select (Atwell, 1987). In the Writers' Workshop, teachers and students establish a supportive writing community that allows writers to work alone and in groups (MacArthur & Schwartz, 1990). The Writers' Workshop is divided into four components: status of the class, minilessons, workshop proper, and sharing (Atwell, 1987). In the status component, teachers work with individual students to identify the project(s) on which students are working, the assistance students will need, and the extent to which students are progressing. Minilessons, brief lessons of approximately five minutes in duration, offer students direct instruction on specific skills such as process skills (idea generation), grammar and spelling skills (capitalization), writing skills (paragraph development), and classroom routines. The majority of the Writers' Workshop centers on the workshop proper, during which teachers and students actively write. In addition to writing, teachers circulate around the room to monitor student progress, and confer with individual students. In the final component, students share their work with others, receive feedback, and publish their work.

The Computer. The computer can aid the revision process. Word processing allows students to delete, add, and move text easily. Graham and MacArthur (cited in Graham & Harris, 1988) found that they could improve both students' revising skills and the quality of their writing by teaching them to compose and revise their essays on a word processor. Specifically, students were taught to do the following:

- Read your essay.
- Find the sentence that tells what you believe—Is it clear?
- Add two reasons why you believe it.
- SCAN each sentence (Does it make *s*ense? Is it *c*onnected to my belief? Can I *a*dd more? *N*ote errors).
- Make changes on the computer.
- Reread the essay and make final changes (Graham & Harris, 1988, p. 509).

Prompting programs have been developed to help students generate ideas (Burns & Culp, 1980), write opinion essays (Woodruff, Bereiter, & Scardamalia, 1981), and compose and revise (Daiute, 1986).

Some word-processing programs have interactive prompting capabilities that help students write effectively. These programs provide students with prompts that appear on the screen to guide the student's product. For example, the Quill writing system (Rubin & Bruce, 1985) has a planner program that presents prompts, such as *Who? What? Where? When?* questions, to assist students in writing a newspaper article. Teachers can tailor these prompts to adapt to the different types of writing assignments. In addition to prompting programs, programs to check punctuation and capitalization, and to identify imprecise words and other signs of poor writing are available.

Publishing

The computer also can be a valuable resource in the fourth stage of the writing process, publishing. Publishing students' written language products presents an excellent opportunity for sharing their work with others and for receiving feedback (Graves & Hansen, 1983).

Feedback. Feedback should facilitate, not frustrate, the writing process. A teacher conference can be an excellent vehicle for providing feedback. By meeting individually with students, teachers serve as both reader and coach to help students learn to correct content, process, and mechanical errors (Whitt, Paul, & Reynolds, 1988). The type and amount of feedback will depend on the students' writing abilities.

Initially, teachers should focus feedback on the positive aspects of the students' written products, and acknowledge and encourage students' writing by praising them, sharing their products with others by reading their stories in class, and posting their writing in the room or the school (Graham & Harris, 1988). As students become more proficient and confident in their writing, corrective feedback can be introduced. Because identifying all errors can frustrate students, teachers' corrective feedback should focus on a limited number of writing problems (no more than two) at a time. Teachers should pinpoint errors that interfere with the writers' abilities to make their products understandable to the reader rather than grammatical, punctuation, spelling, and usage errors (Graham & Harris, 1988). Instruction to correct grammatical and spelling errors should focus on skills that are within the students' repertoire and occur within the context of the students' writing products (Graham, 1992).

Duques (1986) offers strategies teachers can use with students to develop their word choices, sentence structure, and paragraph organization.

Students also should be involved in evaluating their own written products (Harris & Graham, 1985; Hillocks, 1984). Mainstreamed students may have difficulty judging their performance on written tasks (Englert & Raphael, 1988), so the criteria for evaluating written products should be taught explicitly. Hillocks (1984) concluded that allowing students to assess their written products based on clearly defined criteria can improve written expression skills. Similarly, goal setting, in which students establish goals for their writing and graph their performance, has led to positive effects on writing and on motivating students to write (Graham & Harris, 1988).

Hayward and LeBuffe (1985) propose that teachers and students use self-correction codes, a system of symbols that mark various parts of a written product that contain errors. Teachers review students' products and return them to students with codes written in the margins of lines that need to be revised. Students then check the product to identify and correct errors. Finally, teachers praise students for finding and correcting errors.

Cognitive Strategy Instruction in Writing

A teaching approach that introduces students to all subprocesses of writing through use of models and think-alouds is the *Cognitive Strategy Instruction in Writing (CSIW)* program (Englert & Raphael, 1988). In the initial phase of CSIW, students are introduced to a variety of written products and strategies for improving writing through teacher modeling. Teachers use the overhead projector to show well-written and poorly written text, and to model and rehearse for the class text comprehension strategies and ways to expand on text.

When modeling is completed, students are given "think sheets," which offer a list of the steps and questions to guide them in each stage of writing. For example, the planning think sheet structures this phase of the process for students by prompting them to ask themselves the following questions:

- Who am I writing for?
- Why am I writing this?
- What do I know about the topic?
- How can I group my ideas? (Englert & Raphael, 1988, p. 518)

Feedback on drafts is provided through self-evaluation and peer editing, both of which also are structured by think sheets. Peer conferencing is used to discuss peer feedback and to brainstorm ideas to assist in revision.

SPELLING

A skill area that can impact on both writing and reading is spelling (Graham & Miller, 1979). Reading is a decoding process. Spelling is an encoding process; consequently, many students who experience difficulties in reading also are likely to have problems with spelling (Carpenter & Miller, 1982).

Several different approaches have been offered to remediate spelling difficulties (Bos & Vaughn, 1988; Mercer & Mercer, 1985; Miller, 1987). These approaches are described here.

Rule-Governed Approaches

Mercer and Mercer (1985) suggest that rule-governed approaches are appropriate for spelling rules that apply at least 75% of the time.

Rule-governed models are designed to promote spelling skills by teaching students the basic spelling rules. These approaches assume that once students master basic rules, they can apply them to spell unfamiliar words. In rule-governed approaches, teachers help students learn spelling rules and patterns by asking them to analyze words that follow the same grapheme-phoneme correspondence, to discuss similarities and differences in words, to identify the rules that apply, to practice the use of the rule with unfamiliar words, and to learn exceptions to the rule.

One rule-governed model for teaching spelling is the *linguistic* approach, in which spelling instruction focuses on the rules of spelling and patterns that relate to whole words (Mercer & Mercer, 1985). Once the students learn a series of words that follow similar spelling, opportunities to generalize the rule with other words in the family arise. For example, students would be taught the '*oat*' family using the words *boat* and *coat*. Later, students would apply the pattern to words from that family such as *goat, moat,* and *float*.

While the linguistic approach is based on learning spelling patterns within whole words, a ***phonetic*** approach is based on students learning to apply phoneme-grapheme correspondence within parts of words (Mercer & Mercer, 1985). Thus, teachers using a phonetic approach to spelling teach students the sound-symbol correspondence for individual letters and combinations of letters (such as digraphs and dipthongs). Students then apply these rules by breaking words into syllables, pronouncing each syllable, and writing the letter(s) that correspond to each sound. While phonetic approaches to teaching spelling have been successful, several factors limit its use (Graham & Miller, 1979). Hanna, Hanna, Hodges, and Rudorf (1966) reviewed 17,000 words and concluded that only 49 percent could be spelled correctly using a phonetic rule-governed approach. Horn (1960) noted that irregularities in the English language, including multiple-letter sounds, word pronunciations, and unstressed syllables, are deterrents to phonetic spelling.

Cognitive Approaches

Wong (1986) proposes use of a *cognitive* approach to teaching spelling that employs a spelling grid and a seven-step questioning procedure. The five-column spelling grid is designed to teach structural analysis of words. Its use begins with the teacher writing a spelling word, pronouncing it, and discussing its meaning. Next, students complete the spelling grid by reading the word in column one; recording the number of syllables in the word in column two; dividing the word into syllables in column three; breaking the word into its root and suffix and writing the suffix in column four; and writing the modification of the spelling of the root word in column five. The self-questioning strategy entails students asking themselves the following questions:

1. Do I know the word?
2. How many syllables do I hear in this word? (Write down the number.)
3. I'll spell the word.
4. Do I have the right number of syllables down?
5. If yes, is there any part of the word I'm not sure of the spelling? I'll underline that part and try spelling the word again.
6. Now, does it look right to me? If it does, I'll leave it alone. If it still doesn't look right, I'll underline the part of the spelling I'm not sure of and try again. (If the word I spelled does not have the right number of syllables, let me hear the word in my head again, and find the missing syllable. Then I'll go back to steps 5 and 6.)
7. When I finish spelling, I tell myself I'm a good worker. I've tried hard at spelling. (Wong, 1986, p. 172)

Whole Word Approaches

In light of the concerns about the usability of rule-governed approaches to spelling, several educators have advocated using *whole word* approaches to increasing spelling vocabulary (Graham & Miller, 1979). These approaches help students focus on the whole word through a variety of multisensory activities (Miller, 1987). Whole word approaches include test-study-test procedures, corrected test methods, and word study techniques.

Test-Study-Test Procedures

Perhaps the most frequently used method of spelling instruction is the *test-study-test* method. In this method, students receive a pretest on a fixed list of words, study those words they misspell, and take a posttest to assess mastery. Some teachers use a study-test procedure, where students study all the week's spelling words and then take a test. Research indicates that test-study-test procedures are superior to study-test procedures (Stephens, Hartman & Lucas, 1982). When posttesting students with these procedures, Neef, Iwata, & Page (1977) recommend that teachers intersperse known and unknown words into the test.

Teachers can adapt this procedure for mainstreamed students in several ways. Bryant, Drabin, and Gettinger (1981) found that decreasing the number of spelling words given to mainstreamed students from five to three increases their spelling performance. Thus, rather than having students try to master a large list of words each week, teachers can break down the spelling list so that students study and are tested on three words each day.

Teachers also can modify this method by using a flow word list rather than a fixed list (McGuigan, 1975; Mercer & Mercer, 1985). Flow lists can help teachers individualize spelling by allowing students who master spelling words to delete those words from the list and replace them with new words. Whether using a fixed or flow list of spelling words, teachers should allow students the time to work at their own rate, and should require them to demonstrate mastery over a period of time.

Corrected-Test Methods

Feedback on spelling, in-class activities, and tests can have a significant positive impact on spelling performance (Graves, 1977). In addition to receiving feedback from teachers, students should be actively involved in correcting their spelling errors (Graham & Miller, 1979). One method of allowing students to correct their own errors is the *corrected-test* method (Graham & Miller, 1979). Teachers can guide students in correcting their spelling errors by spelling words orally while the student corrects them; spelling words and accentuating each letter as the student simultaneously points to each letter in the word (Allred, 1977); spelling words while the student writes the correct letter above the crossed-out, incorrect letter (Hall, 1964); writing the correct spelling on the student's paper near the incorrectly spelled word, which the student then corrects (Kauffman, Hallahan, Haas, Brame, & Boren, 1978); and copying the student's error, modeling the correct spelling, and observing as the student writes the word correctly (Kauffman et al., 1978).

Nulman and Gerber (1984) found that contingent imitation and modeling was a highly effective procedure for improving spelling performance. Teachers implement contingent imitation and modeling by acknowledging the accuracy of all words spelled correctly, verbalizing and then writing each word the student misspelled, verbalizing and writing the correct spelling for each word misspelled, and asking the student to copy the correct spelling of each misspelled word.

Word Study Techniques

An integral part of spelling programs, *word study* techniques include a wide range of activities that are designed to help students remember spelling words. Graham and Freeman (1985) and Harris, Graham, and Freeman (1988) found that a student-controlled, five-step word study procedure was effective in helping students learn new spelling words. The five-step strategy included verbalizing the word; writing and saying the word; comparing the written word to a model; tracing and saying the word; writing the word from memory and checking it; and repeating prior steps as necessary. Fitzsimmons and Loomer (1978) advocate use of a word study method that encourages students to close their eyes and visualize the spelling word, while others employ strategies that teach students to verbalize the word while writing it. Figure 8.3 presents a summary of several proposed word study techniques.

Radabaugh and Yukish (1982) suggest that teachers match the word study strategies to the learning styles of their students. For visual learners, they recommend the following:

1. Students view the word while the teacher reads the word to them.
2. Students study the word, read it, spell it, and read it again.
3. Students attempt to spell the word orally without the model three times.
4. Students write the word and check its spelling.

FIGURE 8.3
Word study techniques

Fitzgerald Method (Fitzgerald, 1951a)

1. Look at the word carefully.
2. Say the word.
3. With eyes closed, visualize the word.
4. Cover the word and then write it.
5. Check the spelling.
6. If the word is misspelled, repeat steps 1–5.

Horn Method 1 (E. Horn, 1919)

1. Look at the word and say it to yourself.
2. Close your eyes and visualize the word.
3. Check to see if you were right. (If not, begin at step 1.)
4. Cover the word and write it.
5. Check to see if you were right. (If not, begin at step 1.)
6. Repeat steps 4 and 5 two more times.

Horn Method 2 (E. Horn, 1954c)

1. Pronounce each word carefully.
2. Look carefully at each part of the word as you pronounce it.
3. Say the letters in sequence.
4. Attempt to recall how the word looks, then spell the word.
5. Check this attempt to recall.
6. Write the word.
7. Check this spelling attempt.
8. Repeat the above steps if necessary.

Visual-Vocal Method (Westerman, 1971)

1. Say word.
2. Spell word orally.
3. Say word again.
4. Spell word from memory four times correctly.

Gilstrap Method (Gilstrap, 1962)

1. Look at the word and say it softly. If it has more than one part, say it again, part by part, looking at each part as you say it.
2. Look at the letters and say each one. If the word has more than one part, say the letters part by part.
3. Write the word without looking at the book.

Fernald Method Modified

1. Make a model of the word with a crayon, grease pencil, or magic marker, saying the word as you write it.
2. Check the accuracy of the model.
3. Trace over the model with your index finger, saying the word at the same time.
4. Repeat step 3 five times.
5. Copy the word three times correctly.
6. Copy the word three times from memory correctly.

Cover-and-Write Method

1. Look at word. Say it.
2. Write word two times.
3. Cover and write one time.
4. Check work.
5. Write word two times.
6. Cover and write one time.
7. Check work.
8. Write word three times.
9. Cover and write one time.
10. Check work.

References to Other Techniques

Aho, 1967

Bartholome, 1977

Clanton, 1977

Glusker, 1967

Hill & Martinis, 1973

Phillips, 1975

Stowitschek & Jobes, 1977

Source: S. Graham and L. Miller, *Focus on Exceptional Children,* vol. 12 (Denver, CO: Love, 1979), p. 11. Reprinted by permission of the publisher.

For auditory learners, they recommend the following:

1. Students observe the teacher reading, spelling, and reading the word.
2. Students read the word and then attempt to spell it.
3. Students listen to the teacher spell the word, and then repeat after the teacher.
4. Students spell the word without assistance.

Adapting Spelling Instruction

Many mainstreamed students may exhibit problems in spelling (Graham & Miller, 1979). Teachers can adapt their spelling instruction in the following ways:

1. *Teach dictionary skills.* Spelling problems can be minimized by use of the dictionary (Graham & Miller, 1979). Gloeckler & Simpson (1988) note that the dictionary can help students confirm the spelling of irregular words, and can help with spelling demons, confusing rules, and difficult word combinations. Therefore, students need to learn dictionary skills, including alphabetizing, locating words, using guide words, and understanding syllabification and pronunciation. Students in primary grades can use a picture dictionary until they acquire the skills to use a regular dictionary (Mercer & Mercer, 1985).

2. *Teach students to proofread for spelling errors.* Spelling errors can be reduced by students proofreading their work. Teachers can train students to proofread for spelling errors by giving students a list of words and having them identify and correct the misspellings (Hardin, Bernstein, & Shands, 1978), assigning them to find the spelling errors in the assignments of their peers (Rudman, 1973), listing the number of errors in a student's assignment and having students locate and correct the errors, and marking words that may be incorrectly spelled and having students check them (Personkee & Yee, 1971). Posting an alphabetical list of words frequently misspelled in a central location in the room, encouraging students to maintain a list of words they frequently misspell in their notebooks, and assigning peers to serve as a "human dictionary" or "super speller" to assist their classmates can help students learn to identify and vanquish spelling demons (Fagen et al., 1984).

3. *Use spelling games.* Games can motivate students and provide them with the opportunity to practice spelling skills in a nonthreatening environment (Gloeckler & Simpson, 1988). A variety of teacher-made and commercially produced spelling games are available (Gloeckler & Simpson, 1988). Teacher-made games include spelling bingo, hangman, spelling baseball, and spelling lotto, while commercially produced games include Scrabble, Spello, and Boggle.

4. *Employ a combination of approaches.* Graham and Miller (1979) advocate a spelling program that combines several approaches. They propose that spelling instruction encompass a list of common reading and vocabulary words used by students. Spelling words should be selected so that they are

consistent with the students' reading and vocabulary levels (Bos & Vaughn, 1988). These words can then be taught using a variety of methods. Spelling vocabulary should be supplemented by use of rule-governed approaches to teach essential spelling rules and phonetic skills such as prefixes, suffixes, blends, and digraphs. To assist mainstreamed students in learning spelling rules, it is suggested that only one rule be taught at a time.

5. *Teach students to use cues.* Students can employ both mnemonic devices and configuration clues to cue them to correct spelling (Gloeckler & Simpson, 1988). For example, some students may benefit from placing blocks around the outline of the word to remember the configuration of the word.

6. *Have students self-record their progress.* Self-recording motivates students by providing them with a visual representation of their progress. For example, students can keep a cumulative chart or graph of words spelled correctly, or maintain weekly graphs that measure performance on pretests and posttests.

7. *Provide time to review words previously learned.* Since mainstreamed students may experience difficulty remembering words previously mastered, teachers should provide time to review and study previously learned words, and provide students with opportunities to use spelling words in other situations. Graham and Miller (1979) suggest that previously mastered spelling words should be periodically tested during the school year. When assessing mastery of spelling words, students should check their work under the teacher's supervision with the teacher offering feedback (Vallecorsa, Zigmond, & Henderson, 1985).

8. *Model appropriate spelling techniques.* Teachers can facilitate the spelling skills of their students by providing them with oral and written models to imitate (Kauffman, et al., 1978; Stowitschek & Jobes, 1977). When writing on the blackboard, teachers can periodically emphasize the spelling of words, and can occasionally spell words or have peers spell them for the class.

9. *Use the spell checker.* Many word-processing programs come with a spell checker, which can assist students with spelling difficulties (Dalton, Winbury, & Morrocco, 1990). Spell checkers review written text and identify spelling errors and other words that do not match the program's dictionary. Students then correct the spelling errors by typing in the correct spelling or by choosing from a list of alternatives presented by the spell checker. Students can add words to the spell checker's dictionary to tailor it to their unique spelling needs. However, spell checkers cannot identify words that are spelled correctly but used in the wrong context, such as homonyms.

10. *Choose relevant spelling words.* Teachers can motivate students and improve their spelling by focusing initially on a core of frequently used spelling words as well as on those words that are part of the student's listening and spelling vocabulary (Vallecorsa, Zigmond, & Henderson, 1985). Gra-

ham (1992) suggests that students' spelling words be selected by both students and teachers and be those that frequently appear in students' writing products.

11. *Analyze students' spelling errors.* Teachers should observe students while they spell and note the types of errors they make through error analysis. For example, many second language learners may engage in *cross linguistically developed* spelling, incorrectly spelling words by using elements from their first and second languages. Appropriate spelling instruction should be based on the students' error patterns. Teachers also should provide students with time to practice spelling words.

HANDWRITING

Poor handwriting skills can hinder the appearance of written products and may result in mainstreamed students receiving lower grades on their assignments (Hagin, 1983; Markham, 1976).

Students will need to develop the legibility and fluency of their handwriting so that they can express themselves in writing. *Legibility*—the clarity and correctness of letter formation—includes such variables as size, slant, proportion, alignment, and spacing of letters, as well as the thickness and evenness of the lines that constitute the letters. *Fluency* refers to the speed with which students write, and is measured in terms of letters produced per minute.

Initial Handwriting Instruction

Handwriting instruction should be an integral part of the school curriculum. Teachers should schedule time for handwriting instruction for at least 15 minutes each day (Milone & Wasylyk, 1981; Wiederholt, Hamill, & Brown, 1978). Initial instruction in handwriting should focus on helping students develop the prerequisite fine motor, visual motor, and visual discrimination skills needed for handwriting (Mercer & Mercer, 1985). Therefore, early handwriting instruction can include activities such as cutting, tracing, coloring, fingerpainting, discriminating, and copying shapes.

Before receiving formal handwriting instruction, students should be able to draw vertical, horizontal, curved, and slanted lines; make backward and forward circles; discriminate and verbally identify letters and shapes; and reproduce simple shapes when provided with a model. Because instruction is predicated on teachers using directional concepts to verbalize letter formation, students should be able to understand the meaning of such directional terms as *up, down, top, center, bottom, around, left, right, across, middle,* and *diagonal* (Miller, 1987). Initial writing instruction also should focus on teaching students proper posture, writing utensil grip, and paper positioning.

Sitting Correctly

Proper posture is necessary for good handwriting (Milone & Wasylyk, 1981). Poor posture, such as resting the head on the desk, can distort both motor movements and the visual feedback necessary for good handwriting. Therefore, teachers should teach students good posture, including the following:

- sitting upright, with the lower back positioned against the back of the seat and both feet on the floor
- leaning the shoulders and upper back forward in a straight line
- placing the elbows extended slightly at the edge of the writing surface
- using the forearms as a pivot for movements (Graham & Miller, 1980; Milone & Wasylyk, 1981)

Holding the Writing Utensil

In addition to posture, students also need to learn the proper way to hold the writing utensil (Graham & Miller, 1980; Milone & Wasylyk, 1981). The writing utensil should be positioned in the hand so that

- the utensil is held lightly between the index finger and the middle finger with the thumb to the side and index finger on top
- the thumb is bent to hold the pencil high in the hand and the pencil rests near the knuckle of the index finger
- the pinky and ring finger touch the paper (Milone & Wasylyk, 1981)

Righthanders should hold the writing utensil about an inch from the point, and point the eraser toward their right shoulder. Lefthanders should hold their writing utensil 1½ inches from the point, with the eraser pointing toward their left shoulder. The nonwriting hand rests on the desk surface and keeps the paper in place. This hand also moves the page as lines are completed (Hagin, 1983).

Teachers can help students learn the correct way to hold their writing utensil by modeling and demonstrating the correct grip, physically guiding students, and placing the student's fingers in the correct position (Graham & Miller, 1980; Radabaugh & Yukish, 1982). Teachers can cue students on how to hold the writing utensil by using tape, rubber bands, or a rubber device that can be purchased to slip over the writing utensil (Foerster, 1975; Mendoza, Holt, & Jackson, 1978). Some students may require the use of specialized writing utensils, such as large diameter pencils, crayons, holders, and writing frames (Milone & Wasylyk, 1981).

Positioning the Paper

Since the position of the paper also is important in facilitating good handwriting, handwriting instruction should include training in how to position the paper (Milone & Wasylyk, 1981). For manuscript writing, the paper should be located perpendicular to the front of the student, with the left side placed so that it is aligned with the center of the student's body. For cursive writing, righthanders should be taught to slant the paper counterclockwise, while lefthanders should slant it clockwise (Bos & Vaughn, 1988). Harrison (1981) suggests that lefthanders hold their papers more to the right than righthanders and turn their bodies to the right.

For some students, special writing paper helps overcome writing difficulties. Fagen et al. (1984) recommend that teachers adapt writing paper by emphasizing the base lines and marking the starting and end points with green and red dots, respectively. Problems with keeping letters on the writing lines of standard writing paper can be alleviated through use of right-line paper, a specialized writing sheet that allows students to see and feel the baselines that provide the boundaries for forming letters (Mercer & Mercer, 1985). Paper with colored, solid, and dashed lines can be used to help students learn correct letter heights; paper with perpendicular lines can be used to teach proper spacing (Gloeckler & Simpson, 1988).

Manuscript vs. Cursive Writing

Once students possess the readiness skills necessary to begin formal handwriting instruction, they are typically taught manuscript writing, traditionally followed by instruction in cursive writing. Advocates of teaching manuscript writing first argue that it is easy to learn because it consists of simple motor movements, is more legible, promotes reading and spelling skills, resembles book print, and is used to complete applications and documents (Hagin, 1983; Johnson & Myklebust, 1967; Graham & Miller, 1980).

However, some educators propose that students with handwriting difficulties be taught only cursive writing. These proponents note that cursive writing can help some students write faster; decreases the likelihood that students will reverse letters; is easier for many students as the strokes are continuous, rhythmic, and connected; and is the style of handwriting used by peers and required by teachers as students enter the intermediate grades (Bos & Vaughn, 1988; Graham & Miller, 1980; Mercer & Mercer, 1985).

Whether students are learning cursive or manuscript, teachers should individualize instruction and provide feedback to students on their performance. Writing errors should be analyzed and remedial strategies suggested. Mercer & Mercer (1985) offer an excellent framework for linking student errors with remedial strategies (See Figure 8.4).

Transitional Models

In an extensive review of handwriting research, Graham and Miller (1980) suggest that students learn manuscript writing first. Once manuscript writing is mastered, they recommend teaching cursive writing as a distinct but related skill. Mann, Suiter, and McClung (1979) offer a transitional writing model:

1. Students first print words in manuscript.
2. Students then connect the letters within the words with a colored dotted line.
3. Last, students trace over the letters and dotted lines so that the words are converted from manuscript to cursive writing.

FIGURE 8.4
Diagnostic chart for manuscript and cursive writing

Factor	Problem	Possible Cause	Remediation
		Manuscript Writing	
Shape	Letters slanted	Paper slanted	Place paper straight and pull straight line strokes toward center of body.
	Varies from standard	Improper mental image of letter	Have pupil write problem letters on chalkboard.
Size	Too large	Poor understanding of writing lines	Reteach size concept by pointing out purpose of each line on writing paper.
		Exaggerated arm movement	Reduce arm movement, especially on circle and part-circle letters.
		Improper mental image of letter	Have pupil write problem letters on chalkboard.
	Too small	Poor understanding of writing lines	Reteach size concept by pointing out purpose of each line on writing paper.
		Overemphasis on finger movement	Stress arm movement; check hand-pencil and arm-desk positions to be sure arm movement is possible.
		Improper mental image of letter	Have pupil write problem letters on chalkboard.
	Not uniform	Adjusting writing hand after each letter	Stress arm movement; move paper with nonwriting hand so writing hand can remain in proper writing position.
		Overemphasis on finger movement	Stress arm movement; check arm-desk and pencil-hand positions.
Space	Crowded letters in words	Poor understanding of space concepts	Reteach uniform spacing between letters (finger or pencil width).
	Too much space between letters	Improper lowercase letter size and shape	Review concepts of size and shape; provide appropriate corrections under size and shape.
Alignment	Letters not sitting on base line	Improper letter formation	Evaluate work for letter shape; stress bringing straight line strokes all the way down to base line.

FIGURE 8.4
(continued)

Factor	Problem	Possible Cause	Remediation
		Manuscript Writing (continued)	
Alignment (*continued*)		Poor understanding of base line concept	Review purpose of base line on writing paper.
		Improper hand-pencil and paper-desk positions	Check positions to make sure pupil is able to reach base line with ease.
	Letters not of consistent height	Poor understanding of size concept	Review concept of letter size in relationship to lines provided on writing paper.
Line quality	Too heavy or too light	Improper writing pressure	Review hand-pencil position; place wadded paper tissue in palm of writing hand to relax writing grip; demonstrate desired line quality.
		Cursive Writing	
Shape	Letters too oval	Overemphasis of arm movement and poor image of letter size and shape	Check arm-desk position; review letter size and shape.
	Letters too narrow	Finger writing	Check positions to allow for arm movement.
		Overemphasis of straight line stroke	Make sure straight line stroke does not come all the way down to base line in letters like *l*, *b*, and *t*.
		Poor mental image of letter shape	Use transparent overlay for pupil's personal evaluation of shape.
			In all problems of letter shape, review letters in terms of the basic strokes.
Size	Letters too large	Exaggerated arm movement	Check arm-desk position for over-movement of forearm.
		Poor mental image of letter size	Review base and top line concepts in relation to ¼ space, ½ space, and ¾ space; use transparent overlay for pupil's personal evaluation of letter size.
	Letters too small or letters not uniform	Finger movement	Check arm-desk and pencil-hand positions; stress arm movement.

FIGURE 8.4
(continued)

Factor	Problem	Possible Cause	Remediation
		Cursive Writing (continued)	
Size (*continued*)		Poor mental image of letter size	Review concept of letter size (¼ space, ½ space, and ¾ space) in relation to base and top lines; use transparent overlay for pupil's personal evaluation of letter size.
Space	Letters in words crowded or spacing between letters uneven	Finger movement	Check arm-desk, pencil-hand positions; stress arm movement.
		Poor understanding of joining strokes	Review how letters are joined; show ending stroke of one letter to be beginning stroke of following letter; practice writing letters in groups of five.
	Too much space provided between letters in words	Exaggerated arm movement	Check arm-desk position for over-movement of forearm.
		Poor understanding of joining strokes	Review joining strokes; practice writing groups of letters by rhythmic count.
	Uneven space between words	Poor understanding of between-word spacing	Review concept of spacing between words; show beginning stroke in second word starting under ending stroke of preceding word.
Alignment	Poor letter alignment along base line	Incorrect writing position; finger movement; exaggerated arm movement	Check all writing positions; stress even, rhythmic writing movement.
		Poor understanding of base line concept	Use repetitive exercise with emphasis on relationship of base line to written word.
		Incorrect use of joining strokes	Review joining strokes.
	Uneven alignment of letters in words relative to size	Poor understanding of size concept	Show size relationships between lower- and uppercase, and ¼ space, ½ space, and ¾ space lowercase letters; use repetitive exercise with emphasis on uniform height of smaller letters.

FIGURE 8.4
(continued)

Factor	Problem	Possible Cause	Remediation
		Cursive Writing (continued)	
Speed and Ease	Writing becomes illegible under stress and speed (grades 4, 5, and 6)	Degree of handwriting skill is insufficient to meet speed requirements	Improve writing positions; develop more arm movement and less finger movement.
	Writing becomes illegible when writing activity is too long	Handwriting positions have not been perfected to allow handwriting ease	Improve all writing positions, especially hand-pencil position; stress arm movement.
Slant	Back slant	Left-handedness	Correct hand-pencil and paper-desk positions.
	Vertical	Poor positioning	Correct hand-pencil and paper-desk positions.
	Too far right	Overemphasis of finger movement	Make sure pupil pulls slant strokes toward center of body if right-handed and to left elbow if left-handed. Use slant line instruction sheets as aid to teaching slant. Use transparent overlay for pupil's personal evaluation. Review all lowercase letters that derive their shape from the slant line. Write lowercase alphabet on chalkboard; retrace all slant strokes in colored chalk.

Source: C. D. Mercer and A. R. Mercer, *Teaching Students with Learning Problems,* 2nd ed. (New York: Merrill/Macmillan, 1985), pp. 419–422. Reprinted by permission of the publisher.

Another transitional program is Hagin's *Write-Right-or Left* approach, which teaches students to use the vertical downstroke rather than the diagonal slant (Hagin, 1983). Students are taught cursive writing through *letter motifs* (waves, pearls, wheels, and arrows), which are a means for learning the cursive writing strokes. Initially, the letter motifs are introduced to students at the chalkboard. After students practice at the chalkboard, they move to their desks where they trace motifs and letters on an acetate sheet placed over a model; try to write the letters on an acetate without the model; match and compare their letters with the models to determine if additional practice is needed; and produce a final product that is used to assess student progress and mastery.

Brown (1984) and Thurber (1981) offer suggestions for using the D'Nealian method, including slant and letter size, letter spacing, and writing rhythm.

An instructional writing strategy that eases the transition from manuscript to cursive writing is the *D'Nealian* system. In this system, the formation of most manuscript and cursive letters involves similar continuous and slanted strokes.

Instructional Strategies and Models

Several letter formation strategies and models have been used to teach handwriting skills (see Figure 8.5). Writing strategies and models for mainstreamed students should do all of the following:

- teach handwriting directly
- establish the importance of handwriting
- use overlearning to promote automaticity
- encourage students to visualize the task
- teach students to monitor their work and make corrections (Hagin, 1983; Milone & Wasylyk, 1981)

Graham (1983) and S. M. Salend (1984) propose that educators use a combination of procedures, such as modeling, self-instruction, copying, cuing, and teaching basic strokes.

Modeling. A variety of modeling strategies can be employed to teach students handwriting skills. Teachers can introduce students to letter formations by modeling the strokes used to form the letters. Additionally, physically guiding students through the sequence of strokes can help them learn the necessary motor movements. Teacher modeling and physical guidance should be accompanied by verbal descriptions of how to form letters (*We start at the top, swing down to the right and then go up*), as well as by statements that point out the critical and unique features of each letter. Verbal descriptions that create visual images of the letters using real objects can be especially effective in promoting letter formation skills (Bos & Vaughn, 1988). For example, when modeling the letters *j* and *m,* teachers can relate their form to a fishhook and a camel's hump, respectively.

Such visual mnemonics also can be used to assist in remediating reversals in writing (Bos & Vaughn, 1988). Graham and Miller (1980) identified several strategies that can be used to remediate reversals, including teaching students to simultaneously trace and name the letter; write the letter to the right of the paper's midline; write the letter by linking it with a letter that is not typically reversed; use directional cues, such as heavy lines, color coding, and drawings; and employ verbal cues.

In addition to presenting models depicting appropriate letter formations, students should be provided with examples of poorly written letters so that they can learn to compare and assess their writing to identify areas in need of improvement (Mercer & Mercer, 1985). Student evaluation of writing also can be fostered by use of *self-checking transparencies,* overlays of correct letter formations that students can place over their work to examine their letter formation accuracy (Mastropieri & Scruggs, 1987).

FIGURE 8.5
Letter formation strategies

Fauke Approach (Fauke et al., 1973)

1. The teacher writes the letter, and the student and teacher discuss the formational act.
2. The student names the letter.
3. The student traces the letter with a finger, pencil, and magic marker.
4. The student's finger traces a letter form made of yarn.
5. The student copies the letter.
6. The student writes the letter from memory.
7. The teacher rewards the student for correctly writing the letter.

Progressive Approximation Approach (Hofmeister, 1973)

1. The student copies the letter using a pencil.
2. The teacher examines the letter and, if necessary, corrects by overmarking with a highlighter.
3. The student erases incorrect portions of the letter and traces over the teacher's highlighter marking.
4. The student repeats steps 1–3 until the letter is written correctly.

Furner Approach (Furner, 1969a, 1969b, 1970)

1. Student and teacher establish a purpose for the lesson.
2. The student provides the student with many guided exposures to the letter.
3. The student describes the process while writing the letter and tries to write or visualize the letter as another child describes it.
4. The teacher uses multisensory stimulation to teach the letter form.
5. The student compares his or her written response to a model.

VAKT Approach

1. The teacher writes the letter with crayon while the student observes the process.
2. The teacher and student both say the name of the letter.
3. The student traces the letter with the index finger, simultaneously saying the name of the letter. This is done successfully five times.
4. The student copies and names the letter successfully three times.
5. Without a visual aid, the student writes and names the letter correctly three times.

Niedermeyer Approach (Niedermeyer, 1973)

1. The student traces a dotted representation of the letter 12 times.
2. The student copies the letter 12 times.
3. The student writes the letter as the teacher pronounces it.

Handwriting with Write and See (Skinner & Krakower, 1968)

The student traces a letter within a tolerance model on specially prepared paper. If the student forms the letter correctly, the pen writes gray; if it is incorrect, the pen writes yellow.

Source: S. Graham and L. Miller, *Focus on Exceptional Children,* vol. 13 (Denver, CO: Love, 1980), p. 11. Reprinted by permission of the publisher.

A chart presenting lowercase and uppercase letters, the numerals 1 through 10, and their corresponding stroke directions should be placed in the room so that all students can view it. The chart can guide students in forming letters and numerals and can assist them in evaluating their performance. Because the stroke directions are different for lefthanders, those students should be provided with charts and teacher models appropriate for their unique style.

Teachers can use a multisensory approach to provide students with a visual and verbal model that guides their formation of the letters (Mercer & Mercer, 1985). The steps in this approach include the following:

- The teacher writes or presents the letter to the students.
- The teacher states the name of the letter and verbalizes the sequence of the strokes.
- Students trace the letters with their fingers and verbalize their movements.
- Students repeat the step using a pencil.
- Students write the letter while viewing the model.

Mercer & Mercer (1985) also propose a *fading* model to teach handwriting skills. Initially, students are given a model made up of solid, dark, heavy lines, which students trace. Next, parts of the model are gradually and progressively faded, then eliminated, as students trace over them with their writing utensils. Finally, the model is completely eliminated, and the student produces the letter from memory.

Self-Instruction. Self-instructional procedures have been found to be effective for increasing the handwriting skills of students (Graham, 1983; Kosiewicz, Hallahan, Lloyd & Graves, 1982). S. M. Salend (1984) used a combination of cues, tracing, fading and verbal self-instruction to teach appropriate letter formation, alignment, and proportion. Graham (1983) used a six-step, self-instructional procedure to improve handwriting performance:

Step 1: Students watch as the teacher writes the letter. Students and teacher discuss writing the letter, with both outlining the steps in the formation of the letter. Step one concludes after the process is repeated three times.

Step 2: The teacher writes and verbalizes the process while students observe. Students delineate the process in unison with the teacher.

Step 3: Students trace the letters while verbalizing the process with the teacher. Students demonstrate mastery of this phase by verbalizing the steps without teacher assistance.

Steps 4–6: Students learn the self-instructional task. In step four, the teacher writes the letter, traces it, then models the self-instruction, which includes defining the task (*What do I have to do?*), verbalizing the steps in forming the letter (*How do I make this letter?*), correcting errors (*How does it look? Do I need to make any changes?*), and delivering reinforcement (*That looks good. I did a good job*). Steps five and six repeat step four, while fading out teacher assistance.

Robin, Armel, and O'Leary (1975) note that self-instructional techniques may be difficult for younger students to learn and use.

Cuing. S. M. Salend (1984) used a variety of visual and verbal cues to help teach letter formation skills:

IDEAS FOR IMPLEMENTATION

In addition to instruction in posture, writing utensil grip, and paper positioning, teachers can facilitate handwriting for their lefthanded students by enacting the following suggestions:

- Group them together.
- Offer them lefthanded models.
- Teach them to write letters vertically or with a slight backslant.
- Have them eliminate elaborate and excessive loops and curves.
- Have them write on the left side of the blackboard.
- Provide them with lefthanded desks.

Source: Graham & Miller (1980); Harrison (1981).

1. Place a green dot to indicate the correct starting point for each letter.
2. Darken bottom and midlines of the student's paper to assist the student in aligning the letters correctly.
3. Provide one-centimeter blocks, into which the student can write the letters.
4. Put masking tape on the student's desk to indicate the correct position of the paper.
5. Teach the students a rhyme that reminds the student how to perform the task.

Copying. Copying also can be used to improve handwriting skills. Two types of copying activities are available to teachers: near-point and far-point copying. Teachers should begin with *near-point copying,* where students copy a model that is placed on their desks. As students become proficient at near-point copying, *far-point copying*—where the model is placed away from the students' desks—can be employed. Although students may be successful with near-point copying, far-point copying requires them to transfer through space and from different planes, and thus may create problems for many students. Problems in spacing can be minimized by teaching students to establish the space between words and sentences by using their fingers or the size of the lowercase *o* as a guide. For example, teach students that they can determine the space between letters within a word by estimating the size of one lowercase *o,* while the space between words within a sentence would be the size of two of those letters (Miller, 1987).

Research indicates that copying is superior to tracing in promoting letter formation skills (Askov, & Greff, 1975; Hirsch & Niedermeyer, 1973).

Teaching Basic Strokes. Most of the letters in manuscript and cursive writing are made up of a series of basic strokes. Handwriting skills can be facilitated by teaching students these basic strokes (Milone & Wasylyk, 1981). The basic strokes in manuscript writing are the top-bottom line (↓ |), left-to-right line (⇉), backward circle (↺), forward circle (↻) and slant lines (// \\ ). In cursive writing, the basic strokes are the slant stroke (//), understroke (↗), downstroke (↙) and overstroke (↗) (Milone & Wasylyk, 1981).

The *Hanover* method teaches handwriting skills by grouping them in families based on the nature of the strokes that form the letters (Hanover, 1983). In this method, students are taught the similarities and differences between letters within each family.

Assistive Devices

Devices that provide auditory and visual feedback to assist students in improving their handwriting skills are available (Wisniewski & Sedlak, 1992). The *Talking Pen* uses fiber optics to provide auditory feedback to students when the color-sensitive pen goes off the line. Teachers can adjust the pen's sensitivity to the needs of students. The pen can also be connected to a counter to record the number of errors students make. Similarly, the *Auditory Music Converter* plays music on headphones for students when their handwriting skills are appropriate.

Teaching Lefthanders Handwriting

Because writing progresses from left to right, lefthanded students may have difficulties with handwriting (Harrison, 1981; S. M. Salend, 1984). Compared to righthanded students, lefthanded students are more likely to write slower (Burns, 1968), feel awkward and uncomfortable while writing, experience fatigue (Clark, 1959), and reverse letters (Enstrom & Enstrom, 1970).

SUMMARY

This chapter presented guidelines and strategies for adapting instruction in specific content areas. The chapter

- reviewed various approaches and strategies for teaching reading and word recognition skills
- outlined the components in a process-oriented approach to teaching writing
- outlined a variety of approaches and strategies for teaching spelling
- offered suggestions to guide handwriting instruction

RECOMMENDED READINGS

Calkins, L. M. (1986). *The art of teaching.* Portsmouth, NH: Heinemann.

Freeman, Y. S., & Freeman, D. E. (1992). *Whole language for second language learners.* Portsmouth, NH: Heinemann.

Golub, J. (Eds.) (1988). *Focus on collaborative learning.* Urbana, IL: National Council of Teachers of English.

Goodman, K. (1986). *What's whole in whole language?* Portsmouth, NH: Heinemann.

Graham, S. (1992). Helping students with LD progress as writers. *Intervention in School and Clinic, 27*(3), 134–144.

Maldonado-Colon, E. (1991). Development of second language learners' linguistic and cognitive abilities. *The Journal of Educational Issues of Language Minority Students, 9,* 37–48.

Miller, L. J. (1987). Spelling and handwriting. In J. S. Choate, T. Z. Bennett, B. E. Enright, L. J. Miller, J. A. Poteet, & T. A. Rakes (Eds.), *Assessing and programming basic curriculum skills* (pp. 177–204). Boston: Allyn & Bacon.

Milone, M. N., & Wasylyk, T. M. (1981). Handwriting in special education. *Teaching Exceptional Children, 14,* 58–61.

Slavin, R. E., Madden, N. A., & Stevens, R. J. (1990). Cooperative learning models for the 3 R's. *Educational Leadership, 47*(4), 22–28.

Swicegood, P. R., & Parsons, J. L. (1991). The thematic unit approach: Content and process instruction for secondary learning disabled students. *Learning Disabilities Research and Practice, 6,* 112–116.

9 Modifying Mathematics, Science, and Social Studies Instruction

LEARNING BY MANIPULATION

After several lessons on subtraction, Ms. Stanley notices that several of her students still have not mastered the skill. To help these students, Ms. Stanley tries several different strategies. First, Ms. Stanley helps students visualize subtraction of numbers using Cuisenaire rods. Students experiment with the rods and find they are able to compare rods of differing lengths and colors, and compute the differences. Next, Ms. Stanley introduces a counting card, an index card with the numerals 1 through 9 listed in a column followed by a corresponding number of circles. Students use the counting card by identifying the larger number in the subtraction problem and counting down the number of circles in the smaller number to calculate the answer. For example, if the problem is 9 − 2 = , the students locate the line with nine circles and count off two circles to compute the answer. At this point, Ms. Stanley feels that some students still need assistance to perform subtraction problems. She teaches these students to make dots next to the smaller numbers in problems to help them figure out the answer. For example, if the problem is 7 − 5 = , students place 5 dots next to the 5, and use these dots to count down from 7. As students master this technique, Ms. Stanley encourages them to solve problems without the dots.

What additional strategies can Ms. Stanley use to help promote the mathematics skills of her students? After reading this chapter, you should be able to answer this as well as the following questions.

- What approaches and strategies can educators use to adapt instruction of mathematics?
- What approaches and strategies can educators use to adapt instruction of science and social studies?
- How can educators create a multicultural curriculum and use multicultural materials that are meaningful for all students?

Many strategies for adapting classroom instruction to enhance learning, motivation, and social development can be used across academic disciplines (see Chapters 6 and 7). However, teachers may find that they must make adaptations unique to a specific content area to promote learning for mainstreamed students. This chapter offers guidelines for teaching mathematics, science, and social studies. Additionally, we discuss here strategies for transforming the curriculum to make it more inclusive and meaningful to all students.

MATHEMATICS

McKinney and Feagans (1980) found that as many students with disabilities had deficits in mathematics as had deficits in reading.

Math is one of several content areas with which mainstreamed students may experience problems (Bley & Thornton, 1981; Garnett, 1987). McLeod and Armstrong (1982) noted that teachers of intermediate and secondary students with learning disabilities reported that 66 percent of their students had problems with math, indicating that math difficulties may intensify as students age. In particular, mainstreamed students may need assistance in mastering basic math facts and solving word problems (Bley & Thornton, 1981).

Teaching Basic Math Facts

A major portion of the K–8 math curriculum is devoted to mastery of basic math facts—numbers and numeration, addition, subtraction, multiplication, and division of whole numbers, time, measurement, money, percents, decimals, and fractions. Teachers can help mainstreamed students learn this content by carefully planning and organizing instruction according to the following principles.

Organize instruction to follow a developmental sequence. Peterson, Mercer, and O'Shea (1988) suggest that teachers follow an instructional sequence that includes introducing new concepts through use of three dimensional objects such as concrete aids and manipulatives; using semiconcrete aids, such as demonstrations or illustrations on worksheets, overheads, computers, and in textbooks to establish fluency; and promoting speed and accuracy through use of abstract strategies such as mathematical symbols and oral and written language. The *Strategic Math Series* (SMS) employs an instructional sequence based on such an instructional sequence (Mercer & Miller, 1992).

Introduce new concepts through everyday situations to which students can relate. Many math skills are important for functioning in daily life (Johnson & Blalock, 1986). Relating new concepts to everyday situations such as recreational activities can help motivate students to learn them, and can encourage active, purposeful learning (Baroody & Hume, 1991; Bley & Thornton, 1981). For example, percentages and graphing can be introduced by using statistics from the school's sports teams, time concepts can be related to a schedule of favorite television shows, the learning of measurement skills can be facilitated by following recipes. Teachers also should discuss with students the relevance of learning a new skill and the situations in which the skill can be applied (Mercer & Miller, 1992).

Teach key math terms. As with other content areas, math has its own terminology. The math performance of students who are learning English can be hindered by difficulties in understanding English language mathematics vocabulary (Davison & Pearce, 1992). Teachers can help mainstreamed students by teaching them this essential terminology. These key words may then be listed in a math dictionary developed and maintained by the class (Bley & Thornton, 1981). The dictionary could contain definitions and examples of such math terms as *sum, difference, quotients, proper fractions, mixed numbers* and *reciprocals.* A student having difficulty with a term such as *denominator* could locate its definition and view examples. (*The denominator is the bottom part of a fraction that indicates the number of parts. In the fraction* $\frac{5}{6}$, *the 6 is the denominator.*) Teachers also can have students write in their notebooks definitions for mathematical terms using their own words (Davison & Pearce, 1992).

Lists of key math terms that are important for math proficiency have been developed by O'Mara (1981), Cox and Wiebe (1984), and Swett (1978).

Use drawings and diagrams to illustrate new concepts and interrelationships. Oral presentations of math instruction can be supplemented by use of illustrations. Drawings and diagrams of new concepts and interrelationships can help students master many skills; they gain a visual and concrete framework for understanding the foundations of the process as well as the steps necessary to perform the operation. Because material used to present mathematics content is typically difficult to read (Schell, 1982), misunderstandings related to reading mathematical language can be minimized by using drawings and diagrams that depict difficult-to-understand content (Dunlap & McKnight, 1978).

When offering depictions of math concepts, teachers should use colored chalk or marking pens to highlight and delineate important points (Bley & Thornton, 1981). For example, when initially teaching carrying, illustrate the process by highlighting the number to be carried at the top of the next column:

$$\begin{array}{r} \textcircled{1} \\ 48 \\ +\underline{33} \\ 81 \end{array}$$

Cluster math facts to facilitate memory of them. Rather than teaching math facts in isolation, related math facts should be taught together (Thornton, Tucker, Dossey, & Bazik, 1983). For example, students should learn the cluster of multiplying by two together. As students demonstrate mastery, they should practice mixed groups of math facts (Garnett, 1989).

Use manipulatives and concrete teaching aids. The importance of using manipulatives and concrete teaching aids in teaching concepts of varying degrees of difficulty has been recognized (Herbert, 1985; Marzola, 1987). Pieper and Deshler (1985) note that manipulatives can facilitate understanding of abstract and symbolic concepts and should precede drill and practice activities. Parkham (1983) found that students who used manipulatives scored significantly higher on math achievement tests than their counterparts who did not use them. While manipulatives are most frequently used to teach readiness and first-grade math concepts (Suydam, 1986), they have been successful in teaching place value (Beattie & Scheer, 1982), fractions and decimals (Suydam, 1984), money and percentages (Sullivan, 1981), word problem–solving skills (Canny, 1984), probability (Bruni & Silverman, 1986), statistics (Alford, 1985; Bruni & Silverman, 1986), geometry (Clements and Battista, 1986), and algebra (Williams, 1986).

Manipulatives are particularly valuable in helping students with language difficulties acquire math concepts (Garnett, 1989).

When using manipulatives to teach math concepts, teachers should follow several guidelines (Marzola, 1987). Initially, teachers should introduce the manipulatives by modeling their use (Trueblood, 1986) and verbally explaining the concepts illustrated (Garnett & Fleischner, 1987; Thornton & Wilmot, 1986). Next, students should have the opportunity to experiment with the manipulatives and verbalize their actions. Teachers can structure their students' use of the materials by asking questions that guide their experimentation (Thornton & Wilmot, 1986). To promote generalization, teachers should provide students with opportunities to use a variety of manipulatives (Mercer & Miller, 1992).

Marzola (1987) offered a list of commercially produced manipulatives that can be used to teach a variety of concepts including place value, computations, money, time, measurement, fractions, decimals, percent, and geometry. For example, the *Stern Structural Arithmetic Program* (Stern, 1965) employs blocks to teach K–3 arithmetic concepts, while colored Cuisenaire rods of varying lengths have been developed to provide an understanding of many underlying principles of mathematics (Davidson, 1969).

Many manipulatives are available without purchase. These include numberlines, money, and students' fingers. Numberlines can be used to teach a variety of math concepts (Mercer & Mercer, 1985; Thornton et al., 1983). Since many students have difficulty using numberlines, their use should follow experience with other manipulatives such as cubes, popsicle sticks, and chips (Thornton et al., 1983). Additionally, teachers should carefully introduce numberlines and may train students to use them by using a large numberline on which students can walk.

Manipulatives are especially important in teaching money skills. When teaching these skills, it is best to use real money (Bley & Thornton, 1981). If this is not feasible, money substitutes should be as authentic as possible.

Another manipulative aid that students can employ is their fingers. While fingers are often used as an aid in counting and simple addition and subtraction, fingers also can be used to teach basic multiplication facts of nine. Each finger is assigned a consecutive number from one to ten. To multiply four times nine, bend the fourth finger. The number of fingers preceding the bent finger represents the number of tens (in this case, three), and the number of fingers following the bent finger represents the ones (in this case, six). Thus, the answer is 36.

Think About It

Try using the finger method described above to solve 5 × 9, 3 × 9, and 8 × 9.

Use a variety of activities to promote mastery and automaticity. One goal of math instruction in basic facts is for students to respond quickly and accurately. Teachers should offer students a variety of activities that promote mastery and automaticity (Mastropieri & Scruggs, 1987; Thornton et al., 1983). Automaticity can be developed through use of student- or peer-directed flash cards (Mastropieri & Scruggs, 1987), and having students listen to math facts on a Language Master or an audiocassette (Lambie & Hutchens, 1986).

Worksheets and homework also can be used to help students develop automaticity. Rather than giving students a large number of items on worksheets, Parmar and Cawley (1991) suggest that teachers give students worksheets with two sample computation items, discuss the salient features of the items, and ask students to compose and answer new items that resemble the sample items discussed.

Speed and accuracy in basic math facts also can be fostered by use of games (Mercer & Mercer, 1985), interactive videodiscs (Kelly, Carnine, Gersten, & Grossen (1986), and computer software programs (Howell, Sidorenko, & Jurica, 1987). Descriptions of games for teaching a variety of

IDEAS FOR IMPLEMENTATION

Teachers can adapt math assignments for mainstreamed students by enacting the following suggestions:

- Reduce the number of problems on worksheets.
- Increase the time limit students have to complete the assignment.
- Provide adequate space to write out solutions.
- Follow a standard format for developing worksheets.
- Fold worksheets so that students work on one line at a time.
- Cut worksheets into halves or fourths, and have students complete one portion of the sheet before working on the next.
- Allow students to skip certain items, or assign students to work only even- or odd-numbered problems.
- Heighten student awareness of the operation or change in operation by cuing or highlighting each operation, or by grouping problems according to the operational process.
- Increase the number of problems and decrease the time limit as students develop proficiency in a specific skill.

Source: Bley & Thornton (1981); Fagen, Graves, & Tessier-Switlick (1984); Lambie & Hutchens (1986).

math concepts and skills are available (Bley & Thornton, 1981; Mercer & Mercer, 1985; Thornton et al., 1983). Hedley (1987) has compiled a list of computer software games, drill and practice sessions, simulations, and tutorials that can be used to teach basic skills, algebra, geometry, and solving word problems.

Match instruction to students' error types. The instructional strategy selected often will depend on students' error types. Taylor (1992) makes the following suggestions:

- When a step in an algorithm is omitted, teachers should consider teaching students a self-monitoring strategy to check that all steps have been completed.
- When a placement error is made, teachers should focus feedback on and provide students with opportunities to practice the rule.
- When the error involves problems with regrouping, teachers should use manipulatives, concrete materials, and pictorial displays.
- When a step in the process is substituted, teachers should use role playing, where the students review the steps in the process by acting out the role of the teacher.

Ashlock (1986) and Enright (1983, 1986) identify common error patterns that students make and offer strategies that teachers can employ to correct these patterns.

Chiang and Ratajczak (1990) note that when errors are indicative of conceptual misunderstandings, teachers should break down the task into smaller and simpler units, make sure students have mastered prerequisite skills, offer students prompts and cues, and teach students to use self-instruction and self-monitoring techniques.

Offer prompt feedback. The correctness of students' responses should be confirmed by the teacher. Teachers also should acknowledge and reinforce correct responses and alert students to incorrect responses. When incorrect responses are noted, corrective feedback based on analysis of the students' errors should be offered. Chiang and Ratajczak (1990) suggest that teachers use corrective feedback to inform students of the correctness of their response, identify which part of the response is correct or incorrect, and offer students a strategy to obtain the correct response.

Students also should be taught to estimate and check answers. They should learn to locate and correct their errors. Students also can be taught to evaluate their mastery of concepts by graphing their performance on computer programs, worksheets, and followup probes. A checking center equipped with answer keys, teacher's guides, supplementary materials, peer tutors, and recordings of correct responses can facilitate self-checking and minimize the demands on teacher time (Lambie & Hutchens, 1986).

Assess mastery and progress over time. Maintaining skills is important for mainstreamed students, so teachers should periodically conduct cumulative reviews and timed probes to assess mastery of previously learned skills (Thornton et al., 1983). Teachers should provide students with feedback concerning their performance and encourage students to self-record their progress over time.

Cuing Strategies

Cues can help mainstreamed students overcome errors in computation problems that are not related to mastery of basic facts. Attention to computational signs (+, −, ×, ÷) can be accentuated by color coding, boldfacing, and underlining. Attention to signs also can be fostered by listing the sign and its operation at the top of each worksheet (+ = add, 6 + 3 = 9), and teaching students to trace the sign prior to beginning the computation (Enright, 1987a).

Cues also can be used with students who have difficulty remembering the order in which to solve computation items. Arrows can be drawn to indicate the direction in which students should proceed when working on a computation item:

$$\begin{array}{r} \leftarrow \\ 35 \\ -\underline{28} \end{array}$$

Cues such as green and red dots, go and stop signs, and answer boxes can alert students when to proceed or stop when working on a specific computation item.

Another type of cue, *boxing,* or placing boxes around items, can focus students' attention on specific problems within a group (Bley & Thornton, 1981). When boxing items, teachers should leave enough space within the box to do the necessary calculations to solve the item. As students increase their skills, they should be encouraged to assume the responsibility for boxing items.

Boxing also can aid students who have problems aligning their answer in the correct columns. A color-coded, smaller box or broken line can be drawn to delineate columns so that students record their answers in the appropriate column (Gloeckler & Simpson, 1988; Thornton et al., 1983). Problems with aligning answers also can be minimized by having students use centimeter graph paper, which structures the task so that only one digit can be written in each box (Bley & Thornton, 1981), or by turning lined paper so the lines run vertically (Gillet, 1986). Alignment problems also can be lessened by teaching students to estimate and check the reasonableness of their answers. Answers that deviate significantly from their estimate may indicate an alignment problem; students should check their work accordingly.

Providing Models

Some algorithms, such as long division and multiple-digit multiplication, require students to perform a series of different operations in a set sequence to arrive at the correct answer. Many mainstreamed students understand the process and possess the ability to perform these operations, but may need a model to guide them initially through the sequence of calculations (Bley & Thornton, 1981). Worksheets can be coded to provide a correct model for computing the answer. The model provided should vary depending upon the skill level and needs of the students. Sample models are presented in Figure 9.1.

Charts also can be placed in the room to help students. Charts can depict basic computation facts, math terminology, and symbols (*subtract* = *take away* = −) as well as the steps to follow for a specific type of computation problem, such as the steps in dividing fractions (Bley & Thornton, 1981). For example, a fraction strip chart presenting strips divided into halves, thirds, fourths, and so on can be posted to assist students in learning concepts associated with fractions. In addition to class charts, some students may benefit from keeping pocket-size charts of basic math computation facts at their work areas (Garnett, 1989) (see Figure 9.2). A cutout in the shape of a backward *L* can help mainstreamed students find answers, located where the vertical and horizontal rows meet (Garnett, 1989). As these students develop their skills, they can be encouraged to cross out number facts on the chart that they have mastered (Garnett, 1989; Thornton et al., 1983).

Flip charts can be made available to students to offer a model of the correct format and order to approach a task (Bley & Thornton, 1981). Each page of the flip chart represents a step students must perform to complete the task. A sample flip chart for division of fractions is presented in Figure 9.3.

A *demonstration plus model* strategy has been successful in helping students with learning problems develop computational skills (Rivera & Deutsch-Smith, 1988). The strategy involves these steps:

Step 1: The teacher demonstrates the procedures for solving a type of computation problem while verbalizing the key words associated with each step.

FIGURE 9.1
Algorithm models

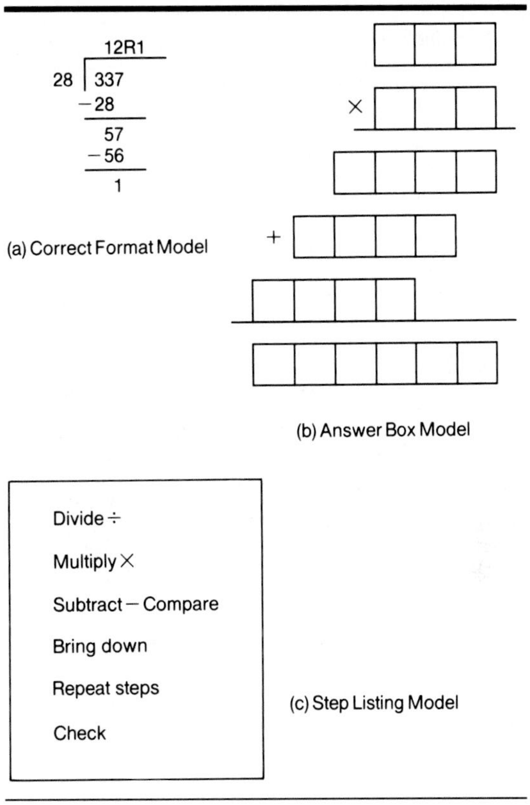

Step 2: The student views the teacher's example, and performs the steps in the computation while verbalizing the key words for each step.

Step 3: The student completes additional problems, referring to the teacher's example if necessary.

Self-Monitoring

Students can learn self-monitoring strategies to guide them in performing a variety of math computations (Frank & Brown, 1992). Self-monitoring checklists can prompt students to remember specific steps necessary to successfully complete a task. In devising self-monitoring checklists, teachers should do the following:

- identify the specific skills necessary to complete the task
- list the skills in sequential order
- create a mnemonic that will help students remember the steps in the process
- develop a self-monitoring checklist, which appears on the students' instructional worksheets
- model use of the self-monitoring checklist and the mnemonic strategy for students while verbalizing each step
- fade out use of the checklist (Frank & Brown, 1992)

FIGURE 9.2
Chart of basic multiplication facts

×	**0**	**1**	**2**	**3**	**4**	**5**	**6**	**7**	**8**	**9**	**10**
0	0	0	0	0	0	0	0	0	0	0	0
1	0	1	2	3	4	5	6	7	8	9	10
2	0	2	4	6	8	10	12	14	16	18	20
3	0	3	6	9	12	15	18	21	24	27	30
4	0	4	8	12	16	20	24	28	32	36	40
5	0	5	10	15	20	25	30	35	40	45	50
6	0	6	12	18	24	30	36	42	48	54	60
7	0	7	14	21	28	35	42	49	56	63	70
8	0	8	16	24	32	40	48	56	64	72	80
9	0	9	18	27	36	45	54	63	72	81	90
10	0	10	20	30	40	50	60	70	80	90	100

FIGURE 9.3
Flip chart for dividing fractions

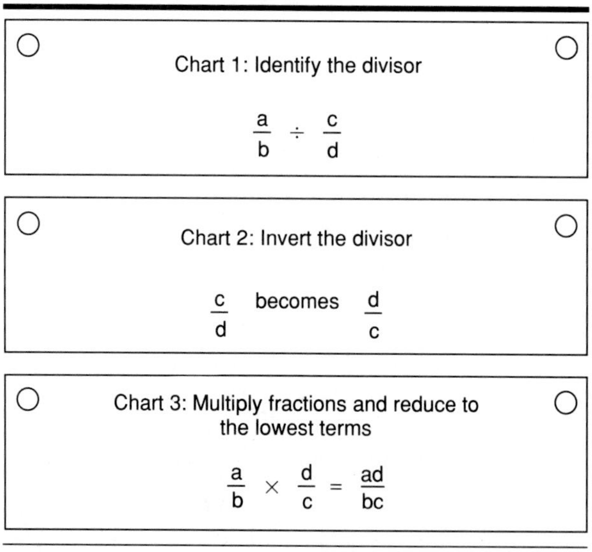
Chart 1: Identify the divisor
$\frac{a}{b} \div \frac{c}{d}$
Chart 2: Invert the divisor
$\frac{c}{d}$ becomes $\frac{d}{c}$
Chart 3: Multiply fractions and reduce to the lowest terms
$\frac{a}{b} \times \frac{d}{c} = \frac{ad}{bc}$

Self-Instruction

Because many mathematical operations involve sequential steps, self-instruction can be highly effective for teaching math skills (Leon & Pepe, 1983). Verbalizing the steps and the signs while performing the computation has resulted in improved mathematical performance (Grimm, Bijou, & Parsons, 1973). The steps for self-instruction of math computation skills are as follows:

Step 1: The teacher models the calculation by demonstrating and overtly stating the steps in the process.

Step 2: The teacher and the student compute the answer and overtly state the steps in the process in unison.

Step 3: The student computes the problem and overtly states the steps in the process while the teacher observes.

Step 4: The student repeats step 3, substituting internal self-instruction for overt verbalizations. If necessary, the teacher provides the student with a cue sheet listing key steps.

Step 5: The student implements the self-instruction procedure internally with no cues and delivers self-reinforcement.

Successful self-instructional techniques for teaching computation skills include equal additions (Sugai & Smith, 1986), count-bys (Lloyd, Saltzman, & Kauffman, 1981), touch math (Miller, Miller, Wheeler, & Selinger, 1989), count-ons, zero facts, doubles, and turn-around (Jones, Thornton, & Toohey, 1985).

Teaching Word Problems

While many students have difficulty solving mathematics word problems (National Council of Teachers of Mathematics, 1980), mainstreamed students may experience particular difficulties in learning to solve these types of problems (Cawley, Miller, & School, 1987; Englert, Culatta, & Horn, 1987). Therefore, in addition to developing computation skills, students will need specialized instruction in approaching and solving word problems.

Such factors as syntactical complexity, amount of extraneous information, sequence, and number of ideas presented can affect students' ability to solve word problems (Bos & Vaughn, 1988; Harris & Sipay, 1985). Teachers can foster their students' abilities by simplifying the syntax used (O'Mara, 1981), deleting extraneous information (Cohen & Stover, 1981), limiting the number of ideas presented, and reordering the presentation of information so that it is consistent with the order students should follow in solving the problem (O'Mara, 1981).

Students who are learning English may fail to understand mathematical language, which can hinder their ability to perform mathematical problem solving tasks, even when they understand the process (Wong-Fillmore, 1986). Teachers can facilitate the word problem–solving skills of such students by encouraging them to work in groups and seek assistance from others to define unknown words, by adding additional information to facilitate their understanding of the problem, and by teaching them to draw pictures to depict information presented in the problem (Fradd, 1987; Leon, 1991).

The problem-solving skills of students, particularly those who are learning English, can be enhanced by incorporating writing tasks into mathematics instruction (Davison & Pearce, 1992). Students can maintain a math journal that contains reactions to and notes on mathematics activities and instruction. Students also can write their story problems, write letters to others outlining a mathematical solution, rule, or concept, and write a mathematical project

IDEAS FOR IMPLEMENTATION

Teachers can facilitate the development of word problem–solving skills by enacting the following suggestions:

- Use field trips, films, and presentations from others to provide students with experiences in a variety of situations.
- Use word problems that interest students and that relate to their cultures and experiences.
- Employ manipulatives and drawings to explain and clarify problems.
- Present word problems orally or on audiocassettes.
- De-emphasize computations and emphasize problem solving by having students write or state mathematical sentences without computing answers to them, and by substituting easier, smaller numbers to minimize the complexity of the calculations.
- Have students act out word problems.
- Encourage students to estimate answers.
- Discuss solutions to word problems.
- Write number cues above specific parts of word problems to alert students to the steps they should follow.
- Ask students to paraphrase problems in their own words.
- Teach students to think about the ideas presented in word problems.
- Allow students to use calculators to assist in computations.
- Have students identify needed and extraneous information by presenting them with problems that have too little or too much information, respectively.
- Ask students to compose problems to be solved by their classmates.
- Supplement textbook problems with teacher-made problems.
- Offer numerous opportunities for practice.

Source: Leon (1991); National Council of Teachers of Mathematics (1980).

that requires students to collect data, compute results, develop graphs and other pictorials, and share conclusions (Davison & Pearce, 1992).

In addition to teacher assistance, students should receive training in identifying the critical elements of word problems, eliminating irrelevant details, and sequencing information in the order it will be needed. These skills can be developed by teaching students to underline the question and circle the given parts of the problem, by providing practice items where students restate the specifics of the problem in their own words, and by having students act out the problem (Enright, 1987a).

Learning Strategies

Several learning strategies have been developed to provide students with a step-by-step approach to solving word problems (Enright & Beattie, 1989; Fleischner, Nuzum, & Marzola, 1987; Montague & Bos, 1986). In general, the steps in these strategies include the following:

Step 1: Read the problem. Initially, read the problem to determine the question and to find unknown words and clue words. Clue words are those words that indicate the correct operation to be used. For example, the words *altogether, both, together, in all, and, plus,* and *sum* suggest that the problem involves addition; words like *left, lost, spent,* and *remain* indicate that the correct operation is subtraction (Mastropieri & Scruggs, 1987; Mercer & Mercer, 1985). When students encounter unknown words, they should ask the teacher to pronounce and define them.

Step 2: Reread the problem. Read the problem a second time so that the students can identify and paraphrase relevant information, which they should highlight by underlining, while deleting extraneous information and irrelevant facts. Focus their attention on determining what mathematical process and unit they should use to express the answer.

Step 3: Visualize the problem. Students visualize the problem and draw a representation of the information given.

Step 4: Make a plan and write the problem. Students hypothesize and write the steps in solving the problem. If there is more than one step, they write each step in order with the appropriate sign.

Step 5: Estimate the answer. Before solving the problem, students estimate the answer. The estimate provides a framework for determining the reasonableness of their response.

Step 6: Solve the problem. Students solve the problem written in step 4 by calculating each step in the process, giving attention to the correctness of the calculations and the unit used to express the answer.

Step 7: Check the answer. Students check their work and compare their answer to their estimate. They examine each step in terms of necessity, order, operation selected, and correctness of calculations.

Choate (1990) and Karrison and Carroll (1991) offer guidelines for teaching students the steps necessary for solving word problems, including studying the problem, devising checklists, identifying clues and key words, and illustrating problems.

Calculators

Calculators can help mainstreamed students develop their math skills by giving them the ability to learn, retrieve, and check computation facts as well as by promoting independence and speed in solving word problems (National Council of Teachers of Mathematics, 1976). Horton, Lovitt, and White (1992) found that when students with disabilities used calculators their performance was equivalent with their regular education peers. Calculators also can help students focus on the problem-solving components of tasks (Cawley, Baker-Kroczynski, & Urban, 1992) and can improve both students' scores on tests and their attitudes toward math (Hembree, 1986).

Horton, Lovitt, and White (1992) offer guidelines for teaching students to use calculators.

Calculators are most useful when students understand basic math operations, so teachers should ensure that students have this understanding before introducing them. Before using the calculator as an alternative to memorizing basic math facts, teachers should provide students with the opportunity to learn these facts over a period of time (Mastropieri & Scruggs, 1987). Once the students are ready, teachers should train them to use calculators (Garnett & Fleischner, 1987). Some students who have difficulty computing with calculators, such as students who reverse numbers, may benefit from use of a "talking calculator," which states the names of the numerals entered and computed (Garnett & Fleischner, 1987). The *Speech Plus Calculator* developed by Telesensory Systems has a 24-word vocabulary that can help students perform addition, subtraction, multiplication, division, square roots, and percentages by stating the function or name of each key as it is pressed.

Calculators can help students focus on the problem-solving components of tasks.

Cognitively Guided Instruction

Students' problem-solving skills can be facilitated through use of *Cognitively Guided Instruction* (*CGI*) (Peterson, Fennema, & Carpenter, 1991). The major elements of the CGI approach are as follows:

Focus on problem solving. Teachers expose students to a variety of problem-solving situations relevant to the students' lives.

An expansive view of children's mathematical knowledge. Teachers believe that their students have mathematical knowledge and they continually assess students' mathematical knowledge.

Encourage and recognize multiple solution strategies for problem solving. Teachers encourage students to use a variety of strategies to solve problems.

Reasoning-Based Arithmetic Program

Resnick, Bill, Lesgold, and Leer (1991) suggest that teachers use a *reasoning-based arithmetic program* to teach students problem solving and computation skills. Their program is based on the following six guidelines.

1: Develop students' trust in their own knowledge. Teachers create a learning environment that explores multiple strategies for solving problems, encourages students to create their own problem-solving strategies, and asks students to explain and justify their strategies in their own words.

2: *Draw students' informal knowledge, developed outside school, into the classroom.* Teachers use events, experiences, and cultural traditions of all students as the basis for understanding and solving problems (Richards, 1991).
3: *Use formal notations as a public record of discussions and conclusions.* Teachers link students' comments and strategies to standard mathematical notation.
4: *Introduce key mathematical structures as quickly as possible.* Teachers introduce students to mathematical structures and build on the development of these skills.
5: *Encourage everyday problem finding.* Teachers encourage students to practice their problem-solving skills in a variety of environments and situations that extend outside the school building.
6: *Talk about mathematics, don't just do arithmetic.* Teachers encourage students to talk about mathematics in large and small groups. Strategies for solving problems are discussed and shared with the whole group.

Mathematics Remedial Programs

Several remedial math programs are available to help mainstreamed students. These remedial programs can be used to supplement the mathematics series that the school district is using. Examples of remedial math programs include Project Math (Cawley, Fitzmaurice, Sedlak, & Althaus, 1976), Computational Arithmetic Program (Smith & Lovitt, 1982), Milliken Wordmath (Coffland & Baldwin, 1985), Corrective Mathematics Program (Engelmann & Carnine, 1982), Distar Arithmetic (Engelmann & Carnine, 1975, 1976), Enright S.O.L.V.E.: Action Problem Solving (Enright, 1987b), Developing Key Concepts for Solving Word Problems (Panchyshyn & Monroe, 1986) and Problem Solving Experiences in Mathematics (Charles, 1984).

SCIENCE AND SOCIAL STUDIES

Mr. Tejada, a social studies teacher, usually collects and grades students' notebooks before all unit tests. He notices that his students are handing in disorganized notebooks that lack many pieces of information he feels are important. As a result, many students are having difficulty with the class and doing poorly on tests.

To help his students retain information, Mr. Tejada decides to use a semantic web. After presenting material to the class, Mr. Tejada helps students review and organize it by drawing a picture outlining the main points and their interrelationships. For example, after discussing the roles of the three branches of government, Mr. Tejada and his students create a treelike semantic web (see Figure 9.4). To further reinforce the concept of checks and balances, Mr. Tejada draws a picture of a seesaw balanced by an equal number of checkmarks on both sides.

Prior to giving his students the unit test, Mr. Tejada collects students' notebooks and is pleased to see that they have copied the webs and pictorials. He also is pleased when his students' exam grades improve.

While the specific content in each area is different, science and social studies share several teaching methods. Both areas use an inquiry approach to teaching. Teachers of both science and social studies rely on lectures and textbooks to present material to students. Because mainstreamed students may experience some difficulty in acquiring information through lectures and textbooks, teachers can adapt these learning formats for mainstreamed students via some key strategies.

Key Word Method

An effective strategy for teaching science and social studies vocabulary is the *key word* method (Fulk, Mastropieri, & Scruggs, 1991; Scruggs & Mastropieri, 1992). The key word method is a mnemonic device that promotes memory of the meanings of new vocabulary words by associating the new word with a word that sounds similar and an illustration that is easy to remember. Mastropieri (1988) outlines the steps in the key word method:

FIGURE 9.4
Semantic web of the three branches of government.

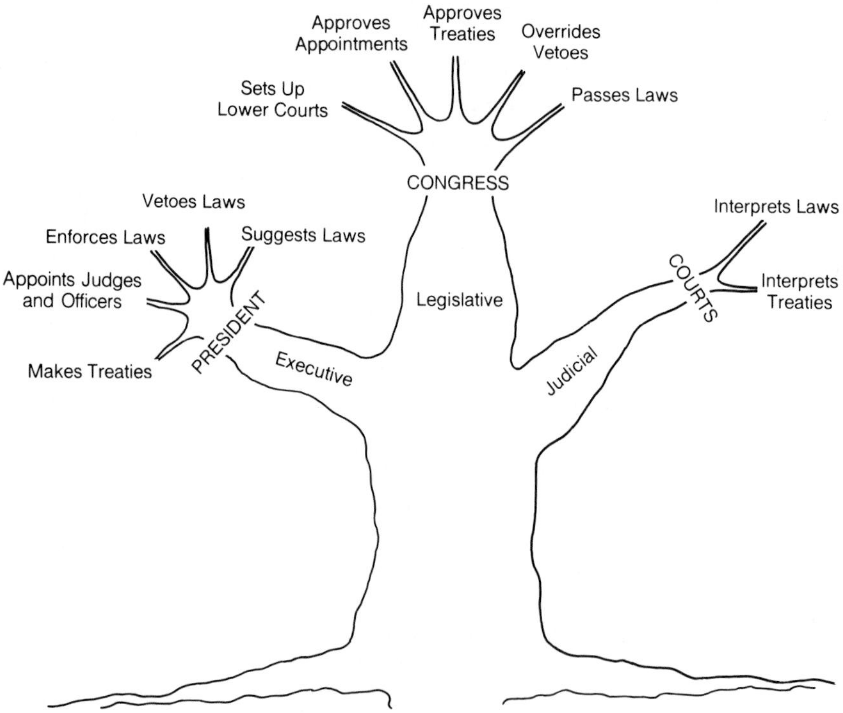

1. *Recoding.* The new vocabulary word is recoded into a key word that sounds similar and is familiar to the student. The key word should be one that students can easily picture. For example, the key word for the word part *Sauro* might be a *saw.*
2. *Relating.* An *interactive illustration*—a mental picture or drawing of the key word interacting with the definition of the vocabulary word—is created. A sentence describing the interaction also is formulated. For example, the definition of *Sauro* and the key word *saw* can be depicted using the sentence *A lizard is sawing.*
3. *Retrieving.* The definition is retrieved by students upon hearing the new vocabulary word by thinking of the key word, creating the interactive illustration and/or its corresponding sentence, and stating the definition.

Definitions of key science and social studies terminology also can be taught by providing students with a list of definitions and asking them to write the correct word, giving students the word and having them write the definition, or matching the word with its definition from lists containing both (Lovitt, Rudsit, Jenkins, Pious, & Bendetti, 1985).

Advance and Post Organizers

Teachers can enhance students' ability to gain information from lectures and textbooks by using *advance* and *post organizers,* which are written or oral statements and illustrations that offer students a framework for determining and understanding the essential information in a learning activity (Darch & Gersten, 1986; Lenz, 1983). Advance organizers can be very effective, and teachers should encourage students to use them (Lenz, Alley, & Schmumaker, 1987). For example, when assigning a reading selection in a science textbook, the teacher could focus students' reading via an advance organizer such as *Read pages 65–68 on mirrors, and find out how a mirror works. Pay careful attention to such terms as plane mirror, virtual image, parabolic mirror, principal axis, principal focus and focal length.* Similarly, a class-developed outline that summarizes the main points of a presentation on the geography of California could serve as a post organizer. In addition to social studies and science, advance and post organizers can be used to facilitate instruction in all content areas. Several types of advance and post organizers are described below.

Structured Overviews

An advance organizer that teachers can use to present science and social studies content is a *structured overview,* also called a *graphic organizer,* which identifies and presents key terms before students encounter them in class lectures and textbooks (Vaca, Vaca, & Gove, 1987). A structured overview is a visual–spatial illustration of the key terms that comprise concepts and their interrelationships. Barron, cited in Vaca et al. (1987) and Allen, Wilson, Cefalo, and Larson (1990) have developed models for constructing structured overviews for students, which include the following procedures:

1. Analyze the curriculum area or textbook to identify key concepts and terms.
2. Arrange the concepts and terms based on their interrelationships.
3. Delete information you want students to contribute.
4. Include additional terms that are important for students to know.
5. Add graphics to motivate students and promote mastery of the information presented.
6. Assess the overview for completeness and organization.
7. Prepare three versions of the graphic organizer: a completed version, a semicompleted version, and a blank version. Use the blank version with students who write quickly. Use the semicompleted version with students who have some difficulty copying and organizing information. Use the completed version with students who have significant difficulties copying and organizing information.
8. Introduce the overview to the students.
9. Include additional information relevant to the overview.

Concept Teaching Routines

Many science and social studies concepts can be taught to students using a *concept teaching routine,* which Bulgren, Schumaker, and Deshler (1988) found improved performance on teacher-made tests, tests of concept acquisition and in note taking when used to teach new concepts. In the concept teaching routine, teachers present new concepts to students through use of a concept diagram that presents the relevant characteristics of the concept. A sample concept diagram is presented in Figure 9.5. Teachers use the concept teaching routine to introduce students to the concept diagram by offering an advance organizer; soliciting from students a list of key words related to the concept, which are recorded on the board; explaining the symbols in the diagram; stating the name of the concept; giving the definition of the concept; discussing the "always", "sometimes", and "never" characteristics of the concept; reviewing an example and then a nonexample of the concept; relating the examples and nonexamples to each of the characteristics; examining examples and nonexamples to determine if they are members of the concept subset; and presenting a post organizer. Each step in the process is recorded by completing a blank concept diagram that has been presented on the blackboard or an overhead transparency. The concept diagram also can be used by students and teachers to review for tests.

Anticipation Guides

Teachers also can orient students to new science and social studies content by using *anticipation guides,* which introduce students to content by having them respond to several oral or written statements or questions concerning the new material (Vaca et al., 1987). For example, an anticipation guide might include a series of true/false statements that the students answer and discuss prior to reading a chapter in the textbook (see Figure 9.6). Vaca et al. (1987) outline the steps in constructing anticipation guides:

FIGURE 9.5
Sample concept diagram

Concept Name: democracy

Definitions: A democracy is a form of government in which the people hold the ruling power, citizens are equal, the individual is valued, and compromise is necessary.

Characteristics Present in the Concept:

Always	Sometimes	Never
form of government	direct representation	king rules
people hold power	indirect representation	dictator rules
individual is valued		
citizens equal		
compromise necessary		

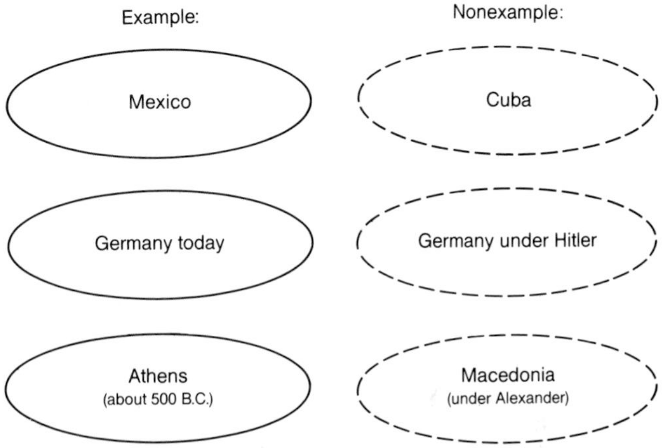

Source: J. Bulgren, J. B. Schumaker, and D. Deshler, *Learning Disability Quarterly, vol. 11* (Overland Park, KS: Council for Learning Disabilities, 1988). Reprinted by permission.

1. Analyze the reading selection and determine the main points.
2. Convert main points into short, declarative, concrete statements that students can understand.
3. Present statements to students in a way that elicits anticipation and predication.
4. Have students discuss their predictions and responses to the statements.
5. Discuss the students' reading of the text selection; compare and evaluate their responses with the information presented in the text.

Semantic Webs

Whereas a structured overview presents critical concepts and terminology before a class lecture or reading a textbook selection, teachers can use semantic webs to foster understanding and retention of information after it has been read or presented (Vaca et al., 1987). *Semantic webs,* like structured overviews, provide a visual depiction of important points as well as the relationships between

FIGURE 9.6
Anticipation guide on energy resources

Working as a group, read the statements and place a *T* next to those that are true and an *F* next to those that are false. Be prepared to explain the reasons for your rating a statement as true or false.

_______ Ninety-five percent of the energy needs of the United States are provided by fossil fuels.
_______ Spacecraft and many homes use solar energy.
_______ Hydroelectric power has no negative effects on the environment.
_______ Fossil fuels produce more energy per gram than nonfossil fuels.
_______ Before the radiation decays, radioactive wastes must be stored for a thousand years.

Wandel, Kennedy, and Kretschmer (1988) delineate the various types of semantic webs teachers can use with their students.

these points, and can be developed by the class (Scanlon, Duran, Reyes, & Gallego, 1992). Semantic webs can be used to introduce, review, and clarify new and previously learned material (Wandel, Kennedy, & Kretschmer, 1988). A semantic web includes a key word or phrase that relates to the main point of the content, which serves as the focal point of the web; web strands, which are subordinate ideas that relate to the key word; strand supports, which include details and information relating each web strand; and strand ties, which establish the interrelationships between different strands (Freedman & Reynolds, 1980). Semantic webs also may take other shapes (see Figure 9.4).

Scanlon et al. (1992) outlined the steps teachers can follow to create a student semantic web:

Step 1: Conduct a content analysis. Teachers analyze the material and determine the relationships between the concepts presented.

Step 2: Lead students in brainstorming. Teachers write a key word or phrase on the blackboard, discuss its meaning, and ask students to brainstorm related concepts.

Step 3: Allow students to develop a clue list. Students survey their text or other resources to identify related ideas and concepts.

Step 4: Develop the web. Students and teachers examine the relationships between ideas discussed during brainstorming, and those identified in clue lists. A semantic web graphically depicting these relationships is developed by the class.

Step 5: Read and revise the web. Students and the teacher read the web and modify it as needed.

Step 6: Review the web. Students review the web, and add new material based on texts and classroom discussions.

Think About It

Develop a structured overview, concept teaching routine, anticipation guide, or semantic web for the content presented in this chapter.

Textbooks

Much of the content in science and social studies is presented through textbooks; therefore, teachers should exercise caution in selecting textbooks. Teachers should avoid using textbooks that employ vague and indirect referents, use concepts that are unknown to the reader, fail to establish relationships between content and within chapters, and include irrelevant information (Harris & Sipay, 1985). Armbruster and Anderson (1988) suggest guidelines for choosing science and social studies textbooks for mainstreamed students in terms of structure, coherence and audience appropriateness:

1. Does the textbook offer informative headings and subheadings?
2. Does the textbook provide signals to highlight main points and key vocabulary (use of marginal notations, graphic aids, pointer words and phrases)?
3. Does the textbook present information in an organized fashion (use of preview or introductory statements, topic sentences, summary statements, lists, enumeration words)?
4. Does the textbook offer transitions that help the reader adjust to changes in topics?
5. Are the accompanying graphic aids easy to read and interpret?
6. Are chronological sequences or events presented in order of occurrence?

It is desirable for science and social studies textbooks to have illustrations. Illustrations that depict content can provide a visual framework for understanding the material and can supplement written presentations. Illustrations are most appropriate for presenting spatial information. Therefore, science and social studies teachers can facilitate the performance of mainstreamed students by selecting textbooks that have numerous illustrations and pictures (Levin, 1981). However, it is also important that illustrations be alluded to and explained in writing in the textbook.

Textbooks also should relate to students' background knowledge (Ruiz, 1989). Franklin and Mickel (in press) and Sadker (1981) examined textbooks and found that many did not address or include the accomplishments or perspectives of individuals from diverse cultural and linguistic backgrounds. Sadker and Sadker (1978) and Shapiro, Kramer, and Hunerberg (1981) noted that many textbooks and instructional materials portrayed other cultures and female students as being invisible, engaged in stereotyping, offered singular interpretations of issues and interpretations, avoided important issues, and presented information about other groups in isolation. Because of the bias in many textbooks, many teachers de-emphasize their use by using hands-on, activity based instructional approaches (Scruggs & Mastropieri, 1992).

Study Guides

Teachers can prepare *study guides* to help students determine critical points and provide activities to aid students in mastering them (Lovitt et al., 1985). Study guides assist students in gaining information from textbooks and lec-

Horton and Lovitt, and Bergerud and Lovitt (both cited in Bergerud, Lovitt, & Horton, 1988) reported that use of study guides led to a significant improvement in the social studies and science performance of mainstreamed students.

tures, and offer students the opportunity to practice and rehearse material (Allen, Wilson, Cefalo, & Larson, 1990).

While the components of study guides vary, they often include objectives, text references, a chapter summary, an outline, study questions, activities, definitions of key terminology, and student evaluation probes (Pauk, 1984). Study guides also can take the form of a *framed outline,* an ordered list of the chapter's main points with key words blanked out. The students fill in the blanks while reading the selection or listening to a lecture in class (Lovitt et al., 1985).

Adapted Textbooks

Many mainstreamed students may have difficulty with reading on-grade science and social studies textbooks (Harris & Sipay, 1985; Johnson & Vardian, 1973). For these students, it may be appropriate to use *adapted textbooks,* which present content that matches the on-grade textbook, but at a lower readability level. For example, Globe's *Pathway to Science* provides junior and senior high chemistry, physics, and biology content to students reading at the fifth- to sixth-grade level. Similarly, Macmillan has adapted their elementary-level social studies textbooks for lower-level readers and created a text called *The Reading Range Plus.* Other science and social studies adapted textbooks include *Science For You* (Steck-Vaughn), *Wonders of Science* (Steck-Vaughn), *American Adventures World History* (Scholastic), *America's Story* (Steck-Vaughn) and *American History* (Follet). Teachers can find

IDEAS FOR IMPLEMENTATION

In devising study guides, teachers should do the following:

1. Create separate study guides for each chapter and unit of content.
2. Review and note the key words, and the main points and concepts of the reading selection.
3. Delete nonessential material.
4. Adjust the readability of the text to each student's needs.
5. Write brief sentences addressing the critical components of the content with a few words missing or state main points as questions.
6. Ensure that the order of the sentences or questions is consistent with the order of the information in the textbook.
7. Present text in shorter lines and narrower columns.
8. Employ pictorial elements to supplement, illustrate, and highlight text.
9. Provide enough space for students to write their answers.
10. Distribute study guides to students and provide enough time for students to complete them.
11. Provide students with cues such as page references to indicate the location of the answer in a textbook.
12. Review answers and offer feedback to students on their performance.

Source: Allen, Wilson, Cefalo, & Larson (1990); Chiappetta, Budd, & Russo (1990).

appropriate adaptive textbooks that correspond to their on-grade textbooks by contacting a representative of their book company.

Parallel Alternative Curriculum

In addition to adapted textbooks, *Parallel Alternative Curriculum* (*PAC*) materials have been developed for mainstreamed students (Mercer & Mercer, 1985). PAC materials are designed to supplement the textbook by providing lower-achieving students with alternative ways to master critical information from content areas. For example, the Livonia (MI) Public Schools District has developed a PAC called *Project PASS* (*Packets Assuring Student Success*) (Mercer & Mercer, 1985) to offer assistance to mainstreamed students taking courses in U.S. history and government. Adapted materials, such as vocabulary lists, glossaries, learning activities, content outlines, and pre- and posttests at a third- to fifth-grade reading level were developed. Similarly, *Project IMPRESS* of the Tallahassee (FL) School District has developed PAC materials for U.S. history (grades eleven and twelve), social studies (grades eight and nine), science (grades seven and eight), basic English, economics, and human biology (Mercer & Mercer, 1986).

Specially designed science programs and science equipment also are available. Malone, Petrucchi, and Thier (1981) developed an activity-based science program for visually impaired students called *Science Activities for the Visually Impaired* (*SAVI*). SAVI takes a laboratory approach to teaching science that stresses observations, manipulation of materials, and the development of science language. Similarly, *Project MAVIS* (*Materials Adaptations for Visually Impaired Students*) has adapted social studies materials to assist in mainstreaming students with visual disabilities. These programs are designed for visually impaired students, but they also can be used with other mainstreamed students. De Avila (1988) has developed a collaborative learning, problem-solving math and science program for second language learners called *Finding Out/Descubrimineto.* Other adapted science curriculum materials include McGraw Hill's *Elementary Science Study Program,* Opportunities for Learning's *IDEAL Science Curriculum,* and Biological Sciences Curriculum Study's *Me in the Future* and Hubbard's *Me and My Environment,* and *Me Now* (Mercer & Mercer, 1985).

Additional information on teaching science to mainstreamed students can be obtained by contacting the Educational Resource Information Center/Science, Math, and Environmental Educational Information Clearing House (ERIC/SMEE).

Graphic Aids

Science and social studies teachers can help mainstreamed students master content by supplementing lectures and textbooks with graphic representations (Darch & Carnine, 1986; Lovitt, Stein, & Rudsit, 1985). Lovitt et al. (1985) reported an increase in mastery of science facts when these facts were taught using a combination of visual displays (charts and diagrams) and direct instruction. For example, comprehension of content presented in a lecture on the brain can be enhanced by displaying a picture of the brain. Similarly, mastery of information concerning comparisons and relationships between events, groups, periods, individuals, countries, and geographical regions in social studies can be fostered through use of charts, tables, graphs, and maps. A chart of important historical events within a period of time, for example, can help students understand the progression of events.

Media

Films, videos, and filmstrips can enhance science and social studies instruction. In addition to providing students with an opportunity to observe unique aspects of the content, these media can motivate students and stimulate their curiosity. To enhance their value as teaching tools, teachers should preview all materials before using them, and orient students to the mediated presentation by focusing their attention on the main points to be presented. After using mediated presentations, main points should be reviewed and discussed.

Field Trips

Class field trips also can make learning more meaningful and real for students. In particular, visits to historical and science museums as well as ecological and historical sites can allow students to experience what they hear and read about. Similarly, many museums offer students hands-on experiences that promote the learning of processes as well as factual information. Many museums are seeking to expand their links with schools by offering teacher training programs and traveling exhibits, and through the development of model curricula and teaching strategies that build on experiences at the museum. Many museums offer special tours, exhibits, and materials for school groups; teachers should contact their local museums to preview these services and arrange student visits.

Experiments

An integral part of science instruction is the use of labs in which students have hands-on learning experiences conducting experiments. Teachers can help mainstreamed students gain information from experiments by demonstrating important aspects of the experiment, pairing students with peers, providing students with a checklist of steps to follow when performing the experiment, monitoring student progress, and having students maintain a log of lab experiences.

Writing Research Papers

Social studies and science teachers often have students write research papers to assess mastery of content and to evaluate student organizational and writing skills. In planning and writing their papers, students should follow several guidelines (Pauk, 1984; Yaggy, 1969), as described here.

Selecting a Topic

The initial step in writing a paper is to choose a topic (Yaggy, 1969). Students should choose a topic that interests them and that relates to the assignment. Before selecting a topic, students also should consider whether they have the capabilities to comprehend it. If undecided, students should try to select a topic that relates to an interest or a hobby. Teacher consultation can help students generate ideas for topics. After choosing a topic, students should try to establish the focus of the paper by narrowing the topic subject. For example, a paper on the general topic of the brain could be narrowed to focus on the left-brain, right-brain theory.

Gaining and Organizing Information

Information on the topic will be available in several resources. The school librarian can help identify and obtain a wide range of these. As students read the material, they should record relevant points and facts on note cards (Yaggy, 1969). Note cards facilitate easy retrieval of information and sources for later use. In preparing notecards, Pauk (1984) recommends that students use a three-by-five inch card; write on only one side of the card; use a separate card for each topic; list the reference at the top of the card and the page number in parentheses; record concise notes in their own words; write neatly; limit the number of direct quotations; employ a system to indicate direct quotes, paraphrased statements, and original notes.*

Outlining the Paper

Notecards also can help students organize their papers into a skeletal outline (Yaggy, 1969). Students should review their notes to determine the focus of the paper as well as the main points and corresponding supporting points. Both main and supporting points should then be organized in an outline that provides a framework for the content and sequence of the paper (Pauk, 1984).

Writing the Paper

Starting with the introductory statement, students should prepare a draft by following their outline sequence. In writing the paper, students should do the following:

- Present each point of the outline in a clear, direct manner.
- Elaborate on and support each point with quotes, statistics, facts, and examples.
- Use transitions to connect related main points.
- Avoid extraneous information (Pauk, 1984).

Once the draft is complete, it is desirable that students wait at least a day before revising and editing their work (Pauk, 1984). In addition to modifying the content of the paper, students should examine it closely for grammar, word usage, spelling, references, and organization. When revision is completed, students should prepare the final paper according to the specifications outlined by the teacher.

---

*Many good general research textbooks are available. One that has proven especially useful and accessible to students is Paul D. Leedy's *Practical Research: Planning and Design,* 5th ed (New York: Macmillan, 1993).

TRANSFORMING THE CURRICULUM

Educators should work toward making the total curriculum meaningful for all students. Means and Knapp (1991) suggest that educators should revise their curricula to focus on complex, meaningful problems, embed instruction in basic skills in the context of global tasks, and make links with students' out-of-school experiences and culture. To implement these curricular reforms, they suggest that teachers model powerful thinking strategies, encourage students to use multiple approaches to solving problems, employ dialogue as an instructional tool, and use scaffolding to assist students in performing complex tasks.

Creating A Multicultural Curriculum

One means of making learning relevant for all students is by creating a *multicultural curriculum,* which acknowledges the voices, histories, experiences, and contributions of all ethnic and cultural groups. A multicultural curriculum has as its goals to help all students do the following:

- understand and view events from various cultural perspectives
- understand and function in their own and other cultures
- engage in personal actions to promote racial and ethnic harmony
- understand various cultural and ethnic alternatives
- develop their academic skills
- improve their ability to make reflective personal and public decisions and actions that contribute to changing society and culture (Banks, 1991a)

Whereas multicultural education is often seen as focusing on the needs of students of color and students who speak languages other than English, a multicultural curriculum should teach information about all groups, and should be directed at all students (Banks, 1991b). In addition to being fully inclusive, the multicultural curriculum should address all content areas. For example, a science lesson on plants can include a discussion of plants in other countries and in various regions of the United States. Similarly, the Native American counting technique that employs knots in a rope can be taught as part of a math lesson.

Banks (1991a) identified four hierarchical curricular models for incorporating multicultural information into existing areas, which he termed the contributions, additive, transformation, and social action approaches. In a *contributions* approach, various ethnic heroes, highlights, and holidays are added to the curriculum. Similarly, in the *additive* approach, content, concepts, and issues related to various cultures are added to the current curriculum. In both the contributions and additive approaches, no substantive changes are made in the organization or goals of the curriculum. As a result, students are often only exposed to a limited amount of information regarding diverse groups.

A *transformation* approach to multicultural curriculum reform seeks to modify the basic structure of the curriculum by encouraging students to examine and explore concepts, issues, problems, and concerns from a variety of cultural perspectives (Banks, 1991b). In this approach, students learn to think critically and reflect upon the viewpoints of a variety of cultural, gender, and social class groups. Banks and Sebesta (1982), for example, developed a lesson that allows students to examine and compare Christopher Columbus and the Arawak Indians from two different perspectives.

The *social action* approach is similar to the transformation approach. However, the social action approach encourages and teaches students to identify and take actions to solve social problems (Banks & Clegg, 1990). Teachers provide students with the opportunities to act consciously to challenge and change practices that they consider inequitable. For example, as part of a mathematics lesson, a class might analyze data concerning the number of female students in advanced mathematics and science classes. They can then propose and evaluate taking action to address identified problems.

Multicultural Instructional Materials

A multicultural curriculum should involve use of multicultural instructional materials. Students from culturally and linguistically diverse backgrounds as well as female and male students will perform better when they learn with inclusive textbooks and instructional materials that reflect their experiences and aspirations. Culturally relevant materials can increase learning for students by establishing a relationship between students' prior knowledge and the instructional materials they are using (McEachern, 1990). Therefore, materials such as textbooks, children's books, books containing rhymes, songs, and stories, media, poetry, toys, puppets, instruments, manipulatives, and art supplies that reflect cultural, ethnic, linguistic, and gender diversity should be used frequently and fully integrated into the curriculum (Foulks, 1991). When selecting multicultural instructional materials, educators should carefully evaluate them in terms of the following questions:

- To what extent do the materials include the various groups that comprise society?
- How are various groups portrayed in the materials?
- Are viewpoints, attitudes, reactions, experiences, and feelings of various cultural groups accurately presented?
- Do the materials present a diverse group of credible individuals to whom students can relate with respect to lifestyle, values, speech and language, and actions?
- Do the materials portray a variety of situations, conflicts, issues, and problems as experienced by a variety of groups?
- Are a wide range of perspectives on situations and issues offered?
- Does the material incorporate the history, heritage, and traditions of various groups?
- Are the experiences of and issues important to various groups presented in a realistic manner that allows students to recognize and understand their complexities?
- Are materials factually correct?

- Are the experiences, contributions, and content of various groups fully integrated into the materials and the curriculum?
- Are graphics accurate, inclusive, and ethnically sensitive?
- Do materials avoid stereotypes and generalizations about ethnic groups?
- Do fictional materials portray strong ethnic characters?
- Is the language of the materials inclusive and reflective of various groups? (Banks, 1991a; Franklin, 1992; Gollnick & Chinn, 1990).

Banks (1991b) offers examples of multicultural materials that teachers can use across a variety of content areas.

The National Seeking Educational Equity and Diversity Project on Inclusive Curriculum (SEED Project) offers educators assistance in developing inclusive and multicultural curriculums that address the issues of race, gender, class, and ethnicity. Information about services offered by the SEED Project can be obtained by writing to

The National SEED Project
Center for Research on Women
Wellesley College
Wellesley, MA 02181

Parallel Lessons

Educators also can make their curriculum multicultural by using *parallel lessons,* which allow students to learn about individuals and content from the mainstream culture and other cultures. For example, a lesson on Abraham Lincoln could be paired with a lesson on Benito Juarez, a liberator in his country (Gonzalez, 1992).

Think About It

Is your curriculum multicultural? What does or does not make it so?

Constructive Controversy

Multiple perspectives on various issues within the curriculum can be examined through use of *constructive controversy,* a cooperative learning technique (Mendez, 1991). In constructive controversy, students are placed in groups of four. Each group of four contains two dyads, with each dyad in the group examining a different perspective on a controversial topic. First, dyads obtain information and prepare arguments to support their perspectives. Each dyad then presents their case, while the other dyad listens, and asks questions to seek clarification. Following the presentations, each dyad challenges the other's case, and questions the facts and logical arguments presented. Dyads then switch roles, and prepare a case for the opposite side of the issue. Next, no longer working in separate dyads, the group agrees on the arguments that are valid from both sides of the issue, and prepares a report or presentation. If the group cannot achieve consensus on the report, a minority report or a report outlining agreements and disagreements is prepared.

Addressing the Needs of Female Students

Studies indicate that female students are frequently underrepresented in advanced math and science classes, and in careers in these fields (Campbell, 1986; Eccles, 1986). There is evidence that teachers engage in differential behaviors that encourage males and discourage females to achieve in math and science. While this underrepresentation is often attributed to math/science

IDEAS FOR IMPLEMENTATION

Teachers can promote the math and science skills of their female students by enacting the following suggestions:

- Provide all students with access to experiences, constructive toys, and materials that promote an interest in how things work, and in the physical world.
- Involve all students in establishing challenging and reasonable learning goals for math and science.
- Give all students opportunities to solve problems.
- Establish a learning environment that allows all students to be active and inquiring participants in science and math tasks.
- Encourage all students to have positive attitudes toward math and science.
- Establish high expectations in math and science for female as well as male students.
- Choose textbooks, instructional materials, and activities that present females in nonstereotypic science and math roles.
- Present word problems and problem-solving activities with female students depicted in active, nonstereotypic ways.
- Communicate to parents and other educators the importance of math and science for female students.
- Demonstrate to students the importance of math and science in their lives.
- Encourage female students to seek advance training and to pursue careers in math and science.
- Present real and pictorial female role models who have been successful in math and science.
- Refrain from using statements, materials, and pictorials that communicate to female students that they are not skilled in math and science.
- Model a positive attitude toward math and science.
- Assign class and school jobs to female students that require them to solve problems and use their math and science skills.
- Deemphasize speed and competition in teaching math and science.
- Emphasize the problem-solving aspects of math and science.
- Teach math and science through cooperative learning groups, science and math projects, games, puzzles, and real-life situations.
- Encourage female students to participate in math and science clubs.

Note: While these suggestions relate to the needs of female students, they are appropriate for all students, including students from culturally and linguistically diverse backgrounds.

Source: Mercer & Miller (1992); Shapiro, Kramer, & Hunerberg (1981).

anxiety, societal expectations and norms make it acceptable for females to ignore or question their abilities in science and math (Bell, 1991; Shapiro, Kramer, & Hunerberg, 1981). Teachers need to be aware of their behavior and of societal pressures so that they can change any such tendencies and create a classroom that encourages math and science competence in all students.

Social Responsibility

An important component of education is the development of *social responsibility,* an interest and concern in the well-being of others and the environment (Berman, 1990). Social responsibility encourages the development of a social consciousness, which helps students explore their hopes for the future and the impact of their actions on others. A curriculum to teach students social responsibility should help students develop an understanding of our social and ecological interdependence, a sense of what it means to be a part of a community, a sense of history, and basic social skills including communication, conflict management, and perspective taking (Berman, 1990). Social responsibility curricula also include opportunities for students to perform community service activities that benefit the lives of others. Social responsibility can be taught throughout the curriculum by examining real-word issues. For example, mathematics classes can explore the impact of math (such as statistics) on the political process, and science classes can examine the relationship between science, technology, and the world (Berman, 1990).

SUMMARY

This chapter presented guidelines and strategies for adapting instruction in mathematics, science, and social studies. Guidelines for transforming the curriculum also were discussed. The chapter

- presented guidelines, strategies, and approaches for teaching mathematics
- described various techniques and approaches for teaching social studies and science
- provided guidelines for creating a multicultural curriculum and using multicultural instructional materials

RECOMMENDED READINGS

Armbruster, B. B., & Anderson, T. H. (1988). On selecting "considerate" content area textbooks. *Remedial and Special Education, 9*(1), 47–52.

Banks, J. A. (1991). *Teaching strategies for ethnic studies* (5th ed.). Boston: Allyn & Bacon.

Bell, L. A. (1991). Changing our ideas about ourselves: Group consciousness raising with elementary school girls as a means to empowerment. In C. Sleeter (Ed.), *Empowerment through multicultural education* (pp. 229–249). Albany, NY.: SUNY Press.

Bergerud, D., Lovitt, T. C., & Horton, S. (1988). The effectiveness of textbook adaptations in life science for high school students with learning disabilities. *Journal of Learning Disabilities, 21,* 70–76.

Berman, S. (1990). Educating for social responsibility. *Educational Leadership, 48*(3), 75–80.

Cawley, J. F., Baker-Krocynski, S., & Urban, A. (1992). Seeking excellence in mathematics for students with mild disabilities. *Teaching Exceptional Children, 24*(2), 40–43.

Fradd, S. H. (1987). Accommodating the needs of limited English proficient students in regular classrooms. In S. H. Fradd & W. J. Tikunoff (Eds.), *Bilingual education and bilingual special education* (pp. 133–182). Boston: College-Hill.

Garnett, K. (1989). Math learning disabilities. *The Forum, 14*(4), 11–15.

Leedy, P. D. (1993). *Practical research: Planning and design* (5th ed.). New York: Macmillan.

Lenz, B. K., Alley, G. R., & Schumaker, J. B. (1987). Activating the inactive learner: Advance organizers in the secondary content classroom. *Learning Disability Quarterly, 10,* 53–67.

Peterson, S., Mercer, C., & O'Shea, L. (1988). Teaching learning disabled students place value using concrete to abstract sequence. *Learning Disabilities Research, 4*(1), 52–56.

10 Modifying Classroom Behavior and the Classroom Environment

JAIME

Just as Ms. McLeod is beginning to read to her students, Jaime approaches her with another book and asks Ms. McLeod if she would read it. Ms. McLeod tells Jaime that she cannot read it now and asks him to please put it away. Jaime goes to the back of the group, sits down, and begins to play with the book. Ms. McLeod again asks him to put the book away. Jaime stands up, walks halfway to his desk, and returns to the group, still carrying the book. Again, Ms. McLeod asks him to put it away, and he finally complies.

The class begins to discuss the book, with Ms. McLeod asking the students various questions. Jaime touches another student's sneakers and makes faces at Maria, who is sitting next to him. Jaime raises his hand to respond to a question but cannot remember what he wants to say when Ms. McLeod calls on him, and starts playing with another classmate.

As Ms. McLeod begins to give directions for independent seatwork, Jaime begins to open and close his velcro sneaker. Ms. McLeod asks him to stop and get to work. He responds by "walking" back to his desk on his knees. When he reaches his desk, he begins to search for a missing crayon, naming each one as he puts it back in the box.

What strategies could Ms. McLeod use to help Jaime modify his classroom behavior? After reading this chapter, you should be able to answer this as well as the following questions.

- Why is it important for educators to understand and interpret behavior and communication within a social/cultural context?
- What strategies can educators use to define and record student behavior?
- How can educators use an antecedents-behavior-consequences (ABC) analysis to plan appropriate strategies to modify classroom behavior?
- What individually oriented strategies can educators use to promote appropriate classroom behavior?
- What individually oriented strategies can educators use to decrease inappropriate classroom behavior?
- What group-oriented behavior management strategies can educators employ to promote appropriate and decrease disruptive behavior?
- How can educators use affective education strategies as part of their classroom management system?
- What classroom design strategies can educators employ to modify their classroom design to accommodate mainstreamed students?

To be successful in mainstreamed settings, mainstreamed students will need to demonstrate classroom behaviors that are consistent with teachers' demands and expectations and that promote socializations with peers (Kauffman, Lloyd, & McGee, 1989; Wheeler, Rubin, & Miller, 1990). Appropriate social and behavioral skills will allow mainstreamed students to fully integrate into the social fabric of the class, the school, and the community. Unfortunately, due to factors both internal and external to the classroom, mainstreamed students may exhibit behaviors that interfere with their learning and socialization and disrupt the learning environment (Alberto & Troutman, 1990). Therefore, teachers may need to employ a variety of strategies to increase appropriate and decrease inappropriate social and behavior skills.

SOCIAL SKILLS

Mr. Green is concerned about Bobby's ability to play with others. During recess, Bobby ignores all requests to walk with the class and runs down the hall to the playground. On the playground, he often provokes other students into fighting by teasing and cursing them. After being separated, he complains, while kicking the wall, that others started the fight. Later when he enters the classroom, he tells Mr. Green that he was very good during recess.

To address Bobby's difficulties in playing with others, Mr. Green uses a variety of activities from the ACCEPTS curriculum. After Bobby observes Mr. Green modeling how to ask others to play, engage in social greetings, and refrain from teasing, Bobby practices these behaviors with him. Next, Mr. Green and Bobby develop and practice a script relating to playing with others, and walk around the playground to identify cues that could prompt Bobby to play with others. Finally, they role play playing with others in the playground during recess. Two weeks later, Mr. Green notices that Bobby is playing with a few classmates and is getting into fewer fights.

Peer Relationships

Many students with disabilities may exhibit behaviors that result in social rejection from their peers who are not disabled (Sabornie & Kauffman, 1985).

Because a major goal of mainstreaming is the social integration of students, mainstreamed students need to be taught appropriate behaviors for establishing and maintaining positive peer relationships. Therefore, students needing social skill training should be taught to employ behaviors that result in peer acceptance (Hollinger, 1987) such as: using praise, social greetings, and affection to positively reinforce others (Masters & Furman, 1981); seeking to enter a group by using low-key techniques, such as standing around a group and waiting to be asked to play rather than commenting on the group's activities or members (Dodge, Schlundt, Schoken, & Delugach, 1983); initiating social interactions at appropriate times, such as playground time rather than during seatwork (Dodge, Coie, & Brakke, 1982); engaging in nonaggressive behaviors (French & Wass, 1985); and demonstrating prosocial behaviors (Hollinger, 1987).

Social Skills Training Programs

Commercial programs to teach social skills are available. One such program, designed to prepare students for the classroom behaviors and the peer relationships that they will encounter in mainstreamed settings, is *A Curriculum for Children's Effective Peer and Teacher Skills (ACCEPTS)* (Walker et al., 1983). ACCEPTS uses techniques such as direct instruction, modeling, and repeated practice to teach appropriate social skills. Field test results of ACCEPTS indicate that it has been effective in increasing classroom on-task behavior and social interactions on the playground. Figure 10.1 lists other instructional programs that can be used to teach social skills to mainstreamed students. Guidelines for evaluating these programs in terms of effectiveness, cost, target group and setting, ease of use, instructional approach, depth of content, and generalization and maintenance are available (Carter & Sugai, 1989; Sabornie & Beard, 1990).

FIGURE 10.1
List of social skills curricula

Camp, B. W., & Bash, M. A. (1985). *Think aloud.* Champaign, IL: Research Press.

Goldstein, A. P., Sprafkin, R. P., Gershaw, N. J., & Klein, P. (1980). *Skillstreaming the adolescent.* Champaign, IL: Research Press.

Hazel, J. S., Schumaker, J. B., Sherman, J. A., & Sheldon-Wildgen, J. (1982). *AS-SET: A social skills program for adolescents.* Champaign, IL: Research Press.

Jackson, J. F., Jackson, D. A., & Monroe, C. (1983). *Getting along with others: Teaching social effectiveness to children.* Champaign, IL: Research Press.

McGinnis, E., & Goldstein, A. P. (1984). *Skillstreaming the elementary school child: A guide for teaching prosocial skills.* Champaign, IL: Research Press.

Stephens, T. M. (1978). *Social skills in the classroom.* Columbus, OH: Cedar Press.

Waksman, S. A., & Messmer, C. L. (1985). *Assertive behavior: A program for teaching social skills to children and adolescents.* Portland, OR: Enrichment Press.

Walker, H. M., Todis, B., Holmes, D., & Horton, G. (1988). *The Walker social skills curriculum: The ACCESS program.* Austin, TX: PRO-Ed.

Zigmond, N., Kerr, M. M., Schaeffer, A. L., Farra, H. E., & Brown, G. M. (1986). *The school survival skills curriculum.* Pittsburgh: University of Pittsburgh.

Problem Solving

Students also may benefit from a problem-solving approach to learning appropriate social skills. Vaughn, McIntosh, and Spencer-Rowe (1991) developed a learning strategy, entitled *FAST,* to teach students interpersonal problem-solving skills. The FAST strategy involves the following:

> *F*reeze and Think: What is the problem? State the problem in behavioral terms.
>
> *A*lternatives: What are the possible behaviors I could do to solve the problem? List the alternatives.
>
> *S*olution: Which alternatives will solve the problem in the long run and are safe and fair? Select the best alternative.
>
> *T*ry: How can I implement the solution? If this does not solve the problem, return to the second step (Vaughn, et al., 1991, p. 85).

Crank (1990) has developed a list of questions that students can use to evaluate problem-solving solutions. Additional strategies for teaching social skills are discussed in Chapter 5.

BEHAVIORAL DEMANDS OF MAINSTREAMED SETTINGS

Several researchers have begun to identify the behavioral demands that contribute to success in regular education programs. Salend and Lutz (1984) surveyed elementary-level regular and special education teachers to identify

Wilkes, Bireley, and Schultz (1979) concluded that a student's behavior was considered more important than academic performance in determining a student's success in a mainstreaming setting.

the behavioral skills these teachers felt a mainstreamed student should possess to be successful in the regular classroom. The teachers surveyed rated 17 behavioral skills as critical for success in the mainstream. These skills, related to the social skill areas of interacting positively with others, obeying class rules, and displaying proper work habits, are presented in Figure 10.2. Furthermore, differences were found between intermediate (third grade through sixth grade) and primary (kindergarten through second grade) teachers, with the intermediate-level behavioral demands being more rigorous than the expectations in primary-level settings.

Salend and Salend (1986) identified the behavioral skills necessary for successful performance in secondary mainstreamed settings (see Figure 10.3). Although similarities arose between elementary- and secondary-level educators in their responses, the findings indicated that there is a more stringent attitude at the secondary level concerning classroom decorum and behavioral expectations. A discrepancy also was noted between the responses of the junior high school educators and the high school educators, with junior high school educators being more stringent than their high school counterparts.

Think About It

What behavioral skills are important for success in your classroom?

FIGURE 10.2
Elementary-level behavioral skills

Each competency is preceded by the competency stem, *To function effectively in elementary-level regular education settings, mainstreamed students should be able to*

1. follow directions.
2. ask for help when it's appropriate.
3. begin an assignment after the teacher gives it to the class.
4. demonstrate an adequate attention span.
5. obey class rules.
6. try to complete a task before giving up.
7. refrain from speaking when others are talking.
8. work well with others.
9. respect the feelings of others.
10. refrain from cursing and swearing.
11. avoid getting in fights with others.
12. play cooperatively with others.
13. respect the property of others.
14. share materials and property with others.
15. refrain from stealing others' property.
16. attend class regularly.
17. tell the truth.

Source: Adapted from S. J. Salend and J. G. Lutz, "Mainstreaming or Mainlining: A Competency-based Approach to Mainstreaming," *Journal of Learning Disabilities* 17 (1984): 27–29.

FIGURE 10.3
Secondary-level behavioral skills

Each competency is preceded by the competency stem, *To function effectively in secondary-level regular education settings, mainstreamed students should be able to*

1. attend class regularly.
2. refrain from stealing others' property.
3. obey class rules.
4. follow directions.
5. respect the property of others.
6. refrain from cutting classes.
7. avoid getting in fights with others.
8. respect adults.
9. tell the truth.
10. bring the necessary materials to class.
11. refrain from cheating on tests.
12. try to complete a task before giving up.
13. ask for help when it is appropriate.
14. complete homework.
15. refrain from cursing and swearing.
16. demonstrate an adequate attention span.
17. refrain from speaking when others are talking.
18. display proper health and hygiene habits.
19. communicate their needs.
20. remember more than one oral direction at a time.
21. exhibit appropriate behavior in large group settings.
22. begin an assignment after the teacher gives it to the class.
23. be aware of the effects of their behavior on others.
24. complete work on time.
25. refrain from boastful comments concerning inappropriate behaviors.
26. respect the feelings of others.
27. seek teacher permission before speaking.
28. avoid distractions.
29. work well with others.

Source: Adapted from S. J. Salend and S. M. Salend, "Competencies for Mainstreaming Secondary-level Learning Disabled Students," *Journal of Learning Disabilities* 19 (1986): 91–94.

Understanding Behavior and Communication Within a Social/Cultural Context

Schools in the United States and therefore the behavioral expectations of teachers are rooted in the Anglo-American culture, but educators need to assess the impact of cultural perspectives and language background on student behavior. Therefore, to effectively assess the behavioral skills of students from culturally and linguistically diverse backgrounds, educators must increase their understanding of behavior and communication within a social/cultural context, and expand their acceptance of individual differences so that it reflects a cross-cultural perspective that promotes bicultural and multicultural rather than monocultural competence.

Hoover and Collier (1985) noted that the behavior of students from nondominant backgrounds often is related to their cultural norms and customs. For example, a Mexican American student may appear passive in class, which may be interpreted by educators as evidence of the student's immaturity and disinterest in the class. However, the behavior may be an indication of the student's respect for the educator whom she or he may perceive as an authority figure (Ramirez & Price-Williams, 1974). This can be acceptable behavior in the Mexican American culture, where parents emphasize respect for authority (Ramirez & Casteneda, 1974).

Similarly, Boykin (1986) noted that African American students may engage in a variety of passive and active behaviors to cope with social institutions primarily based on mainstreamed perspectives. These behaviors may be misinterpreted by educators. For example, to mask their frustration and rage, and maintain a sense of integrity, some African American male students may exhibit a *cool pose,* a series of mannerisms, gestures, language, and movement that is often misinterpreted by educators as a sign of aggressive, intimidating, and irresponsible behavior (Goleman, 1992).

A variety of cultural factors that may affect classroom behavior are discussed in Chapter 2.

MEASURING CLASSROOM BEHAVIOR

Educators can measure students' mastery of behavioral skills in several ways. Data on the student's behavioral skills can be collected and shared with others through observing the student in his or her current classroom setting. Cartwright and Cartwright (1974) suggest several guidelines for conducting an observation:

- Select an individual to serve as the observer.
- Identify the behaviors that will be observed.
- Delineate the setting(s) of the observation(s).
- Determine when the observation will be conducted.
- Decide on a method of recording the observation.

Defining Behavior

First, educators should select the behavioral skill(s) that will be the focus of the observations. Next, these behavioral skills should be operationally defined in observable and measurable terms. For example, the behavioral skill of *demonstrates adequate attention* could be clearly defined as eyes on the teacher or an instructional object, whichever is appropriate for the learning environment.

Choosing a Recording System

After the behavior has been operationally defined, educators must select an appropriate recording strategy and should implement it during a day that is typical and representative. The recording system selected should relate to the nature of the behavior being observed. Examples of different recording systems are presented in Figure 10.4.

Event Recording

If the behavior to be observed has a discrete beginning and ending and occurs for brief time periods, event recording is an appropriate choice (Koorland, Mondla, & Vail, 1988). In *event recording,* the observer counts the number of behaviors that occurred during the observation period as shown in Figure 10.4(a). For example, a teacher could use event recording to count the number of times a student calls out during a thirty-minute teacher-directed activity. Data collected using event recording is displayed as either a frequency (number of times it occurred) or a rate (number of times it occurred per length of observation).

Teachers often use an inexpensive grocery, stitch, or golf counter to assist in event recording. If such a mechanical counter is not available, marks can be made on a pad, index card, chalkboard, or piece of paper taped to the

FIGURE 10.4
Examples of observational recording strategies

Date	Length of Sessions	Number of Events
9/11	30 minutes	𝍸
9/15	30 minutes	𝍸 𝍸 I
9/20	30 minutes	III

(a) Event Recording of Call-outs

Date	Occurence Number	Time Start	Time End	Total Duration
5/8	1	9:20	9:25	5 minutes
	2	9:27	9:30	3 minutes
5/9	1	10:01	10:03	2 minutes
	2	10:05	10:06	1 minute
	3	10:10	10:14	4 minutes

(b) Duration Recording of Out-of-seat Behavior

15 Sec	15 Sec	15 Sec	15 Sec
+	–	–	+
+	+	–	–
+	–	–	–
–	+	+	+
+	+	–	+

(c) Interval Recording of On-task Behavior

wrist. Some teachers use a transfer system where they place small objects (for example, poker chips, paper clips) in one pocket, and transfer an object to another pocket each time the behavior occurs. The number of objects transferred to the second pocket gives an accurate measure of the behavior.

Duration and Latency Recording

If time is an important factor of the observed behavior, an appropriate recording strategy would be either duration or latency recording. *Duration recording,* shown in Figure 10.4(b), involves the observer recording the length of time a behavior lasts. *Latency recording,* on the other hand, is used to determine the delay between receiving instructions and beginning a task. For example, to find out how much time a student spends out of seat during a twenty-five minute independent seatwork period, a teacher would use duration recording. However, to assess how long it took a student to begin an assignment after the directions were presented, the teacher would employ latency recording. Both recording systems can be presented as the total length of time or as an average (Alberto & Troutman, 1990). Duration recording data also can be summarized as a percentage of time in which the student engaged in the behavior by dividing the length of time the behavior occurs by the length of the observation period, and multiplying by 100.

Interval Recording or Time Sampling

Interval recording and time sampling are similar methods that can be used to record behaviors. When using *interval recording,* the observer divides the observation period into equal intervals and records whether the behavior occurred during each of the intervals, with a plus (+) indicating occurrence and a minus (−) indicating nonoccurrence of the behavior. In interval recording systems, the intervals usually do not exceed thirty seconds, while the intervals in *time sampling* are usually defined in terms of minutes (Alberto & Troutman, 1990). A + does not indicate how many times the behavior occurred in that interval, but only that the behavior did occur. Therefore, this system is scored as the percentage of intervals in which the behavior has occurred, rather than as a frequency.

The interval percentage is calculated by dividing the number of intervals in which the behavior occurred by the total number of intervals in the observation period, then multiplying by 100. For example, a teacher might use an interval recording system to measure on-task behavior. After defining the behavior, the teacher would divide the observation period into intervals and construct a corresponding interval score sheet as shown in Figure 10.4(c). The teacher would then record whether the student was on-task or not for each interval. The number of intervals in which the behavior occurred would be divided by the total number of intervals to determine the percentage of intervals in which the student was on-task.

There are three types of interval/time sampling recording systems: whole, partial, and momentary. In *whole interval recording,* the behavior must occur continuously during the entire interval for it to be scored as an occurrence. In *partial interval recording,* the observer records an occurrence of the behavior if the behavior was exhibited at least once during the interval. In *momentary interval recording,* the observer checks to see if the behavior is occurring only toward the end of the interval.

Anecdotal Records

An anecdotal record, also referred to as continuous recording, is often an appropriate method of reporting the results of the observation. An *anecdotal record* is a narrative of the events that took place during the observation. Wright (1967) offers several suggestions for writing narrative anecdotal reports:

- Describe the activities, design, individuals, and their relationships to the setting in which the observation was conducted.
- Report in observable terms all verbal and nonverbal behaviors of the targeted student as well as the responses of others to these behaviors.
- Avoid interpretations.
- Provide an indication of the sequence and duration of events.

A sample anecdotal record is presented in Figure 10.5. Alberto and Troutman (1990) suggest that educators analyze data collected in an anecdotal report by responding to the following questions:

1. What are the behaviors that can be described as inappropriate?
2. Is this behavior occurring frequently, or has a unique occurrence been identified?
3. Can reinforcement or punishment be identified?
4. Is there a pattern to these consequences?
5. Can antecedents to the behavior be identified?
6. Is there a pattern that can be identified for certain events or stimuli (antecedents) that consistently precede the behavior's occurrence? (p. 101)

Checklists and Rating Scales

Checklists and rating scales also can be used to assess a student's behavioral skills. Individuals familiar with the student can be asked to rate the student on

FIGURE 10.5
Sample anecdotal report

The observation of Jack took place on the school playground during a fifteen-minute recess period. The playground is made up of an open space area for group games and an area with typical playground equipment of swings, a jungle gym, and two slides. During the first five minutes of the observation, Jack played by himself on a swing with no interactions with his peers, who were also swinging or waiting for a turn. One of the waiting students asked Jack for a turn on the swing. Jack ignored the request, neither slowing down the swing, making eye contact, or verbally responding to the student. The teacher's aide then intervened, asking Jack to finish his ride so others could have a turn. Jack responded by jumping off the swing in mid-flight and loudly cursing at the aide. The aide then removed Jack from the playground.

each checklist or rating scale item. To ensure that the rating is accurate, several different individuals should rate the student in different settings.

One such rating scale that has been developed is the *SBS Inventory of Teacher Social Behavior Standards and Expectations (SBS Inventory)* (Walker & Rankin, 1983). The SBS Inventory has three sections that are designed to aid educators in determining the behavioral demands of the regular classroom setting. Part 1 asks teachers to rate as *critical, desirable,* or *unimportant* 56 prosocial behaviors of students. Similarly, in Part 2, teachers rate the acceptability of 51 inappropriate behaviors using the choices of *unacceptable, tolerated,* or *acceptable.* In Part 3, teachers determine which skills from Parts 1 and 2 are important for the student to master to be successful in the mainstreamed setting. Examples of items from Parts 1 and 2 of the SBS Inventory are presented in Figure 10.6.

Peer Referencing

Once the student's behavior has been recorded, it can be compared to the levels of the same behavior in the regular classroom through *peer referencing,* whereby data on the performance of students in the regular classroom is collected by recording the behavior of randomly selected students (Brulle, Barton, & Repp, 1984; Deno, 1985). These data then provide a normative baseline for assessing the student's behavior in relation to classroom peers.

Germann and Tindal (1985) provide a formula that educators can use to calculate the discrepancy between the behavioral rates of the mainstreamed students and their classroom peers.

Think About It

How would you operationally define, in observable and measurable terms, and what recording strategies would you use to assess out-of-seat, inattentive, aggressive, tardy, noisy, and disruptive behavior?

Antecedents-Behavior-Consequences (ABC) Analysis

Ms. Hogencamp is concerned about Arnold's out-of-seat behavior. After repeatedly reminding him to stay in his seat, she decides to perform an antecedents-behavior-consequences (ABC) analysis concerning Arnold's behavior. She observes Arnold and lists the events that happen before and after his out-of-seat behavior.

Antecedents	Behavior	Consequences
What happens before?	*Out-of-seat*	*What happens after?*
1. Location of the student's work area		1. Attention from peers and/or adults
2. Placement of peers' work areas		2. Makes friends, antagonizes enemies

3. Type and difficulty level of in-seat activity		3. Avoids unpleasant in-seat activity
4. Proximity of adults		4. Performs pleasant out-of-seat activity
5. Duration of in-seat activity		5. Releases physical energy after sitting for a period of time
6. Prior activity required sitting		
7. Auditory stimuli in the room		
8. Peer out-of-seat behavior		
9. Availability of other activities		

Ms. Hogencamp then examines her ABC analysis to identify strategies for modifying Arnold's out-of-seat behavior. These strategies include placing Arnold's desk near Ms. Hogencamp or her teacher's aide; adjusting the in-seat activity to Arnold's level; allowing Arnold to work in a peer tutoring group; limiting the distractions in the classroom; varying the activity so that Arnold is not required to sit for long periods of time; reprimanding peers that are out of their seats and praising seated peers; praising Arnold for in-seat behavior; circulating around the room to monitor students; and allowing students to perform a desired activity when the in-seat activity is completed.

While recording behavior, teachers also should attempt to perform an *antecedents-behavior-consequences (ABC) analysis,* which can assist a teacher in selecting an appropriate behavior management strategy. *Antecedents* refer to the events, stimuli, objects, actions, and activities that precede and trigger

FIGURE 10.6
Sample items from the SBS Inventory

SAMPLE ITEM FROM PART 1

	Critical	Desirable	Unimportant
Child is flexible and can adjust to different instructional situations.	( )	( )	( )

SAMPLE ITEM FROM PART 2

	Unacceptable	Tolerated	Acceptable
Child disturbs or disrupts the activities of others.	( )	( )	( )

the behavior. *Consequences* relate to the events, stimuli, objects, actions, and activities that follow and maintain the behavior. Questions to guide teachers in performing an ABC analysis are presented in Figure 10.7. The results of the ABC analysis can be used to plan appropriate intervention.

Think About It

Perform an ABC analysis on one of your behaviors such as studying or eating. How could you use the results of your ABC analysis to modify your behavior?

Rules

Rules should be shared with parents, administrators, other teachers, substitute teachers, and other professionals working with students (Curwin & Mendler, 1988).

An important aspect of behavior management is establishing, teaching, and enforcing classroom rules (Herr, 1988). Rules serve as antecedents for appropriate behavior by establishing the expectations for behavior in the classroom, and provide a structure to guide interactions in the classroom (Smith & Misra, 1992). Because it is desirable for students to be involved in developing classroom rules, teachers should solicit input from students concerning rules. Since most important classroom behaviors can be addressed using five to seven rules, teachers should limit the number of rules to those that relate to classroom needs and that help create an environment to facilitate academic and social growth.

FIGURE 10.7
ABC analysis questions

In analyzing each antecedent, consider the following:

1. Is it related to the content area or the task?
2. Is it related to the way the material is presented?
3. Is it related to the way the student responds?
4. Is it related to the physical design of the classroom (location of the students' seats, proximity of the teacher, seating arrangements, furniture, etc.)?
5. Is it related to the behavior of the teacher or the teacher's aide?
6. Is it related to the behavior of peers?
7. Is it related to the time of day?
8. Is it related to events outside the classroom (seeing other students in the halls, etc.)?
9. Is it related to the student's cultural perspective?
10. What other events happen before the behavior?

In analyzing the consequences, consider the following:

1. How do the teacher and the teacher's aide respond to the behavior?
2. How do the other students respond to the behavior?
3. What is the effect of the behavior on the classroom atmosphere?
4. What progress or lack of it is made on the activity or the assigned task?
5. How does the behavior impact on the student's cultural perspective?
6. What has served to encourage the behavior?
7. What has served to stop the behavior?

Once the areas that need to be addressed by the rules have been identified, teachers can follow several guidelines to make their rules meaningful to students (Heward, Dardig, & Rossett, 1979). Phrase rules so that they are concise, simple, and easily understood. Each rule should include a behavioral expectation that is defined in observable terms, and the consequences of following the rules should be explained. When exceptions to rules exist, identify the exceptions and discuss them in advance. Whenever possible, state rules in positive terms. For example, a rule for in-seat behavior can be stated as *Work at your desk* rather than *Don't get out of your seat.*

After teachers select and phrase rules, they should teach them to students. Teachers can help students learn the rules by verbally describing and physically modeling the observable behaviors that make up the rules, and by discussing the rationale and positive aspects of each (Everston, Emmer, Clements, Sanford, & Worsham, 1989). Teachers should initially review the rules frequently with the class, asking students periodically to recite them or practice a particular one. Displaying the rules on a neat, colorful sign in a prominent location in the room also can help students remember them. Some mainstreamed students and younger students may have difficulty reading, so pictorial representations of the rules are often beneficial. Additionally, teachers can foster an understanding of the rules and a commitment to following them by enforcing the rules immediately and consistently, and by reminding students of the rules when a class member has complied with them.

Think About It

What rules would you institute in your classrooms? Why would you select these rules?

Cues

Cues can serve as antecedents for appropriate classroom behavior. For example, color cues can indicate acceptable noise levels in the classroom. Red can alert students that the noise level is excessive, yellow can suggest that a moderate noise level is appropriate, and green can indicate that there are no restrictions on the noise level (D'Zamko & Hedges, 1985). Similarly, using verbal and nonverbal cues such as physical gestures to indicate group or individual response can establish routines and promote efficiency, or signal to students that their behavior is unacceptable and should be changed (Meier, 1992; Smith & Misra, 1992). When working with students from culturally and linguistically diverse backgrounds, teachers should use culturally appropriate cues (Hoover & Collier, 1989).

Scheduling

Proper scheduling also can function as an antecedent that teachers should consider in their classroom management plans. A regular schedule that contains ongoing classroom routines provides students with an understanding of the day's events. Since many mainstreamed students receive supplementary instruction and services from ancillary support personnel, regular classroom teachers should coordinate their schedules with other professionals. Additionally, since these students will miss work and assignments while outside the room, teachers should establish procedures for making up these assignments (Everston, Emmer, Clements, Sanford, & Worsham, 1989). Smith (1985), Meier (1992), and Murray (1991) offered the following guidelines for devising schedules:

- listing all periods dictated by the master schedule;
- considering the priorities in students' IEPs;
- involving students in planning the schedule for negotiable events;
- posting the schedule in a prominent location that is available to all students using a format that is consistent with the students' ages;
- reviewing the schedule periodically with students;
- beginning the school day with a lesson or activity that is motivating and interesting to students;
- planning activities so that less desirable activities are followed by activities students like to perform;
- alternating movement and discussion activities with passive and quiet activities;
- adjusting the length of scheduled activities to the needs of students;
- freeing up the teacher to work individually with students during whole class activities that require limited teacher supervision;
- refraining from changing the schedule;
- providing students with a variety of alternatives when they complete an assigned activity early;
- sharing schedules with parents and other professionals.

Additionally, educators can evaluate mainstreamed students' schedules in these terms:

IDEAS FOR IMPLEMENTATION

To determine if a rule is necessary, teachers should examine their rules in terms of the following:

1. Is the rule necessary to prevent harm to others or their property?
2. Does the rule promote the personal comfort of others?
3. Does the rule facilitate learning?
4. Does the rule encourage the development of friendships in the classroom?
5. Does the rule prevent disrespectful behavior directed at peers, the teacher, the teacher's aide, or others in school?
6. Is the rule logical and reasonable?
7. How will the rule affect the class?
8. Is the rule consistent with the schoolwide rules and procedures students are expected to follow?

Source: Safran and Safran (1985a).

1. Does the schedule allow time for meeting the students' IEP goals?
2. Is the length of time for each component appropriate for the students?
3. Does the sequence of events provide for a variety of learning experiences?
4. Does the sequence flow in a logical progression?
5. Do the components vary from one-to-one to group activities?
6. Are transitions between activities planned to minimize confusion?
7. Does the schedule provide a stable routine? (Lund & Bos, 1981, p. 121)

Making Transitions

Transitions from one period to the next and activities within a class period comprise approximately 15 percent of the school day (Rosenshine, 1980). These times can lead to disruptive behaviors that interfere with student learning (Jones & Jones, 1986). Teachers can minimize problems with transitions by incorporating several adaptations into the classroom routine. At the beginning of the school day or class period, teachers can post and discuss a schedule of events for that day in the class, paying particular attention to schedule modifications that deviate from the typical school day. Many mainstreamed students will be receiving the services of ancillary support personnel (speech and language therapists, guidance counselors, special educators, English as a second language teachers, bilingual educators) on different days of the week; these students should be alerted to the unique aspects of their schedules.

A particularly difficult part of transitions for students may be ending one activity and beginning another. Teachers can facilitate the students' ability to make this change by doing the following:

- establishing and teaching routines
- using a cue to signal students that they have five minutes left to complete their work
- reviewing at the end of an activity several motivating aspects of the next activity
- rewarding groups or individual students for making an orderly and smooth transition
- pairing students together to help each other finish an activity, clean up their work areas, and prepare for the next activity
- modeling appropriate behavior during transitional activities
- giving students lead time for transitions
- providing students with the opportunity to practice making transitions
- examining movement patterns and minimizing congestion in heavily used areas
- having materials for the subsequent lesson prepared in advance
- monitoring students during classroom transitions (Jones & Jones, 1986; Meier, 1992; Prater, 1992)

Giving students specific directions about how to move to the next activity can help them make the transition. For example, rather than telling students *Get ready for physical education class,* the teacher can provide them with specific directions, such as *Finish working on your assignment, put all your materials neatly in your desk or bookbag, check to see that you have your sneakers and gym uniform, and line up quietly.*

Transitional activities also can make transitions smoother (Jones & Jones, 1986). When students come from a less structured social activity like recess to a setting that requires quiet and attention, a transitional activity is important. For example, having students write in a journal one thing that was discussed in social studies class the day before can help prepare students for the day's lesson and facilitate the transition.

PROMOTING POSITIVE CLASSROOM BEHAVIOR

An important goal of a teacher's classroom management system is promoting positive classroom behavior. Teachers can use a variety of strategies to increase students' appropriate classroom behavior.

Positive Reinforcement

A widely used, highly effective method of maintaining and increasing compliance with rules is *positive reinforcement,* the contingent presentation of a stimulus after a behavior occurs that increases the rate of the behavior or the likelihood that the behavior will occur again. Stimuli and/or consequences that serve to increase the probability of the occurrence of a behavior are called *positive reinforcers.* For example, many teachers use praise as a positive reinforcer to increase a variety of classroom behaviors, such as raising hands to speak, staying in seat, and paying attention.

One form of positive reinforcement used by many classroom teachers is the *Premack Principle* (Premack, 1959). Teachers can apply the Premack Principle by making a desired activity available to students contingent on the completion of an undesired activity. For example, a student who works on an in-seat assignment for a period of time can earn an opportunity to work on the computer.

IDEAS FOR IMPLEMENTATION

When using positive reinforcement, teachers should do the following:

1. Make sure that reinforcers are delivered after the desired behavior occurs.
2. Be consistent in the delivery of reinforcement.
3. Deliver reinforcement immediately after the behavior occurs, especially when the behavior is being learned.
4. Gradually decrease the frequency and immediacy of the delivery of reinforcement.
5. Gradually increase the behavioral expectations that students must demonstrate to receive reinforcement.
6. Use reinforcers that are desired by the students.

Classroom Lottery

A positive reinforcement system that can motivate students to demonstrate appropriate behavior is the *classroom lottery,* where teachers acknowledge appropriate behavior of class members by writing a student's name on a lottery ticket and placing it in a jar located in full view of the class (George, 1975). At the end of the class or at various times during the day, the teacher or a designated student draws names from the jar, and those selected receive prizes. Students can earn several tickets in the lottery to increase the probability of winning the lottery. The lottery system can be modified by having the class earn a group reward when the number of tickets accumulated exceeds a pre-established number specified by the teacher.

Selecting Reinforcers

A key component in the success of positive reinforcement and other behavior management systems is the reinforcers that students receive. Teachers can use a variety of culturally relevant edible, tangible, activity, social, and group reinforcers.

Edible Reinforcers. Edible reinforcers are the least sophisticated of reinforcers because they are highly intrusive. Teachers should exercise caution in choosing this form of reinforcement as students can be easily satiated. However, edibles have the advantages of being highly desirable, available, and able to be dispensed in varying quantities.

Edible reinforcers include a pizza party, a fast food coupon, pretzels, potato chips, candy, and cookies. When possible, teachers should select more nutritious alternatives such as raisins, peanuts, popcorn, fruit, sugar-free gum, or cereal.

Many edible reinforcers have limited nutritional value and can have negative effects, so educators, parents, and health professionals should carefully evaluate them with respect to student health needs and allergic reactions.

Tangible Reinforcers. Tangible reinforcers, such as pins, stickers, posters, magazines, bumper stickers, stencils, bookcovers, t-shirt transfers, records, comic books, and books that reflect the current fads or heroes and heroines can be powerful reinforcers. Tangible reinforcers that are not directly related to current fads are also a good idea. These potential reinforcers include frisbees, mechanical pencils, magic markers, and bracelets. Additional tangible items can be identified by visiting a toy store, novelty shop, or the school store.

Activity Reinforcers. Activity reinforcers, which allow students to perform a desired task or activity, are highly motivating alternatives to tangible and edible reinforcers. One flexible activity reinforcer is free time, which can be varied according to individual preference to provide students with the opportunity to work alone, with a peer, or with the teacher. Free time also can be used by students to go to the library, play a favorite game, sit in a location of their choice in the room, make an arts project, or perform a supervised activity in the gymnasium.

Class jobs also can motivate students. Initially, teachers may assign class jobs—handing out and collecting papers, cleaning the classroom, making class announcements, taking attendance, running errands, and so on. As students demonstrate the skill to perform these jobs, they can be given jobs that require more responsibility, such as working in the main office, assisting the janitorial staff, running media, tutoring peers and younger students, and helping teachers grade papers.

Another activity that can be a reinforcing event is access to media and technology (Salend & Santora, 1985). The opportunity to listen to music on headphones, play an electronic keyboard, have extra time at the computer, watch a video on the VCR, or view a filmstrip can positively motivate students.

Reinforcement Surveys

Mr. Gordon is growing increasingly frustrated by Priscilla's frequent calling out in class. Having been taught positive reinforcement strategies at a recent inservice program, Mr. Gordon decides to use them to modify Priscilla's behavior. Mr. Gordon meets with Priscilla and they discuss her behavior and plan a positive reinforcement system to reward Priscilla for raising her hand in class. On the first two days of the program, Mr. Gordon notices a significant improvement in Priscilla's behavior, and rewards her by giving her stickers. Unfortunately, after several days Priscilla seems disinterested in the program and resorts to her old ways. Mr. Gordon decides to examine the program to see what caused it to break down. First, Mr. Gordon examines his own behavior, and determines that he has clearly defined the target behavior and has communicated it to Priscilla, and has been consistent in implementing the program. Next, Mr. Gordon examines other aspects of the program and concludes that he may be using the wrong reinforcer. He notices that when given the stickers, Priscilla quickly puts them away in her book.

Mr. Gordon decides to try the program with some new reinforcers. He and Priscilla meet again, but this time he asks her to complete a reinforcement survey. The survey includes the following completion items:

The things I like to do at school are______________________.
I am proudest in this class when I______________________.
When I have free time in class, I like to______________________.
The best reward the teacher could give me is______________________.
Something that I would work hard for is______________________.

Mr. Gordon is surprised by Priscilla's responses. Rather than wanting tangible items such as stickers, Priscilla states that she would prefer a class job, and extra time to spend with the teacher or two of her friends. Mr. Gordon decides to revise the system and tells Priscilla if she is successful at raising her hand in class, she may choose a reward from among a class job, free time with Mr. Gordon, free time with a friend, and the opportunity to work with a friend. Priscilla's hand raising increases and she seems to be a happier student. Mr. Gordon also is a happier teacher.

Many behavior management systems fail because teachers do not identify appropriate and effective reinforcers. One way to help ensure that reinforcers are motivating is by soliciting student preferences through a *reinforcement survey* (Raschke, 1981; Swanson & Reinert, 1979). While a variety of reinforcement surveys exist (Fox & Wise, 1981; Phillips, Fischer, & Singh, 1977), teachers can develop their own surveys to encompass the special characteristics of their students and classrooms.

Excellent examples of a variety of reinforcement surveys are available (Raschke, 1981).

Raschke (1981) identified three formats for reinforcement surveys: open ended, multiple choice, and rank order. The *open-ended* format asks students to identify reinforcers by completing statements concerning their preferences (*If I could choose the game we will play the next time we go to recess, it would be*____________.). The *multiple-choice* format allows students to select one or more choices from a list of potential reinforcers (*If I had 15 minutes of free time in class, I'd like to (a) work on the computer; (b) play a game with a friend; (c) listen to music on the headphones*). For the *rank order* format, students grade their preferences from strong to weak through a number system.

Teachers should consider several factors when developing reinforcement surveys. Items should be phrased using student language rather than professional jargon (*reward* rather than *reinforcer*) and should reflect a range of reinforcement. In addition, the availability (*Will I be able to provide the reinforcer at the appropriate times?*), practicality (*Is the reinforcer consistent with the class and school rules?*), cultural relevance (*Is the reinforcer consistent with the student's cultural background?*), and cost (*Will the reinforcer prove too costly to maintain?*) of reinforcers on the survey should be examined. Finally, since students may have reading and/or writing difficulties, teachers may need to read items for students as well as record their responses.

Contingency Contracts

Downing (1990) and Cooper, Heron, and Heward (1987) offer guidelines of planning and developing contingency contracts.

Students and teachers may formalize agreements concerning specific behavior and the exchange of reinforcers by a *contingency contract,* a written agreement that outlines the behaviors and consequences of a specific behavior management system. Swanson (1992) proposes an *ICAN* strategy, whereby teachers and students develop a contract that outlines students' academic and behavioral goals in terms of *I*ndependence, *C*ompletion (levels), *A*ccuracy, and *N*eatness. Homme (1970) suggests that contracts should provide for immediate and frequent reinforcement, be structured for success by initially calling for small changes in behavior, be perceived as fair by both parties, and be stated in language the student can read and understand.

A contract should include the following elements:

- a statement of the behavior(s) the student(s) are to increase/decrease in observable terms
- a statement of the environmental conditions during which the strategy will be implemented
- a listing of the type and amount of reinforcers that will be provided and who will provide them

- a schedule of when the delivery of reinforcers will take place
- a listing of the roles teachers and students can perform to increase the success of the system
- a time frame for the length of the contract, including a date for renegotiation
- signatures of the students and teacher

Figure 10.8 presents an outline of a sample contingency contract.

Think About It

Is positive reinforcement bribery?

Self-Management Interventions

Kris, a mainstreamed sixth grader, is having difficulty completing assignments because she is frequently off task—leaving her seat, talking to classmates, playing with objects, and looking around the room. Kris's teacher, Mr. Bevier, is concerned about this behavior and decides that Kris could benefit from a strategy that increases her awareness of it. Mr. Bevier meets with Kris. They discuss her behavior and the use of a self-management strategy, which Kris agrees to try. Before starting, they meet again to discuss the system and the behavior. Initially, Mr. Bevier explains that on-task behavior means eyes on the materials and/or on the teacher. Next, he demonstrates specific observable examples of on-task and off-task behaviors, emphasizing the salient features of each. After this demonstration, he asks Kris to present examples and nonexamples of on-task behavior. Finally, they role play the intervention.

The intervention involves placing on Kris's desk a 4 by 6-inch index card that contains 10 drawings of eyes. When Kris fails to engage in on-task behavior, she crosses out one of the eyes on the index card. If Kris has any eyes remaining at the end of the class period, she receives 15 minutes free time. Through this system, Kris is able to increase her on-task behavior and Mr. Bevier notices that Kris is attempting more assignments and completing these assignments with greater accuracy.

Self-management strategies are superior to adult-managed strategies in that they promote consistency, increase motivation and awareness, don't require a large communication network, and can be applied in settings where adults are not available (Kazdin, 1975).

Teachers have successfully used a variety of student-management interventions to modify a wide range of student behaviors (Alberto & Troutman, 1990). *Self-management intervention* strategies teach students how to monitor and control their behavior. These strategies can be used unobtrusively in a variety of settings to encourage development of appropriate behavior and promote independence (Alberto & Troutman, 1990). Several self-management strategies are described here. Where possible, teachers may want to use combinations of these strategies.

Self-Recording

Self-recording techniques have been successful in modifying a variety of classroom behaviors including staying seated, talking out, time on task, and aggression toward others (Alberto & Troutman, 1990). Because self-recording strategies are often effective in maintaining behaviors that have been learned via externally managed systems, they are particularly appropriate for promoting the transition to regular education settings. *Self-recording* involves the student monitoring specific behaviors by measuring them using a data-collection system such as event recording, duration recording, perma-

FIGURE 10.8
Sample contingency contract outline

This is a contract between ______________________________ and
Students's or class's name

______________________________. The contract starts on __________ and ends
Teacher's name

on __________. We will renegotiate it on __________.

During ______________________________,
Environmental conditions (times, classes, activities)

I (we) agree to ______________________________.
Behavior student(s) will demonstrate

If I (we) do, I (we) will ______________________________.
Reinforcer to be delivered

The teacher will help by ______________________________.

The class will help by ______________________________.

____
Teacher's Signature

____
Student or Class Representative's Signature

____
Date

nent product, or time sampling. For example, Broden, Hall, and Mitts (1971) taught a student to increase her on-task behavior during a lecture class by placing a + in a box when she paid attention for several minutes, and a − if she was off task. Sample self-recording systems are presented in Figure 10.9.

Teachers can help strengthen the student's ability to monitor behavior by using a *countoon* (Jones & Jones, 1986), a recording sheet that includes a visual depiction of the behavior being recorded and space for students to record each occurrence of the behavior. Countoons can increase student awareness and motivation. A countoon for in-seat behavior for example, would include a drawing of a student sitting in a chair with a box under the chair for recording.

FIGURE 10.9
Self-recording examples

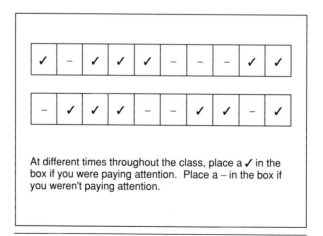

Student's name ____________ Class period ________
Date __________

卌 卌 ||

Place a mark on the card each time you leave your seat.

✓	–	✓	✓	✓	–	–	–	✓	✓

–	✓	✓	✓	–	–	✓	✓	–	✓

At different times throughout the class, place a ✓ in the box if you were paying attention. Place a – in the box if you weren't paying attention.

Source: Adapted from M. Broden, R. V. Hall, and B. Mitts, *Journal of Applied Behavior Analysis* 4 (1971), pp. 193, 496. Copyright 1971 by the Society for the Experimental Analysis of Behavior, Inc.

Self-Reinforcement

Because the effects of self-recording can be short term, educators also should consider using self-reinforcement (O'Leary & Dubey, 1979). In *self-reinforcement,* the student is taught to evaluate her or his behavior and then deliver reinforcement if it is appropriate. Rhode, Morgan, and Young (1983) found that self-reinforcement was successful in transferring behavior from a special education to a regular education classroom. Since the reinforcers available in the regular classroom may be different from those used in other educational settings, the reinforcers used in self-reinforcement should be consistent with those available in the regular classroom.

Self-Managed Free-Token Response-Cost

One system, combining elements of self-recording and self-reinforcement, that has been successfully employed by mainstreamed students in regular classrooms is a *student-managed free-token response-cost* system (Salend, Tintle, & Balber, 1988). In this system, the teacher gives students an index card with a fixed number of symbols on it. The symbols represent the number of inappropriate behaviors the student may exhibit before losing the agreed-upon reinforcement. Each time an inappropriate behavior occurs, the student crosses out one of the symbols on the index card. If any symbols remain at the end of the class time, the student receives the agreed-upon reinforcement.

Self-Evaluation

A self-management system that has been used to promote appropriate behavior in the regular classroom is *self-evaluation* (Rhode, Morgan, & Young, 1983), in which students are taught to evaluate their in-class behavior using a rating scale. For example, Smith, Young, West, Morgan, & Rhode (1988) had students rate their on-task and disruptive behavior using a 0 to 5 point (unacceptable to excellent) rating scale. Students earned points, which they exchanged for reinforcers based on both their behavior and the accuracy of their rating.

Self-Instruction

Another effective self-management technique is *self-instruction* (Burron & Bucher, 1978), which teaches students to solve problems by verbalizing to themselves the questions and responses necessary to 1) identify problems (*What am I being asked to do?*), 2) generate potential solutions (*What are the ways to do it?*), 3) evaluate solutions (*What is the best way?*), 4) implement appropriate solutions (*Did I do it?*), and 5) determine if the solutions were effective (*Did it work?*) (Mastropieri & Scruggs, 1987). Students are usually taught to employ self-instruction by having them do the following:

- Observe the teacher performing and verbalizing the steps in a task.
- Perform the task under the guidance of the teacher.
- Execute and verbalize the task without guidance from the teacher.

- Whisper while performing the task.
- Implement the task by covertly verbalizing the steps (Meichenbaum & Goodman, 1971).

Students' ability to use self-instruction can be fostered by using *cuing cards* (Palkes, Stewart, & Kahana, 1968), index cards with visual stimuli depicting self-instruction steps for following directions (*stop, look, listen,* and *think*) that are placed on the student's desk to guide them.

Teaching Self-Management Skills

Students will need instruction to implement self-management strategies successfully. Salend (1983b) has developed a six-step model for teaching students the specifics of a self-managed program, including the behavior to be changed and the intervention.

Step 1: Explanation. The teacher explains to the student the need for rules in general and, in particular, the need for a rule related to the target behavior.

Step 2: Identification. The teacher and student identify the target behavior and discuss its effect on the student and others.

Step 3: Demonstration. The teacher demonstrates examples and nonexamples of the target behavior. While demonstrating, the teacher accentuates and verbalizes the observable, salient features that characterize the behavior to be changed.

Step 4: Differentiation. The teacher presents examples and nonexamples of the target behavior, and the student decides whether the target behavior did occur. As the student becomes proficient in differentiating the behavior, the teacher increases the difficulty of the task by presenting incidents that require finer discriminations and having students present examples and nonexamples of the target behavior.

Step 5: Role playing. The student and the teacher role play the intervention in the environmental milieu where it will be implemented. Following the role play, the teacher provides feedback to the student concerning her or his use of the system.

Step 6: Assessment. The teacher assesses the student's mastery of the intervention. Assessment questions should relate to the following areas: the target behavior, the rationale for the behavior change, the daily and weekly goals, the data recording system, the environmental conditions in which the system will be in effect, the consequences of appropriate and inappropriate behavior, and the roles of the student and the teacher.

Think About It

Choose a behavior you would like to increase or decrease. Select one of the self-management strategies and keep track of your progress. Were you successful? If so, why? If not, why?

DECREASING INAPPROPRIATE CLASSROOM BEHAVIOR

While educators certainly care about students' positive behaviors, they tend to be more concerned with the inappropriate behaviors of students (Kauffman et al., 1989). In particular, they are worried about how these inappropriate behaviors impact on the learning environment and spill over to other students in the class (Safran & Safran, 1985a).

Teachers can use several strategies to decrease inappropriate classroom behavior. When selecting a procedure to decrease inappropriate behavior, educators should consider the following questions:

- Is the strategy aversive?
- Does the strategy produce undesirable side effects?
- Is the strategy effective?
- Does the strategy provide for the teaching of a new, functional alternative behavior to replace the behavior that has been decreased? (Alberto & Troutman, 1990)

Positive Reductive Procedures/Differential Reinforcement Techniques

Positive reductive procedures, also called *differential reinforcement techniques,* decrease inappropriate behaviors by increasing appropriate behaviors that serve as positive alternatives to the inappropriate behaviors targeted for behavior reduction (Deitz & Repp, 1983). In other words, educators reinforce and increase the occurrence of a positive behavior that cannot coexist with the negative behavior that educators want to decrease, this reinforcement reducing the incidence of inappropriate behavior. Positive reductive procedures have been effective in decreasing a wide range of inappropriate classroom behaviors (Webber & Scheuerman, 1991).

Three strategies comprise the positive reductive procedures: differential reinforcement of other behaviors (DRO), differential reinforcement of incompatible behavior (DRI), and differential reinforcement of lower rates of responding (DRL). *Differential reinforcement of other behaviors (DRO),* also referred to as differential reinforcement of zero rates of behavior or differential reinforcement of the omission of behavior, involves reinforcing students for not engaging in the inappropriate behavior for a specific period of time. For example, to decrease a student's use of profanity, the teacher could reinforce the student at 30-minute intervals for *not* swearing.

Differential reinforcement of incompatible behavior (DRI), sometimes referred to as differential reinforcement of alternative behavior (DRA), refers to reinforcing a behavior that is incompatible with the behavior to be decreased. For example, a teacher could use DRI to decrease a student's out-of-seat behavior by reinforcing a student for being in his or her seat.

Differential reinforcement of lower rates of behavior (DRL) is used to decrease behaviors that are tolerable or desirable at low rates of occurrence, and can be reduced gradually or are habitual (Alberto & Troutman, 1990;

IDEAS FOR IMPLEMENTATION	When implementing differential reinforcement techniques, teachers should do the following: 1. Identify the behavior to be decreased. 2. Select positive alternatives that are incompatible with the behavior to be decreased. 3. Choose an appropriate differential reinforcement technique. 4. Determine a variety of appropriate reinforcers. 5. Establish a reasonable criterion for the behavior. 6. Evaluate the effectiveness of the technique.

Source: Webber & Scheuermann (1991).

Webber & Scheuermann, 1991). DRL entails reinforcing students when the number of behaviors that occur in a prescribed time period does not exceed a pre-established criteria. As students successfully reduce their behavior, teachers gradually reinforce progressively lower rates of behavior (Webber & Scheuermann, 1991). For example, a student can be reinforced if his or her rate of calling out is less than, or equal to three per 45-minute class. A description of differential reinforcement techniques for dealing with classroom problem behaviors are presented in Figure 10.10.

Think About It

Identify behaviors that may serve as positive, incompatible alternatives to the following inappropriate behaviors: calling out, being off task, being out of seat, and swearing.

Interspersed Requests

Interspersed requests, also known as pretask requests and behavioral momentum, can be strategically used to decrease avoidance and challenging behaviors of students (Sprague & Horner, 1990). Interspersed requests are used to motivate students to perform a difficult or unpleasant task by initially asking them to perform several easier tasks. Teachers implement the strategy by asking students to perform two to five easy tasks prior to presenting a task that might trigger a negative or noncompliant response from students. Easy tasks are defined as tasks that the student can successfully complete in a short period of time.

Storey and Horner (1988) suggest that educators use interspersed requests to help students make transitions, learn difficult material, and refrain from engaging in a series of escalating behaviors.

Extinction

When teachers can identify and withhold all sources of reinforcement that are maintaining inappropriate classroom behavior, extinction may be an appropriate behavior reduction strategy (Cooper, Heron, & Heward, 1987). *Extinction* is a strategy in which the positive reinforcers maintaining a behavior are

FIGURE 10.10
Problem classroom behaviors and differential reinforcement strategies

Undesired Behavior	Reinforced Alternative
Talking back	Positive response such as "Yes Sir" or "OK" or "I understand"; or acceptable questions such as "May I ask you a question about that?" or "May I tell you my side?"
Cursing	Acceptable exclamations such as "Darn," "Shucks."
Being off task	Any on-task behavior: looking at book, writing, looking at teacher, etc.
Being out of seat	Sitting in seat (bottom on chair, with body in upright position).
Noncompliance	Following directions within _______seconds (time limit will depend upon age of student); following directions by second time direction is given.
Talking out	Raising hand and waiting to be called on.
Turning in messy papers	No marks other than answers; no more than_____ erasures; no more than three folds or creases.
Hitting, pinching, kicking, pushing/shoving	Using verbal expression of anger; pounding fist into hand; sitting or standing next to other students without touching them.
Tardiness	Being in seat when bell rings (or by desired time).
Self-injurious or self-stimulatory behaviors	Sitting with hands on desk or in lap; hands not touching any part of body; head up and not touching anything (desk, shoulder, etc.).
Inappropriate use of materials	Holding/using materials appropriately (e.g., writing *only* on appropriate paper, etc.).

Source: J. Webber and B. Scheuermann, *Teaching Exceptional Children,* vol. 24 (Reston, VA: Council for Exceptional Children, 1991), p. 15. Reprinted by permission of the publisher.

withheld or terminated, resulting in a reduction in the behavior to preinforcement levels (Alberto & Troutman, 1990). For example, a teacher may be inadvertently maintaining a student's calling out by reminding the student to raise his or her hand, and by responding to the student's comments. Rather than giving the student attention through these reminders, the teacher could decrease the behavior by ignoring the student's calling out.

Teachers should be aware of several problems associated with the use of extinction (Heron & Harris, 1987). Because extinction takes time to be effective, and often results in an initial increase in the rate and/or intensity of inappropriate behavior, educators should use it only for behaviors that can be changed gradually. Teachers can increase the speed in which extinction will be effective by combining it with reinforcing appropriate alternative behaviors. Similarly, educators also should not use extinction for behaviors that are maintained by reinforcers they cannot withdraw, such as peer attention. Finally, there also may be an increase in aggressive behavior when teachers use extinction.

Verbal Reprimands

Educators can use verbal reprimands to deal with inappropriate classroom behavior. Verbal reprimands have been effective in decreasing the inappropriate behavior of reprimanded students and students sitting next to them (Van Houten, Nau, Mackenzie-Keating, Sameoto, & Calavecchia, 1982).

GROUP-ORIENTED BEHAVIOR MANAGEMENT STRATEGIES

Frustrated by her students' frequent calling out, which is interfering with their lessons, Ms. Davila introduces her students to the Good Behavior Game. She divides the students into three groups, Group A, Group B, and Group C. She divides the chalkboard so that each team has a separate area designated by the group's name. Each calling out exhibited by a team member was recorded by a mark on the board in the group's designated area. If the group's total marks at the end of class do not exceed six, the group receives the agreed-upon reinforcement. At the end of the first class period, the result of the Good Behavior Game is as shown in Figure 10.11.

Groups A and C are allowed 20 minutes of extra recess, while Group B loses the opportunity to receive reinforcement because they receive more than six marks. Throughout the next four weeks, Ms. Davila modifies the game by moving students to different groups, decreasing the criteria necessary to receive reinforcement, and changing the reinforcer.

One behavior management strategy that employs the group's influence to promote appropriate behavior and decrease disruptive behavior is the *group-oriented management system,* which has been used successfully in a variety of educational settings to modify a wide range of behaviors including hyperactivity, calling out, obscene gestures and verbalizations, on-task behavior, and academic performance (Gresham & Gresham, 1982; Nelson, 1981; Sal-

FIGURE 10.11
The good behavior game

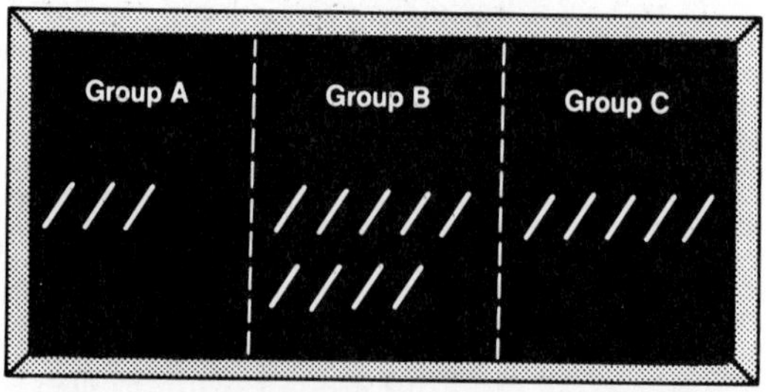

Source: S. J. Salend, *Teaching Exceptional Children,* vol. 20 (Reston, VA: Council for Exceptional Children, 1987), p. 54. Reprinted by permission of the publisher.

IDEAS FOR IMPLEMENTATION	Teachers can increase the effectiveness of their verbal reprimands by enacting the following suggestions: • Employ reprimands immediately after the inappropriate behavior occurs. • Deliver reprimands in close proximity to the student in a firm, matter-of-fact, even-tempered voice. • Make reprimands brief and specific. • Reprimand one behavior at a time. • Use precise, age-appropriate language that students can understand. • State reprimands as statements (*Stop now, and do your work.*) rather than as questions (*Why aren't you doing your work?*). • Refrain from repeating reprimands. • Phrase reprimands to include a statement that directs students to engage in an appropriate, alternative behavior. • Combine reprimands with nonverbal behaviors such as eye contact and a firm grasp. • Avoid the use of judgmental language (*You're a bad boy/girl*), which can create self-concept problems and precipitate negative comments toward reprimanded students from peers. • Use positive reinforcement when students engage in appropriate behavior.

Source: Abramowitz, O'Leary, & Futtersak (1988); Smith & Misra (1992), Van Nouten et al. (1982).

end, 1987). Group systems have several advantages over traditional methods for managing classroom behavior: they foster group cohesiveness and cooperation among members; they teach responsibility to the group and enlist the support of the class in solving classroom problems; they allow the teacher to manage behavior effectively and efficiently; they are adaptable to a variety of behaviors and classrooms; and they offer peers a positive, practical, and acceptable method of dealing effectively with peer-related problems. Because group-oriented management systems emphasize group solidarity, they may be particularly appropriate for students from cultural backgrounds that value responsibility to the group (Li, 1992).

Interdependent Group Systems

When a behavior problem is common to several students in a class, an appropriate intervention strategy is an *interdependent* group system, where the contingency is applied to the entire group and is dependent upon the behavior of the group (Hayes, 1976; Litow & Pumroy, 1975). Some potential reinforcers that can be highly motivating to groups of students are free time; a class trip; a party for the class; time to play a group game in class, the gymnasium, or the schoolyard; or a special privilege, such as renting a video. Because the success of an interdependent system depends on the behavior of the class, a single classmate can prevent the class from receiving reinforcement by repeatedly engaging in disruptive behavior. If one student continually prevents the group from achieving its goal, the offender can be removed from the group system and dealt with individually.

Group Free-Token Response-Cost System

One interdependent group system that has been effective is a *group response-cost* system mediated by free tokens (Salend & Allen, 1985; Salend & Kovalich, 1981). In this group system, the group is given a predetermined number of tokens, which are placed in full view of the students and within easy access of the teacher (such as paper strips on an easel, or checks or marks on the chalkboard). A token is removed each time a class member displays an inappropriate behavior. If any tokens remain at the end of the time period, the agreed-upon reinforcement (for example, 10 minutes free time) is delivered to the whole group.

Initially, the number of tokens should guarantee success for the group. As the group is successful, the number of tokens given should gradually be decreased. Adaptations to this system include allowing students within the class to be responsible for removing the tokens (Salend & Lamb, 1986) and making each token worth a set amount. An illustration of the group response-cost system is presented in Figure 10.12.

Good Behavior Game

Salend, Reynolds, and Coyle (1989) individualized the Good Behavior Game to account for the differences in the types and frequencies of inappropriate behaviors engaged in by class members.

The *Good Behavior Game* is an interdependent group system where class members are divided into two or more groups. Each inappropriate behavior is recorded by a slash on the blackboard (see Figure 10.11). If a group's total slashes are fewer than the number specified by the teacher, the group earns special privileges (Barrish, Saunders, & Wolf, 1969).

Group Evaluation

Teachers can use a variety of group-evaluation systems to promote appropriate classroom behavior. Salend, Whittaker, Raab, and Giek (1991) documented the effectiveness of an interdependent group-evaluation system that employed group averaging. In the group average group-evaluation system, teachers distribute an evaluation form to each student in the group, and ask each student to rate the group's behavior using the form. The teacher then

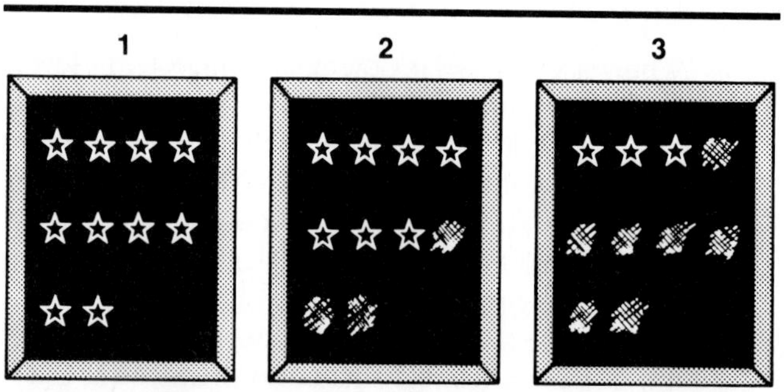

FIGURE 10.12 Illustration of a group response-cost system. The class is given free tokens (chalkboard 1), which are removed when a disruptive behavior occurs (chalkboard 2). If any tokens remain at the end of the class, the group receives reinforcement (chalkboard 3).

Source: S. J. Salend, *Teaching Exceptional Children* 20 (Reston, VA: Council for Exceptional Children, 1987), p. 54. Reprinted by permission of the publisher.

determines a group rating by computing an average of the students' ratings. Teachers also individually rate the group's behavior using the same form, and the group rating is compared to the teacher's rating. The group earns points, which are exchanged for reinforcers, based on their behavior and accuracy in rating their behavior.

Salend, Whittaker, and Reeder (1993) found that a consensus based interdependent group-evaluation system was an effective strategy for modifying classroom behavior. The consensus based group-evaluation system consists of the following elements:

- dividing the class into teams and giving each team an evaluation form
- having each team employ a consensus method for collaboratively determining the team's ratings of the class's behavior
- having the teacher rate the class's behavior using the same evaluation form that the groups are using
- comparing each team's ratings to the teacher's rating
- delivering reinforcement to each team based on the behavior of the class and the team's accuracy in rating the class's behavior

Group evaluation also can be adapted for use as a dependent group system, where one student's evaluation of the behavior of the whole group determines the extent to which all members of the class receive reinforcement (Salend, Reeder, Katz, & Russell, 1992). In such a system, each student in the class and the teacher rate the class's behavior using the same evaluation form. The teacher then randomly selects a student whose rating represents the class's rating. The teacher's rating is compared to the randomly selected student's rating and the group receives reinforcement based on the class's behavior and the selected student's congruence with the teacher's rating.

Group Timeout Ribbon

The *group timeout ribbon* employs a ribbon, leather string, piece of rope, or piece of colored paper placed where all students can see it and within easy access of the teacher. While the class is behaving appropriately, the ribbon remains in its location and the class earns tokens that can be exchanged for reinforcers (Salend & Gordon, 1987). As the class is successful, the time interval for receiving a token should be increased.

If a group member exhibits an inappropriate behavior, the ribbon is removed for one to five minutes, during which time the group loses the opportunity to earn tokens. After the group has behaved appropriately for a specified brief period of time, the ribbon is returned and the group can earn tokens again. However, if a group member engages in inappropriate behavior while the ribbon is removed, the timeout period is extended. As the class becomes acquainted with the system, students can assume responsibility for removing the ribbon and dispensing tokens. An example of a group timeout ribbon system is presented in Figure 10.13.

FIGURE 10.13
Illustration of a group timeout ribbon system. When the timeout ribbon is in place (easel 1), the group earns tokens. However, when the timeout ribbon is removed (easel 2), no tokens are delivered to the group.

Source: S. J. Salend, *Teaching Exceptional Children* vol. 20 (Reston, VA: Council for Exceptional Children, 1987), p. 55. Reprinted by permission of the publisher.

Dependent Group Systems

A *dependent* group system is used when an individual student's behavior problem is reinforced by his or her peers. In the dependent group system, the contingency is applied to the whole class dependent upon the behavior of one of the class's members (Nelson, 1981).

Hero Method

The *hero method* is a dependent group system where one student earns special privileges for the whole class by improving his or her behavior (Patterson, 1965). For example, a student can earn extra recess time for the class by reducing the number of call outs during teacher-directed instruction. However, because failure to earn the reward for the class can have a negative impact on the social status of the "hero," the teacher must carefully structure this system to ensure success.

Peer Confrontation

Another group-oriented management procedure that possesses characteristics of both interdependent and dependent systems is *peer confrontation* (Salend, Reid-Jantzen, & Giek, 1992). Whenever a behavior is deemed inappropriate, it and its consequences on others are verbally acknowledged by the group (Bellafiore & Salend, 1983). The procedure can be initiated by the teacher or a class member by asking the class to respond to the following questions:

- "(Helena) seems to be having a problem. Who can tell (Helena) what the problem is?"
- "Can you tell (Helena) why that is a problem?"
- "Who can tell (Helena) what (she) needs to do to solve the problem?"

Independent Group Systems

In an *independent* group system, teachers deliver reinforcers to individual students based on their individual performance or behavior. Thus, reinforcement is available to each student in the class contingent upon that student's behavior.

Token Economy Systems

One widely used independent group system that has been effective in decreasing a wide range of behaviors in a variety of educational settings is a *token economy* system (McLaughlin, 1981; Wolf, Giles, & Hall, 1968). Students earn tokens for demonstrating appropriate behavior and can redeem these tokens for social, activity, tangible, and edible reinforcers. The steps teachers can follow to implement token economy systems are as follows:

Step 1: Determine a set of rules and behaviors that students must demonstrate in order to receive tokens.

Step 2: Obtain tokens that are safe, attractive, durable, inexpensive, easy to handle and dispense, and that can be controlled by the teacher. When selecting tokens, educators also should consider the age and cognitive abilities of students (Myles, Moran, Ormsbee, & Downing, 1992). Determine the number of tokens needed per student.

Step 3: Identify reinforcers that students desire and determine how many tokens each item is worth. Many teachers establish a store where students may go to purchase items with their tokens. Teachers keep records of what items students purchase and stock the store with those items. Some teachers use an auction system, whereby students bid for available items (Polloway & Polloway, 1979), while others exchange tokens for lottery chances to win items in a class raffle (Schilling & Cuvo, 1983).

Step 4: Collect other materials needed to implement the token economy system such as a container for students to store their tokens. Some teachers establish a bank where students can store their tokens and earn interest for saving them for a period of time.

Step 5: Arrange the room for effective and efficient implementation of the system. For example, desks should be arranged so that the teacher has easy access to all students when dispensing tokens.

Step 6: Introduce and explain the specifics of the token system to students.

Step 7: Implement the token system. Initially, dispense large amounts of tokens to students by catching students being appropriate, and allow students to exchange their tokens for reinforcers on a regular basis to show students that tokens have real value. Tokens should be given out quickly and unobtrusively to individual students and groups of students. Pair the delivery of tokens with verbal praise and a statement informing students of the specific appropriate behavior(s) exhibited. Some teachers use a timer to assist them in dispensing tokens.

Step 8: Determine how to handle inappropriate behavior. Some teachers use a timeout card, which is placed on students' desks for a brief period of time to indicate that no tokens can be earned. When students are appropriate for a brief, specified time period, the timeout card is removed and students can earn tokens. Other teachers use a response-cost system, whereby students are fined a specific amount of tokens for engaging in inappropriate behavior. A response-cost system should not be used when students do not have a sufficient number of tokens.

Step 9: Field test the token system and revise the system to correct any problems. For example, if a student is suspected of stealing tokens from others, give the student tokens that are unique in terms of shape or color.

Step 10: Begin to fade out the token system by increasing the number of appropriate responses necessary to earn a token, increasing the number of tokens needed for a specific reinforcer, dispensing tokens on an intermittent schedule, decreasing the number of times students are allowed to exchange tokens for reinforcers, and moving toward the use of naturally occurring reinforcers.

Peer Mediation

One method for involving students in resolving classroom and school related conflicts, particularly conflicts that are based on age and cultural differences, is *peer mediation* (Johnson & Johnson, 1991). Peer mediation is "an approach to resolve conflicts in which disputants, or people who disagree, have the chance to sit face to face and talk uninterrupted so each side of the dispute is heard. After the problem is defined, solutions are created and then evaluated" (Schrumpf, Crawford, & Usadel, 1991, p. 41). Students are trained to serve as peer mediators, who attempt to facilitate conflict resolution through communication, problem solving, and critical thinking through role plays and practice (Johnson & Johnson, 1991). The peer mediation process involves the following steps.

Step 1: Initiate the session. Peer mediators introduce themselves and the peer mediation process, welcome disputants, and establish the ground rules for the process.

Step 2: Gather information. Peer mediators collect information regarding the conflict by asking disputants to discuss the event from their perspective. After disputants discuss what happened, the peer mediator summarizes their statements, solicits additional information, seeks clarification through questioning, and validates the concerns of all parties.

Step 3: Focus on common interests. Peer mediators use questioning to help disputants discover common interests (*How do you think the other person feels? What happens if no agreement is reached?*).

Step 4: Create options. Peer mediators use brainstorming and questioning to help disputants generate options for solving the conflict.

Step 5: Evaluate options and choose a solution. Peer mediators ask disputants to evaluate the options and select those they feel might be successful. If disputants agree on a solution, peer mediators help them examine the solution's components and summarize the main points of the agreement.

Schrumpf, Crawford, and Usadel (1991) offer guidelines for establishing peer mediation programs and dealing with students who fail to reach an agreement, break an agreement, or repeatedly request peer mediation.

Step 6: Write the agreement and close. Peer mediators write out the agreement, share it with the disputants, ask disputants to acknowledge their agreement, encourage disputants to shake hands, and thank disputants for their participation (Schrumpf, Crawford, & Usadel, 1991).

AFFECTIVE EDUCATION STRATEGIES

Appropriate classroom behavior can be promoted by use of affective education strategies and programs, which help students gain insights into their feelings, attitudes, and values (Epanchin & Monson, 1982). These strategies are designed to enhance students' emotional, behavioral, and social development through enhancing their self-esteem and their ability to engage in positive emotional expression (Abrams, 1992).

Values Clarification

One affective education strategy that teachers can use in their classrooms is *values clarification,* which views inappropriate classroom behavior as a function of confused values (Raths, Harmin, & Simon, 1978). Through values clarification activities that are integrated throughout the curriculum, teachers help students examine their attitudes, interests, and feelings, and learn how these values affect their behavior. As students discover their values, teachers engage in *clarifying responses,* which aid students in reflecting upon their

Teachers can use a variety of strategies to promote positive classroom behavior.

attitudes, choices, values, and feelings. For example, after students have expressed their attitudes or opinions, or engaged in a specific behavior, teachers might ask students, *How did that affect you and others? Why is that important to you?* and *Did you consider any alternatives?* In addition to clarifying responses, teachers implement values clarification by creating a nonjudgmental, open, and trusting environment that encourages all students to share their values and beliefs and respect the feelings and beliefs of others (Adams, 1992).

Many strategies and activities for implementing values clarification in the classroom are available (Hawley & Hawley, 1975; Howe & Howe, 1975; Simon, Howe, & Kirschenbaum, 1972; Simon & Olds, 1976; Smith, 1977).

Life Space Interviewing

Teachers also can employ *Life Space Interviewing,* which involves talking empathetically with students who are experiencing school-related problems (Long, 1990). Life Space Interviewing may take the form of either or both Emotional First Aid and Clinical Exploitation of Life Events. Emotional First Aid seeks to provide temporary emotional support by helping students deal with frustration, anger, panic, and hostility. Through Clinical Exploitation of Life Events, teachers assist students in examining a behavioral incident by conducting a reality check, focusing on the students' behavior, and helping students assuage their guilt as well as understand and develop their self-control system. Wood and Long (1990) suggest that teachers can implement Life Space Interviewing by using the following six steps:

Step 1: Focus on the incident. Try to focus students' attention on the behavioral incident.

Step 2: Encourage the student to talk about the incident. Encourage students to talk through questioning. Seek clarification about the event and the students' reactions to and perceptions of what happened.

Step 3: Find the central issue and select a therapeutic goal. Sort out the information presented and determine the critical issue as well as the intervention goal.

Step 4: Choose a solution based on values. Select with the student an intervention that will address all components of the problem.

Step 5: Plan for success. Create a plan that allows students to rehearse new behaviors, understand how to apply the new behaviors in new situations, and receive support from others.

Step 6: Help the student return to the activity. Assist the student in making the transition to the activity.

Teacher Effectiveness Training

Teacher Effectiveness Training, which facilitates communication between students and teachers, also can enhance teachers' classroom management skills (Gordon, 1974). Teacher Effectiveness Training employs several strategies to minimize conflicts between teachers and students, including *active listening,* which involves the following:

Using door openers—Teacher comments that encourage students to express their feelings and ideas. (*It looks like you're feeling sad about something. Would you like to talk about it?*)

Engaging in reflective comments—Teacher comments that attempt to reflect back the feelings and experiences shared by students. (*When the other students said bad things about your friend, it made you sad.*)

Acknowledging comments—Teacher comments that show understanding of students' comments and encourage students to continue to share their feelings. (*Yes, I see. What else would you like to tell me?*)

Avoiding roadblocks to communication—Teachers encourage communication and refrain from questioning, directing, threatening, advising, lecturing, labeling, analyzing, consoling, and criticizing students, moralizing to students, and changing the focus of the discussion.

Resolving problems through a no-lose approach—Teachers and students focus on the problem and seek and agree to solutions that are acceptable to all parties.

Gordon (1974) also proposes that teachers respond to students' appropriate and inappropriate behaviors through use of *I-statements,* which express teachers' feelings about student behavior. I-statements usually include the following:

- a review of the student's behavior (*When you* ______________)
- a mention of how the behavior made the teacher feel (*It made me feel* ______________)
- a comment directed at the reasons why the teacher felt that way (*Because* ______________) (Curwin & Mendler, 1988)

Class Meetings

Students, as a group, also can share their opinions and brainstorm solutions to class behavior problems, concerns about school work, and general topics that are of concern to students during *class meetings* (Glasser, 1969). Because class meetings are designed to help students understand the perspectives of others, it is an especially good technique for resolving conflicts between students that are based on differences in cultural perspectives (Meier, 1992). Class meetings are typically scheduled at the end of the day, with students seated in an arrangement that promotes discussion. Teachers facilitate discussion by presenting open-ended topics through use of *defining* questions (*What does it mean to interrupt the class?*); *personalizing* questions (*How do you feel when someone interrupts the class?*); and *creative thinking* questions (*How can we stop others from interrupting the class?*). In classwide discussions, all class members must have a right to share their opinions without being criticized by others, and only positive, constructive suggestions should be presented.

Classroom problems and tensions between students can be identified and dealt with through use of a *gripe box* located in the classroom, where students and teachers submit descriptions of problems and situations that made them feel upset, sad, annoyed, or angry (Curwin & Mendler, 1988). These descriptions can relate to events or individuals in or out of school. At classroom meetings, gripes can be shared with the class, and all students can brainstorm possible solutions. The concept can be expanded to include submissions that reflect positive classroom events that made students feel happy.

Class discipline committees also can be used to deal with classroom problems and help students assume responsibility for their behavior (Swarthout, 1988). For example, a committee of students and teachers can meet to set classroom and school rules, and determine appropriate actions when individuals fail to comply with the rules.

USING NONVERBAL COMMUNICATION

Teachers can modify and respond to student behavior through use of appropriate nonverbal communication (Banbury & Hebert, 1992). Nonverbal communication includes physical distance and personal space, eye contact and facial expressions, and gestures and body movements. Teachers' nonverbal messages should be consistent with teachers' behavioral expectations, should facilitate positive interactions, and should communicate attitudes (Miller, 1986; Woolfolk & Brooks, 1985). Nonverbal behaviors also should be consistent with students' cultural backgrounds. For example, individuals from some cultures may feel comfortable when they interact with others at a close proximity, while individuals from other cultures may view this same nonverbal behavior as a sign of aggressiveness (Curwin & Mendler, 1988). Similarly, physical gestures may have different meanings in different cultures. For example, to some Southeast Asian groups, crossed fingers to indicate good luck is viewed as obscene, while hand gestures are considered rude as they are used with animals or to challenge others to a fight (National Coalition of Advocates for Students, 1991).

Grant and Hennings (1971) noted that approximately 80% of the messages that teachers convey to students are nonverbal.

Teachers who are aware of the nonverbal behavior of their students can respond to these behaviors with appropriate and congruent nonverbal and verbal messages. When verbal and nonverbal messages are not congruent, students tend to respond to the nonverbal message (Curwin & Mendler, 1988). A series of congruent nonverbal and verbal messages that teachers can use to promote positive classroom behaviors are presented in Figure 10.14.

Think About It

Observe several individuals with whom you interact regularly. What nonverbal communication strategies do they employ when interacting with others? Are their nonverbal behaviors congruent with their verbal behaviors? When their nonverbal and verbal behaviors are incongruent, on which type of behavior do you rely?

USING HUMOR

In addition to defusing a difficult classroom situation, humor can help teachers and students develop relationships and a positive classroom atmosphere, help students see a situation from another perspective, and decrease the likelihood of conflicts (Curwin & Mendler, 1988; Meier, 1992). Humor can be

FIGURE 10.14
Congruency of verbal and nonverbal messages

	Approving/ Accepting	Disapproving/ Critical	Assertive/ Confident	Passive/ Indifferent
Verbal message	"I like what you are doing."	"I don't like what you are doing."	"I mean what I say."	"I don't care."
Physical distance	Sit or stand in close proximity to other person.	Distance self from other person; encroach uninvited into other's personal space.	Physically elevate self; move slowly into personal space of other person.	Distance self from other person.
Facial expressions	Engage in frequent eye contact; open eyes wide; raise brows; smile.	Engage in too much or too little eye contact; open eyes wide in fixed, frozen expression; squint or glare; turn corners of eyebrows down; purse or tightly close lips; frown; tighten jaw muscle.	Engage in prolonged, neutral eye contact; lift eyebrows; drop head and raise eyebrow.	Avert gaze; stare blankly; cast eyes down or let them wander; let eyes droop.
Body movements	Nod affirmatively; "open" posture; uncross arms/legs; place arms at side; show palms; lean forward; lean head and trunk to one side; orient body toward other person; grasp or pat shoulder or arm; place hand to chest.	Shake head slowly; "close" posture; fold arms across chest; lean away from person; hold head/trunk straight; square shoulders; thrust chin out; use gestures of negation, e.g., finger shaking, hand held up like a stop signal.	Place hands on hips; lean forward; touch shoulder; tap on desk; drop hand on desk; join fingers at tips and make a steeple.	Lean away from other person; place head in palm of hand; fold hands behind back or upward in front; drum fingers on table; tap with feet; swing crossed leg or foot; sit with leg over chair.

Source: M. M. Banbury and C. R. Hebert, *Teaching Exceptional Children,* vol. 24, no. 2 (Reston, VA: Council for Exceptional Children, 1992), p. 36. Reprinted by permission of the publisher.

employed by agreeing with students instead of being defensive, responding in an improbable fashion, and behaving paradoxically. When using humor in the classroom, teachers should make sure that their jokes are not directed toward students, and are free of racial, ethnic, religious, sexual orientation, and gender bias.

MODIFYING THE CLASSROOM ENVIRONMENT

Ms. O'Hara and Mr. Butler teach in classrooms next door to each other. Ms. O'Hara has decided that she wants to rearrange her room to make it more consistent with her teaching style. She asks Mr. Butler to observe several of her classes, and note her and her students' movements on a map of the classroom. After several observations, Ms. O'Hara and Mr. Butler meet to analyze the map, and revise Ms. O'Hara's classroom.

Because Ms. O'Hara uses a variety of instructional strategies, they decide to try seating students in a horseshoe arrangement, which facilitates lecturing and group discussions, and can easily be transformed into a setting for cooperative learning groups. Next, they discuss the placement of Ms. O'Hara's desk, deciding to move it to the front of the room so that Ms. O'Hara can see all students. So that Ms. O'Hara could store her materials (teacher's edition of textbooks, assessment instruments, instructional programs) near her desk, they place a cabinet adjacent to it.

Mr. Butler notes that students' movements are mostly to obtain materials to complete assignments. However, because these materials are not centrally located, students often must go to several locations, and these movements often result in the distraction of others. To cut down on these movements, Ms. O'Hara and Mr. Butler create a labeled materials storage area accessible to all students.

Mr. Butler also observes that Harry, a student seated in the back of the room near the pencil sharpener, is frequently off task. When students use the pencil sharpener, Harry always has a comment for them or something to show them. Similarly, since Ms. O'Hara spends a lot of time in the front of the room, Harry often plays with his materials rather than focusing on his work. Ms. O'Hara decides to move Harry's work area to a location near Ms. O'Hara's desk, away from the pencil sharpener and other high-traffic areas.

Everston, Emmer, Clements, Sanford, and Worsham (1989) suggest that teachers assess the effectiveness of their room arrangements by simulating the various movements that they make during a typical day, and by pretending to be a student and examining the visibility, movement patterns, and accessibility of materials from the perspective of the students.

An important variable for teachers to consider in adapting instruction for mainstreamed students is the design of the classroom environment, which should complement the teachers' teaching style and accommodate the students' unique learning needs. In planning their classroom's design, teachers should consider several variables: objects and areas in the room that cannot be altered easily (doors, windows, lights, outlets, cabinets, shelves, chalkboards, and bulletin boards), unique classroom and student needs and problems, and teaching style and educational philosophy (Hayes, 1986).

Seating Arrangements

The seating arrangement of the classroom will depend on the type of instruction the teacher employs. Generally, students should be seated in areas that allow clear sightlines to instructional presentations and displays (Everston et al., 1989). When using small-group teacher-directed instruction, students should be seated in a semicircle facing the teacher (Carnine & Silbert, 1979).

In a larger-group teacher-directed activity, such as lecturing, it is most conducive for learning if all students are facing the teacher sitting in row, circular, or horseshoe arrangements. When the instructional format requires students to work in groups (role plays, simulations, cooperative learning arrangements), teachers should have students arrange their desks in groups so that they face each other and can share information efficiently and quietly.

Since some students may perform better in different settings, for appropriate assignments, teachers should allow students the chance to select the location in the room in which they can best complete their work (Hoover, 1986). For example, a mainstreamed student may feel more comfortable working on a seatwork assignment on a rug-covered floor than at a desk. To encourage academic performance and neatness, students who work in areas other than their desks should be given a clipboard or another hard surface on which to mount and secure their work (Jones & Jones, 1986). Teachers use a variety of instructional formats, so the design of their classrooms should allow for flexibility in seating arrangements. Students should be taught how to move their desks into the appropriate layout.

Each student's desk should be of the correct size and should be placed to ensure that the student can participate in all classroom activities and maintain good posture and body alignment (Kerr & Nelson, 1983; Rikhye, Gothelf, & Appell, 1989).

Teachers should pay special attention to the seating location of their mainstreamed students. Teachers should seat their mainstreamed students to facilitate those students' discussion participation, on-task behavior, listening and attending skills, and academic performance (Delefes & Jackson, 1972; Schwebel & Cherlin, 1972). It is easier for teachers to monitor student performance, deliver cues and nonverbal feedback, and assess understanding when students are sitting near them. Sitting students near the teacher also allows for proximity control and can make implementation of a behavior management system easier.

The space around students' desks should be large enough for teachers to have easy access to students in order to monitor performance and distribute papers. Space also should be provided so that students have a place to store their materials. When students' desks do not provide adequate storage, tote trays can be used to store their supplies (Everston et al., 1989).

Teacher's Desk

An important factor in managing the classroom is the location of the teacher's desk, which should allow teachers to monitor behavior and progress and to move quickly if a situation warrants teacher intervention. In order to monitor students, the teacher's desk should be placed in an area that provides teachers with a barrier-free view of the whole classroom. Any obstacles that prevent teachers from periodically scanning different parts of the room should be removed. Similarly, when teachers are working with students at other parts of the room, teachers should sit facing the other students in the class.

Instructional Materials

An important element of the classroom design is the organization of the teacher's instructional materials. Paine, Radicchi, Rossellini, Deutchman, and Darch (1983) suggest that a materials area should be located in the front or center of the room and include room for storing extra pencils, papers, and other supplies students will need to complete classroom activities.

Employing a system for storing, organizing, and categorizing materials can make the classroom a more orderly, efficient place and facilitate student independence and the individualization of instruction. Teachers can help organize their instructional materials in the classroom by keeping frequently used materials together in a location that is visible and accessible to all adults and students, and labeling storage areas and materials so that students can find them easily (Lund & Bos, 1981). Cohen and de Bettencourt (1988) offer teachers a system for categorizing their instructional materials:

1. Create a file box of all classroom materials with each card including the material's name, objectives, level of difficulty, and potential modifications.
2. Develop a code and label each material by the type of activity. For example, a * could indicate a software program while a # can indicate a role play.
3. Assign each material a level of difficulty.
4. Color code and place materials in separate locations by content areas.
5. Individualize assignments for students using the system.

Bulletin Boards and Walls

Including bulletin boards in the classroom design can help teachers create a pleasant, visually appealing environment that promotes learning and class pride. Hayes (1985) delineated four types of bulletin boards: decorative, motivational, instructional, and manipulative. *Decorative* bulletin boards make the room attractive and interesting, and often relate to a theme. *Motivational* bulletin boards encourage students by providing a place where teachers acknowledge student progress and publicly display students' work. *Instructional* bulletin boards, or *teaching walls,* (Cummins & Lombardi, 1989) often include an acquisition wall, which introduces new concepts and material, and a maintenance wall, which emphasizes review of previously learned concepts (Creekmore, 1987). *Manipulative* bulletin boards also promote skill mastery by using materials that students can manipulate to learn new skills.

Since it is the students' room as well as the teacher's, displays should be planned so that they are at the students' eye level. Whenever possible, students should be involved in decorating areas of the room. Mobiles, posters, pictures, and other forms of student artwork (for example, a class collage that includes a contribution from each class member) can make the walls and ceiling of the classroom colorful and attractive.

When planning how to use wall space around the room, teachers also should include a space for displaying students' academic work. Such a space can help motivate students to produce exemplary products because seeing their work posted is a visible reminder of their success. Posting the daily assignment schedule and examples of products on a part of the bulletin board or wall can help students remember to perform all assigned tasks. Wall displays can include a clock and calendar large enough to be seen from all parts of the classroom, and a list of class rules (Everston et al., 1989).

Specialized Areas

A location of the room that is available to groups of students to read together or share time with a peer can be valuable in promoting socialization (Jones & Jones, 1986).

Teachers also may want to establish specialized areas of the room for specific functions. For example, an old couch or rocking chair can be placed in a quiet part of the room to offer students a place they can go to relax when the classroom pace is hectic, to process what they have just learned, to be alone, or to gain control of their behavior (Hayes, 1985).

High traffic areas, such as learning centers, small-group instruction areas, the teacher's desk, and the pencil sharpener area, should be free from congestion, separated from each other, easily accessible, and spacious (Everston et al., 1989).

Learning Centers

Learning centers can provide variety in the classroom and help teachers individualize instruction. They also can help students develop independent skills and learn to work in small groups.

Gearheart et al. (1988) delineated four types of learning centers: skill centers, discovery/enrichment centers, listening centers, and creativity centers. *Skill centers* allow students to practice skills such as math facts, spelling words, alphabetizing, and defining vocabulary. *Discovery/enrichment centers* employ a variety of learning activities (science experiments, math applications) that require students to add to their knowledge base. A *listening center* is designed to offer students instruction or recreation through listening. Arts and crafts, music, creative writing, and poetry are often the focus of activities in a *creativity center*.

Study Carrels

Some students may have difficulty screening out noise and visual distractions in the classroom. When these students are working on individualized assignments that require concentration, teachers might allow them to move to a

IDEAS FOR IMPLEMENTATION

Teachers can establish learning centers by doing the following:

1. Identify students' academic levels, abilities, interests, and needs.
2. Determine relevant objectives.
3. Offer students a variety of activities that allow them to explore new skills and practice previously learned skills.
4. Develop appropriate materials that students can use independently or in small groups.
5. Train students to work at learning centers.
6. Provide students with directions that are easily understood and guidelines for using the materials and accompanying media.
7. Explain to the students appropriate times for using the center and the number of students that the center can accommodate at one time.
8. Monitor student progress and change materials and activities as students master new skills.

quiet area of the room, away from the teacher's desk and other high-traffic, visually loaded areas of the room. When it is necessary for students to work in such a self-contained area, students should be continuously monitored. Consequently, the barriers around the area should be low enough to allow an unobstructed view of the students, but high enough to eliminate distractions. Although some educators advocate use of a study carrel for students with attention problems (Hewett, 1967), teachers should be careful to avoid frequent use of study carrels because they may isolate or stigmatize the students that use them. Teachers can lessen the potential problems associated with study carrels by discussing how individuals learn and function best in different ways, allowing all students to use the study carrel, referring to the study carrel area in a positive manner, and using the study carrel for several purposes such as a relaxation area, and a computer or media center.

Classroom Design Modifications

Teachers should design the classrooms to affirm the value of students and education. Therefore, teachers should welcome students by creating a cheerful and pleasant environment that is clean, orderly, well lit, odor free, and colorful. The classroom design also should be set up to ensure safety; teachers should check to make sure that electrical wires are anchored and covered, dangerous materials and equipment are locked in cabinets, sharp edges and broken furniture are removed, and walls, floors, and equipment are in good condition (Rikhye, Gothelf, & Appell, 1989).

Many mainstreamed students will require specific classroom design modifications in order to perform at their optimal levels. Guidelines for adapting regular classroom physical environments to address the needs of students with a variety of disabilities are outlined here. (Also see Chapter 2 for further discussion of the educational needs of these students.)

Students with Hearing Impairments

Because students with hearing impairments have difficulty receiving auditory stimuli, classroom design adaptations for this group should promote their ability to gain information from teachers and interact with peers. The placement of students with hearing impairments' desks can affect their performance in the mainstreamed setting (Salend, 1983a). To facilitate lip reading and the use of residual hearing, the desks of students with hearing impairments should be in a central location, about two rows from the front, where these students can have visual access to the teacher's and other students' lips. Hearing and lip reading also can be fostered by having the student sit on a swivel chair on casters, giving easy movement and the ability to follow the flow of the conversation. If students with hearing impairments have an obstructed view of the speaker's lips, they should be allowed to leave their seat to assume a position that will maximize their lip reading skills. During lectures or other teacher-directed activities, the student should be seated near the teacher and to one side of the room, where he or she has a direct line of sight to the lips of peers and teachers. A semicircular seating arrangement can facilitate lip reading during small-group instruction (Gearheart, Weishahn, Gearheart, 1988).

Teachers also should consider lighting and noise levels in determining the location of the work areas of their students with hearing impairments (Salend, 1983a). Light glaring into the eyes of students with hearing impairments can hinder lip reading; therefore, avoid locating the teacher or source of information in a poorly lighted area or where the light is behind the speaker. Noise can also interfere with the residual hearing abilities of students with hearing impairments. Internal structure-borne noises, such as heating units, footsteps, furniture movements, and external airborne noises, such as cars or construction outside the school, can be lessened by use of carpets and acoustic tiles on the floor, draperies on windows, and sound-absorbent room dividers (Niemoller, 1968; Rikhye, Gothelf, & Appell, 1989), as well as by locating classes containing students with hearing impairments in rooms that are situated in quiet locations and away from noise centers such as gymnasiums, cafeterias, and busy hallways and corridors (D'Alonzo, D'Alonzo, & Mauser, 1979).

Students with hearing impairments can benefit from sitting next to an alert and competent peer. During verbal conversations, peers can help students with hearing impairments follow along by indicating changes in the speaker. A peer also can be assigned the role of alerting students when and what information is being conveyed on the intercom system. Peers also can be responsible for assisting students in reacting to fire drills. However, as students with hearing impairments make the adjustment to the regular classroom, the assistance they receive from peers should be faded out, if possible.

Teachers should exercise caution in the use of media with students with hearing impairments. The overhead projector allows teachers to present content visually and orally while standing in one place facing students, so it is a valuable instructional apparatus for students with hearing impairments. However, other media, such as audiocassette recorders, films, and filmstrips, can cause frustration (Salend, 1983a). When using these types of media, teachers can reduce the potential frustration students with hearing impairments may encounter by providing students with a script of the audio segments of the media, stopping periodically and explaining the content of the material, and illuminating the lips of the speaker with a flashlight when the lights are dimmed.

The Florida State Department of Education (1986) offers suggestions for placing the educational interpreter when interpreting for several students in a class and when interpreting for students who have hearing impairments but who also have full or partial speech capacities.

When designing classrooms to accommodate students with hearing impairments who require the services of an educational interpreter, teachers also should consider the positioning of the interpreter, which will depend on the nature of the instructional activity (Florida State Department of Education, 1986). When teachers are employing a lecture format, the interpreter should stand or sit to the side and slightly in front of the teacher with the student's desk located three to five feet from the interpreter. In a one-to-one instructional setting, the interpreter should be located adjacent to the individual with hearing and facing the student from a distance of approximately four to six feet. During group activities, the group should be seated in a circle with the interpreter located across from the student.

Students with Visual Impairments

Several classroom design adaptations can help students with visual impairments function successfully in mainstreamed settings. Because students with visual impairments should be encouraged to use their residual vision (Barraga, 1964), their work area should be glare free and well lighted (Salend, 1983a). Teachers can reduce problems associated with glare by using a gray-green chalkboard, placing translucent shades on windows (Wolf, 1967), installing furniture and equipment with matte finishes (Abend, 1974), and positioning desks so that the light comes over the shoulder of the student's nondominant hand (Salend, 1983a). During teacher-directed activities, the student should not have to look directly into the light to see the teacher. To reduce the fatigue associated with bending over, desks should have adjustable tops.

The work area for students with visual impairments should offer the students an unobstructed and direct trail to the major parts of the room, including the teacher's desk, learning centers, storage areas, media, chalkboards, bookshelves, and wastebaskets. When students with visual impairments are initially placed in the regular classroom setting, they should be taught how to move around the room and from their desk to the major classroom locations. Students can be taught to navigate the classroom by using *trace trailing,* directing them to the routes between their desks and major classroom landmarks by having them touch the surfaces of objects on the path. Visual descriptions of the room and routes also can supplement trace trailing and help students develop a mental picture of the room. When the room is rearranged, teachers should again provide time so that the students can learn to adjust to the new arrangement.

Because of the unique needs of students with visual impairments, teachers should locate these students' work areas in a quiet place, away from potentially harmful objects, such as hot radiators, half-open doors, and paper cutters. To enhance students' abilities to compensate for their visual impairment by increased attention to verbal information, students should be seated where they can hear others well. Masking tape markers on the floor can assist students with visual impairments in keeping their desks in the proper alignment.

Students with visual impairments may require the use of cumbersome prosthetic devices and optical aids, such as large-print books, braillers, and magnifiers, to benefit from instruction in the mainstream setting. Therefore, teachers should consider the placement and storage of these aids when designing their classrooms to accommodate these students. A music stand or drafting table can be placed adjacent to the students' work areas to lessen the problems related to the use of large-print books. When the devices students use are electrically powered, students with visual impairments should be positioned near electrical outlets. Teachers also should provide these students with a sufficient, convenient, safe space to store these aids when not using them.

Students with Physical Disabilities

Students with physical disabilities who use wheelchairs or prostheses will need several classroom design modifications (Salend, 1983a). Wheelchair-bound students should be provided space to maneuver in the classroom. Place desks and classroom furniture if possible in a configuration with aisles that can accommodate crutches, canes, and adequate turning for wheelchair-bound students. Additionally, some wheelchair-bound students may need space in which to recline during the school day. Students whose wheelchairs are electrically charged should be seated near an electrical outlet.

The abilities of wheelchair-bound students also will be affected by the types of floor coverings in the classroom (Salend, 1983a). Floors should have a nonslip surface, but deep pile, shag, or sculptured rugs can limit mobility. Floors should be covered with tightly looped, commercial-grade carpet smooth enough to allow wheelchairs to move easily and strong enough to withstand frequent use. To keep the rug from fraying or rippling, tape it down from wall to wall without padding underneath it.

The type and size of the furniture in the classroom also can be a critical factor in meeting the needs of students with physical disabilities in the regular education setting. The height of the student's work area should be adjusted to accommodate wheelchairs or to allow prostheses to function properly (Gearheart, Weishahn, & Gearheart, 1988). Some students with cerebral palsy may require stand-up desks; students in wheelchairs may use desk tops or lap boards placed on the wheelchair (Gearheart, Weishahn, & Gearheart, 1988). Furniture that is rounded with padding on the edges and with no protrusions is appropriate for students with physical disabilities (Abend, 1974). Work areas should be at least 28 inches high to allow students in wheelchairs to get close to them. Because the reach of wheelchair-bound students is restricted, work tables should not be wider than 42 inches. For comfortable seating, chairs should be curvilinear, have seat heights at least 16 inches above the ground, and be strong enough to offer support to students to pull up on and out of the chairs (Salend, 1983a). Work areas of students with physical disabilities should include space for computers or other adaptive devices that they may need.

In addition to working at their desks, students with physical disabilities also will be required to work at the chalkboard. Therefore, at least one chalkboard in the classroom should be lowered to 24 inches from the floor. To assist students in working at the chalkboard, attach a sturdy vertical bar as a handrail (Wolf, 1967).

When working with students who use wheelchairs, teachers should be aware of the importance of positioning, and should know how to move and transfer these students (Parette & Hourcade, 1986). To prevent pressure sores and help students maintain proper positioning, the position of wheelchair-bound students should be changed every 20 to 30 minutes. Posting photographs and descriptions of suggested positions for students with physical disabilities can remind and assist staff to use appropriate positioning and transferring techniques (Rikhye, Gothelf, & Appell, 1989).

Parette and Hourcade (1986) offer specific guidelines for moving students forward, backward, and sideways in their wheelchairs and transferring students to toilets and the classroom floor.

Glazzard (1980) identified several classroom adaptations that can assist students whose movements are limited. Buddies can be assigned the role of bringing assignments and materials to the students' desks. Teachers should consider allowing these students to leave class early to get to their next class

IDEAS FOR IMPLEMENTATION

When transferring wheelchair-bound students, educators should do the following:

1. Wear comfortable footwear that minimizes the likelihood of slipping on the school's floor surfaces.
2. Encourage students who are able to bear some weight by standing to wear footwear that will not slip off or slide on the school's floor surfaces and to wear sturdy belts.
3. Make sure that their muscles are ready to be exerted.
4. Lift with the legs, not the back, and keep the back straight.
5. Maintain a smooth and steady movement.
6. Maintain a wide base of support by locating one foot in front of the other, and by getting close to the student.
7. Move feet in short steps when changing directions.
8. Avoid becoming twisted when changing directions.
9. Inform students of what is going to happen before moving them.
10. Use walls or sturdy objects to assist in maintaining balance.
11. Encourage students who are being transferred to assist in the transfer.
12. Consult with a physical or occupational therapist.

Source: Parette & Hourcade (1986).

and avoid the rush in the hallway. Securing papers by taping them to the students' desks can help with writing. Similarly, connecting writing utensils to strings taped to students' desks can help students retrieve them when dropped. Desks with textured surfaces or with a barrier around the periphery of the student's desk also can help prevent papers, books, and writing utensils from falling (D'Zamko & Hedges, 1985). Gearheart et al. (1988) suggest that students with restricted arm movement can benefit by using paper holders, such as a clipboard attached to the work area or an unbleached muslin cloth sprayed with a nonskid liquid and glued to the desk. Rikhye, Gothelf, and Appell (1989) note that built-up utensils, velcro fasteners, cut-out cups, switches, and nonslip placemats can be used as adaptations for students with physical disabilities.

Students with Behavior Disorders

An important factor to consider in designing the classroom for students who exhibit inappropriate behaviors is the location of their desks. In addition to seating students with behavior disorders near teachers for proximity control, placing these students near positive peer models can help them learn appropriate classroom behaviors. To enhance the effectiveness of the model, teachers should praise the model periodically in the presence of the behaviorally disordered students. The praise can function as vicarious reinforcement and promote positive behaviors in behaviorally disordered students (Kazdin, 1979; Strain & Timm, 1974).

Teachers also should examine the movement patterns within the classroom when determining the work areas for students with behavior disorders

IDEAS FOR IMPLEMENTATION	Teachers can adapt their classroom organization to reduce off-task behavior by enacting the following suggestions: • Locate the teacher's desk near the front of the room and position it so that it faces the class. • Use borders and partitions to minimize distractions in the room. • Place teaching stations and centers in corners of the room so that they can be more easily monitored. • Establish activity centers for special projects. • Use bulletin boards to post scores and showcase materials. • Establish systematic routines for performing nonacademic tasks (free time, attendance, lunch money) • Organize and arrange teacher and student materials before class begins.

Source: Reith and Everston (1988); Paine et al. (1983).

(Salend, 1983a). Teachers should avoid putting the desks of students with behavior disorders in parts of the room that have a lot of activity, such as near learning centers, media, and pencil sharpeners. Since many students with behavior disorders may experience problems with staying on task, avoid sitting them near open doors and windows.

Students from Culturally and Linguistically Diverse Backgrounds

The classroom design, including the seating and materials arrangement, should promote social and academic interactions and the full integration of all students. Toward this end, bulletin boards should display the work of all students, and should also display pictures, posters, and art forms that reflect the students' families, homes, and neighborhoods, and illustrations of other cultural groups that may not be represented in the classroom (Foulks, 1991). Teachers can arrange the classroom environment to promote the acquisition of language by second language learners by doing the following:

- making language an integral part of all classroom routines
- providing students with access to relevant and motivating materials and learning activities
- labelling work areas and objects in the classroom
- establishing social and work areas
- setting up listening and meeting areas
- offering students opportunities to sit next to and work with peer models (Enright & Gomez, 1984; Ostrosky & Kaiser, 1991)

Think About It

Sketch a classroom plan. Consider such factors as seating arrangements, the teacher's and students' desks, instructional materials, bulletin boards and walls, specialized areas, and learning centers. How does your classroom design relate to your educational philosophy and teaching style? How has your classroom been adapted for students with disabilities and students from culturally and linguistically diverse backgrounds?

SUMMARY

This chapter was designed to offer guidelines for promoting appropriate classroom behavior, and modifying the classroom design to address the needs of mainstreamed students. The chapter

- presented a rationale for understanding and interpreting behavior and communication within a social/cultural context
- outlined strategies educators can use to define and record student behavior
- provided guidelines for conducting an antecedent-behavior-consequences (ABC) analysis to plan appropriate strategies to modify classroom behavior
- offered strategies to promote appropriate classroom behavior
- presented strategies to decrease inappropriate classroom behavior
- outlined group-oriented behavior management strategies to promote appropriate and decrease disruptive behavior
- described affective education strategies that can be used as part of their classroom management system
- offered classroom design strategies to modify the classroom design to accommodate mainstreamed students

RECOMMENDED READINGS

Alberto, P. A., & Troutman, A. C. (1990). *Applied behavior analysis for teachers (3rd ed).* New York: Merrill/Macmillan.

Banbury, M. M., & Hebert, C. R. (1992). Do you see what I mean? Body language in classroom interactions. *Teaching Exceptional Children, 24*(2), 32–38.

Curwin, R. L., & Mendler, A. N. (1988). *Discipline with dignity.* Alexandria, VA: Association for Supervision and Curriculum Development.

Everston, C. M., Emmer, E. T., Clements, B. S., Sanford, J. P., & Worsham, M. E. (1989). *Classroom management for elementary teachers (2nd ed.).* Englewood Cliffs, NJ: Prentice-Hall.

Jones, V. F., & Jones, L. S. (1986). *Comprehensive classroom management: Creating positive learning environments.* Boston: Allyn and Bacon.

Parette, H. P., & Hourcade, J. J. (1986). Management strategies for orthopedically handicapped students. *Teaching Exceptional Children, 18,* 282–286.

Rikhye, C. H., Gothelf, C. R., & Appell, M. W. (1989). A classroom environment checklist of students with dual sensory impairments. *Teaching Exceptional Children, 22*(1), 44–46.

Schrumpf, F., Crawford, D., & Usadel, H. C. (1991). *Peer mediation: Conflict resolution in schools.* Champaign, IL: Research Press.

Smith, M. A., & Misra, A. (1992). A comprehensive management system for students in regular classrooms. *The Elementary School Journal, 92*(3), 354–371.

Webber, J., & Scheuermann, B. (1991). Accentuate the positive . . . Eliminate the negative! *Teaching Exceptional Children, 24*(1), 13–19.

11 Evaluating the Progress of Mainstreamed Students

EXAMINING MONA'S PROGRESS

The multidisciplinary team is meeting to determine Mona's progress in her mainstreamed classes. To assess Mona's academic performance, the team examines data from a curriculum-based assessment relating to Mona's math and a portfolio assessment addressing Mona's reading performance. Curriculum-based assessment data indicate that Mona is benefitting from her current math instructional program. Portfolio assessment data collected via think-alouds, interviews, and an analysis of oral reading, initially indicated that Mona's reading was characterized by a failure to consider meaning and the message being communicated by the author. However, her current reading performance indicates that she is beginning to pay more attention to the author's meaning. She also is beginning to read with more confidence and enthusiasm.

The team also examines her grades in each subject area. Since teachers are using a multiple grading system that is supplemented with descriptive statements, the team examines Mona's grades in terms of ability, effort, and achievement. Her grades indicate that she is experiencing some problems in social studies. Ms. Carlos, Mona's social studies teacher, notes that Mona has not been completing her homework regularly, and is doing poorly on some tests. Mona confirms Ms. Carlos's observation, and tells the team, "I'm trying, but it's hard to get everything done. I'm in two afterschool clubs, and sometimes I'm so tired I just go home and collapse. I do the worst on her essay tests. Sometimes, I just go blank and don't know what she wants."

While the team is pleased with Mona's overall progress, the members discuss how they can help Mona complete her homework and improve her performance on tests. To assist Mona in completing her homework, the team devises a communication system between Mona's parents and teachers to assist and monitor Mona's completion of her homework. The team asks the resource room teacher to teach Mona test-taking skills and how to study for tests. Ms. Carlos also agrees to adapt the essay questions on her tests by dividing open-ended essay questions into smaller sequential subquestions that guide students' responses, and listing on the test important concepts that students should mention in writing their essays.

What additional components of Mona's educational experience should the multidisciplinary team examine to evaluate her progress in the mainstream? After reading this chapter, you should be able to answer this as well as the following questions.

- What types of informal and formal testing procedures can educators use to monitor and assess student performance?
- What alternative procedures are available to assess the progress of students from culturally and linguistically diverse backgrounds?
- How can educators adapt grading systems for mainstreamed students?
- How can educators adapt teacher-made tests to assess the performance of mainstreamed students accurately?
- What alternative testing techniques can educators employ to help mainstreamed students perform at their optimal level?
- How can educators teach students a variety of test-taking skills?
- How can parents, teachers, and students be involved in evaluating the progress of mainstreamed students?
- What factors should educators consider in evaluating the effectiveness of instructional modifications, adaptive devices, and medical interventions?

Once students are placed in the mainstream, the planning team should monitor their progress to determine if the mainstreamed placement is achieving its intended academic and social outcomes (Bender, 1987; Hundert, 1982; Ledeber & Azzara, 1980). If problems are found, the team can then gather followup information to develop new strategies to intervene in and minimize the identified problem areas. Additionally, a followup examination of students' progress should be directed at providing educators with data to evaluate the school district's mainstreaming procedures (Bender, 1987). Such data can help educators validate successful mainstreaming policies that should be continued, as well as pinpoint procedures that need to be revised.

DESIGNING EVALUATION OF MAINSTREAMING PLACEMENTS

Wang, Anderson, and Bram (1985) identified three aspects of student performance that should be assessed in evaluating mainstream programs: performance, attitude, and process. *Performance* measures relate to achievement in the content areas. *Attitudinal* measures include the mainstreamed student's self-concept as well as attitudes toward school and peers. The attitudes of peers, teachers, and parents toward mainstreaming and mainstreamed students also are important attitudinal variables. *Process* measures encompass the types of interactions mainstreamed students have with their teachers and peers.

Bender (1988) proposes that teachers, administrators, and multidisciplinary teams—or a combination of these three groups—periodically assess student progress in the mainstream. The frequency of followup evaluations will depend on the needs and skill levels of the students, parents and educators (Salend, 1983c).

The followup evaluation of student progress should be carefully planned and implemented by the multidisciplinary IEP planning team. The team should determine the areas to be evaluated, the specific criteria to guide the evaluation, as well as the procedures for measuring student progress. They can obtain information on student progress via norm-referenced and criterion-referenced testing, curriculum-based assessment, portfolio assessments, error analysis, think-alouds, student journals, observation, and interviews with educators, parents, and students. These assessments can be performed by special educators, regular educators, and placement team members with specific areas of expertise.

ASSESSING STUDENT PROGRESS

Educators make many critical decisions about student educational programs based on data collected from informal testing, and norm-referenced and criterion-referenced standardized tests. Both types of testing can be used to assess student progress in the mainstreamed setting. This chapter presents discussions of various formal and informal assessment strategies.

Norm-Referenced Testing

Norm-referenced tests provide measures of performance that allow educators to compare an individual's score to the scores of others (McLoughlin & Lewis, 1990). Norms are determined by analyzing the scores of students from different ages, grades, geographical regions, cultural and economic backgrounds, and settings (such as urban, suburban, and rural). These norms are then used to compare students, schools, school districts, and geographical regions in terms of such variables as age and grade level (Wallace & Larsen, 1978). For example, norm-referenced testing may yield that a student is reading at a third-grade level and performing at a fifth-grade level in mathematics.

Norm-referenced tests are used as the basis for many educational decisions. They can be employed in the initial screening of students to determine if their performance warrants a more extensive evaluation. They also can be employed to determine if a student's performance makes him or her eligible for special education services. Norm-referenced tests can help educators determine the general curricular areas in which students excel or need remedial instruction as well as evaluate whether or not the instructional program has resulted in a change in the students' performance. The advantages and disadvantages of norm-referenced testing are summarized in Figure 11.1.

Criterion-Referenced Testing

As opposed to norm-referenced testing, *criterion-referenced testing* compares an individual's performance to a specific level of mastery in relation to a curriculum. Rather than giving a grade level at which students are functioning, criterion-referenced testing yields information to determine the specific skills mastered and not mastered by students. For example, the results of a criterion-referenced test may show that a student can add and subtract decimals and fractions, but cannot multiply or divide them. The advantages and disadvantages of using criterion-referenced testing are presented in Figure 11.2.

FIGURE 11.1
Advantages and disadvantages of norm-referenced testing

Advantages	Disadvantages
1. Provides basis for comparison with other students.	1. Fails to provide data for teaching and planning an instructional program.
2. Offers general measures of progress.	2. Findings can be overgeneralized and used to make incorrect decisions.
3. Reliability and validity are usually reported in the manual.	3. Often lacks adequate reliability and validity.
4. Provides educators with a capsule description of a student's performance.	4. Provides global information rather than looking at each item.
5. Can pinpoint areas where student needs remediation or more intensive assessment.	5. Format of test can be difficult for many students.
6. Usually easy to administer, score, and interpret.	6. Test items and standardization do not reflect a multicultural perspective.
	7. Can be biased with respect to curriculum content.
	8. Test content and items often conflict with developmentally appropriate practices.

McCormack (1978) provides guidelines for constructing teacher-made, criterion-referenced tests.

Many criterion-referenced tests measuring a range of content areas are available, but educators may need to develop their own criterion-referenced tests tailored to their unique curriculum.

Think About It

Examine a standardized test for gender, race, social class, and linguistic bias. Look at the pictures, and content and language of items. Are they free of bias?

Curriculum-Based Assessment

Although student progress traditionally has been assessed via norm-referenced and criterion-referenced testing, it can also be examined in relation to the curriculum of the class, grade, school, or district through use of *curriculum-based assessment* (*CBA*) (Germann & Tindal, 1985; Tucker, 1985). Gickling and Thompson (1985) define CBA as "a procedure for determining the instructional needs of students based on the student's on-going performance in existing course content" (p. 206).

CBA provides individualized, direct, and repeated measures of students' levels of proficiency and progress in the curriculum. The content of CBA is derived directly from students' instructional programs (Salvia & Hughes, 1990). For example, a CBA to assess progress in reading would require students to read selections from the reader they use everyday. Rather than assessing students at irregular intervals, teachers using CBA regularly sample student performance of typical classroom tasks. Because CBA is an ongoing dynamic process, it provides teachers with a continuous measurement of student progress.

CBA has several advantages over other methods of assessment including linking testing, teaching, and evaluation; improving communication among professionals; being sensitive to changes in student performance over brief

FIGURE 11.2
Advantages and disadvantages of criterion-referenced testing

Advantages	Disadvantages
1. Students are judged on their own strengths and weaknesses.	1. Content of commercially produced tests may not match the teachers' curriculum.
2. Facilitates teaching and the planning of instructional programs.	2. Teacher-made criterion-referenced tests can be time consuming to construct and are only as good as the teachers' competence.
3. Allows for ongoing assessment of students' progress.	3. The behavioral levels for mastery and the skill sequence may be inappropriate.
4. Teacher-made criterion-referenced tests can be adapted to a variety of curricular areas, and have a direct link to the curriculum.	

IDEAS FOR IMPLEMENTATION

Educators can follow these guidelines when devising teacher-made criterion-referenced tests:

1. Determine the curriculum area to be assessed (for example, addition and subtraction of decimals).
2. Develop a skill sequence for the curriculum area. Make sure the skill sequence is complete and ordered from easiest to hardest.
3. Task analyze each skill into subskills, if necessary.
4. State each skill as a behavioral objective.
5. Determine a level of mastery for each objective.
6. Construct items to reflect the objectives. Consider the following:

   - Do items match the objectives?
   - Are there a sufficient number of items per objective?
   - What materials are needed?
   - What is the teacher's role?
   - Are the presentation and response modes consistent with the objectives?
   - How are items scored?

7. Construct a scoring and descriptive data sheet.
8. Conduct the assessment.
9. Revise assessment device.

periods of time; facilitating decisions regarding student progress in the mainstream curriculum and instructional placement; increasing student performance and being cost effective in terms of ease of administration and economics (Deno & Fuchs, 1988; Frank & Gerken, 1990). CBA provides teachers with information on the demands of instructional tasks, allowing them to determine the content and pace of an instructional program. Thus, in addition to providing data on student progress, CBA can help teachers match specific instructional practices and materials to mainstreamed students' learning needs, which results in improved performance on school-related tasks (Gickling & Thompson, 1985). CBA also can be used to develop norms for school districts to provide a database for decisions to classify students and develop IEPs (Germann & Tindal, 1985; Peterson, Heistad, Peterson, & Reynolds, 1985).

Blankenship (1985), Deno and Fuchs (1988), and Salvia and Hughes (1990) offer educators guidelines for conducting a CBA:

1. *Identify the content area(s) to be assessed.* CBA has been used to assess a variety of content areas including speech, vocational education, secondary content areas, independent living skills, and reading, math, and social skills (Germann & Tindal, 1985).

2. *Define the school-related tasks that will constitute the assessment and the sample duration.* For example, measure reading by having students read aloud from their readers for a sample duration of one minute, spelling

by the number of words from the spelling list spelled correctly, and writing by the number of words in a story during a sample duration of five minutes (Deno & Fuchs, 1988). The level of the content will vary depending on the ability of the individual student.

3. *Determine if performance or progress measurement will be used.* Performance measurement involves changes on a specific task over a period of time, while progress measurement evaluates student progress on sequentially ordered levels/objectives within the curriculum (Deno & Fuchs, 1988; Germann & Tindal, 1985). If performance measurement is selected, then the task that comprises the assessment will remain constant throughout the CBA. If progress measurement is chosen, then the objectives in the curriculum should be placed in sequential order, mastery levels determined, and corresponding tasks identified.

4. *Prepare and organize the necessary materials.*

5. *Administer the CBA.* Students should be informed that the goal of the assessment is to help teachers decide what needs to be taught, and that they may not know the answers to every question, but should just do their best (Blankenship, 1985).

6. *Decide how frequently the CBA will be readministered.* Depending on teacher time, student skill, and the nature of the task, educators should decide how frequently to readminister the CBA to students.

7. *Graph student performance.* A sample graph is presented in Figure 11.3. The vertical axis measures the student's performance on the school-related task (such as the number of words read, or the number or words spelled). The horizontal axis indicates the day on which the measurement is taken. Data points on the graph should provide a measure of the correct and

FIGURE 11.3
Graph of curriculum-based spelling assessment

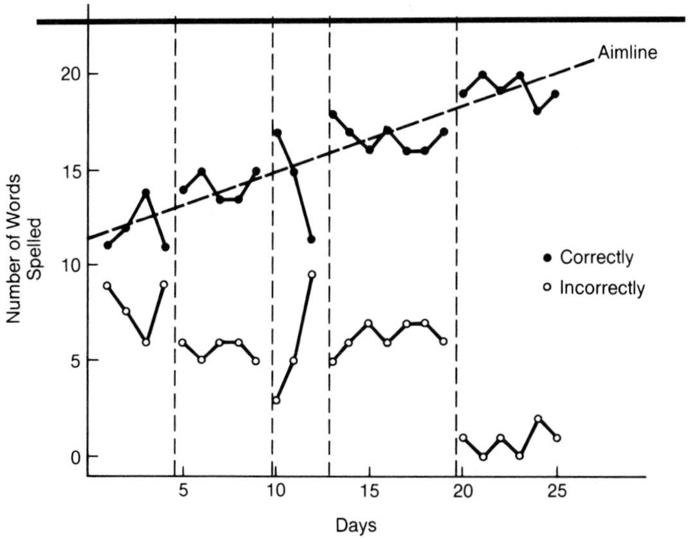

incorrect responses. The diagonal broken line starting at the left and ending on the right side of the graph is called the *aimline.* Germann and Tindal (1985) define aimlines as "visual illustrations of estimated or predicted progress/performance and indicate the general trend and direction that the data must take" (p. 246). Aimlines provide educators with a reference point for judging student progress and making decisions about students' instructional program (Shinn & Hubbard, 1992). The vertical broken lines indicate changes in the instructional program.

8. *Analyze the results to determine student progress in terms of skills mastered and not mastered.* Identify the students who evidence mastery of the skills and are ready for new instructional objectives; those who are progressing but need additional instruction to demonstrate mastery of skills; and those who have not progressed and need modifications in their instructional program (Blankenship, 1985).

9. *Compare the efficacy of different instructional strategies.* Several rules for using CBA to determine the need for changes in instructional strategies have been suggested (Germann & Tindal, 1985; White & Haring, 1981). White and Haring (1981) recommend that educators use a different instructional program when students' levels of performance are below the predicted performance level (aimline) for three consecutive days. Similarly, Mirkin et al. (1981) propose that teachers examine performance for a period of 7 to 10 days before modifying the instructional program. Germann & Tindal (1985) believe that teachers should change their instructional strategies every three weeks to determine the effectiveness and efficiency of a variety of instructional procedures.

Portfolio Assessment

In addition to receiving ESL instruction, Chin Lee is placed in a mainstreamed classroom upon her arrival in the United States. Though she has received an education in her homeland, her English skills are limited to a few words and sentences. Rather than charting her progress in developing writing proficiency in English through use of a standardized test, Chin Lee's teachers decide to maintain a portfolio of her written products, such as writing samples and written responses in journals. Chin Lee's teachers also keep anecdotal records of their observations of Chin Lee during writing time. An analysis of these records over 12 months reveals the following observations:

"Initially, Chin Lee's writing is characterized by scribbling and drawing. Her stories contain pictures, and she attempts to tell her story by using scribble."

"While Chin Lee is still expressing her stories through use of pictures and scribbling, she has started to learn the correct directional movement of English writing."

"Chin Lee today wrote a story containing random letters and symbols in addition to pictures and scribbling."

"Chin Lee's story was noteworthy for its use of approximations of words through use of beginning and ending letters. Her story also included various sight words and she began to leave spaces between words. She continues to use scribble for words or sounds she doesn't know."

"Chin Lee's stories are longer, containing four attempted sentences. The stories also show an increase in the use of sight words, which are now usually spelled correctly."

"Chin Lee has stopped using scribbling. She is inventing spellings of words based on her phonetic skills."

"Chin Lee is writing on a greater variety of topics. She is starting to include periods and capital letters in her stories."

Portfolio assessment involves a collection of a variety of student products across a range of content areas throughout the school year. Portfolios are archival in nature and contain samples over time that are periodically reviewed by educators, parents, and students to document progress, process, effort, achievement, and development. The use of portfolios is especially important for students who may be making progress, but who may appear to be limited in comparison to peers. While portfolio assessment is appropriate for all students, it is particularly meaningful for students from culturally and linguistically diverse backgrounds whose progress may not be accurately measured by traditional testing strategies. For example, a series of audio recordings of language samples over time can be included in the portfolio for second language learners to measure students' progress in learning English by examining the amount of description provided, the use of more complex sentence structures, and vocabulary.

Samples that may be placed in portfolios include checklists, journals, selected daily work samples, projects, tests, tape recordings, reports, homework assignments, artwork, awards, language proficiency tests, lists of after school clubs, teacher observations, and parent and student interviews and surveys.

The items that are selected for the portfolio are jointly determined by teachers and students and should be related to the goals of the student's instructional program. Some teachers involve students in the selection process by asking students to identify products with which they are satisfied and dissatisfied. Over time, products that were originally identified as dissatisfied evolve into satisfied products and vice versa. When selecting products to be part of a portfolio, educators and students should determine what the selected piece demonstrates about the student's learning and how the piece provides information about the instruction needed for this student.

Once an item has been selected to be part of a portfolio, the information it presents regarding the student's performance should be noted by including a caption statement (Valencia, 1990). *Caption statements* are brief descriptions that identify the document, provide the context in which the document was produced, and explain why the item was selected. A sample caption statement is presented in Figure 11.4. Portfolios also contain *summary sheets,* which synthesize the information presented in the portfolio, and allow educators to organize the contents of the portfolio to facilitate the instructional decisionmaking process (Wolf, 1990). Portfolios also should include a statement from the student reflecting upon his or her products.

FIGURE 11.4
Sample caption statement

Date: 10/2/94

Context: Writing

Description: This is an example of a piece of writing from draft to publication. Included are a semantic map used for brainstorming during prewriting, an initial draft, two revisions, anecdotal comments from two conferences with the teacher, and the published piece. This product demonstrates the student's first attempts at revision.

Portfolios should be reviewed periodically by teachers, students, parents, and administrators throughout the school year. Portfolios can be shared with others during conferences, which allow participants to examine the student's portfolio in comparison to the goals of the student's instructional program. Additionally, portfolios can be shared with the student's new teacher(s) at the end of each school year (Gropper, n.d.).

Error Analysis

Educators using both formal and informal assessment techniques to evaluate student progress in mainstreamed settings can increase the amount of information obtained from these procedures by employing *error analysis* (Gickling & Thompson, 1985; Grimes, 1981). Data provided via error analysis can help teachers make decisions that significantly improve student performance (Grimes, 1981). Error analysis allows teachers to examine students' responses to identify areas of difficulty and patterns in the ways students approach a task.

IDEAS FOR IMPLEMENTATION

Teachers can implement portfolio assessments by doing the following:

1. *Determine the goals that the portfolio will address.* Goals should cover an extended period of time, be broadly stated, and related directly to the curriculum.
2. *Select a variety of real classroom products that address the goals of the portfolio.* Students and teachers select a range of items that relate to the goals of the portfolio to be included in the students' portfolios.
3. *Establish procedures for collecting student's products.* Teachers store students' products in individualized folders that are located in a convenient location. As teachers enter products into folders, caption statements are placed on the products.
4. *Review portfolios periodically.* Teachers examine students' portfolios and prepare summary statements to synthesize information presented in the portfolio. Portfolios are reviewed with students and plans to facilitate student progress are made.
5. *Share portfolios with others.* Portfolios are shared with parents, other teachers and administrators. At the end of the school year, parts of the portfolio can be shared with students' new teachers.

Source: Gropper (n.d.); Pike, Compain, & Mumper (in press).

Error analysis usually focuses on identifying errors related to inappropriate applications of rules and concepts, rather than careless random errors or errors caused by lack of training (Cox, 1975). For example, an error analysis of the subtraction problem

$$\begin{array}{r} 4265 \\ -\ \underline{3197} \\ 1132 \end{array}$$

may indicate that the student has mastered the subtraction facts, but subtracts the smaller number from the larger number rather than the subtrahend from the minuend. Rather than teaching the student subtraction facts, the teacher would then focus instruction on subtracting the subtrahend from the minuend.

Think-Aloud Techniques

Information on the ways students approach a task also can be obtained through use of *think-aloud techniques,* which ask students to state the process they are employing while working on a task (Meyers & Lytle, 1986). For example, Meyers and Lytle (1986) propose think-aloud techniques to assess reading comprehension. Students are instructed to read each sentence individually, then state their thoughts, which are then categorized as indicating understanding, expressing doubt or lack of understanding, analyzing text features, expanding on text, or judging the text and reasoning. These data are then used to assist students in improving their reading comprehension skills.

Andrews and Mason (1991) employed think-aloud techniques to assess the reading strategies of deaf and hearing readers.

Because students do not spontaneously think aloud, they must be taught to do so. Teachers can encourage students to think aloud by modeling the procedure and talking as they work through tasks and situations. In addition, teachers can prompt students to think-aloud by employing probing questions such as *Tell me, what are you doing now?; What are you thinking about?;* and *Tell me, how did you come up with that answer?* (Andrews & Mason, 1991).

IDEAS FOR IMPLEMENTATION

Educators can conduct an error analysis by doing the following:

1. Give the student a series of problems or questions.
2. Record the student's responses so that they can be analyzed. When a written response is not produced by the student, such as when reading, teachers should convert the student's response to a permanent product.
3. Analyze errors by looking for patterns in the student's responses.
4. Probe further to confirm error patterns by having the student respond to additional items.
5. Review with the student how she or he approached the task and arrived at answers.
6. Provide instruction to the student to remediate the error pattern.

Student Journals/Learning Logs

Davison and Pearce (1992) used student journals to assess and increase the math performance of students from culturally and linguistically diverse backgrounds.

Students also can be involved in the assessment process through use of *journals,* or *learning logs.* Periodically, students can write comments in their journals concerning what they learned; how they learned it; what they do not understand; why they are confused; and what help they would like to receive. Teachers and students can then examine the logs to identify instructional goals and modifications. Students also can place entries in their journals relating to specific information covered in class or attitudes toward a content area.

Self-Evaluation Questionnaires/Interviews

Data from students concerning their performance also can be obtained by using *self-evaluation questionnaires* or *interviews.* Self-evaluation questionnaires or interviews can provide data concerning students' perceptions of their educational needs, progress in learning new material, and strategies for completing a task. For example, according to Pike, Compain, and Mumper (in press), a questionnaire or interview might focus on asking students to respond to the following questions: *What are some things you do well when you read? What are some areas in reading that cause you difficulty? In what ways is your reading improving? What areas of your reading would you like to improve?*

Assessing the Progress of Students from Culturally and Linguistically Diverse Backgrounds

Educators should exercise caution when using standardized tests to assess the progress of students from culturally and linguistically diverse backgrounds (Laosa, 1977; Oakland, 1980).

Nondiscriminatory Testing

While the IDEA mandates that assessment materials and procedures be selected and administered so that they are not racially and culturally discriminatory, research indicates that standardized tests *are* culturally and socially biased, resulting in a disproportionate number of students from culturally and linguistically diverse backgrounds being misclassified as having disabilities (Heller, Holtzman, & Messick, 1982). Additionally, several court cases have established the need for nondiscriminatory testing (Galagan, 1985). In the landmark case relating to nondiscriminatory assessment, *Diana v. California State Board of Education* (1970), nine Spanish-speaking Mexican American students were classified as mentally retarded as a result of their performance on English-language standardized tests. The students' attorneys argued that the evaluation procedures were discriminatory in terms of standardization and their dependence on English-language skills. To support this contention, they produced evidence which showed that when seven of the nine students were retested in Spanish, they scored in the average range. In an out-of-court settlement, it was agreed that students must be assessed in their native language in addition to English; assessments should include a measure of student performance on nonverbal subtests; Mexican American students in classes for the Educable Mentally Retarded must be retested, and plans for placing students no longer eligible for these services in regular education classrooms must be developed; educators will develop an IQ test that is consistent with the Mexican American culture and normed using Mexican American students; and school districts must examine the racial and ethnic balance in their classes for students with mental retardation and establish plans for any inequities that are found to exist. The findings of *Diana* were extended to African American students in *Larry P. v. Riles* (1979) and to Asian American students in *Lau v. Nichols* (1974). In *Arreola v. Santa Anna Board of Education* (1968), parents were granted the right to have a hearing prior to their child's placement in special education. Similarly, in *Covarrubias v. San Diego Unified School District* (1971), the right to informed consent prior to special education placement was established. While *Jose P. v. Ambach* (1983) dealt with complying with timelines for evaluation and placement in special education, this case also established that if a bilingual student is experiencing a learning problem that may lead to special education placement, personnel fluent in the student's home language and bicultural in the student's home culture should be involved in assessment and instruction. Similar cases have been initiated in other states (Fradd, Vega, & Hallman, 1985; Galagan, 1985).

Standardized testing is particularly problematic for second language learners, whose learning needs are often viewed as learning problems rather than language and cultural differences (Duran, 1989; Figueroa, 1989; Rueda, 1989). Researchers note that the use of inappropriate assessment instruments and ineffective instructional strategies leads to inaccurate placements that fail to address the specific learning needs of second language learners. Furthermore, Duran (1989) points out that the performance of second language learners on standardized tests is often hindered by their limited proficiency in English, their lack of familiarity with the tests' content and with test-taking strategies, and the failure of test administrators to understand the social and cultural factors associated with the assessment process. To address these inappropriate placements, researchers have proposed that assessment procedures include strategies for measuring first and second language proficiency, examining achievement and intelligence testing in the students' primary languages, documenting students' language use in natural environments, promoting prereferral interventions, and linking assessment with effective instruction (Rueda, 1989).

Several alternatives to traditional assessments for students from culturally and linguistically diverse backgrounds have been proposed: culture-free/ -fair tests, culture-specific tests, translations, pluralistic assessment, measuring adaptive behavior, and dynamic assessment (Duran, 1989; Guerin & Maier, 1983; McLoughlin & Lewis, 1990).

Culture-Free/ Culture-Fair Tests. Culture-free or culture-fair tests seek to measure aspects of growth that are presumed to be unrelated to culture, such as perceptual and motor growth. For example, the *Cattell Culture-Free Test of Intelligence* (Cattell & Cattell, 1963) attempts to minimize the influences of language and school learning in assessing intelligence by asking students to select the appropriate visual stimuli that completes a visual pattern. However, research on these types of tests indicates they are *not* free of bias (Galagan, 1985; Gonzales, 1982) because perceptual and test-taking skills *are* related to culture (Guerin & Maier, 1983).

Culture-Specific Tests. Culture-specific tests measure knowledge of and competence within a nondominant culture (McLoughlin & Lewis, 1990). These tests give a measure of the student's understanding of the culture, but their use is limited because their relationship to school learning is minimal and their content is only related to a small region (Guerin & Maier, 1983).

Test Translation. The IDEA (PL 101-476) requires school districts to establish procedures so that students from linguistically diverse backgrounds are administered tests in their native language or preferred mode of communication. As a result, some educators have sought to minimize the bias in English-language assessments by translating them into the student's dominant language. However, translations do not remove the bias in tests that are related to item, picture, and task selection. For example, some concepts may not exist in other cultures and languages, such as certain time and color concepts. In addition, because words may have different levels of difficulty across languages and dialects, test translations may change the psychometric properties of the original test. For example, Figueroa (1989) noted that words in English do not have the same levels of difficulty as Spanish words that have the same meaning. Additionally, translation does not account for experiences and words that have different or multiple meanings in different cultures. Thus, despite the translation, the constructs on which the test items are based still reflect the dominant culture and may not be appropriate for students from other cultures.

Pluralistic Assessment. Pluralistic assessment seeks to reduce the bias in testing by assessing several domains and using norms developed for multicultural populations. Pluralistic assessment provides data on students' medical status, social performance, and learning potential using standardized tests with norms established on students from linguistically and culturally diverse students (Mercer & Lewis, 1977).

Measurements of Adaptive Behavior. A key component of nondiscriminatory assessment is the measurement of adaptive behavior, the "effectiveness with which individuals can cope with the social and cultural demands of their environments" (Knapp & Salend, 1983, p. 63). Because adaptive behavior instruments examine domains outside the traditional educational setting, they can be instrumental in giving a more accurate and diverse profile of student performance (Coulter & Morrow, 1978). This is especially important for students whose lifestyles provide them with a range of experiences and create a demand for them to perform a variety of roles, which may differ significantly from their middle-class peers. However, educators should interpret the results of adaptive behavior measurements with care, as behavior is culture bound (Trueba, 1983) and these instruments are based on a cultural perspective of adaptive behavior. They are therefore not completely free of cultural bias. Additional potential problems in the administration and interpretation of adaptive behavior measurements have been identified, and solutions offered (Knapp & Salend, 1983).

Dynamic Assessment. Dynamic assessment seeks to establish a direct relationship between assessment and instruction by employing a test-train-test model (Duran, 1989). While students work on a task, educators observe and offer feedback to students designed to increase students' performance and skill levels. As students master skills, the educators offer less assistance and feedback and seek to increase students' problem solving abilities. One example of dynamic assessment is Feuerstein's (1979) *Learning Potential Assessment Model,* where educators use their clinical judgment to offer students prompts and cues to facilitate skill acquisition.

ADAPTING GRADING AND TESTING FOR MAINSTREAMED STUDENTS

Grading procedures are affected by students' gender and past performance as well as disability labels (Carpenter, 1985).

Testing and grading student mastery of specific material are necessary components of evaluating student progress. However, for mainstreamed students, traditional testing and grading procedures can be an obstacle to successful functioning in the regular classroom milieu (S.M. Salend & S.J. Salend, 1985). Therefore, in addition to modifying the instructional program for mainstreamed students, teachers may need to adapt their grading and testing systems.

Educators must be careful that the grading and testing modifications they institute do not compromise the integrity of the test, course, or curriculum. Therefore, the need for adaptations in testing and grading should be determined by the multidisciplinary placement team and should be outlined in the student's IEP.

Grading

After numerous complaints about the school district's grading procedures for mainstreamed students, the district forms a committee of teachers, parents, administrators, and students to devise a new grading system for mainstreamed students. Initially, the committee debates the purposes of grading. One member states, "Grades should indicate how much students know in comparison to others." Another member feels that "grades should give students and parents an indication of student growth and effort." A third member argues that "grades should identify strengths and weaknesses."

After much discussion, the committee decides that the district needs an individualized, flexible, grading system that acknowledges student competence, progress, and effort, and proposes two alternative grading systems. One system, based on students' IEPs, uses the objectives and performance criteria in the IEP to measure the students' performance and achievements during the marking period. The students' grades are a function of the number of objectives mastered and the level of mastery demonstrated for each objective. To ensure the consistency of this grading system with the school district's policies for grading, the criteria levels specified in the IEP reflect the performance standards specified in the district's grading procedures. For example, students who master all their objectives by obtaining a mastery level of 80 percent are assigned a grade of B, while students who achieve a mastery level of 90 percent or greater on all their objectives are assigned a grade of A.

The committee also suggests that the district consider a level grading system, whereby a subscript is used to indicate students' grades and the levels at which students are working. They devised a subscript system so that a B_1, B_2, and B_3, indicate that the student grade is a B based on content above grade level, at grade level, or below grade level, respectively. In addition to using subscripts, they suggest that teachers also can supplement these quantitative report card grades by writing comments concerning the students' performance and effort.

Although grading presents a problem for many educators, it may be particularly problematic for teachers dealing with mainstreamed students (Carpenter, 1985; Harrington & Morrison, 1981). The major responsibility for assigning grades will lie with the regular classroom teacher, but because mainstreamed students may receive the services of other teachers, the roles of these professionals regarding the assigning of grades should be discussed and delineated (Cohen, 1983). This discussion should include the following considerations:

1. Who is responsible for assigning the report card grade?
2. Should the grade be based on the discrepancy between the student's actual and potential performance or between the actual performance and grade level expectancy?
3. What type of grading feedback should be given on a daily basis?
4. What type of descriptive annotation will best complement the system's report card grading procedure?
5. Whom should the parent contact to discuss a grade? (Cohen, 1983, p. 86)

Alternative Grading Systems

Most teachers use a traditional grading system whereby students are compared and assigned letter or numerical grades based on their performance on tests (Marsh & Price, 1980). However, this system may not be appropriate for many mainstreamed students, as it does not allow for grades to be assigned on an individualized scale (Cohen, 1983). Point systems can be made fairer for mainstreamed students by weighting a variety of activities to determine students' grades (Kinnison, Hayes, & Acord, 1981). For example, rather than grades being based solely on test scores, points toward the final grade can be divided so that 40 percent of the grade is related to projects, 30 percent to test performance, 10 percent to class participation, 10 percent to homework and 10 percent to effort.

When grading students, teachers should consider using alternative grading systems. (The discussion that follows, concerning individual alternative systems, is adapted from the work of Cohen, 1983; Jones & Jones, 1986; Kinnison, Hayes, & Acord, 1981; Rojewski, Pollard, & Meers, 1992; and Vasa, 1981.)

Individual Educational Program. Students' IEP goals and performance criteria serve as the foundation for grading, and teachers assign grades that acknowledge student progress in meeting goals established at a certain skill level.

Student Self-Comparison. Students and teachers meet and determine appropriate instructional goals within the curriculum for students, and then keep track of the students' progress toward meeting the identified goals, which are reported on the students' report cards.

Contract Grading. Teachers and students determine the amount and quality of the work students must complete to receive a specific grade. In framing the contract, both teachers and students should agree on the content the students hope to learn; activities, strategies, and resources that will help them acquire the skills; products students will produce to demonstrate mastery; strategies for evaluating their products; timelines for assignments including penalties for lateness; and procedures for assigning a grade.

Pass/Fail Systems. Minimum course competencies are specified and any student who demonstrates mastery receives a P grade, while students who fail to meet the minimum standards are given an F grade. Some schools have modified traditional Pass/Fail grading to include such distinctions as honors (HonorP), high pass (HP), pass (P), and low pass (LP).

Mastery Level/Criterion Systems. Students and teachers meet to divide the material into a hierarchy of skills and activities based on individual needs and abilities as measured by a pretest. After completing learning activities, the students take a posttest or perform an activity to demonstrate mastery of the content. When students demonstrate mastery via the posttest or the activity, they receive credit for that accomplishment and proceed to the next skill to be mastered. This process is repeated until students master all skill levels.

Checklists. Teachers develop checklists that delineate the competencies associated with their courses and evaluate each student according to mastery of these competencies.

Multiple Grading. Teachers grade students in the areas of ability, effort, and achievement. The ability grade is based on the students' expected improvements in content area. The effort grade is a measure of the time and energy the students devoted to learning the content. The achievement grade assesses the students' mastery of the material in relation to others. Students' report cards can then include a listing of the three grades for each content area, or grades can be computed by averaging the three areas.

Level Grading. Teachers individualize the grading system by using a subscript to indicate the level of difficulty at which the students' grades are based. For example, a grade of B_6 can be used to note that a student is working in the B range at the sixth-grade level.

Shared Grading. Teachers who are working together to instruct students collaborate to assign students their grades based on both teachers' observations of performance and establish guidelines for determining and weighting valid criteria and measuring performance.

Descriptive Grading. Teachers write descriptive comments and give examples regarding student performance that provide parents, students, and other educators with information on the students' skills, learning styles, effort, and attitudes.

Think About It

Should mainstreamed students be graded using the same grading systems as their peers? Should grades be assigned to mainstreamed students only by the regular classroom teacher or through collaboration with support staff? Should grades measure student competence? Should grades reflect student growth, progress, and effort? Should they identify students' strengths and weaknesses?

Adapting Teacher-Made Tests

Ms. McNair is surprised and disturbed by students' grades on her tests. Though students seem to understand the material in class, many students make C's, D's and F's on her tests. In an attempt to rectify the situation, Ms. McNair asks students to write confidentially the reasons they feel they do so poorly on her tests. Students write the following:

"You teach things one way and test them another way."

"The book has a lot of facts but your tests don't ask for them."

"I studied the textbook, but the majority of the test was from the class notes."

"The test covers too much information. It's hard to memorize all that."

"We spent a lot of time discussing photosynthesis in class, but very few test questions dealt with it."

"The tests are too long."

"The directions are unclear."

"The essay questions are vague. I never really know what answer you're looking for."

"You're always trying to trick us."

"The fill in the blank questions are too hard."

"You never give us enough space to write our answers."

While alternative grading systems are available to teachers, most grades are based on data from traditional teacher-made tests (Putnam, 1992). Lee and Alley (1981) found that performance on teacher-made unit tests constituted 60 percent of students' grades. However, use of teacher-made tests to evaluate performance may be an obstacle for mainstreamed students whose ability to function within the parameters of such tests may be limited (Adelman, 1982). Therefore, teachers should consider several factors when constructing tests to accurately assess the performance of mainstreamed students. Questions that can guide teachers in adapting their tests for mainstreamed students are presented in Figure 11.5. A sample test evaluated using the guidelines presented in Figure 11.5 is presented in Figure 11.6.

Test Content

The academic component of a teacher-made test should be directly related to the objectives of the instructional program. Prior academic instruction should serve as a guide to the formation of test items. The test should reflect not only *what* but also *how* content has been taught. Since many mainstreamed students may experience difficulty with generalization (Rose, Lesson, & Gottlieb, 1982; Vaughn, Bos, Lund, 1986), the application of skills to other conditions should not be tested unless specifically taught. For example, after teaching basic multiplica-

Student progress is often assessed by use of teacher-made tests.

FIGURE 11.5
Teacher-made test construction evaluation questions

Questions to ask in devising and evaluating teacher-made tests:

CONTENT

- Is the content of the test directly related to the objectives taught?
- Does the test require students to apply skills that they have not been specifically taught?
- Are the types of questions consistent with the strategies used to help students learn the content?
- Are the language and terminology used in both test directions and items consistent with that used in class?
- Is the percentage of items devoted to specific content areas commensurate with the amount of class time spent on those areas?
- Is the scope of the material being tested too broad? Too narrow?
- Is the readability of the test appropriate?

FORMAT

- Are directions understandable?
- Are cues provided to indicate a change in directions? To alert students to the specifics of each item?
- Is the test too long?
- Is the test neat and free of distracting features?
- Is the test legible?
- Are there a reasonable number of items per page?
- Do items on a page have proper spacing?
- Are items sequenced correctly?
- Do students have to transfer their responses to a separate answer sheet?
- Do students have enough space to record their responses?

MULTIPLE-CHOICE ITEMS

- Are the choices grammatically correct and free of double negatives?
- Is the stem longer than the answer alternatives?
- Does the stem relate to only one point and include only relevant information?
- Are all the choices feasible and of the same length?

MATCHING ITEMS

- Does the matching section include no more than 10 items?
- Are there an equal number of choices in both columns?
- Is an example embedded?
- Is there only one correct response for each pair?
- Are the directions and the columns presented on the same page?
- Are columns labeled?
- Do students respond by writing the letter or number in a blank rather than drawing lines from column to column?
- Are the longer item statements listed in the righthand column and the shorter statements in the lefthand column?

FIGURE 11.5
(continued)

TRUE-FALSE ITEMS

- Are questions phrased clearly without double negatives?
- Do items relate to relevant information?
- Do students respond by circling their choice of *True* or *False* rather than writing out their response?

SENTENCE COMPLETION ITEMS

- Do questions relate to meaningful information?
- Are questions understandable to students?
- Are response choices or word banks provided for students?

ESSAY QUESTIONS

- Is the readability of the question appropriate?
- Are key words highlighted?
- Are open-ended questions divided into smaller sequential questions?
- Are students provided with a list of important concepts that should be discussed in the essay?

tion facts with numbers only, it would be counterproductive to attempt to test these facts through word problems. Similarly, the types of items should relate to the ways in which students acquired the information (Bloom, 1956; Gagne, 1970). Content taught via analysis, synthesis, or problem-solving techniques is best tested through essay questions, whereas factual and rote memory material can be tested by multiple-choice, true-false, matching, and short-answer items. Additionally, the language and terminology used in both test directions and items should be consistent with that used in class.

Another aspect of previous academic instruction to consider in determining the content of a test is the amount of time spent on instructional units. The percentage of test questions related to specific content areas should be commensurate with the amount of class time spent on these topics (S. M. Salend & S. J. Salend, 1985). For example, a test following a unit during which 30 percent of class time was spent on the U.S. Constitution, should have an equal proportion of test items (30 percent) assessing mastery of material related to the Constitution. Shorter and more frequent tests that focus on more specific content rather than fewer comprehensive tests of broader scope can assist mainstreamed students who have difficulty remembering large amounts of information. Frequent testing can allay the apprehension produced by unit testing and provide opportunities to develop proper test-taking behaviors.

Test Format

Even though many mainstreamed students can master the academic content necessary for successful performance on a test, they may experience unusual

FIGURE 11.6
Sample teacher-made test evaluation

Sample Teacher-Made Test Evaluation

This composite of teacher-made tests has been evaluated using the questions presented in Figure 11.5 to consider which factors and design considerations would enhance student performance and which would hinder student performance.

NO DIRECTIONS GIVEN

POORLY WORDED ITEM

Multiple Choice

MULTIPLE CHOICE SHOULD USE VERTICAL FORMAT

1. What is the least amount of hours of daylight?

   (a) Winter (b) Summer (c) Spring (d) Fall (e) None of the above

KEY WORDS HIGHLIGHTED

2. Which state is in the northeast?
   (a) Kansas (b) Illinois (c) California (d) New York (e) A & D

POOR SPACING BETWEEN LINES AND CHOICES

AVOID CHOICES SUCH AS "NONE OF THE ABOVE" OR "A&D"

Sentence Completion

Directions: Complete the following statements using the words provided below.

WORD BANK PROVIDED

Words: continent west 50 island north 57

east 48 south inlet 32 peninsula

Statements:

1. The United States has ________ states.
2. The sun rises in the ________ and sets in the ________.
3. A large body of land is called a ________.

Matching

Write the letter from column 2 in the blank next to the best answer in column 1. The first one is done for you as an example.

COLUMNS ARE LABELED

EXAMPLE GIVEN

RESPONSE SPACE PROVIDED

LONGER ITEMS IN LEFT COLUMN

Column 1	Column 2
E 1. A small, raised part of the land, lower than a mountain.	A. Peninsula
__ 2. Land surrounded by water on three sides.	B. Plateau
__ 3. An area of high, flat land.	C. Reservoir
__ 4. A lake where a large water supply is	D. Valley

FIGURE 11.6
(continued)

MATCHING ITEMS AND DIRECTIONS SHOULD ALL BE ON THE SAME PAGE

stored.

__ 5. Low land between mountains or hills. E. Hill

__ 6. Low and wet land. F. Swamp

True or False

Directions: Read each statement. If the statement is true, circle the T. If the statement is false, circle the F.

WRITE OUT "TRUE" AND "FALSE" TO AVOID CONFUSION

T F 1. The bee that lays all the eggs in the colony is called the queen.

KEY WORDS HIGHLIGHTED

T F 2. A living thing that lives on or in another organism and gets food from it is a host.

T F 3. A cloud does not always have water in it.

POORLY STATED ITEM

Essay

When writing this essay, some terms you may want to mention include minerals, vitamins, protein, carbohydrates, and fats.

IMPORTANT CONCEPTS TO BE DISCUSSED ARE IDENTIFIED

1. Why is it important to eat different kinds of foods and have a balanced diet? In writing your answer, discuss the following:

What are the four food groups?

What are examples of the foods that make up the four food groups?

SUB-QUESTIONS PROVIDED

What nutrients does each food group provide?

How many servings from each group should one have?

How does the body use nutrients?

NO ROOM FOR STUDENT RESPONSE

difficulty with the test format (Beattie, Grise, & Algozzine, 1983). Tests for mainstreamed students should be designed to correspond not only to the testing purpose, but also to the characteristics of the students to be tested. Therefore, to promote optimal student performance, educators should consider several aspects of a test's format (S. M. Salend & S. J. Salend, 1985).

The appearance and organization of a test may affect students' scores. Tests that seem overwhelmingly long or that cause confusion and distraction because of poor appearance or spatial design can defeat students before they begin. The test should be neat and free of distracting features. Only information relevant to the test items should appear on the pages. Because many mainstreamed students have reading problems, legibility of items is essential. Therefore, items should be clearly and darkly printed on a solid, nondistracting background. A piece of dark paper can be placed under the test to serve as a background (Wood, 1988). Ideally, tests should be typed but if they must be written, the writing should be in the style (manuscript or cursive) to which the student is accustomed. Finally, making more than one master copy of a test will reduce the number of tests being run from one master, so that printing clarity is preserved. If, however, a ditto of the test does not provide a copy clear enough for mainstreamed students, teachers should provide them with a photocopy of the master sheet.

Many students with specific learning problems lack appropriate organizational skills, which can adversely affect their test performance (Hammill & Bartel, 1978; Wallace & McLoughlin, 1979). The number and types of items on a page, as well as how they are displayed, can have an impact on student performance. Too many items on a page can cause confusion, as can items that are begun on one page and continued on another. Inadequate spacing between items or poor spacing within items can make a test seem overwhelming. Tests that cannot be written on and that require students to transfer answers to a separate paper may be especially difficult for mainstreamed students.

Potential organizational confusion can be minimized by proper spacing and sequencing of items. A minimum of three spaces between items and one and one-half spaces within lines of an item can help delineate boundaries between items for students. Similarly, presenting items in a fixed, predictable symmetrical sequence that emphasizes the transition from item to item can ensure that mainstreamed students do not skip lines or fail to complete test items. Allowing students to write on the test itself rather than transferring answers to a separate page can lessen confusion for those students with organizational difficulties. Providing adequate space for responses will allow students to complete an answer without continuing on another page, and can structure the length of student responses.

Teachers also should consider the order in which items are presented, as well as the variety of items presented on a test. Items that measure similar skills should be ordered so that they reflect a progression from easiest to hardest (Beattie, Grise, & Algozzine, 1983). Objective items, such as multiple-choice, true-false, or matching, are best suited to the response modes of some students; subjective essays and short answers are best for others. For this reason, a test that requires a variety of responses within a reasonable amount of time will be most fair.

An important aspect of the format of the test is the manner in which test items are presented to students. Therefore, teachers also should consider the needs of their mainstreamed students in phrasing and structuring objective and essay type questions. Guidelines teachers should consider in writing questions are discussed here.

Multiple-Choice Items. The most frequently used test item type is the multiple-choice question (Putnam, 1992). Teachers can promote student performance on multiple-choice items by considering several factors relating to the stem and the choices. A well-written multiple-choice item has the following characteristics:

- the choices are grammatically correct and free of double negatives
- the stem is longer than the answer alternatives
- the stem has only one major point and includes only relevant information
- the choices are all feasible
- the choices are presented to students using a vertical format, with the answer bubble located to the right of each alternative
- the correct choice is the best answer (Beattie, Grise, & Algozzine, 1983; Pauk, 1984; New York State Department of Education, 1986)

Multiple-choice items also can be tailored to the needs of mainstreamed students by reducing the number of choices, and by eliminating more difficult choices, such as having to select *all of the above* or *none of the above.* Furthermore, allowing students to circle their choice selection can alleviate problems students may encounter in recording their answers (Wood, 1988).

Matching Items. The organization of matching-item questions can have a significant impact on students' test scores. When constructing matching items, teachers should consider several variables, including number and organization of items (Wood, 1988). Each matching section of the test should contain a maximum of 10 items. When the need arises for more than 10 items, group the additional items by content area in a separate matching section. There should be an equal number of choices in both columns, with only one correct response for each pair. Because students usually approach matching items by reading an item in the lefthand column and then reading all the available choices in the righthand column, teachers can help students save time and work in a coordinated fashion by listing the longer items in the lefthand column (Shanley, 1988). For example, a matching item designed to assess mastery of vocabulary would have the definitions in the lefthand column and the vocabulary words in the righthand column.

The matching section should be organized to avoid confusion. Placing the directions and both columns on the same page can prevent the frustration some students encounter when matching questions are presented on more than one page. To avoid the disorganization that can occur when students respond by drawing lines connecting their choices from both columns, direct students to record the letter or number of their selection in the blank provided. Teachers also can facilitate student performance on this type of test question by composing choices that are clear and concise, embedding an example into the matching question, labeling both columns, and organizing columns in a sensible fashion (such as identifying items in one column in numerical order, and in the other in alphabetical order).

True-False Items. Many students may have difficulty responding to the true-false part of a test. In particular, they may experience problems responding to items that require students to correct all false choices. Teachers can help students perform on true-false items by doing the following:

- phrasing questions clearly, briefly and without double negatives
- highlighting critical parts of the true-false statements such as words like *always* and *never*
- eliminating items that assess trivial information or that serve to mislead students
- avoiding items that are stated negatively
- avoiding items that ask students to change false statements into true statements
- limiting the number of this type of question per test (Wood, 1988)

Since some students may inadvertently fail to discriminate the *T* and the *F* when working in the pressure situation of a test, the response choices of *True* or *False* should be written out completely. Rather than writing out their response, students should be afforded the opportunity to record their response by circling either *True* or *False.*

Sentence Completion Items. Sentence completion items can be especially difficult for mainstreamed students who have memory deficits. Teachers can lessen the memory requirements of these items by providing several response choices, or a word bank that includes a listing of choices from which students select to complete the statement. For example, the sentence completion question *The outer layer of the atmosphere is called the* __________ can be modified by listing the choices of *stratosphere, exosphere,* and *ionosphere* under the blank. Where possible, the words in word banks should be categorized and placed together in the list. Because statements to be completed that come directly from print materials such as textbooks can be too vague when taken out of the context of the paragraph or chapter, teachers should clearly phrase sentence completion items so that students can understand them (Wood, 1988).

Essay Questions. Essay questions present unique problems for many mainstreamed students because of the numerous skills necessary to answer them. Teachers can adapt essay questions by making sure that the questions are appropriate for students in terms of readability and level of difficulty. Key words that guide students in analyzing and writing the essay can be highlighted and defined for students. If it is inconvenient to define a large number of words and concepts on the test itself, students can be allowed to use a word list or dictionary (Sarda, 1988). Similarly, important concepts that students should include in their essays should be listed, highlighted, and located in a prominent place so that students will read them before writing their essays. For example, an essay on the different food groups might include a listing of the concepts of calories, sugars, vitamins, proteins, and carbohydrates as terms students should mention in writing their response.

Teachers can structure students' essays by providing an outline or an answer checklist to serve as a format for writing and sequencing the response (Wood, 1988).

Teachers also can help students interpret the question correctly and guide the essay in several ways. Rather than using a single, open-ended essay question, teachers can direct the organization and completeness of the response by employing subquestions that divide the open-ended question into smaller sequential questions that can elicit all the components of an accurate, well structured, detailed answer. As an example, an essay question that teachers at Paramus (New Jersey) High School adapted for an English test follows:

> In *By the Waters of Babylon,* John's father says, "If your dreams do not eat you, some day you will be a great man." Using *2* of the following characters—Arthur, Jack, Ralph, and John—discuss:
>
> 1. What does each character dream of doing?
> 2. What must each character do to fulfill his dream?
> 3. How do the attempts of each character to realize his dream change him as a person?
> 4. Does each achieve his dream? Explain.
> 5. Does each character's dream eat up that character? Explain.
> 6. In what ways does his success or failure make his life better or worse, happier or sadder? (Walla, 1988)

Readability of Items

Another factor to consider when composing tests is the readability of its items. Putnam (1992) reviewed tests in mainstreamed secondary classrooms across all content areas and found that the average test had approximately 35 questions and a readability level at the 8.9 grade level. Teachers can adjust the readability of each item in several ways. Abstract sentences can be simplified by reducing the complexity of the language and adding examples that illustrate the statements. For example, the essay terms requiring students to compare and contrast two concepts can be simplified by asking students to identify how the concepts are alike and different (Wood, 1988). Similarly, understanding of critical, complicated terms can be facilitated by the use of synonyms and jargon-free explanations. The readability of sentences that are too long can be enhanced by eliminating unnecessary clauses and phrases or by dividing the sentence into two or more sentences. Misunderstandings can be avoided in reading test items by decreasing the number of pronouns used to refer to important points, objects, or events (Simpson, n.d.).

Think About It

Obtain a textbook relating to content area or grade you would like to teach. Using the content in the textbook, develop a teacher-made test that includes multiple-choice, matching, true-false, sentence completion, and essay items. How did you adapt the content and format of the test for mainstreamed students?

Alternative Testing Techniques

Mainstreamed students' performance on teacher-made and standardized commercially produced tests may be affected by their specific learning needs. For example, students with reading difficulties may perform below their capabilities on a math test if the test problems and directions are presented solely through reading. The IDEA mandates the use of alternative testing techniques so that "when a test is administered to a child with impaired sensory, manual, or speaking skills, the test results accurately reflect the child's aptitude or achievement level or whatever other factors the test purports to measure, rather than reflecting the child's impaired sensory, manual, or speaking skills (except where those skills are the factors which the test purports to measure)."

Alternative testing techniques are adaptations in testing administration and procedures that provide students with the opportunity to perform at their optimal level (New York State Education Department, 1986). The type of testing modification needed will depend on the individual student's needs, as well as the nature of the test. The multidisciplinary team should determine specific alternative testing techniques that are appropriate for students and list them in the students' IEP. Alternative testing techniques should only be used when necessary, and students should be weaned from their use as they demonstrate success in the mainstreamed setting.

Alternative testing techniques include adaptations in the manner in which test questions and directions are presented to students, or changes in the manner students respond to test items or determine their answers. *Any* modification in the procedures used to administer and score the test also is considered an alternative testing technique. When using commercially produced, standardized tests, educators should consult the test's manual to determine if the test modification is consistent with the administration procedures outlined by the test developers. Because alternative testing techniques prohibited in the manual may invalidate a student's test results in comparison to the norm group, educators should exercise caution when interpreting these results.

Presentation of Items and Directions

Cues can be incorporated into the test to facilitate the mainstreamed students' understanding and following of test directions. For example, to indicate a change in directions among types of items, teachers should provide a sample of each type of problem set off in a box with each change of test directions (Beattie, Grise, & Algozzine, 1983). Similarly, cues such as color coding, underlining, enlarging key words, or highlighting changes in mathematical symbols will alert students to the specifics of each item. If appropriate, key terms can be highlighted and defined for students on the test. For example, the directions for a section of a test asking students to find the least common denominator can include a definition of that term. Cues, such as arrows, can be placed at the bottom of the test pages to indicate those pages that are a continuous part of a section of the test; stop signs can be placed to indicate ending pages (Beattie, Grise, & Algozzine, 1983).

Some students will require the use of school personnel to assist them in discerning the test's directions and items. An adult—the teacher, resource room teacher, bilingual education teacher, or teacher's aide—can be an individualized proctor to read the test directions and questions to students. When using this alternative, it may be necessary to read the fixed directions at the beginning of the test repeatedly, and review them when a new set of directions is introduced (New York State Education Department, 1986). In reading test parts to students, adults should be careful not to provide students with cues and additional information that may affect their performance.

In addition to assistance from school personnel, some mainstreamed students may need the help of specialized equipment to gain information about test directions and items. Students with visual impairments may benefit from use of visual magnification aids, while devices that amplify auditory stimuli can help maximize the performance of students with hearing impairments. Audiotapes of tests and markers to focus the students' attention and maintain place during reading can aid students with reading disabilities (New York State Department of Education, 1986).

Responses to Items

Some mainstreamed students, particularly those that have problems with writing and speaking, may require the use of alternative testing techniques to respond to test items. Spelling problems can be minimized by spelling on the chalkboard difficult words necessary for essays or short-answer items. Students who have difficulty with handwriting can be helped in several ways. Use of multiple-choice items instead of sentence completion and essay questions can minimize the writing requirements necessary to complete the test. When grammar, punctuation, and spelling are not essential aspects of the response,

IDEAS FOR IMPLEMENTATION

Educators can help students who have difficulty decoding printed matter to understand the test's directions and items by enacting the following suggestions:

- Rewrite the test's directions in terminology that the student can read and understand.
- Offer directions for each new section of the test.
- Present directions in the sequence in which they should be followed.
- Translate the test directions and items into sign language, Braille, large print, and/or the students' native language.
- Structure the reading so that each sentence is placed on a single line.
- Avoid double negatives when phrasing questions.
- Omit items that cannot be modified to address the students' unique needs.
- Give additional examples and provide models to assist students.
- Define unfamiliar, abstract, or difficult-to-understand words.

Source: New York State Education Department (1986); Wood (1988).

students can tape-record answers or take an oral test. If the mechanics of written language are important in evaluating the response, students can dictate their response to an adult recorder. Students can then review their response in written form, and direct their recorder on the correct grammar, punctuation, and word choices. Devices such as word processors, pointers, communication boards, and typewriters can help students who have difficulties communicating their answers orally or in writing to respond to test items (New York State Department of Education, 1986).

Because of their unique conditions, some mainstreamed students may need to employ aids to determine their responses to items. Computational aids, such as calculators, software programs, arithmetic tables, word lists, an abacus, and numberlines, can be useful for students who have the requisite problem solving abilities to complete items but lack the necessary memory skills to remember facts or word definitions. For example, a list of arithmetic tables can help students who understand the process of solving word problems but lack the mastery of the math facts necessary to compute the correct answer.

Scoring

Teachers also can modify the scoring of tests to address the unique needs of mainstreamed students. Teachers can adapt their scoring procedures by scoring only items that are completed, omitting certain questions, and prorating credit (Banbury, 1987; New York State Department of Education, 1986). For example, mainstreamed students' scores can be determined by computing the percentage correct out of the number attempted (Gillet, 1986). Tests can be scored so that students who give incorrect answers receive partial credit for showing correct work. For example, when completing math tests, students can earn credit for performing and listing the operations necessary to solve the problem. When grammar, spelling, and punctuation are not the elements being tested, teachers can consider not penalizing students for these errors or giving students separate grades for content and mechanics. For example, if an essay response on a social studies test is correct but contains many misspelled words, the teacher could give the student separate grades for content and spelling. On essay tests, students initially can be given credit for an outline, web, diagram, or chart in lieu of writing a lengthy response (Fagen et al., 1984).

Testing Procedures

Although tests are typically administered in large groups during one timed session, educators may need to adjust the procedures they employ to test mainstreamed students. One such testing procedure is the scheduling of tests. Mainstreamed students may not work as fast as their peers because of 1) difficulties processing information and staying on task, 2) the time constraints associated with the use of specialized testing techniques (such as dictating answers), and 3) physical needs that cause them to tire easily (New

York State Education Department, 1986). Therefore, when planning testing for some mainstreamed students, educators should consider scheduling alternatives:

- allocating more time to complete tests
- eliminating the time limits on tests
- reducing the length of the test
- providing the opportunity for students to take frequent breaks as needed
- dividing the testing sessions into separate, short periods within a day
- completing the test over a period of several days (Banbury, 1987; New York State Education Department, 1986)

Guidelines for using microcomputers to design, construct, administer, and score teacher-made tests are available (S. J. Salend & S. M. Salend, 1985b).

One alternative testing technique that can be appropriate for some mainstreamed students is changing the setting of the test. Students who are easily distracted, have difficulty remaining on task, and are anxious about taking tests may perform better if they take the test individually in a quiet place free of distractions, such as the resource room. Similarly, students who have difficulty maintaining on-task behavior should be seated in a nondistracting area of the room (Wood, 1988). Students with physical disabilities may require adaptive furniture or devices, while students with sensory impairments may need specific environmental arrangements, such as specialized lighting or acoustics (Banbury, 1987).

Two-Tiered Testing

Some teachers use a two-tiered testing system to assess student mastery of course content (Gajria, Giek, Hemrick, & Salend, 1992). In such a system, students working in collaborative groups take a test, with each student receiving the group grade. Following the group test, students work individually on a second test that covers similar material. Students can be given two separate grades, their two grades can be averaged together into one grade, or they can be given the opportunity to select the highest grade.

Student Involvement

Teacher-made tests can be made fairer by involving students in the testing process. Curwin and Mendler (1988) suggest that teachers incorporate input from students in devising and scoring tests by asking students to submit possible test questions, having students test each other, and allowing students to score each others' exams. Students also can be given a choice concerning the type of test they take (Gajria, Giek, Hemrick, & Salend, 1992). Teachers can devise several versions of a test: a multiple-choice test, an essay test, and a sentence completion test. Students can then select the test that best fits their response style and study habits. Similarly, teachers can structure their tests to allow students to have some choice in responding to items (L. Sarda, personal communication, May 18, 1988). For example, a test section can comprise twenty items of varying format; students can be directed to respond to any fifteen questions within that section. Those students who are proficient at multiple-choice items but have difficulty with true-false questions can select more of the former and fewer of the latter.

Test Adaptations for Second Language Learners

Teachers also may need to adapt their tests for use with second language learners. While assessment of language proficiency may not be the stated objective of the test, language proficiency can affect students' abilities to understand the test's directions, respond to the test's items, expand on knowledge in content areas, and seek assistance from and interact with the test administrator (Wolfram, 1990). Teachers can modify their tests for second language learners and students who speak vernacular dialects of English by doing the following:

- using items that are high in comprehension and simple in terms of language level
- providing context clues
- allowing students to demonstrate mastery of test material in alternative ways, such as with projects developed by cooperative learning groups or through use of manipulatives
- presenting items and directions through use of graphics and pictorial representations
- accounting for differences in English dialects when scoring tests
- defining key words both in English and in students' native languages
- allowing students to use a language dictionary
- allowing students to respond in their native language or dialect
- having students give oral presentations or theatrical/dramatic performances
- using a translator to assist in the administration of the test

Fradd and Wilen (1990) provide guidelines for using interpreters and translators to assess the performance of second language learners on tests.

Think About It

Do alternative testing techniques give mainstreamed students an advantage over other students? Would alternative testing techniques violate the integrity of your tests?

Minimum Competency Testing

While *minimum competency testing* (*MCT*) has been employed by many school districts to ensure that students exit high school with a minimum set of skills to function successfully in society, it also has been used to measure the progress of students and determine their promotion to the next grade (McCarthy, 1980). Gallagher and Hall (1979) note that competency testing can assess the extent to which mainstreamed students have mastered the basic skills that comprise the regular education curriculum. However, the advent of MCT creates several problems for mainstreamed students. First, if promotion to the next grade is contingent on passing MCT rather than identifying instructional needs, then many mainstreamed students face the prospect of not being promoted or being segregated into special education classes (McCarthy, 1980). Second, use of tests that reflect middle-class norms and that lack reliability and validity can prevent students from culturally and linguistically diverse backgrounds from receiving a high school diploma and thus limit their employability (Safer, 1980).

In light of the problems MCT can create for mainstreamed students, educators must consider several procedures to lessen its potential deleterious effects. While mainstreamed students should be granted exemptions from MCT when it can have a negative impact on the students' families and self-concept and when they lack the skills to pass the test (Amos, 1980), all mainstreamed students should have an opportunity to take the test using any alternative testing techniques they require (McCarthy, 1980). Mainstreamed students who fail the test should receive remedial instruction and be allowed to retake the test as many times as necessary (McCarthy, 1980).

Multidisciplinary teams also can address issues related to students' performance on MCT through the IEP process (Amos, 1980; Safer, 1980). The IEP could contain information on which MCT requirements are valid for a specific mainstreamed student, as well as the best procedures to assess mastery of these requirements (Safer, 1980). Amos (1980) suggests several modifications that multidisciplinary teams can consider when adapting the MCT process for mainstreamed students:

1. Review the MCT and select the test items that will best evaluate the objectives of the student's plan.
2. Choose a test that will best evaluate the child's mastery of basic skills.
3. Develop a comparable test that will clearly demonstrate the outcome of her or his objectives or goals (Amos, 1980, p. 197).

TEACHING TEST-TAKING SKILLS

Research indicates that many students with learning problems fail to use appropriate test-taking skills to enhance their test performance (Scruggs & Lifson, 1986; Tolfa & Scruggs, 1986).

The ability of students to demonstrate mastery of classroom content covered on tests can be affected by their test-wiseness (Scruggs & Mastropieri, 1988). Millman and Pauk (1969) define *test-wiseness* as "the ability to use the characteristics of tests and test-taking situations to reach the full potential of one's knowledge and aptitude" (p. xiii).

Mainstreamed students can learn a variety of test-taking skills to increase their test-wiseness and to maximize their performance on tests (Scruggs & Mastropieri, 1988; and Scruggs, Mastropieri & Tolfa-Veit, 1986). Lee and Alley (1981) increased students' performance on teacher-made tests by teaching them to use the *SCORER* strategy, a first-letter cue strategy that facilitates test performance:

S = Schedule your work
C = Clue words
O = Omit difficult questions
R = Read carefully
E = Estimate your answers
R = Review your work
(Carman & Adams, 1972, p. 125)

Similarly, Hughes and Schumaker (cited in Putnam, 1992) improved students' test performance by teaching them to use *PIRATES:*

P = Prepare to succeed
I = Inspect the instructions
R = Read, remember, reduce
A = Answer or abandon
T = Turn back
E = Estimate
S = Survey

Several test-taking behaviors that can be taught to students are discussed here.

Study for the Test

Appropriate studying behaviors also can ensure that students perform to the best of their abilities on tests. Students should be encouraged to do the following:

- Review content to be studied over a spaced period of time rather than cramming.
- Determine the specific objectives to be accomplished in each study session.
- Study the most difficult content areas first.
- Set up the study area so that it is conducive to studying.
- Gather all the materials necessary to facilitate the process, including notebook, textbooks, paper, writing utensils, reference books, and calculators.
- Write out from memory the main points to be remembered after studying and compare them with notes and textbooks for discrepancies.
- Learn content-related terminology by creating a word file (Chapman, 1969; Farquhar, Krumboltz, & Wrenn, 1969; Spargo, 1977).

When preparing to study for a test, students should determine the type(s) of questions that will comprise the test (Spargo, 1977). Since teachers often use tests that have similar formats and that repeat questions, teachers can help students prepare for tests by providing them with the opportunity to review prior tests and quizzes (Millman & Pauk, 1969). The review could offer students an explanation of the purpose and format of the test, and should cover the length of the test, response types, and the completeness of the responses required; examples of actual student responses also are helpful.

In addition to knowing the type of test, it also is helpful for students to have an idea of the test's content. One indication of the likelihood of a content area being covered on a test is the amount of class time the teacher spends in teaching it. Typically, important topics that will be covered on tests are those on which the teacher has spent significant amounts of time. Examining their notes and textbooks also can help students determine the content of a test (Farquhar, Krumboltz, & Wrenn, 1969). Those topics that appear in *both* notes and textbooks are likely to appear on the test. To ensure that

Humphrey, Hoffman, and Crosby (1984) suggest that teachers give students a written outline or review sheet of material that will be covered on the test at least one week before the test.

students study relevant content, teachers should offer students specific information regarding the chapters and notes that will be covered on the test (Mercer & Mercer, 1985).

Teachers also can provide students with time to work in small groups to prepare for tests. For example, small groups can review notes and chapters, predict possible questions, and quiz members on specific facts, terms, and concepts (Bos & Vaughn, 1988). Similarly, students can work together to develop and study lists of terms that are relevant to the subject matter (Devine, 1981).

Survey the Test

Before beginning a test, students should be taught to survey it (Millman & Pauk, 1969). This survey or preview should help students to determine both the number and nature of test items. If unsure, students also should ask the test administrator how much time they will have to complete the test.

Establish a Plan

Based on the information obtained in surveying the test and reading the directions, students should develop an order and timeline for working on the test. In establishing the plan, students should consider the total time allotted to the test, the point values of sections, and the level of difficulty of the items. To ensure that they cover each section of the test, students should allot a certain amount of time for each section based on point values and length. They should work on those sections worth the most points in descending order (Spargo, 1977).

In addition to working on the sections with respect to their point values, students may also categorize items according to their level of difficulty, and work on the easiest items first. Thus, it is recommended that students make three passes through the test (Spargo, 1977). In the first pass, students should read all questions and respond to those they know how to answer, noting those that are somewhat difficult or very difficult by placing a symbol next to them. During the second pass, students respond to those questions skipped in the first pass that have been identified as somewhat difficult. All unanswered questions should be answered during the third and final pass.

Read the Directions

It is essential that students carefully and purposefully read the directions to all parts of the test. In reading the directions, students should identify the nature of the response that is required, the aids that they will be allowed to use to assist them in answering questions (reference books, calculators, computers), the sequence to be followed in completing the test, the point values of items and sections of the test, and the time and space constraints (Millman & Pauk, 1969). Underlining important components of test directions and questions can be helpful (Putnam, 1992).

To ensure that students understand the test's directions, teachers can, at the beginning of the test, assign several practice items relating to the various types of questions on the test. These practice items can be reviewed with students prior to allowing them to proceed with the rest of the test. Once students start the test, teachers can check their understanding of test directions by periodically monitoring the student's answer sheet (Fagen, et al., 1984).

Seek Clarification

During the test, students may forget directions, encounter words that they do not understand, or find questions that can be interpreted in several ways. For example, in the question *Discuss four differences between the ideas of Jefferson and Hamilton,* students may need additional clarification concerning how extensively they should discuss these differences. When these instances arise, students should be allowed to seek clarification from the teacher concerning the specifics of the question or section. Teachers willing to answer questions concerning the test should establish specific procedures for doing so beforehand.

Jot Down Essential Facts

Most tests require memorization of information, so students initially should write down on the test paper essential facts and formulas that they will use throughout the test (Millman & Pauk, 1969). When studying, students should develop and then memorize a list of essential information likely to appear on the test.

Use Key Words

The need for assistance from teachers during testing can be minimized by teaching students to identify key words in question stems and giving the definitions of these words. It is recommended that students learn to circle or underline key words as they encounter them, and then determine their definition. A list of key words that are typically used in phrasing essay test questions and their meanings with respect to test items is presented in Figure 11.7.

Check Answers

If time remains at the end of the test, students should check that their responses are correct, complete, and neat (Millman & Pauk, 1969). After a page of the test has been reviewed, students should note that it has been checked so they do not waste time reviewing it again. Students should be taught that when they are unsure of an answer, it is best to stay with their first choice (Spargo, 1977). Rather than leaving questions unanswered, students should attempt to answer all questions. However, when they lose additional points for incorrect responses, students should be taught to answer only those questions that have a high probability of being correct.

Review Returned Tests

Teachers should offer corrective feedback on items in addition to providing students with a score on their tests (Cohen, 1983). When the test is graded and returned to students, it should be reviewed carefully by the class. In

FIGURE 11.7
Key words in essay questions

Clue Words	Meaning
1. describe define trace discuss examine analyze	Give in words a picture of an idea, a concept, or an object. Give clear, concise definitions. Record careful observation. Give the important ideas and show how they are related.
2. compare and contrast differentiate distinguish	Give likenesses and differences. Show differences between items, groups, or categories.
3. enumerate outline	Use lists, outlines, main and subordinate points, and details.
4. state relate	Write concisely and clearly, connecting ideas or concepts. Use chronology of events or ideas where it applies.
5. prove justify	Use facts, or logic, or cite authorities to justify your thesis.
6. evaluate criticize	Make value judgments but use logic to explain. Criticize, pro or con, the merits of a concept or a theory.
7. review summarize synthesize	Summarize main points concisely, restate judgments or conclusions, integrate arguments from different sources.

Source: M. J. Tonjes and M. V. Zintz, *Teaching Reading/Thinking/Study Skills in Content Classrooms* (Dubuque, IA: Wm. C. Brown, 1981), p. 246. Reprinted by permission.

addition to checking for scoring errors, students should analyze tests to determine the frequency and types of errors made. If patterns of errors are noted, preparation for upcoming tests should address the error trends. Error trends also can provide teachers with information for adapting tests to meet students' skills and preparing students for tests. For example, if a student's test showed problems with true-false items, the classroom or resource room teacher could assess mastery of this content using other types of items or review with the student the suggested strategies for optimizing performance on true-false items.

Skills for Specific Test Types

Objective Tests

While several test-taking strategies are relevant for all types of tests (Mastropieri & Scruggs, 1987), taking an objective test is very different from an essay test. Objective tests include multiple-choice, true-false, matching, and sentence completion items. Because objective tests cover a wide range of content areas, students will need to review all specifics that will be covered.

When working on any type of item in an objective test, students should identify and analyze critical words, look for word clues such as *always* and *never,* which indicate extremes and (usually) incorrect answers, and rephrase questions in language they can understand (Spargo, 1977).

Multiple-Choice Items. One of the most popular objective test formats is the multiple-choice item, which gives a question stem and then requires that the best answer be selected from a series of alternatives. In multiple-choice questions, it is often best to read the question and think of the answer before reading and carefully analyzing all the choices. If the anticipated response is not one of the answer alternatives, students should delete obviously incorrect choices and analyze the other available choices.

Students should examine each response alternative and eliminate choices that are obviously false or incorrect statements, not related to the content covered in class, or that are silly and deal with nonsense or irrelevant material (Pauk, 1984). However, in choosing correct options, students should examine all the alternatives and select the one that is the most complete and inclusive (Langan, 1982). Students should be aware that the choices of *all of the above, none of the above,* and numbers that represent the middle range often are correct (Pauk, 1984). Similarly, alternatives that are unusually long or short also are frequently the correct answer (Bragstad & Stumpf, 1987). When response alternatives present contradictory answers, one of them is likely to be the correct response (Langan, 1982). However, when options provide information that is similar, both of them should be eliminated from consideration (Scruggs & Mastropieri, 1988).

Examining other elements of multiple-choice items can provide clues to students in selecting the correct alternative. Subject-verb agreement, verb tense, and modifiers such as *a* or *an* can assist students in determining the correct response. Sometimes information from one question can assist in determining the correct answer to another question. Occasionally, the stems of questions contain the answer to other questions.

Occasionally, multiple-choice tests are machine graded and require the student to use a special writing utensil and record responses in a grid on a separate answer sheet. Since the transfer of responses from one document (test questions) to another (answer sheet) can be problematic, students should exercise caution to ensure that they do not lose credit because of this unique format. Therefore, in taking machine scored tests, students should do the following:

- Use the correct writing tool.
- Mark completely the grid that indicates their response.
- Erase changes or mistakes thoroughly.
- Fill in only one answer grid per item.
- Record answers in the correct space and follow the correct sequence (Carman & Adams, 1972).

Matching Items. Matching tests require students to establish a relationship between information presented in left and right columns. Initially, students should determine the parameters of the matching tasks to note if each column has an equal number of items and if they can use an alternative more than once (Langan, 1982).

True-False Items. Some true-false tests require students to respond by listing whether a statement is correct or incorrect, while others require students to correct false responses. Since their performance on the test will suffer if students do not read the directions to discern this difference, students should be instructed to determine the type of true-false items on the test before beginning. When working on true-false items, students should examine the questions for *specific determiners,* which are words that modify or limit a statement (rarely, usually) (Millman & Pauk, 1969). In general, false statements often include a qualifier that suggests the statement is extreme, or true 100 percent of the time (such as *no, never, every, always, all*). Words that moderate a statement (such as *sometimes, most, many, generally, usually*) often indicate that a statement is true. Similarly, if true-false statements lack a specific determiner, the question should only be marked *True* if it is always true (Millman & Pauk, 1969).

Some true-false items have several parts. When answering these types of items, students should be careful to read all parts of the statement. If any part of the statement is false, then the statement should be marked *False* (Pauk, 1984).

True-false statements that have negative words or prefixes in them can be particularly difficult. In responding to these items, students should highlight the negative terms and identify the meaning of the item while deleting the negatives. Then, they should examine the sentence to determine whether the statement is true or false (Pauk, 1984).

Sentence Completion Items. Sentence completion or fill in the blank items require students to write the missing word, phrase, or number that correctly

IDEAS FOR IMPLEMENTATION

When answering matching questions, it is helpful for students to do the following:

1. Survey both lists to get an idea of the choices.
2. Read the initial item in the lefthand column first.
3. Read each choice in the righthand column before answering.
4. Determine and record the correct answer if the answer is readily known.
5. Circle or underline the choice in the righthand column that has been used.
6. Skip items that are difficult.
7. Repeat steps 1–7 while proceeding down the lefthand column.
8. Avoid guessing until answering all other items, as an incorrect match can multiply the number of errors by using a possible correct choice from the righthand column.

Source: Pauk (1984).

completes a sentence. Students can be taught to approach these types of items by converting them into a question (Wood, 1988). For example, the sentence completion question *A large mass of moving air is called a* ________, can be transformed into the question *What is a large mass of moving air called?* In responding to these questions, students should use the grammatical structure of the item to assist in formulating the answer (Millman & Pauk, 1969). For example, if the stem ends in *a* or *an,* then students can deduce that the correct answer starts with a vowel or a consonant, respectively. Examining the verb form also can cue students to whether the answer is singular or plural (Hook, 1969). Sometimes a hint about the correct answer to this type of item is provided by examining the number and length of the blanks provided by the teacher. Often, two blanks with no words between them indicates that a two-word answer, such as an individual's name, is the answer; two blanks separated by words should be approached as two separate statements. Similarly, a long blank tends to suggest that the correct answer is a phrase or a sentence. Students should be encouraged to choose responses that are logical and consistent with the stem of the question.

Essay Tests

Essay tests necessitate that students write a response to a question. The degree of detail of the response will vary, but students can employ several strategies to improve their performance on this type of test. Millman and Pauk (1969) propose that students answer essay questions by using a three-step method. In the first step, students read the questions and record relevant points to be mentioned or addressed next to each question. This technique allows students to make sure that they don't forget essential information from one question as they work on another. Second, students start with the easiest questions first, rereading them and adding new or deleting irrelevant information recorded during the first pass. At this time, students also should organize their response into an outline before writing. The outline should use a combined number and letter system to indicate main points (1, 2, 3) and secondary supporting arguments (1a, 1b, 1c).

During the final step, students use the outline as a guide for composing their answer. In writing responses to essay questions, students should do the following:

- rephrase the question as the initial sentence of the answer
- present the answer in a logical order with transitions from paragraph to paragraph
- give specifics when necessary
- use examples to support statements
- summarize the main points at the end of the essay

In terms of appearance of their final product, students should leave room in the lefthand margin for the teacher's comments, provide space between responses, and record their answer on one side of the page (Pauk, 1984).

Finally, since the scoring of most essay questions allows for partial credit, students should try to respond to each question in some fashion. Therefore, if they are running out of time, students should be taught to put down their outline rather than leaving the question blank.

Open-ended Tests

Though not as prevalent as objective or essay tests, open-ended tests are used by some teachers. In an open-ended test, students are allowed to use reference books, usually their textbooks, to complete the exam. Since open-ended tests measure the ability to organize and interpret information, preparation for taking these type of tests is critical for success (Millman & Pauk, 1969). Therefore, rather than trying to memorize content, students should spend time organizing and reviewing their notes from class and textbooks.

Millman and Pauk (1969) suggest that students develop an outline to index information from their notes and textbooks when preparing for open-ended tests, for example, one that contains main points and secondary points, or key questions and the corresponding pages from textbooks, class notes, and worksheets that address these topics (see Figure 11.8). When working from reference materials during the test, students should phrase their responses in their own words, rather than copying sentences or quotations verbatim.

Oral Exams

A test modification that some mainstreamed students may need is the use of an oral exam, which is particularly relevant for students who may have difficulty writing responses to test questions (New York State Department of

FIGURE 11.8
Sample open-ended test study outline

Content area	Textbook pages	Class notes	Worksheets	Other materials
1. Matter				
a. Definition	81–82	10/11	Matter	
b. Characteristics	83–84	10/11	Matter	
2. States of matter				
a. Solid	85–86	10/12	Solids	
b. Liquid	87–89	10/13	Liquids	
c. Gas	90–93	10/14	Gases	
3. Changing states of matter				
a. Freezing Points	100–103	10/17	Freezing Points	
b. Boiling Points	104–106	10/18		Experiment #4
c. Evaporation	107–111	10/20		Experiment #5

Education, 1986). However, oral exams can be intimidating and students may have limited experience with this type of situation, so students should be taught to engage in several behaviors that can aid them in performing on oral exams. These behaviors include determining what content will be covered on the exam, listening carefully to the examiner, seeking clarification from the examiner concerning ambiguous questions and terminology, recording on a pad (if possible) key points to make in answering a question, thinking prior to responding, allowing time for the examiner to respond, distinguishing opinions from facts, staying on task, and displaying appropriate manners (Millman & Pauk, 1969). Allowing students to supplement their oral responses with visual aids and manipulatives also may facilitate their performance on oral tests (Fagen et al., 1984).

Think About It

What studying and test-taking strategies do you use? Are they successful? How did you learn these strategies?

OBTAINING FOLLOWUP INFORMATION

Followup information on a student's progress in the mainstreamed setting can be obtained from regular educators, parents and mainstreamed students.

Information from Regular Educators

Students' regular classroom teachers are a primary source of information concerning their progress in mainstreamed settings (Salend, 1983c). Through observation, teachers can obtain valuable data that can pinpoint existing or potential problems in the academic, behavioral, social, and emotional adjustment of mainstreamed students that can be shared with special educators, parents, and other members of the mainstreaming communication network (see Chapter 3). For example, a teacher may notice that a mainstreamed student is performing well academically but has few social interactions with peers during free time, recess, and lunch. Interventions to increase the mainstreamed student's social interactions with peers can then be initiated.

Recordkeeping

An essential component of monitoring student progress is efficient recordkeeping. An effective recordkeeping system should relate directly to the specific skills outlined in the curriculum, be easy to complete, and should promote communication concerning student progress among educators, parents, and students (Giek, 1992). Figure 11.9 presents a sample recordkeeping system.

FIGURE 11.9
Sample recordkeeping system

Record Sheet for Second Grade Mathematics

Student:	Ronnie Smith
Teacher:	Ms. Jones
Testing Modifications:	Extended Time

Skill Area	Objective	Progress	Comments
2M1	Read numbers to 12 with 100% accuracy.	9/10 9/13 9/26 10/1 10/2 11/4 1/20 2/8	10/1 - Back after chicken pox 2/8 - Writes 5 backwards
2M2	Write numbers to 12 with 100% accuracy.	10/1 10/18 10/23 11/1 11/6 12/4 1/13 3/18	11/1 - Provide model of numbers
2M3	Recall addition facts through sums to 5 with 90% accuracy.	10/12 11/2 11/30 12/18 2/7 3/2 4/18 6/1 6/23	4/18 - Use of flashcards with peer
2M4	Recall addition facts where 1 addend is 0,1,2,3, with 90% accuracy.	12/6 12/21 1/6 1/18 2/1 3/2 3/18 3/26 4/18 4/27	3/18 - Had fight with classmate
2M5	Recall subtraction facts related to sums of 5 with 80% accuracy.	1/22 2/3 2/17 2/28 3/7 4/22 5/19	
2M6	Recall subtraction facts for which subtrahend is 0,1,2,3, with 80% accuracy.	3/4 3/12 3/30 4/7 4/12 5/1 5/17 5/22 5/30 6/3 P	
2M7	Read and write 2-digit numbers for objects grouped by 10s and 1s with 80% accuracy.	4/2 4/17 4/28 5/6 6/13	
2M8	Read, write, and count numbers through 100 with 100% accuracy.	N	
2M9	Skip count by 2,3,5,10 with 80% accuracy.	N	

Key to symbols:

- ▭ - objective introduced
- ◯ - unsuccessful attempt
- 9/26 - successful probe
- P - partially mastered
- N - not introduced

Source: K. A. Giek, *Teaching Exceptional Children,* vol. 24 (Reston, VA: Council for Exceptional Children, 1992), p. 23. Reprinted by permission of the publisher.

IDEAS FOR IMPLEMENTATION

Information on the progress of mainstreamed students can be obtained by asking teachers to respond to the following questions:

- How is the student performing academically in your class?
- Does the student complete classwork, homework, or other assigned projects?
- Was the student academically ready for entry into your class?
- How does the student's linguistic abilities affect performance in your classroom?
- In what behavioral areas does the student demonstrate proficiency?
- With what behavioral areas does the student experience difficulty?
- What study skills and work habits does the student have?
- How does the student react to your classroom management system?
- Was the student behaviorally prepared for entry into your class?
- How does the student get along with his or her peers?
- In what school clubs or extracurricular activities does the student participate?
- How do you think the new placement is affecting the student's self-concept?
- Was the student socially and emotionally prepared for entry into your class?
- How are the student's hygiene and health-related habits?
- What, if any, architectural barriers exist in your classroom?
- Is the student receiving the necessary services from ancillary support personnel?
- How is the communication system between school personnel functioning?
- How is the communication system with the student's parents functioning?
- Are you satisfied with the student's progress in your class?
- What solutions would you suggest to remediate identified problem area?
- What schoolwide mainstreaming policies would you like to see retained? What policies would you like to see revised?

Source: Salend (1983c).

Information from Parents

Parents are often a good source of information concerning their children's reactions to the mainstreamed setting and relationships with classroom peers (Salend, 1983). Parents can be especially informative concerning the social and emotional adjustment of the student. For example, parents may notice that a recently mainstreamed student is now reluctant to go to school, and has little contact with classmates outside of school. Similarly, parents can inform educators that their child is spending excessive amounts of time on homework and thus having difficulty with the academic requirements of the mainstreamed setting. Therefore, followup evaluation should also assess parent satisfaction with respect to their child's social and emotional adjustment and academic progress as well as the communication between home and school.

Student attitudes and reactions to the social and academic environment of the mainstreamed placement can be assessed by asking students to complete a classroom climate inventory, which examines the student's satisfaction with specific aspects of the classroom (Wallace & Larsen, 1978).

Information from Mainstreamed Students

Feedback from mainstreamed students can provide a novel perspective on student progress and serve to validate the perceptions of others (Salend, 1983c). Students can be interviewed regarding their perceptions of their academic, behavioral, and social-emotional adjustment to the regular classroom.

IDEAS FOR IMPLEMENTATION

Parents can provide useful information concerning the progress of a mainstreamed student by responding to the following questions:

- What is your reaction to your child's new class placement?
- How do you think your child feels about her or his new class placement?
- How is your child coping with the academic demands of the new class placement?
- How would you rate your child's progress in interacting with his/her peers?
- Do you notice any changes in your child since she or he has been placed in the mainstreamed setting?
- Are you satisfied with your role in the mainstreaming process?
- How is the communication system between you and the school personnel working?
- Could you suggest any strategies that would be helpful in facilitating the child's adjustment to her or his new setting?
- What schoolwide mainstreaming policies would you like to see retained? What policies would you like to see revised?

Source: Salend (1983c).

Examining the Effectiveness of Instructional Modifications, Adaptive Devices, and Medical Interventions

Because mainstreamed students may require the use of instructional modifications, adaptive devices, and medical interventions to be successful in the mainstream, information to examine the effectiveness of these adaptations should be an integral part of the followup evaluation.

Implementing Instructional Modifications

Although many students will require specific instructional procedures and modifications to function successfully in mainstreamed settings, research indicates that many elementary and secondary teachers are not instituting these accommodations for their mainstreamed students (Ammer, 1984; Zigmond, Levin, & Laurie, 1985). Therefore, data should be collected on the types of instructional strategies and adaptations teachers are employing (Bender, 1987). For example, the *Bender Classroom Structure Questionnaire* (*BCSQ*) can be used by educators to assess their use of effective instructional strategies with mainstreamed students (Bender, 1992). Educators can help teachers who are not employing planned modifications by offering assistance to help regular classroom teachers implement the strategy and providing praise and recognition to teachers for strategy use (Margolis & McGettigan, 1988).

Biklen, Lehr, Searl, and Taylor (1987) developed an LRE checklist that school districts can use to evaluate their mainstreaming policies.

Teachers and planning teams should evaluate the effectiveness and efficiency of using suggested instructional practices and adaptations. Since a positive relationship exists between academic learning time and student achievement (Rosenberg, Sindelar, & Stedt, 1985), this learning time is one factor to consider when evaluating interventions for mainstreamed students. Wilson (1987) defines *academic learning time* as the "amount of time students spend successfully performing relevant academic tasks" (p. 13). Aca-

IDEAS FOR IMPLEMENTATION

Educators can assess mainstreamed students' perspectives of their progress by asking them the following questions:

- How do you feel about your new class?
- Were you academically prepared for entry into your new class?
- In what academic areas are you doing well?
- With what academic areas are you having difficulty?
- How are your language skills affecting your performance?
- Are the academic modifications and adaptations that are being implemented helping you?
- Are you receiving the necessary services and assistance from ancillary support personnel (specify support personnel for the student)?
- How would you rate your behavior in the new class (be specific)?
- Briefly describe your study skills and work habits.
- Are you completing all classwork, homework, and assigned projects? If not, why not?
- How do you get along with other students in your class?
- In what school clubs or activities do you participate? If none, why?
- Could you suggest any strategies that would help your adjustment to your new class?

Source: Salend (1983c).

demic learning time is usually measured by determining the actual instructional time, student's on-task behavior, and student success rate. Actual instruction time is determined by recording the length of time students spend learning. On-task behavior relates to the time a student is engaged looking at the teacher or the instructional materials that make up the lesson. Student success rate is examined by calculating the percentage of correct responses to oral or written questions and problems.

Adaptive Device Monitoring

The progress of some mainstreamed students, particularly those with sensory and physical disabilities, also will depend on the use of adaptive and prosthetic devices. Since failure of these devices to work properly can limit the likelihood of success for mainstreamed students, educators will need to monitor their working condition. For example, a malfunctioning hearing aid can hinder the academic progress of a student with a hearing impairment; the wear and tear on a wheelchair or other prostheses can limit a student's mobility and ability to interact with peers. Information concerning prostheses and adaptive devices can be obtained by consulting students, parents, special educators, ancillary support personnel, and medical personnel.

Educators can periodically examine a student's hearing aid by using an inexpensive plastic stethoscope, which may be obtained from the speech and hearing specialist. The stethoscope allows the educator to hear what the student using the hearing aid hears, and can help detect malfunctions and

Madell (cited in Cartwright, Cartwright, & Ward, 1985) provides guidelines for determining and solving problems with hearing aids.

their causes. A whistling sound may indicate that the earmold doesn't fit, the battery or the receiver is malfunctioning, or the volume control is too loud. No sound often suggests that the cord or the battery is not working. If a faint sound is heard from the aid, it may be the result of a worn down or incorrect battery, a broken cord, or an incorrect setting for the volume or tone control. When the sound varies from on to off, the battery and cord connections may be loose or corroded. If the battery and cord are connected properly, the fluctuating signal may be caused by a broken receiver. Finally, a sound that is distorted or too loud can be caused by a weak battery, improper battery or cord connections, incorrect tone control setting, damaged earphone, or a wax-clogged earmold or earphone.

Teachers can help maintain the hearing aid in working condition for students by keeping it out of excessively hot or cold locations and making sure it does not get wet (Gearheart, Weishahn, & Gearheart, 1988). When teachers suspect that an aid is malfunctioning and they cannot correct the problem, they should immediately contact the student's parents and speech and language therapist for assistance.

Venn, Morganstern, and Dykes (1979) suggest that teachers examine ambulatory devices used by students. If they note problems, they should contact parents or appropriate medical personnel. They provide a series of checklists to assist teachers in determining the condition of students' lower extremity braces, prostheses, and wheelchairs.

Medication Monitoring

Some mainstreamed students may be taking prescription drugs to enhance their school performance. For example, physicians may prescribe medication for students with epilepsy to control seizures, and for students with attention deficits to increase their ability to pay attention (Courtnage, Stainback, & Stainback, 1982). Educators serving these students should be aware of the school district's policies regarding drug management. Specifically, educators should consider the following questions:

1. Who is allowed to administer drugs to students?
2. Does the school district have a form that empowers school personnel to dispense medications?
3. Does the school district have a form for obtaining the approval of physicians to dispense medications to students?
4. Does the school district have a procedure for obtaining information from physicians and parents concerning the name of medication, dosage, frequency, duration and possible side effects?
5. Does the school district have a format for maintaining records of medications administered to students?
6. Does the school district have established procedures for receiving, labeling, storing, dispensing, and disposing of medications?
7. Does the school district have procedures concerning the self-administration of drugs? (Courtnage, Stainback, & Stainback, 1982).

Educators serving mainstreamed students who require medication should carefully monitor student progress and behavior throughout the drug treatment, and maintain communication with parents and medical professionals. To effectively monitor students, teachers should receive information from the student's doctor, school physician, or school nurse concerning the name or type of medication; dosage, frequency, and duration of the administration; and anticipated symptoms and side effects (Courtnage, Stainback, & Stainback, 1982). Teachers should be informed of changes in students' medication schedule and dosage level.

Because side effects are possible with many medications, Courtnage, et al. (1982) suggest that teachers maintain an anecdotal record of student behavior in school, including statements concerning the students' academic performance, social skills, notable changes in behavior, and possible symptoms associated with the use of medications (Sprague & Gadow, 1976). This record should be shared with parents and medical personnel with the consent of parents to assist them in evaluating the efficacy and need for continued use of the medication (Courtnage et al., 1982). A sample anecdotal record is presented in Figure 11.10.

Educators should avoid dispensing medications, but occasionally the drug treatment schedule may necessitate the school nurse administering medication to students during school hours. If the school nurse cannot dispense the medication, teachers may be asked to give students their medication. However, before dispensing medication, educators should obtain the permission of parents and the appropriate medical personnel. All medica-

FIGURE 11.10
Sample drug anecdotal record

Name of Student Henry Jones **Grade** 6
School Pine Lake Elementary **Recorded by** Ms. Healy

Date	Observations
10-8-81	Henry seems to have lost his appetite. He didn't eat much of his lunch Tuesday and Wednesday. Today he did manage to eat everything, but it did demand encouragement on my part. If this continues much longer I will contact the parents.
10-12-81	Henry was not very accepting of the idea of taking medication but since my contact with the parents on October 8th, he seems to be less resistant.
10-15-81	Henry did eat his lunch today. He also did attend better in his morning reading and social studies classes, but had two fights with his classmates at lunch break and was irritable during the afternoon.

Source: L. Courtnage, W. Stainback, and S. Stainback, *Teaching Exceptional Children,* vol. 15 (Reston, VA: Council for Exceptional Children), p. 9. Reprinted by permission of the publisher.

tions should be stored together in a secured location that is open to only school personnel involved in their administration. To avoid confusion, each students' medication should be clearly labeled, including the name of the student, physician, pharmacy, and the medication; the telephone number of the physician and the pharmacy; the date; and the dosage and frequency of administration (Kinnison & Nimmer, 1979). A record of the medications dispensed also should be maintained (see Figure 11.11).

GRADUATION REQUIREMENTS

As mainstreamed students achieve success in and progress through the regular education system, the likelihood that they will graduate with a diploma or some type of recognition will increase. While variations exist in the ways mainstreamed students demonstrate mastery of graduation requirements, Ross and

FIGURE 11.11
Record of drug administration

Name of Student	Henry Jones	**Birthdate**	July 25, 1970
Address	Holcomb Avenue Des Moines, Iowa	**Phone**	(515) 832-6111
School	Pine Lake Elementary	**Grade**	6

Date	Time	Name of medication	Dosage	Signature of person administering medication	Comments
10-5-81	11:20	*Ritalin Initiated*	20 mg.	H. Healy	Henry questioned the need for medication. Parents notified.
10-6-81	11:20	Ritalin	20 mg.	H. Healy	—
10-7-81	11:20	Ritalin	20 mg.	H. Healy	—
10-8-81	11:20	Ritalin	20 mg.	H. Healy	—
10-9-81	Absent				—
10-12-81	11:20	Ritalin	20 mg.	H. Healy	—
10-13-81	11:20	Ritalin	20 mg.	H. Healy	—
10-14-81	11:20	Ritalin	20 mg.	H. Healy	Henry spit out pill. Said said didn't need it—took it a second time
10-15-81	11:20	Ritalin Discontinued	—	H. Healy	—
10-15-81	9:15	Cylert Initiated	37.5 mg.	H. Healy	Hesitant about taking new medication.

Source: L. Courtnage, W. Stainback, and S. Stainback, *Teaching Exceptional Children,* vol. 15 (Reston, VA: Council for Exceptional Children), p. 8. Reprinted by permission of the publisher.

Weintraub (1980) have identified several approaches to granting some type of diploma to acknowledge completion of graduation requirements:

1. *Pass/Fail Approach.* Upon completing their individualized course of study, all students receive a standard diploma. Individualized achievements, courses completed, and scores on minimum competency tests are specified on the students' transcripts.

2. *Certificate of Attendance Approach.* Students who do not meet graduation requirements receive a certificate to document that they participated in and attended a specific educational program for a specified period of time. In using this alternative, educators should be careful that it does not demean students, lessen the availability of services to them, or limit the post-secondary opportunities for mainstreamed students and students from culturally and linguistically diverse backgrounds.

3. *IEP Approach.* Students' IEPs act as the framework for establishing and individualizing eligibility for graduation and receipt of a diploma. The goals and objectives of the IEP parallel the standard diploma requirements and serve as a document listing the minimum competencies a mainstreamed student must complete in order to graduate. Students who complete the goals and objectives specified in their IEPs earn a diploma. Diplomas can be supplemented by a transcript indicating courses taken, IEP objectives mastered, and instructional adaptations employed.

4. *Special Education Diploma Approach.* Students who do not complete the standardized graduation requirements receive a specialized diploma based on mastery of goals and objectives outlined in their IEP. A transcript listing mastery of objectives and goals could accompany the diploma to provide additional information to prospective employers.

5. *Curricular Approach.* Students and parents with the assistance of educators select a course of study related to their needs and career goals (college preparation, vocational education, basic skills, life management). Each course of study has a prescribed set of requirements and strategies for assessing mastery of identified competencies. When requirements are met, students receive a diploma documenting their mastery of the competencies of the plan of study they have selected.

6. *Work Study Approach.* Students work in various community settings while simultaneously earning credits toward graduation.

SUMMARY

This chapter offered educators a variety of strategies for evaluating the progress of mainstreamed students. The chapter

- presented various types of informal and formal testing procedures educators can use to monitor and assess student performance
- outlined alternative procedures to assess the progress of students from culturally and linguistically diverse backgrounds

- reviewed various alternative grading systems for use with mainstreamed students
- provided guidelines for adapting teacher-made tests to assess the performance of mainstreamed students accurately
- reviewed a variety of alternative testing techniques that can help mainstreamed students perform at their optimal level
- provided suggestions for teaching students a variety of test-taking skills
- outlined a variety of strategies for involving parents, teachers, and students in evaluating the progress of mainstreamed students
- identified factors to consider when evaluating the effectiveness of instructional modifications, adaptive devices, and medical interventions

RECOMMENDED READINGS

Bender, W. N. (1992). The Bender Classroom Structure Questionnaire: A tool for placement decisions and evaluation of mainstream learning environments. *Intervention in School and Clinic, 27*(5), 307–312.

Carpenter, D. (1985). Grading handicapped pupils: Review and position statement. *Remedial and Special Education, 6,* 54–59.

Figueroa, R. A. (1989). Psychological testing of linguistic-minority students: Knowledge gaps and regulations. *Exceptional Children, 56*(2), 145–153.

Giek, K. A. (1992). Monitoring student progress through efficient record keeping. *Teaching Exceptional Children, 24*(3), 22–26.

Kinnison, L. R., Hayes, C., & Acord, J. (1981). Evaluating student progress in mainstream classes. *Teaching Exceptional Children, 13,* 97–99.

Mastropieri, M. A., & Scruggs, T. E. (1987). *Effective instruction for special education.* Boston: College-Hill.

Putnam, M. L. (1992). Characteristics of questions on tests administered by mainstream secondary classroom teachers. *Learning Disabilities Research and Practice, 7,* 129–136.

Salvia, J., & Hughes, C. (1990). *Curriculum-based assessment: Testing what is taught.* New York: Macmillan.

Valencia, S. (1990). A portfolio approach to classroom reading assessment: The whys, whats, and hows. *The Reading Teacher, 43,* 338–340.

Venn, J., Morganstern, L., & Dykes, M. K. (1979). Checklists for evaluating the fit and function of orthoses, prostheses, and wheelchairs in the classroom. *Teaching Exceptional Children, 11,* 51–56.

Appendix: Parental, Professional, and Advocacy Organizations*

Advocates * Resources * Counseling
ARC of King County
2230 Eighth Avenue
Seattle, WA 98121 206–622–9324

Maintains a Parent-to-Parent Support Program, trains parents to work with parents whose children have similar disabilities. Disseminates a newsletter for parents and for grandparents of children with special needs.

Alexander Graham Bell Association for the Deaf
3417 Volta Place, NW
Washington, DC 20007 202–337–5220

Answers inquiries from parents, offers information on educational options and consultation services, disseminates a journal and newsletter.

American Association on Mental Retardation
1719 Kalorama Road, NW
Washington, DC 20009 800–424–3688

Distributes information about programs and research, sponsors conferences, and serves as a clearinghouse on various aspects of mental retardation. A publications list and newsletter are available.

*Compiled by Lynn Sarda, Lynne Crockett, Veronica Lazzaro, Cathy Mastrocola, Susan Richmann, Joan Neugebauer, and Merrilly Warren-Blum.

American Cancer Society
90 Park Avenue
New York, NY 10016 212–599–8200

Provides information, direct services, and referrals. Some materials are available in Spanish.

American Cleft Palate Association
331 Salk Hall, University of Pittsburgh
Pittsburgh, PA 15213 412–681–9620

Provides publications, referrals for services, and free pamphlets for parents. Puts parents in touch with others who have children with cleft palates.

American Council for the Blind
1010 Vermont Avenue, NW, Suite 1100 800–424–8666, 3–5 P.M.
Washington, DC 20005 202–393–3666

Serves people who are visually impaired or deaf/blind. Offers a parent organization, legal assistance, a newsletter, and free magazine. Some information is available in Braille, Spanish.

American Council on Rural Special Education
National Rural Development Institute
Western Washington University
Bellingham, WA 98225 206–676–3576

Focuses on improving services for students with disabilities living in rural areas.

American Foundation for the Blind, Inc.
15 West 16th Street 800-AFBLIND
New York, NY 10011 212-620-2000

Serves people who are visually impaired or deaf/blind. Provides information on education and employment and daily living activities. Pamphlets, films, and publications are available including some in Braille and Spanish.

American Heart Association
7320 Greenville Avenue
Dallas, TX 75231 214–750–5300

Provides information and referral services for individuals with cardiovascular disorders, stroke, and aphasia. There is a small charge for some materials. Some materials are available in Spanish.

American Lung Association
1740 Broadway
New York, NY 10019 212–315–8700

Provides information on respiratory conditions, tuberculosis, and asthma. Most resources and materials are free. Several pamphlets in Spanish are available.

American Physical Therapy Association
1111 North Fairfax Street
Alexandria, VA 22314 703–684–2782

Provides pamphlets, newsletter, and free bibliographies. Refers to facilities offering physical therapy services.

American Printing House for the Blind
P.O. Box 6085, 1839 Frankfort Avenue
Louisville, KY 40206–0085 502–895–2405

Offers lists of books, brochures, catalogues in Braille and large print publications. Serves as the largest publishing house for people who are blind or visually impaired.

American Society for Deaf Children
814 Thayer Avenue
Silver Spring, MD 20910 301–585–5400

Provides parents and families of children who are hard of hearing or deaf with support and information. Offers networking referral and advocacy services. Publishes a newsletter, legislative information, and position papers.

American Speech, Language & Hearing Association
10801 Rockville Pike
Rockville, MD 20852 301–897–5700

A professional organization that disseminates research and information on communication disorders. Publishes journals and serves as an advocacy group.

Association of Birth Defects Children, Inc. (ABDC)
3526 Emerywood Lane
Orlando, FL 32806 407–859–2821

Provides information about birth defects associated with environmental factors and disseminates information related to effects of environmental agents. Publishes a quarterly newsletter.

Association for Children and Adults with Learning Disabilities
4156 Library Road
Pittsburgh, PA 15234 412–341–1515/8077

Provides general information and referrals. Offers free pamphlets, lists of special schools, colleges, and camps for students with learning disabilities.

Association for Persons with Severe Handicaps
7010 Roosevelt Way, N.E.
Seattle, WA 98115 206–523–8446

Offers parent-to-parent support and communication network. Assists with referrals and publishes a journal, newsletter, and bibliographies.

Association for Retarded Citizens of the United States
National Headquarters
2501 Avenue J 800–433–5255
Arlington, TX 76006 817–640–0204

Provides services and referrals. Publishes pamphlets, books, and a newsletter. There is a nominal charge for publications. Some publications in Spanish are available.

Bilingual Special Education
Department of Special Education
EDB 306
University of Texas
Austin, TX 78710

Provides newsletter and bulletin board for information on the identification, assessment, placement, and educational planning for special needs bilingual students.

Blind Children's Fund
International Institute for Visually Impaired, 0–7, Inc.
230 Central Street
Auburndale, MA 02166–2399

Develops and disseminates information, materials, and services for individuals with visual impairments. Provides support services to parents and professionals, programs, a newsletter, publications. Some publications in Spanish are available.

The Candlelighters
Childhood Cancer Foundation
Suite 1001
1901 Pennsylvania Avenue, NW
Washington, DC 20006 202–659–5136

For parents and their children with cancer. Produces a quarterly newsletter and a youth newsletter. Provides support, information services, and lobbying groups.

Children's Defense Fund
122 C Street NW
Washington, DC 20001

Attends to the needs of children and children with special needs through public education, awareness, and preventive programs. Provides information on legislation and specific projects. Charges for some publications and newsletter.

Children with Attention Deficit Disorders (CHADD)
1859 North Pine Island Road
Suite 185 305–384–6869
Plantation, FL 33322 305–792–8100

Serves parents of children with attention deficit disorders by offering informational meetings, a support group, and newsletters.

Citizens Alliance to Uphold Special Education (CAUSE)
313 South Washington Square, Suite 040
Lansing, MI 48917 Voice/TDD 800–221–9105

Provides information and training for parents interested in helping other parents through workshops and support groups. Maintains a resource library, transition and outreach programs, and a program of parents training parents.

Clearinghouse on the Handicapped
Office of Special Education and Rehabilitative Services
U.S. Department of Education
Switzer Building, Room 3132
Washington, DC 20202–2319 202–732–1214

Answers inquiries regarding programs, housing, transportation, legislation, funding, etc. A newsletter, referrals to parents, publication list are some of the free services available.

Collaboration Among Parents and Health Professionals Project (CAPP)
P.O. Box 992
Westfield, MA 01086 413–562–5521

Promotes communication among parents and health care providers. Encourages parent involvement in the health care of their children with special needs. Provides listings of regional and national parent centers.

Coordinating Council for Handicapped Children
20 East Jackson Boulevard, Room 900
Chicago, IL 60604 312–939–3513

Publishes pamphlets, training manuals, fact sheets, and newsletters for parents of children with special needs. Provides an information and referral service and an outreach program for parents. Materials are available in Spanish.

Council for Exceptional Children
1920 Association Drive
Reston, VA 22091 703–620–3660

Provides an information service on special education, laws, and policy. Advocates for legislation and services to benefit individuals with special needs and their families. Materials and bibliographies are available.

Council for Learning Disabilities
P.O. Box 40303
Overland Park, KS 66204 913–492–8755

Functions as a professional organization that publishes journals and disseminates information and research concerning individuals with learning disabilities.

Easter Seal Society
National Headquarters
2023 West Ogden Avenue 800–211–6827
Chicago, IL 60612 312–243–8400

Provides services, journals, newsletters, and bibliographies for parents. There is a small charge for some information. Some materials in Spanish are available.

Epilepsy Foundation of America
4351 Garden City Drive, Suite 406 800–EFA–1000
Landover, MD 20785 301–459–3700

Serves individuals with epilepsy or seizure disorders. Provides services, programs, as well as information on education, health, and employment. Pamphlets, newsletters and bibliographies are available in Braille, Spanish, and other languages.

Father's Program
Merrywood School
16120 NE 8th Street
Bellevue, WA 98008 206–747–4004

Provides training for forming support groups to meet the needs of fathers of children with special needs. Suggests developmentally appropriate activities that fathers and their children can enjoy together. Lists current related books and materials and publishes a newsletter.

Federation for Children with Special Needs
312 Stuart Street 2nd Fl.
Boston, MA 02116 617–482–2915

Provides child advocacy and information centers for parents and parent organizations. Conducts workshops and provides technical assistance for parents.

The Genesis Fund
30 Warren Street
Brighton, MA 02135 800–225–5995

Provides genetic counseling; funding for diagnosis, care and treatment of children born with genetic diseases, birth defects, and mental retardation.

HEATH Resource Center
Higher Education and Adult Training for People with Handicaps
One Dupont Circle, Suite 670 800–544–3284
Washington, DC 20036–1193 202–939–9320

Serves as an information center for higher education and people with special needs. Publications, fact sheets, and newsletters are available at no cost.

Helen Keller National Center for Deaf-Blind Youths and Adults
111 Middle Neck Road
Sands Point, NY 11050 516–944–8900

Serves students aged 18 and up. Provides information on communication, mobility, and life skills. Pamphlets, articles, and bibliographies are available for a nominal fee.

International Rett Syndrome Association
8511 Rose Marie Drive
Fort Washington, MD 20744 301–284–7031

Provides information and referral services and offers direct and parent-to-parent support systems. Encourages research, promotes awareness, disseminates information through brochures and a quarterly newsletter.

Juvenile Diabetes Foundation
60 Madison Avenue
New York, NY 10010 212–689–2860

Disseminates research and information on juvenile diabetes.

The Kids on the Block, Inc.
9385-C Gerwig Lane
Columbia, MD 21045

Provides educational puppeteering programs that include topics on disability awareness, medical issues, and social concerns.

KIDS Project, Inc.
1720 Oregon Street
Berkeley, CA 94703 415–548–4121

Develops and presents inclusive, non-discriminatory materials dealing with individuals with disabilities in society. Provides free informational brochures, pamphlets, articles, and a price list of other games, books, and materials.

Leukemia Society of America
733 Third Avenue
New York, NY 10017 212–573–8484

Disseminates research and information and offers a variety of services to individuals with leukemia and their families.

March of Dimes Birth Defects Foundation
1275 Mamaroneck Avenue
White Plains, NY 10605 914–428–7100

Provides information for the public as well as prospective parents on how to protect mother's and baby's health. Printed materials are available.

Ronald McDonald House
500 North Michigan Avenue
Chicago, IL 60611

Offers temporary housing near hospitals for families of children who are seriously ill and must be hospitalized or receive outpatient care for an extended period of time at a site far from home.

Migrant Education Resource List Information Network (MERLIN)
Pennsylvania Department of Education
8th Floor, 333 Market Street 800–233–0306
Harrisburg, PA 17018 717–783–7121

Provides information on migrant education. Identifies and links national resources that support the educational needs of migrant children.

Muscular Dystrophy Association
810 Seventh Avenue
New York, NY 10019 212–586–0808

Provides services, materials, magazine, and free brochures.

National Amputation Foundation
12–45 150th Street
Whitestone, NY 11367 718–767–8400

Provides assistance and legal, financial, and employment information.

National Association for Bilingual Education
Room 407, 1201 16th Street, NW
Washington, DC 20036 202–822–7870

Addresses educational needs of bilingual populations. Programs, materials, and newsletters are available.

National Association of the Deaf
814 Thayer Avenue
Silver Spring, MD 20910 301–587–1788

Serves individuals who are deaf or hearing impaired. Provides information on programs and services, legislation and legal rights. Newsletter, books, publications lists are available.

National Association for the Education of Young Children
1834 Connecticut Avenue, NW
Washington, DC 20009 202–323–8777

Focuses on improving the quality and availability of child care and early education for young children (0–8 years). Provides referrals, books, kits, brochures, bibliographies, and directories.

National Association for Hearing and Speech Action
10801 Rockville Pike
Rockville, MD 20855 800–638–TALK

Disseminates brochures on hearing, listening devices, communication disorders, and on role of speech pathologists and audiologists. Publishes a newsletter on services, products, programs, and activities for individuals and families. Provides information on legislation and insurance coverage for speech/language pathology and audiology services. Some materials in Spanish are available.

National Association for Parents of the Visually Impaired, Inc.
P.O. Box 562
Camden, NY 13316 800–562–6265

Promotes the development of state and local organizations of, by, and for parents of children who are visually impaired. Provides support and increases public awareness. Publishes quarterly newsletter.

National Association of Protection and Advocacy Systems (NAPAS)
300 I Street, NE
Suite 212
Washington, DC 20002 202–546–8202

Provides a listing of advocacy agencies by state.

National Association for Sickle Cell Disease, Inc.
4221 Wilshire Boulevard, Suite 360 800–421–8453
Los Angeles, CA 90010 213–936–7205

Provides services, fact sheets, brochures, and a newsletter. Most materials are available at no charge.

National Association for the Visually Handicapped
22 West 21st Street
New York, NY 10010 212–889–3141

Serves those with partial vision. Provides information, referrals, services, materials, and newsletters. Some materials in Spanish are available.

National Ataxia Foundation
600 Twelve Oaks Center
15500 Wayzata Boulevard
Wayzata, MN 55391 612–473–7666

Offers counseling, support, and referrals. Free booklets, brochures, and fact sheets are disseminated.

National Birth Defects Center
c/o Kennedy Memorial Hospital
30 Warren Street
Brighton, MA 02135 800–322–5014

Offers diagnostic and evaluation clinics. Maintains parent support groups. Houses the Pregnancy Environmental Hotline for information about drugs, medications, chemicals, and other environmental agents that are potentially harmful to a pregnant woman and her child.

National Captioning Institute
5203 Leesburg Pike
Falls Church, VA 22041 Voice/TTY 703–998–2400

Provides cable and network listings two times a year for closed-captioned programming and a closed-captioned videocassette listing six times a year.

National Center for Education in Maternal and Child Health
38th and R Streets, NW
Washington, DC 20007 202–625–8400

Provides research, information services, and educational materials on pregnancy, high risk infants, nutrition, genetics, and disabling conditions. Some publications are available in Spanish.

National Center for Research in Vocational Education
University of California at Berkeley
1995 University Avenue
Suite 375 800–762–4093
Berkeley, CA 94704 510–642–4004

Provides publications list, data bases, catalogs of products, and services for professionals in employment-related education and training.

National Clearinghouse for Bilingual Education
11501 Georgia Avenue, Suite 102 800–647–0123
Wheaton, MD 20902 301–933–9448

Has information on bilingual education programs and legislation.

National Committee for Citizens in Education
10840 Little Patuxent Parkway, Suite 301 800–NET–WORK
Columbia, MD 21044–3199 301–997–9300

Focuses on improving quality of public schools through increased public involvement. Publications, newsletter, special education checklist, parents' rights, and legal information are available.

National Cystic Fibrosis Foundation
6000 Executive Boulevard — 800–FIGHTCF
Rockville, MD 20855 — 301–881–9130

Has information on local chapters, materials, publications list, and publishes a newsletter. Most information is available free.

National Down Syndrome Congress
1800 Dempster Street — 800–232–NDSC
Park Ridge, IL 60068–1146 — 312–823–7550

Provides opportunities for parents and professionals to work towards improving education, stimulating research, and promoting the rights and welfare of individuals with Down syndrome. Sponsors national and international conferences, publishes a monthly newsletter, fact sheets, brochures, and bibliographies.

National Down Syndrome Society
141 Fifth Avenue — 800–221–4602
New York, NY 10010 — 212–460–9330

Provides information, services and referrals, booklets, materials, bibliography, fact sheets, and a newsletter. Some materials in Spanish are available. Maintains 24-hour hotline.

National Head Injury Foundation, Inc.
1776 Massachusetts Avenue
Suite 100 — 800–444-NHIF
Washington, DC 20036 — 202–296–6443

Increases public, family, and professional awareness. Publishes a newsletter and brochures. Provides a resource center and disseminates legislative information.

National Hearing Aid Society
20361 Middlebelt
Livonia, MI 48152 — 800–521–5247

Provides listing of professional hearing instrument specialists, informational booklet on signs and types of hearing loss, recommendations for choosing and evaluating a specialist, and consumer information on hearing aids. Maintains a hotline for further information.

National Hemophilia Foundation
The Soho Building
110 Greene Street, Room 406
New York, NY 10012 — 212–219–8180

Provides referrals, materials, publications and a newsletter.

National Information Center for Children and Youth With Handicaps
(NICHCY)
PO Box 1492 — 800–999–5599
Washington, DC 20013 — Voice/TDD 703–893–6061

Answers questions, connects individuals with similar needs, provides advice, and directories of agencies and organizations. Some materials in Spanish are available.

National Institute of Neurological and Communicative Disorders and Stroke
National Institute of Health
U.S. Department of Health and Human Services
Building 31, Room 8A–16
Bethesda, MD 20814 301–496–5751

Serves people with neurological and communicative disorders, cerebrovascular disease, metabolic disorders, head and spinal cord injury. Answers question, provides publications, pamphlets, and fact sheets. Maintains publications list and single pamphlets free.

National Legal Resource Center for Child Advocacy
1800 M Street, NW
Washington, DC 20036 202–331–2250

Provides information and educational services on issues relating to children with special needs and their parents.

National Library Service for the Blind and Physically Handicapped
Library of Congress
1291 Taylor Street, NW 800–424–8567
Washington, DC 20011 212–287–5100

Has a collection of Braille, talking books, magazines, and playback equipment that is loaned. Articles, fact sheets, brochures, bibliographies, and directories are free.

National Mental Health Association
1021 Prince Street
Alexandria, VA 22314

Serves people with mental and emotional disorders. Provides information on services, research, rehabilitation, legislation, and employment. Publications and materials list are available.

National Rehabilitation Information Center
4407 Eighth Street, NE 800–43–NARIC
Washington, DC 20017 202–635–5826

Provides brochures, publications, newsletter, information, and catalogs on products and equipment. Most resources are available at no cost.

National Rural Development Institute
Western Washington University
Bellingham, WA 98225 206–676–3576

Provides copies of published and unpublished articles on specific topics, notices of upcoming conferences of possible interest, and personnel recruitment services. Supports parental and professional involvement in research, program, and staff development.

National Society for Children and Adults with Autism
1234 Massachusetts Avenue, NW, Suite 1017
Washington, DC 20005–4599 202–783–0125

Provides information, services, referrals, parent support groups, public education, and advocacy. Offers a catalog of books, pamphlets on autism, and a newsletter. Some materials in Spanish are available.

National Spinal Cord Injury Association
149 California Street
Newton, MA 02158 617–965–0521

Disseminates fact sheets on spinal cord injury, publications list, newsletter, and a list of state chapters.

National Tay-Sachs and Allied Diseases Association, Inc.
385 Elliot Street
Newton, MA 02164 617–964–5508

Provides information and education about Tay-Sachs and allied diseases. Promotion of carrier screening, a parent support group, and research are other activities sponsored by this organization.

National Wheelchair Athletic Association—Junior Division
3617 Betty Drive, Suite S
Colorado Springs, CO 80907

Provides organized athletic opportunities for youth with physical disabilities and listings of videotapes including integrated recreation. A newsletter is available.

New Eyes for the Needy
549 Milburn Avenue
Short Hills, NJ 07078 201–376–4903

Provides funds to individuals not eligible for other sources of financial aid for glasses, artificial eyes, and contact lenses for cataract patients.

Orton Dyslexia Society
724 York Road
Baltimore, MD 21204 301–296–0232

Provides information and guidance to resources. Pamphlets and articles are available at a small charge.

PACER Center, Inc.
Parent Advocacy Coalition for Educational Rights
4826 Chicago Avenue South 800–53–PACER
Minneapolis, MN 55417 612–827–2966

Provides information on infants, toddlers, and preschoolers with special needs. Offers a free newsletter, workshops, lists, and brochures. Disseminates information about laws, parents' rights and responsibilities. Some materials in Spanish are available.

Parent Information Center
P.O. Box 1422
Concord, NH 03301 603–224–7005

Provides support, information, and training to families of children with disabilities. Provides technical assistance to parents/parent groups interested in establishing parent training and information programs.

Parents Helping Parents, Inc.
535 Race Street, # 220
San Jose, CA 95126 408–288–5010

Offers services to special needs families. Includes information packets, peer counseling, home visits, public meetings, social gatherings, family support sessions, training, advocacy, and sibling support groups. Publishes a quarterly newsletter.

PEAK Parent Center, Inc.
6055 Lehman Drive, Suite 101 800–426–2466 ex. 423
Colorado Springs, CO 80918 713–531–9400

Provides parents with answers to questions about children, location of services/resources, parent networks, state and federal laws, educational issues, and integration.

Perkins School for the Blind
175 N. Beacon Street
Watertown, MA 02172 617–924–3434

Serves people who are blind, deaf/blind, or multihandicapped/blind. Lists of curriculum materials and publications, brochures, books, newsletters are available in Braille, large type, and Spanish.

Pilot Parents
Central Palm Plaza
2005 N. Central Avenue, Suite 100
Phoenix, AZ 85004 602–271–4012

Offers family-to-family support, information, and education for families of children with disabilities. Publishes a newsletter and maintains a lending library.

Prader-Willi Syndrome Association
6439 Excelsior Boulevard, E-102
St. Paul, MN 55426 612–926–1947

Provides a bimonthly newsletter, a materials list, and information for persons interested in Prader-Willi syndrome. Local chapters of the organization have been formed throughout the United States and Canada. A national annual conference is held.

Shriners Hospitals for Crippled Children
2900 Rocky Point Drive
Tampa, FL 33607 813–885–2575

Offers free orthopedic and severe burn care to children.

Sibling Information Network
Connecticut's University Affiliated Facility
University of Connecticut
249 Glenbrook Road U-64
Storrs, CT 06268 203–486–4034

Serves as a clearinghouse for information, research and activities relating to siblings of children with special needs.

Speech Foundation of America
5139 Lingle Street NW
Washington, DC 20016

Publishes current information on prevention and treatment of speech disorders; some for parents, some for professionals. Some materials are available in Spanish, French, and Vietnamese.

Spina Bifida Association of America
1700 Rockville Pike, Suite 540 — 800-621-3141
Rockville, MD 20852 — 301-770-SBAA

Provides public education, research, referrals. Disseminates publications, newsletter, and manuals. Some materials are available in Spanish.

Tourette Syndrome Association
42-40 Bell Boulevard
Bayside, NY 11361 — 718-224-2999

Serves persons interested in Tourette syndrome. Programs, brochures, research materials, videotapes and films, and legal aid publications are available.

Travel Information Center
Moss Rehabilitation Hospital
12th Street and Tabor Road
Philadelphia, PA 19141

Provides a listing of airlines and trains having accommodations for individuals with special needs. Offers a listing of hotel chains that offer accommodations for people with special needs.

United Cerebral Palsy Association
666 E. 34th Street
New York, NY 10016 — 212-947-5770

Disseminates information and delivers services to individuals with cerebral palsy and their families.

Very Special Arts
1825 Connecticut Avenue, NW, Suite 417
Washington, DC 20009 — 202-662-8899

Provides information on curriculum and instruction in arts for individuals with special needs. Lists of organizations with art programs, brochures, and a newsletter are available.

References

Aaron, P. G., Phillips, S., & Larsen, S. (1988). Specific reading disability in historically famous persons. *Journal of Learning Disabilities, 21,* 523–538.

Abend, A. C. (1974). Criteria for selecting school furniture and equipment for the disabled. *CEFP Journal, 12,* 4–7.

Abramowitz, A. J., O'Leary, S. G., & Futtersak, M. W. (1988). The relative impact of long and short reprimands on children's off-task behavior in the classroom. *Behavior Therapy, 18,* 243–247.

Abrams, B. J. (1992). Values clarification for students with emotional disabilities. *Teaching Exceptional Children, 24*(3), 28–33.

Adelman, H. S., & Taylor, L. (1983). Enhancing motivation for overcoming learning and behavior problems. *Journal of Learning Disabilities, 16,* 384–392.

Adelman, M. J. (1982, April). *Making mainstreaming work: A collaborative consulting model for secondary schools.* Paper presented at the meeting of the Council for Exceptional Children, Houston, TX.

Adger, C., Wolfram, W., Detwyler, J., & Harry, B. (1992, November). *The place of African American English in the classroom.* Paper presented at the Council for Exceptional Children's Topical Conference on Culturally and Linguistically Diverse Exceptional Children, Minneapolis, MN.

Adler, M. (1969). How to mark a book. In F. L. Christ (Ed.), *SR/SE resource book* (pp. 41–45). Chicago: Science Research Associates.

Adolescent Pregnancy Prevention Clearinghouse (1990). *Latino youth at crossroads.* Washington, DC: Children's Defense Fund.

Agard, J. A., Veldman, D. J., Kaufman, M. J., & Semmel, M. I. (1978). *How I feel toward others: An instrument of the PRIME instrument battery.* Baltimore: University Park.

Ahmann, E., & Lipski, K. A. (1991). Early intervention for technology-dependent infants and young children. *Infants and Young Children, 3*(4), 67–77.

Ahn, H., Prichep, L., John, E. R., Baird, H., Trepetin, M., & Kaye, H. (1980). Developmental equations reflect brain dysfunctions. *Science, 210*(12), 1259–1262.

Aiello, B. (1979). Hey, what's it like to be handicapped? *Education Unlimited, 1,* 28–31.

Alberto, P. A., & Troutman, A. C. (1990). *Applied behavior analysis for teachers.* New York: Merrill/Macmillan.

Alexander, C. F. (1985). Black English dialect and the classroom teacher. In C. K. Brooks (Ed.), *Tapping potential: English and language arts for the black learner* (pp. 20–29). Urbana, IL: National Council of Teachers of English.

Alford, I. (1985). Manipulating mathematics. *Mathematics Teaching. 114.* 44–45.

Allen, K., Wilson, J., Cefalo, B., & Larson, C. (1990). *Effective instruction—Regular education—Special education: A perfect marriage.* Paper presented at the meeting of the Council for Exceptional Children, Toronto.

Allen, L., & Majidi-Ahi, S. (1989). Black American children. In J. Taylor Gibbs and L. Nahme Huang (Eds.). *Children of color: Psychological interventions with minority youth* (pp. 148–178). San Francisco: Jossey-Bass.

Alley, G., & Deshler, D. (1979). *Teaching the learning disabled adolescent: Strategies and methods.* Denver: Love.

Alleyne, M. (1980). *Comparative Afro-American.* Ann Arbor: Karoma.

Allington, R. L., & Broikou, K. A. (1988). Development of shared knowledge: A new role for classroom and specialist teachers. *The Reading Teacher, 41,* 806–811.

Allington, R. L., & Shake, M. C. (1986). Remedial reading: Achieving curricular congruence in classroom and clinic. *The Reading Teacher, 39,* 648–654.

Allred, R. (1977). *Spelling: The application of research findings.* Washington, DC: National Education Association.

Almanza, H. P., & Mosley, W. J. (1980). Curriculum adaptations and modifications for culturally diverse handicapped children. *Exceptional Children, 46,* 608–613.

Alper, S., & Ryndak, D. L. (1992). Educating students with severe handicaps in regular classes. *The Elementary School Journal, 92*(3), 373–387.

Ambert, A. N., & Dew, N. (1982). *Special education for exceptional bilingual students: A handbook for educators.* Milwaukee, WI: Midwest National Origin Desegregation Assistance Center.

American Council on Education. (1987). *American freshman: National norms for 1987.* Washington, DC: Author.

American Psychiatric Association. (1987). *Diagnostic and statistical manual of mental disorders* (3rd. ed., rev.). Washington, DC: Author.

Ammer, J. J. (1984). The mechanics of mainstreaming: Considering the regular educators' perspective. *Remedial and Special Education, 5,* 15–20.

Amos, K. M. (1980). Competency testing: Will the LD student be included? *Exceptional Children, 47,* 194–197.

Anderegg, M. L., & Vergason, G. A. (1988). An analysis of one of the cornerstones of the regular education initiative. *Focus on Exceptional Children, 20*(6), 1–7.

Anderson, L. M. (1984). The environment of instruction: The function of seatwork in a commercially developed curriculum. In G. G. Duffy, I. R. Roehler, & J. Mason (Eds.), *Comprehension instruction: Perspectives and suggestions* (pp. 93–103). New York: Longman.

Anderson, P. P., & Fenichel, E. S. (1989). *Serving culturally diverse families of infants and toddlers with disabilities.* Washington, DC: National Center for Clinical Infant Programs.

Anderson-Inman, L. (1986). Bridging the gap: Student-centered strategies for promoting the transfer of learning. *Exceptional Children, 52,* 562–572.

Andrews, J. F., & Mason, J. M. (1991). Strategy usage among deaf and hearing readers. *Exceptional Children, 57,* 536–545.

Antonak, R. F., & Livneh, H. (1988). *The measurement of attitudes toward people with disabilities: Methods, psychometrics and scales.* Springfield, IL: Charles C. Thomas.

Antonak, R. F. (1981). *Development and psychometric analysis of the Scale of Attitudes Toward Disabled Persons (Technical Report #1).* Durham, NH: University of New Hampshire, Education Department.

Aragon, J. (1974). Cultural conflict and cultural diversity in education. In L. A. Bransford, L. Baca, & K. Lane (Eds.), *Cultural diversity and the exceptional child* (pp. 24–31). Reston, VA: Council for Exceptional Children.

Aramburo, D. J. (1989, August). Cultural pluralism—The numbers are still growing. *Exceptional Times,* 3.

Archer, A. L. (1988). Strategies for responding to information. *Teaching Exceptional Children, 20,* 55–57.

Argulewicz, E. N. (1983). Effects of ethnic membership, socioeconomic status, and home language on LD, EMR, and EH placements. *Learning Disability Quarterly, 6,* 195–200.

Arlin, M., Scott, M., & Webster, J. (1979). The effects of pictures on rate of learning sight words: A critique of the focal attention hypothesis. *Reading Research Quarterly, 14*(4), 645–660.

Armbruster, B. B., & Anderson, T. H. (1988). On selecting "considerate" content area textbooks. *Remedial and Special Education, 9*(1), 47–52.

Aronson, E., Blaney, N., Stephan, C., Sikes, J., & Snapp, M. (1978). *The jigsaw classroom.* Beverly Hills, CA: Sage.

Arreola v. Santa Anna Board of Education. No. 160–577, (Orange County, California, 1968).

Arter, J. A., & Jenkins, J. R. (1979). Differential diagnosis-prescriptive teaching: A critical appraisal. *Review of Educational Research, 49,* 517–555.

Asante, M. (1990). American elements in African-American English. In J. Holloway (Ed.), *Africanisms in American Culture* (pp. 19–33). Bloomington, IN: Indiana University Press.

Ashcroft, L. (1987). Defusing "empowering": The what and the why. *Language Arts, 64,* 142–156.

Asher, J. J. (1977). *Learning author language through actions: The complete teacher's guide.* Los Gatos, CA: Sky Oaks.

Asher, S. R., & Taylor, A. R. (1981). Social outcomes of mainstreaming: Sociometric assessment and beyond. *Exceptional Education Quarterly, 1,* 13–30.

Ashlock, R. B. (1990). *Error patterns in computation: A semi-programmed approach* (4th ed.). New York: Merrill/Macmillan.

Askov, E., & Greff, K. (1975). Handwriting: Copying versus tracing as the most effective type of practice. *Journal of Educational Research, 69,* 96–98.

Astin, A. (1977). *Four critical years: Effects of college on beliefs, attitudes and knowledge.* San Francisco: Jossey-Bass.

Atwell, N. (1987). *In the middle: Reading, writing, and learning from adolescents.* Portsmouth, NH: Heinemann.

Aune, E. P., & Ness, J. E. ((1991). *Tools for transition: Preparing students with learning disabilities for postsecondary education.* Circle Pines, MN: American Guidance Service.

Ayres, B., Belle, C., Green, K., O'Connor, J., & Meyer, L.H. (n.d.). *Examples of curricular adaptations for students with severe disabilities in the elementary classroom—Study Group Report Series No. 3.* Syracuse, NY: Division of Special Education, Syracuse University.

Baca, L. M., & Cervantes, H. T. (1984). *The bilingual special education interface.* St. Louis: Times Mirror/Mosby.

Baca, L. M., & Cervantes, H. T. (1989). *The bilingual special education interface* (2nd ed.). New York: Merrill/Macmillan.

Baca, L. M. & Harris, K. C. (1988). Teaching migrant exceptional students. *Teaching Exceptional Children,* 20, 32–35.

Bacon, E. H., & Schulz, J. B. (1991). A survey of mainstreaming practices. *Teacher Education and Special Education, 14*(2), 144–149.

Bagley, M. T., & Greene, J. F. (1981). *Peer attitudes toward the handicapped scale.* Austin, TX: Pro-Ed.

Baldwin, B. A. (1989). The cornucopia kids. *US Air Magazine, 11*(10), 30–34.

Ball, T. S., Coyne, A., Jarvis, R. M., & Pease, S. F. (1984). Parents of retarded children as teaching assistants for other parents. *Education and Training of the Mentally Retarded, 19,* 64–69.

Banbury, M. M. (1987). Testing and grading mainstreamed students in regular education subjects. In A. Rotatori, M. M. Banbury, & R. A. Fox (Eds.), *Issues in special education* (pp. 177–186). Mountain View, CA: Mayfield.

Banbury, M. M., & Hebert, C. R. (1992). Do you see what I mean? Body language in classroom interactions. *Teaching Exceptional Children, 24*(2), 32–38.

Banks, J. A. (1987). *Teaching strategies for ethnic studies* (4th ed). Boston: Allyn & Bacon.

Banks, J. A. (1991a). A curriculum for empowerment, action, and change. In C. E. Sleeter (Ed.), *Empowerment through multicultural education* (pp. 125–141). Albany, NY: State University of New York Press.

Banks, J. A. (1991b). *Teaching strategies for ethnic studies* (5th ed.). Boston: Allyn & Bacon.

Banks, J. A., & Clegg, A. A. (1990). *Teaching strategies for social studies: Inquiry, valuing, and decision-making* (4th ed.). White Plains, NY: Longman.

Banks, J.A., & Sebesta, S. L. (1982). *We Americans: Our history and people* (Vols. 1–2). Boston: Allyn & Bacon.

Banta, E. M. (1979). Siblings of deaf-blind children. *Volta Review, 81,* 363–369.

Barclay, K. D. (1990). Constructing meaning: An integrated approach to teaching reading. *Intervention in School and Clinic, 26*(2), 84–91.

Barnes, D. M. (1986). Brain function decline in children with AIDS. *Science, 232,* 1196.

Barnes, E., Berrigan, C., & Biklen, D. (1978). *What's the difference? Teaching positive attitudes toward people with disabilities.* Syracuse, NY: Human Policy.

Baron, R. M., Tom, D. Y., & Cooper, H. M. (1985). Social class, race and teacher expectations. In J. B. Dusek (Ed.), *Teacher expectancies* (pp. 251–269). Hillsdale, NJ: Lawrence Erlbaum Associates.

Baroody, A. J., & Hume, J. (1991). Meaningful mathematics instruction: The case for fractions. *Remedial and Special Education, 12*(3), 54–68.

Barr, R. (1975). Influence of reading materials on response to printed words. *Journal of Reading Behavior, 7,* 123–135.

Barraga, N. C. (1964). *Increased visual behavior in low vision children.* New York: American Foundation for the Blind.

Barraga, N. C. (1983). *Visual handicaps and learning.* Austin, TX: Exceptional Resources.

Barringer, F. (1992, May 29). New census data reveal redistribution of poverty. *The New York Times,* p. A14.

Barrish, H. H., Saunders, M., & Wolf, M. M. (1969). Good behavior game: Effects on individual contingencies for group consequences on disruptive behavior in the classroom. *Journal of Applied Behavior Analysis, 2,* 119–124.

Bartalo, D. B. (1983). Calculators and problem solving instruction: They are made for each other. *Arithmetic Teacher, 30,* 18–21.

Bartel, N. R., & Meddock, T. D. (1989). AIDS and adolescents with learning disabilities: Issues for parents and educators. *Journal of Reading, Writing and Learning Disabilities, 5,* 299–311.

Bassuk, E., & Rubin, L. (1986). Homeless children: A neglected population. *American Journal of Orthopsychiatry, 57,* 279–286.

Bauman, K. E., & Iwata, B. A. (1977). Maintenance of independent housekeeping skills using scheduling plus self-rewarding procedures. *Behavior Therapy, 8,* 554–560.

Baumann, J. F. (1982). Research on children's main idea comprehension: A problem of ecological validity. *Reading Psychology, 3,* 167–177.

Bauwens, J., Hourcade, J. J., & Friend, M. (1989). Cooperative teaching: A model for general and special education integration. *Remedial and Special Education, 10*(2), 17–22.

Beach Center on Families and Disability. (1989). The Americans with disabilities act. *Families and Disability Newsletter, 1*(2), pp. 6, 8.

Bean, R. M., & Eichelberger, R. T. (1985). Changing the role of the reading specialists: From pull-out to in-class programs. *The Reading Teacher, 38,* 648–653.

Beattie, I. D., & Scheer, J. K. (1982). *Using the diagnostic stamp kit.* Port Roberts, WA: Janian Educational Materials.

Beattie, S., Grise, P., & Algozzine, B. (1983). Effects of test modification on minimum competency performance of learning disabled students. *Learning Disability Quarterly, 6,* 75–77.

Beaty, M. (1990, April). *LEP students, monolingual teacher: Hot to!* Paper presented at the meeting of the Council for Exceptional Children, Toronto.

Beck, I. L. (1984). Developing comprehension: The impact of the directed reading lesson. In R. Anderson, J. Osburn, and R. Tierney (Eds.), *Learning to read in American schools: Basal readers and context texts* (pp. 3–20). Hillsdale, NJ: Lawrence Erlbaum Associates.

Beck, I. L., & McKeown, M. C. (1981). Developing questions that promote comprehension: The story map. *Language Arts, 58,* 913–918.

Becker, W. C. (1971). *Parents as teachers.* Champaign, IL: Research.

Beckoff, A. G., & Bender, W. M. (1989). Programming for mainstream kindergarten success in preschool: Teachers' perceptions of necessary prerequisite skills. *Journal of Early Intervention, 13,* 269–280.

Beech, M. C. (1983). Simplifying text for mainstreamed students. *Journal of Learning Disabilities, 16,* 400–402.

Beirne-Smith, M., & Johnson, L. (1991, April). *Regular and special teachers' perceptions of effective teaching strategies with students with learning disabilities.* Paper presented at the Council for Exceptional Children's International Conference, Atlanta, GA.

Bell, L. A. (1991). Changing our ideas about ourselves: Group consciousness raising with elementary school girls as a means of empowerment. In C. Sleeter (Ed.), *Empowerment through multicultural education* (pp. 229–250). Albany, NY: State University of New York Press.

Bellafiore, L., & Salend, S. J. (1983). Modifying appropriate behaviors through a peer confrontation system. *Behavioral Disorders, 8,* 274–279.

Benavides, A. (1980). Cultural awareness training for exceptional teachers. *Teaching Exceptional Children, 13,* 8–11.

Bender, W. N. (1987). Effective educational practices in the mainstream setting: Recommended model for evaluation of mainstream teacher classes. *Journal of Special Education, 20,* 475–488.

Bender, W. N. (1988). The other side of placement decisions: Assessment of the mainstream learning environment. *Remedial and Special Education, 9*(5), 28–33.

Bender, W. N. (1992). The Bender Classroom Structure Questionnaire: A tool for placement decisions and evaluation of mainstream learning environments. *Intervention in School and Clinic, 27*(5), 307–312.

Benton, S., & Blohm, P. (1986). Effect of question type and position on measures of conceptual elaboration in writing. *Research in the Teaching of English, 20,* 98–108.

Berg, F. S. (1986). Characteristics of the target population. In F. S. Berg, J. C. Blair, S. H. Viehweg, & A. Wilson-Vlotman (Eds.), *Educational audiology for the hard of hearing child* (pp. 1–24). Orlando, FL: Grune & Stratton.

Bergan, J. R. (1977). *Behavioral consultation.* New York: Merrill/Macmillan.

Berger, E. H. (1981). *Parents as partners in education.* St. Louis: C. V. Mosby.

Bergerud, D., Lovitt, T. C., & Horton, S. (1988). The effectiveness of textbook adaptations in life science for high school students with learning disabilities. *Journal of Learning Disabilities, 21,* 70–76.

Berkell, D. E. (1991). Working toward integration. *The Forum, 17*(2), 3.

Berkell, D. E., & Brown, J. M. (1989). *Transition from school to work for persons with disabilities.* White Plains, NY: Longman.

Berkell, D. E. & Gaylord-Ross, R. (1989). The concept of transition: Historical and current developments. In D. E. Berkell & J. M. Brown (Eds.), *Transition from school to work for persons with disabilities* (pp. 1–21). White Plains, NY: Longman.

Berliner, D. C., & Rosenshine, B. V. (1977). The acquisition of knowledge in the classroom. In R. C. Anderson, F. J. Spiro, & W. E. Montague (Eds.). *Schooling and the acquisition of knowledge* (pp. 375–396). Hillsdale, NJ: Erlbaum.

Berman, A., & Jobes, D. (1991). *Adolescent suicide: Assessment and intervention.* Arlington, VA: American Psychological Association.

Berman, S. (1990). Educating for social responsibility. *Educational Leadership, 48*(3), 75–80.

Berne, E. (1964). *Games people play.* New York: Grove.

Bernstein, S. L., & McGuire, K. L. (1992). *The effect of peer tutoring on the acquisition of written English words in Japanese speaking students' daily journal writing.* Unpublished manuscript, State University of New York at New Paltz.

Bernthal, J., & Bankson, N. (1988). *Articulation and phonology disorders* (2nd ed.). Englewood Cliffs, NJ: Prentice-Hall.

Best, S., Bigge, J. L., & Sirvis, B. (1990). Physical and health impairments. In N. G. Haring & L. McCormick (Eds.), *Exceptional children and youth* (5th ed.) (pp. 283–324). New York: Merrill/Macmillan.

Biemiller, A. (1970). Changes in the use of graphic and contextual information as functions of passage difficulty and reading achievement level. *Journal of Reading Behavior, 11,* 308–318.

Biklen, D. (1990). Communication unbound: Autism and praxis. *Harvard Educational Review, 60,* 291–314.

Biklen, D., & Schubert, A. (1991). New words: The communication of students with autism. *Remedial and Special Education, 12*(6), 46–57.

Biklen, D., Lehr, S., Searl, S., & Taylor, S. J. (1987). *Purposeful integration ... Inherently equal.* Boston: Technical Assistance for Parent Programs.

Billings, H. K. (1963). An exploratory study of the attitudes of non-crippled children toward crippled children in three selected elementary schools. *Journal of Experimental Education, 31,* 381–387.

Billows, R. M. (1977). Metaphor: A review of the psychological literature. *Psychological Bulletin, 84,* 81–92.

Bittle, R. G. (1975). Improving parent-teacher communication through recorded telephone messages. *Journal of Educational Research, 69,* 87–95.

Blackhurst, A. E., & Berdine, W. H. (1981). *An introduction to special education.* Boston: Little, Brown.

Blackhurst, A. E., & Shupping, M. B. (1991). A philosophy for the use of technology in special education. *Back-to-school special education technology resource guide,* pp. 3–4.

Blalock, G. (1991). Paraprofessionals: Critical team members in our special education programs. *Intervention in School and Clinic, 26,* 200–214.

Blankenship, C. S. (1985). Using curriculum-based assessment data to make instructional decisions. *Exceptional Children, 52,* 233–238.

Blau, H., & Blau, H. (1968). A theory of learning to read. *The Reading Teacher, 22,* 126–129, 144.

Bley, N. S., & Thornton, C. A. (1981). *Teaching mathematics to the learning disabled.* Rockville, MD: Aspen.

Bloom, B. (1956). *Taxonomy of educational objectives: Handbook 1: Cognitive domain.* New York: David McKay.

Bloomfield, L., & Barnhart, C. L. (1961). *Let's read—A linguistic approach.* Detroit: Wayne State University Press.

Blumenthal, S. (1985, April 30). Testimony before the United States Senate Subcommittee on Juvenile Justice. Washington, DC: U.S. Department of Health and Human Services.

Board of Education of the Hendrick Hudson Central School District v. Rowley, 102 S. Ct. 3034 (1982).

Boehm, A. E. (1986). *Boehm Test of Basic Concepts—Revised.* New York: Psychological Corporation.

Bogdan, R. (1983). A closer look at mainstreaming. *Educational Forum, 47,* 425–434.

Bookbinder, S. R. (1978). *Mainstreaming: What every child should know about disabilities.* Boston: Exceptional Parent.

Boomer, L. W. (1980). Special education paraprofessionals: A guide for teachers. *Teaching Exceptional Children, 12,* 146–149.

Boomer, L. W. (1981). Meeting common goals through effective teacher-paraprofessional communication. *Teaching Exceptional Children, 13,* 51–54.

Borkowski, J. G., Weyhing, R. S., & Carr, M. (1988). Effects of attributional retraining on strategy-based reading comprehension in learning-disabled students. *Journal of Educational Psychology, 80,* 46–53.

Borton, L. (1984). *Sensing the enemy: An American woman among the boat people of Vietnam.* New York: Doubleday.

Bos, C. S. (1982). Getting past decoding: Assisted and repeating readings as remedial methods for learning disabled students. *Topics in Learning Disabilities, 1,* 51–57.

Bos, C. S. (1988). Process-oriented writing: Instructional implications for mildly handicapped students. *Exceptional Children, 54,* 521–527.

Bos, C. S. (1991). Reading–writing connections: Using literature as a zone of proximal development for writing. *Learning Disabilities Research and Practice, 6*(4), 251–256.

Bos, C. S., & Vaughn, S. (1988). *Strategies for teaching students with learning and behavior problems.* Boston: Allyn & Bacon.

Bos, C. S., & Vaughn, S. (1991). *Strategies for teaching students with learning and behavior problems* (2nd ed). Boston: Allyn & Bacon.

Bos, C. S., Anders, P. L., Filip, D., & Jaffe, L. E. (1989). The effects of an interactive instructional strategy for enhancing reading comprehension and content area learning for students with learning disabilities. *Journal of Learning Disabilities, 22,* 384–390.

Bowd, A. D. (1987). Knowledge and opinions about AIDS and related education issues among special education teachers. *Canadian Journal of Public Health, 78,* 88–90.

Bowers, E. M. (1980). *The handicapped in literature: A psychosocial perspective.* Denver: Love.

Boykin, A. W. (1982). Task variability and the performance of black and white children: Vervistic explorations. *Journal of Black Studies, 12*(4), 469–485.

Boykin, A. W. (1986). The triple quandary and the schooling of Afro-American children. In U. Neisser (Ed.), *The school achievement of minority children* (pp. 57–92). Hillsdale, NJ: Lawrence Erlbaum Associates.

Bradstad, B. J., & Stumpf, S. M. (1987). *A guide book for teaching study skills and motivation* (2nd ed.). Boston: Allyn & Bacon.

Brady, R. C. (1988). Physical and health handicaps. In E. W. Lynch & R. B. Lewis (Eds.), *Exceptional children and adults: An introduction to special education* (pp. 136–179). Boston: Scott, Foresman.

Brandenburg, S. A., & Vanderheiden, C. G. (1987). *Rehab/education technology resource book series: Communication, control and computer access for disabled elderly individuals, Resource book 1: Communication aids.* Boston: College-Hill.

Brandenburg-Ayres, S. (1990). *Working with parents.* Gainesville, FL: Bilingual/ESOL Special Education Collaboration and Reform Project, University of Florida.

Brandt, M. D., & Berry, J. O. (1991). Transitioning college bound students with LD. *Intervention in School and Clinic, 26,* 297–301.

Brischetto, R., & Arciniega, T. (1980). Examining the examiners: A look at educators' perspectives on the Chicano student. In M. Cotera & L. Hufford (Eds.), *Bridging two cultures: Multidisciplinary readings in bilingual bicultural education* (pp. 145–167). Austin, TX: National Educational Laboratory.

Britton, G., Lumpkin, M., & Britton, E. (1984). The battle to imprint citizens for the 21st century. *The Reading Teacher, 37,* 724–733.

Broden, M., Hall, R. V., & Mitts, B. (1971). The effects of self-recording on the classroom behavior of two eighth-grade students. *Journal of Applied Behavior Analysis, 4,* 191–199.

Brody, J. E. (1992, June 16). Suicide myths cloud efforts to save children. *The New York Times,* pp. C1, C3.

Bronheim, S. (n.d.). *An educator's guide to Tourette Syndrome.* Bayside, NY: Tourette Syndrome Association.

Brolin, D. (1982). Life-centered career education for exceptional children. *Focus on Exceptional Children, 14*(7), 1–15.

Brophy, J. E. (1981). Teacher praise: A functional analysis. *Review of Educational Research, 5,* 301–318.

Brophy, J. E. (1982). Classroom organization and management. *Elementary School Journal, 83,* 254–285.

Brophy, J. E. (1987). Synthesis of research on strategies for motivating students to learn. *Educational Leadership, 45,* 40–48.

Brophy, J. E., & Everston, C. (1976). *Learning from teaching: A developmental perspective.* Boston: Allyn & Bacon.

Brophy, J. E., & Good, T. (1974). *Teacher-student relationships: Causes and consequences.* New York: Holt, Rinehart & Winston.

Browder, D. (1983). Guidelines for inservice planning. *Exceptional Children, 49,* 300–306.

Brown v. Board of Education of Topeka, 347 U.S. 483 (1954).

Brown, A. L., Campione, J. C., & Day, J. D. (1981). Learning to learn: On training students to learn from texts. *Educational Researcher, 10,* 14–21.

Brown, J. (1988, March). *Preventing classroom failure: Small modifications make a big difference.* Paper presented at the meeting of the Council for Exceptional Children, Washington, DC.

Brown, S., Fruehling, R., & Hemphill, N. J. (1982). *The smallest minority: Adapted regular education social studies curricula for understanding and integrating severely disabled students. Upper elementary grades: Understanding prejudice.* Honolulu: University of Hawaii/Manoa, Hawaii Integration Project.

Brown, S., Hemphill, N. J., & Voeltz, L. (1982). *The smallest minority: Adapted regular education social studies curricula for understanding and integrating severely disabled students. Lower elementary grades: Understanding self and others.* Honolulu: University of Hawaii/Manoa, Hawaii Integration Project.

Brown, V. L. (1984). D'Nealian handwriting: What it is and how to teach it. *Remedial and Special Education, 5,* 48–52.

Bruininks, R. H., Thurlow, M. L., Lew, D. R., & Larson, N. W. (1988). Post-school outcomes for students in special education and other students in special education and other students one to eight years after high school. In R. H. Bruininks, D. R. Lewis, & M. L. Thurlow (Eds.), *Assessing outcomes, costs, and benefits of special education programs* (pp. 9–111). Minneapolis, MN: University of Minnesota.

Bruininks, R. H., & Warfield, G. (1978). The mentally retarded. In E. L. Meyen (Ed.), *Exceptional children and youth: An introduction* (pp. 162–216). Denver: Love.

Bruininks, R. H., Rynders, J. E., & Gross, J. C. (1974). Social acceptance of mildly retarded pupils in resource rooms and regular classes. *American Journal of Mental Deficiency, 78,* 377–383.

Brulle, A. R., Barton, L. E., & Repp, A. C. (1984). Evaluating LRE decisions through social comparison. *Journal of Learning Disabilities, 17,* 462–466.

Bruni, J. V., & Silverman, H. J. (1986). Developing concepts in probability and statistics—and much more. *Arithmetic Teacher, 33,* 34–37.

Bryan, T. H. (1974). Peer popularity of learning disabled children. *Journal of Learning Disabilities, 7,* 621–625.

Bryan, T. H. (1977). Learning disabled children's comprehension of nonverbal communication. *Journal of Learning Disabilities, 10,* 501–506.

Bryan, T. H., Bay, M., Lopez-Reyna, N., & Donahue, M. (1991). Characteristics of students with learning disabilities: The extant database and its implications for educational programs. In J. W. Lloyd, N. N. Singh, & A. C. Repp (Eds.), *The regular education initiative: Alternative perspectives on concepts, issues, and models* (pp. 113–132). Sycamore, IL: Sycamore.

Bryan, T., & Bryan, J. H. (1978). Social interactions of learning disabled children. *Learning Disabilities Quarterly, 1,* 33–38.

Bryan, T., Pearl, R., Donahue, M., Bryan, J. H., & Pflaum, S. (1983). The Chicago institute for the study of learning disabilities. *Exceptional Educational Quarterly, 4*(1), 1–22.

Bryant, N. D., Drabin, I. R., & Gettinger, M. (1981). Effects of varying unit size on spelling achievement in learning disabled children. *Journal of Learning Disabilities, 14*(4), 200–203.

Budoff, M., & Gottlieb, J. (1976). Special class EMR children mainstreamed: A study of an aptitude (learning potential) X treatment interaction. *American Journal of Mental Deficiency, 81,* 1–11.

Buffer, L. C. (1980). Recruited retired adults as volunteers in special education. *Teaching Exceptional Children, 12,* 113–115.

Bulgren, J., Schumaker, J. B., & Deshler, D. (1988). Effectiveness of a concept teaching routine in enhancing the performance of LD students in secondary-level mainstream classes. *Learning Disability Quarterly, 11,* 3–17.

Bullard, S. (1992). Sorting through the multicultural rhetoric. *Educational Leadership, 49*(9), 4–7.

Burnette, J. M. (1987). *Adapting instructional materials for mainstreamed students.* Reston, VA: Council for Exceptional Children.

Burns, H., & Culp, G. H. (1980). Stimulating invention in English composition through computer-assisted instruction. *Educational Technology, 20*(8), 5–10.

Burns, P. C. (1968). *Improving handwriting instruction in elementary schools.* Minneapolis, MN: Burgess.

Burron, D., & Bucher, B. (1978). Self-instructions as discriminative cues for rule-breaking or rule-following. *Journal of Experimental Psychology, 26,* 46–57.

Butler, A. (n.d.). *The elements of the whole language program.* Crystal Lake, IL: Rigby.

Byrne, C. E. (1981, September). *Diabetes in the classroom.* Washington, DC: National Education Association.

Byrom, E. (1990). Hypermedia (Multimedia). *Teaching Exceptional Children, 23*(4), 47–48.

Byrom, E., & Katz, G. (1991). *HIV prevention and AIDS education: Resources for special educators.* Reston, VA: Council for Exceptional Children.

Calderon, M. E., Hertz-Lazarowitz, R., & Tinajero, J. V. (1991). Adapting CIRC to multiethnic and bilingual classrooms. *Cooperative Learning, 12*(1), 17–20.

Calderon, M. E., Tinajero, J. V., & Hertz-Lazarowitz, R. (1992). Adapting cooperative integrated reading and composition to meet the needs of bilingual students. *The Journal of Educational Issues of Language Minority Students, 10,* 79–106.

Calhoun, G., & Elliot, R. (1977). Self-concept and academic achievement of educable retarded and emotionally disturbed pupils. *Exceptional Children, 44,* 379–380.

Calkins, L. M. (1986). *The art of teaching.* Portsmouth, NH: Heinemann.

Calvert, D. R. (1969). *Dimensions of family involvement in early childhood education.* Reston, VA: Council for Exceptional Children. (ERIC Document Reproduction Service No. ED 013 371).

Campbell, P. (1986). What's a smart girl like you doing in a math class? *Phi Delta Kappan, 67*(7), 516–520.

Canfield, J., & Wells, H. C. (1976). *100 ways to enhance self-concept in the classroom.* Englewood Cliffs, NJ: Prentice-Hall.

Cartwright, C. A., & Cartwright, G. P. (1974). *Developing observational skills.* New York: McGraw-Hill.

Canny, M. E. (1984). The relationship of manipulative materials in achievement in three areas of fourth-grade mathematics: Computation, concept development and problem-solving. *Dissertation Abstracts International, 45a,* 775–776.

Caparulo, B., & Zigler, E. (1983). The effects of mainstreaming on success expectancy and imitation in mildly retarded students. *Peabody Journal of Education, 60,* 85–98.

Carbo, M., Dunn, R., & Dunn, K. (1986). *Teaching students to read through their individual learning styles.* Reston, VA: Reston Publishing. (ERIC Document Reproduction Service No. ED 281 171).

Carbo, M., & Hodges, H. (1991, May). *Learning styles strategies can help students at risk.* Reston, VA: Clearinghouse on Handicapped and Gifted Children at the Council for Exceptional Children.

Carlberg, C., & Kavale, K. (1980). The efficacy of special versus regular placements for exceptional children: A meta-analysis. *Journal of Special Education, 14,* 295–309.

Carlin, J., & Sokoloff, B. (1985). Mental health treatment issues for Southeast Asian refugee children. In T. Owan (Ed.), *Southeast Asian mental health: Treatment, prevention, services, training, and research* (pp. 91–112). Washington, DC: U.S. Department of Health and Human Services.

Carlson, L. B., & Potter, R. E. (1972). Training classroom teachers to provide in-class educational services for exceptional children in rural areas. *Journal of School Psychology, 10,* 147–150.

Carman, R. A., & Adams, W. R. (1972). *Study skills. A student's guide for survival.* New York: John Wiley & Sons.

Carnine, D. W. (1989). Designing practice activities. *Journal of Learning Disabilities, 22,* 603–607.

Carnine, D. W., Silbert, J., & Kameenui, E. (1990). *Direct instruction reading* (2nd ed.). New York: Merrill/Macmillan.

Carpenter, D. (1985). Grading handicapped pupils: Review and position statement. *Remedial and Special Education, 6,* 54–59.

Carpenter, D., & Miller, L. J. (1982). Spelling ability of reading disabled students and able readers. *Learning Disability Quarterly, 5,* 65–70.

Carter, J., & Sugai, G. (1988). Teaching social skills. *Teaching Exceptional Children, 20,* 68–71.

Carter, J., & Sugai, G. (1989). Social skills curriculum analysis. *Teaching Exceptional Children, 21,* 36–39.

Cartwright, C. A., & Cartwright, G. P. (1974). *Developing observational skills.* New York: McGraw-Hill.

Cartwright, G. P., Cartwright, C. A., & Ward, M. E. (1985). *Educating special learners* (2nd ed.). Belmont, CA: Wadsworth.

Castle, D. (1988). *Oral interpreting: Selections from papers by Kirsten Gonzalez.* Washington, DC: Alexander Graham Bell Association for the Deaf.

Cattell, R. B., & Cattell, A. K. S. (1963). *Culture fair intelligence test: Scale 3.* Champaign, IL: Institute for Personality and Ability Testing.

Cawley, J. F., Baker-Kroczynski, S., & Urban, A. (1992). Seeking excellence in mathematics for students with mild disabilities. *Teaching Exceptional Children, 24*(2), 40–43.

Cawley, J. F., Fitzmaurice, A. M., Sedlak, R., & Althaus, V. (1976). *Project math.* Tulsa, OK: Educational Progress.

Cawley, J. F., Miller, J. H., & School, B. A. (1987). A brief inquiry of arithmetic word-problem-solving among learning disabled secondary students. *Learning Disabilities Focus, 2*(2), 87–93.

Celis, W. (1991, November 27). Bilingual teaching: A new focus on both tongues. *The New York Times,* p. B6.

Center for Recreation and Disability Studies. (1991). *Leisure education folder.* University of North Carolina at Chapel Hill: Author.

Ceprano, M. A. (1981). A review of selected research on methods of teaching sight words. *The Reading Teacher, 35,* 314–322.

Chadsey-Rusch, J., Rusch, F. R., & O'Reilly, M. F. (1991). Transition from school to integrated communities. *Remedial and Special Education, 12*(6), 23–33.

Chalfant, J. C., Pysh, M. V., & Moultrie, R. (1979). Teacher assistance teams: A model for within building problem solving. *Learning Disability Quarterly, 2,* 85–95.

Chalmers, L. (1991). Classroom modifications for the mainstreamed student with mild handicaps. *Intervention in School and Clinic, 27*(1), 40–42, 51.

Chamot, A. U. (1985). *English language development through a content-based approach.* In *Proceedings of the Information Exchange co-sponsored by the National Clearinghouse for Bilingual Education and the Georgetown University Bilingual Education Service Center* (pp. 49–56). Rosslyn, VA: National Clearinghouse for Bilingual Education.

Chamot, A. U., & O'Malley, J. M. (1989). The cognitive academic language learning approach. In P. Rigg & V. G. Allen (Eds.), *When they don't all speak English: Integrating the ESL student into the regular classroom* (pp. 108–125). Urbana, IL: National Council of Teachers of English.

Chapman, E. N. (1969). The time message. In F. L. Christ (Ed.), *SR/SE resource book* (pp. 3–8). Chicago: Science Research Associates.

Chapman, J. E., & Heward, W. L. (1982). Improving parent-teacher communication through recorded phone messages. *Exceptional Children, 49,* 79–81.

Charles, R. I. (1984). *Problem solving experiences in mathematics.* Menlo Park, CA: Addison-Wesley.

Chavez, D. (1985). Perpetuation of gender inequality: A content analysis of comic strips. *Sex Roles, 13*(1–2), 93–102.

Chavkin, N. F. (1991). *Family lives and parental involvement in migrant students education.* Charleston, WV: Appalachia Educational Laboratory.

Chiang, B., & Ratajczak, L. (1990). Analyzing computational errors for instruction. *LD Forum, 15*(2), 21–22.

Chiappetta, R. J., Budd, C. R., & Russo, J. H. (1990, April). *The collaboratively re-organized middle school.* Paper presented at the meeting of the Council for Exceptional Children, Toronto.

Chigier, E., & Chigier, M. (1968). Attitudes to disability of children in the multi-cultural society of Israel. *Journal of Health and Social Behavior, 9,* 310–317.

Chilcoat, G. W. (1987). Teacher talk: Keep it clear. *Academic Therapy, 22,* 263–271.

Children with Attention Deficit Disorders. (n.d.). *Attention deficit disorders: A guide for teachers.* Plantation, FL: Author.

Children's Defense Fund. (1988). *A children's defense fund budget.* Washington, DC: Author.

Children's Defense Fund. (1989). *A vision for America's future.* Washington, DC: Author.

Children's Defense Fund. (1990). *Latino youths at a crossroads.* Washington, DC: Author.

Choate, J. S. (1990). Study the problem. *Teaching Exceptional Children, 22*(4), 44–46.

Cisneros, R., & Leone, B. (1991, Fall). *ESL in bilingual education: Reflecting on issues for the '90s, 1,* 2.

Clark, C. R., & Bott, D. A. (1991). Issues in implementing the Adaptive Learning Environments model. *Teacher Education and Special Education, 14*(1), 57–65.

Clark, F., Deshler, D., Schumaker, J., Alley, G., & Warner, M. (1984). Visual imagery and self-questioning: Strategies to improve comprehension of written material. *Journal of Learning Disabilities, 17*(3), 145–149.

Clark, G. M. & Kolstoe, O. (1990). *Career development and transition education for adolescents with disabilities.* Boston: Allyn & Bacon.

Clark, M. M. (1959). *Teaching left-handed children.* New York: Philosophical Library.

Clary, L. M. (1986). Help for the homework hassle. *Academic Therapy, 22,* 57–60.

Clements, D. C., & Battista, M. (1986). Geometry and geometric measurement. *Arithmetic Teacher, 33,* 29–32.

Clore, G. L., & Jeffrey, K. M. (1972). Emotional role-playing, attitude change and attraction toward a disabled person. *Journal of Personality and School Psychology, 23,* 105–111.

Cloud, N., & Landurand, P. M. (n.d.). *Multisystem: Training program for special educators.* New York: Teachers College.

Coballes-Vega, C., & Salend, S. (1988). Guidelines for assessing migrant handicapped students. *Diagnostique, 13,* 64–75.

Cobb, S. (1978, February). *Social support and health through the life cycle.* Paper presented at the meeting of the American Association for the Advancement of Sciences, Washington, DC.

Coffland, J. A., & Baldwin, R. S. (1985). *Wordmath.* St. Louis: Milliken.

Cohen, R., King, W., Knudsvig, G. P., Markel, G., Patten, D., Shtogren, J., & Wilhelm, R. W. (1973). *Quest: Academic skills program.* New York: Harcourt Brace Jovanovich.

Cohen, S. A., & Stover, G. (1981). Effects of teaching sixth-grade students to modify format variables of math word problems. *Reading Research Quarterly, 16*(2), 175–200.

Cohen, S. B., (1983). Assigning report card grades to the mainstreamed child. *Teaching Exceptional Children, 15,* 86–89.

Cohen, S. B., & de Bettencourt, L. V. (1988). Teaching children to be independent learners: A step by step strategy. In E. L. Meyen, G. A. Vergason, & R. J. Whelan (Eds.), *Effective instructional strategies for exceptional children* (pp. 319–334). Denver: Love.

Cohen, S. B., & de Bettencourt, L. V. (1991). Dropouts: Intervening with the reluctant learner. *Intervention in School and Clinic, 26,* 263–271.

Cohen, S. B., & Lynch, D. K. (1991). An instructional modification process. *Teaching Exceptional Children, 23*(4), 12–18.

Cohen, S. B., Perkins, V. L., & Newmark, S. (1985). Written feedback strategies used by special education teachers. *Teacher Education and Special Education, 8,* 183–187.

Cohen, S., & Plakson, P. (1978). Selecting a reading approach for the mainstreamed child. *Language Arts, 55,* 966–970.

Coles, G. S. (1980). Evaluation of genetic explanations of reading and learning problems. *Journal of Special Education, 14,* 365–383.

Coles, R. (1971). *Migrants, sharecroppers, mountaineers (Volume II of Children of Crisis).* Boston: Little, Brown.

Collicott, J. (1991). Implementing multi-level teaching: Strategies for classroom teachers. In G. L. Porter & D. Richler (Eds.), *Changing Canadian schools: Perspectives on disability and inclusion* (pp. 191–218). Toronto: Roeher Institute.

Collier, C., & Kalk, M. (1989). Bilingual special education curriculum development. In L. M. Baca and H. T. Cervantes (Eds.), *The bilingual special education interface* (2nd ed.) (pp. 205–229). New York: Merrill/Macmillan.

Colson, S. E., & Colson, J. K. (1992). *HIV/AIDS education for students with special needs.* Paper presented at the meeting of the Council for Exceptional Children, Baltimore, MD.

Comer, J. P. (1989). Racism and the education of young children. *Teachers College Record, 90,* 352–361.

Comer, J. P., & Poussant, A. F. (1975). *Black child care.* New York: Simon & Schuster.

Commission on the Education of the Deaf (1988). *Toward equality: Education of the deaf. A report to the President and the Congress of the United States.* Washington, DC: U.S. Government Printing Office.

Communication Briefings. (1989a). *Listening tips.* Pitman, NJ: Author.

Communication Briefings. (1989b). *Teamwork tips.* Pitman, NJ: Author.

Compton, C., & Kaplan, H. (1988). Up close and personal: Assistive devices increase access to speech and sound. *Gallaudet Today, 18*(4), 18–23.

Cone, J. D., Delawyer, D. D., & Wolfe, V. V. (1985). Assessing parent participation: The parent/family involvement index. *Exceptional Children, 51,* 417–424.

Cone, T. E., Wilson, L. R., Bradley, C. M., & Reese, J. H. (1985). Characteristics of LD students in Iowa: An empirical investigation. *Learning Disability Quarterly, 8,* 211–220.

Conture, E. G., & Fraser, J. (1990). *Stuttering and your child: Questions and answers.* Memphis, TN: Speech Foundation of America.

Conway, R. N. F., & Gow, L. (1988). Mainstreaming special students with mild handicaps through group instruction. *Remedial and Special Education, 9*(5), 34–41.

Cook, R. E., Tessier, A., & Klein, M. D. (1992). *Adapting early childhood curricula for children with special needs* (3rd ed.). New York: Macmillan.

Cooper, J. O., Heron, T. E., & Heward, W. L. (1987). *Applied behavior analysis.* New York: Merrill/ Macmillan.

Copeland, J. S., & Lomax, E. D. (1988). Building effective student writing groups. In J. Golub (Ed.), *Focus on collaborative learning* (pp. 99–104). Urbana, IL: National Council of Teachers of English.

Cornett, C. E. (1983). *What you should know about teaching and learning.* Bloomington, MN: Phi Delta Kappa Education Foundation.

Corporation for Public Broadcasting. (1990). *Old harvest new shame.* Alexandria, VA: Author.

Coulter, F. (1980). *Secondary school network. Cooperative research report No. 7.* Perth, Australia: University of Western Australia Education Department and Perth Department of Education. (ERIC Document Reproduction Service No. ED 209200).

Coulter, W. A., & Morrow, H. W. (1978). *Adaptive behavior.* New York: Grune & Stratton.

Council for Exceptional Children. (1991). Some statistical clues to today's realities and tomorrow's trends. *Teaching Exceptional Children, 24,* 80.

Council on Interracial Books for Children. (1980). *Guidelines for selecting bias-free textbooks and storybooks.* New York: Author.

Courtnage, L., Stainback, W., & Stainback, S. (1982). Managing prescription drugs in schools. *Teaching Exceptional Children, 15,* 5–9.

Covarrubias v. San Diego Unified School District, No. 70394-T (San Diego, CA, 1971).

Cox, J., & Wiebe, J. H. (1984). Measuring reading vocabulary and concepts in mathematics in the primary grades. *The Reading Teacher, 37,* 402–410.

Cox, L. S. (1975). Diagnosing and remediating systematic errors in addition and subtraction computations. *The Arithmetic Teacher, 22,* 151–157.

Cox, S., & Galda, L. (1990). Multicultural literature: Mirrors and windows on a global community. *The Reading Teacher, 43,* 582–589.

Coyle-Williams, M. (1991). The 1990 Perkins Amendments: No more "business as usual." *TASPP Brief, 3*(1), 1–4.

Crank, J. N., & Keimig, J. (1988, March). *Learning strategies assessment for secondary students.* Paper presented at the meeting of the Council for Exceptional Children, Washington, DC.

Crank, J. N. (1990, April). *Teaching learning disabled students a strategy to evaluate and choose acceptable solutions to their personal problems.* Paper presented at the meeting of the Council for Exceptional Children, Toronto.

Cratty, B. J. (1971). *Active learning.* Englewood Cliffs, NJ: Prentice-Hall.

Creekmore, W. N. (1987). Effective use of classroom walls. *Academic Therapy, 22,* 341–348.

Crnic, K. A., & Pym, H. A. (1979). Training mentally retarded adults in independent living skills. *Mental Retardation, 17,* 13–16.

Cronin, M. E., Slade, D. L., Bechtel, C., & Anderson, P. (1992). Home–school partnerships: A cooperative approach to intervention. *Intervention in School and Clinic, 27*(5), 286–292.

Crosby, M. E. (1963). *Reading ladders for human relations.* Washington, DC: American Council on Education.

Cullinan, D., & Epstein, M. H. (1990). Behavior disorders. In H. G. Haring & L. McCormick (Eds.), *Exceptional children and youth* (5th ed.) (pp. 153–192). New York: Merrill/Macmillan.

Cummins, G. J., & Lombardi, T. P. (1989). Bulletin board learning center makes spelling fun. *Teaching Exceptional Children, 21,* 33–35.

Cummins, J. (1981). Four misconceptions about the language proficiency in bilingual children. *Jour-*

nal of the National Association of Bilingual Education, 5(3), 31–45.

Cummins, J. (1984). *Bilingualism and special education: Issues in assessment and pedagogy.* San Diego, CA: College-Hill.

Cummins, J. (1986). Empowering minority students: A framework for intervention. *Harvard Education Review, 56,* 18–36.

Cummins, J. (1989). A theoretical framework for bilingual special education. *Exceptional Children, 56,* 111–119.

Cuninggim, W. (1980). Recruited volunteers: A growing resource for teachers and students. *Teaching Exceptional Children, 12,* 108–112.

Curtis, M. J., & Watson, K. (1980). Changes in consultee problem clarification skills following consultation. *Journal of School Psychology, 18,* 210–221.

Curwin, R. L., & Mendler, A. N. (1988). *Discipline with dignity.* Alexandria, VA: Association for Supervision and Curriculum Development.

Cziko, G. A. (1992). The evaluation of bilingual education from necessity and probability to possibility. *Educational Researcher, 21*(2), 10–15.

D'Alonzo, B. J., D'Alonzo, R. L., & Mauser, A. J. (1979). Developing resource rooms for the handicapped. *Teaching Exceptional Children, 11,* 91–96.

D'Zamko, M. E., & Hedges, W. D. (1985). *Helping exceptional students succeed in the regular classroom.* West Nyack, NY: Parker.

Dahl, P. R. (1979). An experimental program for teaching high speed word recognition and comprehension skills. In J. E. Button, T. C. Lovitt, & T. D. Rowland (Eds.), *Communications research in learning disabilities and mental retardation* (pp. 633–655). Baltimore: University Park.

Daiute, C. A. (1986). Physical and cognitive factors in revising: Insights from studies with computers. *Research in Teaching of English, 20,* 141–159.

Dalton, B., Winbury, N. E., & Morocco, C. C. (1990). "If you could just push a button": Two fourth grade boys with learning disabilities learn to use a computer spelling checker. *Journal of Special Education Technology, 10,* 177–191.

Danielson, L. C., & Bellamy, G. T. (1989). State variation in placement of children with handicaps in segregated environments. *Exceptional Children, 55,* 448–455.

Dank, M. (1977). What effect do reading programs have on the oral reading behavior of children? *Reading Improvement, 14,* 66–69.

Darch, C., & Carnine, D. (1986). Teaching content area materials to learning disabled students. *Exceptional Children, 53,* 240–246.

Darch, C., & Gersten, R. (1986). Direction setting in reading comprehension: A comparison of two approaches. *Learning Disability Quarterly, 9,* 235–243.

Dattilo, J., & St. Peter, S. (1991). A model for including leisure education in transition services for young adults with mental retardation. *Education and Training in Mental Retardation, 26*(4), 420–432.

Davidson, J. (1969). *Using the Cuisenaire rods.* New Rochelle, NY: Cuisenaire.

Davies, D. (1991). Restructuring schools: Increasing parent involvement. In K. Kershner & J. Connolly (Eds.), *At-risk students and school restructuring* (pp. 89–100). Philadelphia, PA: Research for Better Schools.

Davis, R. B., Allen, T., & Sherman, J. (1989). The role of the teacher: Strategies for helping. Get info from mental health. In National Association for Children of Alcoholics (Ed.), *It's elementary: Meeting the needs of high risk youth in the school setting* (p. 11–12). South Laguna, CA: National Association for Children of Alcoholics.

Davison, D. M., & Pearce, D. L. (1992). The influence of writing activities on mathematic learning of American Indian students. *The Journal of Educational Issues of Language Minority Students, 10,* 147–157.

De Avila, E. A. (1988). *Finding Out/Descubrimiento.* Northvale, NJ: Santillana.

de Bettencourt, L. V. (1987). How to develop parent relationships. *Teaching Exceptional Children, 19,* 26–27.

Deboer, A. L. (1986). *The art of consulting.* Chicago: Arcturus.

Decker, S. N., & DeFries, J. C. (1980). Cognitive abilities in families of reading-disabled children. *Journal of Learning Disabilities, 13,* 517–522.

Degnan, S. C. (1985). Word processing for special education students: Worth the effort. *Technological Horizons in Education Journal, 12,* 80–82.

Deitz, D. E., & Repp, A. C. (1983). Reducing behavior through reinforcement. *Exceptional Education Quarterly, 3,* 34–46.

Delefes, P., & Jackson, B. (1972). Teacher-pupil interaction as a function of location in the classroom. *Psychology in the Schools, 9,* 119–123.

Denburg, S. D. (1976). The interaction of picture and print in reading instruction. *Reading Research Quarterly, 12*(2), 176–189.

Deno, E. (1970). Special education as developmental capital. *Exceptional Children, 37,* 229–237.

Deno, S. L. (1985). Curriculum-based assessment: The emerging alternative. *Exceptional Children, 52,* 219–232.

Deno, S. L., & Fuchs, L. S. (1988). Developing curriculum-based measurement systems for data-based special education problem solving. In E. L. Meyen, G. A. Vergason, & R. J. Whelan (Eds.), *Effective instructional strategies for exceptional children* (pp. 481–504). Denver: Love.

Derman-Sparks, L. (1989). *Anti-bias curriculum.* Washington, DC: National Association for the Education of Young Children.

Derman-Sparks, L., Higa, C., & Sparks, B. (1980). Children, race, and racism: How racism awareness develops. *Interacial Books for Children Bulletin, 11*(3–4), 3–9.

Deshler, D. D., & Graham, S. (1980). Tape recording educational materials for secondary handicapped students. *Teaching Exceptional Children, 12,* 52–54.

Deutsch-Smith, D. (1981). *Teaching the learning disabled.* Englewood Cliffs, NJ: Prentice-Hall.

Devine, T. G. (1981). *Teaching study skills.* Boston: Allyn & Bacon.

Diamond, G. W. (1989). Developmental problems in children with HIV infection. *Mental Retardation, 27,* 213–217.

Diana v. California State Board of Education, No. C-70-37, RFP, (N.D. Cal., 1970).

Diaz, J., Trotter, R., & Rivera, V. (1989). *The effects of migration on children: An ethnographic study.* Harrisburg, PA: Pennsylvania Department of Education, Division of Migrant Education.

Dillard, J. L. (1977). *Lexicon of black English.* New York: Seabury.

DiMeo, J., Ryan, L., & DeFanti, A. (1989, April). *Activating collective expertise through collaborative consultation: Classroom alternatives support teams.* Paper presented at the meeting of the Council for Exceptional Children, San Francisco, CA.

Dinkmeyer, D., & McKay, G. (1976). *Systematic training for effective parenting.* Circle Pines, MN: American Guidance Services.

Dishon, D., & O'Leary, P. W. (1985). *A guidebook for cooperative learning.* Holmes Beach, FL: Learning Publications.

Dishon, D., & O'Leary, P. W. (1991). Tips for heterogeneous group selection. *Cooperative Learning, 12*(1), 42–43.

Dodge, K. A., Coie, J. D., & Brakke, N. P. (1982). Behavior patterns of socially rejected and neglected preadolescents: The roles of social approach and aggression. *Journal of Abnormal Psychology, 10,* 389–410.

Dodge, K. A., Schlundt, D. C., Schocken, I., & Delugach, J. D. (1983). Social competence and children's social status: The role of peer group entry strategies. *Merrill-Palmer Quarterly, 29,* 309–326.

Donahue, M. (1987). Interactions between linguistic and pragmatic development in learning disabled children: Three views of the state of the union. In S. Rosenberg (Ed.), *Advances in applied psycholinguistics* (Vol. 1) (pp. 126–179). Cambridge, England: Cambridge University Press.

Donaldson, J. (1980). Changing attitudes toward handicapped persons: A review and analysis of research. *Exceptional Children, 46,* 504–512.

Donaldson, J. (1981). The visibility and image of handicapped people on television. *Exceptional Children, 47,* 413–416.

Donaldson, J., & Martinson, M. C. (1977). Modifying attitudes toward physically disabled persons. *Exceptional Children, 43,* 337–341.

Doorlag, D. H. (1988). Behavior disorders. In E. W. Lynch & R. B. Lewis (Eds.), *Exceptional children and adults: An introduction to special education* (pp 407–455). Boston: Scott, Foresman.

Dorr, D. (1977). Some practical suggestions on behavioral consultation with teachers. *Professional Psychology, 8,* 95–102.

Downing, J. A. (1990). Contingency contracts: A step-by-step format. *Intervention in School and Clinic, 26*(2), 111–113.

Driscoll, A. (1989, August 13). Enlarging the world of disabled. *The New York Times,* p. 48.

Dufflemeyer, F. A. (1982). Introducing words in context. *Wisconsin Reading Association Journal, 26,* 4–6.

Dugger, C. W. (1992, March 31). Tiny incomes, little help for single mothers. *The New York Times,* pp. A1, B8.

Dunlap, K. H., Stoneman, Z., & Cantrell, M. H. (1980). Social interaction of exceptional and other children in a mainstreamed preschool classroom. *Exceptional Children, 47,* 132–141.

Dunlap, W. P., & McKnight, M. B. (1978). Vocabulary translations for conceptualizing math word problems. *The Reading Teacher, 32,* 183–189.

Dunn, L. M. (1968). Special education for the mildly retarded—is much of it justifiable? *Exceptional Children, 35,* 5–22.

Dunn, R. (1990). Bias over substance: A critical analysis of Kavale and Forness' Report on modality-based instruction. *Exceptional Children, 56,* 352–356.

Dunn, R., & Dunn, K. (1978). *Teaching students through their individual learning styles: A practical approach.* Reston, VA: Reston.

Dunn, R., Dunn, K., & Price, G. E. (1989). *Learning Style Inventory.* Lawrence, KS: Price Systems.

Duques, S. L. (1986). An oral language bridge to writing. *Teaching Exceptional Children, 18,* 214–219.

Duran, R. P. (1989). Assessment and instruction of at-risk Hispanic students. *Exceptional Children, 56*(2), 154–159.

Durgin, R. W., Lindsay, M. A., & Hamilton, B. S. (1985). *A guide to recreation, leisure and travel for the handicapped: Vol. 1. Recreation and sports.* Toledo, OH: Resource Directories.

Durkin, D. (1978). *Teaching them to read.* Boston: Allyn & Bacon.

Dweck, C. S. (1975). The role of expectations and attributions in the alleviation of learned helplessness. *Journal of Personality and Social Psychology, 31,* 674–685.

Dweck, C., Davidson, W., Nelson, S., & Enna, B. (1978). Sex differences in learned helplessness: The contingencies of evaluative feedback in the classroom; An experimental analysis, *Developmental Psychology, 14,* 268–276.

Eccles, J. (1986). Gender-roles and women's achievement. *Educational Researcher, 15*(6), 15–19.

Edelman, M. W. (1987). *Families in peril: An agenda for social change.* Cambridge, MA.: Harvard University Press.

Edelsky, C., Altwerger, B., & Flores, B. (1991). *Whole language: What's the difference?* Portsmouth, NH: Heinemann.

Edwards, C., & Stout, J. (1990). Cooperative learning: The first year. *Educational Leadership, 47*(4), 38–41.

Edwards, P. (1973). Panorama: A study technique. *Journal of Reading, 17,* 132–135.

Edyburn, D. L. (1990/1991). Locating information about software. *TAM Newsletter, 6*(1), 14–15.

Elbow, P. (1981). *Writing with power.* New York: Oxford University Press.

Ellis, E. S. (1989). A metacognitive intervention for increasing class participation. *Learning Disabilities Focus, 5*(1), 36–46.

Ellis, E. S., & Lenz, B. K. (1987). A component analysis of effective learning strategies for LD students. *Learning Disabilities Focus, 2,* 94–107.

Ellis, E. S., Lenz, B. K., & Sarbornie, E. J. (1987). Generalization and adaptation of learning strategies to natural environments: Part 2: Research into practice. *Remedial and Special Education, 8*(2), 6–23.

Ellis, E. S., & Sarbornie, E. J. (1988). Effective instruction with microcomputers: Promises, practices, and preliminary findings. In E. L. Meyen, G. A. Vergason, & R. J. Whelan (Eds.), *Effective instructional strategies for exceptional children* (pp. 355–379). Denver: Love.

Elmquist, D. L. (1991). School-based alcohol and other drug prevention programs: Guidelines for the special educator. *Intervention in School and Clinic, 27,* 10–19.

Emery, R. E., Hetherington, E. M., & Fisher, L. (1984). Divorce, children and social policy. In H. Stevenson & A. Siegal (Eds.), *Social policy and children* (pp. 189–266). Chicago: University of Chicago Press.

Englemann, S., & Carnine, D. (1975). *Distar arithmetic level 1.* Chicago: Science Research Associates.

Englemann, S., & Carnine, D. (1976). *Distar arithmetic level 2.* Chicago: Science Research Associates.

Englemann, S., & Carnine, D. (1982). *Corrective mathematics program.* Chicago: Science Research Associates.

Englert, C. S. (1984). Measuring teacher effectiveness from the teacher's point of view. *Focus on Exceptional Children, 17*(2), 1–14.

Englert, C. S., Raphael, T. E., Anderson, L. M., Anthony, H. M., Fear, K. L., & Gregg, S. L. (1988). A case for writing intervention: Strategies for writing informational text. *Learning Disabilities Focus, 3,* 98–113.

Englert, C. S., Culatta, B. E., & Horn, D. G. (1987). Influence of irrelevant information in addition word problems on problem solving. *Learning Disability Quarterly, 10,* 29–36.

Englert, C. S., & Raphael, T. E. (1988). Constructing well-formed prose: Process, structure, and metacognitive knowledge. *Exceptional Children, 54,* 513–520.

Englert, C. S., & Chase Thomas, C. (1982). Management of task involvement in special education classrooms. *Teacher Education and Special Education, 5,* 3–10.

Enright, B. E. (1983). *Enright diagnostic inventory of basic arithmetic skills.* N. Billerica, MA: Curriculum Associates.

Enright, B. E. (1986). *Enright computation series.* N. Billerica, MA: Curriculum Associates.

Enright, B. E. (1987a). Basic mathematics. In J. S. Choate, T. Z. Bennett, B. E. Enright, L. J. Miller, J. A. Poteet, & T. A. Rakes (Eds.), *Assessing and programming basic curriculum skills* (pp. 121–145). Boston: Allyn & Bacon.

Enright, B. E. (1987b). *Enright S.O.L.V.E.: Action problem solving series.* N. Billerica, MA: Curriculum Associates.

Enright, B. E., & Beattie, J. (1989). Problem solving step by step in math. *Teaching Exceptional Children, 22*(1), 58–59.

Enright, D. S., & Gomez, B. (1984). Pro-Act: Strategies for organizing peer interaction in elementary classrooms. *Journal of the National Association for Bilingual Education, 9,* 5–24.

Enstrom, E. A., & Enstrom, D. (1970). Right writing. *Grade Teacher, 87,* 105–106.

Epanchin, B. C., & Monson, L. B. (1982). Affective education. In J. L. Paul & B. C. Epanchin (Eds.), *Emotional disturbance in children* (pp. 405–426). New York: Merrill/Macmillan.

Epilepsy Foundation of America. (1987). *The teacher's role: Children and epilepsy—A guide for school personnel.* Landover, MD: Author.

Epps, S., Prescott, A. L., & Horner, R. H. (1990). Social acceptability of menstrual-care training methods for young women with developmental disabilities. *Education and Training in Mental Retardation, 25*(1), 33–44.

Epstein, L. G., Sharer, L. R., & Goudsmit, J. (1988). Neurological and neuropathological features of human immunodeficiency virus infection in children. *Annals of Neurology, 23,* 19–23.

Espin, C. A., & Deno, S. L. (1988). Characteristics of individuals with mental retardation. In P. J. Schloss, C. A. Hughes, & M. A. Smith (Eds.), *Mental retardation: Community transition* (pp. 35–55). Boston: College-Hill.

Espin, C. A., & Sindelar, P. T. (1988). Auditory feedback and writing: Learning disabled and nondisabled students. *Exceptional Children, 55,* 45–51.

Esposito, B. G., & Peach, W. (1983). Changing attitudes of preschool children toward handicapped persons. *Exceptional Children, 49,* 361–363.

Esposito, B. G., & Reed, T. M. (1986). The effects of contact with handicapped persons on young children's attitudes. *Exceptional Children, 53,* 224–229.

Everston, C. M., & Emmer, E. T. (1982). Effective management in the beginning of the school year in junior high classes. *Journal of Educational Psychology, 74,* 485–498.

Everston, C. M., Emmer, E. T., & Brophy, J. E. (1980). Predictors of effective teaching in junior high mathematics classrooms. *Journal of Research in Mathematics Education, 11,* 167–178.

Everston, C. M., Emmer, E. T., Clements, B. S., Sanford, J. P., & Worsham, M. E. (1989). *Classroom management for elementary teachers* (2nd ed.). Englewood Cliffs, NJ: Prentice-Hall.

Everston, J., & Heshusius, L. (1985). Feedback in secondary mainstreaming. *Teaching Exceptional Children, 17,* 223–224.

Fagen, S. A., Graves, D. L., & Tessier-Switlick, D. (1984). *Promoting successful mainstreaming: Reasonable classroom accommodations for learning disabled students.* Rockville, MD: Montgomery County Public Schools.

Fairchild, T. N. (1987). The daily report card. *Teaching Exceptional Children, 19,* 72–73.

Falty, J. E. (1965). *Attitudes toward physical disability in Costa Rica and their determinants: A pilot study.* Unpublished dissertation, Michigan State University.

Farquhar, W. W., Krumboltz, J. D., & Wrenn, C. G. (1969). Prepare for examinations. In F. L. Christ (Ed.), *SR/SE resource book* (pp. 63–69). Chicago: Science Research Associates.

Fassler, D. (1990). Children's perceptions of AIDS. *Journal of the American Academy of Child and Adolescent Psychiatry, 29,* 459–462.

Federal Register. (1985, July 1). Washington, DC: U.S. Government Printing Office.

Feldman, M. J. (1985). Evaluating pre-primer basal readers using story grammar. *American Educational Research Journal, 22,* 527–547.

Fernald, G. (1943). *Remedial techniques in basic school subjects.* New York: McGraw-Hill.

Feuerstein, R. (1979). *The dynamic assessment of retarded performers: The Learning Potential Assessment Device. Theory, instruments and techniques.* Baltimore: University Park.

Fielder, C. R., & Simpson, R. L. (1987). Modifying attitudes of nonhandicapped high school students toward handicapped peers. *Exceptional Children, 53,* 342–349.

Figueroa, R. A. (1989). Psychological testing of linguistic-minority students: Knowledge gaps and regulations. *Exceptional Children, 56,* 145–153.

Figueroa, R. A., Fradd, S. H., & Correa, V. I. (1989). Bilingual special education and this special issue. *Exceptional Children, 56,* 174–178.

Fine, M. (1988). Sexuality, schooling and adolescent females: The missing discourse of desire. *Harvard Educational Review, 58,* 29–53.

Fisher, J. A. (1967). *Learning and study skills: A guide to independent learning.* Des Moines, IA: Drake University Reading and Study Skills Clinic.

Fishman, J. A. (1979). Bilingual education: What and why? In H. T. Trueba & C. Barnett-Mizrachi (Eds.), *Bilingual multicultural education and the professional: From theory to practice* (pp. 11–19). New York: Newbury House.

Fitzgerald, G. E., Bauder, D. K., & Werner, J. G. (1992). Authoring CAI lessons: Teachers as developers. *Teaching Exceptional Children, 24*(2), 15–21.

Fitzsimmons, R. J., & Loomer, B. M. (1978). *Excerpts from spelling: Learning and instruction—research and practice.* Wellesley, MA: Curriculum Associates.

Flax, E. (1990, February 7). Special problems of homosexual students need attention, advocates urge. *Education Week, 9*(20), 1, 24.

Flaxman, E., & Inger, M. (1991). Parents and schooling in the 1990s. *The ERIC Review, 1*(3), 2–6.

Fleischner, J. E., Nuzum, M. G., & Marzola, E. S. (1987). Devising an instructional program to teach arithmetic problem-solving skills to students with learning disabilities. *Journal of Learning Disabilities, 20,* 214–217.

Fleming, M. B. (1988). Getting out of the writing vacuum. In J. Golub (Ed.), *Focus on collaborative learning* (pp. 77–84). Urbana, IL: National Council of Teachers of English.

Florida State Education Department (1986). *Interpreting in the educational setting.* Tallahassee, FL: Author.

Flower, L., & Hayes, J. R. (1981). A cognitive process theory of writing. *College Composition and Communication, 32,* 365–387.

Flynn, G., & Kowalczyk-McPhee, B. (1989). A school system in transition. In S. Stainback, W. Stainback, & M. Forest (Eds.), *Educating all students in the mainstream of regular education* (pp. 29–41). Baltimore: Paul H. Brookes.

Foerster, L. (1975). Sinistra power! Help for lefthanded children. *Elementary English, 52,* 213–215.

Ford, B. A., & Jones, C. (1990). Ethnic feelings book: Created by students with developmental handicaps. *Teaching Exceptional Children, 22*(4), 36–39.

Fordham, S., & Ogbu, J. (1986). Black students' school success: Coping with the burden of "acting white." *The Urban Review, 18,* 176–206.

Forest, M., & Lusthaus, E. (1989). Promoting educational equality for all students: Circles and maps. In S. Stainback, W. Stainback, & M. Forest (Eds.), *Educating all students in the mainstream of regular education* (pp. 43–57). Baltimore, MD: Paul H. Brookes.

Forest, M., & Lusthaus, E. (1990). Everyone belongs with MAPS action planning system. *Teaching Exceptional Children, 22*(2), 32–35.

Forest, M., & Pierpoint, J. (1991, October). Two roads: Inclusion and exclusion in schools and society. Presented Paper, Kingston, NY.

Foulks, B. (1991, November). *Promoting multicultural acceptance within the elementary classroom.* Paper presented at the meeting of the New York Federation of Chapters of the Council for Exceptional Children, Buffalo, NY.

Fowler, S. A., Schwartz, I., & Atwater, J. (1991). Perspectives on the transition from preschool to kindergarten for children with disabilities and their families. *Exceptional Children, 58,* 136–145.

Fox, L. (1977). *The effects of sex role stereotyping on mathematics participation and achievement of women in mathematics: Research perspectives for change.* Washington, DC: National Institute of Education.

Fox, R., & Wise, P. S. (1981). Infant and preschool reinforcement survey. *Psychology in the Schools, 18,* 92.

Fradd, S. H. (1987). Accommodating the needs of limited English proficient students in regular classrooms. In S. H. Fradd & W. J. Tikunoff (Eds.), *Bilingual education and bilingual special education* (pp. 133–182). Boston: College-Hill.

Fradd, S. H. (June 29, 1992). Personal communication.

Fradd, S. H., Barona, A., & Santos de Barona, M. (1988). Implementing change and monitoring progress. In S. H. Fradd & M. J. Weismantel (Eds.), *Meeting the needs of culturally and linguistically different students* (pp. 63–105). Austin, TX: Pro-Ed.

Fradd, S. H., & Bermudez, A. B. (1991). POWER: A process for meeting the instructional needs of handicapped language-minority students. *Teacher Education and Special Education, 14*(1), 19–24.

Fradd, S. H., & Vega, J. E. (1987). Legal considerations. In S. H. Fradd & W. J. Tikunoff (Eds.), *Bilingual education and bilingual special education* (pp. 45–74). Boston: College-Hill.

Fradd, S. H., Vega, J. E., & Hallman, C. L. (1985). *Meeting the educational needs of limited english proficient students policy issues and perspectives.* Gainesville, FL: College of Education.

Fradd, S. H., & Wilen, D. K. (1990). *Using interpreters and translators to meet the needs of handicapped language minority students and their families.* Washington, DC: National Clearinghouse for Bilingual Education.

Fraenkel, J. R. (1973). *Helping students think and value: Strategies for teaching social studies.* Englewood Cliffs, NJ: Prentice-Hall.

Frank, A. R., & Brown, D. (1992). Self-monitoring strategies in arithmetic. *Teaching Exceptional Children, 24*(2), 52–53.

Frank, A. R., & Gerken, K. C. (1990). Case studies in curriculum-based measurement. *Education and Training in Mental Retardation, 25*(2), 113–119.

Frank, D. A., Zuckerman, B. S., Amaro, H., Aboagye, K., Baucher, H., Cabral, H., Fried, L., Hingson, R., Kayne, H., Levenson, S. M., Parker, S., Reece, H., & Vinvi, R. (1988). Cocaine use during pregnancy: Prevalence and correlates. *Pediatrics, 82,* 888–895.

Franklin, E. A. (1992). Learning to read and write the natural way. *Teaching Exceptional Children, 24*(3), 45–48.

Franklin, M. E. (1992). Culturally sensitive instructional practices for African-American learners with disabilities. *Exceptional Children, 59,* 115–122.

Franklin, M. E. (n.d.). *On developing culturally competent special education teachers.* Manuscript submitted for publication.

Franklin, M. E., & Mickel, V. (in press). Are publishers of reading textbooks for intermediate-grade students sensitive to the learning characteristics of African-American students? *SENGA.*

Fredericks, A. D. (1986). Mental imagery activities to improve comprehension. *The Reading Teacher, 40,* 78–81.

Freedman, G., & Reynolds, E. G. (1980). Enriching basal reader lessons with semantic webbing. *The Reading Teacher, 33,* 677–684.

Freedman, P. I., Gotti, M., & Holtz, G. (1981, February). In support of direct teaching to counter ethnic stereotypes. *Phi Delta Kappan,* p. 456.

Freeman, D. E., & Freeman, Y. S. (1989). A road to success for language-minority high school students. In P. Rigg & V. G. Allen (Eds.), *When they don't all speak English: Integrating the ESL student into the regular classroom* (pp. 126–138). Urbana, IL: National Council of Teachers of English.

Freeman, Y. S., & Freeman, D. E. (1992). *Whole language for second language learners.* Portsmouth, NH: Heinemann.

Freire, P. (1970). *Pedagogy of the oppressed.* New York: Continuum.

French, C. D., & Wass, G. A. (1985). Behavior problem of peer-neglected and peer-rejected elementary aged children: Parent and teacher perspectives. *Child Development, 56,* 246–252.

Friedlander, M. (1991). *The newcomer program: Helping immigrant students succeed in US schools.* Washington, DC: National Clearinghouse for Bilingual Education.

Friend, M., & Bauwens, J. (1988). Managing resistance: An essential consulting skill for learning disabilities teachers. *Journal of Learning Disabilities, 21,* 556–561.

Friend, M., & Cook, L. (1992). *Interactions: Collaboration skills for school professionals.* White Plains, NY: Longman.

Fries, C. C. (1963). *Linguistics and reading.* New York: Holt, Rinehart & Winston.

Fritz, M. F. (1990). A comparison of social interaction using a friendship awareness activity. *Education and Training in Mental Retardation, 25,* 352–359.

Froschl, M., Colon, L., Rubin, E., & Sprung, B. (1984). *Including all of us: An early childhood curriculum about disability.* New York: Educational Equity Concepts.

Fruehling, R., Hemphill, N. J., Brown, S., & Zukas, D. (1981). *Special alternatives: A learning system for generating unique solutions to problems of special education in integrated settings.* Honolulu: University of Hawaii/Manoa, Hawaii Integration Project.

Fuchs, D., & Fuchs, L. S. (1988). Evaluation of the adaptive learning environments model. *Exceptional Children, 55,* 115–127.

Fuchs, D., Fuchs, L. S., Fernstrom, P., & Hohn, M. (1991). Toward a responsible reintegration of behaviorally disordered students. *Behavioral Disorders, 16,* 133–147.

Fuhler, C. J. (1991). Searching for the right key: Unlocking the doors to motivation. *Intervention in School and Clinic, 26,* 217–220.

Fulk, B. J., & Mastropieri, M. A. (1990). Training positive attitudes: "I tried hard and did well!" *Intervention in School and Clinic, 26*(2), 79–83.

Fulk, B. J., Mastropieri, M. A., & Scruggs, T. E. (1992). Mnemonic generalization training with learning disabled adolescents. *Learning Disabilities Research and Practice, 7*(1), 2–10.

Gagne, R. (1970). *The conditions of learning.* New York: Holt, Rinehart & Winston.

Gajria, M. (1988). *Effects of a summarization technique on the text comprehension skills of learning disabled students.* Unpublished doctoral dissertation, Pennsylvania State University.

Gajria, M., & Hughes, C. A. (1988). Introduction to mental retardation. In P. J. Schloss, C. A. Hughes, & M. A. Smith (Eds.). *Mental retardation: Community transition* (pp. 35–55). Boston: College-Hill.

Gajria, M., Giek, K., Hemrick, M., & Salend, S. J. (1992). *Teacher acceptability of testing modifications for mainstreamed students.* Paper presented at the meeting of the Council for Exceptional Children, Baltimore, MD.

Galaburda, A. (1983). Developmental dyslexia: Current anatomical research. *Annals of Dyslexia, 33,* 41–51.

Galagan, J. E. (1985). Psychological testing: Turn out the lights, the party's over. *Exceptional Children, 52,* 288–299.

Galda, L., & Cotter, J. (1992). Exploring cultural diversity. *The Reading Teacher, 45*(6), 452–460.

Gallagher, J. J., & Hall, J. (1979). The benefits of competency testing for the exceptional student. *Education Unlimited, 1,* 71–72.

Garate, D., Sen, P., Thien, H. T., & Chaleunrath, V. (1987). *Involving LEP parents.* Washington DC: Trinity College (ERIC Document Reproduction Service No. ED 275 213).

Garber, H. L., & McInerney, M. (1982). Sociobehavioral factors in mental retardation. In P. Cegelka & H. Prehm (Eds.). *Mental retardation: From categories to people* (pp. 111–145). New York: Merrill/Macmillan.

Garcia, R. L. (1978). *Fostering a pluralistic society through multi-ethnic education.* Bloomington, IN: Phi Delta Kappa Educational Foundation.

Garcia, S. B., & Ortiz, A. A. (1988). Preventing inappropriate referrals of language minority students to special education. *New Focus, 5,* 1–12.

Garnett, K. (1987). Math learning disabilities: Teaching and learners. *Journal of Reading Writing and Learning Disabilities, 3,* 1–8.

Garnett, K. (1989). Math learning disabilities. *The Forum, 14*(4), 11–15.

Garnett, K., & Fleischner, J. E. (1987). Mathematical disabilities. *Pediatric Annals, 16,* 159–176.

Garrido, L. (August 10, 1991). Personal communication.

Gaylord-Ross, R., & Haring, T. (1987). Social interaction research for adolescents with severe handicaps. *Behavioral Disorders, 12,* 264–275.

Gearhart, B. R., & Weishahn, M. W. (1984). *The exceptional student in the regular classroom.* St. Louis: C. V. Mosby.

Gearheart, B. R., Weishahn, M. W., & Gerheart, C. J. (1988). *The exceptional student in the classroom* (4th ed.). New York: Merrill/Macmillan.

George, N. L., & Lewis, T. J. (1991). EASE: Exit assistance for special educators—Helping students make the transition. *Teaching Exceptional Children, 23*(2), 34–39.

George, P. (1975). *Better discipline: Theory and practice.* Gainesville, FL: Florida Educational Research and Development Council.

George, P. (1986). Teaching handicapped children with attention problems: Teacher verbal strategies make the difference. *Teaching Exceptional Children, 18,* 172–175.

Gerber, M. (1977). Awareness of handicapping conditions and sociometric status in an integrated preschool setting. *Mental Retardation, 15,* 24–25.

Gerber, M. A., & Kauffman, J. M. (1981). Peer tutoring in academic settings. In P. S. Strain (Ed.), *The utilization of classroom peers as behavior change agents* (pp. 155–187). New York: Plenum.

Germann, G., & Tindal, G. (1985). An application of curriculum-based assessment: The use of direct and repeated measurement. *Exceptional Children, 52,* 244–265.

Gersten, R., Carnine, D., & Woodward, J. (1987). Direct instruction research: The third decade. *Remedial and Special Education, 8*(6), 48–56.

Giangreco, M. F., Cloninger, C. J., & Iverson, V. S. (1990). *Cayuga-Onondaga assessment for children with handicaps.* Burlington, VT: Center for Developmental Disabilities, University of Vermont.

Gickling, E. E., & Thompson, V. P. (1985). A personal view of curriculum-based assessment. *Exceptional Children, 52,* 205–218.

Giek, K. A. (1990). Diary of a consulting teacher. *The Forum, 16*(1), 5–6.

Giek, K. A. (1992). Monitoring student progress through efficient record keeping. *Teaching Exceptional Children, 24*(3), 22–26.

Gilbert, S. E., & Gay, G. (1989). *Improving the success in school of poor black children.* In B. J. Shade (Ed.), *Culture style and the educative processes* (pp. 275–283). Springfield, IL: Charles C. Thomas.

Gillespie, D. (1976). Processing questions: What they are and how to ask good ones. In M. L. Silberman, J. S. Allender, & J. M. Yanoff (Eds.), *Real Learning: A sourcebook for teachers* (pp. 235–238). Boston: Little, Brown.

Gillet, P. (1981). *Career education for exceptional youth. Of work and worth: Career education for the handicapped.* Salt Lake City: Olympus.

Gillet, P. (1986). Mainstreaming techniques for LD students. *Academic Therapy, 21,* 389–399.

Gillingham, A., & Stillman, B. W. (1973). *Remedial training for children with specific disability in reading, spelling and penmanship.* Cambridge, MA: Educators Publishing Service.

Ginott, H. (1965). *Between parent and child.* New York: Macmillan.

Glasser, W. (1969). *Schools without failure.* New York: Harper & Row.

Glazzard, P. (1979). Simulation of handicaps as a teaching strategy for pre-service and in-service training. *Teaching Exceptional Children, 11,* 101–104.

Glazzard, P. (1980). Adaptations for mainstreaming. *Teaching Exceptional Children, 13,* 26–29.

Gleason, M. M. (1988). Study skills. *Teaching Exceptional Children, 20,* 52–53.

Glick, O. (1969). Person-group relationships and the effect of group properties on academic achievement in the classroom. *Psychology in the Schools, 1,* 197–203.

Gloeckler, T., & Simpson, C. (1988). *Exceptional students in regular classrooms: Challenges, services and methods.* Mountain View, CA: Mayfield.

Goldhammer, K. A., & Taylor, R. E. (1972). *Career education: Perspective and promise.* New York: Merrill/Macmillan.

Goldstein, H., Moss, J., & Jordan, L. (1965). *The efficacy of special class training on the development of mentally retarded children* (U.S. Office of Education Cooperative Project No. 619). Urbana, IL: University of Illinois Press.

Goldstein, S., & Turnbull, A. P. (1982). Strategies to increase parent participation in IEP conferences. *Exceptional Children, 48,* 360–361.

Goleman, D. (1992, April 21). Black scientists study the pose of the inner city. *The New York Times,* pp. C1, C7.

Golightly, C. J. (1987). Transdisciplinary training: A step in special education teacher preparation. *Teacher Education and Special Education, 10*(3), 126–130.

Gollnick, D. M., & Chinn, P. C. (1990). *Multicultural education in a pluralistic society* (3rd ed.). New York: Merrill/Macmillan.

Gonzales, E. (1982). Issues in the assessment of minorities. In H. L. Swanson & B. L. Watson (Eds.), *Educational and psychological assessment of exceptional children* (pp. 375–389). St. Louis: C. V. Mosby.

Gonzalez, G. (1974). Language, culture, and exceptional children. In L. A. Bransford, L. Baca, & K. Lane (Eds.), *Cultural diversity and the exceptional child* (pp. 2–11). Reston, VA: Council for Exceptional Children.

Gonzalez, L. A. (1992). Tapping their language—A bridge to success. *The Journal of Educational Issues of Language Minority Students, 10,* 27–39.

Good, T. L., & Grouws, D. A. (1979). The Missouri mathematics effectiveness project. *Journal of Educational Psychology, 71,* 143–155.

Goodman, G. (1979). From residential treatment to community based education: A model for reintegration. *Education and Training of the Mentally Retarded, 14*(2), 95–100.

Goodman, H., Gottlieb, J., & Harrison, R. H. (1977). Social acceptance of EMRs integrated into a nongraded elementary school. *American Journal of Mental Deficiency, 76,* 412–417.

Goodman, K. (1986). *What's whole in whole language?* Portsmouth, NH: Heinemann.

Gordon, T. (1970). *Parent effectiveness training.* New York: Peter H. Wyden.

Gordon, T. (1974). *Teacher effectiveness training.* New York: Peter H. Wyden.

Gottesman, R. L., Croen, L. G., & Rotkin, L. G. (1982). Urban second grade children: A profile of good and poor readers. *Journal of Learning Disabilities, 15,* 268–272.

Gottlieb, J. (1980). Improving attitudes toward retarded children by using group discussion. *Exceptional Children, 47,* 106–111.

Gottlieb, J. (1981). Mainstreaming: Fulfilling the promise? *American Journal of Mental Deficiency, 86,* 115–126.

Gottlieb, J., Alter, M., & Gottlieb, B. W. (1983). Mainstreaming mentally retarded children. In J. L. Matson & J. A. Mulich (Eds.) *Handbook of mental retardation* (pp. 67–77). New York: Pergamon.

Gottlieb, J., & Budoff, M. (1973). Social acceptability of retarded children in nongraded schools differing in architecture. *American Journal of Mental Deficiency, 78,* 15–19.

Gottlieb, J., & Leyser, Y. (1981). Friendships between mentally retarded and nonretarded children. In S. Asher & J. Gottman (Eds.), *The development of children's friendships* (pp. 150–181). Cambridge, England: Cambridge University Press.

Graden, J. L., Casey, A., & Bonstrom, O. (1985). Implementing a prerefferal system: Part 2. The data. *Exceptional Children, 51,* 487–496.

Graden, J. L., Casey, A., & Christenson, S. L. (1985). Implementing a prereferral intervention system: Part 1. The model. *Exceptional Children, 51,* 377–384.

Graham, S. (1982). Composition research and practice: A unified approach. *Focus on Exceptional Children, 14,* 1–16.

Graham, S. (1983). The effect of self-instructional procedures on LD students' handwriting performance. *Learning Disability Quarterly, 6,* 231–234.

Graham, S. (1992). Helping students with LD progress as writers. *Intervention in School and Clinic, 27*(3), 134–144.

Graham, S., & Freeman, S. (1985). Strategy training and teacher vs. student—controlled study conditions: Effects on LD students' spelling performance. *Journal of Learning Disabilities, 8,* 267–274.

Graham, S., & Harris, K. R. (1986, April). *Improving learning disabled students' compositions via story grammar training: A component analysis of self-control strategy training.* Paper presented at the Annual Meeting of the American Educational Research Association, San Francisco, CA.

Graham, S., & Harris, K. R. (1988). Instructional recommendations for teaching writing to exceptional students. *Exceptional Children, 54,* 506–512.

Graham, S., & Harris, K. R. (1989). Improving learning disabled students' skills at composing essays: Self-instructional strategy training. *Exceptional Children, 56,* 201–214.

Graham, S., Harris, K. R., & Sawyer, R. (1987). Composition instruction with learning disabled students: Self-instructional strategy training. *Focus on Exceptional Children, 20,* 1–11.

Graham, S., & Johnson, L. A. (1989). Teaching reading to learning disabled students: A review of research-supported procedures. *Focus on Exceptional Children, 21*(6), 1–12.

Graham, S., MacArthur, C., Schwartz, S., & Page-Voth, V. (1992). Improving the compositions of students with learning disabilities using a strategy involving product and process goal setting. *Exceptional Children, 58*(4), 322–334.

Graham, S., & Miller, L. (1979). Spelling research and practice: A unified approach. *Focus on Exceptional Children, 12*(2), 1–16.

Graham, S., & Miller, L. (1980). Handwriting research and practice: A unified approach. *Focus on Exceptional Children, 13*(2), 1–16.

Grant, B. W., & Hennings, D. G. (1971). *The teacher moves: An analysis of nonverbal activity.* New York: Teachers College.

Grasso-Ryan, A., & Price, L. (1992). Adults with LD in the 1990s. *Intervention in School and Clinic, 28*(1), 6–20.

Graves, D. H. (1977). Spelling texts and structural analysis. *Language Arts, 54,* 86–90.

Graves, D. H. (1983). *Writing: Teachers and children at work.* Exeter, NH: Heinemann.

Graves, D. H. (1985). All children can write. *Learning Disabilities Focus, 1,* 36–43.

Graves, D. H., & Hansen, J. (1983). The author's chair. *Language Arts, 60,* 176–183.

Green, J. (1991, October 13). This school is out. *The New York Times Magazine,* pp. 32–33, 36, 59–60, 68.

Green, W. W. (1981). Hearing disorders. In A. E. Blackhurst & W. H. Berdine (Eds.), *An introduction to special education* (pp. 154–205). Boston: Little, Brown.

Greenan, J. (1989). Identification, assessment, and placement of persons needing transition assistance. In D. E. Berkell & J. M. Brown (Eds.), *Transition from school to work for persons with disabilities* (pp. 64–107). White Plains, NY: Longman.

Greenbaum, J., Varas, M., & Markel, G. (1980). Using books about handicapped children. *The Reading Teacher, 33,* 416–419.

Greenwood, C. R. (1991). Classwide peer tutoring: Longitudinal effects on the reading language, and mathematics achievement of at-risk students. *Reading, Writing, and Learning Disabilities International, 7,* 105–123.

Greer, J. V. (1988). No more noses to the glass. *Exceptional Children, 54,* 294–296.

Gresham, F. M. (1982). Misguided mainstreaming: The case for social skills training with handicapped children. *Exceptional Children, 48,* 422–433.

Gresham, F. M., & Gresham, G. N. (1982). Interpendent, dependent and interdependent group contingencies for controlling disruptive behavior. *Journal of Special Education, 16,* 101–110.

Gresham, F. M., & Reschly, D. J. (1986). Social skill deficits and low peer acceptance of mainstreamed learning disabled children. *Learning Disability Quarterly, 9,* 23–32.

Grimes, L. (1981). Error analysis and error correction procedures. *Teaching Exceptional Children, 14,* 17–21.

Grimm, J. A., Bijou, S. W., & Parsons, J. A. (1973). A problem solving model for teaching remedial arithmetic to handicapped children. *Journal of Abnormal Child Psychology, 1,* 26–39.

Gronlund, N. E. (1990). *Measurement and evaluation in teaching* (6th ed.). New York: Macmillan.

Gropper, N. (n.d.). *Steps in conducting portfolio assessments.* New Paltz, NY: Department of Elementary Education, State University of New York at New Paltz.

Gropper, N., & Shuster, A. (1981, Winter–Spring). Separate is not equal: Intended and implicit messages about the disabled in children's literature. *Equal Play,* 5–9.

Grossnickle, D. R. (1986). *High school dropouts: Causes, consequences, and cure.* Bloomington, IN: Phi Delta Kappa Educational Foundation.

Guerin, G. R., & Maier, A. S. (1983). *Informal assessment in education.* Palo Alto, CA: Mayfield.

Guerin, G. R., & Male, M. (1988, March). *Models of best teaching practices.* Paper presented at the meeting of the Council for Exceptional Children, Washington, DC.

Guerin, G. R., & Szatlocky, K. (1974). Integration programs for the mildly retarded. *Exceptional Children, 41,* 173–179.

Guetzloe, E. (1988). Suicide and depression: Special education's responsibility. *Teaching Exceptional Children, 20,* 25–28.

Guetzloe, E. (1989). *Youth suicide: What the educator should know.* Reston, VA: Council for Exceptional Children.

Guralnick, M. J. (1982). Pediatrics, special education, and handicapped children: New relationships. *Exceptional Children, 48,* 294–295.

Guskin, S. L., & Spicker, H. H. (1968). Educational research in mental retardation. In N. R. Ellis (Ed.), *International review of research in mental retardation* (Vol. 3) (pp. 217–278). New York: Academic.

Gutierrez, M., Whittington-Couse, M., & Korycki, L. (1990). *Meeting the needs of culturally and linguistically diverse students.* New Paltz, NY: Ulster County Bilingual Education Technical Assistance Center.

Gutkin, T. B. (1980). Teacher perceptions of consultation services provided by school psychologists. *Professional Psychology: Research and Practice, 11,* 637–642.

Gutkin, T. B., Singer, J. H., & Brown, R. (1980). Teacher reactions to school-based consultation: A multivariate analysis. *Journal of School Psychology, 18,* 126–134.

Guy, E. (1991). Vocational rehabilitation services for American Indians. *OSERS News in Print, 3*(4), 10–15.

Haber, L. R., Haber, R. N., & Furlin, K. R. (1983). Word length and word shape as sources of information in reading. *Reading Research Quarterly, 18,* 165–189.

Haber, R. N., & Haber, L. R. (1981). The shape of a word can specify its meaning. *Reading Research Quarterly, 16*(3), 334–345.

Hagerman, R. J., & Sobesky, W. E. (1989). Psychopathology in fragile X syndrome. *American Journal of Orthopsychiatry, 59,* 142–152.

Hagin, R. A. (1983). Write right or left: A practical approach to handwriting. *Journal of Learning Disabilities, 16*(5), 266–271.

Hale-Benson, J. E. (1986). *Black children: Their roots, culture, and learning style* (2nd ed.). Baltimore: Johns Hopkins University Press.

Hall, M. (1981). *Teaching reading as a language experience* (3rd ed.). New York: Merrill/Macmillan.

Hall, N. (1964). The letter mark-out corrected test. *Journal of Educational Research, 58,* 148–157.

Hallahan, D. P. (1989). Attention disorders: Specific learning disabilities. In T. Husen & N. Postlethwaite (Eds.), *The international encyclopedia of education: Research and studies* (Suppl. Vol 1, pp. 98–100). New York: Pergamon.

Hallahan, D. P., & Kauffman, J. M. (1988). *Exceptional children: Introduction to special education* (4th ed.). Englewood Cliffs, NJ: Prentice-Hall.

Hallahan, D. P., Keller, C. E., McKinney, J. D., Lloyd, J. W., & Bryan, T. (1988). Examining the research base of the regular education initiative: Efficacy studies and the adaptive learning environments model. *Journal of Learning Disabilities, 21,* 29–34, 55.

Hallenback, M. J., & McMaster, D. (1991). Disability simulation for regular education students. *Teaching Exceptional Children, 24*(1), 12–15.

Halpern, A. S. (1985). Transition: A look at the foundations. *Exceptional Children, 51,* 479–502.

Haman, T. A., & Issacson, D. K. (1985). Sharpening organizational skills. *Academic Therapy, 12*(1), 45–50.

Hamayan, E. V., & Perlman, R. (1990). *Helping language minority students after they exit from Bilingual/ESL programs: A handbook for teachers.* Washington, DC: National Clearinghouse for Bilingual Education.

Hammill, D., & Bartel, N. R. (1978). *Teaching children with learning and behavior problems.* Boston: Allyn & Bacon.

Hammill, D. D., Leigh, J. E., McNutt, G., & Larsen, S. C. (1981). A new definition of learning disabilities. *Learning Disability Quarterly, 4,* 336–342.

Hamre-Nietupski, S., McDonald, J., & Nietupski, J. (1992). Integrating elementary students with multiple disabilities into supported regular classes: Challenges and solutions. *Teaching Exceptional Children, 24*(3), 6–9.

Hancock, I. (1986). The domestic hypothesis, diffusion, and componentiality: An account of Atlantic Anglophone Creole origins. In P. Muysken & N. Smith (Eds.), *Substrata versus universals in creole genesis* (pp. 71–102). Amsterdam: John Benjamins.

Handscombe, J. (1989). A quality program for learners of English as a second language. In P. Rigg & V. G. Allen (Eds.), *When they don't all speak English: Integrating the ESL student into the regular classroom* (pp. 1–14). Urbana, IL: National Council of Teachers of English.

Hanna, P., Hanna, J., Hodges, R., & Rudorf, E. (1966). *Phoneme-grapheme correspondences as cues to spelling improvement.* Washington, DC: U.S. Government Printing Office.

Hanover, S. (1983). Handwriting comes naturally? *Academic Therapy, 18,* 407–412.

Hansell, S. (1981). Ego development and peer friendship networks. *Sociology of Education, 54,* 51–63.

Hansen, C. L., & Eaton, M. D. (1978). Reading. In N. G. Haring, T. C. Jones, H. A. Lovitt, M. D. Eaton, & C. L. Hansen (Eds.), *The fourth R: Reading in the classroom* (pp. 41–92). New York: Merrill/Macmillan.

Hansen, J. (1981). The effect of inference training and practice on young children's reading comprehension. *Reading Research Quarterly, 16*(3), 391–417.

Hardin, B., Bernstein, B., & Shands, F. (1978). The "Hey what's this?" approach to teaching spelling. *Teacher, 94,* 64–67.

Hare, B. R. (1985). Reexamining the achievement central tendency: Sex differences within race and race differences within sex. In H. P. McAdoo & J. L. McAdoo (Eds.), *Black children: Social, educational, and parental environments* (pp. 139–158). Beverly Hills, CA: Sage.

Haring, N. G., & Krug, D. A. (1975). Placement in regular programs: Procedures and results. *Exceptional Children, 41,* 413–417.

Haring, N. G., & McCormick, L. (1990). *Exceptional children and youth* (5th ed.). New York: Merrill/Macmillan.

Harness, B., Epstein, R., & Gordon, H. (1984). Cognitive profile of children referred to a clinic for reading disabilities. *Journal of Learning Disabilities, 17*(5), 346.

Harrington, A. M., & Morrison, R. A. (1981). Modifying classroom exams for secondary LD students. *Academic Therapy, 16,* 571–577.

Harris, A. J., & Sipay, E. R. (1985). *How to increase reading ability: A guide to developmental and remedial approaches* (8th ed.). New York: Longman.

Harris, C. R. (1991). Identifying and serving the gifted new immigrant. *Teaching Exceptional Children, 23,* 26–30.

Harris, G. A. (1985). Considerations in assessing English language performance of Native American children. *Topics in Language Disorders, 5*(4), 42–52.

Harris, K. R., & Graham, S. (1985). Improving learning disabled students' composition skills: Self-control strategy training. *Learning Disability Quarterly, 8,* 27–36.

Harris, K. R., & Graham, S. (1988). Self-instructional strategy training. *Teaching Exceptional Children, 20,* 35–37.

Harris, K. R., Graham, S., & Freeman, S. (1988). Effects of strategy training on metamemory among learning disabled students. *Exceptional Children, 54,* 332–338.

Harrison, R., & Edwards, J. (1983). *Child abuse.* Portland, OR: Ednick.

Harrison, S. (1981). An open letter from a left handed teacher: Some sinistral ideas on the teaching of handwriting. *Teaching Exceptional Children, 13,* 116–120.

Harry, B. (1992). *Culturally diverse families and the special education system.* New York: Teachers College.

Hart, V. (1977). The use of many disciplines with severely and profoundly handicapped. In E. Sontag, J. Smith, & N. Certo (Eds.), *Educational programming for the severely and profoundly handicapped.* Reston, VA: Council for Exceptional Children, Division of Mental Retardation.

Harth, R. (1971). Attitudes toward minority groups as a construct in assessing attitudes toward the mentally retarded. *Education and Training of the Mentally Retarded, 6,* 142–147.

Hartse, J. C., Short, K. G., & Burke, K. G. (1988). *Creating classrooms for authors: The reading-writing connection.* Portsmouth, NH: Heinemann.

Harvey, D., & Greenway, A. (1984). The self-concept of physically handicapped children and their nonhandicapped siblings: An empirical investigation. *Journal of Child Psychology and Psychiatry, 25,* 273–284.

Hasazi, S. B., Gordon, L. R., & Roe, C. A. (1985). Factors associated with the employment status of handicapped youth exiting high school from 1979 to 1983. *Exceptional Children, 51,* 455–469.

Hasazi, S. B., Johnson, R. E., Hasazi, J. E., Gordon, L. R., & Hull, M. (1989). Employment of youth with and without handicaps following high school: Outcomes and correlates. *The Journal of Special Education, 23,* 243–255.

Hawkins, J. (1988). Antecedent pausing as a direct instruction tactic for adolescents with severe behavioral disorders. *Behavioral Disorders, 13,* 263–272.

Hawley, R., & Hawley, I. (1975). *Human values in the classroom: A handbook for teachers.* New York: Hart.

Hayek, R. A. (1987). The teacher assistance team: A pre-referral support system. *Focus on Exceptional Children,* 20(1), 1–7.

Hayes, L. A. (1976). The use of group contingencies for behavioral control: A review. *Psychological Bulletin, 83,* 628–648.

Hayes, M. L. (1985). Materials for the resource room. *Academic Therapy, 20,* 289–297.

Hayes, M. L. (1986). Resource room: Space and concepts. *Academic Therapy, 21,* 453–464.

Hayward, L. R., & LeBuffe, J. R. (1985). Self-correction: A positive method for improving writing skills. *Teaching Exceptional Children, 18,* 68–72.

Heckelman, R. G. (1969). A neurological-impress method of remedial reading instruction. *Academic Quarterly, 4,* 277–282.

Hedges, H. G. (1972). *Volunteer parental assistance in elementary schools.* Unpublished doctoral dissertation, University of Toronto.

Hedley, C. N. (1987). Software feature: What's new in software? Computer programs in math. *Journal of Reading Writing and Learning Disabilities, 3,* 103–107.

Heilman, A. W., Blair, T. R., & Rupley, W. H. (1990). *Principles and practices of teaching reading* (7th ed.). New York: Merrill/Macmillan.

Helge, D. (1984). The state of the art of rural special education. *Exceptional Children, 50,* 294–305.

Helge, D. (1987a). Effective partnership in rural America. *OSERS News in Print, 1,* 2–3.

Helge, D. (1987b). Strategies for improving rural special education programs. *Remedial and Special Education, 8*(4), 53–60.

Heller, K., Holtzman, W. H., & Messick, N. (1982). *National Research Council Special Task Force Report.* Washington, DC: National Academy Press.

Hembree, R. (1986). Research gives calculators a green light. *Arithmetic Teacher, 34,* 18–21.

Hemphill, N. J., Zukas, D., & Brown, S. (1982). *The smallest minority: Adapted regular education social studies curricula for understanding and integrating severely disabled students. The secondary grades (7–12): Understanding alienation.* Honolulu: University of Hawaii/Manoa, Hawaii Integration Project.

Henk, W. A. (1983). Adapting the NIM to improve comprehension. *Academic Therapy, 19,* 97–101.

Henk, W. A., Helfedt, J. P., & Platt, J. M. (1986). Developing reading fluency in learning disabled student. *Teaching Exceptional Children, 18,* 202–206.

Henry, S. L., & Pepper, F. C. (1990). Cognitive, social, and cultural effects on Indian learning style: Classroom implications. *Journal of Educational Issues of Language Minority Students,* 7, 85–97.

Herbert, E. (1985). One point of view: Manipulatives are good mathematics. *Arithmetic Teacher, 32,* 4.

Hermann, K. (1959). *Reading disability: A medical study of word-blindness and related handicaps.* Springfield, IL: Charles C. Thomas.

Hernandez, H. (1989). *Multicultural education: A teacher's guide to content and process.* New York: Merrill/Macmillan.

Heron, T. E., & Harris, K. C. (1987). *The educational consultant: Helping professionals, parents, and mainstreamed students* (2nd ed.). Austin, TX: Pro-Ed.

Heron, T. E., & Kimball, W. H. (1988). Gaining perspective with the educational consultation research base: Ecological considerations and further recommendations. *Remedial and Special Education, 9*(6), 21–28, 47.

Herr, D. E. (1988, March). *Behavior management techniques effective for both the regular and special educator.* Paper presented at the meeting of the Council for Exceptional Children, Washington, DC.

Herreman, D. (1988). None of us is as smart as all of us. In J. Golub (Ed.), *Focus on collaborative learning* (pp. 5–12). Urbana, IL: National Council of Teachers of English.

Hetherington, E. M., Cox, M., & Cox, C. R. (1982). Effects of divorce on parents and children. In M. Lamb (Ed.), *Nontraditional families* (pp. 223–288). Hillsdale, NJ: Lawrence Erlbaum Associates.

Hetrick, E. S., & Martin, A. D. (1987). *Developmental issues and their resolution for gay and lesbian adolescents.* New York: Haworth.

Heward, W. L., & Orlansky, M. D. (1992). *Exceptional children* (4th ed.). New York: Merrill/Macmillan.

Heward, W. L., Dardig, J. C., & Rossett, A. (1979). *Working with parents of exceptional children.* New York: Merrill/Macmillan.

Hewett, F. M. (1967). Educational engineering with emotionally disturbed children. *Exceptional Children, 33,* 459–467.

Hickman, J. (1989). Bookwatching: Notes on children's books. *Language Arts, 66,* 564–570.

Higgins, K., & Boone, R. (1990). Hypertext: A new vehicle for computer use in reading instruction. *Intervention in School and Clinic, 26*(1), 26–31.

Hildreth, B. L., & Candler, A. (1992). Learning about learning disabilities through general public literature. *Intervention in School and Clinic, 27*(5), 293–296.

Hilliard, A. G. (1980). Cultural diversity and special education. *Exceptional Children, 46,* 584–588.

Hillocks, G. (1984). What works in teaching composition: A meta-analysis of experimental treatment studies. *American Journal of Education, 93,* 133–170.

Hillocks, G. (1986). *Research on written composition: New directions for teaching.* Urbana, IL: National Conference for Research in English.

Hirsch, E., & Niedermeyer, F. C. (1973). The effects of tracing prompts and discrimination training on kindergarten handwriting performance. *Journal of Education Research, 67*(2), 81–86.

Hoben, M. (1980). Toward integration in the mainstream. *Exceptional Children, 47,* 100–105.

Hobson v. Hansen, 269 F. Supp. 401 (1967) (D.C.C., 1967).

Hochman, B. (1979). *Simulation activities handout.* Bethlehem, PA.: Project STREAM.

Hocutt, A., Martin, E., & McKinney, J. D. (1991). Historical and legal context of mainstreaming. In J. W. Lloyd, N. N. Singh, & A. C. Repp (Eds.), *The regular education initiative: Alternative perspectives on concepts, issues and models* (pp. 17–28). Sycamore, IL.: Sycamore.

Hoemann, H. W., & Briga, J. S. (1981). Hearing impairments. In J. M. Kauffman & D. P. Hallahan (Eds.), *Handbook of special education* (pp. 222–247). Englewood Cliffs, NJ: Prentice-Hall.

Hoff, M. K., Fenton, K. S., Yoshida, R. K., & Kaufman, M. J. (1978). Notice and consent: The school's responsibility to inform parents. *Journal of School Psychology, 16,* 265–273.

Hofferth, S. L. (1987). Implications of family trends for children: A research perspective. *Educational Leadership, 45,* 78–84.

Holdaway, D. (1979). *The foundations of literacy.* Portsmouth, NH: Heinemann.

Holliday, B. C. (1985). Towards a model of teacher-child transactional processes affecting black children's academic achievement. In M. B. Spencer, G. K. Brookins, & W. R. Allen (Eds.), *Beginnings: The social and affective development of black children* (pp. 117–131). Hillsdale, NJ: Lawrence Erlbaum Associates.

Hollinger, J. D. (1987). Social skills for behaviorally disordered children as preparation for mainstreaming: Theory, practice, and new directions. *Remedial Education and Special Education, 8,* 17–27.

Hollingsworth, P. M., & Reutzel, D. R. (1988). Whole language with the LD child. *Academic Therapy, 23,* 477–488.

Homme, L. (1970). *How to use contingency contracting in the classroom.* Champaign, IL: Research.

Hook, J. N. (1969). Read carefully. In F. L. Christ (Ed.), *SR/SE resource book* (pp. 55–62). Chicago: Science Research Associates.

Hoover, J. J. (1986). *Teaching handicapped students study skills.* Lindale, TX: Lindale.

Hoover, J. J., & Collier, C. (1985). Referring culturally different children: Sociocultural considerations. *Academic Therapy, 20,* 503–509.

Hoover, J. J., & Collier, C. (1986). *Classroom management through curricular adaptations: Educating minority handicapped students.* Lindale, TX: Hamilton.

Hoover, J. J., & Collier, C. (1989). Methods and materials for bilingual special education. In L. M. Baca & H. T. Cervantes (Eds.), *The bilingual special education interface* (2nd ed.) (pp. 231–255). New York: Merrill/Macmillan.

Hoover, J. J., & Collier, C. (1991). Meeting the needs of culturally and linguistically diverse exceptional learners: Prereferral to mainstreaming. *Teacher Education and Special Education, 14*(1), 30–34.

Hoover, K. H. (1972). *The professional teacher's handbook: A guide for improving instruction in today's middle and secondary schools.* Boston: Allyn & Bacon.

Horn, E. (1960). *Encyclopedia of educational research* (4th ed.). New York: Macmillan.

Horne, M. D. (1981). *Assessment of classroom status: Using the perception of social closeness scale.* (ERIC Document Reproduction Service No. 200 616).

Horne, M. D. (1985). *Attitudes toward handicapped students: Professional, peer, and parent reactions.* Hillsdale, NJ: Lawrence Erlbaum Associates.

Horne, M. D., & Powers, J. E. (1983). Teacher's ratings of aggression and students' own perceived status. *Psychological Reports, 53,* 275–278.

Horton, S. V., Lovitt, T. C., & White, O. R. (1992). Teaching mathematics to adolescents classified as educable mentally handicapped: Using calculators to remove the computational onus. *Remedial and Special Education, 13*(3), 36–60.

Hough, R. A., Nurss, J. R., & Enright, D. S. (1986). Story reading with limited English speaking children in the regular education classroom. *The Reading Teacher, 39,* 510–515.

Houlton, D. (1986). *Cultural diversity in the primary school.* London: B. T. Balsford.

Howe, L., & Howe, M. M. (1975). *Personalizing education: Values clarification and beyond.* New York: Hart.

Howe-Murphy, R., & Charboneau, B. G. (1987). *Therapeutic recreation intervention: An ecological perspective.* Englewood Cliffs, NJ: Prentice-Hall.

Howell, R., Sidorenko, E., & Jurica, J. (1987). The effects of computer use on the acquisition of multiplication facts by a student with learning disabilities. *Journal of Learning Disabilities, 20,* 336–341.

Hudson, F. G., & Graham, S. (1978). An approach to operationalizing the IEP. *Learning Disability Quarterly, 1,* 13–32.

Hughes, C. A., Hendrickson, J. M., & Hudson, P. J. (1986). The pause procedure: Improving factual recall from lectures by low and high achieving middle school students. *International Journal of Instructional Media, 13,* 217–226.

Hughes, J., & Falk, R. (1981). Resistance, reluctance, and consultation. *Journal of School Psychology, 19,* 130–142.

Humphrey, J. H. (1969). Active games as a learning medium. *Academic Therapy, 5,* 15–24.

Humphrey, M. J., Hoffman, E., & Crosby, B. M. (1984). Mainstreaming LD students. *Academic Therapy, 19,* 321–327.

Hundert, J. (1982). Some considerations of planning the integration of handicapped children into the mainstream. *Journal of Learning Disabilities, 15,* 73–80.

Hunter, B. (1982). Policy issues in special education for migrant students. *Exceptional Children, 48,* 469–472.

Hunter, M. (1981). *Increasing your teaching effectiveness.* Palo Alto, CA.: Learning Institute.

Ide, J. K., Parkerson, J., Haertel, G. D., & Walberg, H. J. (1981). Peer group influence on educational outcomes: A quantitative synthesis. *Journal of Educational Psychology, 73,* 472–484.

Idol, L. (1987a). A critical thinking map to improve content area comprehension of poor readers. *Remedial and Special Education, 8*(4), 28–40.

Idol, L. (1987b). Group story mapping: A comprehension strategy for both skilled and unskilled readers. *Journal of Learning Disabilities, 20,* 196–205.

Idol, L. (1988). A rationale and guidelines for establishing special education consultation programs. *Remedial and Special Education, 9*(6), 48–58.

Idol, L., & Croll, V. J. (1987). Story-mapping training as a means of improving reading comprehension. *Learning Disability Quarterly, 10,* 214–229.

Idol, L., Paolucci-Whitcomb, P., & Nevin, A. (1986). *Collaborative consultation.* Rockville, MD: Aspen Systems.

Idol, L., West, J. F., & Lloyd, S. R. (1988). Organizing and implementing specialized reading programs: A collaborative approach involving classroom, remedial, and special education teachers. *Remedial and Special Education, 9*(2), 54–61.

Idol-Maestas, L. A. (1981). A teacher training model: The resource/consulting model. *Behavioral Disorders, 6,* 108–121.

Idol-Maestas, L. A. (1985). Getting ready to read: Guided probing for poor comprehenders. *Learning Disability Quarterly, 8,* 243–254.

Imber, S. C., Imber, R. B., & Rothstein, C. (1979). Modifying independent work habits: An effective teacher-parent communication program. *Exceptional Children, 46,* 218–221.

Interstate Migrant Education Council. (1987). *Migrant education: A consolidated view.* Denver: Author.

Irvine, J. J. (1990). *Black students and school failure: Policies, practices and prescriptions.* New York: Praeger.

Irvine, J. J. (1991, May). *Multicultural education: The promises and obstacles.* Paper presented at the Sixth Annual Benjamin Matteson Invitational Conference of the State University of New York at New Paltz, New Paltz, NY.

Irving Independent School District v. Tatro, 104 S. Ct. 3371, 82 L.Ed. 2d 664 (1984).

Isaacson, S. (1988). Assessing the writing product: Qualitative and quantitative measures. *Exceptional Children, 54,* 528–534.

Isaacson, S. (1989). Teaching written expression to mildly handicapped students. *The Forum, 14*(3), 5–7.

Israelson, J. (1980). I'm special too—A classroom program promotes understanding and acceptance of handicaps. *Teaching Exceptional Children, 13,* 35–38.

Jackson, R. M., Cleveland, J. C., & Merenda, P. F. (1975). The longitudinal effects of early identification and counseling of underachievers. *Journal of School Psychology, 13,* 119–128.

Jacobs, M. C. (1989). Head injured students in the public schools: A model program. *The Forum, 14*(4), 9–11.

Jason, L. A., & Ferone, L. (1978). Behavioral v. process consultation interventions in school settings. *American Journal of Community Psychology, 6,* 531–543.

Jenkins, J. R., Heliotis, J. D., Stein, M. L., & Haynes, M. C. (1987). Improving reading comprehension by using paragraph restatements. *Exceptional Children, 54,* 54–59.

Jenkins, J. R., & Jenkins, L. M. (1981). *Cross-age and peer tutoring: Help for children with learning problems.* Reston, VA: Council for Exceptional Children.

Jenkins, J. R., Larson, K., & Fleisher, L. (1983). Effects of error correction on word recognition and reading comprehension. *Learning Disability Quarterly, 6,* 139–145.

Johnson, D., & Blaylock, J. (1986). *Adults with learning disabilities: Clinical studies.* Orlando, FL: Grune & Stratton.

Johnson, D. J., & Myklebust, H. R. (1967). *Learning disabilities: Educational principles and practices.* New York: Grune & Stratton.

Johnson, D. R., & Thompson, S. J. (1989). Enhancing opportunities for parent participation in interagency planning for transition: A case study. *The Forum, 15*(2), 5–10.

Johnson, D. W. (1988). *The power of positive interdependence.* Paper presented at the conference on Designing the Future Together: Cooperative Learning, Team Building and Collaboration at Work, New Paltz, NY.

Johnson, D. W., & Johnson, R. T. (1980). Integrating handicapped students into the mainstream. *Exceptional Children, 47,* 90–98.

Johnson, D. W., & Johnson, R. T. (1986). Mainstreaming and cooperative learning strategies. *Exceptional Children, 52,* 553–561.

Johnson, D. W., & Johnson, R. T. (1990). Social skills for successful group work. *Educational Leadership, 47*(4), 29–33.

Johnson, D. W., & Johnson, R. T. (1991). *Teaching students to be peacemakers.* Edina, MN: Interaction.

Johnson, D. W., Johnson, R., Holubec, E., & Roy, P. (1984). *Circles of learning.* Alexandria, VA: Association for Supervision and Curriculum Development.

Johnson, L. J., Cook, M., & Yongue, C. P. (1990). *Capstone transition process.* Unpublished manuscript, University of Alabama.

Johnson, L. J., Pugach, M. C., & Hammitte, D. J. (1988). Barriers to effective special education consultation. *Remedial and Special Education, 9*(6), 41–47.

Johnson, R., & Vardian, E. R. (1973). Reading, readability, and the social studies. *The Reading Teacher, 26,* 483–488.

Johnston, P., Allington, R., & Afflerbach, P. (1985). The congruence of classroom and remedial reading instruction. *Elementary School Journal, 83,* 465–477.

Jones, G. A., Thornton, C. A., & Toohey, M. A. (1985). A multioption program for learning basic addition facts: Case studies and an experimental report. *Journal of Learning Disabilities, 18,* 319–325.

Jones, H. (1991). HIV related beliefs, knowledge, and behaviors of ninth and eleventh grade public school students. *Journal of Health Education, 22*(1), 12–19.

Jones, H. A., & Warren, S. F. (1991). Enhancing engagements in early language teaching. *23*(4), 48–50.

Jones, J. D., Van Fossen, B. E., & Spade, J. Z. (1987, April). *Individual and organizational predictors of high school track placement.* Paper presented at the meeting of the American Educational Research Association, Washington, DC.

Jones, R. L., & Sisk, D. A. (1967). Early perceptions of orthopedic disability. *Exceptional Children, 34,* 551–556.

Jones, T. W., Sowell, V. M., Jones, J. K., & Butler, G. (1981). Changing children's perceptions of handicapped people. *Exceptional Children, 47,* 365–368.

Jones, V. F., & Jones, L. S. (1986). *Comprehensive classroom management: Creating positive learning environments.* Boston: Allyn & Bacon.

Jordan, J. B., & Zantal-Wiener, K. (1987). *1987 special education yearbook.* Reston, VA: Council for Exceptional Children.

Jose P. v. Ambach, 557 F. Supp. 11230 (E.D.N.Y., 1983).

Kagan, S. (1988). *Cooperative learning: Resources for teachers.* Riverside, CA: University of California.

Kagan, S. (1990). The structural approach to cooperative learning. *Educational Leadership, 47*(4), 12–15.

Karl, D. (1992, November). *The special education needs of children treated for cancer.* Paper presented at the meeting of the New York State Federation of Chapters of the Council for Exceptional Children, Albany, NY.

Kansas-National Education Association. (1984). Shape the future as a teacher: A manual for beginning teachers. In S. Fenner (Ed.), *Student teaching and special education* (pp. 4–9). Guilford, CT: Special Learning Corporation.

Karp, S. (1991, June). Is all black and all male all right? *Z Magazine,* pp. 87–91.

Karrison, J., & Carroll, M. K. (1991). Solving word problems. *Teaching Exceptional Children, 23*(4), 55–56.

Kasl, S. (1975). Issues in patient adherence to health care regimens. *Journal of Human Stress. 1,* 5–17.

Kauffman, J. M. (1989). The Regular Education Initiative as Reagan-Bush education policy: A trickle-down theory of education of the hard-to-teach. *The Journal of Special Education, 23*(3), 256–278.

Kauffman, J. M., & Hallahan, D. P. (1981). *Handbook of special education.* Englewood Cliffs, NJ: Prentice-Hall.

Kauffman, J. M., Gerber, M. M., & Semmel, M. I. (1988). Arguable assumptions underlying the regular education initiative. *Journal of Learning Disabilities, 21,* 6–11.

Kauffman, J., Hallahan, D., Haas, K., Brame, T., & Boren, R. (1978). Imitating children's errors to improve spelling performance. *Journal of Learning Disabilities, 11,* 33–38.

Kauffman, J. M., Lloyd, J. W., & McGee, K. A. (1989). Adaptive and maladaptive behavior: Teachers' attitudes and their technical assistance needs. *The Journal of Special Education, 23,* 185–200.

Kaufman, M., Gottlieb, J., Agard, J., & Kukic, M. (1975). Mainstreaming: Toward an explanation of the concept. In E. Meyen, G. Vergason, & R. Whelan (Eds.), *Alternatives for teaching exceptional children* (pp. 35–54). Denver: Love.

Kaufman, T. (1988, April). *Computers, composition and the LD writer.* Paper presented at the conference on Writing Models and Programs the Learning Disabled College Student, New Paltz, NY.

Kavale, K. A. (1980). Learning disability and cultural-economic disadvantage: The case for a relationship. *Learning Disability Quarterly, 3*(3), 97–112.

Kavale, K. A., & Forness, S. A. (1990). Substance over style: A rejoinder to Dunn's animadversions. *Exceptional Children, 56,* 357–361.

Kazdin, A. E. (1975). Behavior modification in applied settings. Homewood, IL: Dorsey.

Kazdin, A. E. (1979). Vicarious reinforcement and punishment in operant programs for children. *Child Behavior Therapy, 1,* 13–26.

Kazdin, A. E. (1980). Acceptability of alternative treatments for deviant child behavior. *Journal of Applied Behavior Analysis, 13,* 259–297.

Keene, S., & Davey, B. (1987). Effects of computer-presented text on LD adolescents reading behaviors. *Learning Disability Quarterly, 10,* 283–290.

Keith, T. (1982). Time spent on homework and high school grades: A large-sample path analysis. *Journal of Educational Psychology, 74,* 248–253.

Kelly, B., Carnine, D., Gersten, R. S., & Grossen, B. (1986). The effectiveness of videodisc instruction in teaching fractions to learning disabled and remedial high school students. *Journal of Special Education Technology, 8,* 5–17.

Kelly, B. W., & Holmes, J. (1979). The guided lecture procedure. *Journal of Reading, 22,* 602–604.

Kennedy, B. (1968). *Motivational effect of individual conferences and goal setting on performances and attitudes in arithmetic.* Madison, WI: University of Wisconsin. (ERIC Document Reproduction Service No. ED 032 113).

Kerr, M. M., & Nelson, C. M. (1989). *Strategies for managing behavior problems in the classroom* (2nd ed.). New York: Merrill/Macmillan.

Kinnison, L. R., Hayes, C., & Acord, J. (1981). Evaluating student progress in mainstream classes. *Teaching Exceptional Children, 13,* 97–99.

Kinnison, L. R., & Nimmer, D. (1979). An analysis of policies regulating medication in schools. *The Journal of School Health, 49,* 280–287.

Kirk, S. A., & Gallagher, J. J. (1989). *Educating exceptional children* (6th ed.). Boston: Houghton Mifflin.

Knapp, S., & Salend, S. J. (1983). Adapting the adaptive behavior scale. *Mental Retardation, 21,* 63–67.

Knoff, H. M. (1983). Investigating disproportionate influence and status in multidisciplinary child study teams. *Exceptional Children, 49,* 367–369.

Kokaska, C. J., & Brolin, D. E. (1985). *Career education for handicapped individuals* (2nd ed.). New York: Merrill/Macmillan.

Koorland, M. A., Monda, L. E., & Vail, C. O. (1988). Recording behavior with ease. *Teaching Exceptional Children, 21,* 59–61.

Kosiewicz, M. M., Hallahan, D., Lloyd, J., & Graves, A. (1982). Effects of self-instruction and self-correction procedures on handwriting performance. *Learning Disability Quarterly, 5,* 71–78.

Kozol, J. (1991). *Savage inequalities: Children in American schools.* New York: Crown.

Krashen, S. D. (1982). *Principles and practice in second language acquisition.* New York: Pergamon.

Kroth, R. L. (1980). The mirror model of parental involvement. *The Pointer, 25,* 18–22.

Kroth, R. L., & Simpson, R. (1977). *Parent conferences as a teaching strategy.* Denver: Love.

Kugel, R. B., & Wolfensberger, W. (1969). *Changing patterns in residential services for the mentally retarded.* Washington, DC: President's Committee on Mental Retardation.

Kulhavy, R. W. (1977). Feedback in written instruction. *Review of Educational Research, 47,* 211–232.

Kunisawa, B. (1988). A nation in crisis: The dropout dilemma. *NEA Today, 6*(6), 61–65.

LaFromboise, T. D., & Graff-Low, K. (1989). American Indian children and adolescents. In J. Taylor Gibbs & L. Nahme Huang (Eds.), *Children of color: Psychological interventions with minority youth* (pp. 114–147). San Francisco: Jossey-Bass.

Lagomarcino, T. R., Hughes, C., & Rusch, F. R. (1989). Utilizing self-management to teach independence on the job. *Education and Training of the Mentally Retarded, 24,* 139–148.

Lakein, A. (1973). *How to get control of your time and your life.* New York: New American Library.

Lambie, R. A., & Hutchens, P. W. (1986). Adapting elementary school mathematics instruction. *Teaching Exceptional Children, 18,* 185–189.

Landau, E. D., Epstein, S. E., & Stone, A. P. (1978). *The exceptional child through literature.* Englewood Cliffs, NJ: Prentice-Hall.

Landerholm, E. (1990). The transdisciplinary team approach in infant intervention programs. *Teaching Exceptional Children, 22*(2), 66–70.

Langan, J. (1982). *Reading and study skills* (2nd ed.). New York: McGraw-Hill.

Langdon, H. W. (1989). Language disorder or difference? Assessing the language skills of Hispanic students. *Exceptional Children, 56,* 160–167.

Langer, J. A. (1981). From theory to practice: A prereading plan. *Journal of Reading, 25*(2), 152–156.

Laosa, L. M. (1977). Nonbiased assessment of children's abilities: Historical antecedents and current issues. In T. Oakland (Ed.), *Psychological and education assessment of minority children* (pp. 1–20). New York: Brunner/Mazel.

Larry P. v. Riles, 495 F. Supp. 96 (N.D. Cal., 1979).

Larson, C. (1981). *EBCE State of Iowa dissemination model for MD and LD students.* Fort Dodge, IA: Iowa Central Community College.

Lau v. Nichols, 414 U.S. 563 (1974).

Lazar, A. L., Gensley, J. T., & Orpet, R. E. (1971). Changing attitudes of young mentally gifted children toward handicapped persons. *Exceptional Children, 37,* 600–602.

Leal, L., & Rafoth, M. A. (1991). Memory strategy development: What teachers do makes a difference. *Intervention in School and Clinic, 26,* 234–237.

Learning Resource Center (n.d.). *Study skills handouts.* New Paltz, NY: Learning Resource Center, State University of New York at New Paltz.

Ledeber, J., & Azzara, C. (1980, April). *Mainstreaming for emotionally disturbed students.* Paper presented at the annual meeting of Council for Exceptional Children, Philadelphia, PA.

Lee, F. R. (1991, October 16). Immunization of children is said to lag. *The New York Times,* pp. B1, B5.

Lee, J. F., & Pruitt, K. W. (1979). Homework assignments: Classroom games or teaching tools? *The Clearing House, 53,* 31–37.

Lee, P., & Alley, G. R. (1981). *Training junior high LD students to use a test-taking strategy* (Research Report No. 38). Lawrence, KS: University of Kansas, Institute for Research in Learning Disabilities.

Leinhardt, G. (1980). Transition rooms: Promoting maturation or reducing education? *Journal of Educational Psychology, 72,* 55–61.

Leinhardt, G., & Pallay, A. (1982). Restrictive educational settings: Exile or haven? *Review of Educational Research, 52,* 557–578.

Lenz, B. K. (1983). Using advance organizers. *The Pointer, 27,* 11–13.

Lenz, B. K., Alley, G. R., & Schumaker, J. B. (1987). Activating the inactive learner: Advance organizers in the secondary content classroom. *Learning Disability Quarterly, 10,* 53–67.

Lenz, B. K., Deshler, D. D., Schumaker, J. B., & Beals, V. C. (1984). *The word identification strategy.* Lawrence, KS: University of Kansas.

Leon, J. A., & Pepe, H. J. (1983). Self-instructional training: Cognitive behavior modification for remediating arithmetic deficits. *Exceptional Children, 50,* 54–60.

Leon, R. E. (1991, March). *Mathematical word problems.* Paper presented at the New York State Association for Bilingual Education Conference, Tarrytown, NY.

Leone, P. E., Greenburg, J. M., Trickett, E. J., & Spero, E. (1989). A study of the use of cigarettes, alcohol, and marijuana by students identified as seriously emotionally disturbed. *Counterpoint, 9*(3), 6–7.

Lerner, J. (1985). *Children with learning disabilities: Theories, diagnosis, and teaching strategies* (4th ed.). Boston: Houghton Mifflin.

Leung, E. K. (1980). Evaluation of a children's literature program designed to facilitate the social integration of handicapped children into regular elementary classrooms. (Doctoral dissertation, The Ohio State University). *Dissertation Abstracts, 40,* 4528A.

Leung, E. K. (1988). Cultural and acculturational commonalities and diversities among Asian Americans: Identification and programming considerations. In A. A. Ortiz & B. A. Ramirez (Eds.), *Schools and the culturally diverse exceptional student: Promising practices and future directions* (pp. 86–95). Reston, VA: Council for Exceptional Children.

Levin, J. R. (1981). On functions of pictures in prose. In F. Pirozzolo & M. Wittrock (Eds.), *Neuropsychological and cognitive processes in reading* (pp. 203–228). New York: Academic.

Levin, J. R., & Allen, V. L. (1976). *Cognitive learning in children: Theories and strategies.* New York: Academic.

Levine, M. D. (1982). The child with school problems: An analysis of physician participation. *Exceptional Children, 48,* 296–305.

Levitt, H. (1989). Technology and speech training: An affair to remember. *Volta Review, 91*(5), 1–6.

Lewandowski, G. (1979). A different look at some basic sight-word lists and their use. *Reading World, 18,* 333–341.

Lewis, R. B., & Doorlag, D. H. (1987). *Teaching special students in the mainstream* (2nd ed.). New York: Merrill/Macmillan.

Li, A. K. F. (1992). Peer relations and social skill training: Implications for multicultural classroom. *The Journal of Educational Issues of Language Minority Students, 10,* 67–78.

Lindley, L. (1990, August). Defining TASH: A mission statement. *TASH Newsletter, 16*(8), 1.

Lindsey, J. D., & Frith, G. H. (1983). The effects of nonhandicapped students' personal characteristics on their attitude toward handicapped peers. *Journal for Special Educators, 20,* 64–69.

Lipsky, D. K., & Gartner, A. (1991). Restructuring for quality. In J. W. Lloyd, N. N. Singh, & A. C. Repp (Eds.), *The regular education initiative: Alternative perspectives on concepts, issues and models* (pp. 43–56). Sycamore, IL: Sycamore.

Litow, L., & Pumroy, D. K. (1975). A brief review of classroom group-oriented contingencies. *Journal of Applied Behavior Analysis, 8,* 341–347.

Litton, F. W., Banbury, M. M., & Harris, K. (1980). Materials for educating handicapped students about their handicapped peers. *Teaching Exceptional Children, 13,* 39–43.

Lloyd, J. W., Saltzman, N. J., & Kauffman, J. M. (1981). Predictable generalization in academic learning as a result of preskills and strategy training. *Learning Disability Quarterly, 4,* 203–216.

Loban, W. (1976). *Language development: Kindergarten through grade twelve* (Research Report #18). Urbana, IL: National Council of Teachers of English.

Lock, C. (1981). *Study skills.* West Lafayette, IN: Kappa Delta Pi.

Lockavitch, J. F. (1983). The teaching connection. *Academic Therapy, 19,* 199–203.

Locust, C. (1990). *Handicapped American Indians: Beliefs and behaviors.* Paper presented at the Council for Exceptional Children's Symposium on Culturally Diverse Exceptional Children, Albuquerque, NM.

Loeb, R., & Sarigiani, P. (1986). The impact of hearing impairments on self-perceptions of children. *The Volta Review, 88*(2), 89–100.

Loescher, G., & Scanlan, J. (1986). *Calculated kindness: Refugees and America's half-open door, 1945 to the present.* New York: Free Press.

Long, N. (1990). Life space interviewing. *Beyond Behavior, 2*(1), 10–15.

Lora v. Board of Education of the City of New York, 587 F. Supp. 1572 (E.D.N.Y., 1984).

Lorber, N. M. (1973). Measuring the character of children's peer relations using the Ohio social acceptance scale. *California Journal of Educational Research, 24,* 71–77.

Los Angeles Unified School District. (1990). *Today's challenge: Teaching strategies for working with young children at risk due to prenatal substance exposure.* Los Angeles: Author.

Lovaas, O. I. (1987). Behavioral treatment and normal educational and intellectual functioning in young autistic children. *Journal of Consulting and Clinical Psychology, 55,* 3–9.

Lovaas, O. I., & Newsom, C. D. (1976). Behavior modification with psychotic children. In H. Leitenberg (Ed.), *Handbook of behavior modification and behavior therapy* (pp. 303–360). Englewood Cliffs, NJ: Prentice-Hall.

Lovitt, T. C. (1975). Operant conditioning techniques for children with learning disabilities. In S. A. Kirk & J. M. McCarthy (Eds.), *Learning disabilities: Selected ACLD papers* (pp. 248–254). Boston: Houghton Mifflin.

Lovitt, T. C., Rudsit, J., Jenkins, J., Pious, C., & Benedetti, D. (1985). Two methods of adapting science materials for learning disabled and regular seventh graders. *Learning Disabilities Quarterly, 8,* 275–285.

Lovitt, T. C., Rudsit, J., Jenkins, J., Pious, C., & Benedetti, D. (1986). Adapting science materials for regular and learning disabled seventh graders. *Remedial and Special Education,* 7(1), 31–39.

Lovitt, T. C., & Smith, J. O. (1972). Effects of instructions on an individual's verbal behavior. *Exceptional Children, 38,* 685–693.

Lowenbraun, S., & Thompson, M. D. (1990). Hearing impairments. In N. G. Haring & L. McCormick (Eds.), *Exceptional children and youth* (5th ed.) (pp. 365–401). New York: Merrill/Macmillan.

Lowenthal, B. (1987). Mainstreaming—Ready or not. *Academic Therapy, 22,* 393–397.

Lucas, T., Henze, R., & Donato, R. (1990). Promoting the success of Latino language-minority students: An exploratory study of six high schools. *Harvard Educational Review, 60,* 315–340.

Ludlow, B. L., Turnbull, A. P., & Luckasson, R. (1988). *Transition to adult life for people with severe disabilities: Principles and practices.* Baltimore: Paul H. Brookes.

Lund, K. A., & Bos, C. S. (1981). Orchestrating the preschool classroom: The daily schedule. *Teaching Exceptional Children, 14,* 120–125.

Lyman, F. (1987). Think-Pair-Share: An expanding teaching technique. *MAACIE Cooperative News. 1*(1), 1–2.

Lynch, E. W. (1988). Mental retardation. In E. W. Lynch & R. B. Lewis (Eds.), *Exceptional children and adults* (pp. 96–135). Boston: Scott, Foresman.

Lynch, E. W., Lewis, R. B., & Murphy, D. S. (1992). Educational services for children with chronic illnesses: Perspectives of educators and families. *Exceptional Children, 59,* 210–220.

Lynch, E. W., & Stein, R. C. (1987). Parent participation by ethnicity: A comparison of hispanic, black, and anglo families. *Exceptional Children, 54,* 105–111.

MacArthur, C. A. (1988). The impact of computers on the writing process. *Exceptional Children, 54,* 536–542.

MacArthur, C. A., Graham, S., & Skarvoed, J. (1986). *Learning disabled students' composing with three methods: Handwriting, dictation, and word processing* (Technical Report No. 109). College Park, MD: Institute for the Study of Exceptional Children and Youth.

MacArthur, C. A., & Schneiderman, B. (1986). Learning disabled students' difficulties in learning to use a word processor: Implications for instruction and software evaluation. *Journal of Learning Disabilities, 19,* 248–253.

MacArthur, C. A., & Schwartz, S. S. (1990, April). *The computers and writing instruction project: A model curriculum.* Paper presented at the meeting of the Council for Exceptional Children, Toronto.

MacArthur, C. A., Schwartz, S. S., & Graham, S. (1991). A model for writing instruction: Integrating word processing and strategy instruction into a process approach to writing. *Learning Disabilities Research and Practice, 6*(4), 230–236.

Mack, C. (1988). Celebrate cultural diversity. *Teaching Exceptional Children, 21,* 40–43.

MacMillan, D. L., & Semmel, M. I. (1977). Evaluation of mainstreaming programs. *Focus on Exceptional Children, 9,* 1–14.

Macy, D. J., & Carter, J. L. (1978). Comparison of a mainstream and self-contained special education program. *Journal of Special Education, 12,* 303–313.

Madden, N., & Slavin, R. (1983). Mainstreaming students with mild handicaps: Academic and social outcomes. *Review of Educational Research, 53,* 519–569.

Maheady, L., & Algozzine, B. (1991). The regular education initiative—Can we proceed in an orderly and scientific manner? *Teacher Education and Special Education, 14*(1), 66–73.

Maheady, L., Harper, G. F., & Mallette, B. (1991). Peer-mediated instruction: A review of potential applications for special education. *Reading, Writing, and Learning Disabilities International, 7,* 75–103.

Maheady, L., Harper, G. F., & Sacca, M. K. (1988). Classwide peer tutoring programs in secondary self-contained programs for the mildly handicapped. *Journal of Research and Development in Education, 21*(3), 76–83.

Maher, C. A., & Hawryluk, M. K. (1983). Framework and guidelines for utilization of teams in schools. *School Psychology Review, 12,* 180–185.

Majsterek, D. J. (1990). Writing disabilities: Is word processing the answer? *Intervention in School and Clinic, 26*(2), 93–97.

Majsterek, D. J., & Wilson, R. (1989). Computer-assisted instruction for students with learning disabilities: Considerations for practitioners. *Learning Disabilities Focus, 5*(1), 18–27.

Majsterek, D. J., Wilson, R., & Mandlebaum, L. (1990). Computerized IEPs: Guidelines for product evaluation. *Journal of Special Education Technology, 10,* 207–219.

Maldonado-Colon, E. (1990, October). *Successful strategies for enhancing language arts instruction for exceptional second language learners.* Paper presented at the Symposium on Culturally Diverse Exceptional Children, Albuquerque, NM.

Maldonado-Colon, E. (1991). Development of second language learners' linguistic and cognitive abilities. *The Journal of Educational Issues of Language Minority Students, 9,* 37–48.

Mallette, B., Pomerantz, D., & Sacca, D. (1991, November). *Getting mainstreamed students with special needs to perform as well as their peers: Peer-mediated instructional strategies.* Paper presented at the meeting of the New York State Federation of Chapters of the Council for Exceptional Children, Buffalo, NY.

Malone, L. D., & Mastropieri, M. A. (1992). Reading comprehension instruction: Summarization and self-monitoring training for students with learning disabilities. *Exceptional Children, 58,* 270–279.

Malone, L., Petrucchi, L., & Thier, H. (1981). *Science activities for the visually impaired (SAVI).* Berkeley, CA: Center for Multisensory Learning, University of California.

Mann, P. H., Suiter, P. A., & McClung, R. M. (1979). *Handbook in diagnostic-prescriptive teaching* (2nd ed., Abridged). Boston: Allyn & Bacon.

Manning, A. L., & Wray, D. (1990). Using figurative language in the classroom. *Teaching Exceptional Children, 22*(4), 18–21.

Manzo, A. (1969). The request procedure. *Journal of Reading, 13,* 123–126.

Manzo, A. (1975). Guided reading procedure. *Journal of Reading, 18,* 287–291.

Manzo, A., & Manzo, U. (1990). *Content area reading: A heuristic approach.* New York: Merrill/Macmillan.

Margolis, H., & McGettigan, J. (1988). Managing resistance to instructional modifications in mainstreamed environments. *Remedial and Special Education, 9*(4), 15–21.

Marino, J., Gould, S., & Haas, L. (1985). The effects of writing as a prereading activity on delayed recall of narrative text. *Elementary School Journal, 86,* 199–205.

Markham, L. (1976). Influence of handwriting quality on teacher evaluation of written work. *Educational Research Journal, 13,* 277–283.

Marotz-Ray, B. (1985). Measuring the social position of the mainstreamed handicapped child. *Exceptional Children, 52,* 57–62.

Marrs, L. W. (1984). A bandwagon without music: Preparing rural special educators. *Exceptional Children, 50,* 334–342.

Marsh, G. E., & Price, B. J. (1980). *Methods for teaching the mildly handicapped adolescent.* St. Louis: C. V. Mosby.

Marsh, V., & Friedman, R. (1972). Changing public attitudes toward blindness. *Exceptional Children, 38,* 426–428.

Martens, B. K., Peterson, R. L., Witt, J. C., & Cirone, S. (1986). Teacher perceptions of school-based interventions. *Exceptional Children, 53,* 213–223.

Martin, D. S. (1987). Reducing ethnocentrism. *Teaching Exceptional Children, 20*(1), 5–8.

Martin, R. (1978). Expert and reference power: A framework for understanding and maximizing consultation effectiveness. *Journal of School Psychology, 16,* 49–55.

Marzola, E. S. (1987). Using manipulatives in math instruction. *Journal of Reading Writing and Learning Disabilities, 3,* 9–20.

Massachusetts Commission for the Deaf and Hard of Hearing. (1988). *An information guide related to standards for educational interpreting for deaf and severely hard of hearing students in elementary and secondary schools.* Boston: Author.

Masters, J. C., & Furman, W. (1981). Popularity, individual friendship selection, and specific peer interaction among children. *Developmental Psychology, 17,* 344–350.

Masters, L. F., & Mori, A. A. (1986). *Teaching secondary students with mild learning and behavior problems: Methods, materials, strategies.* Rockville, MD: Aspen.

Mastropieri, M. A. (1988). Using the keyword method. *Teaching Exceptional Children, 20,* 4–8.

Mastropieri, M. A., & Scruggs, T. E. (1987). *Effective instruction for special education.* Boston: College-Hill.

Mastropieri, M. A., Scruggs, T. E., McLoone, B., & Levin, J. R. (1985). Facilitating the acquisition of science classifications in LD students. *Learning Disabilities Quarterly, 8,* 299–309.

May, J., & Davis, P. (1990). Service delivery issues in working with fathers of children with special needs. *Association for the Care of Children's Health Network, 8*(2), 4.

McCann, S. K., Semmel, M. I., & Nevin, A. (1985). Reverse mainstreaming: Nonhandicapped students in special education classrooms. *Remedial and Special Education, 6,* 13–19.

McCarthy, M. (1980). Minimum competency testing and handicapped students. *Exceptional Children, 47,* 166–173.

McCauley, J. K., & McCauley, D. S. (1992). Using choral reading to promote language learning for ESL students. *The Reading Teacher, 45*(7), 526–533.

McClelland, D. C. (1977). Power, motivation and impossible dreams. *Wharton Magazine, 1,* 33–39.

McCormack, J. E. (1978). The assessment tool that meets your needs: The one you construct. *Teaching Exceptional Children, 8,* 106–109.

McCormick, L. (1990). Cultural diversity and exceptionality. In N. G. Haring & L. McCormick (Eds.), *Exceptional children and youth* (5th ed.) (pp. 47–75). New York: Merrill/Macmillan.

McCormick, V. (1988). The sound of music: A harmonious meeting of minds. In J. Golub (Ed.), *Focus on collaborative learning* (pp. 117–122). Urbana, IL: National Council of Teachers of English.

McCormick, L., & Haring, N. G. (1990). Technological applications for children with special needs. In N. G. Haring & L. McCormick (Eds.), *Exceptional children and youth* (5th ed.) (pp. 42–69). New York: Merrill/Macmillan.

McCoy, K. M., & Prehm, H. J. (1987). *Teaching mainstreamed students: Methods and techniques.* Denver: Love.

McEachern, W. R. (1990). *Supporting emergent literacy among young American Indian students.* Charleston, WV: Appalachia Educational Laboratory.

McGookey, K. (1992). Drama, disability, and your classroom. *Teaching Exceptional Children, 24*(2), 12–14.

McGuigan, C. A. (1975). *The effects of a flowing words list vs. fixed word lists and the implementation of procedures in the add-a-word spelling program* (Working paper No. 52). Seattle: University of Washington Experimental Education Unit.

McIntyre, T. (1992). The invisible culture in our schools: Gay and lesbian youth. *Beyond Behavior, 3*(3), 6–12.

McKenzie, R. G., & Houk, C. S. (1986). The paraprofessional in special education. *Teaching Exceptional Children, 18,* 246–252.

McKinney, J. D., & Feagans, L. (1980). *Learning disabilities in the classroom* (Final project report). Chapel Hill, NC: University of North Carolina, Frank Porter Graham Child Development Center.

McKinney, J. D., & Hocutt, A. M. (1982). Public school involvement of parents of learning disabled and average achievers. *Exceptional Education Quarterly, 3,* 64–73.

McKinney, J. D., & Hocutt, A. M. (1988). The need for policy analysis in evaluating the regular education initiative. *Journal of Learning Disabilities, 21,* 12–18.

McLanahan, S. (1986). Family structure and the reproduction of poverty. *American Journal of Sociology, 90,* 873–901.

McLaughlin, T. F. (1981). The effects of classroom token economy system on math performance in an intermediate grade school class. *Education and Treatment of Children, 4,* 139–147.

McLeod, T. M., & Armstrong, S. W. (1982). Learning disabilities in mathematics skill deficits and remedial approaches at the intermediate and secondary level. *Learning Disability Quarterly, 5,* 305–311.

McLoughlin, J. A., Edge, D., & Strenecky, B. (1978). Perspective on parental involvement in the diagnosis and treatment of learning disabled children. *Journal of Learning Disabilities, 13,* 295–300.

McLoughlin, J. A., & Lewis, R. B. (1986). *Assessing special students* (2nd ed.). New York: Merrill/Macmillan.

McLoughlin, J. A., & Lewis, R. B. (1990). *Assessing special students* (3rd ed). New York: Merrill/Macmillan.

McMath, J. S. (1990). Multicultural literature for young children. *Democracy and Education, 5*(2), 5–10.

McNamara, B. E. (1986). Parents as partners in the IEP process. *Academic Therapy, 21,* 309–315.

McNeil, J., & Donant, L. (1982). Summarization strategy for improving reading comprehension. In J. Niles and L. A. Harris (Eds.), *New inquiries in reading: Research and instruction* (pp. 215–219). Rochester, NY: National Reading Conference.

McNeil, M., Thousand, J., & Bove, M. (1989, April). *The powers of partnerships: Adults and children collaborating in education.* Paper presented at the meeting of the Council for Exceptional Children, San Francisco, CA.

McNergney, R., & Haberman, M. (1988). Dropouts: Time for solutions. *NEA Today, 6*(10), 27.

Means, B., & Knapp, M. S. (1991). Models for teaching advanced skills to educationally disadvantaged children. In B. Means & M. S. Knapp (Eds.), *Teaching advanced skills to educationally disadvantaged students* (pp. 1–20). Washington, DC: U.S. Department of Education.

Meese, R. L. (1992). Adapting textbooks for children with learning disabilities in mainstreamed classrooms. *Teaching Exceptional Children, 24*(3), 49–51.

Meichenbaum, D. H., & Goodman, J. (1971). Training impulsive children to talk to themselves: A means of developing self-control. *Journal of Abnormal Psychology, 77,* 115–126.

Meier, F. E. (1992). *Competency-based instruction for teachers of students with special learning needs.* Boston: Allyn & Bacon.

Mendelsohn, S. R., & Jennings, K. D. (1986). Characteristics of emotionally disturbed children referred for special education assessment. *Child Psychiatry and Human Development, 16,* 154–170.

Mendez, G. (1991). Constructive controversy: The bilingual dilemma. *Cooperative Learning, 12*(1), 22–23.

Mendoza, M., Holt, W., & Jackson, D. (1978). Circles and tapes: An easy teacher-implemented way to teach fundamental writing skills. *Teaching Exceptional Children, 10,* 48–50.

Mental Retardation Institute. (1991). *Assessment and educational planning for students with severe disabilities.* Valhalla, NY: Author.

Mercer, C. D. (1990). Learning disabilities. In L. McCormick & N. G. Haring (Eds.), *Exceptional children and youth* (5th ed.) (pp. 119–160). New York: Merrill/Macmillan.

Mercer, C. D., & Mercer, A. R. (1990). *Teaching students with learning problems* (3rd ed.). New York: Merrill/Macmillan.

Mercer, C. D., & Miller, S. P. (1992). Teaching students with learning problems in math to acquire, understand, and apply basic math facts. *Remedial and Special Education, 13*(3), 19–35, 61.

Mercer, J. R. (1973). *Labelling the mentally retarded.* Berkeley, CA: University of California Press.

Mercer, J. R., & Denti, L. (1989). Obstacles to integrating disabled students in a "two-roof" elementary school. *Exceptional Children, 56,* 30–38.

Messerer, J., & Lerner, J. W. (1989). Word processing for learning disabled students. *Learning Disabilities Focus, 5*(1), 13–17.

Meunier, C., & Rule, B. (1967). Anxiety, confidence and conformity. *Journal of Personality, 35,* 498–504.

Meyer, B. J. F. (1984). Organizational aspects of text: Effects of reading comprehension and applications for the classroom. In J. Flood (Ed.), *Promoting reading comprehension* (pp. 113–138). Newark, DE: International Reading Association.

Meyer, B. J. F., Brandt, D., & Bluth, G. (1979). Use of top-level structure in text: Key for reading comprehension of ninth-grade students. *Reading Research Quarterly, 16,* 72–103.

Meyer v. Nebraska 262 U.S. 390 (1923).

Meyer, D. J., Vadasy, P. F., & Fewell, R. (1985). *Living with a brother or sister with special needs: A book for sibs.* Seattle: University of Washington Press.

Meyers, J., & Lytle, S. (1986). Assessment of the learning process. *Exceptional Children, 53,* 138–144.

Michael, R. J. (1992). Seizures: Teacher observations and record keeping. *Intervention in School and Clinic, 27*(4), 211–214.

Mid-Hudson Library System. (n.d.). *Now that we've met what do I say?: General guidelines for communicating with persons who have disabilities.* Poughkeepsie, NY: Author.

Miles, A. S., Russo, C. J., & Gordon, W. M. (1991, October 10). The reasonable accommodations provisions of the Americans with Disabilities Act. *West's Education Law Reporter,* pp. 1–8.

Miller, G. A., (1956). The magical number seven, plus or minus two: Some limits on our capacity for processing information. *Psychological Review, 63,* 81–97.

Miller, L. J. (1987). Spelling and handwriting. In J. S. Choate, T. Z. Bennett, B. E. Enright, L. J. Miller, J. A. Poteet, & T. A. Rakes (Eds.), *Assessing and programming basic curriculum skills* (pp. 177–204). Boston: Allyn & Bacon.

Miller, M., Hagan, M., & Armstrong, S. (1980). Nonhandicapped students' attitudes as assessment variables. *Diagnostique,* 5, 20–25.

Miller, M., & Loukellis, I. (1982, April). *Assessment of rural elementary students' attitudes toward the handicapped.* Paper presented at the meeting of the Council for Exceptional Children, Houston, TX.

Miller, M., Miller, S. R., Wheeler, J., & Selinger, J. (1989). Can a single-classroom treatment approach change academic performance and behavioral characteristics in severely behaviorally disordered adolescents: An experimental inquiry, *Behavioral Disorders, 14*(4), 215–225.

Miller, M., Richey, D. D., & Lammers, C. A. (1983). Analysis of gifted students' attitudes toward the handicapped. *The Journal for Special Educators, 19,* 14–21.

Miller, P. W. (1986). *Nonverbal communication* (2nd ed.). Washington, DC: National Education Association.

Miller, T. L., & Sabatino, D. (1978). An evaluation of the teacher consultant model as an approach to mainstreaming. *Exceptional Children, 45,* 86–91.

Miller, W. (1989, July). *Obstetrical issues.* Paper presented at the Conference on Drugs, Alcohol, Pregnancy and Parenting: An Intervention Model, Spokane, WA.

Millman, J., & Pauk, W. (1969). *How to take tests.* New York: McGraw-Hill.

Mills v. D.C. Board of Education, 348 F. Supp. 866 (D.D.C., 1972).

Milone, M. N., & Wasylyk, T. M. (1981). Handwriting in special education. *Teaching Exceptional Children, 14,* 58–61.

Mims, R. M., & Gholson, B. (1977). Effects and type and amount of feedback upon hypothesis sampling systems among 7 and 8 year old children. *Journal of Experimental Psychology, 24,* 358–371.

Minner, S., Beane, A., & Porter, G. (1986). Try telephone answering machines. *Teaching Exceptional Children, 19,* 62–63.

Miramontes, O. B. (1991). Organizing for effective paraprofessional services in special education: A multilingual/multiethnic instructional service team model. *Remedial and Special Education, 12*(1), 29–36.

Mirkin, P., Deno, S. L., Fuchs, L., Wesson, C., Tindal, G., Marston, D., & Kuehnle, K. (1981). *Procedures to monitor student progress on IEP goals.* Minneapolis, MN: University of Minnesota, Institute for Research on Learning Disabilities.

Misra, A., & Smith, M. A. (1991, November). *How do I discipline special education students in regular education settings? A question consulting teachers must answer.* Paper presented at the meeting of New York State Federation of Chapters of the Council for Exceptional Children, Buffalo, NY.

Mithaug, D. E., Martin, J. E., Agran, M., & Rusch, F. R. (1988). *Why special education graduates fail: How to teach them to succeed.* Colorado Springs, CO: Ascent.

Moe, L. (1980). *Guidelines for evaluating books about individuals with handicaps.* Bethlehem, PA: Project STREAM.

Mohr, M. M. (1984). *Revision: The rhythm of meaning.* Upper Montclair, NJ: Boynton/Cook.

Monroe, J. D., & Howe, C. E. (1971). The effects of integration and social class on the acceptance of retarded adolescents. *Education and Training of the Mentally Retarded, 6,* 20–24.

Montague, M., & Bos, C. S. (1986). The effect of cognitive strategy training on verbal math problem solving performance of learning disabled adolescents. *Journal of Learning Disabilities, 19,* 26–33.

Montague, M., Graves, A., & Leavell, A. (1991). Planning, procedural facilitation, and narrative composition of junior high school students with learning disabilities. *Learning Disabilities Research and Practice, 6*(4), 219–224.

Moore, B. C. (1982). Biomedical factors in mental retardation. In P. Cegelka & H. Prehm (Eds.), *Mental retardation: From categories to people* (pp. 76–110). New York: Merrill/Macmillan.

Moore, D. W., Moore, S. A., Cunningham, P. M., & Cunningham, J. W. (1986). *Developing teachers and writers in the content areas.* White Plains, NY: Longman.

Moore, P. (1990). Voice disorders. In G. H. Shames & E. H. Wiig (Eds.), *Human communication disorders* (3rd ed.) (pp. 266–305). New York: Merrill/Macmillan.

Moores, D. (1982). *Educating the deaf: Psychology, principles, practices* (2nd ed.). Boston: Houghton Mifflin.

Moores, D. F., & Maestas y Moores, J. (1988). Hearing disorders. In E. W. Lynch & R. B. Lewis (Eds.), *Exceptional children and adults: An introduction to special education* (pp. 276–317). Boston: Scott, Foresman.

Moran, M. R. (1988). Rationale and procedures for increasing the productivity of inexperienced writers. *Exceptional Children, 54,* 552–558.

Morocco, C. C., & Neuman, S. B. (1986). Word processors and the acquisition of writing strategies. *Journal of Learning Disabilities, 19,* 243–247.

Morrow, R. D. (1987). Cultural differences—Be aware. *Academic Therapy, 23,* 143–149.

Morse, W. C., Cutler, R. L., & Fink, A. H. (1964). *Public school classes for the emotionally handicapped: A research analysis.* Washington, DC: Council for Exceptional Children.

Morsink, C. V. (1981). Learning disabilities. In A. E. Blackhurst & W. H. Berdine (Eds.), *An introduction to special education* (pp. 354–390). Boston: Little, Brown.

Morsink, C. V., Chase Thomas, C., & Correa, V. I. (1991). *Interactive teaming: Consultation and collaboration in special programs.* New York: Merrill/Macmillan.

Morton, T. (1988). Fine cloth, cut carefully: Cooperative learning in British Columbia. In J. Golub (Ed.), *Focus on collaborative learning* (pp. 35–42). Urbana, IL: National Council of Teachers of English.

Murray, M. (1991). The role of the classroom teacher. In G. L. Porter & D. Richler (Eds.), *Changing Canadian schools: Perspectives on disability and inclusion* (pp. 173–189). Toronto: Roeher Institute.

Mutch, T. A. (1989, November). *Instructional procedures for teaching strategies to learning disabled adolescents: A component of a SIRCL model.* Paper presented at the meeting of the New York State Federation of Chapters of the Council for Exceptional Children, Saratoga Springs, NY.

Myers, J. K. (1976). *The special day school placement for high IQ and low EMR pupils.* Paper presented at the annual meeting of the Council for Exceptional Children, Chicago. (ERIC Document Reproduction Services No. ED 125 197).

Myers, P. I., & Hammill, D. D. (1982). *Learning disabilities: Basic concepts, assessment practices, and instructional strategies.* Austin, TX: Pro-Ed.

Myklebust, H. R. (1973). *Development and disorders of written language. Vol. 2: Studies of normal and exceptional children.* New York: Grune & Stratton.

Myklebust, H. R., & Boshes, B. (1969). *Minimal brain damage in children.* Washington, DC: Neurological and Sensory Disease Control Program, Department of Health, Education, and Welfare.

Myles, B. S., Moran, M. R., Ormsbee, C. K., & Downing J. A. (1992). Guidelines for establishing and maintaining token economies. *Intervention in School and Clinic, 27,* 164–169.

Nagata, D. K. (1989). Japanese American children and adolescents. In J. Taylor Gibbs & L. Nahme Huang (Eds.), *Children of color: Psychological interventions with minority youth* (pp. 67–113). San Francisco: Jossey-Bass.

Nagel, D. R., Schumaker, J. B., & Deshler, D. D. (1986). *The FIRST-Letter mnemonic strategy.* Lawrence, KS: University of Kansas Institute for Research in Learning Disabilities.

Nahme Huang, L. (1989). Southeast Asian refugee children and adolescents. In J. Taylor Gibbs and L. Nahme Huang (Eds.), *Children of color: Psychological interventions with minority youth* (pp. 278–321). San Francisco: Jossey-Bass.

Nahme Huang, L., & Taylor Gibbs, J. (1989). Multicultural perspectives on two clinical cases. In J. Taylor Gibbs & L. Nahme Huang (Eds.), *Children of color: Psychological interventions with minority youth* (pp. 351–374). San Francisco: Jossey-Bass.

Nahme Huang, L., & Ying, Y. (1989). Chinese American children and adolescents. In J. Taylor Gibbs and L. Nahme Huang (Eds.), *Children of color: Psychological interventions with minority youth* (pp. 30–68). San Francisco: Jossey-Bass.

National Coalition of Advocates for Students. (1989). *Immigrant students: Their legal right to access to public schools: A guide for advocates and educators.* Boston: Author.

National Coalition of Advocates for Students. (1990). *On the road to healthy living: A bilingual curriculum on AIDS and HIV prevention for migrant students.* Boston: Author.

National Coalition of Advocates for Students. (1991). *New voices: Immigrant students in U.S. public schools.* Boston: Author.

National Council of Teachers of Mathematics. (1976). Minicalculators in schools. *The Arithmetic Teacher, 23,* 72–74.

National Council of Teachers of Mathematics. (1980). *An agenda for action: Recommendations for school mathematics of the 1980s.* Reston, VA: Author.

National Institute of Education. (1985, February). *Research in brief.* Washington, DC: Author.

National School Boards Association. (1989). *A equal chance: Educating at-risk children to succeed.* Alexandria, VA: Author.

National Society for the Prevention of Blindness. (1977). *Signs of possible eye trouble in children.* New York: Author.

Neef, N., Iwata, B., & Page, T. (1977). The effects of known-item interspersal on acquisition and retention of spelling and sight word reading. *Journal of Applied Behavior Analysis, 10,* 738.

Nelson, C. M. (1981). Classroom management. In J. M. Kaufman & D. P. Hallahan (Eds.), *Handbook of special education* (pp. 663–687). Englewood Cliffs, NJ: Prentice-Hall.

Nelson, R., & Cummings, J. (1981). Basic concept attainment of educable mentally handicapped children: Implications for teaching concepts. *Education and Training of the Mentally Retarded, 16*(4), 303–306.

New York State Education Department. (1986). *Alternative testing techniques for students with handicapping conditions.* Albany, NY: Author.

New York State Education Department. (1989). *Bilingual education: Regents policy paper and proposed action plan for bilingual education.* Albany, NY: Author.

New York State Education Department. (n.d.). *The identification and reporting of child abuse and maltreatment.* Albany, NY: Author.

New Zealand Department of Education. (1988). *New voices: Second language learning and teaching: A handbook for primary teachers.* Wellington, NZ: Department of Education.

Newcomb, M. D., & Bentler, P. M. (1989). Substance abuse and abuse among children and teenagers. *American Psychologist, 44,* 242–248.

Newell, R. C. (1981). Giving good weight to black English. *Perspectives: The Civil Rights Quarterly, 13,* (1), 25–29.

Newman, J. M. (1985). *Whole language: Theory in use.* Portsmouth, NH: Heinemann.

Nguyen, D. (1987). Presentation at the multicultural issues track session of the Topical Conference of the Technical Assistance for Parent Programs (TAPP) Project, Crystal City, VA.

Nicol, S. E., & Erlenmeyer-Kimling, L. (1986). Genetic factors in psychopathology: Implications for prevention. In B. A. Edelstein & L. Michelson (Eds.), *Handbook of prevention* (pp. 21–41). New York: Plenum.

Nicolau, S., & Ramos, C. L. (1990). *Together is better: Building strong partnerships between schools and Hispanic parents.* New York: Hispanic Policy Development Project.

Nidorf, J. (1985). Mental health and refugee youths: A model for diagnostic training. In T. Owan (Ed.), *Southeast Asian mental health: Treatment, prevention, services, training, and research* (pp. 391–429). Washington, DC: U.S. Department of Health and Human Services.

Niemoeller, A. F. (1968). Acoustical design of classrooms for the deaf. *American Annals of the Deaf, 113,* 1040–1045.

Nirje, B. (1969). The normalization principle and its human management implications. In R. B. Kugel

& W. Wolfensberger (Eds.), *Changing patterns in residential services for the mentally retarded* (pp. 231–240). Washington, DC: U. S. Government Printing Office.

Noar, M., & Milgram, R. M. (1980). Two preservice strategies for preparing regular class teachers for mainstreaming. *Exceptional Children, 47,* 126–127.

Northcutt, L., & Watson, D. (1986). *Sheltered English teaching handbook.* Carlsbad, CA: Northcutt, Watson, Gonzales.

Nulman, J. A., & Gerber, M. M. (1984). Improving spelling performance by imitating a child's errors. *Journal of Learning Disabilities, 17,* 328–333.

Nuzum, M. (1987). Teaching the arithmetic story problem process. *Journal of Reading, Writing and Learning Disabilities, 3,* 53–61.

O'Brien, J., Forest, M., Snow, J., Pearpoint, J., & Hasbury, D. (1989). *Action for inclusion: How to improve schools by welcoming children with special needs in regular classrooms.* Toronto: Inclusion.

O'Connor, K. (1989). *Homeless children.* San Diego, CA: Lucent.

O'Donnell, H. (1974). Black communicative styles. *Elementary English, 51,* 1091–1095.

O'Leary, S. G., & Dubey, D. R. (1979). Applications of self-control procedures by children: A review. *Journal of Applied Behavior Analysis, 12,* 449–465.

O'Mara, D. H. (1981). The process of reading mathematics. *Journal of Reading, 25,* 22–30.

Oakland, T. (1980). Nonbiased assessment of minority group children. *Exceptional Education Quarterly, 1*(3), 31–46.

Ogbu, J. U. (1978). *Minority education and caste.* New York: Academic.

Ogbu, J. U., & Matute-Bianchi (1986). Understanding sociocultural factors: Knowledge, identity, and school adjustment. In Bilingual Education Office, California State Department of Education, *Beyond Language: Social and cultural factors in schooling language minority students* (pp. 73–142). Los Angeles: California State University, Evaluation, Dissemination and Assessment Center.

Ogden, E. H., & Germinario, V. (1988). *The at-risk student: Answers for educators.* Lancaster, PA: Technomic.

Ogle, D. M. (1986). K-W-L: A teaching model that develops active reading of expository text. *The Reading Teacher, 39,* 562–570.

Okolo, C., Bahr, C. M., & Gardner, J. E. (1992, April). *Strategies for increasing the achievement motivation of students with mild disabilities.* Paper presented at the meeting of the Council for Exceptional Children, Baltimore, MD.

Ortiz, A. A. (1984). Choosing the language of instruction for exceptional bilingual children. *Teaching Exceptional Children, 16,* 208–212.

Ortiz, A. A., & Wilkinson, C. Y. (1989). Adapting IEPs for limited English proficient students. *Academic Therapy, 24,* 555–568.

Ortiz, A. A., & Wilkinson, C. Y. (1991). Assessment and intervention model for bilingual exceptional student (Aim for the Best). *Teacher Education and Special Education, 14*(1), 35–42.

Ortiz, A. A., & Yates, J. R. (1989). Staffing and the development of individualized educational programs for the bilingual exceptional student. In L. M. Baca and H. T. Cervantes (Eds.), *The Bilingual special education interface* (2nd ed.) (pp. 183–203). New York: Merrill/Macmillan.

Osguthorpe, R. T., & Scruggs, T. E. (1986). Special education students as tutors: A review and analysis. *Remedial and Special Education, 7*(4), 15–26.

Ostrosky, M. M., & Kaiser, A. P. (1991). Preschool classroom environments that promote communication. *Teaching Exceptional Children, 23*(4), 6–10.

Ovando, C. J., & Collier, V. P. (1985). *Bilingual and ESL classrooms: Teaching in multicultural contexts.* New York: McGraw-Hill.

Oxford, R., Pol, L., Lopez, D., Stupp, P., Gendell, M., & Peng, S. (1981). Projections of non-English language background and limited English proficient persons in the United States to the year 2000: Educational planning in the demographic context. *NABE Journal, 5,* 1–30.

Page, E. (1958). Teacher comments and student performance. *Journal of Educational Psychology, 49,* 172–181.

Paine, S. C., Radicchi, J., Rossellini, L. C., Deutchman, L., & Darch, C. B. (1983). *Structuring your classrooms for academic success.* Champaign, IL: Research.

Paivio, A. (1971). *Imagery and verbal processes.* New York: Holt, Rinehart and Winston.

Palinscar, A., & Brown, A. L. (1983). *Reciprocal teaching of comprehension-monitoring activities. Technical Report No. 269.* Champaign, IL: Center for the Study of Reading, University of Illinois.

Palinscar, A. S., & Klenk, L. J. (1991). Learning dialogues to promote text comprehension. In B. Means & M. S. Knapp (Eds.), *Teaching advanced skills to educationally disadvantaged students—Final Report* (pp. 20–34). Washington, DC: U.S. Department of Education.

Palkes, H., Stewart, M., & Kahana, K. (1968). Porteus maze performance of hyperactive boys after training in self-directed verbal commands. *Child Development, 39,* 817–826.

Panchyshym, R., & Monroe, E. E. (1986). *Developing key concepts for solving word problems.* Baldwin, NY: Barnell Loft.

Pang, O. (1991). Teaching children about social issues: Kidpower. In C. Sleeter (Ed.), *Empowerment through multicultural education* (pp. 179–197). Albany, NY: State University of New York Press.

Parette, H. P., & Hourcade, J. J. (1986). Management strategies for orthopedically handicapped students. *Teaching Exceptional Children, 18,* 282–286.

Parish, T. S., Ohlsen, R. L., & Parish, J. G. (1978). A look at mainstreaming in light of children's attitudes toward the handicapped. *Perceptual and Motor Skills, 46,* 1019–1021.

Parish, T. S., & Taylor, J. (1978). The Personal Attribute Inventory for Children: A report on its validity and reliability as a self-concept scale. *Educational and Psychological Measurement, 38,* 565–569.

Parkham, J. L. (1983). A meta-analysis of the use of manipulative materials and student achievement in elementary school mathematics. *Dissertation Abstracts International, 44a,* 96.

Parmar, R. S., & Cawley, J. F. (1991). Challenging the routines and passivity that characterize instruction for children with mild handicaps. *Remedial and Special Education, 12*(5), 23–32, 43.

Pasanella, J. (1980). A team approach to educational decision making. *Exceptional Teacher, 1,* 1–2, 8–9.

Patterson, G. R. (1965). An application of conditioning techniques to the control of a hyperactive child. In L. P. Ullman & L. Krasner (Eds.), *Case studies in behavior modification* (pp. 370–375). New York: Holt, Rinehart & Winston.

Pauk, W. (1984). *How to study in college.* Boston: Houghton Mifflin.

Pear, R. (1991, September 9). Homeless children challenge schools. *The New York Times.* p. A10.

Pearl, R., Bryan, T., & Donahue, M. (1980). Learning disabled children's attributions for success and failure. *Learning Disabilities Quarterly, 3,* 3–9.

Peck, M. L. (1985). Crisis intervention treatment with chronically and acutely suicidal adolescents. In M. L. Peck, N. L. Farberow, & R. Litman (Eds.), *Youth suicide* (pp. 112–122). New York: Springer.

Pecoraro, J. (1970). *The effect of a series of special lessons in Indian history and culture upon the attitudes of Indian and non-Indian students.* Augusta, ME: Maine State Department of Education. (ERIC Document Reproduction Service No. ED 043 556).

Pediatric Research and Training Center (1988). *An introduction to cultural sensitivity: Working with Puerto Rican families in early childhood special education.* Farmington, CT: Author.

Pelham, W. E., & Murphy, H. A. (1986). Attention deficit disorders. In M. Herson (Ed.), *Pharmacological and behavioral treatment: An integrative approach* (pp. 108–148). New York: Wiley.

Pennsylvania Association for Retarded Children v. Commonwealth of Pennsylvania. 343 F. Supp. 279 (E.D. Pa., 1972).

Pepper, F. (1976). Teaching the American Indian child in mainstream settings. In R. Jones (Ed.), *Mainstreaming and the minority child* (pp. 133–158). Reston, VA: Council for Exceptional Children.

Perl, S. (1983). How teachers teach the writing process: Overview of an ethnographic research project. *Elementary School Journal, 84,* 19–24.

Perlmutter, B. F., Crocker, J., Corday, D., & Garstecki, D. (1983). Sociometric status and related personality characteristics of mainstreamed learning disabled adolescents. *Learning Disability Quarterly, 6,* 20–30.

Perreira, D., Franke, S., & Woych, J. (1988). *Aiding the writing skills of learning disabled college students.* Paper presented at the conference on Writing Models and Programs for the Learning Disabled College Student, New Paltz, NY.

Perske, R., & Perske, M. (1988). *Friendship.* Nashville, TN: Abington.

Personkee, C., & Yee, A. (1971). *Comprehensive spelling instruction: Theory, research, and application.* Scranton, PA: Intext Educational Publishers.

Peterson, D., (1989). *Parent involvement in the educational process.* Urbana, IL: ERIC Clearinghouse on Educational Management, University of Illinois.

Peterson, J., Heistad, D., Peterson, D., & Reynolds, M. (1985). Montevideo individualized prescriptive instructional management system. *Exceptional Children, 52,* 239–243.

Peterson, P. L., Fennema, E., & Carpenter, T. (1991). Using children's mathematical knowledge. In B. Means & M. S. Knapp (Eds.), *Teaching advanced skills to educationally disadvantaged students* (pp. 103–128). Washington DC: U.S. Department of Education.

Peterson, S., Mercer, C., & O'Shea, L. (1988). Teaching learning disabled students place value using concrete to abstract sequence. *Learning Disabilities Research, 4*(1), 52–56.

Petty, W. T., Petty, D. C., & Becking, M. F. (1985). *Experiences in language: Tools and techniques for language arts methods.* Boston: Allyn & Bacon.

Phillips, D., Fischer, S. C., & Singh, R. (1977). A children's reinforcement survey schedule. *Journal of Behavior Therapy and Experimental Psychiatry, 8,* 131–134.

Pieper, B. (1991). *Traumatic brain injury: What the teacher needs to know.* Albany, NY: New York State Head Injury Association.

Pieper, E., & Deshler, D. D. (1985). Intervention considerations in mathematics for the LD adolescent. *Focus on Learning Problems in Mathematics, 7*(1), 35–47.

Pike, K., Compain, R., & Mumper, J. (in press). *Passport to literacy: Becoming readers and writers.* NY: HarperCollins.

Pinkerton, D. (1992). Preparing children with disabilities for school. *The ERIC Review, 2*(1), 21–23.

Plata, M., & Santos, S. L. (1981). Bilingual education: A challenge for the future. *Teaching Exceptional Children, 14,* 97–100.

Platt, J. M., & Platt, J. S. (1980). Volunteers for special education: A mainstreaming support system. *Teaching Exceptional Children,* 13, 31–36.

Plumb, I. J., & Brown, D. C. (1990). SPAN: Special peer action network. *Teaching Exceptional Children, 22*(1), 22–24.

Polloway, E. (1984). The integration of mildly retarded students into the schools: A historical review. *Remedial and Special Education, 5,* 18–28.

Polloway, E., Payne, J., Patton, J., & Payne, R. (1985). *Strategies for teaching learners with special needs* (4th ed.). New York: Merrill/Macmillan.

Polloway, E. A., & Polloway, C. H. (1979). Auctions: Vitalizing the token economy. *Journal for Special Educators, 15,* 121–123.

Polloway, E. A., & Smith, J. D. (1983). Changes in mild mental retardation: Population, programs, and perspectives. *Exceptional Children, 50,* 149–159.

Ponti, C. R., Zins, J. E., & Graden, J. L. (1988). Implementing a consultation-based service delivery system to decrease referrals for special education: A case study of organizational considerations. *School Psychology Review, 17,* 89–100.

Popp, R. A. (1983). Learning about disabilities. *Teaching Exceptional Children, 15,* 78–81.

Powell, T. H., & Moore, S. C. (1992). Benefits and incentives for students entering supported employment. *Teaching Exceptional Children, 24*(3), 16–19.

Powers, D. A. (1983). Mainstreaming and the inservice education of teachers. *Exceptional Children, 49,* 432–439.

Prasse, D. P., & Reschly, D. J. (1986). Larry P.: A case of segregation, testing or program efficacy? *Exceptional Children, 52,* 333–346.

Prater, M. A. (1992). Increasing time-on-task in the classroom. *Intervention in School and Clinic, 28*(1), 22–27.

Premack, D. (1959). Toward empirical behavior laws. *Psychological Review, 66*(4), 219–233.

Pressman, S. (1991, October). *Drinking, drugging, smoking: Schools do make a difference.* Workshop presented at the Roundout School District staff development day, Accord, NY.

Price, B. J., & Marsh, G. E. (1985). Practical guidelines for planning and conducting parent conferences. *Teaching Exceptional Children, 17,* 274–278.

Price, J. P. (1990, April). *Communication during consultation.* Paper presented at the meeting of the Council for Exceptional Children, Toronto.

Prillaman, D. (1981). Acceptance of learning disabled students in the mainstream environment: A failure to replicate. *Journal of Learning Disabilities, 14,* 344–368.

Putnam, M. L. (1992). Characteristics of questions on tests administered by mainstream secondary classroom teachers. *Learning Disabilities Research and Practice, 7,* 129–136.

Quay, H. C. (1979). In H. C. Quay & J. S. Werry (Eds.), *Psychopathological disorders of childhood* (2nd ed.). New York: John Wiley.

Quay, H., & Werry, J. (1986). *Psychopathological disorders of children.* New York: John Wiley.

Radabaugh, M. T., & Yukish, J. F. (1982). *Curriculum and methods for the mildly handicapped.* Boston: Allyn & Bacon.

Ramafedi, G. (1987). Homosexual youth: A challenge to contemporary society. *Journal of the American Medical Association, 258,* 222–225.

Ramirez, M., & Casteneda, A. (1974). *Cultural democracy, bicognitive development, and education.* New York: Academic.

Ramirez, M., & Price-Williams, D. (1974). Cognitive styles in children: Two Mexican communities. *Inter-American Journal of Psychology, 8,* 93–100.

Ramirez, O. (1989). Mexican American children and adolescents. In J. Taylor Gibbs & L. Nahme Huang (Eds.), *Children of color: Psychological interventions with minority youth* (pp. 224–250). San Francisco: Jossey-Bass.

Randolph, A. H., & Harrington, R. M. (1981). Fifth graders' projected responses to physically handicapped classmate. *Elementary School Guidance and Counseling, 16,* 31–35.

Raschke, D. (1981). Designing reinforcement surveys—Let the student choose the reward. *Teaching Exceptional Children, 14,* 92–96.

Raschke, D., & Dedrick, C. (1986). An experience in frustration: Simulations approximating learning difficulties. *Teaching Exceptional Children, 18,* 266–271.

Rasky, S. F. (1989, September 17). How the disabled sold Congress on a new Bill of Rights. *The New York Times,* p. E5.

Raths, L., Harmin, M., & Simon, S. (1978). *Values and teaching* (2nd ed.). New York: Merrill/Macmillan.

Redden, M. R., & Blackhurst, A. E. (1978). Mainstreaming competency specifications for elementary teachers. *Exceptional Children, 44,* 615–617.

Reetz, L. J., & Crank, J. (1988). Include time management and learning strategies in the ED curriculum. *Perceptions, 23*(2), 26–27.

Reeve, R. E. (1990). ADHD: Facts and fallacies. *Intervention in School and Clinic, 26*(2), 70–78.

Reeves, B. (1990). Individual differences: Literature about people with special needs. *Democracy and Education, 5*(2), 11–15.

Regional Support and Technical Assistance Centers Coordination Office. (1976). *The game bag.* Raleigh NC: Author.

Rehder, K. V. (Ed.) (1986). *Rehabilitation Research and Training Center Newsletter, 3*(3). Richmond, VA: Virginia Commonwealth University.

Reimer, K. M. (1992). Multiethnic literature: Holding fast to dreams. *Language Arts, 69,* 14–21.

Reiss, A. L., & Freund, L. (1990). Fragile X syndrome. *Biological Psychiatry, 27,* 223–240.

Reissman, R. (1992). Multicultural awareness collages. *Educational Leadership, 49*(4), 51–52.

Reith, H., & Everston, C. (1988). Variables related to the effective instruction of difficult-to-teach children. *Focus on Exceptional Children, 20*(5), 1–8.

Reschly, D. J. (1988). Minority MMR overrepresentation and special education reform. Exceptional Children, *54,* 316–323.

Research and Training Center on Independent Living. (1987). *Guidelines for reporting and writing about people with disabilities* (2nd ed.). Lawrence, KS: University of Kansas.

Research for Better Schools (1978). *Clarification of PL 94-142 for the classroom teacher.* Philadelphia, PA: Author.

Resnick, L. B., Bill, V., Lesgold, S., & Leer, M. (1991). Thinking in arithmetic class. In B. Means & M. S. Knapp (Eds.), *Teaching advanced skills to educationally disadvantaged students* (pp. 137–159). Washington, DC: U.S. Department of Education.

Reyes, M. de la L. (1987). Comprehension of content passages: A study of Spanish/English readers in third and fourth grade. In S. R. Goldman and H. T. Trueba (Eds.), *Becoming literate in English as a second language.* Norwood, NJ: Ablex.

Reynolds, C. J., & Salend, S. J. (1989). Using cooperative learning in special education teacher training programs. *Teacher Education and Special Education, 12,* 91–95.

Reynolds, C. J., & Salend, S. J. (1990a). Issues and programs in the delivery of special education services to migrant students with disabilities. *The Journal of Educational Issues of Language Minority Students, 7,* 69–83.

Reynolds, C. J., & Salend, S. J. (1990b). Teacher-directed and student-mediated textbook comprehension strategies. *Academic Therapy, 25,* 417–427.

Reynolds, C. J., Salend, S. J., & Behan, C. (1989). Motivating secondary students: Bringing in the reinforcements. *Academic Therapy, 25,* 81–90.

Reynolds, C. J., & Volkmar, J. N. (1984). Mainstreaming the special educator. *Academic Therapy, 19,* 585–591.

Reynolds, M. C., & Birch, J. W. (1988). *Adaptive mainstreaming: A primer for teachers and principals* (3rd ed.). New York: Longman.

Rhode, G., Morgan, D. P., & Young, K. R. (1983). Generalization and maintenance of treatment gains of behaviorally disordered handicapped students from resource rooms to regular classrooms using self-evaluation procedures. *Journal of Applied Behavior Analysis, 16,* 171–188.

Rhodes, L. E., & Valenta, L. (1985). Industry-based supported employment: An enclave approach. *The Journal of The Association for Persons with Severe Handicaps, 10,* 12–20.

Richards, J. J. (1991). Discussion: Appreciating children's mathematical knowledge and thinking in ethnically, linguistically, and economically diverse classrooms. In B. Means & M. S. Knapp (Eds.), *Teaching advanced skills to educationally disadvantaged students* (pp. 129–136). Washington, DC: U.S. Department of Education.

Richardson, L. (1992, January 2). New York schools falling behind homeless. *The New York Times,* pp. A1, B2.

Richardson, S. A., Goodman, N., Hastorf, A. H., & Dornbusch, S. M. (1961). Cultural uniformity in reaction to physical disabilities. *American Sociological Review, 26,* 241–247.

Rikhye, C. H., Gothelf, C. R., & Appell, M. W. (1989). A classroom environment checklist of students with dual sensory impairments. *Teaching Exceptional Children, 22*(1), 44–46.

Rist, M. C. (1990). The shadow children. *American School Board Journal, 177,* 18–24.

Rivera, D., & Deutsch-Smith, D. (1988). Using a demonstration strategy to teach middle school students with learning disabilities how to compute long division. *Journal of Learning Disabilities, 21,* 77–81.

Robbins, D. R., & Alessi, N. E. (1985). Depression symptoms and suicidal behavior in adolescents. *American Journal of Psychiatry, 142*(5), 588–592.

Roberson, W. H., Gravel, J. S., Valcante, G. C., & Maurer, R. G. (1992). Using a picture task analysis to teach students with multiple disabilities. *Teaching Exceptional Children, 24*(4), 12–16.

Roberts, G. W., Bell, L. A., & Salend, S. J. (1991). Negotiating change for multicultural education: A consultation model. *Journal of Educational and Psychological Consultation, 2*(4), 323–342.

Robin, A., Armel, S., & O'Leary, K. (1975). The effects of self-instruction on writing deficiencies. *Behavior Therapy, 6,* 178–187.

Robinson, F. P. (1969). Survey Q3R method of reading. In F. L. Christ (Ed.), *SR/SE resource book* (pp. 35–40). New York: Harper Brothers.

Robinson, S. M., & Kasselman, C. J. (1990). Feedback strategies: Instructional techniques for increasing student time-on-task (Technical Report #2). Lawrence, KS: Department of Special Education at the University of Kansas.

Robinson, S. M., & Smith, D. D. (1981). Listening skills: Teaching learning disabled students to be better listeners. *Focus on Exceptional Children, 13,* 1–15.

Robinson, S. M., & Smith, D. D. (1983). Listening skills: Teaching learning disabled students to be better listeners. In E. L. Meyen, G. A. Vergason, & R. J. Whelan (Eds.), *Promising practices for exceptional children: Curriculum practices* (pp. 143–166). Denver: Love.

Rodin, J., & Janis, I. (1979). The social power of health-care practitioners as agents of change. *Journal of Social Issues, 35,* 60–81.

Roe, B. D., Stodt, B. D., & Burns, P. C. (1983). *Secondary school reading instruction: The content areas* (2nd ed.). Boston: Houghton Mifflin.

Rojewski, J. W., Pollard, R. R., & Meers, G. D. (1992). Grading secondary vocational special education students with disabilities: A national perspective. *Exceptional Children, 59*(1), 68–76.

Ronan, P. (1991). Writing conferences in a secondary classroom. In L. Badger, P. Cormack, & J. Hancock (Eds.), *Success stories from the classroom* (pp. 134–138). Roselle, Australia: Primary English Teaching Association.

Roos, P. D. (1984). *The handicapped limited English proficient student: A school district's obligation.* Tallahassee, FL: Florida State Education Department.

Rose, M. C., Cundick, B. P., & Higbee, K. L. (1983). Verbal rehearsal and visual imagery: Mnemonic aids for learning disabled children. *Journal of Learning Disabilities, 16,* 352–354.

Rose, T. L. (1984a). Effects of previewing on the oral reading of mainstreamed behaviorally disordered students. *Behavioral Disorders, 10,* 33–39.

Rose, T. L. (1984b). The effects of two prepractice procedures on oral reading. *Journal of Learning Disabilities, 17,* 544–548.

Rose, T. L., McEntyre, E., & Dowdy, C. (1982). Effects of two-error correction procedures on oral reading. *Learning Disability Quarterly, 5,* 100–105.

Rose, T. L., Lesson, E. I., & Gottlieb, J. (1982). A discussion of transfer of training in mainstreaming programs. *Journal of Learning Disabilities, 15,* 162–165.

Rose, T. L., & Sherry, L. (1984). Relative effects of two previewing procedures on LD adolescents' oral reading performance. *Learning Disability Quarterly, 7,* 39–44.

Rosegrant, T. J. (1986, April). *It doesn't sound right: The role of speech output as a primary form of feedback for beginning text revision.* Paper presented at the annual meeting of the American Research Association, San Francisco, CA.

Rosenberg, M., Sindelar, P., & Stedt, J. (1985). The effects of supplemental on-task contingencies upon the acquisition of simple and difficult academic tasks. *Journal of Special Education, 19,* 189–203.

Rosenshine, B. V. (1980). How time is spent in elementary classrooms. In C. Denham & A. Lieberman (Eds.), *Time to learn* (pp. 107–126). Washington, DC: National Institute of Education.

Rosenshine, B. V. (1983). Teaching functions in instructional programs. *Elementary School Journal, 83,* 335–352.

Rosenshine, B. V. (1986). Synthesis of research on explicit teaching. *Educational Leadership, 43*(7), 60–69.

Rosenthal, G., & Tetel-Hanks, J. (1981). Socidrama: A program for intervention in the schools. *Education Unlimited, 3,* 9–16.

Ross, J. W., & Weintraub, F. J. (1980). Policy approaches regarding the impact of graduation requirements on handicapped students. *Exceptional Children, 47,* 200–203.

Rothstein, A. S., & Levine, J. (1992, November). *Ventilator dependent children in school.* Paper presented at the meeting of the New York State Federation of Chapters of the Council for Exceptional Children, Albany, NY.

Rowe, M. (1974). Wait-time and rewards as instructional variables, their influence on language, logic, and fate control: Part one, wait-time. *Journal of Research in Science Teaching, 11,* 81–94.

Rubin, A., & Bruce, B. (1985). *Learning with QUILL: Lessons for students, teachers and software designers* (Reading Report No. 60). Washington, DC: National Institute of Education.

Rudman, M. (1973). Informal spelling in the classroom: A more effective approach. *Reading Teacher, 26,* 602–604.

Rueda, R. (1989). Defining mild disabilities with language-minority students. *Exceptional Children, 56,* 121–129.

Rueda, R., & Mercer, J. R. (1985). *Predictive analysis of decision-making with language minority handicapped children.* Paper presented at the BUENO Center Third Annual Symposium on Bilingual Education, Boulder, CO.

Ruhl, K. L., Hughes, C. A., & Schloss, P. J. (1987). Using the pause procedure to enhance lecture recall. *Teacher Education and Special Education, 10*(1), 14–18.

Ruiz, N. T. (1989). An optimal learning environment for Rosemary. *Exceptional Children, 56*(2), 130–144.

Rusch, F. R. (1990). *Supported employment models, methods, and issues.* Sycamore, IL: Sycamore.

Russell, C. (1983). Putting research into practice: Conferencing with young writers. *Language Arts, 60,* 333–340.

Russo, D. C., & Koegel, R. L. (1977). A method for integrating an autistic child in a normal public-school classroom. *Journal of Applied Behavior Analysis, 10,* 579–590.

Sabornie, E. J., & Beard, G. H. (1990). Teaching social skills to students with mild handicaps. *Teaching Exceptional Children, 22,* 35–38.

Sabornie, E. J., & Kauffman, J. M. (1985). Regular classroom sociometric status of behaviorally disordered adolescents. *Behavioral Disorders,* 268–274.

Sadker, M. P. (1981). Diversity, pluralism, and textbooks. In J. Y. Cole and T. G. Sticht (Eds.), *The textbook in American society* (pp. 41–42). Washington, DC: Library of Congress.

Sadker, M. P., & Sadker, D. (1978). *The teacher educator's role. Implementing Title IX and attaining sex equality: A workshop package for postsecondary educators.* Washington, DC: Council of Chief State School Officers. (ERIC Document Reproduction Service No. ED 222 466)

Sadker, M. P., & Sadker, D. (1985, March). Sexism in the schoolroom of the 80s. *Psychology Today,* 54–57.

Sadker, M. P., & Sadker, D. (1990). Confronting sexism in the college classroom. In S. Gabriel & I. Smithson (Eds.), *Gender in the classroom* (pp. 176–187). Chicago: University of Illinois Press.

Safer, N. (1980). Implications of minimum competency standards and testing for handicapped students. *Exceptional Children, 46,* 288–290.

Safilios-Rothschild, C. (1979). *Sex-role socialization and sex discrimination: A synthesis and critique of the literature.* Washington, DC: National Institute of Education.

Safran, J. S., & Safran, S. P. (1985a). A developmental view of children's behavioral tolerance. *Behavioral Disorders, 10,* 87–94.

Safran, J. S., & Safran, S. P. (1985b). Organizing communication for the LD teacher. *Academic Therapy, 20,* 427–435.

Sailor, W. (1991). Special education in the restructured school. *Remedial and Special Education,* 12(6), 8–22.

Sailor, W., Anderson, J. L., Halvorsen, A. T., Doering, K., Filler, J., & Goetz, L. (1989). *The comprehensive local school: Regular education for all students with disabilities.* Baltimore: Paul H. Brookes.

Salend, S. J. (1979a). Active academic games: The aim of the game is mainstreaming. *Teaching Exceptional Children, 12,* 3–6.

Salend, S. J. (1979b). New kids in school. *Instructor, 89,* 142.

Salend, S. J. (1980). How to mainstream teachers. *Education Unlimited, 2,* 31–33.

Salend, S. J. (1980, October). Using cues and clues. *Early Years,* 32–33.

Salend, S. J. (1981a). Cooperative games promote positive student interactions. *Teaching Exceptional Children, 13,* 76–80.

Salend, S. J. (1981b). The treasure hunt game: A strategy for assimilating new students into the mainstream of the school culture. *Education Unlimited, 3,* 40–42.

Salend, S. J. (1983a). Classroom design adaptations for mainstreamed settings: Making the least restrictive environment less restrictive. *Journal for Special Educators, 20,* 51–57.

Salend, S. J. (1983b). Guidelines for explaining target behaviors to students. *Elementary School Guidance and Counseling, 18,* 88–93.

Salend, S. J. (1983c). Mainstreaming: Sharpening up follow-up. *Academic Therapy, 18,* 299–304.

Salend, S. J. (1983d). Using hypothetical examples to sensitize nonhandicapped students to their handicapped peers. *The School Counselor, 30,* 306–310.

Salend, S. J. (1984). Factors contributing to the development of successful mainstreaming programs. *Exceptional Children, 50,* 409–416.

Salend, S. J. (1987). Group-oriented behavior management strategies. *Teaching Exceptional Children, 20,* 53–55.

Salend, S. J. (1990). A migrant education guide for special educators. *Teaching Exceptional Children, 22*(2), 18–21.

Salend, S. J., & Allen, E. M. (1985). A comparison of self-managed response-cost systems on learning disabled children. *Journal of School Psychology, 23,* 59–67.

Salend, S. J., Brooks, L., & Salend, S. (1987). Identifying school districts' policies for implementing mainstreaming. *The Pointer, 32,* 34–37.

Salend, S. J., & Giek, K. (1987). The availability of follow-up services to landlords renting to individuals who are retarded. *Education and Training in Mental Retardation, 22,* 91–97.

Salend, S. J., & Gordon, B. (1987). A group-oriented timeout ribbon procedure. *Behavioral Disorders, 12,* 131–137.

Salend, S. J., & Hankee, C. (1981). Successful mainstreaming: A form of communication. *Education Unlimited, 3,* 47–48.

Salend, S. J., & Johns, J. (1983). Changing teacher commitment to mainstreaming. *Teaching Exceptional Children, 15,* 82–85.

Salend, S. J., & Knops, B. (1984). Hypothetical examples: A cognitive approach to changing attitudes toward the handicapped. *The Elementary School Journal, 85,* 229–236.

Salend, S. J., & Kovalich, B. (1981). A group response-cost system mediated by free tokens: An alternative to token reinforcement in the classroom. *American Journal of Mental Deficiency, 86,* 184–187.

Salend, S. J., & Lamb, E. M. (1986). The effectiveness of a group-managed interdependent contingency system. *Learning Disability Quarterly, 9,* 268–274.

Salend, S. J., & Longo, M. (in press). The roles of the educational interpreter in mainstreaming. *Teaching Exceptional Children.*

Salend, S. J., & Lutz, G. (1984). Mainstreaming or mainlining?: A competency-based approach to mainstreaming. *Journal of Learning Disabilities, 17,* 27–29.

Salend, S. J., Michael, R., Veraja, M., & Noto, J. (1983). Landlords' perceptions of retarded individuals as tenants. *Education and Training of the Mentally Retarded, 18,* 232–234.

Salend, S. J., & Moe, L. (1983). Modifying nonhandicapped students' attitudes toward their handicapped peers through children's literature. *Journal for Special Educators, 19,* 22–28.

Salend, S. J. & Nowak, M. R. (1988). Effects of peer-previewing on LD students' oral reading skills. *Learning Disability Quarterly, 11,* 47–54.

Salend, S. J., Reeder, E., Katz, N., & Russell, T. (1992). The effects of a dependent group-evaluation system. *Education and Training of Children, 15*(1), 32–42.

Salend, S. J., Reid-Jantzen, N., & Giek, K. (1992). Using a peer confrontation system in a group setting. *Behavioral Disorders, 17*(3), 211–218.

Salend, S. J., Reynolds, C. J., & Coyle, E. M. (1989). Individualizing the good behavior game across type and frequency of behavior with emotionally disturbed adolescents. *Behavior Modification, 13,* 108–126.

Salend, S. J., & Salend, S. M. (1984). Consulting with the regular teacher: Guidelines for special educators. *The Pointer, 28,* 25–28.

Salend, S. J., & Salend, S. M. (1985a). Competencies for mainstreaming secondary learning disabled students. *Journal of Learning Disabilities, 19,* 91–94.

Salend, S. J., & Salend, S. M. (1985b). Implications of using microcomputers in classroom testing. *Journal of Learning Disabilities, 18,* 51–53.

Salend, S. J., & Salend, S. M. (1986). Competencies for mainstreaming secondary level learning disabled students. *Journal of Learning Disabilities, 19,* 91–94.

Salend, S. J., & Santora, D. (1985). Employing access to the computer as a reinforcer for secondary students. *Behavioral Disorders, 11,* 30–34.

Salend, S. J., & Schliff, J. (1988). The many dimensions of homework. *Academic Therapy, 23,* 397–404.

Salend, S. J., & Schliff, J. (1989). An examination of the homework practices of teachers of students with learning disabilities. *Journal of Learning Disabilities, 22,* 621–623.

Salend, S. J., & Schobel, J. (1981). Coping with name-calling in the mainstreamed setting. *Education Unlimited, 3,* 36–37.

Salend, S. J., & Schobel, J. (1981, October). Getting the mainstreamed into the mainstream. *Early Years,* 66–67.

Salend, S. J., Tintle, L., & Balber, H. (1988). Effects of a student-managed response-cost system on the behavior of two mainstreamed students. *Elementary School Journal, 89,* 89–97.

Salend, S. J., & Viglianti, D. (1982). Preparing secondary students for the mainstream. *Teaching Exceptional Children, 14,* 137–140.

Salend, S. J., & Washin, B. (1988). The effects of team-assisted individualization on the academic, behavioral, and social skills of handicapped adjudicated youth. *Exceptional Children, 55,* 174–180.

Salend, S. J., Whittaker, C. R., Raab, S., & Giek, K. (1991). Using a self-evaluation system as a group contingency. *Journal of School Psychology, 29,* 319–329.

Salend, S. J., Whittaker, C. R., & Reeder, E. (1992). Group evaluation: A collaborative peer mediated behavior management system. *Exceptional Children,* 59(3), 203–209.

Salend, S. M. (1984). A multidimensional approach to remediating sinistral handwriting deficits in a gifted student. *The Pointer, 29,* 23–28.

Salend, S. M., & Salend, S. J. (1985). Adapting teacher-made tests for mainstreamed students. *Journal of Learning Disabilities, 18,* 51–53.

Salvia, J., & Hughes, C. (1990). *Curriculum-based assessment: Testing what is taught.* New York: Macmillan.

Sandburg, L. D. (1982). Attitudes of nonhandicapped elementary school students toward schoolaged trainable mentally retarded students. *Education and Training of the Mentally Retarded, 17,* 30–34.

Sanders, N. M. (1966). *Classroom questions: What kinds?* New York: Harper & Row.

Santos, K. E. (1992). Fragile X syndrome: An educator's role in identification, prevention, and intervention. *Remedial and Special Education, 13*(2), 32–39.

Sarda, L., Salend, S. J., Crockett, L., Lazzaro, V., Mastrocola, C., Richmann, S., Neugebauer, J., & Warren-Blum, M. (1991). *Early intervention with special needs children: Resources for parents, caregivers, and professionals.* Tucson, AZ: Communication Skill Builders.

Sargent, L. R., Swartzbaugh, T., & Sherman, P. (1981). Teaming up to mainstream in English: A successful secondary program. *Teaching Exceptional Children, 13,* 100–104.

Saski, J., Swicegood, P., & Carter, J. (1983). Notetaking formats for learning disabled adolescents. *Learning Disability Quarterly, 6,* 265–272.

Savage, R. C. (1987). Educational issues for head injured adolescent and young adult. *Journal of Head Trauma Rehabilitation, 2,* 1–10.

Saville-Troike, M. (1991). *Teaching and testing for academic achievement: The role of language development.* Washington, DC: National Clearinghouse for Bilingual Education.

Scandary, J. (1981). What every teacher should know about due process hearings. *Teaching Exceptional Children, 13,* 92–96.

Scanlon, C., Arick, J., & Phelps, N. (1981). Participation in the development of the IEP: Parents' perspective. *Exceptional Children, 47,* 373–376.

Scanlon, D. J., Duran, G. Z., Reyes, E. I., & Gallego, M. A. (1992). Interactive semantic mapping: An interactive approach to enhancing LD students' content area comprehension. *Learning Disabilities Research and Practice, 7,* 142–146.

Scardamalia, M., & Bereiter, C. (1985). Research on written composition. In M. C. Wittrock (Ed.), *Handbook of research on teaching* (3rd ed.) (pp. 778–803). New York: Macmillan.

Scharfenaker, S. K. (1990, September). The fragile X syndrome. *American Speech-Language-Hearing Association,* 45–47.

Schell, V. J. (1982). Learning partners: Reading and mathematics. *The Reading Teacher, 35,* 544–548.

Schilling, D., & Cuvo, A. J. (1983). The effects of a contingency-based lottery on the behavior of a special education class. *Education and Training of the Mentally Retarded, 18,* 52–58.

Schloss, P. J. (1986). Sequential prompt instruction for mildly handicapped learners. *Teaching Exceptional Children, 18,* 181–184.

Schloss, P. J., & Sedlak, R. A. (1986). *Instructional methods for students with learning and behavior problems.* Boston: Allyn & Bacon.

Schneider, W., Schmeisser, G., & Seamone, W. (1981). A computer-aided robotic arm/worktable system for high level quadriplegics. *Computer, 14,* 41–47.

Schniedewind, N., & Davidson, E. (1983). *Open minds to equality: A sourcebook of learning activities to promote race, sex, class and age equity.* Englewood Cliffs, NJ: Prentice-Hall.

Schniedewind, N., & Davidson, E. (1987). *Cooperative learning: Cooperative lives.* Dubuque, IA: William. C. Brown.

Schniedewind, N., & Salend, S. J. (1987). Cooperative learning works. *Teaching Exceptional Children, 19,* 22–25.

Schoen, S. F. (1989). Teaching students with handicaps to learn through observation. *Teaching Exceptional Children, 22,* 18–21.

Schram, L., Semmel, M. I. (1984). *Problem solving teams in California: Appropriate responses by school site staff to students who are difficult to teach and manage.* Santa Barbara, CA: University of California, Graduate School of Education. (ERIC Document Reproduction Service No. ED 255 485)

Schrumpf, F., Crawford, D., & Usadel, H. C. (1991). *Peer mediation: Conflict resolution in schools.* Champaign, IL: Research Press.

Schulz, J. B. (1987). *Parents and professionals in special education.* Boston: Allyn & Bacon.

Schulz, J. B., & Turnbull, A. P. (1983). *Mainstreaming handicapped students* (2nd ed.). Boston: Allyn & Bacon.

Schumaker, J. B., Denton, P. H., & Deshler, D. D. (1984). *The paraphrasing strategy.* Lawrence, KS: University of Kansas.

Schumaker, J. B., Deshler, D. D., Alley, G. R., & Warner, M. M. (1983). Toward the development of an intervention model for learning disabled adolescents: The University of Kansas Institute. *Exceptional Education Quarterly, 4,* 45–74.

Schumaker, J. B., Deshler, D. D., Denton, P. H., Alley, G. R., Clark, F. L., & Warner, M. M. (1982) Multipass: A learning strategy for improving reading comprehension. *Learning Disability Quarterly, 5,* 295–304.

Schumaker, J. B., Nolan, S. M., & Deshler, D. (1985). *Learning strategies curriculum: The error monitoring strategy.* Lawrence, KS: University of Kansas.

Schwebel, A., & Cherlin, D. (1972). Physical and social distancing in teacher-pupil relationships. *Journal of Educational Psychology, 63,* 543–550.

Scranton, T. R., & Ryckman, D. B. (1979). Sociometric status of learning disabled children in integrative programs. *Journal of Learning Disabilities, 12,* 49–54.

Scruggs, T. E., & Lifson, S. (1986). Are learning disabled students "test-wise"?: An inquiry into reading comprehension test items. *Educational and Psychological Measurement, 46,* 1075–1082.

Scruggs, T. E., & Mastropieri, M. A. (1988). Are learning disabled students "test-wise"?: A review of recent research. *Learning Disabilities Focus, 3*(2), 87–97.

Scruggs, T. E., & Mastropieri, M. A. (1992). Effective mainstreaming for mildly handicapped students. *The Elementary School Journal, 92*(3), 389–409.

Scruggs, T. E., & Tolfa, D. (1985). Improving the test-taking skills of learning disabled students. *Perceptual and Motor Skills, 60,* 847–850.

Scruggs, T. E., Mastropieri, M. A., & Tolfa-Veit, D. (1986). The effects of coaching on the standardized test performance of learning disabled and behaviorally disordered students. *Remedial and Special Education, 7,* 37–41.

Self, H., Benning, A., Marston, D., & Magnusson, D. (1991). Cooperative teaching project: A model for students at risk. *Exceptional Children, 58*(1), 26–34.

Seligman, M. (1983). *The family with a handicapped child: Understanding and treatment.* New York: Grune & Stratton.

Semmel, M. I., Abernathy, T. V., Butera, G., & Lesar, S. (1991). Teacher perceptions of the regular education initiative. *Exceptional Children, 58,* 9–24.

Shanley, D. (1988, November). *Techniques and strategies for secondary level resource rooms.* A paper presented at the meeting of the New York State Federation of Chapters of the Council for Exceptional Children, Buffalo, NY.

Shapiro, J., Kramer, S., & Hunerberg, C. (1981). *Equal their chances: Children's activities for non-sexist learning.* Englewood Cliffs, NJ: Prentice-Hall.

Sharan, S. (1980). Cooperative learning in teams: Recent methods and effects on achievement, attitudes, and ethnic relations. *Review of Educational Research, 50,* 241–272.

Shell, D. F., Horn, C. A., & Severs, M. K. (1989). Computer-based compensatory augmentative communications technology for physically disabled, visually impaired, and speech impaired students. *Journal of Special Education Technology, 10*(1), 29–43.

Shields, J. M., & Heron, T. E. (1989). Teaching organizational skills to students with learning disabilities. *Teaching Exceptional Children, 21,* 8–13.

Shinn, M. R., & Hubbard, D. D. (1992). Curriculum-based measurement and problem-solving assessment: Basic procedures and outcomes. *Focus on Exceptional Children, 24*(5), 1–20.

Short, D. J. (1991). *Integrating language and content instruction: Strategies and techniques.* Washington, DC: National Clearinghouse for Bilingual Education.

Shotland J. (1989). *Full fields, empty cupboard: The nutritional status of migrant farmworkers in America.* Washington, DC: Public Voice for Food and Health Policy.

Simon, S., Howe, L., & Kirschenbaum, H. (1972). *Values clarification: A handbook of practical strategies for teachers and students.* New York: Hart.

Simon, S., & Olds, S. W. (1976). *Helping your child learn right from wrong: A guide to values clarification.* New York: McGraw-Hill.

Simpson, M. (n.d.). *Writing effective teacher-made tests for slow learning and mainstreamed students.* Unpublished manuscript.

Simpson, R. L. (1980). Modifying the attitudes of regular class students toward the handicapped. *Focus on Exceptional Children, 13*(3), 1–11.

Siperstein, G. N., Bak, J. J., & Gottlieb, J. (1977). Effects of group discussion on children's attitudes toward handicapped peers. *The Journal of Educational Research, 70,* 131–134.

Siperstein, G. N., Bopp, M., & Bak, J. (1978). Social status of learning disabled children. *Journal of Learning Disabilities, 11,* 98–102.

Sirvis, B. (1988). Students with special health care needs. *Teaching Exceptional Children, 20,* 40–44.

Skrtic, T., Knowlton, H. E., & Clark, F. L. (1979). Action versus reaction. A curriculum development approach to inservice education. *Focus on Exceptional Children, 11,* 1–16.

Slapin, B., Lessing, J., & Belkind, E. (1987). *Books without bias: A guide to evaluating children's literature for handicapism.* Berkeley, CA: KIDS Project.

Slavin, R. E. (1980). *Using student team learning.* Baltimore: Johns Hopkins University.

Slavin, R. E. (1990). *Cooperative learning: Theory, research, and practice.* Englewood Cliffs, NJ: Prentice-Hall.

Slavin, R. E., Madden, N. A., & Leavey, M. (1984). Effects of cooperative learning and individualized instruction on mainstreamed students. *Exceptional Children, 50,* 434–443.

Slavin, R. E., Madden, N. A., & Stevens, R. J. (1990). Cooperative learning models for the 3 R's. *Educational Leadership, 47*(4), 22–28.

Slavin, R. E., Sharan, S., Kagan, S., Hertz-Lazarowitz, R., Webb, C. W., & Schmuck, R. (1985). *Learning to cooperate, cooperating to learn.* New York: Plenum.

Sleeter, C. E. (1991). Introduction: Multicultural education and empowerment. In C. E. Sleeter (Ed.), *Empowerment through multicultural education* (pp. 1–23). Albany, NY: State University of New York Press.

Sleeter, C. E., & Grant, C. A. (1987). An analysis of multicultural education in the U.S. *Harvard Education Review, 57,* 421–444.

Slingerland, B. H. (1976). *A multi-sensory approach to language arts for specific language disability children: A guide for primary teachers.* Cambridge, MA: Educators Publishing Service.

Small Special Education Program Caucus. (1991). *The Caucus News,* 1(29).

Smith, D. D., & Lovitt, T. C. (1982). *The computational arithmetic program.* Austin, TX: Pro-Ed.

Smith, D. J., Young, K. R., West, R. P., Morgan, D. P., & Rhode, G. (1988). Reducing the disruptive behavior of junior high school students: A classroom self-management procedure. *Behavioral Disorders, 13,* 231–239.

Smith, G., & Smith, D. (1985). A mainstreaming program that really works. *Journal of Learning Disabilities, 18,* 369–372.

Smith, J. B. (1988). Connecting WP and LD: Students write! *The Forum, 14*(3), 12–15.

Smith, L., & Land, M. (1981). Low-inference verbal behaviors related to teacher clarity. *Journal of Classroom Interaction, 17,* 37–42.

Smith, M. (1977). *A practical guide to value clarification.* La Jolla, CA: University Associates.

Smith, M. A. (1985). Scheduling for success. *Perspectives for Teachers of the Hearing Impaired, 3*(3), 14–16.

Smith, M. A., & Misra, A. (1992). A comprehensive management system for students in regular classrooms. *The Elementary School Journal, 92*(3), 354–371.

Smitherman, G. (1977). *Talkin and Testifyin: The language of black America.* Boston: Houghton Mifflin.

Smitherman, G. (1985). What go round come round: King in perspective. In C. K. Brooks (Ed.), *Tapping potential: English and language arts for the black learner* (pp. 41–62). Urbana, IL: National Council of Teachers of English.

Smithson, I. (1990). Introduction: Investigating gender, power, and pedagogy. In S. L. Gabriel & I. Smithson (Eds.), *Gender in the classroom: Power and Pedagogy* (pp. 1–27). Chicago, IL: University of Illinois Press.

Spargo, E. (1977). *The now student: Reading and study skills.* Jamestown, RI: Jamestown.

Sparks, B. (1980). Children, race, and racism: How racism awareness develops. *Interacial Books for Children Bulletin, 11*(3–4), 3–9.

Sparks, D. (1991). Migrant farmworkers in south Texas. *OSERS News in Print, 3*(4), 16–19.

Spector, S., Decker, K., & Shaw, S. F. (1991). Independence and responsibility: An LD resource room at South Windsor High School. *Intervention in School and Clinic, 26,* 238–245.

Spekman, N. J., & Roth, F. P. (1984). Intervention strategies for learning disabled children with oral communication disorders. *Learning Disability Quarterly, 7,* 7–18.

Spivack, G., Platt, J. J., & Shure, M. B. (1976). *The problem-solving approach to adjustment: A guide to research and intervention.* San Francisco: Jossey-Bass.

Sprague, J. R., & Horner, R. H. (1990). Easy does it: Preventing challenging behaviors. *Teaching Exceptional Children, 23*(1), 13–15.

Sprague, R., & Gadow, K. (1976). The role of the teacher in drug treatment. *School Review, 85,* 109–140.

Sprung, B. (1975). *Non-sexist education for young children.* New York: The Women's Action Alliance.

Stainback, S., & Stainback, W. (1988). Educating students with severe disabilities. *Teaching Exceptional Children, 21,* 16–19.

Stainback, W., Stainback, S., & Bunch, G. (1989). A rationale for the merger of regular and special education. In S. Stainback, W. Stainback, & M. Forest (Eds.), *Educating all students in the mainstream of regular education* (pp. 15–26). Baltimore: Paul H. Brookes.

Stainback, W., Stainback, S., Courtnage, L., & Jaben, T. (1985). Facilitating mainstreaming by modifying the mainstream. *Exceptional Children, 52,* 144–152.

Stainback, W., Stainback, S., & Wilkinson, A. (1992). Encouraging peer supports and friendships. *Teaching Exceptional Children, 24*(2), 6–11.

Stalker, A. (1990). Multicultural resources for adolescents. *Democracy and Education, 5*(2), 25–28.

Stephens, T. M., Blackhurst, A. E., & Magliocca, L. A. (1982). *Teaching mainstreamed students.* New York: John Wiley & Sons.

Stephens, T. M., Hartman, A. C., & Lucas, V. H. (1982). *Teaching children basic skills: A curriculum handbook* (2nd ed.). New York: Merrill/Macmillan.

Stern, C. (1965). *Structural arithmetic.* Boston: Houghton Mifflin.

Sternglanz, S., & Lyberger-Ficek, S. (1977). Sex differences in student-teacher interactions in the college classroom. *Sex Roles, 3,* 345–352.

Stevens, K. B., & Schuster, J. W. (1988). Time delay: Systematic instruction for academic tasks. *Remedial and Special Education, 9*(5), 16–21.

Stevens, R., & Rosenshine, B. V. (1981). Advances in research on teaching. *Exceptional Education Quarterly, 2,* 1–9.

Stokes, S., & Axelrod, P. (1980). Staff support teams: Critical variables. In L. Burello (Ed.), *What works in inservice* (pp. 15–23). Bloomington, IN: National Inservice Network.

Stokes, T. F., & Baer, D. M. (1977). An implicit technology of generalization. *Journal of Applied Behavior Analysis, 10,* 349–369.

Storey, K., & Horner, R. H. (1988). Pretask requests help manage behavior problems. *Association for Direct Instruction News, 7*(2), 1–3.

Stowitschek, C. E., & Jobes, N. K. (1977). Getting the bugs out of spelling—Or an alternative to the spelling bee. *Teaching Exceptional Children, 9,* 74–76.

Strain, P. S., & Shores, R. E. (1977). Social reciprocity: A review of research and educational implications. *Exceptional Children, 43,* 526–530.

Strain, P. S., & Timm, M. A. (1974). An experimental analysis of social interaction between a behaviorally disordered preschool child and her classroom peers. *Journal of Applied Behavior Analysis, 7,* 583–590.

Straus, M. A., Gelles, R. J., & Steinmetz, S. K. (1980). *Behind closed doors: Violence in the American family.* New York: Anchor.

Strickland, B. B. & Turnbull, A. P. (1990). *Developing and implementing individualized education programs* (3rd ed.). New York: Merrill/Macmillan.

Strully, J. L., & Strully, C. F. (1989). Friendship as an educational goal. In S. Stainback, W. Stainback, & M. Forest (Eds.), *Educating all students in the mainstream of regular education* (pp. 59–70). Baltimore: Paul H. Brookes.

Sugai, G. A., & Smith, P. (1986). The equal additions method of subtraction taught with a modeling technique. *Remedial and Special Education, 7,* 40–48.

Sullivan, K. (1981). Money: A key to mathematical success. *Arithmetic Teacher, 29,* 34–35.

Summers, M., Bridge, J., & Summers, C. R. (1991). Sibling support groups. *Teaching Exceptional Children,* 23(4), 20–25.

Supancheck, P. (1989). Language acquisition and the bilingual exceptional child. In L. M. Baca & H. T. Cervantes (Eds.), *The bilingual special education interface* (2nd ed.) (pp. 101–123). New York: Merrill/Macmillan.

Suydam, M. N. (1984). Research report: Manipulative materials. *Arithmetic Teacher, 31,* 27.

Suydam, M. N. (1986). Manipulative materials and achievement. *Arithmetic Teacher, 33,* 10, 32.

Suzuki, B. H. (1984). Curriculum transformation for multicultural education. *Education and Urban Society, 16,* 294–322.

Swanson, D. P. (1992). ICAN: An acronym for success. *Teaching Exceptional Children, 24*(2), 22–26.

Swanson, H. L., & Reinert, H. R. (1979). *Teaching strategies for children in conflict.* St. Louis: C. V. Mosby.

Swarthout, D. W. (1988). Enhancing the moral development of behaviorally/emotionally handicapped students. *Behavioral Disorders, 14,* 57–68.

Swett, S. C. (1978). Math and LD: A new perspective. *Academic Therapy, 14,* 5–13.

Swicegood, P. R., & Parsons, J. L. (1991). The thematic unit approach: Content and process instruction for secondary learning disabled students. *Learning Disabilities Research and Practice, 6,* 112–116.

Swick, K. J., Flake-Hobson, C., & Raymond, G. (1980). The first step—Establishing parent-teacher communication in the IEP conference. *Teaching Exceptional Children, 12,* 144–145.

Swift, C. A. (1988). Communication disorders. In E. W. Lynch & R. B. Lewis (Eds.), *Exceptional children and adults: An introduction to special education* (pp. 318–351). Boston: Scott, Foresman.

Taber, F. M. (1984). The microcomputer—Its applicability to special education. In E. L. Meyer, G. A. Vergason, & R. J. Whelan, *Promising practices for exceptional children: Curriculum implications.* Denver: Love.

Taylor Gibbs, J. (1989). Black American adolescents. In J. Taylor Gibbs and L. Nahme Huang (Eds.), *Children of color: Psychological interventions with minority youth* (pp. 179–223). San Francisco: Jossey-Bass.

Taylor Gibbs, J., & Nahme Huang, L. (Eds.). (1989). *Children of color: Psychological interventions with minority youth.* San Francisco: Jossey-Bass.

Taylor, D. F. (1989, November). *Portfolio evaluation and group share: Making the most of your students' best.* Paper presented at the meeting of the National Council of Teachers of English, Baltimore, MD.

Taylor, L. S. (1992). *Adult remedial mathematics: Diagnostic and teaching strategies.* Manuscript submitted for publication.

Taylor, L., & Salend, S. J. (1983). Reducing stress-related burnout through a network support system. *The Pointer, 27,* 5–9.

Taylor, L. S., Stefannisko, R. M., Peck, K. M., & Schlissel, M. (1991). The use of cooperative learning by teachers in more restrictive settings. *The Forum, 17*(3), 16–21.

Taylor, O. (1990). Language and communication differences. In G. Shames & E. Wiig (Eds.), *Human communication disorders* (3rd ed.) (pp. 126–158). New York: Merrill/Macmillan.

Taylor, S. J. (1988). Caught in the continuum: A critical analysis of the principle of the least restrictive environment. *Journal of the Association for Persons with Severe Handicaps, 13*(1), 41–53.

Teltsch, K. (1991, October 30). To teach distant pupils, educators in Kentucky turn on interactive TV. *The New York Times,* p. B7.

Terranova, L. (1984). Instructor's terrific timesaver tips. In S. Fenner (Ed.), *Readings in student teaching and special education* (p. 21). Guilford, CT: Special Learning.

Terrell, T. D. (1981). The natural approach to bilingual education. In *Schooling and language minority students: A theoretical framework.* Los Angeles: Evaluation, Dissemination and Assessment Center, California State University.

Terzieff, I. S. (1988). Visual impairments. In E. W. Lynch & R. B. Lewis (Eds.), *Exceptional children and adults: An introduction to special education* (pp. 227–275). Boston: Scott, Foresman.

Thistlethwaite, L. L. (1991). Summarizing: It's more than just finding the main idea. *Intervention in School and Clinic, 27,* 25–30.

Thomas, A., & Chess, S. (1984). Genesis and evolution of behavioral disorders: From infancy to early adult life. *American Journal of Psychiatry, 141,* 1–9.

Thomas, C. C., Englert, C. S., & Gregg, S. (1987). An analysis of errors and strategies in the expository writing of learning disabled students. *Remedial and Special Education, 8,* 21–30.

Thompson, D. P. (1990). From "it easy" to "it is easy": Empowering the African-American student in the racially mixed classroom. *The Clearing House, 63,* 314–317.

Thorkildsen, R. J., & Friedman, S. G. (1986). Interactive videodisc: Instructional design of a beginning reading program. *Learning Disability Quarterly, 9,* 111–117.

Thornton, C. A., & Wilmot, B. (1986). Special learners. *Arithmetic Teacher, 33,* 38–41.

Thornton, C. A., Tucker, B. F., Dossey, J. A., & Bazik, E. F. (1983). *Teaching mathematics to children with special needs.* Menlo Park, CA: Addison-Wesley.

Thousand, J. S., Fox, T. J., Reid, R., Godek, J., & Williams, W. (1986). *The homecoming model: Educating students who present intensive educational challenges within regular education environments.* Burlington, VT: Center for Developmental Disabilities, University of Vermont.

Thousand, J. S., & Villa, R. A. (1990). Strategies for educating learners with severe disabilities within their local home schools and communities. *Focus on Exceptional Children, 23*(3), 1–24.

Thurber, D. N. (1981). *Teacher's edition. D'Nealian handwriting.* Glenview, IL: Scott, Foresman.

Tierney, R. J., & Cunningham, J. W. (1984). Research on teaching reading comprehension. In P. D. Pearson (Ed.), *Handbook of reading research* (pp. 609–655). New York: Longman.

Tiffany, J., Tobias, D., Raqib, A., & Ziegler, J. (1991). *Talking with kids about AIDS.* Ithaca, NY: Department of Human Services Studies at Cornell University.

Tikunoff, W. J., Ward, B. A., van Broekhuizen, L. D., Romero, M., Vega-Casteneda, L., Lucas, T., & Katz, A. (1991). *Final report: A descriptive study of significant features of exemplary special alternative instructional programs.* Los Alamitos, CA: Southwest Regional Educational Laboratory.

Tindal, G. (1985). Investigating the effectiveness of special education: An analysis of methodology. *Journal of Learning Disabilities, 18,* 101–112.

Tobias, T. (1977). *Easy or hard? That's a good question.* Chicago: Children's Press.

Tolfa, D., & Scruggs, T. E. (1986). Can LD students effectively use separate answer sheets? *Perceptual and Motor Skills, 63,* 155–160.

Tompkins, G. E., & Friend, M. (1986). On your mark, get set, write!, *Teaching Exceptional Children, 18,* 82–89.

Tompkins, G. E., & Friend, M. (1988). After the students write: What's next? *Teaching Exceptional Children, 20,* 4–9.

Tonjes, M. J., & Zintz, M. V. (1981). *Teaching reading/thinking/study skills in content classrooms.* Dubuque, IA: William C. Brown.

Torgesen, J. K. (1977). The role of nonspecific factors in the task performance of learning disabled children: A theoretical assessment. *Journal of Learning Disabilities, 10,* 27–34.

Torres, I., & Corn, A. L. (1990). *When you have a visually handicapped child in your classroom: Classroom suggestions for teachers.* New York: American Foundation for the Blind.

Toscano, J. A. (1985). *Autism: A guide to its understanding and early identification.* Albany, NY: Statewide Services for the Autistic.

Tower, C. C. (1987). *How schools can help combat child abuse and neglect* (2nd ed.). Washington, DC: National Education Association.

Tracy, J., & Mann, E. (1992). The program for success at Londonberry junior high school. *Intervention in School and Clinic,* 28(1), 49–53.

Tracy, L. (1990, September). School gayze. *Outweek,* 36, 39, 85–86.

Traub, N. (1982). Reading, spelling, handwriting: Traub systematic holistic method. *Annals of Dyslexia, 32,* 135–145.

Tringo, J. L. (1970). The hierarchy of preference toward disability groups. *Journal of Special Education, 4,* 295–306.

Trueba, H. T. (1983). Adjustment problems in Mexican and Mexican-American students: An anthropological study. *Learning Disability Quarterly, 6,* 395–415.

Trueblood, C. R. (1986). Hands on: Help for teachers. *Arithmetic Teacher, 33,* 48–51.

Trybus, R. (1985). *Today's hearing impaired children and youth: A demographic and academic profile.* Washington, DC: Gallaudet Research Institute.

Tsujimoto, S. E. (1988). Partners in the writing process. In J. Golub (Ed.), *Focus on collaborative learning* (pp. 85–92). Urbana, IL: National Council of Teachers of English.

Tucker, J. A. (1985). Curriculum-based assessment: An introduction. *Exceptional Children, 52,* 199–204.

Tucker, J. A. (1989). Less required energy: A response to Danielson and Bellamy. *Exceptional Children, 55,* 456–458.

Tucker, J., Stevens, L. J., & Ysseldyke, J. E. (1983). Learning disabilities: The experts speak out. *Journal of Learning Disabilities, 16,* 6–14.

Turnbull, A. P., & Schulz, J. B. (1979). *Mainstreaming handicapped students.* Boston: Allyn & Bacon.

Turnbull, H. R. (1986). Appropriate education and Rowley. *Exceptional Children, 52*(4), 347–352.

Turner, T. (1984). The joy of homework. *Tennessee Education, 14,* 25–33.

Tymitz-Wolf, B. L. (1982). Extending the scope of in service training for mainstreaming effectiveness. *Teacher Education and Special Education, 5,* 17–23.

United States Bureau of the Census. (1987). *Statistical abstract of the United States: 1987* (107th ed.). Washington, DC: U.S. Department of Commerce.

United States Department of Education. (1977, August 23). Implementation of Part B of the Education of the Handicapped Act. *Federal Register, 42,* 42474–42518.

United States Department of Education. (1988a). *AIDS and the education of our children.* Washington, DC: Author.

United States Department of Education. (1988b). *Tenth annual report to Congress on the implementation of Public Law 94-142: The Education of All Handicapped Children Act.* Washington, DC: U.S. Government Printing Office.

United States Department of Education. (1989). *What works: Schools without drugs.* Washington, DC: Author.

United States Department of Education (1991a). *America 2000.* Washington, DC: Author.

United States Department of Education. (1991b). *Thirteenth annual report to Congress on the implementation of the Individuals with Disabilities Education Act.* Washington, DC: U.S. Government Printing Office.

Vaca, J. L., Vaca, R. T., & Gove, M. K. (1987). *Reading and learning to read.* Boston: Little, Brown.

Vacc, N. N. (1987). Word processor versus handwriting: A comparative study of writing samples produced by mildly mentally handicapped students. *Exceptional Children, 54,* 156–165.

Valencia, S. (1990). A portfolio approach to classroom reading assessment: The whys, whats, and hows. *The Reading Teacher, 43,* 338–340.

Vallecorsa, A. L., Zigmond, N., & Henderson, L. M. (1985). Spelling instruction in special education classrooms. *Exceptional Children, 52,* 19–24.

Van Houten, R., Nau, P., Mackenzie-Keating, S., Sameoto, D., & Calavecchia, B. (1982). An analysis of some variables influencing the effectiveness of reprimands. *Journal of Applied Behavior Analysis, 15,* 65–83.

Van Reusen, A. K., & Bos, C. (1990). I PLAN: Helping students communicate in planning conferences. *Teaching Exceptional Children, 22*(4), 30–32.

Van Reusen, A. K., Bos, C. S., Schumaker, J. B., & Deshler, D. D. (1987). *I PLAN: An education planning strategy.* Lawrence, KS: Edge.

Van Reusen, A. K., Deshler, D., & Schumaker, J. B. (1989). Effects of a student participation strategy in facilitating the involvement of adolescents with learning disabilities in the individualized educational program planning process. *Learning Disabilities, 1*(2), 23–34.

Vanderslice, V., Cherry, F., Cochran, M., & Dean, C. (1984). *Communication for empowerment: A facilitator's manual of empowering teaching techniques.* Ithaca, NY: Family Matters Project at Cornell University.

Vasa, S. F. (1981). Alternative procedures for grading handicapped students in the secondary schools. *Education Unlimited, 3,* 16–23.

Vasquez, J. A. (1975). Locus of control: Learning and implications for educators. In *School desegregation and cultural pluralism: Perspectives on progress.* San Francisco: Far West Laboratory for Education Research and Development.

Vasquez, J. A. (1988). Contexts of learning for minority students. *The Educational Forum, 6,* 243–253.

Vaughn, S., Bos, C. S., & Lund, K. A. (1986). . . . But they can do it in my room: Strategies for promoting generalization. *Teaching Exceptional Children, 18,* 176–180.

Vaughn, S., McIntosh, R., & Spencer-Rowe, J. (1991). Peer rejection is a stubborn thing: Increasing peer acceptance of rejected students with learning disabilities. *Learning Disabilities Research and Practice, 6,* 83–88.

Venn, J., Morganstern, L., & Dykes, M. K. (1979). Checklists for evaluating the fit and function of orthoses, prostheses, and wheelchairs in the classroom. *Teaching Exceptional Children, 11,* 51–56.

Violand-Sanchez, E., Sutton, C. P., & Ware, H. W. (1991). *Fostering home-school cooperation: Involving language minority families as partners in education.* Washington, DC: National Clearinghouse for Bilingual Education.

Vitello, S. (1986). The Tatro case: Who gets what and why. *Exceptional Children, 52*(4), 353–356.

Voeltz, L. M. (1980). Children's attitudes toward handicapped peers. *American Journal of Mental Deficiency, 84,* 455–464.

Vogel, S. (1988). *Characteristics of LD college writers.* Paper presented at the conference on Writing Models and Programs for the Learning Disabled College Student, New Paltz, NY.

Wade-Lewis, M. (December 2, 1991). Personal communication.

Wagner, M. (1989). *Youth with disabilities during transition: An overview of descriptive findings from the National Longitudinal Transition Study.* Stanford, CA: SRI International.

Waldron, M. B., Diebold, T. J., & Rose, S. (1985). Hearing impaired students in regular classrooms: A cognitive model for educational services. *Exceptional Children, 52,* 39–43.

Walker, H. M., & Bullis, M. (1991). Behavior disorders and the social context of regular class integration: A conceptual dilemma? In J. W. Lloyd, N. N. Singh, & A. C. Repp (Eds.), *The regular education initiative: Alternative perspectives on concepts, issues, and models* (pp. 75–94). Sycamore, IL: Sycamore.

Walker, H. M., & Rankin, R. (1983). Assessing the behavioral expectations and demands of less restrictive settings. *School Psychology Review, 12,* 274–284.

Walker, H. M., McConnell, S., Holmes, D., Todis, B., Walker, J., & Golden, N. (1983). *The Walker social skills curriculum: The ACCEPTS program.* Austin, TX: Pro-Ed.

Walker, M. L. (1991). Rehabilitation service delivery to individuals with disabilities: A question of cultural competence. *OSERS News in Print, 4*(2), 7–10.

Walker, V. S. (1974). The efficacy of the resource room for educating retarded children. *Exceptional Children, 40,* 288–289.

Walla, D. (1988, April). *A secondary modified program in English/Language Arts.* Paper presented at the conference on Writing Models and Programs for the Learning Disabled College Student, New Paltz, NY.

Wallace, G., Cohen, S. B., & Polloway, E. A. (1987). *Language arts: Teaching exceptional students.* Austin, TX: Pro-Ed.

Wallace, G., & Kauffman, J. M. (1986). *Teaching students with learning and behavior problems* (3rd ed.). New York: Merrill/Macmillan.

Wallace, G., & Larsen, S. C. (1978). *Educational assessment of learning problems: Testing for teaching.* Boston: Allyn & Bacon.

Wallace G., & McLoughlin, J. A. (1988). *Learning disabilities concepts and characteristics* (3rd ed.). New York: Merrill/Macmillan.

Wallerstein, J. S., & Blakeslee, S. (1989). *Second chances: Men, women and children a decade after divorce. Who wins, who loses—and why.* New York: Ticknor & Fields.

Wandel, J. E., Kennedy, K. L., & Kretschmer, R. E. (1988). *Linguistics in the classroom: Semantic mapping for hearing impaired students.* New York: Teachers College, Columbia University.

Wang, M. C., Anderson, K. A., & Bram, P. (1985). *Toward an empirical data base on mainstreaming: A research synthesis of program implementation and effects.* Pittsburgh: Learning Research and Development Center, University of Pittsburgh.

Wang, M. C., & Birch, J. W. (1984a). Comparison of a full-time mainstreaming program and a resource room approach. *Exceptional Children, 51,* 33–40.

Wang, M. C., & Birch, J. W. (1984b). Effective special education in regular classes. *Exceptional Children, 50,* 391–398.

Wang, M. C., Reynolds, M. C., & Walberg, H. J. (1986). Rethinking special education. *Educational Leadership, 44*(1), 26–31.

Ward, M. J., Arkell, R. N., Dahl, H. G., & Wise, J. H. (1979). *Everybody counts! A workshop manual to increase awareness of handicapped persons.* Reston, VA: Council for Exceptional Children.

Warren, S. F. (1991). Enhancing engagement in early language teaching. *Teaching Exceptional Children, 23*(4), 48–50.

Weaver, C. (1990). *Understanding whole language.* Portsmouth, NH: Heinemann.

Webb-Johnson, G. (1992, April). *Using cultural frameworks to educate African American youth who demonstrate educational/behavioral problems.* Paper presented at the meeting of the Council for Exceptional Children, Baltimore, MD.

Webber, J., & Scheuermann, B. (1991). Accentuate the positive . . . Eliminate the negative! *Teaching Exceptional Children, 24*(1), 13–19.

Wehman, P., & Kregel, J. (1985). A supported work approach to competitive employment of individuals with moderate and severe handicaps. *The Journal of The Association for Persons with Severe Handicaps, 10,* 3–11.

Weinberg, N., & Santana, R. (1978). Comic books: Champions of the disabled stereotype. *Rehabilitation Literature, 39,* 327–331.

Weiner, H. (1988, April). *Collaborative models revised.* Paper presented at the conference on Writing Models and Programs for the Learning Disabled College Student, New Paltz, NY.

Welsh, P. (1986). *Tales out of school.* New York: Viking.

Wesson, C., & Mandell, C. (1989). Simulations promote understanding of handicapping conditions. *Teaching Exceptional Children, 21*(1), 32–35.

West, J. F., & Cannon, G. S. (1988). Essential collaborative consultation competencies for regular and special educators. *Journal of Learning Disabilities, 21,* 56–63.

West, J. F., & Idol, L. (1987). School consultation (Part 1): An interdisciplinary perspective on theory, models, and research. *Journal of Learning Disabilities, 20,* 388–408.

West, J. F., & Idol, L. (1990). Collaborative consultation in the education of mildly handicapped and at-risk students. *Remedial and Special Education, 11*(1), 22–31.

West, M., Kregel, J., & Wehman, P. (1991). Assisting young adults with severe TBI to get and keep employment through a supported work approach. *OSERS News in Print, 1*(4), 25–30.

Westby, C. E. (1992). Whole language and learners with mild handicaps. *Focus on Exceptional Children, 24*(8), 1–16.

Westby, C. E., & Rouse, G. R. (1985). Culture in education and the instruction of language learning-disabled speakers. *Topics in Language Disorders, 5*(4), 29–41.

Westervelt, V. D., & McKinney, J. D. (1980). Effects of a film on nonhandicapped children's attitudes toward handicapped children. *Exceptional Children, 46,* 294–296.

Westling, D. L. (1986). *Introduction to mental retardation.* Englewood Cliffs, NJ: Prentice-Hall.

Wheeler, J. J., Rubin, J. J., & Miller, S. R. (1990, April). *The relationship of social skills to the transition of students with SED from restrictive to least restrictive settings.* Paper presented at the meeting of the Council for Exceptional Children, Toronto.

White, O. R., & Haring, N. G. (1981). *Exceptional teaching.* New York: Merrill/Macmillan.

White, W. J., Alley, G. R., Deshler, D. D., Schumaker, J. B., Warner, M. M., & Clarke, F. L. (1982). Are there learning disabilities after high school. *Exceptional Children, 49,* 273–274.

Whitt, J., Paul, P. V., & Reynolds, C. J. (1988). Motivate reluctant learning disabled writers. *Teaching Exceptional Children, 20,* 36–39.

Whittaker, C. R. (1991). *The cooperative learning planner.* Ann Arbor, MI: Exceptional Innovations.

Whittaker, C. R., & Salend, S. J. (1991). Collaborative peer writing groups. *Journal of Reading, Writing, and Learning Disabilities, 7*(2), 125–136.

Wiederholt, J. L., Hammill, D. D., & Brown, V. (1978). *The resource teacher: A guide to effective practices.* Boston: Allyn & Bacon.

Wiig, E. H., Freedman, E., & Secord, W. A. (1992). Developing words and concepts in the classroom: A holistic-thematic approach. *Intervention in School and Clinic, 27*(5), 278–285.

Wiig, E. H., & Semel, E. M. (1984). *Language assessment and intervention for the learning disabled* (2nd ed.). New York: Merrill/Macmillan.

Wilcox, B., & Sailor, W. (1982). Service delivery issues: Integrated educational systems. In B. Wilcox & R. York (Eds.), *Quality education for the severely handicapped* (pp. 277–302). Falls Church, VT: Quality Handicrafted Books.

Wilkes, H. H., Bireley, J. K., & Schultz, J. J. (1979). Criteria for mainstreaming the learning disabled child into the regular classes. *Journal of Learning Disabilities, 12,* 46–51.

Wilkinson, C. Y., & Ortiz, A. A. (1986). *Reevaluation of learning disabled Hispanic students: Changes over three years.* Bilingual Special Education Newsletter. Austin, TX: Bilingual Special Education Training Program at the University of Texas at Austin.

Will, M. C. (1984). *OSERS program for transition of youth with disabilities: Bridges from school to working life.* Washington, DC: U.S. Department of Education, Office of Special Education and Rehabilitation Services (OSERS).

Will, M. C. (1986). Education children with learning problems: A shared responsibility. *Exceptional Children, 52,* 411–415.

William T. Grant Foundation (1988). *The forgotten half: Pathways to success for America's youth and young families.* Washington, DC: Author.

Williams, B. F. (1992). Changing demographics: Challenges for educators. *Intervention in School and Clinic, 27*(3), 157–163.

Williams, D. E. (1986). Activities for algebra. *Arithmetic Teacher, 33,* 42–47.

Willis, M. G. (1989). Learning styles of African American children: A review of the literature and interventions. *The Journal of Black Psychology, 16*(1), 47–65.

Wilson, J. J. (1981). Notetaking: A necessary support for hearing-impaired students. *Teaching Exceptional Children, 14,* 38–40.

Wilson, R.
learni
19, 1

Winter, R.
Umbr
pairm
York:

Wisniewsk
for s
Schoo

Witman, C
mess
readi

Wolery, M. (1991). Instruction in early childhood special education: "Seeing through a glass darkly . . . Knowing in part." *Exceptional Children, 58,* 127–135.

Wolf, D. (1990). Portfolio assessment: Sampling student work. *Educational Leadership, 46,* 35–39.

Wolf, J. M. (1967). Physical facilities guidelines for handicapped children: Fitting facilities to the child, Part 3. *School Management, 11,* 38–40.

Wolf, J. S., & Troup, J. (1980). Strategy for parent involvement: Improving the IEP process. *The Exceptional Parent, 10,* 31–32.

Wolf, M. M., Giles, D. K., & Hall, V. R. (1968). Experiments with token reinforcement in remedial classroom. *Behavior Research and Therapy, 6,* 305–312.

Wolfensberger, W. (1972). *The principle of normalization in human services.* Toronto: National Institute on Mental Retardation.

Wolff, J. (1991). *A program to train professionals and parents in the use of facilitated communication.* Kingston, NY: Children's Annex.

Wolfram, W. (1990). *Dialect differences and testing.* Washington, DC: Center for Applied Linguistics.

Wolman, C., Bruininks, R., & Thurlow, M. (1989). Dropouts and dropout programs: Implications for special education. *Remedial and Special Education, 10*(5), 6–20.

Wolock, I., & Horowitz, B. (1984). Child maltreatment as a social problem: The neglect of neglect. *American Journal of Orthopsychiatry, 54,* 530–543.

Wong, B. Y. L. (1982). Understanding learning disabled students' reading problems: Contributions from cognitive psychology. *Topics in Learning and Learning Disabilities, 1,* 43–50.

Wong, B. Y. L. (1986). A cognitive approach to spelling. *Exceptional Children, 53,* 169–173.

… (1982). Increasing metacom… …earning disabled and normally … …udents through self-questioning … *…earning Disability Quarterly, 5,* 228–

… Y. L., Wong, R., & LeMare, I. (1982). The ef…cts of knowledge of criterion task on comprehension and recall in normally achieving and learning disabled children. *Journal of Educational Research, 76,* 119–126.

Wong, B. Y. L., Wong, R., Perry, N., & Sawatsky, D. (1986). The efficacy of a self-questioning summarization strategy for use by underachievers and learning disabled adolescents in social studies. *Learning Disabilities Focus, 2,* 20–35.

Wong-Fillmore, L. (1985). Teaching bilingual learners. In M. C. Wittrock (Ed.), *Handbook of research on teaching* (3rd ed.) (pp. 648–685). New York: The Free Press.

Wood, B. J. (1976). *Children and communication.* Englewood Cliffs, NJ: Prentice-Hall.

Wood, J. W. (1988, March). *Adapting instruction for the mildly handicapped student: A national perspective.* Paper presented at the meeting of the Council for Exceptional Children, Washington, DC.

Wood, J. W. (1992). *Adapting instruction for mainstreamed and at-risk students* (2nd ed.). New York: Merrill/Macmillan.

Wood, J. W., & Miederhoff, J. W. (1989). Bridging the gap. *Teaching Exceptional Children, 21,* 66–68.

Wood, J. W., & Rosbe, M. (1985). Adapting the classroom lecture for the mainstreamed student in the secondary schools. *The Clearing House, 58,* 354–358.

Wood, J. W., & Wooley, J. A. (1986). Adapting textbooks. *The Clearing House, 59,* 332–335.

Wood, M., & Long, N. (1990). *Life space intervention: Talking to children and youth in a crisis.* Austin, TX: Pro-Ed.

Woodruff, E., Bereiter, C., & Scardamalia, M. (1981). On the road to computer assisted compositions. *Journal of Educational Technology Systems, 10,* 133–148.

Woodward, J., & Gersten, R. (1992). Innovative technology for secondary students with learning disabilities. *Exceptional Children, 58*(5), 407–421.

Woolfolk, A. E., & Brooks, D. M. (1985). The influence of teachers' nonverbal behaviors on students' perceptions and performance. *The Elementary School Journal, 85,* 513–528.

Wright, B. (1978). The coping framework and attitude change: A guide to constructive role-playing. *Rehabilitation Psychology, 25,* 177–183.

Wright, H. F. (1967). *Recording and analyzing child behavior.* New York: Harper & Row.

Wysocki, D., & Harrison, R. (1991). AIDS and the media: A look at how periodicals influence children and teenagers in their knowledge of AIDS. *Journal of Health Education, 22*(1), 20–23.

Yaggy, E. (1969). Writing a research paper. In F. L. Christ (Ed.), *SR/SE resource book.* (pp. 79–84). Chicago: Science Research Associates.

Yates, J. R. (1973). A model for preparing regular classroom teachers for mainstreaming. *Exceptional Children, 39,* 471–472.

Yates, J. R. (1988). Demography as it affects special education. In A. A. Ortiz & B. A. Ramirez (Eds.), *Schools and the culturally diverse exceptional student: Promising practices and future directions* (pp. 1–5). Reston, VA: Council for Exceptional Children.

Yates, J. R., & Ortiz, A. A. (1991). Professional development needs of teachers who serve exceptional language minorities in today's schools. *Teacher Education and Special Education, 14*(1), 11–18.

Ysseldyke, J. E. (1987). Classification of handicapped students. In M. Wang, M. Reynolds, & H. Walberg (Eds.), *Handbook of special education research: Research and practice* (Vol. 1) (pp. 253–271). New York: Pergamon.

Ysseldyke, J. E., & Algozzine, B. (1982). *Critical issues in special and remedial education.* Boston: Houghton Mifflin.

Yuker, H., Block, J., & Young, J. (1970). *The measurement of attitudes toward disabled persons.* Albertson, NY: Human Resources Center.

Zentall, S. S., & Kruczek, T. (1988). The attraction of color for active attention-problem children. *Exceptional Children, 54,* 357–362.

Zigler, E., & Muenchow, S. (1979). Mainstreaming: The proof is in the implementation. American Psychologist, *34,* 993–996.

Zigmond, N., Levin, E., & Laurie, T. E. (1985). Managing the mainstream: An analysis of teacher attitudes and student performance in mainstream high school programs. *Journal of Learning Disabilities, 18,* 535–541.

Zigmond, N., Vallecorsa, A., & Leinhardt, G. (1980). Reading instruction for students with learning disabilities. *Topics in Language Disorders, 1,* 89–98.

Zins, J. E., Curtis, M. J., Graden, J. L., & Ponti, C. R. (1988). *Helping students succeed in the regular classroom.* San Francisco: Jossey-Bass.

Zirkel, P. A. (1978). *A digest of Supreme Court decisions affecting education.* Bloomington, IN: Phi Delta Kappa.

Zirpoli, T. J. (1990). Physical abuse: Are children with disabilities at greater risk? *Intervention in School and Clinic, 26,* 6–11.

Subject Index

Author Index

ISBN 0-02-405331-7